The Federal Bureau of Investigation before Hoover

The federal Bureau of Investigation before Hoover

Volume II:
The fBI and American Neutrality, 1914-1917

by

Heribert von Feilitzsch and Charles H. Harris III

Copyright ©2024 by Heribert von Feilitzsch and Charles H. Harris III

All rights reserved. No part of this book may be reproduced or transmitted in any form or by any means, electronic or mechanical, including photography, recording, or by any other information storage and retrieval system, without permission in writing from the authors.

First published in the United States of America in 2024 by Henselstone Verlag LLC
First Edition

Every effort has been made to locate and contact all holders of copyright to material reproduced in this book. For information about permission to reproduce selections from this book, contact info@henselstoneverlag.com or send mail to Henselstone Verlag, P.O. Box 201, Amissville, VA 20106

Library of Congress Control Number: 2024948366
Keyword Data

Harris, Charles Houston, 1937-
von Feilitzsch, Heribert, 1965-

The federal Bureau of Investigation before Hoover: Volume II: The fBI and American Neutrality, 1914-1917 / Heribert von Feilitzsch, Charles Houston Harris
p. cm.
Includes biographical references and index.

ISBN 978-1-7349324-7-8 (hardcover) | 978-1-7349324-8-5 (paperback) | 978-1-7349324-2 (e-book)

1. United States – History – Law Enforcement
2. United States – History – 20th Century
3. United States – History – Bureau of Investigation
4. United States – History – Foreign Policy - Mexico
5. Mexico – History – Revolution, 1910-1920 – Diplomatic History
6. United States – Foreign Relations – Mexico
7. Mexico – Foreign Relations – United States
8. United States - Intelligence History – 20th Century
9. Mexico – History – Revolution, 1910-1920 – Diplomatic History
10. Mexico – Foreign Relations – United States
11. Mexico – Intelligence History – 20th Century
12. Germany – Intelligence History – 20th Century
I. von Feilitzsch, Heribert; Harris, Charles Houston. Title.

www.fbibeforehoover.com
www.feilitzsch.com
Printed in the United States of America

> Germany does not want one faction dominant in Mexico; therefore we must recognize one faction as dominant in Mexico ... It comes down to this: our possible relations with Germany must be our first consideration, and all our intercourse with Mexico must be regulated accordingly.

Robert Lansing, Diary Entry, October 10, 1915

Praise for

The federal Bureau of Investigation
Volume II: The fBI and American Neutrality, 1914-1917

"Excellence describes this book. The manuscript demonstrates exceptional characteristics in three major ways: the research demonstrates superior historical skills, including an acceptance of the sources that exist rather than attempt to determine what sources will work in one methodology or another; a fresh interpretation of the significance of the Bureau of Investigation in the years when the US remained officially neutral in World War I, ignoring previous conclusions, reached as the authors show through political motives, and careful discussion of programs imagined, dismissed or ignored in previous monographs.

The authors used sources ignored or only sampled by other authors, even official FBI ones. Here the authors have reviewed the official Bureau of Investigation's files on the Mexican Revolution that include more than 70,000 pages of reports, correspondence, and files for the Neutrality Period and World War I, 1914 to 1918, an additional 450,000 pages of case files known as the "Old German Files," all declassified in 1977. This investigation alone makes the book stand out.

Reviewing the massive archive of documents, the authors decided to organize the manuscript topically so that readers do not become confused with overlapping cases and events. The topics divided into fifteen chapters that focus on such themes as attacks on Canada (1914 to 1916), conspiracies involving the Hindu-German and Irish groups (1915-1918), the campaign of firebombing and sabotage (1915-1917), Pancho Villa and his attacks on US interests (1915-1916), and the Carranza and Wilson administrations' conflicts (1915-1917). This topical organization gives the text a clarity of narrative.

It is this narrative that moves the book beyond the simple explication of international politics or government administrative policies to a sophisticated analysis of the development taken for granted by other authors. For example, the Bureau built and successfully prosecuted many legal cases against German plotters. Still the bureau missed some major actions such as the unprecedented attack on the United States in July 1916, when the German sabotage cell of Paul Hilken and Friedrich Hinsch caused the explosion at Black Tom Island in the New York Harbor. It was only resolved after World War II.

Moreover the case of the Albert portfolio provides the most striking theme in the book. President Wilson permitted the British to campaign for US entry into the war on the side of the Allies. The publication of the contents of Heinrich Albert's briefcase is linked to the president in support of British propaganda efforts. The authors show clearly the Albert affair, despite accounts by a dozen or so historians, never happened as told.

The conclusion is clear: read this book for a clear explanation of what took place during the period when the US remained out of World War I! It is excellent!"

— William H. Beezley, *University of Arizona*

"This superbly researched history is all the more fascinating in the parallels it illuminates to our present situation and challenges. When considered together with the authors' earlier works on the periods just before and during WWI, the result is an amazing sequence of subversion, espionage, struggle and reaction. For readers such as myself who are much more familiar with WWII or Cold War history, this book and its companions provide vital history and essential context to what began and followed in intelligence and counterintelligence."

— Lieutenant Colonel Frank Stearns, *US Army (retired)*

"You won't find a better history of how the FBI developed during the First World War and the influence the intelligence war in the US exerted on its creation. The authors tap into neglected archival collections to bring to life the battle on American soil between an Imperial Germany desperate to keep the US from joining the Allies and a new and untried group of federal agents. This work clears up long-standing misinterpretations and restores long-missing parts of the historical record. It is essential reading for anyone interested in the history of espionage and for those who want a fuller understanding of the United States' role in The Great War."

— Mark Benbow, *Marymount University*
Retired Associate Professor of American History
Visiting Lecturer in American History, George Washington University

To the two B's,
Betty and Berkley

Table of Contents

	Acknowledgments	vii
	Preface	ix
1	Wartime Staffing in The US	1
2	The Great Supply Mission	13
3	Passport Fraud	25
4	Attacks on Canada	37
5	The Enemy of The Enemy	51
6	A Massive German Iceberg	69
7	Huerta Comeback	97
8	The Wolf and The Tiger	133
9	The Great Cover-Up	153
10	From Friend to Foe	177
11	The Chief Manipulator	205
12	War Crisis	221
13	Trust is Good — Control is Better	261
14	If He Just Had Money	281
15	Descent Into War	317
	Epilogue	341
	Bibliography	347
	Endnotes	359
	Index	415

List of Figures

Figure 1. Alexander Bruce Bielaski, 1917 xii
Figure 2. HMS *Centurion*, 1918 2
Figure 3. Virginia Mackay-Smith, c. 1910-1915 3
Figure 4. Captain Franz von Papen, 1915 4
Figure 5. Johann Heinrich Count von Bernstorff. 5
Figure 6. Paul Koenig, aka P. K. 7
Figure 7. Emanuel Viktor Voska, before 1921. 8
Figure 8. Bernhard Dernburg, c. 1910-1915 9
Figure 9. John R. Rathom, 1917 11
Figure 10. Karl Boy-Ed. c. 1910-1915 14
Figure 11. Karl (Carl) Gottlieb Bünz (Buenz), c. 1910-1915. ... 15
Figure 12. Black Tom Island explosion, 1916. 17
Figure 13. Heinrich Friedrich Albert, 1916 21
Figure 14. Captain Horst von der Goltz, before 1919 26
Figure 15. Werner Horn, c. 1910-1915. 27
Figure 16. Captain Hans Walter Luigi Boehm 29
Figure 17. Hans von Wedell and his Wife, c. 1914. 31
Figure 18. Hans Adam von Wedell, c. 1914 33
Figure 19. Carl Ruroede, c. 1914 34
Figure 20. Franz von Papen, December 12, 1915 41
Figure 21. Werner Horn and Deputy Sheriff, George W. Ross, 1915. 45
Figure 22. Peabody Overall Company Explosion, 1915. 48
Figure 23. Special Agent in Charge Jay Herbert Cole, c. 1910 .. 49

Figure 24. Sikhs on the *Komogata Maru*, Vancouver, Canada. 1914 53

Figure 25. Johanna and Lotte Gadski, 1911 55

Figure 26. Captain Hans Tauscher, 1916 56

Figure 27. Felix A. Sommerfeld and Pancho Villa, 1915 60

Figure 28. Wolf von Igel, c. 1915-1920 61

Figure 29. Franz Rintelen, 1915 72

Figure 30. Portrait of Walter T. Scheele, April 13, 1916 77

Figure 31. Herrmann, drawing of cigar bomb 79

Figure 32. Forrest Currier Pendleton, 1920 81

Figure 33. Robert Fay, c. 1917-1918 84

Figure 34. Franz Rintelen, c. World War II 86

Figure 35. Captain Charles von Kleist, 1916 89

Figure 36. Richmond Mortimer Levering 94

Figure 37. Venustiano Carranza, 1913 98

Figure 38. Harry Berliner at the border 99

Figure 39. José C. Delgado, Victoriano Huerta, Abraham Z. Ratner 101

Figure 40. Brigadier General John J. Pershing and 10th US Cavalry Staff . 107

Figure 41. Hotel Astor, New York, c. 1900-1910 109

Figure 42. Heinrich Albert at his Desk 110

Figure 43. Francisco "Pancho" Villa, Possibly Battle of Ojinaga, 1914 111

Figure 44. Bernhard Dernburg, 1931 113

Figure 45. Zach Lamar Cobb, 1916 119

Figure 46. Stephen Lee Pinckney, 1912 121

Figure 47. Pascual Orozco, c. 1910-1915 128

Figure 48. David Lamar, c. 1917-1918 134

Figure 49. Labor's National Peace Council Meeting, c. 1915 136

Figure 50. Samuel Gompers, c. 1908 138

Figure 51. U-*Deutschland*, 1916 146

Figure 52. Frederico Stallforth with Daughters, c. 1925 148

Figure 53. Frank I. Cobb. 155

Figure 54. Samuel Untermeyer, c. 1915 156

Figure 55. Vanceboro Bridge, 1915 157

Figure 56. William J. Flynn, 1919. 159

Figure 57. US Attorney General Thomas Watt Gregory, 1917. 160

Figure 58. William Gibbs McAdoo, c. 1914 161

Figure 59. Agent Frank Burke upon retirement. 162

Figure 60. Heinrich Friedrich Albert 164

Figure 61. George Sylvester Viereck, 1922 167

Figure 62. James Francis Jewell Archibald, c. 1915. 169

Figure 63. "Those Idiotic Yankees," September 24, 1915 170

Figure 64. Villa Voska, 1920. 171

Figure 65. Sir Guy Reginald Archer Gaunt 172

Figure 66. Ralph Van Deman. 173

Figure 67. Constantin Dumba, c. 1910-1915 174

Figure 68. Sinking of the *Lusitania*, May 1915 175

Figure 69. Stephen Pinckney, 1912. 181

Figure 70. Charles E. Jones, mother and father, and brother Winfield. . . . 190

Figure 71. John Killian Wren 207

Figure 72. Ramón P. DeNegri. 209

Figure 73. William M. Offley, c. 1912-1919. 210

Figure 74. Victor and Bessie Weiskopf, June 1921. 232

Figure 75. Arthur Alva Hopkins 241

Figure 76. Harry Berliner at the Border 246

Figure 77. Manuel Sorola 256

Figure 78. Robert Lee Barnes, May 1919 257

Figure 79. Emilio Kosterlitzky. 268

Figure 80. General Félix Díaz, 1915 282

Figure 81. Harry Berliner. 293

Figure 82. William Earl Dodge Stokes, 1917 299
Figure 83. Arthur Zimmermann, 1918 338
Figure 84. Horst von der Goltz, 1914 340

Acknowledgments

The idea for this book started many years ago when Charles Harris and Louis Sadler received and analyzed the microfilm reels containing the Case Files of the Bureau of Investigation, 1908-1922, "Old Mexican Files" from the National Archives. Sadly, before the first word could be committed to paper, Louis Sadler, best friend and 50-year research and writing partner of Charles Harris, passed away. Heribert von Feilitzsch and Charles Harris continued the project. The initial book The fBI and Mexican Revolutionists, 1908-1914 took shape over a period of two years and expanded into a four-volume study titled The federal Bureau of Investigation before Hoover.[1] Volume 2, The fBI and American Neutrality, 1914-1917 continues on the path of creating the first comprehensive history of the early federal law enforcement agency. This momentous task did not come to fruition in a vacuum. First and foremost, Betty Harris deserves heartfelt thanks for coaching and patiently assisting in virtual meetings twice-a-week, which are still on-going. Berkley von Feilitzsch supported several research trips and provided great advice as a flow editor.

Several scholars, researchers, and descendants of federal agents have supported our insatiable thirst for details and information. We would like to give special thanks to John Fox Jr., the historian of the FBI, who forwarded to us valuable files and information. To a large measure, John helped us bring A. Bruce Bielaski to life in our story. Thank you! The editors of Studies in Intelligence gave us a great break by peer-reviewing and publishing the most controversial chapter in this book, the Albert briefcase affair. The publication of this article allowed us to stake a claim for our research a year before the current volume was published. Thank you! Frank Stearns, Mark Benbow, and Roberto Cantú read the manuscript early on and provided valuable insights.

We also want to thank the archivists in the US National Archives in Maryland and St. Louis for their dedication and assistance. Thank you!

Lastly, we would like to thank Rosa DeBerry King for her patience and challenging questions. Rosa edited this manuscript and prepared the publishable document you hold in your hands (or on your e-reader) today.

Preface

THE FBI IS ARGUABLY the most famous law enforcement organization in the world, ranking ahead of Scotland Yard, the Royal Canadian Mounted Police, and the Texas Rangers. The prevailing view is that the federal Bureau of Investigation was of little account prior to J. Edgar Hoover becoming Director in 1924. A prime example is Athan G. Theoharis with Tony G. Poveda, Susan Rosenfeld and Richard Gid Powers, *The FBI: A Comprehensive Reference Guide from J. Edgar Hoover to the X-Files* (New York: Checkmark Books, 2000). This view is also found in more recent works, such as Rhodri Jeffreys-Jones, *The FBI: A History*,[2] and Garrett M. Graff, *Watergate: A New History*.[3]

Hoover remained as Director until his death in 1972.[4] He was a master of public relations, drawing a stark picture of how terrible conditions were until he took over. Using techniques such as commissioning the official history of the FBI, Don Whitehead, *The FBI Story: A Report to the People* (New York: Random House, 1956), argues that Hoover adroitly built the image of the Bureau as an organization composed of highly trained professionals who were unswervingly committed to enforcing the law. In reality, as a law enforcement arm of the Executive Branch, the FBI by its very nature has always operated within a political framework.[5] The timing, sources, and subjects of investigations have frequently led to political controversies to this day.[6]

The origins of the FBI date back to July 26, 1908, when Attorney General Charles J. Bonaparte created the federal Bureau of Investigation, the BI or Bureau, as the investigative and law enforcement arm of the Department of Justice. On July 1, 1935, the BI received the capital "F" in its name, the Federal Bureau of Investigation, or the FBI. The Hoover myth has been so ingrained in the Bureau's historiography that one reads things such as "No one remembers the force's first chief, Stanley W. Finch, or his successor, A. Bruce Bielaski, who had worked for him. Until J. Edgar Hoover became director in 1924, the bureau was faceless."[7] As we shall see, Bielaski especially merits a much more prominent place in the history of the FBI.

The nascent Bureau devoted much of its energies to matters such as enforcing the Mann Act against white slavery and combatting other varieties of white-collar and interstate crime. The organization did reach its low point in the early 1920s, before Hoover, but during the preceding decade some of its enduring features and characteristics developed. Prominent among these was the emergence of the Bureau as a national law enforcement agency oriented around investigative techniques, intelligence gathering, and tradecraft as core doctrines.

Historian Raymond J. Batvinis in his book *The Origins of* FBI *Counterintelligence* stated that the FBI's counterintelligence capability developed "in the critical years before the Second World War."[8] Counterintelligence became a critical part of the Bureau's mission much earlier. Historian Ronald Kessler in *The Bureau: The Secret History of the* FBI postulated that when the United States entered World War I in 1917, "Overnight, the bureau had been transformed from an agency that merely investigated violations of criminal law to one that investigated spying and was responsible for the internal security of the country."[9] There was nothing "overnight" about it — the Bureau cut its counterintelligence eyeteeth beginning in 1908 against Mexican revolutionists, whose activities paralleled and intersected with the challenges the US faced during the Neutrality Period of World War I (1914-1917), especially starting in 1915 as a result of German activities. By the time the US entered the war, the Bureau was this country's premier intelligence agency. This important but neglected aspect of the Bureau's activities involved enforcing the neutrality laws in the Federal Penal Code: Section 10 prohibited anyone from being hired or retained or entering or enlisting himself in the service of any foreign prince, state, colony, district or people; and Section 13 prohibited any military expedition against the territory or dominion of any foreign prince or state or of any colony, district, or people with whom the United States was at peace.[10] The Bureau was not merely enforcing the laws of the United States, but was rapidly building a highly effective counterintelligence capability.

The United States helped shape the Mexican Revolution by extending or withholding diplomatic recognition of various Mexican regimes. No Mexican government could feel secure unless it had been recognized because, otherwise, the United States had the option of supporting that regime's enemies. Recognition also dictated the enforcement of the neutrality laws. By the selective enforcement of these laws, the Bureau was implementing United States foreign policy. The State Department decided who was, or was not, a "friendly" foreign government. Hence, how the Bureau enforced the laws with regard to the Mexican Revolution was impacted fundamentally by changes in US foreign policy. Among other things, the agency had to adjust to the sporadic arms embargos the US placed on shipments to Mexico, and on two occasions, to American military intervention in Mexico. Besides dealing with various Mexican factions struggling for power, the Bureau also dealt with the activities in the United States of reputable businesses and businessmen whose endeavors had a profound impact on the course of the Mexican Revolution. As if all this were not enough, the Bureau had to deal with agents of foreign powers. In short, the fledgling Bureau of Investigation faced a steep learning curve, and was operating in stormy and uncharted waters.

Yet, remarkably enough, under the leadership of A. Bruce Bielaski, by 1917 the Bureau of Investigation had become the pre-eminent intelligence agency of the United States government. World War I saw close cooperation between the War Department's Military Intelligence Division, the Bureau and the State Department to maximize counterintelligence capabilities for the war effort. Bielaski resigned in February 1919 once the war ended, and left the Bureau in the hands of less capable leaders. In the early 1920s, the agency lacked a clear mission and succumbed to corruption and mismanagement until 1924 when J. Edgar Hoover established his forty-eight-year reign as Director.

The current volume, *The fBI and American Neutrality, 1914-1917*, continues to recount the efforts of the Bureau to enforce the Neutrality Laws. While in the previous volume the Bureau contended with the ever-changing US foreign policy and factionalism of the Mexican Revolution, the outbreak of World War I in August 1914 added a new dimension to the agency's challenges: Agents of Germany, Great Britain, France, and Russia first competed with each other on US soil, then dragged the US into the conflict. German agents attacked Canadian logistics and infrastructure targets and resupplied the remnants of its fleet from US soil. By 1915, the US had become a major supplier of war materiel for the Allies, which prompted German agents to engage in propaganda, sabotage, and labor unrest, mainly in the rust belt and major port cities. This campaign to prevent the US from supplying Germany's enemies included efforts to stoke the fires of the Mexican Revolution and provoke cross-border incidents.

Under the leadership of A. Bruce Bielaski, the Bureau managed rapid growth of both personnel, signal intelligence (SIGINT) and human intelligence (HUMINT). Operating as a national counterintelligence agency with field offices across the country, and centralizing intelligence collection and analysis, the Bureau rapidly increased its capabilities to become the US government's premier intelligence agency. This development did not come without its challenges and failures. Local resistance to federal prosecutions, tampered juries, and hostile judges remained hindrances to field offices bringing lawbreakers to justice. Despite significant increases in funding, the Bureau still lacked necessities such as timely translation of correspondence, automobiles, and funding for informants. These challenges notwithstanding, Bielaski's organization produced remarkable successes and fielded several outstanding agents, some of whom operated internationally. By 1916, the Bureau had unraveled most of the German conspiracies and had sent scores of German agents to jail. The two main successes of German intrigue during the Neutrality Period, however, the *villista* attack on Columbus, New Mexico in March 1916, and the explosion on Black Tom Island in the New York harbor in July 1916, slipped through the Bureau's investigative dragnet.

Figure 1. Alexander Bruce Bielaski, 1917
Source: Harris & Ewing Collection
Library of Congress Prints and Photographs Division

This monograph does not attempt to describe every one of the thousands of the Bureau's investigations into German intrigue during the Neutrality Period. The selected investigations into German activities in the US represent the most significant cases, and illustrate the successes and failures of the Bureau during this period, its interaction with foreign clandestine services, especially those of Great Britain, and the gradual shift of the Bureau from neutrality law enforcement to counterintelligence. Many of the investigations happened in parallel, such as the investigations into German firebombing of ships and factories, sabotage of Allied shipping, the outfitting of revolutionary movements against Great Britain from US soil, continuous attacks on Canada from the US, and the manipulation of the US labor and peace movements. In the spring of 1916 as many as five grand juries simultaneously investigated German intrigue.

To streamline the historical analysis, we decided to present the Bureau investigations into German and Mexican intrigue by topic rather than chronologically, such as attacks on Canada (1914 to 1916), the Hindu-German and Irish conspiracies (1915-1918), the firebombing and sabotage campaign (1915-1917), the *villista* attacks on US interests (1915-1916), and the conflict between the Carranza and Wilson administrations (1915-1917). Yet, the reader should note that A. Bruce Bielaski and a handful of administrative staff oversaw all these investigations, court cases, and manhunts, which literally often happened at the same time. The distillation of hundreds of thousands of pages of reports, not including the many more filings from grand jury investigations which to a large extent remain sealed to this day, all crossed the desk of Chief Bielaski, and by and large were acted upon.

Sources for this volume are primarily based on the Bureau of Investigation's files on the Mexican Revolution—some 70,000 pages of documents of agents' reports, correspondence, and case files declassified in 1977. During the Neutrality Period and World War I, 1914 to 1918, the Bureau files include some 450,000 pages of case files collectively named "Old German Files," also declassified in 1977. Special Agents' reports have two dates: for the period covered and for the date the report was submitted. We cite the second date.[11]

1
WARTIME STAFFING IN THE US

THE BEGINNING OF WORLD WAR I in Europe had an immediate effect on the United States and posed new challenges for the Bureau. As the great European powers, Germany, Austro-Hungary, Great Britain, France, and Russia plunged into war in 1914, President Wilson declared that the United States remained "impartial in thought as well as in action."[12] To escape marauding British warships, fifty-four German merchant ships and passenger liners sought refuge in US harbors, mainly in New York and Philadelphia.[13] The internment of the German merchant fleet required sailors to remain within the confines of the harbors. The Imperial German Navy's representative in the US, Naval Attaché Karl Boy-Ed, took care of pay and provisions, as well as maintenance of the ships. Most of the crews of the German ships were reservists who now were activated for the war effort.

The most pressing issues at the outbreak of the war for the Allies and the Central Powers were fund-raising and sourcing of supplies, supply of their respective naval assets in both the Atlantic and Pacific oceans, repatriating reservists, and propaganda, which in German was called "Aufklärungsarbeit," an "educational" effort.[14] Clandestinely, both the Allies and Germany also had "hurting the enemy" on their agenda. The Allies had distinct advantages in pursuing all of these goals: The day after Great Britain declared war on Germany, its navy cut Germany's transatlantic cables, effectively severing Germany's access to international finance, international communications, and its ability to transmit information such as war news to the United States. The UK also blockaded access to the North Sea in the first weeks of the war. Merchant ships destined for Europe had to submit to British searches and be guided through extensive minefields. Although illegal by international law, the British sea blockade effectively choked off German access to world markets by sea.[15]

Within a month, both warring camps swarmed the US with purchasing agents, spies, and propagandists. Command and control over these wartime personnel lay with the diplomatic corps of each nation. The respective ambassadors managed their accredited foreign service staff and regional consuls. Their respective governments also assigned attachés for specific departmental expertise, such as commerce, navy, and army affairs. Control over intelligence assets of the European powers overseas rested with the naval departments, thus elevating the role of the naval attachés to prime importance. Prior to the war, Washington was a backwater assignment as compared to representing the navy in the capital of a major European power. The Imperial German government, for example, before the war only assigned one naval attaché and one military attaché to all of North America.

Two months before the beginning of the war, Great Britain had assigned Naval Commander Guy Reginal Archer Gaunt to become naval attaché under Ambassador Sir Cecil Spring-Rice. The forty-five-year-old Gaunt, born in Ballarat, Australia, was one of the rising stars in the British Navy. He had joined the merchant marine at age fourteen and progressed to the Royal Navy in 1895.[16] His career as a naval officer progressed rapidly until a fateful night in December 1912, when he was in command of a new dreadnought, the HMS *Centurion*. While undergoing sea trials in the English Channel, the *Centurion* collided with and sank an Italian steamer, the SS *Derna*. All thirty-six souls on board perished.[17] Gaunt was subsequently court martialed, but found not guilty.[18] Still, his navy career was in tatters. The assignment to Washington in

Figure 2. HMS Centurion, 1918
Source: Creative Commons

1914 sought to allow the navy commander to cool his heels in the backwaters of the British empire. He had neither staff, nor any idea of how to pass the time. According to his memoirs, he "made himself agreeable in the society [...] and write voluminous reports to your Admiralty superiors, which are usually shelved and forgotten."[19] His assignment would assume a pivotal wartime role within a few months.

Guy Gaunt's German counterpart was the forty-two-year-old Commander Karl Boy-Ed.[20] The career naval officer began his assignment in North America in 1912. He spent the first year as naval attaché in Jamaica, the Panama Canal Zone, and Mexico, collecting information. While Gaunt had scant experience in intelligence matters, Boy-Ed had spent years in that realm. He collected and assessed intelligence in China just before the Boxer Rebellion caused an international military intervention in 1900. Working directly under Grand Admiral Alfred von Tirpitz between 1906 and 1909, Boy-Ed headed the Nachrichtenabteilung N, Germany's department of naval intelligence. Before his assignment to North America, Boy-Ed went back to sea and sailed as first officer on the German battle cruisers SMS *Deutschland* and SMS *Preussen*.[21]

Boy-Ed and Gaunt knew and, according to Gaunt, liked each other before the war. Gaunt wrote in his memoirs: "He was a big, heavily built fellow, speaking excellent English, and we quickly contracted a friendship [...]."[22] Boy-Ed, just like his British counterpart, enjoyed the social life of Washington, DC, and New York. While more reserved and shyer, the German naval commander was popular and well respected

Figure 3. Virginia Mackay-Smith, c. 1910-1915
Source: Library of Congress Prints and Photographs Division

among American naval officials before the war, who perceived him to be funny, cosmopolitan, and intellectual. In the beginning of 1914, the until-then-single naval officer began dating Virginia Mackay-Smith, the daughter of a prominent Episcopal bishop in Pennsylvania. The couple would eventually marry in 1921 in Germany.[23]

The German embassy also assigned a representative of the Imperial War Department to North America. Franz von Papen, seven years Boy-Ed's junior, came to North America in the spring of 1914. Just as Boy-Ed had, the military attaché spent his first months in Mexico, where he witnessed firsthand the American occupation of Veracruz in April as the guest of General Frederick Funston. The ambitious young military attaché reported perceptively and in voluminous detail on the military organization and preparedness of the US expeditionary force. Traveling with the Mexican military factions battling the federal government in the civil war gripping Mexico, von Papen witnessed the fall of Mexico City, marking the last throes of President Huerta's rule; Huerta fled into exile on July 14, 1914.[24] The military attaché also reported on the amounts, types, and origins of the weapons and ammunition that had precipitated the American occupation of Veracruz.[25] The military supplies did not represent, as many historians have alleged, German military support for the Huerta regime, but rather originated in the United States and were privately funded.[26] In the battle for Mexico City in June, von Papen spearheaded the self-defense of the German community of Mexico City, which earned him accolades, not only among the Germans in Mexico, but also

Figure 4. Captain Franz von Papen, 1915
Source: Underwood and Underwood
US National Archives and Records Administration

from the Imperial Foreign Office.²⁷ He rushed to the United States in August to assume his wartime responsibilities.

Von Papen, scion of a prominent and wealthy Westphalian noble family, was an archetypal Prussian Junker. In line with primogeniture rules, von Papen's older brother took over the family estate, while he served in the military. The young officer joined the cavalry, became an expert equestrian and competed internationally for the German army. Many competitions in the early 1900s took place in Great Britain, and is there that von Papen learned English. In 1908, he went and briefly joined the Great General Staff of the Imperial Army with the rank of captain before he received his overseas assignment.²⁸ Although married since 1905 with four children, the dashing, overly self-assured, and charming German military attaché was rumored to be especially popular with young ladies.

As soon as the European war started in August 1914, the German government dispatched two more government agents to execute the wartime assignments in the United States. One of them, Heinrich Friedrich Albert officially worked for HAPAG (the Hamburg-Amerikanische-Paketfahrt-Aktien-Gesellschaft) shipping line on loan to the German Interior Ministry as head of the "Purchasing Agency" in New York. Only in May 1915 did Albert become Commercial Attaché, a move largely motivated to protect him with diplomatic cover for criminal activities. Within days of Albert's arrival, Bernhard Dernburg, former colonial secretary of Germany, disembarked at New York, together with German Ambassador Johann Heinrich Count von Bernstorff, who returned from his summer vacation. Dernburg brought with him millions of dollars'

Figure 5. *Johann Heinrich Count von Bernstorff*
Source: Library of Congress Prints and Photographs Division

worth of German war bonds to be sold in the United States to finance operations during the war. Albert's job was to invest these funds in supplies for the German war effort, propaganda, and clandestine work. As the German forces became bogged down in a two-front war, the war bonds found fewer and fewer investors in the US. Thus, fundraising became the fourth major pillar of Albert's mission.

Both Gaunt and the two German attachés in New York had to establish clandestine capabilities as quickly as possible to gather intelligence, disseminate propaganda, and thwart the other side's missions. For Gaunt, finding secret agents was more of a challenge since the British government had no such personnel in the US. He turned to private detective agencies, most notably the William J. Burns International Detective Agency of New York, an organization until then mostly involved in strike-breaking and union-busting. Burns operated a large group of agents along the waterfront, which now hosted dozens of interned German ships with thousands of reservists whom Gaunt needed to monitor closely.[29] Also important for the British naval attaché was the security of British freighters and passenger liners, arriving and departing daily from Boston, New York, and Philadelphia. The Mooney and Boland Detective Agency and several smaller private detective companies shadowed German agents and provided intelligence on US labor organizations suspected of cooperating with German agents.

Bill Burns's nemesis was a heavy-set ruffian who headed the police department of the HAPAG shipping line. In New York, Paul König, or P. K. as he was known in the docks, ran a group of detectives estimated to comprise twenty-five men. They provided security for German ships and investigated theft, smuggling, stowaways, and such.[30] The HAPAG police also conducted background checks of German crews. P. K. thus had files on hundreds of HAPAG employees, knew US and Latin American harbors like the back of his hand, and, according to journalist John Price Jones, "was a sort of boss, an unmerciful autocrat in the lower world, physically fearless, trusting no man and driving every man to work by the use of violent, abusive language[...]."[31] In short, just the man von Papen needed to counter the Burns operatives on the docks. P. K. headed the "Bureau of Investigation," with a Pier Division (security in the harbor), a Special Detail Division (security for embassy, consulates, attaché offices, HAPAG offices), and the Secret Service (intelligence-gathering, sabotage, shadowing of enemy personnel).[32] Despite the rough edges of von Papen's intelligence head, P. K. was an effective secret agent: He was a trained and disciplined investigator and intelligence analyst, who quickly weaponized his existing detective agency to become an effective counterintelligence and intelligence-gathering organization for the German government.

Karl Boy-Ed benefitted from P. K.'s organization, but also maintained his own intelligence assets. One of the most important agents working directly for Boy-Ed was Felix A. Sommerfeld, who reported on arms contracts the Allies were concluding in the US.[33] Sommerfeld also kept the naval attaché up-to-date with respect to the Mexican Revolution and the disposition of the US government vis-à-vis certain factions and events. Gaston B. Means, officially an employee of Bill Burns, but a career conman and "spectacular rogue," signed up with Boy-Ed as an agent, promising information on British activities.[34] It is doubtful whether Boy-Ed trusted a self-proclaimed double agent. Means lasted only a few months and was fired when he overstepped his orders and acted as a German agent provocateur.[35] As virtually all the crews on the interned German ships were naval reservists, Boy-Ed also had a large contingent of personnel for secret missions at his disposal, which came in handy in the spring of 1915.

Figure 6. Paul Koenig, aka P. K.
Source: US National Archives and Records Administration

An organization that remained largely in the shadows during the war, but proved to be a highly effective source of intelligence and counterintelligence for Gaunt and his superiors was the Bohemian National Alliance, founded on September 6, 1914.[36] Headed by a Czech-American businessman, Emanuel Viktor Voska, the Alliance sought to organize Czech (and after October 1915 also Slovak) nationalists in the US to support the Allied war effort and to eventually achieve statehood in case of the Central Powers's defeat.

Voska organized a highly effective intelligence organization using the human resources of the Alliance. He fielded over eighty agents in New York and Chicago, the largest Czech immigrant communities in the US.[37] Born in Kutna Hora, Bohemia, fifty miles east of Prague, the now thirty-eight-year-old stonemason and sculptor had emigrated from Bohemia to the US in 1894.[38] He became an American citizen in 1902.[39] Five-foot, seven inches tall, broad shouldered with brown eyes, a large square, determined chin, and a "rather flat and large nose," Voska cut a powerful figure, brimming with determination and grit to succeed in his chosen country.[40] In New York, Voska started virtually penniless. From street vending and dish washing, he worked himself up to become the owner of a decorative marble business. Attending college business classes at night, Voska expanded his business to own not only a workshop but also several quarries, from which he extracted marble.[41]

Figure 7. Emanuel Viktor Voska, before 1921
Source: Creative Commons

Voska arrived in New York on September 4, 1914, from London. He was returning from a four-month trip to Prague, where he had met the future president of Czechoslovakia, Thomas Masaryk, as well as Brussels and London, where he synchronized his plans with exiled Czech, Slovak, and Serbian nationalist leaders. His task was to support the global efforts of the Slavic peoples to help defeat the Austro-Hungarian Empire and achieve statehood after the war.

Voska founded regional organizations in the US that supported Czech language newspapers and Czech and Slovak businesses to unify in support of the Allies. His intelligence organization successfully infiltrated German and Austrian businesses and organizations. Nominally, Voska's agents were

Austro-Hungarian nationals and spoke German either as their primary or secondary language. As a result, Voska placed Czech and Slovak agents and informants in the Austro-Hungarian consulate in New York, HAPAG, and in the office of Heinrich F. Albert, to name a few.[42] In the fall of 1914, Voska offered his organization's services to the British government, just as his fellow patriots in Europe had. Guy Gaunt was only too glad to accept.[43] It was a good deal for the British. Selling his marble quarries, Voska financed his organization from personal funds for the first two years.[44]

With secret agencies in place, able to monitor each other's activities, the next big task was to establish effective propaganda. For Gaunt and the British ambassador, this task had succeeded to a large degree with the cutting of Germany's transatlantic cables. Virtually all news from the front came to the US through British censors. Not entirely undeserved, but helped along by British propaganda, Germany appeared on the front pages of American dailies in a decidedly bad light. The invasion of neutral Belgium in mid-August and the subsequent brutal suppression of its resistance, as well as the destruction of invaluable cultural treasures exacerbated the losses in the field with an utter propaganda defeat in the US. The American public, lapping up the one-sided British news, rooted for the underdog Belgian resistance fighters standing tall against the overwhelming "Hun" forces.

In the absence of German ambassador Count Johann Heinrich von Bernstorff until well into September, without a plan, and without an organization to counter the effective British

Figure 8. Bernhard Dernburg, c. 1910-1915
Source: Library of Congress Prints and Photographs Division

propaganda, well-respected professors at Ivy League universities took charge of Germany's messaging. Psychologist Hugo Muensterberg, Germanist Kuno Franke, historian Edmund von Mach, and political scientist John Burgess published editorials espousing a superior German "Kultur" and race that would make a German victory a foregone conclusion.[45] If the American public had still been open-minded and nuanced about war guilt, the illegal British sea blockade, and a German side to explain the disastrous war, the professors' racial, cultural, and historical German superiority argument killed whatever sympathies still existed in the US. The first month of German propaganda was an unmitigated disaster.

Slowly digging out of the mess but arguably never recovering from the bad image of the first month of the war, Bernhard Dernburg took the responsibility for organizing German propaganda. He hired staff, controlled the message, and sent German-friendly newsletters to American editors across the country. The former colonial secretary also spoke English well and made a good impression on audiences when he gave talks. The task of turning the propaganda tide in the US, however, was insurmountable: The atrocities of an aggressive war, the imperialist, anti-democratic Prussian system of government, a largely Anglophile educated class in the US, including the president and most of his cabinet, all worked against the German cause, even if British propaganda had not been so effective.

Despite the tremendous advantages British propagandists had in the US, Guy Gaunt wanted more. While sympathizing with the Allies for the most part, the American public was weary of the British sea blockade restricting trade with Central Europe. The fall of 1914 saw a severe recession in the United States with unemployment rising and industrial production slumping. Especially farmers and businesses in the South saw the British blockade as a major blow to exporting cotton to Central and Northern Europe. Gaunt recognized the potential for German propagandists to capitalize on the rumblings in the business community and among American labor. Great Britain wanted the American public to pressure its government to join the war on the side of the Allies. Gaunt had his work cut out for himself. He needed editorial control of the British message in order to succeed, and an outlet for precisely targeted intelligence that exposed German activities in the US. His prayers were answered in the person of John Revelstone Rathom, editor of the *Providence Journal*.

When and under what circumstances Rathom and Gaunt met remains unclear. Rathom's biographer, Mark Arsenault, doubts that Rathom met Gaunt at the onset of the war, but does not have an alternative set of facts.[46] The Bureau investigated Rathom's background and exposed his fraudulent

Figure 9. John R. Rathom, 1917
Source: Creative Commons

resumé, as well as the many invented stories he had published during the war.⁴⁷ In a lengthy undated memorandum, likely a brief for Attorney General Thomas Gregory in 1918, the investigators established that at the beginning of the war, the Providence Journal was in dire financial straits. As a result, Rathom and two executives of the paper traveled to Washington, DC, and had a meeting with "a member of the British Government, at which time it was alleged a fund was set aside by the British Government, guaranteeing the 'Providence Journal' against loss through publishing articles exposing German propaganda…"⁴⁸ British Naval Attaché Guy Gaunt confirmed the story in his memoirs, the meeting in the British embassy (albeit "by chance"), and the deal that he would provide Rathom with the "low-down."⁴⁹ Rathom personally was also hard-up for cash but miraculously, within months of the beginning of World War I, his debts in Chicago vanished.⁵⁰

A year younger than Gaunt, Rathom was of dubious character sporting an invented name and past. Born as John Solomon in Melbourne, Australia, Rathom's early career is still a mystery. His claims of serving in the Chinese navy and being a war correspondent in Sudan in the 1890s proved to be untrue. It seems that he lived in Astoria, BC, came to the US sometime around 1898, and worked in San Francisco and Chicago. In each of these locations, he left a trail of unpaid bills and criminal accusations.⁵¹ He became an American citizen in 1906. As a newspaperman in San Francisco and Chicago, he appeared to have distinguished himself as an investigative journalist, a talent which, despite being fired from a San Francisco newspaper, enabled him to join the Providence Journal as editor in 1906. By 1912 he had become editor and general manager.

He met Gaunt in the fall of 1914, likely as a result of the British military attaché disputing one of Rathom's scoops about him.[52] Rathom offered to be Gaunt's editorial outlet, under the cover of operating his own "army" of agents and informers. The real "army" was composed of Voska's men, the Burns detectives, and Gaunt. Rathom also had close contact with the editors of the New York Times, which would famously publish his stories with the introductory sentence "The Providence Journal will report today[...]" or even "The Providence Journal will report tomorrow[...]."[53] Most importantly for Guy Gaunt, Rathom established close contact with Bureau Chief A. Bruce Bielaski in late 1915 and became a prime conduit of British intelligence for the Bureau.[54]

2

THE GREAT SUPPLY MISSION

THE MOST PRESSING TASK for Commander Karl Boy-Ed at the beginning of the war was to supply the battered remnants of the German fleet in both the Atlantic and Pacific oceans. The British Navy had effectively bottled up the German High Seas Fleet at Wilhelmshaven and Kiel, and patrolled international waters off the US, Central and South America. German men-of-war could not resupply in neutral harbors in the Americas, while British warships received supplies from Canada, British Honduras, various British domains in the Caribbean, the Falklands, and Australia. The first clandestine and illegal operation German officials undertook in the United States in 1914 was to procure coal and supplies, then hire ships in American harbors, and send the materiel under false manifests to rendezvous with German warships in international waters. The logistics of this operation were complex and vulnerable to discovery by US customs and law enforcement. Indeed, it only took weeks for the scheme to come to light, when British officials furiously complained to the US government and alerted the press.[55] Despite the publicity, the Bureau did not start an investigation until well after the supply mission had ended with the sinking of the German fleet in the Battle of the Falklands in December 1914, and the self-internment in Norfolk, Virginia, of the last German raiders in the Atlantic, the *Prinz Eitel Friedrich* in March, and the *Kronprinz Wilhelm* in April, 1915.[56]

The supply of the German fleet was profitable business for the US and did not rise to a serious national security issue. It was also a massive operation for which German Naval Attaché Boy-Ed had received $1.2 million in funding (approximately $25.4 million in today's value).[57] After the German commercial fleet either made it back to home stations, or self-interned in neutral harbors overseas in the first weeks of the war, several navy cruisers remained at sea:[58] The SMS *Dresden*, SMS *Scharnhorst*, SMS *Gneisenau*, SMS *Karlsruhe*, and the SMS

Leipzig initially covered the Caribbean and South American regions before sailing into the Pacific theatre. The SMS *Leipzig* joined the SMS *Nürnberg*, and SMS *Emden*, and raided the Pacific coasts of the United States, Mexico, Central and South America.

Two converted liners, *Prinz Eitel Friedrich*, and *Kronprinz Wilhelm*, also roamed international waters off North America as auxiliary cruisers. These battle cruisers outfitted several German merchant ships with deck guns, and sent them to sink unsuspecting enemy steamers. They were the "gunboat *Eber* and the converted cruisers *Santa Luccia*, *Cape Trafalgar*, *Eleanor*, *Wörmer*, and *Pontus*."[59] The unarmored cruiser, *Geier*, self-interned on October 15, 1914 in Hawaii with engine trouble after raiding in the Pacific for months.[60] The SMS *Planet*, a German surveying ship self-interned in Guam and was also supported by Boy-Ed's finances. Both ships are listed in Boy-Ed's accounts.[61]

The extent of Boy-Ed's supply operation was revealed in the eventual trial of HAPAG (in the US known as the Hamburg-America Line) managers who were involved in the false manifesting of supply cargo. The Hamburg-America Line was Germany's largest commercial shipping line. Its founder was Danish-German Albert Ballin, a visionary leader who built his company from a small mail transport line to become a giant in transatlantic shipping and luxury cruising. Interned in the New York harbor among dozens of HAPAG's ships, lay Albert Ballin's pride and joy, the largest luxury liner ever built at that time, the SS *Vaterland*. Launched in January 1914, she had crossed the Atlantic only a few times before she became stranded in New York.

Figure 10. Karl Boy-Ed. c. 1910-1915
Source: Bain News Service Collection
Library of Congress Prints and Photographs Division

Through the US affiliate of HAPAG, and under the authority and collaboration of its managing director, Dr. Karl Bünz, Boy-Ed leased a fleet of merchant ships. Deliberately misstating their destination and purpose to American authorities, these ships met with German raiders on the high seas and transferred coal and other supplies, including arms, to the warships.[62]

Boy-Ed's accounting dated November 7, 1914, lists $43,290 for "coals and supplies for D. Patagonia, D. Spreewald, D. Präsident, D. Stadt Schleswig."[63] Officers of HAPAG signed these shipping documents under oath with fictitious destinations and cargoes.

In addition to seconding HAPAG to help the German navy, Boy-Ed also activated the North German Lloyd, HAPAG's competitor headquartered in Bremen. The representative of the North German Lloyd was the A. Schumacher and Co. firm, owned by Henry Gerhard Hilken and his son, Paul. The Hilken family was a respected German-American family that had

Figure 11. Karl (Carl) Gottlieb Bünz (Buenz), c. 1910-1915
Source: Bain News Service Collection
Library of Congress Prints and Photographs Division

lived in Baltimore since 1868. The A. Schumacher and Co. offices were located in the Hansa Haus at the northwest corner of Charles and German (now Redwood) Streets. The Hansa Haus also housed the German and Swedish consulates. The junior partner, Paul Hilken, "a boyish looking man in his mid-thirties with a mustache," had attended Lehigh University and MIT to study ship building.[64] Paul was slated to run the North German Lloyd's business in North America as managing director starting in January 1915.[65] It was not to be. The British sea blockade stopped all German shipping starting in September 1914. Hilken, a reservist of the Etappendienst (German naval intelligence), was summoned by Boy-Ed to help save the German navy in the Atlantic. Hilken would play a more notorious role in the destruction of Black Tom Island in 1916.

The naval attaché's fleet consisted of twenty-seven documented ships.[66] Without a doubt, a host of additional ships sailed under Boy-Ed's direction and finance. An article in *The New York Times*, dated August 22, 1914, illustrates the semi-public operation:

> Philadelphia, Aug. 21. — The North German Lloyd steamship *Brandenburg* today took out clearance papers for Bergen, Norway, but was still anchored below this city at a late hour tonight. It is said that she has taken aboard 10,000 tons of coal. This has been placed everywhere, even being piled in the staterooms and on deck. The Captain explains that this big supply is necessary because it will require two months to steam to Bergen. It is also stated that enough provisions have been taken on board to feed the crew for a year. Considerable comment was caused by the character of the cargo, which shipping men declare contains many articles never before exported from this port for Norway. It includes sauerkraut, würst [sic], canned herring, canned sardines, and fifteen half barrels of beer. Canned goods of every description and other provisions, with smoking tobacco, cigars, pipes, wines, and liquors compose the bulk of the cargo in addition to the coal.[67]

She sailed on the 22nd, cunningly evaded the three British cruisers lying in wait, and offloaded her supplies to a German raider just off the coast of Delaware.[68] Neither customs officials nor the Bureau appear to have investigated the reports.

The German navy had far more assets in the Pacific, which had to be supplied. The German agent in charge of leasing and manning the German supply ships on the US west coast for Boy-Ed was Frederick Jebsen. The *Mazatlán* and another supply ship, the *Alexandria*, belonged to Jebsen's front company for the German government, the "Northern and Southern Navigation Company."[69]

Jebsen was a shipping magnate in San Francisco with a colorful history. Born on May 21, 1881 in Appenrade, Denmark, son of Michael Jebsen, a wealthy German ship owner, Jebsen joined the German navy in 1898. He left as a lieutenant (*Fähnrich zur See*) in 1902 and emigrated to the US. His father's business transferred to Jebsen's three siblings after Jebsen, Sr. passed away in 1899. A high-risk gambler, Jebsen invested in commercial steamers in the recession of 1908 just when investors exited the industry in droves. The money for his ventures came from his German brothers who had financial interest in all of his undertakings in the US. According to the official German navy obituary,

"[...] after working for a few years as a [commercial] captain, he started his own business first in Seattle then in San Francisco, and after a few disappointments became very successful [...] At the beginning of the 1. World War he supplied the German squadron of Count Spee with coal..."[70]

Young, six-foot, six-inches tall, slim, with curly hair, single, and highly social, the flamboyant German-American investor turned the Jebsen Line into a fabulous success.[71] San Francisco papers marveled at Jebson's business acumen and eagerly reported on lavish parties the shipping magnate hosted on

Figure 12. Black Tom Island explosion, 1916
Source: Mixed Claims Commission

his vessels.[72] The "Adonis of the local shipping world" was hands-on, sailing on his ships to round up business in the middle of the Mexican Revolution.[73] His ships called mostly on the Pacific coast harbors of Mexico and Central America. Jebsen lived in a "palatial" home in one of the nicest neighborhoods of San Francisco, sharing the residence with Baron von Berckheim, a diplomat attached to the German consulate general.[74] For pleasure, he competed in the California horse show circuit and was a member of all the right country clubs.

Throughout his career, the shipping tycoon maneuvered through recession, revolution, and attempts of competitors in the coffee trade to outwit him.[75] His business flourished in the face of adversity, mainly because of its idealistic, dedicated, risk-taking, and creative leader. Jebsen, a naval reserve officer at the outbreak of the war, came under the command of Karl Boy-Ed. Immediately, his fleet of a dozen steamers, tenders, and schooners joined the supply organization of the German navy. Jebsen's supply operations not only encompassed the Pacific coasts of the United States, Mexico, and Central America, but also fueled and supplied German battle cruisers as far away as Singapore and the Philippines.

Jebsen's ships typically sailed under the American flag. He also maintained several vessels under the Mexican flag for his business there. The leased steamer *Jason* flew the Norwegian colors. Jebsen purchased the ship in the spring of 1914, and renamed her *Mazatlán*. One of his first business ventures using the large steamer was with the German government. When fighting in the Mexican Revolution threatened the German expatriate communities of Guaymas and Mazatlán, the German envoy to Mexico, Admiral Paul von Hintze, leased the *Mazatlán* to take German refugees to San Francisco. She took not only Germans on board, but on April 25, 1914 also carried ninety-two American refugees, an operation that endeared the German skipper to the San Francisco print media.

The German navy turned Jebsen's fleet into the supply armada for the Pacific squadron when the war started.[76] Through a mishap, or through the manipulation of British intelligence agents, the *Mazatlán* and her colorful owner briefly crowned the headlines of US papers. When the SMS *Leipzig*, a light cruiser of the German navy, docked at San Francisco on August 18, 1914 to take on coal, she was only permitted a small amount as a result of the US neutrality laws.[77] Jebsen and the *Mazatlán* received orders secretly to rendezvous with the warship off the coast of Mexico and top off the battle cruiser's hold. While loading 9,000 tons of coal in San Francisco, the "[...] *Mazatlán* mysteriously caught fire while he [Jebsen] was cavorting with girlfriends, allowing firefighters and port authorities to discover the illegal cargo. Nevertheless, Jebsen got [the] *Mazatlán* out of US waters with two prostitutes aboard and rendezvoused with [the] *Leipzig* at the Mexican port of Guaymas. There British naval intelligence observed the coal transfer from shore, having been informed by the *Mazatlán*'s disgruntled telegrapher, an Englishman who had notified his country's consulate upon arrival in Guaymas."[78]

The next day, the British chargé d'affaires voiced a determined protest against the activities of the *Mazatlán* for openly supplying the SMS *Leipzig* and SMS *Nürnberg* just outside San Francisco Bay and further south along the Mexican coast.[79] Returning to her berth at San Francisco harbor a few months later, on October 5, Jebsen allegedly was arrested and detained for "violating the 'white slavery' act."[80] Not a single newspaper carried the story. If it was true, it might just have been the latest effort of British intelligence to discredit

Jebsen. Whether British propaganda or the embellishment of a historian, this nasty rumor entered the historiography as fact.[81] Jebsen sailed again within two weeks, further dispelling the rumor of legal troubles. Despite the risk and British attempts of sabotaging the effort, supplying the German fleet was a boon for Jebsen.

Another cog in the wheel of Germany's secret supply scheme were US-based businesses with international reach. Large international corporations such as HAPAG, North German Lloyd, and Bayer & Company provided badly needed cash for German missions at the beginning of the World War. German-owned US companies provided "loans" to the German government overseas, which then were reimbursed by the home offices in Germany. Using company cash from US sources to finance German government schemes, while receiving reimbursements in Germany, made the money flow virtually untraceable. With offices and banking connections in Berlin, New York, as well as in Central and South America, the senior partner of the prominent, New York-based coffee trading company, Wessels, Kulenkampff and Company, Gustav Kulenkampff, disbursed money for Boy-Ed's supply scheme in the fall of 1914. He secretly transferred an estimated $600,000 (approximately $12.6 million in today's value) to Jebsen in San Francisco, earmarked for supplying the German navy in the Pacific.[82] Boy-Ed's accounts also show a payment of $151,500 marked "for Manila" around the end of October.[83] With Jebsen's help, the German naval squadron under Admiral von Spee resupplied in the Philippines, then a US possession, in November for her last battle off the Falkland Islands.

Disguised as company investments, Kulenkampff also sent money to buy supply ships. Jebsen's companies acted as fronts to arrange for these purchases.[84] The *Mazatlán* was one of those ships. Originally, Jebsen had bought her in the spring of 1914 for $135,000. The low price resulted from the repairs she had undergone after she suffered extensive damage from a fire in March 1913.[85] When the war started, he turned the freighter over to the German navy for $80,000, $35,000 below his cost.[86] She registered under Jebsen's Lloyd Mexicano S.A. as SS *Mazatlán*, and made two voyages in 1914 for the German navy.

It took the Bureau until March of 1915 to become interested in the German supply operation, after the German Pacific fleet was destroyed and the supply mission had ended. By then, unrestricted German submarine war threatened US steamers, and German clandestine activities targeted the US and threatened national security. Although Boy-Ed's central role in the supply scheme quickly became obvious, diplomatic immunity prevented his indictment. Instead, prosecutors homed in on the seventy-two-year-old Dr. Karl Bünz, the Managing Director of HAPAG in New York. The estimated value of supplies, defined by British authorities as conditional contraband, amounted to more than $1.4 million (approximately $30 million in today's value), carried on twelve ships American investigators had identified.[87]

This was only a fraction of the total value of supplies. Heinrich Albert's accounts for Karl Boy-Ed additionally listed the expenditures for coal for the SMS *Dresden* in Veracruz, Mexico. Amazingly, the German manager of HAPAG in Mexico, Carl Heynen, who ran Boy-Ed's supply operation from Veracruz, was never implicated in the scheme. Heynen kept the operation going with Boy-Ed's generous financial support until the last German ship had been swept from the Atlantic. That Heynen remained under the Bureau's radar is especially astonishing since he joined the Albert office in 1915 and became one of the key German agents in the United States. Paul Hilken, as well, did not arouse the Bureau's interest in 1914. As investigators of the Mixed Claims Commission (established in 1922) showed in the late 1920s and 1930s, Hilken was one of the key conspirators in the explosion of Black Tom Island in July 1916.[88]

Jebsen eventually was indicted in 1915 for violating US neutrality laws, and the Bureau looked for him all the way into 1919,[89] to no avail. He fled the United States early in 1915 before he could be apprehended, volunteered for submarine service, and died on his first voyage.

The British government used the Burns Detective Agency and other local informants to uncover the German efforts, and applied public pressure through leaks to US papers, such as *The New York Times*. Within weeks of Boy-Ed and HAPAG's leasing of ships and purchasing of supplies, US papers broke the story based on British leads.[90] Regional British consuls also filed official complaints with local customs officials. Furthermore, the British Foreign Office threatened the Cuban government with severe consequences if it did not stop supplying the German raiders.[91] The money obviously was too good to pass up, and the supply mission from Cuba continued unabated. The HAPAG liner, *Präsident*, called at Havana for supplies on a regular basis. The British navy finally sank her on January 17, 1915, much to the consternation of the local population.[92]

The public and official American backlash the British had envisioned as a result of the frequent newspaper leaks did not materialize. The US economy had slipped into a hard recession in the fall of 1914, which lasted into the spring of 1915. It is plausible that US government officials informed law enforcement agencies, in this case customs and the Bureau, to "slow walk" their investigations, just as had happened many times in the enforcement of neutrality laws on the Mexican border. Supplying the warring fleets was good money, after all. The inaction of law enforcement was also supported by jurisdictional complexity—customs issues fell under the Treasury Department. The falsified manifests presented a minor violation of the law and involved no real damages; purchasing and storing supplies was not illegal and did not constitute a neutrality law violation. That may have kept the Bureau from prioritizing the issue; resupplying ships in international waters also was not illegal in itself and did not trigger the US Navy or State Department to intervene, especially given the strict neutrality orders from the commander-in-chief.

When the Justice Department finally indicted senior HAPAG executives and several supercargoes (HAPAG officials on board of the ships directing the captain and crew) in March 1915, German officials were caught by surprise. Heinrich Albert, a lawyer, had assessed that falsifying manifests would present a minor infraction and would likely be ignored by the US government. Albert wrote that the US government expressed "extremely sensitive feelings of neutrality [...]. A false clearance is without a doubt an evasion of the American statistical authorities [...] there is no material damage [...]."[93] He was badly mistaken.

German officials from Ambassador Count Johann Heinrich von Bernstorff on down considered the US reaction to the naval supply missions and to attempts to ship non-military supplies (in the British definition conditional contraband, which indirectly could support the war effort, such as cotton, rubber, oil, and foodstuffs) as fundamentally biased towards British interests.

Figure 13. Heinrich Friedrich Albert, 1916
Source: Genthe Photograph Collection
Library of Congress Prints and Photographs Division

Karl Boy-Ed also assumed that the British fleet received supplies from US harbors, which fed into the argument that "everyone is doing it." After the indictment of the HAPAG executives in November 1914, Boy-Ed made it a priority to find proof of British naval supply missions from US soil in anticipation of American investigations. Evidence was hard to come by, however. Paul König and his investigators were tasked with finding out, but returned empty-handed. In his plight P. K. hired Gaston B. Means of the Burns Detective Agency in February of 1915.

Means, a disreputable character who will reappear prominently in a later volume of this series, promised to produce proof of British supply ships leaving from US harbors. That proof did not exist. So Means, likely with the knowledge and financial support of P. K., devised a scheme by which he would produce affidavits from collier and lighter captains, claiming that they had carried freight for the British and supplied the British Navy one mile off the shore of New York.[94] Together with a fellow Burns detective, Frank Garger, he went around the New York harbor and hired lighter captains who were willing to carry supplies to British ships. In all, he signed five boats, and had them stand by in the New York harbor. Although they never carried supplies to British ships, Means convinced the captains to sign affidavits to that effect.[95] Means had the documents typed up and witnessed by a Burns Agency lawyer, a man by the name of Holden, in a room in the Eastern Hotel in Whitehall Street.[96] He then submitted complaints with the false affidavits to the Collector of the Port in New York, Dudley Field Malone, an energetic thirty-three-year-old lawyer, who had received the job for working on President Wilson's campaign.

Instead of investigating the allegations, Malone took the affidavits at face value and went public with the claim that the British navy engaged in an "elaborate plot in violation of neutrality laws."[97] Newspapers quoted Malone as having requested to bring the case before a grand jury. According to the papers, he also received investigative support from Washington, DC, which implied that the Bureau was involved. Nothing of the sort happened. The New York District Attorney Hudson Snowden Marshall quickly announced that no charges would be filed in this case.[98] The Bureau records also do not show a case file for either Gaston B. Means or the false affidavit case.[99]

There are several reasons why a thorough investigation did not commence as the ruse became public. First and foremost, the false affidavits were not filed in a court or official proceeding and, therefore, did not rise to the level of a federal investigation. As thinly spread as the Bureau was in the spring and summer of 1915, it seems unlikely that Chief Bielaski would have invested significant resources into this tit-for-tat game between British and German interests in New York. In hindsight, however, the Bureau's lack of interest in this case was regrettable. Only months after the false affidavits became public, some of the same lighter captains participated in a devastating firebomb campaign that damaged or sank dozens of freighters. Gaston Means publicly declared that he was a German agent, even after Boy-Ed fired him.

Collector of Customs Dudley Field Malone likely had little interest in furthering the investigation, either. Within a day of the story breaking, the British Consul General in New York publicly denied that any of the alleged supply missions ever happened.[100] Several of the captains recanted their affidavits and admitted that they had not supplied the British navy.[101] As a political appointee, and already in trouble with Tammany Hall because of congestion in the harbor, Malone quietly closed the case. Like many other victims of Gaston B. Means, he had been had.

Heinrich Albert met Malone on a regular basis to discuss freight heading to Europe on neutral ships. It was at Malone's sole discretion to issue or withhold clearance papers on any ship. Tasked with circumventing the British blockade, which included hiding the origin and destination of German supplies, Albert really needed the friendly disposition of the powerful customs collector. Albert noted in his diary on July 1, 1915, "Breakfast with collector Malone. He is the head of the local port officials and thereby occupies one of the most important positions in the civil service[...] A very likable man[...] admires Bernstorff; Irish extraction."[102]

Not interested in a public scandal linking him to the fraud, and hoping to preserve the good graces of the collector of customs, Boy-Ed fired Means. Means, however, refused to go away and used his dubious role to gain notoriety. He continued to attract public attention in May 1915 with claims of being able to prove British neutrality violations, this time sourcing submarine parts in the US.[103] Not getting his job back with Boy-Ed, he then started to feed "information" about the German clandestine war to Rathom and Chief Bielaski between 1915 and 1917. Whether he continued to work for Burns during his stint as a German agent and British informer is unclear. Burns distanced himself, and steadfastly proclaimed that Means was acting on his own.[104] The fraudster's role as propagandist and informer ended abruptly in 1917, when he was accused of murdering an elderly lady for her inheritance. The subsequent trial ended in an acquittal for Means for lack of evidence that he shot his victim or that it was just an unfortunate accident.[105] One would think that his career may have ended there, but Means resurfaced in 1921 as a Bureau special agent, working for his old boss Bill Burns, who had become chief of the Bureau of Investigation. A Bureau case file on Means, which surely must have existed given his activities during the World War and would have served well in any sort of vetting process, conveniently disappeared and has not surfaced to this day.

The prosecution of the top HAPAG managers in the US was swift and surprisingly harsh. The project turned into Managing Director Karl Bünz's personal nightmare. He was indicted in March 1915, tried, and sentenced to penitentiary in November for conspiracy to defraud the United States involving false manifests.[106] The proud diplomat and business executive remained free at first, and later under house arrest, as his case wound its way to the Supreme Court. Finally, in bad health, Bünz started his sentence in 1918 but died of influenza in the Atlanta penitentiary two months after he was committed.[107] Karl Boy-Ed, on account of his diplomatic status, was never prosecuted. His managing role in the supply conspiracy presented clear violations of several US statutes; mainly conspiracy to commit fraud. He dedicated his memoirs to Dr. Bünz and included a chapter on the trial itself.[108] One can sense the regret the naval attaché must have felt for having brought such trouble upon his friend. Boy-Ed's involvement with this and other infringements of American law eventually caused his expulsion from the United States in December of 1915. German officials in the US and Germany saw the Bünz trial as an indication that the US, from the beginning of the war, sympathized with the Allies.

The Bureau's lack of interest in the matter until Germany engaged in a sabotage campaign against the US beginning in 1915 indicates that the US response to the activities of foreign agents on US soil was hampered by unclear divisions of jurisdiction. Just as on the Mexican border, the precise moment when neutrality laws were violated remained in dispute. The lack of aggressive investigations also indicated another lesson learned in neutrality law enforcement along the Mexican border: Federal law enforcement agencies acted within a political framework. In this case, the Bureau and customs favored American business interests over strict law enforcement and elected to stand back. Arguably, this lenient attitude emboldened the German officials to test the US's resolve.

3

Passport Fraud

BESIDES HAVING TO SUPPLY the remnants of the German fleet from overseas harbors, the Central Powers faced another challenge. With the outbreak of war, the German and Austrian governments called up reservists worldwide. Citizens had to report to the closest consulate and register for military service. Military Attaché Franz von Papen had responsibility for the German army call-up in North America. In response to questions from regional German consulates regarding what to do with the reservists, von Papen issued a circular in the first week of August requesting consulates in his jurisdiction to send reservists to his offices in New York. His Austrian colleague and he seemed to have planned to give these recruits some traveling money and place them on leased neutral liners for their journey to Germany.[109] As the reality of an effective British sea blockade became apparent, von Papen rescinded his orders on August 6. Too late. Tens of thousands of eager German reservists singing, "Die Wacht am Rhein" clogged the streets around his office at 11 Broadway.[110] New York police had to keep German and Allied supporters apart and break up fights that erupted between the two groups.[111] The enthusiastic German crowds thinned quickly as it became clear that there would be no transportation. There were also insufficient shelters willing to take in the reservists or feed them.

Von Papen's plan, even if the US had been willing to allow neutral liners to carry German reservists to Europe, a clear challenge to American neutrality, was doomed. Not allowing his enthusiasm to fall victim to pesky details, the German military attaché underestimated the sheer number of people he had planned on transporting to Germany. An employee at Oelrichs and Co., a freight forwarding company and agent of the North German Lloyd in New York, estimated that after von Papen's call to come to New York, "between 60,000 and 100,000 German reservists" waited to be shipped to the front.[112]

In addition to the impossible logistics, British authorities were already boarding any ship heading to Northern Europe as part of the blockade and would have pulled any male passenger with a German passport between the ages of sixteen and eighty off the ships for wartime internment.

Von Papen quickly shifted gears. Before the throngs of German reservists scattered and returned home, the German military attaché painstakingly had them registered with information as to their military value and skills. P. K. was in charge of vetting the candidates, a process with questionable results, as we will see. Von Papen selected several reservists to serve as potential clandestine agents, mostly in and around New York, but he also detailed some to regional German consulates in Baltimore, Chicago, San Francisco, and Seattle. One of the more notorious of such recruits in New York was Horst von der Goltz, who had come to New York from Chihuahua, Mexico. Another was the sabotage agent Werner Horn, who had come from Guatemala.

Figure 14. *Captain Horst von der Goltz, before 1919*
Source: International Film Service
US National Archives and Records Administration

Von Papen also decided to find a way to send army officers with special skills or war experience on their way to Germany. The most notorious of such officers was Hans Walter Luigi Boehm, who would conduct sabotage missions, carry top secret messages from Berlin to the US and Spain, and train Irish military prisoners in Germany for the 1916 Easter Rising.

The German military attaché used regional consulates not only to send agents on specific reconnaissance and intelligence gathering missions. Von Papen also asked the consuls for some "special" favors, such as helping to procure American passports for German agents and recruits to travel to the Fatherland. The most well-known example is the case of Horst von der Goltz, alias Bridgeman Taylor, alias Franz Robert Wachendorf, alias Otto Goltz. After he abandoned an assigned mission to dynamite the Welland Canal, which connected strategic shipping lanes between Lake Ontario and Lake Erie and circumventing the Niagara Falls, the German agent returned to New York. Whether von Papen planned for von der Goltz to go to Germany and be assigned elsewhere, or whether von der Goltz requested permission to leave for Germany is not known. Von Papen certainly had reason to get rid of the agent since he had utterly failed to carry out his mission and now possessed compromising information on the military attaché's role in the sabotage plot. Von der Goltz, according to his statement filed with British authorities, also was extremely paranoid and afraid to be discovered, which was the stated reason for his abandonment of the sabotage mission.[113] That could have been his motivation to leave the US. The third possibility, one that remains the most plausible and is supported by von der Goltz's activities before the war and from 1915 on, was that the German agent was not a German agent, after all. He was a soldier of fortune, willing to work for anyone on anything in his quest for recognition and fame.

Figure 15. Werner Horn, c. 1910-1915
Source: Bain News Service Collection
Library of Congress Prints and Photographs Division

At von Papen's behest, von der Goltz went to the German Consul, Carl August Lüderitz, in Baltimore in August 1914. Under the radar of American officials, the German consul, who worked for the A. Schumacher and Co., the North German Lloyd representative in Baltimore owned by the German-American Hilken family, had played an important role of registering and vetting the crews of interned German liners. Lüderitz also funneled agents to and from von Papen and the German sabotage cell around Paul Hilken that took shape in 1915. Using his secretary as a notary public, Lüderitz procured an American passport for von der Goltz under the name of Bridgeman Taylor, born in San Francisco of German and American parentage, and signed an affidavit as to the veracity of Taylor's identity.[114] He also took possession of von der Goltz's trunk containing a Mexican army uniform and a saber among other personal effects.

British authorities arrested von der Goltz on November 4, 1914, in London. British Ambassador in Washington, Sir Cecil Spring-Rice, filed an official complaint with the State Department that British authorities had captured von der Goltz traveling on a fraudulent American passport. "I have informed the State Department of all the facts, and they state that the Department of Justice is making enquiries with a view to apprehending and punishing the accomplices of von der Goltz."[115] The State Department indeed confirmed that a passport had been issued to Bridgeman Taylor based on an application made in Baltimore on August 29, 1914.[116] Department officials also notified the Justice Department and requested an investigation. It did not happen.

How the British lead could not have triggered an investigation is not documented. However, the pattern of the Bureau's lackadaisical approach to suspected German intrigue in the fall of 1914 until the declaration of unrestricted submarine warfare in February 1915, seems to repeat itself in this case. While it is documented that the British lead made it to the State Department, and from there to the Attorney General, whether Chief Bielaski was notified is not documented. Counselor Robert Lansing at least assumed that he was, when on December 23, 1914, he forwarded further proof of falsified passports to Attorney General Thomas Gregory. He wrote, "You are requested to have this matter investigated in connection with the investigations already being made by agents of your department concerning the fraudulent procurement of passports."[117] An investigation into fraudulent passports was indeed underway, just not in Baltimore.

If Attorney General Gregory discussed the issue with Bielaski, they may have decided that surveilling a German person under diplomatic protection was politically too hot. Especially in a case based on hearsay with a witness in England, who was unreliable from the onset. Lying on an affidavit was a peccadillo offense at best, especially when it involved a foreign diplomat. The other reason for not investigating the German consul could have been the agent in charge of the Baltimore field office. Billups Harris had recently taken over the office after transferring from the New Orleans field office. Bielaski had cleaned house there and installed the thirty-four-year-old Special Agent Forrest Currier Pendleton to take over. The ineffective Harris arrived in Baltimore in the spring of 1915 to a field office deemed mostly unimportant as compared to those in New York, Chicago, New Orleans, Los Angeles, or San Antonio, where Bielaski placed his best agents in charge. Considering Baltimore not important, and failing to pursue Lüderitz turned out to be a grave mistake as subsequent events showed.

One of the German reserve officers who successfully returned to the *Fatherland* in the early fall of 1914 was Hans Walter Luigi Boehm. Boehm, a first lieutenant of the Reserve, had settled in the United States in 1904. From a prominent family—his father had been the governor of Alsace-Lorraine and a close confidante of Kaiser Wilhelm II— young Hans, upon reaching the age of 21, inherited $55,000 from his grandmother, an Italian countess and likely the reason for Luigi in his array of first names.[118] The fortune (close to $2 million in today's value[119]) did not last very long. Boehm lost all his deposits when one of Germany's largest banks, the Dresdner Bank, crashed in 1898. Reeling from this setback, the twenty-five-year-old volunteered for the Imperial army. As a first lieutenant he served in an artillery unit, saw combat in China during the Boxer Rebellion, and ended with an assignment to the Imperial General Staff in Berlin. He retired in 1903 and emigrated to the US in search of the American dream.

Figure 16. *Captain Hans Walter Luigi Boehm*
Source: *www.irishbrigade.eu*

After living in New Jersey, Montana, and Illinois, the young reserve officer settled in Portland, Oregon, where he married and fathered two boys. Far from recreating his lost fortune, Boehm worked as a hotel clerk and manager of an athletic club. When the World War started, the reserve officer immediately applied to Military Attaché von Papen to return to active service and travel to Germany. Von Papen activated Boehm in September 1914 and arranged for his return to Germany in October. Boehm traveled on the passport of his lawyer friend, Joseph D. Woerndle of Portland, a German-American and naturalized citizen. Von Papen apparently had arranged for Boehm's photograph to be affixed instead of the image of the bespectacled young lawyer. Boehm, five-foot, eleven inches tall, blue eyes, with a pencil mustache, who spoke American English, French, and Italian fluently and without an accent, was destined to play a role in German intelligence.

While American authorities did not uncover the existence of Boehm, alias Woerndle, until 1917, the British submitted an important lead to the State Department in the fall of 1914, this time concerning criminal activities in New York rather than in Baltimore. That information triggered a successful counterintelligence investigation, interrupted an active conspiracy, and resulted in successful criminal prosecutions. In the middle of December, the British Foreign Office submitted to US ambassador to Great Britain, Walter Hines Page, the papers of a certain Charles Raoul Chattilon, an American citizen born in San Francisco and traveling to Italy. While Chattilon indeed existed, lived in San Francisco, and had been issued a legal American passport on November 12, 1914, he was not the man British authorities discovered on the SS *Duca de Aosta* in Gibraltar. Suspecting the American passport to be a forgery, British agents questioned Charles Chattilon. He turned out to be a Dr. Stark, a German reservist on his way to "report on conditions in Italy for *The New York Herald*."[120] The American Charles Chattilon had sold his passport to a good friend, a certain Hans Adam von Wedell in New York.[121]

At the beginning of November 1914, on the recommendation of Ambassador Count Bernstorff, Franz von Papen recruited a young New York lawyer from a prominent northern German noble family to work on a false passport scheme. Hans Adam von Wedell was born on July 7, 1880, in Marseille, France, where his father was the German consul. He came to the United States in 1907 as a student.[122] Three years later he married the German-American Lida Weiman in New York, then took her to Germany on their honeymoon, and presumably introduced his bride to family at his ancestral home in Schleswig-Holstein.[123] The couple returned in July 1910.[124] Von Wedell took out his papers and became an American citizen in May 1913.[125] While he studied law at Columbia Law School, the young baron worked as a "dramatic editor" and music critic.[126] In the spring of 1914, von Wedell, who clerked for Wise and Seligsburg, a prominent law firm in New York, was admitted to the New York bar.[127]

Von Wedell had good credentials; not only was he the scion of a prominent noble family in Germany, but he had also provided valuable services to the German ambassador Count Bernstorff. In the middle of September 1914, von Wedell made use of his own, legal American passport, and went to Germany as a messenger on behalf of the embassy.[128] He returned at the end of October with important messages from senior HAPAG officers and advisers of the emperor, Albert Ballin, and Admiral Henning von Holtzendorff, as well as personal letters from Ida Albert (Heinrich Albert's wife) and other embassy personnel.[129] At that point, von Papen entrusted the courageous young nobleman to devise a scheme by which German reservists could travel home on American and neutral passports.

Figure 17. Hans von Wedell and his Wife, c. 1914
Source: Project Gutenberg

Von Wedell set out to contact primarily German-Americans, who could legally apply for American passports. Providing them with blank applications, and using a notary to certify the signatures, but providing the photographs of travel-thirsty German reserve officers, von Wedell sent the papers to the State Department. He paid the volunteers $50 for their services. The operation quickly expanded from falsifying passports to include the purchasing of travel documents outright. In a newly established office on Bridge Street in Brooklyn, only blocks from the Navy Yard, von Wedell had a handful of employees match the acquired passports with reserve officer names provided by von Papen's office. The reservist's photograph was exchanged for the original, carefully matching age, height, and other details. Through the office of

Oelrichs and Company, von Wedell then obtained tickets on neutral steamers for the "American travelers."

The list of reserve officers desiring one of these passports was lengthy. Finding legal passports became the top priority. Soon, von Wedell trusted people he had not thoroughly vetted with sourcing the documents, not only from German-Americans, but also Swiss, Scandinavian, and Latin-American citizens. The endeavor quickly turned into a nightmare for the inexperienced young lawyer. Rather than bringing new passports and collecting on finder's fees, his buyers started blackmailing von Wedell. And, afraid of discovery, he complied. Predictably, the blackmailers increased their demands, and von Wedell paid. Within a few weeks, the German-American lawyer was in way over his head. Terrified of being discovered, he hid in his Manhattan apartment and around December 20 turned the business over to his main contact at Oelrichs and Co., Carl Ruroede.

It was on December 23, that the Counselor of the State Department, Robert Lansing, officially requested Attorney General Thomas Gregory to investigate the fraudulent passport of Dr. Stark. Gregory in turn notified Chief Bielaski.[130] The investigation had already begun in the middle of December. At Bielaski's request, Lansing sent to the Bureau a passport for a fictitious American citizen which could be offered for sale to whomever bought American passports in New York to falsify. The investigator assigned to the New York case was the thirty-three-year-old agent, Albert Garfield Adams. Adams, a tough Irish-American with blue eyes and blond hair, was born and raised in New York. Scars on his chest and a "cracked spine" attest to his having seen his fair share of violence.[131] With a broad Irish accent, he seemed a good fit for undercover work as John Aucher, of an Irish mother and German father, and undoubtedly, given the parentage, with strong German sympathies.[132]

Dr. Stark's fraudulent passport led to a notary public in Kings County, New York, Isidore Weckstein, and a lawyer named Maurice Deiches, as well as Carl Ruroede, a freight forwarding and booking agent for Oelrichs and Co. Agent Adams, who was already following leads into a rumored scheme that a German agent was buying passports for $50 apiece, learned that von Wedell had rented a room in the Elks Lodge No. 1 at 108 West 43rd Street in Manhattan a month earlier, on November 24.

Agent Adams quickly determined that the Hans Adam von Wedell identified in the British lead regularly bought passports in his one-room office at the Elks Lodge and had them modified to fit German reservists at an office in 8 & 10 Bridge Street in downtown Brooklyn. That was the office of the Oelrichs and Co. manager, Carl Ruroede, Sr. Ruroede, a man in his mid-50s, seemed an unlikely criminal. Working in the booking department at Oelrichs, he had a solid job, a nice home, was married, and had three children, the oldest of whom, Carl Jr., seventeen years old, helped him in the office.

As it later became clear, von Wedell had been warned of his impending discovery and arrest warrant. While the British government forwarded the Stark papers to the State and Justice Departments, German Military Attaché von Papen received a telegram from someone who had witnessed the arrest of Stark. Von Papen advised von Wedell on December 16 to stop work and, if possible, flee, which he did ten days later.[133] Division Superintendent William Offley decided to throw all available investigative resources into the mix. He put Assistant Superintendent Baker in charge of the investigation. Baker summoned Agents Scully, Adams, Jentzer, McGee, and Tucker to work the case. Agent Tucker was in charge of following von Wedell, while Adams and the others shadowed Ruroede. When Agent Tucker finally tried to contact von Wedell on December 29, he found out that the German agent had left his apartment (and wife) in a hurry three days before, carrying luggage. With von Wedell gone, the investigation took on additional urgency. Were the other conspirators about to flee, as well?

Figure 18. Hans Adam von Wedell, c. 1914
Source: Project Gutenberg

Agent Adams, under cover as John Aucher, had Ruroede under control. In a brilliant move, Adams took advantage of a huge problem that von Wedell had left behind: the blackmailers. Adams was able to identify one of von Wedell's blackmailers as a man named Correll. His real name was John Patrick

Corrigan, an Irish American listed in the US Census of 1910 as an "office boy," in 1920 as a "huckster," and in 1940 as a "collector" and jewelry store owner.[134] Ruroede had paid Correll $100 of von Papen's money to get rid of him.[135] Agent Adams alias John Aucher approached Ruroede as one of Correll's sources of passports, badmouthed the blackmailer, and ingratiated himself with the German agent who desperately needed a new source of passports on December 24. The two met at Davidson's Coffee Room on Broad Street in Brooklyn.[136] As luck would have it, Aucher had a fresh American passport issued to a Howard Paul Wright, which he promptly sold to Ruroede in front of Agents Tucker, McGee, and Jentzer, who occupied several nearby tables in the restaurant. The passport was the one the State Department had provided to the Bureau in New York.[137]

The working relationship progressed quickly as Aucher produced four more pristine American passports on December 28.[138] The German trusted the burly Irishman and showed him the falsification process at Bridge Street. The other agents assigned to the case closely shadowed Ruroede who went back and forth between his Oelrichs office in the Maritime Building and Bridge Street where he worked on the passports. On December 30 and again on December 31, the agents who shadowed Ruroede and Aucher witnessed the transfer of four more passports and the exchange of money.[139] The plan was in place. Chief Bielaski sent Agent John J. Grgurevic from Baltimore as a reinforcement on January 1, 1915.[140] Agents Scully, Klawans, and Tucker covered the lawyer Maurice Deiches, two of the people that had procured passports for von Wedell, and Baroness von Wedell. Agents McGee and Scully shadowed Ruroede,

Figure 19. Carl Ruroede, c. 1914
Source: Project Gutenberg

his son, and John Aucher. Agent Jentzer procured the passenger list of the SS *Bergensfjord*, a Norwegian liner, on which Ruroede had booked passage for the fake passport holders.[141] Agents LoMedico and Pigniuolo stayed at the harbor and awaited the Norwegian liner.[142]

At 1:05 p.m. on January 2, Assistant Bureau Superintendent Baker, Agents Grgurevic, Cantrell, McGee, and Tucker arrested Ruroede, his son, and Agent Adams (who remained undercover as John Aucher) at his office in the Maritime building in Brooklyn.[143] The attempt to nab lawyer Maurice Deiches failed, since he had left for Germantown, Pennsylvania to visit family.[144] Agents Tucker and Klawans, however, were able to arrest the two suspects who had procured passports for von Wedell.[145] Using a customs cutter, Agents Grgurevic and Jentzer boarded the Norwegian-America liner, SS *Bergensfjord*, on its way to Europe, and arrested the four reservists who held the fake passports issued by the State Department. They missed Hans Adam von Wedell. Without a photograph of the German agent, Grgurevic and Jentzer could not identify von Wedell using a fake passport in the lineup. Passenger "Rosato Sprio" was allowed to proceed.[146]

The operation was a resounding success for the Bureau, nonetheless. In light of the voluminous secondary literature about this time period claiming a counterintelligence role for the US Secret Service, it was not even peripherally involved in these counterfeit passport cases.[147] Eleven defendants including Ruroede, his son, Maurice Deiches, the two passport buyers, and the four reservists were indicted and sentenced in March 1915. Ruroede received three years in the penitentiary. The reservists received a $200 slap on the wrist for traveling on fake documents. The only one who got away was Hans Adam von Wedell. British officers identified him when they boarded the *Bergensfjord* off Northampton. Taken prisoner, he was being transferred to the mainland when the British auxiliary cruiser hit a mine and sank, taking with it the hapless Hans Adam von Wedell.[148]

4

Attacks on Canada

The Great Armada

NOVEMBER 4, 1914, a young man, age twenty-seven, five-foot, eight-and-a-half inches tall, with brown hair and blue eyes, clean shaven, disembarked from the SS *Batavia* steamer on the Tilbury Docks in London.[149] He had come from Rotterdam. The American passport he traveled under identified him as Bridgeman Taylor, born in San Francisco and on a business trip. He checked into a hotel. The next day, Taylor walked into a local police station and requested to be connected to the British Foreign Office as he had important intelligence to relay. The local police officer obviously was unimpressed and jailed him.[150] Upon further interrogation, Taylor admitted to being a German citizen with the name Horst von der Goltz.[151] His statements proved unreliable. The only fact that was undeniably true was his fraudulent American passport. Unable to prove that he was a spy, British authorities charged von der Goltz with having failed to register as an enemy alien, and sentenced him to a six-month prison term on November 13.[152]

While von der Goltz was cooling his heels in "the Villa," the Pentonville prison in North London, British authorities investigated further. Von der Goltz admitted to having left papers in a safe deposit box in Rotterdam, which an MI6 agent recovered a few days later.[153] The papers included his commission as a major in the Mexican army, and a "leave of absence" permission signed by Raúl Madero, a general in Pancho Villa's *División del Norte*.[154] British Foreign Secretary Sir Edward Grey asked the British minister to Mexico to substantiate von der Goltz's claims that he was a Mexican citizen and officer. While his army commission proved to be true, a certain Dr. Robert Emerson in Chihuahua, who had treated von der Goltz in prison in Chihuahua in 1913, also was convinced that the man was a "professional" German spy.[155]

A simple violation of immigration rules turned into a prison sentence, with deportation to Germany after having served. As will become obvious, von der Goltz definitely did not want to be deported to Germany. He decided to try once more to use his knowledge of German activities in the US, especially the information he had about Military Attaché Franz von Papen, to get out of prison and avoid deportation. He offered to work for British intelligence. On January 4, 1915, he petitioned to see Admiral Reginald "Blinker" Hall, the chief of British Naval Intelligence, on a "matter of great consequence."[156]

Von der Goltz promised to share vital information about German operations in the United States. Hall initially refused to see the agent. The naval intelligence chief requested that von der Goltz submit a sworn statement before agreeing to meet.[157] Von der Goltz filed a seven-page affidavit, detailing his work for the German military attaché von Papen in New York. He described the failed plot to blow up the Welland Canal, a critical Canadian waterway connecting Lake Ontario with Lake Erie. He told investigators how he had obtained dynamite from the Krupp representative in New York, Hans Tauscher, and how he had received the fraudulent passport from Consul Lüderitz, on which he had traveled back to Europe after the failed Welland Canal mission.[158] Hall agreed to a personal visit at Pentonville on January 18, after reviewing von der Goltz's statement.[159] Regrettably, the original transcript of the interview was not preserved. Still, as subsequent British propaganda in the US showed, the German agent had implicated von Papen as the mastermind of the conspiracy, the editor of the *Gaelic American* newspaper and Irish nationalist John Devoy, who supplied critical communication links for the plotters, and Hans Tauscher.[160] "Blinker" Hall, the wily intelligence master with a nervous twitch in his eyes, decided to use von der Goltz as a propaganda weapon against German interests in the United States.

By April 1915, von der Goltz had signed on to work for British intelligence, and his deportation order was duly rescinded.[161] The issue for Admiral Hall was that he did not have enough proof to disgrace von Papen and the rest of the German officials in the US. Von der Goltz was a shadowy character, at best, and other than his word, there was no physical proof that he had worked for von Papen or German military intelligence. Hall ordered his man in the US, Naval Attaché Guy Gaunt, to start disseminating details of the failed Welland Canal plot. The provincial, and hitherto unimportant *Providence Journal* suddenly broke major news.[162] For actual proof, Hall had to wait for more concrete details to surface.

The British Foreign Office also alerted the US State Department of the arrest and fraudulent passport. Despite repeated prodding by the British

Ambassador in Washington, Cecil Spring-Rice, to vigorously investigate this and other passport frauds in Baltimore, the Justice Department investigation into the strange case of Horst von der Goltz never happened.[163]

During the interrogations of von der Goltz in England, his story evolved. According to von der Goltz, he arrived in New York from the Mexican border at the end of August 1914.[164] Consul Otto Kueck of Chihuahua had sent him to report to Military Attaché von Papen. Once in New York, von der Goltz indeed met von Papen and offered his services.[165] The German military attaché assigned his young volunteer to a sabotage mission he was just organizing. The task was to prevent the Canadian expeditionary forces, some 83,000 men strong, from leaving for the European battlefields.[166] Troops from all over Canada assembled in Valcartier Camp just outside Quebec and awaited ships to take them down the Saint Lawrence River and across the Atlantic.

According to von der Goltz, the German plan was to sabotage the Welland Canal. Sabotaging the canal would interrupt a vital supply line for the troops in Quebec. Von Papen had also planned to send a second team, under P. K.'s command, to go to Quebec and sink several large barges in the middle of the Saint Lawrence River, which would render Quebec harbor unsuitable as a launching point for troop transport ships. Finally, German submarines and raiders were to lie in wait for the vessels as they entered the Atlantic to sink as many of them as possible.[167]

Von der Goltz's team of five under the leadership of Alfred Fritzen, a reserve lieutenant, was charged with dynamiting the locks in the Welland Canal. The second team of three agents under the command of Paul König would render Quebec harbor unusable. Both teams left in the middle of September. Von Papen provided money and Hans Tauscher suitcases packed with dynamite. Both teams reconnoitered their targets for a week. But around September 24, both teams returned to New York without having accomplished their tasks. Von der Goltz claimed that the German military attaché had cancelled the mission due to objections from German Ambassador to the US, Johann Heinrich Count Bernstorff.[168] There is no evidence for that, however. It seems more likely that, in view of the formidable protection of their targets by Canadian troops and police, the teams got cold feet. P. K. abandoned his mission, as well, and returned to New York, likely preferring his work in the US to virtually guaranteed discovery and court martial in Canada.

On October 3 and 24, 1914 "[...] the entire Armada, containing the largest military force which had ever crossed the Atlantic at one time, set sail for England. In three long parallel lines of about a dozen ships each, with flags flying and signals twinkling, it made an imposing sight for the handful of people who saw it off. On October 6 the convoy was joined at sea by a ship carrying the Newfoundland Regiment."[169] There were no raiders or submarines lying in wait for the ships. The German attempt to block the Canadian Expeditionary Force had totally collapsed.

Upon von der Goltz's return to New York, von Papen sent him to Germany. Using the Bridgeman Taylor passport, the agent left the United States on a neutral Italian steamer to Genoa on October 3, 1914, and arrived in Italy around October 20. Von der Goltz claimed that he proceeded from Italy to Berlin. What he did in Berlin, or whether he ever was even there, is unclear.[170] Casimir Pilenas, a British agent who had interviewed von der Goltz extensively in 1916, published an exposé two years later, in which he claimed that the German agent never went to Berlin, but offered intelligence to German agents in Rotterdam. When they refused, he went to England to peddle his information there. There is no further substantiation of this claim, but it seems plausible given that von der Goltz had only fifteen days between his arrival in Europe and appearance in England. It is a fact that von der Goltz travelled from Rotterdam to England on November 4, where he offered his services and intelligence to the British government, most likely expecting to be paid. Instead, he went to jail.

He did, however, become a British asset. His conviction and sentence included a deportation order back to Germany. Clearly, he did not want to go there, especially if he had offered intelligence to German agents and, after being unsuccessful, had gone on to England. After the interview with Admiral Hall, he made an agreement with British Naval Intelligence to provide information and, when called upon, to testify against German officials in the United States. In return, he would not be deported, but remain in British custody until the war's end. He was transferred to the more comfortable Brixton prison in South London, where inmates typically awaited trial.[171]

There is no record of von der Goltz's Welland Canal story to have made it to the Bureau of Investigation in 1915. The only official notification about the case had to do with the passport. It took British intelligence until January 1916 to find corroboration for von der Goltz's story. When Military Attaché von Papen, expelled from the United States in December 1915, was on his way back to Germany, British authorities seized his luggage at Falmouth and found cancelled checks to von der Goltz, as well as others on the sabotage teams.[172] Finally, Great Britain could prove that von der Goltz's story was true.

Admiral Hall now had what he needed to send von der Goltz to the US as a star witness against Hans Tauscher, and by extension, the entire German organization. British authorities published von der Goltz's prison statement a

ATTACKS ON CANADA

year later.[173] Von der Goltz testified in the trial of Hans Tauscher in May 1916. It did not go well. The prosecution's "star witness" had given widely publicized press interviews, exaggerating his role as a German spy, even suggesting that he reported to the Kaiser personally.[174] Tauscher's lawyer, Herbert C. Smyth, made mincemeat of von der Goltz's testimony and secured the acquittal of his client.[175] Yet, in a big win for von der Goltz, he was a free man after the trial and remained in New York during and after the war. He continued to fashion himself as a spy, and provided information to anyone looking for it, including on occasion to the Bureau of Investigation.

Interestingly, the Bureau never opened an investigation into von der Goltz. His case file, containing three sheets of paper, started in 1917, and contains no investigative results.[176] Neither is there a case file on Consul Carl Lüderitz, nor are there any reports about Lüderitz and the falsified passport issue from agents in Baltimore. It took eighteen months for Bureau agents to finally raid the residence of the German consul in Baltimore. Furthermore, the agents raided his residence, but not his offices in the center of Baltimore, the well-known (and now historical landmark) Hansa Haus. The building not only was the headquarters of A. Schumacher and Company, a front operation for German naval intelligence run by the German-American Paul Hilken, but also the German and Swedish consulates. The Hansa Haus was the center of German

Figure 20. Franz von Papen, December 12, 1915
Source: Underwood and Underwood
US National Archives and Records Administration

41

intrigue in Baltimore and in 1916, the place from where the conspiracy to blow up the Allied loading terminals in the New York harbor emanated. It seemed to have been blissfully ignored by the agent in Baltimore, Billups Harris.

Bureau agents raiding Lüderitz's home found a trunk belonging to von der Goltz, but no other incriminating evidence.[177] The investigation found no credible evidence that could dispute Lüderitz's steadfast denials of willfully having lied on the affidavit verifying Bridgeman Taylor as an American citizen known to the consulate. Lüderitz claimed that he never knew a Horst von der Goltz, and certified the veracity of Bridgeman Taylor's claims based on information he received from Franz von Papen. Von Papen, of course, was long gone by then and beyond the reach of American prosecutors. A grand jury indicted the German consul with an accusation that was based entirely on the testimony of von der Goltz.[178] It was a weak case, and records indicate that Lüderitz was never convicted. He continued to plot freely with Paul Hilken, his business partner, who with other conspirators blew up Black Tom Island just two months later.[179]

Britain used the von der Goltz testimony largely for propaganda purposes to influence the US public to support the American entry into the war. From the Bureau's perspective, the German agent who now was a British agent, did not commit any serious crimes. There was no law against reconnoitering Canadian installations. The dynamite the teams had with them never surfaced, although an investigation could have uncovered that Hans Tauscher, indeed, was the source, as cancelled checks in von Papen's captured luggage later proved.[180] To the Bureau, the Welland Canal was a Canadian affair. When asked what would be done with von der Goltz after he arrived in New York as a star witness on March 28, 1916, Bureau Superintendent William Offley bluntly stated that the German was "not wanted by the Department of Justice. He may be questioned as to the manner in which he obtained his passport [...], but I do not think he can be prosecuted here for anything he has done."[181]

The Canadian Pacific Railroad

The day after the German government announced unrestricted submarine warfare against all commerce shipping in the Atlantic, and while von der Goltz desperately pondered his fate in Pentonville prison, an explosion ripped through the night just after 1:30 a.m. on Tuesday, February 2, 1915, in the little town of Vanceboro, Maine.[182] A few windows shattered in several houses on both sides of the Saint Croix River under the railroad bridge connecting Vanceboro with Saint Croix, New Brunswick, Canada, exposing the unsuspecting residents to the cold gusts and precipitation of a major nor'easter. Bureau Chief Bielaski later wrote in a memo to the Alien Property Custodian, "The wind was blowing an eighty-mile gale and the thermometer registered 30 degrees below zero."[183] The 110-foot-long bridge connected the Canadian Pacific Railway with the Maine Central Railway, an important passenger and freight link between the harbor of Bangor, Maine, and the city of Saint John, New Brunswick.

The detonation, while sufficient to bend one of the main pillars of the bridge, was not sufficient to rouse local Deputy Sheriff George W. Ross from his bed. Chief Bielaski wrote in a report to his boss, "He heard the explosion but did not get up until half past five Tuesday."[184] However, the proprietor of the Vanceboro Exchange Hotel, Aubrey Tague, whom the explosion startled awake, did get out of bed. When Tague came out of his room, he encountered one of his guests, registered as a Dane, in the common bathroom thawing his frozen hands under warm water. "I freeze my hands," he stammered in broken English. Tague noticed the Imperial German armband on his coat sleeve and suggested to the man he "better take it off."[185] Tague and other residents looked around the area and discovered some damage to the railroad bridge, mostly a few splintered beams and a bent steel girder, and notified the sheriff.

That morning, a special agent of the Maine Central Railroad, two constables of the Canadian Pacific Railroad, and Deputy Sheriff Ross inspected the area where the explosion had occurred. About three feet from the ground on the American bank of the Saint Croix River, one of the main pillars of the bridge had suffered significant damage and left little doubt that something more than teenager mischief must have been at play. The men proceeded to the Vanceboro Exchange Hotel, where proprietor Tague informed them of a German occupying a room on the top floor. Sheriff Ross knocked on the door and encountered a 37-year-old man identifying himself as Werner Horn. Ross proceeded to arrest Horn after a short scuffle during which the German saboteur tried to get to his revolver still in a coat pocket from the previous night's activities. When Ross identified himself as an American official, Horn surrendered, relieved that he was not facing Canadian police. "I thought you were all Canadians," he explained to the sheriff. "I would not harm any one [sic] from here."[186]

In addition to a .38 revolver and a "jack knife," the German agent had in his possession a blasting cap, a railroad schedule, $115, and the Imperial German colors on two armbands. His handlers had told him to wear the armbands in order to be considered a prisoner of war in case of capture. Throughout the next days, Canadian border officials tried their best to convince Sheriff Ross to let them have possession of Horn. Ross refused on the grounds that there was no damage to the bridge on the Canadian side, and that he doubted "that Horn could secure a fair and impartial trial in Canada at this time."[187] The sheriff was acutely aware that Horn would have been executed as a German spy without much ado. The offer of a $100 bribe from one of the Canadians did not change his mind.

Horn fully cooperated with the sheriff and confessed to having received nitroglycerin in New York, transported it via Boston and Bangor to Vanceboro, and attempted to blow up the bridge. The original plan had been to place the explosives in the middle of the tracks on top of the bridge to rip the structure and rails apart. Navigating the unforgiving storm and cold, and after having fallen off the icy bridge twice, Horn decided to just blow up a lower pillar. He claimed to Sheriff Ross that he wanted to disable the bridge, but had not wanted a train to crash and cause human casualties.[188]

Horn would not divulge who had furnished the explosives. The question of who was behind this attack not only gained importance because the source in New York surely would have the capability of more such attacks, but also because of the sheer recklessness of sending a low-ranking amateur through Grand Central and Boston South Stations on some of the busiest rail lines in the US with a suitcase containing sixty vials of nitroglycerin. The volatile liquid could easily have produced a mass casualty event if the suitcase was damaged or impacted in any way, for example if it had simply fallen out of the luggage compartment in the railcar.

Sheriff Ross pitied the honest, naïve, patriotic, and, as it later turned out, mentally handicapped German saboteur.[189] He took Horn before District Judge George H. Smith in Machias, Maine. The German agent received a quick trial for breaking "between three and thirteen windows" in Vanceboro and was sentenced to thirty days in the local jail.[190]

The day of Horn's sentencing, on February 5, 1915, as a result of an official British request for Horn's extradition, Attorney General Gregory asked Chief Bielaski to investigate the case and report back with a recommendation. Bielaski decided to take the task on personally. He travelled to Machias, Maine, the next day and started interviewing witnesses.

Bielaski's first interview was with the suspect.[191] In the presence of the local sheriff, Bielaski advised Horn that Great Britain demanded his extradition and that anything he said could be used in both criminal prosecution in the United States and in extradition proceedings. The German saboteur agreed to talk to Bielaski candidly for more than three hours, and again the next day when the Chief brought the transcript of the previous conversation for him to sign. Just as was the case with Sheriff Ross a week before, Bielaski took a liking to the German lieutenant. Horn had been in Guatemala working on a coffee plantation when the war started. He, like so many other German reservists, heeded the call of von Papen to report to New York for transportation to Germany. And like so many others, found when he arrived in New York that there was no transportation.

Disappointed and on his way back to Guatemala he heard that his previous job was filled while passing through Mexico City. With limited financial assistance from German consuls along the way—he came through Veracruz and New Orleans—Horn returned to New York around New Year's Eve. He begged Military Attaché von Papen to send him back to Germany. Instead, the military attaché with fresh orders from the German general staff to blow up Canadian railroads, decided to recruit Horn as a sabotage agent. At this point in the interview, Horn recounted that a man named "Tommy" had given him the explosives. When prompted to describe "Tommy," Horn stammered and tried to evade the questions. Bielaski immediately recognized that Horn was lying. The next day he made Horn swear to have told the truth about everything. His officer's honor challenged, Horn admitted that the nitroglycerin had come from German sources in New York. But again, he refused to divulge the names of his superiors.

Figure 21. Werner Horn and Deputy Sheriff, George W. Ross, 1915
Source: International Film Service
US National Archives and Records Administration

Despite Horn's caginess on this subject, Bielaski was satisfied with the information he had received. He probably also suspected that von Papen and his people had not given much information to Horn since he was sent on a virtual suicide mission. The Chief went on to Calais, Maine to interview Sheriff Ross who confirmed Horn's statements. Ross also told Bielaski about the bribery attempt by the Canadian officials. In Vanceboro, the Chief interviewed the Hotel owner, the Canadian railroad constables, a few witnesses to the explosion, and secured the blasting cap that Horn had in his possession when he was arrested. Agent Schmid was tasked to research its origin. Bielaski also dispatched agents in Boston to interview the porter and train personnel who had been in contact with Horn on his way to Vanceboro.

On February 13, the Chief submitted his full report to Attorney General Gregory. He recommended that Horn be tried in federal court for transporting explosives across state lines. Bielaski strongly advised against extraditing the German agent. Once in Canada, Horn would not be able to help identify the German suspects in New York who had organized the mission. The Attorney General accepted Bielaski's judgment. Horn spent thirty days in the Machias jail, then was indicted in Boston for transporting explosives across state lines. He served a two-year sentence in Massachusetts. In June 1917, Horn was tried in federal court and sentenced to another eighteen months and a $1,000 fine. He served his time in the penitentiary in Atlanta.

British authorities never stopped their pursuit of extraditing Horn, and Bielaski never quit thwarting their efforts. Saving Horn from certain execution in 1915, Bielaski came into contact with Horn's German family. He periodically updated Horn's siblings about his condition. In 1917 Horn was indicted again, and Bielaski actively supported the German's lawyers, even collecting new witness statements using Bureau agents.[192] The Horn case was personal to the Chief. In 1917 he had petitioned Leland Harrison of the Bureau of Secret Intelligence in the State Department to forward two letters from Horn to his family. Harrison declined with a stern reference to being in a state of war with Germany.

The Chief had promised Horn's family to get him home safely, and he tried. Preempting Horn's extradition to Canada, Bielaski wrote to Assistant Attorney General John Lord O'Brian in 1918 that he strictly opposed it, and believed that von Papen had duped Horn into believing that his actions were not a crime. "I must confess to a feeling of some sympathy for Horn [...]. I think he is the most decent German that I have had anything to do with since the European war started. This and the fact that the Canadian officers tried to bribe the deputy marshal at the time of Horn's arrest to put him across the border may account for the feeling of hesitancy that I have about the advisability of turning him over to the British without restriction."[193] When in October 1918 Horn's prison sentence ended and the British government once more sought his extradition and requested his file, Bielaski conveniently had "lost" the Horn case. However, in August 1919, eight months after Bielaski had left the Bureau, Horn was extradited to Canada and sentenced to ten years in prison. He finally returned to Germany, released on humanitarian grounds with failing health in August 1921.[194]

By the time Horn had finished his sentence in 1918, the Bureau knew of course that German Military Attaché von Papen had ordered the attack, and that German bombmaker Dr. Walter T. Scheele of Hoboken had provided the suitcase with the explosives. Paul König's diary also proved that he had provided the explosives, maps, armband, knife, and pistol to Horn.[195] Von Papen's checkbook, which British authorities seized in January 1916, showed that he had personally issued check #87 for $700 to Horn on January 18, 1915, two weeks before the bombing.[196] Neither von Papen, nor P. K., nor Horn himself ever disclosed the scope of the mission.

The leader of the coordinated attack on Canada remained in the shadows until the late 1920s, when messages dated December 1914 and January 1915 between the German General Staff, von Papen and Count Bernstorff surfaced: "January 3, 1915 [...] vigorous effort should be taken to destroy the Canadian Pacific [Railway] in several places[...] Captain BOEHM who is well known in America and will soon be returning, is informed[...] Acquaint the Military Attaché with the above and furnish the sums required for the enterprise. ZIMMERMANN."[197] Hans Boehm, who had gone to Germany in October 1914 on a false passport, returned to the US in January 1915, with a promotion to Captain of the Reserve, as an agent of the General Staff intelligence division, *Abteilung* IIIb. His orders were to blow up the Canadian Pacific Railroad, then recruit, train, and supply German brigades to attack Canada from the US. Boehm received $50,000 ($1 million in today's value) for his missions from German Naval Attaché Karl Boy-Ed.[198]

The first mission included Werner Horn's sabotage in Vanceboro. Horn was one of three sabotage teams to destroy bridges in Vanceboro, near Lac Mégantic (which Boehm himself headed), and between Andover and Perth.[199] All three bombings failed because of the same nor'easter that pummeled the Eastern US-Canadian border in February of 1915. Neither the Bureau nor British intelligence ever discovered who the other bombers were, or the significant scope of the sabotage mission.

The second mission never came to fruition, at least not under Boehm's command. German-Americans proved unwilling to join the *Fatherland* on crazy military adventures in Canada. Military Attaché von Papen kept trying to no avail, even after Boehm received new orders. He repaid the $50,000 and returned to Germany undetected in March 1915. There, he was in charge of salvaging the raising and training of Irish prisoners of war to be inserted into the Emerald Isle and defeat British rule there.²⁰⁰

On June 21, 1915, an explosion ripped through the Peabody Leather Label Overall Company in Walkertown, Ontario. No one was injured, but the building suffered significant damage. Canadian police quickly identified nightwatchman William Lefler of Detroit as the person who had placed a timed dynamite bomb in a space under the factory. Lefler implicated Karl "Charles" F. Respa, a twenty-eight-year-old German citizen, also of Detroit, as the source of the dynamite. Respa, whom Canadian authorities apprehended in August 1915 on another sabotage mission, confessed to also having placed dynamite in the Windsor Armory, housing 200 British soldiers at the time. The same night when the Peabody factory exploded, a nightwatchman discovered the timebomb in Windsor, which had failed to detonate. Respa later claimed that he had purposely disabled the timing device because of the many souls in the building at the time.²⁰¹ Canadian authorities identified Respa's father, Franz, and his business partner, German citizen Albert C. Kaltschmidt of Detroit, as the leaders of a sabotage cell with orders to attack Canadian installations. Kaltschmidt, a thirty-six-year-old mechanical engineer and president of the

Figure 22. Peabody Overall Company Explosion, 1915
Source: Windsor Public Library

Marine City Salt Company with offices in the prestigious Kresge building in downtown Detroit, was the local secretary of the "Deutscher Bund" and a leader of the German-American community in the city.²⁰² He laughed off the Canadian accusations, professed his innocence to the press, and called the Canadian claims a "joke."²⁰³ The "Deutscher Bund" seemed to have thought the accusations sufficient enough to demand Kaltschmidt's resignation, which he tendered on September 3, 1915.²⁰⁴

A grand jury in Ontario indicted Kaltschmidt and Respa in October 1915.²⁰⁵ Canadian authorities could not provide any physical evidence of Kaltschmidt's role, making his indictment a non-extraditable offence.²⁰⁶ The witness confessions alone, likely under duress, were not sufficient to warrant extradition. Karl Respa was sentenced to life in prison, Wiliam Lefler received a ten-year sentence in August 1915. On the day the US entered the war on the side of the Allies, April 6, 1917, Bureau agents arrested Kaltschmidt and ten others for "set[ting] on foot from the United States an attack against the Dominion of Canada." Special Agent J. Herbert Cole, an experienced Bureau agent who had served in the San Antonio and El Paso field offices before the war, led the investigation into the saboteurs. Special Agent Keene discovered a $1,000 payment that came from von Papen's office in New York to the German consul in Chicago, Kurt von Reiswitz, who deposited it for Kaltschmidt in Detroit.²⁰⁷ Albert's financial records show that von Reiswitz had repeatedly received funds from Heinrich Albert. The files, however, do not contain enough information to link the payments to Kaltschmidt. The last and highest payment of $16,000 ($336,000 in today's value) in January 1917 from Albert to von Reiswitz is

Figure 23. Special Agent in Charge Jay Herbert Cole, c. 1910
Source: FBI Media

marked "reimbursement" from the Imperial War Department, which paid for sabotage efforts.[208]

Canadian authorities made Respa and Lefler available for Kaltschmidt's court case as star witnesses for the prosecution. Respa testified of having scouted the Lake Huron tunnel for sabotage, as well as a number of railroad bridges under the orders from Kaltschmidt for $18 per day. None of these plans came to fruition. Respa, who had come to the US in 1908 to evade the military draft in Germany, claimed that Kaltschmidt knew of Respa's past and blackmailed him into working as a sabotage agent.[209] Respa also claimed that Kaltschmidt never paid him a $200 bonus for dynamiting the factory. Kaltschmidt was finally convicted of all charges and received a four-year penitentiary sentence and $20,000 fine.[210] Throughout the entire period between the attacks in June 1915 and the arrest of Kaltschmidt and his associates in April 1917, the Kaltschmidt case file contains not a single page of investigative work by the Bureau. The Bureau did not consider the attack on Canadian installations from US soil sufficiently important to warrant a neutrality law investigation.

Bielaski's protection of Horn is heartwarming, and paints the Chief in a caring, humane, and sympathetic light. Yet, Horn never told all he knew, and the Bureau failed to take seriously the violations of US neutrality laws that had occurred in both the Welland Canal plot and the Canadian Pacific Railroad bombing. Just as was the case with Horst von der Goltz and the British evidence that a larger, coordinated attack on Canada from US soil had been planned, the Bureau seemed uninterested in investigating. That attitude would change rapidly, when some of the same agents who engaged in the early attacks on Canada a few months later attacked the United States. Possibly spurred on by the lack of investigative vigor of American authorities, attacks on Canada also continued. P. K. undertook a second, unsuccessful attack on the Welland Canal in the fall of 1915, for which he was finally convicted in American courts (his sentence, however, was suspended). Attacks against Canada continued sporadically. The most devastating attack occurred in February 1916, when the Canadian parliament in Ottawa went up in flames. The origin of the fire has never been proven to have been an arson attack. Circumstantial evidence shows that the conflagration originated from a Scheele-type pencil bomb. Hans Boehm most likely was the sabotage agent who executed the attack.[211]

5

THE ENEMY OF THE ENEMY

EARLY IN JANUARY 1915, the Constitutionalist consul general at San Francisco, Ramón P. DeNegri, notified the Bureau that a massive arms and munitions shipment, allegedly to be used to equip a military expedition into Mexico, was in violation of Section Thirteen of the Federal Penal Code. Chief Bielaski immediately instructed Agent Ely Murray Blanford to investigate. Blanford assigned Agent Frank P. Webster to the matter. But illustrating the agency's difficulty in keeping all the Mexican players straight, Webster was instructed to call on Los Angeles consul Adolfo Carrillo and learn whether he belonged to the same faction as DeNegri. If so, Webster was to determine what information Carrillo had concerning the shipment. Carrillo was also a Constitutionalist, but he knew nothing about the shipment. Agent Webster learned from a Santa Fe freight agent that four boxcars containing 4,000,000 rounds of ammunition and 5,000 rifles (561 cases of rifles, 3,759 cases of cartridges) were coming from New York through Galveston to San Diego, consigned by a Walter C. Hughes to a certain Juan Bernardo Bowen. And, an additional boxcar was on the way.

The Bureau agents assumed, logically enough, that the munitions were destined for Baja California, where the military governor, Colonel Esteban Cantú, was fighting to retain control. The Constitutionalist consul at San Diego wired Carranza at Veracruz, and was informed that the shipment was not for their faction. Bureau agents were surprised, therefore, when the deputy US marshal at San Diego telephoned that he had heard a rumor that the arms were really for Germany, and were to be transferred to a German warship at sea. Blanford immediately dispatched Agent Webster to San Diego to follow up this sensational lead.[212]

Webster reported that the five boxcars had arrived in San Diego on January 27. Not only that, but five additional boxcars were expected the following day. No one seemed to know anything about W. C. Hughes. The firm of M. Martínez and Co. was handling the huge shipment, consigned to Juan Bernardo Bowen at the Constitutionalist-held port of Topolobampo on the west coast of Mexico. There were indications that the rumors involving the Germans were true. The Bureau learned from the Los Angeles arms broker R. L. Hall that about three weeks earlier the German consular agent in Los Angeles had asked him about purchasing 4,000,000 cartridges and a large quantity of rifles, not to exceed 9,000. It turned out, though, that the munitions were not going to Topolobampo, after all, but were to be shipped out on the three-masted schooner *Annie Larsen*.[213]

The Martínez firm had chartered the *Annie Larsen* at San Francisco for $1,250 a month for an indefinite period. Martínez stated that the only instructions received had been from Juan Bernardo Bowen to forward the shipment to Topolobampo, and that Bowen's local attorney, J. Hizar, handled the finances. Webster interviewed Hizar, "who was a German by descent" [underlined in the agent's report], who said he had given Martínez $1,750 for expenses, and was going to place in the bank three months' charter money. Hizar also mentioned that the American National Bank in San Francisco had instructed the local American National Bank to place $14,000 in Hizar's account. When Webster spoke with the Collector of Customs in San Diego, that official said that since there was no arms embargo on Mexico, if clearance papers were in order, he had no authority to hold the *Annie Larsen*. The schooner sailed from San Francisco on January 24 and arrived in San Diego on February 3. She began loading immediately. By this time, the arms shipment had grown to eleven boxcars' worth: "Springfield rifles, ammunition to fit, bayonets and belts. It is old stuff which has been condemned by the United States."[214] Webster kept the *Annie Larsen* under surveillance until she sailed on February 11.[215]

By keeping track of this major shipment of army surplus munitions that the United States had been trying to sell for a decade, the Bureau found itself investigating one of the most audacious operations of World War I. Although the meat grinder that was the Western Front was the principal theater of war, Germany was anxious to weaken the Allies by supporting revolutionary movements in British and French colonies. India and Ireland were the main targets.

A group of expatriate Indians founded the Ghadar party in Oregon in 1913 with the goal of ending British rule in India. The Ghadar party split in 1914 into a Sikh and a Hindu faction, the latter being headquartered in San Francisco. Under the leadership of the charismatic Har Dayal, the group published a revolutionary newspaper called *Hindustan Ghadar*, calling for armed resistance against the British. Har Dayal, a member of the IWW (Industrial

THE ENEMY OF THE ENEMY

Workers of the World) and avowed anarchist, ran afoul of the authorities in April 1914 and fled to Europe. He found sanctuary in Germany and founded the "Indian Independence Committee," which the German government enthusiastically supported.

The Ghadar party continued to flourish in the United States under the leadership of Ram Chandra with headquarters in San Francisco. Two of the leaders of the movement, Haramba L. Gupta and Dr. Chandra Chakraberty, coordinated Germany's support of the movement in the US. Funding from

Figure 24. Sikhs on board the "Komogata Maru" denied landing in Vancouver, Canada. 1914
Source: Library and Archives Canada

Germany arrived from the military attaché's office in New York and the German Consul General Franz Bopp, vice-consul Eckhard von Schack, and military attaché Wilhelm Brincken in San Francisco.[216] In the fall of 1914, hundreds of Indian resistance fighters left the West Coast for India. The Ghadar party and the "Indian Independence Committee" had called for an uprising against the British to commence in February 1915. Germany promised to support the uprising with arms and munitions that were to arrive in India as the revolt was unfolding. Germany's military attaché in New York, Franz von Papen, tasked the representative in the United States of the Krupp munitions firm, Hans Tauscher, in September 1914 to procure the necessary arms.[217] Tauscher purchased $159,049.48 (approximately $3.3 million in today's value) worth of US army surplus munitions.[218] Tauscher shipped them from New York in January 1915, only one month before the planned uprising in India.

While the munitions were on their way to San Diego consigned to Tauscher's freight forwarder, Walter C. Hughes, the German admiralty was organizing their transportation to the Indian resistance movement. German agent Frederick Jebsen secured at Los Angeles a battered, old oil tanker, the *Maverick*, which was to rendezvous with the *Annie Larsen* and take on the cargo.[219] The plan was for the tanker to meet the schooner at San José del Cabo at the tip of Baja California. The transfer completed, the *Maverick* would then head out across the Pacific and the *Annie Larsen* would return to the United States.

Things went awry. The *Annie Larsen* had to wait at San José del Cabo for two months, until April 1915, while the *Maverick* was overhauled in drydock and made its leisurely way down the coast of California.[220] Eluding a shadowing British cruiser, the *Maverick* made a run to the alternative rendezvous, Socorro Island, some 400 miles off the Mexican coast. She failed to find the *Annie Larsen* there. The schooner had indeed been at Socorro Island, but without a fresh water source, and after waiting a month for the tanker to arrive, had sailed to the port of Acapulco for supplies. There she landed most of her cargo, and the Carranza authorities held her in port. Ironically, it was through the good offices of the captain of the American cruiser, *Yorktown*, also at Acapulco, that the *Annie Larsen* was allowed to continue on her way.[221]

Alleging "bad weather," the schooner made no attempt to return to the Socorro Island rendezvous, but sailed up the California coast to her home base at Gray's Harbor in Hoquiam, Washington, arriving on June 29, 1915. The local collector of customs impounded the vessel and what remained of her cargo: 4,000 rifles and 1,000,000 cartridges. The government was unwilling to take any course that would permit the sale of these munitions.[222] The US marshal, however, conducted a sale of the munitions in 1917, which were purchased by W. Stokes Kirk, the arms dealer with stores in Seattle, Los Angeles, Pittsburg, Philadelphia, and Portland. He had sold the arms and ammunition to Tauscher in the first place.[223] Ambassador Count Bernstorff had tried in vain to have the arms released back to the German government with a claim that their destination had been German West Africa.[224]

The Bureau now had Hans Tauscher on its radar who, as it turned out, had been one of the most important secret agents of the by then disgraced German military attaché, Franz von Papen.[225] Tauscher certainly had not hidden in the shadows in New York. The New York phone book advertised H.

Tauscher, 320 Broadway, as the "sole agent" of Waffenfabrik Mauser, Georg Luger, and Deutsche Waffen and Munitions Fabriken for the United States, Canada and Mexico.[226] His most important representation was the Friedrich Krupp AG, one of the world's most powerful arms manufacturers.

The six-foot, two-inch tall, suave, and well-connected German reserve officer established his business in New York around 1900. Born in Prenzlau, Germany in 1867, Tauscher served in the German army in the 1890s, ending his military career as a captain in the Reserve. The German military attaché, Franz von Papen, called him into active service in August 1914, as an agent of the Imperial government in New York. Sporting a goatee with the ends of his mustache slightly turned upwards in Prussian fashion, posture straight as an arrow, and always dressed in a fashionable three-piece suit with expensive silk ties, Tauscher cut an impressive figure. Within a few years of establishing his business, he had amassed a fortune. The Washington Post estimated his annual income in 1905 to have exceeded $450,000 (close to ten million dollars in today's value).[227]

That, however, was likely not the main source of Tauscher's wealth. His wife, Johanna Gadski, one of the most famous sopranos in history, was far better known in New York. The couple married in 1892 in Berlin. Gadski subsequently received an invitation to perform at the New York Metropolitan Opera in 1898. The famous diva took the offer, and the Tauschers moved to New York, where Gadski stayed at the Opera until 1904, and again from 1907 to 1917 after an interlude in London. Her renditions

Figure 25. Johanna and Lotte Gadski, 1911
Source: Bain News Service Collection
Library of Congress Prints and Photographs Division

of Richard Wagner's bombastic operas were legendary, but she also shone in Verdi's "Aida," and other challenging Italian operas. Tickets to Madame Gadski's star-studded performances were as coveted as were invitations to the after-parties at the Tauscher home, where champagne flowed freely among the social crème de la crème of New York.

For the Bureau, this meant that investigations into this power couple had to be by the book. Tauscher had powerful friends, and not only within the German diplomatic corps. The Bureau's investigations had run across Tauscher on multiple occasions in the past. Agents Barnes and Matthews tracked rumors of an order of 50,000 Mauser rifles for the Mexican government in May 1913. It turned out to be 500 rifles, and agents learned that the shipment had been impounded in Hamburg. But Tauscher's New York business name was on the contract.[228] The reason the German government stopped the order could have been fear of bad publicity in case the shipment became public knowledge. More likely, the Mexican president Huerta had not made the required down payment.

Figure 26. Captain Hans Tauscher, 1916
Source: Bain News Service Collection
Library of Congress Prints and Photographs Division

The shipment was moved to a warehouse in Hamburg until further notice.[229] In the summer of 1913, agents probed the role of the German-owned Gans Steamship line, as well as shipments of munitions from New York via New Orleans to Mexico. Although the investigation into neutrality law violations came up short, the Bureau again encountered Tauscher's name, as he had sold this order of 300 cases of 7-millimeter Mauser cartridges to Alfonso Madero.[230] His name appeared on the shipping documents of the Gans steamship, El Norte, that had delivered the munitions to Mexico. These investigations took place before the World War, and as such likely did not rise to the level that Chief Bielaski would risk antagonizing the Tauschers. Yet, despite the lack of follow up, Bureau agents had their eye on Tauscher.

The Bureau in 1915 neither knew the true destination of the surplus weapons and munitions, nor was it aware of the Hindu conspiracy against Great Britain in the US. In keeping with the many arms smuggling plots that the Bureau had investigated in the years since the outbreak of the Mexican Revolution, agents assumed that the *Annie Larsen* shipment had to do with Mexico. The fact that the *Annie Larsen* called at Acapulco and sold parts of its cargo to Mexican revolutionaries seemed to confirm the theory. As late as 1917, Bureau agents maintained that the *Maverick* was transporting arms to Mexican revolutionaries.[231]

The truth was quite different, as a massive trial of Hindu conspirators in 1917 and 1918 would demonstrate. Bielaski proudly proclaimed in August 1917 that his department's investigations led to indictments in "New York, Chicago and San Francisco [...] amounting to at least 100 defendants."[232] Yet, no serious investigation into the matter had commenced in 1915.

As soon as the *Annie Larsen* discovery hit the news in June 1915, Fred Jebsen, the key witness and purported owner of the *Maverick*, disappeared.[233] Bureau and British intelligence agents pursued him all the way into 1919. A German captain reported in 1918 that he had seen Jebsen in Hamburg, alive and well. In March 1919, immigration officers arrested a German crossing illegally from Mexico into the US at Calexico, California, under the name Albert Klein. Klein was suspected of being Fred Jebsen. He turned out to be a shoemaker.[234] British intelligence reported to Agent Blanford in Los Angeles a few months later that they had found Jebsen hiding under a false name in Dutch East Borneo. It turned out to be someone else, a man who was "a hard worker, lives within his salary, does not drink[...]," a description that clearly did not fit the flamboyant socialite of 1915.[235] Indeed, Jebsen had reached Germany in July and joined the submarine force. He died just a few weeks later, when his submarine, the U-36, sank on July 24, 1915, just off the coast of the Shetland Islands.[236] US papers reported his demise at the time, but British intelligence and the Bureau either did not pay attention to the reports or, more likely, distrusted their veracity.

The *Maverick* had orders to take the *Annie Larsen* consignment from Socorro to Karachi, India, via Java, Indonesia at the end of June. Once the cargo was discharged in India, the tanker would return to Java to meet another steamer, the *Djember*. Von Papen leased the *Djember* in April 1915 in New York to transport a second shipment of arms and ammunition from New York to Indonesia. The Maverick would then take the shipment to its final destination, the resistance movement in India. Not knowing that the Maverick never met the Annie Larsen, and that the arms and ammunition would end up back on US soil and impounded by US authorities, Tauscher spent $134,595.22 (about $2.8 million in today's value) on the second shipment.[237] The second attempt to funnel arms and ammunition to the Indian resistance did not go much better than the first.

On Monday morning, June 14, 1915, Tauscher's freight forwarder, Walter C. Hughes, moved the cargo from a warehouse in upper New York to the Holland Line pier, where the Djember was to be loaded. As carriers stacked a virtual mountain of boxes on the dock, 10 Gatling guns, 2,000,000 45/70 cartridges, 5,300 Springfield rifles with bayonets, 2,000 Colt .45 revolvers with 384,000 cartridges, the captain suddenly refused to accept the cargo. Tense negotiations followed. Tauscher tried everything to convince the shipping company, Funch, Edye and Co., to honor their contracts, but to no avail. The negotiations dragged on into nightfall. The boxes could not remain in the open on the dock. In a pinch, Tauscher found a warehouse nearby on West Houston Street, where to take the munitions overnight. One of the drivers for Hughes, Morris J. Ahearn, however, was stopped by Officer Bernard Maguire of the New York police. Residents opposite the warehouse called the police, displaying a certain unease over having mountains of arms and ammunition stored across the street. The policeman determined that the driver did not have the necessary permits from the New York Fire Department to carry or to store the volatile material in the neighborhood. He was ticketed and ordered to appear in court.[238] The police also notified the Bureau. Superintendent Offley dispatched Agent Albert G. Adams to the case.[239]

The case ballooned. The prosecutor demanded to know the source of the weapons and munitions, and summoned Hughes, who identified Henry Muck as the owner of the weapons. Muck, as it turned out, was Hans Tauscher's general manager.[240] Muck testified that the shipment was destined for Surabaya, Java, Indonesia. A few days later, with his lawyer in tow, Tauscher submitted to a "voluntary" interview. While freely admitting to having purchased the weapons, he steadfastly refused to answer questions as to where the money had come from or what the destination of the arms cache was. Tauscher had retained one of New York's highest paid lawyers, Felix H. Levy of the Stanchfield and Levy law firm and former Deputy Attorney General.[241] Levy provided "proof" that a permit to store weapons in the Houston Street warehouse had indeed been applied for on June 15, three days before the police were called, but had only been received on June 20.[242] Since Tauscher had not known that the *Djember* captain would refuse the cargo on June 18, the permit must have been the result of Tauscher calling in a favor with someone at the Fire Department. After promising not to move the boxes from the current warehouse, the prosecutor released Tauscher. Von Papen's name, the German origin of the money used to buy the material, and its final destination never came to light.[243]

With the cargo stuck in the New York warehouse, Tauscher threatened to sue the holding company that owned the *Djember* for damages. As it turned out, British intelligence had figured out that the *Djember* was to sail with German-paid arms to the Far East. The British by then had crushed the uprising in India and had arrested many of the revolutionaries; hence the interest in the cargo of the *Djember*, and its destination. After discovering the German origin of the military supplies, the British consul in New York went to the shipping line that owned the steamer and threatened dire consequences if the cargo was accepted. Hence the sudden refusal by the captain.[244]

Tauscher did not abandon his mission. Neither did Agent Adams stop his investigation. He reported on August 21, 1915, that "six [railroad] carloads of arms and ammunition had yesterday arrived at Jersey City from Philadelphia, consigned by W. Stokes Kirk to H. Tauscher."[245] The destination of the shipment was "Soerabaya," a misspelling of the Indonesian city Surabaya on the island of Java. The arms never left New York harbor, but added to Tauscher's inventory of arms and ammunition. The Bureau investigation into Tauscher stalled.

The British government tried their best to reinvigorate the investigation into Tauscher. When Franz von Papen was compelled to leave the United States in January 1916, British authorities at Falmouth seized his luggage which contained letters and check stubs. In February 1916, the Admiralty authorized the publication of a pamphlet titled, "Miscellaneous. No 6. 1916. Selection from Papers found in the Possession of Captain von Papen, Late German Military Attaché at Washington, Falmouth, January 2 and 3, 1916."[246] The pamphlet not only contained the check written to Horst von der Goltz, alias Bridgeman Taylor, but also various references to Hans Tauscher's involvement in the Bridgeport Projectile Company. In addition to the published content of von Papen's letters, British intelligence also forwarded other letters from Tauscher to the Imperial War Department in Berlin.[247]

The New York Sun published an article on January 20, based on British sources, that showed specific payments Military Attaché von Papen had made to Tauscher for purchasing arms and ammunition. Chief Bielaski asked Superintendent Offley to follow up on the information. Agent Adams interviewed Tauscher at his office at 320 Broadway on February 9, 1916. Tauscher maintained that he had not purchased military supplies for von Papen but rather had helped with investigations, for example whether U.M.C. Cartridge Company was producing illegal dum-dum bullets (which explode upon impact and cause horrible injuries) for the British military. Through his lawyer, Felix Levy, he refused to share his entire customer list, which included sales "obviously made for sporting purposes."[248] The list he provided to the Bureau, however, included sales to Francisco Elías and Alfredo Caturegli, both *carrancista* consuls, as well as Felix Sommerfeld, purchasing agent for Pancho Villa. The shipments destined for the Far East, which Adams had personally investigated in the summer of 1915, were not on the list.[249]

Figure 27. Felix A. Sommerfeld (left) and Pancho Villa (second from left), 1915
Source: El Paso Public Lbrary

The case against Tauscher took on another dimension in April 1916. The British government sent Horst von der Goltz to New York to testify in the case of the first Welland Canal attack. Von der Goltz had implicated Tauscher as the source of the dynamite. Tauscher was arrested and charged with violating the neutrality laws. In the subsequent trial in June 1916, lawyer Felix H. Levy worked his legal magic once more. Tauscher admitted to buying 300 pounds of dynamite, but the purpose had been to blow up some pesky tree stumps in his backyard, not the Welland Canal. How von der Goltz had gotten the dynamite was not his problem, especially since there was no evidence that the German agent ever had the explosives. Tauscher was acquitted.

In the course of investigating the activities of the disgraced German military attaché von Papen, his successor in New York, twenty-seven-year-old Wolf Walter Franz von Igel came into the Bureau's crosshairs. After British authorities published some of the papers they had taken from von Papen in January at Falmouth, the New York prosecutor's office assembled a grand jury, which on April 17, 1916, indicted von Papen, Tauscher, Alfred Fritzen, and Constante Covani in the 1914 Welland Canal conspiracy. While these indictments were publicized, a fifth indictment remained under seal. Von Papen was safely in Germany, Covani was serving in the Italian army, and Fritzen had disappeared to California on $200 travel money he received from von Igel.[250] Agent Adams joined the New York police in the arrest of Tauscher.[251] The latter was immediately released on $25,000 bail. Von Igel fell into a clever trap set by Division Superintendent William Offley. Offley decided not to arrest von Igel at his apartment on East 57th Street, but delayed the arrest until the next day to make sure the German would be in his office. Suspecting that he might be the fifth indictee, the military attaché busied himself on the morning of April 18 with cleaning out his safe and packaging compromising papers to be shipped to the German embassy for safekeeping.[252]

Figure 28. Wolf von Igel, c. 1915–1920
Source: Library of Congress Prints and Photographs Division

As soon as the grand jury handed down the sealed indictment and arrest warrant for von Igel, a US marshal deputized Assistant Division Superintendent Joseph A. Baker that same evening to serve the warrant and arrest von Igel.[253] Agents Adams and Kemp had staked out von Igel's apartment

61

on East 57th Street for several days to report when the German left for his office.²⁵⁴ At 11:00 a.m. agents Baker, Grgurevich, Storck (an accountant), and Underhill descended on the military attaché's offices, rooms 2501 and 2502 at 60 Wall Street. As the agents barged in past one of P. K.'s goons and von Igel's assistant, George von Skal, von Igel was caught completely by surprise—the large safe in his office wide open and the compromising contents stacked all over his desk and nearby tables.

In a report forwarded to the German chancellor, Wolf von Igel reported on April 21 to Ambassador Count Bernstorff:

> On Tuesday morning, 18 April 1916, at a quarter to eleven, [...] the messenger at my office [...] announced that Mr. Baker wished to speak to me. As I did not know the name, I told the messenger to say that I did not know the gentleman, and therefore could not receive him without knowing the reason of his visit [...]. I quietly went on working. Suddenly my door opened, I saw the messenger being pushed aside, and two men entered. One of them said: 'I am Mr. Baker [...]. You are arrested, here is the warrant for your arrest' [...]. I [...] replied: 'You are mistaken; you cannot arrest me, as I am a member of the Staff of the German Embassy.' As I spoke, I seized the telephone which was standing on my desk. Before I had time to take down the receiver, Baker seized me from behind, and pulled me backwards, while the second man [Grgurevich] tried to break the telephone wires. He only succeeded, however, in tearing down the bell-box from the wall[...] Mr. Baker called to his assistance three [sic] more men from outside, who forcibly prevented Herr von Skaal [sic] and the messenger Schüssler, from telephoning to anybody or leaving the office. There was a moment's respite, of which I availed myself to rush to the open safe, in which most of the papers were kept, and to close the doors [...]. The five officials fell upon us, to prevent us from carrying out our intention. I was the nearest to the safe and succeeded in shutting the two handles with my right hand, which was free. Before I could turn the button to the combination, however, I was dragged back. At this moment, Baker gave the order: 'Draw your revolvers, boys,' at the same time shouting: 'Hands up, hold your hands up!' The official who had seized me, let me go for an instant, and pointed

the revolver at me, and I seized the opportunity to turn the combination of the lock [...]. Baker then gave the order to his men: 'Take all the papers you can find and put them in our suitcase.' [...] and while I was again held firmly, the officials put all the papers which were lying on my writing table, into the bag [...]. A pause followed, and Herr von Skaal [sic] seized the opportunity to leave the office and communicate with the lawyers and the Imperial Embassy. In the meantime, I myself packed into the bag all the papers remaining on the table, so as to prevent any of them disappearing. I closed the bag, and held it firmly by the handle, repeating once more: 'All these papers are the property of the German Embassy [...]. Under no circumstances shall I give up the papers.' Mr. Baker replied: 'We shall not take orders from you; give me the suitcase.' I replied: 'No,' and Mr. Baker said to his men: 'All right, take the suitcase.'

[...] Two of the men held me, while others tried to take the bag away from me. A struggle ensued [...]. One of men succeeded in snatching the bag away from me, and immediately hurried out of the office with it. When he had left, the others let me go, and I took my hat and coat, saying: 'I follow immediately. I must see where the papers went to.' I then went to the Court accompanied by the four officials and arrived there at a quarter to twelve. At twelve o'clock I was called before the judge [...]. The State Attorney asked me if I pleaded Guilty or Not Guilty. I did not reply [...]. At the sitting which followed, [...] I was released, on the motion of my lawyers, on bail of $20,000 [...]. Signed Igel."[255]

The New York Sun reported the details of the raid the next day and concluded, "The Federal agents were considerably bruised in their various wrestling matches."[256]

The raid was one of the great counterintelligence triumphs for the Bureau in the Neutrality Period. The insistence of Offley to arrest von Igel at his office in midday, catching him while cleaning out the safe, yielded a staggering amount of confidential German files.[257] Although von Igel managed to close the safe, it appears that it may have been largely emptied. The papers on his desk, side table, and in drawers and file cabinets provided devastating evidence of German intrigue. Among them was an invoice Tauscher had given to von Papen for the purchase of 300 pounds of dynamite. Von Igel's papers also contained letters from John Devoy, the editor of the *Gaelic-American* and one of the Clan na Gael (the prominent Irish republican organization in the US) leaders in the US, showing that the German government supported Irish agitation against Great Britain.[258] Correspondence with and payments to Dr. Chakraberty provided evidence that Germany supported a large-scale conspiracy to assist the Indian resistance.[259] Most devastating was the discovery of several cipher books, which allowed the Bureau to decipher telegrams and other messages between von Papen, Albert, and Count Bernstorff.[260]

Ambassador Count Bernstorff immediately sent Prince Hatzfeld, Councilor of the German embassy, to lodge a formal complaint with the State Department and demand the release of the military attaché and his papers. The personal entreaty followed a written demand. Bernstorff wrote on April 18, "Although I have as yet no knowledge of the special circumstances, this is without doubt a violation of the extraterritorial rights which belong to me under the law of nations, and I therefore have the honor to ask of your excellency that the necessary orders be issued for the immediate release of Mr. von Igel and of such things as were seized together with him, as well as to direct that the responsible officials be reprimanded."[261] Von Igel had already been released on $20,000 bail at the time of Prince Hatzfeld's entreaty. After some back and forth—the State Department claimed the German embassy had not properly registered von Igel as a German diplomat—the indictment was finally dropped in recognition of his diplomatic immunity. Attorney General Gregory still refused to release the confiscated papers.

Agent Grgurevich, who spoke German, translated and interpreted the papers for the Bureau between April 21 and 25.[262] Attesting to their importance, Superintendent William Offley and several of his agents personally transported von Igel's papers to Washington, DC in the middle of the night of April 25/26. Offley met Chief Bielaski at 9:00 a.m. and huddled with the Chief until 2:00 p.m.[263] Secretary of State Lansing suggested that the ambassador verify every document as belonging to the German government. Bernstorff would have had to admit that the Welland Canal plot, support for the Easter Rising in Ireland, and for the Indian resistance all were sanctioned by the German government.[264] Count Bernstorff declined and quietly decided to drop his demands to return the papers to the embassy.[265]

The British government did all it could to assist the Bureau in the investigation and prosecution of Tauscher, von Igel, and the others. Captain Gaunt provided maps of the Welland Canal and even offered to ferry in Canadian witnesses.[266] Working closely with the Bureau in general and William Offley in particular, he most certainly also gained access to the evidence in von Igel's papers regarding the German support and timing of the Easter Rising, which started on Monday, April 24, a week after the raid. British authorities captured the German SS *Libau* with 20,000 rifles and 5,000,000 cartridges on April 21, and arrested Roger Casement, whom the German submarine U-19 had carried from Germany to Kerry.[267]

Unbeknownst to the Bureau, Roger Casement had gone to Germany in October 1914 to raise funds and create an Irish brigade in support of an armed uprising against Great Britain. The German government envisioned a force of "no less than 25,000 men."[268] Casement recruited members for the brigade from the approximately 2,000 Irish prisoners of war interned in the first months of the war. A mere fifty-five volunteered to risk their lives for Irish independence.[269] The preparations did not go well, and the German government lost faith in Casement's ability to organize a disciplined invasion force. In February 1915, Hans Boehm, the German agent dispatched in December 1914 to blow up Canadian installations, received orders to assist with the Irish brigade in Limburg, Germany. Boehm worked with the soldiers for only a few months, but was heralded for putting the effort back on track. He returned to the US in July to lead German sabotage efforts along the Canadian border and the rustbelt. Casement had promised the active support of Irish republicans for the sabotage effort in the US. Per Casement's reference, the sabotage order of January 24, 1915, which only surfaced years after the war, ordered the German military attaché von Papen to contact Joseph McGarrity, John Keating, and Jeremiah O'Leary for organizing sabotage missions across the US.[270]

The Irish republican leaders of the Clan na Gael in the US coordinated with the Imperial government and Casement, which allows for the assumption that British intelligence had information about the plotters on both sides of the Atlantic. According to most scholars, it was Admiral Hall's Room 40 that had intercepted messages between John Devoy, Joseph McGarrity (the leader of the Clan na Gael in the US), Roger Casement, Ambassador Count Bernstorff, and others in the run-up to the Easter Rising. Specific messages from Daniel Cohalan, John Devoy, and Joseph McGarrity to Roger Casement in von Igel's cache of papers were transmitted to the Admiralty, providing proof that the Bureau shared intelligence relevant to British interests.[271]

Headlined "Von Igel Papers—Relating to Casement and Ireland," the Admiralty files included a list of names contained in von Igel's cache, among them John Devoy, Roger Casement, Dr. Chakravarty, John Ryan (a Clan na Gael member in Buffalo, New York), Hans Boehm, and Hans Tauscher. Most importantly, a message from Judge Daniel F. Cohalan, an Irish nationalist and judge on the New York Supreme Court, forwarded by von Igel's assistant George von Skal on April 17, 1916, the day before the raid on the military attaché's office, read: "Irish request to telegraph Berlin—Delivery of arms must not in any case take place before (corrected to 'must take place exactly on' – Pr.) Sunday the 23rd p.m., because smuggling is impossible. They must be unloaded quickly; this is most important. Detachment of troops, even if small, must follow at once. Messenger brings complete text. Skal."[272]

The page with date and origin of the transmission of von Igel's papers to the Admiralty was likely destroyed (the file starts with page 2), but was nestled in interceptions dated mostly between January and April 1916. A second telegram from Judge Cohalan, listed in the British file of von Igel documents, also dated April 17 and marked "very secret," found its way into President Wilson's papers. A plausible assumption is that Secretary Lansing shared some of the most sensitive pieces of information in the von Igel papers with the president and possibly the British government.[273] If either the Justice or State Departments shared the von Igel papers immediately after the raid (since it was actionable intelligence), the Cohalan messages may have provided the specific intelligence about the imminence of the uprising and contributed to the subsequent defeat of the Irish revolutionaries.[274]

The discovery of evidence in von Igel's papers that Tauscher and von Papen had attempted to ship arms and ammunition to India from the US finally shone a light on the mysterious *Annie Larsen* and the Indian nationalist organization in the US. It took another year for the Bureau to seriously investigate the Ghadar party. In May 1917, with the US now officially in the war on the side of the Allies, the first indictments were handed down.

In the run-up to the trial, the Bureau received significant help from British intelligence. British agents in August 1917 presented Mrs. Camille De Berri, who "was at one time very thick with the Indians" to Agent Blanford. She provided letters from members of the Ghadar party in San Francisco, as well as incriminating documents such as the copy of "bomb manual."[275] When she asked to be paid for her information, maybe even become a Bureau employee, Agent Blanford demurred.[276] In November, British agents coordinated with the field office in San Francisco the arrival of six Hindu witnesses from Vancouver, BC, on a steamer.[277] Chief Bielaski also dispatched Agent Gershon from San Diego to San Blas and Topolobampo, Mexico, to interview the consignee of the *Annie Larsen* shipment, Juan Bernardo Bowen.[278] Agent in charge of the San Francisco field office, Ely Blanford, at one point accompanied British Secret Service Agent G. C. Denham to help analyze immigration service records, since "he has lived in India for years [and] is entirely familiar with the Hindus of this case and the various aliases under which they have gone or may have gone and would more quickly recognize one of the parties indicted, under a false name."[279] Denham also joined Agent Feri F. Weise of the Boston field office on the hunt for a German suspect allegedly involved in the Hindu conspiracy.[280] In hundreds of memos, British intelligence Agent Hale also worked closely with Agent Blanford, identifying Hindu conspirators and helped him to understand the relationships between the suspects. With his assistance, Blanford tracked several Hindu suspects who had come from Japan to San Francisco in January 1917.[281]

The Bureau was joined at the hip with British intelligence as the November 1916 trials of the conspirators approached. British help in this case succeeded in focusing the investigation and overcoming the lack of understanding of Indian culture, names, and organizations. Just as its agents had struggled with Mexican revolutionists' names, affiliations, and language, the Bureau in 1917 did not have agents of Indian heritage. The British government also most certainly seemed eager to decapitate the Hindu organizations in the US, therefore eagerly sharing intelligence, resources, and manpower with the Bureau.

After interviews with W. Stokes Kirk managers, the investigation showed that the arms of the *Annie Larsen* had definitely come from Hans Tauscher in New York. He, meanwhile, had returned to Germany. The investigation into German support for the Hindu conspiracy quickly focused on the German consulates in San Francisco and Chicago. San Francisco Consul General Franz Bopp, his assistant Eckhard von Schack, and Military Attaché Wilhelm von Brincken had already been implicated in sabotage cases in Seattle and Vancouver in 1915. Consul Kurt von Reiswitz was accused in two attacks on Canada from Detroit. It now became clear that both consulates had financed and supported the Hindu conspiracy.[282] The German government stripped all four of their diplomatic immunity after the indictments in March and June 1917. Von Reiswitz was acquitted, but four conspirators in Chicago and the three former diplomats in San Francisco were sentenced in November 1917 to serve up to 48 months in Leavenworth penitentiary between 1917 and 1921.[283]

By the beginning of the official Hindu conspiracy trial in November 1917 in San Francisco, the Bureau had assembled over 1,000 pages of investigative material (not including the investigative files of the various grand juries). After indicting 105 Indian nationalists in New York, Chicago, and San Francisco, Bureau agents rounded up the suspects in August and September 1917, making the Ghadar case the single largest investigation for the Bureau during World War I.[284] The trial lasted for five months. The court found twenty-nine conspirators, including Dr. Chakraberty, implicated in the von Igel papers, guilty of violating the neutrality laws, and launching an armed insurrection from US soil. The sentences ranged from a few months to two years. Causing a national sensation, the leader of the Ghadar party in the US, Ram Chandra, on the last day of the trial was assassinated in the courtroom. The shooter, a fellow defendant and suspected British agent, died when a US marshal opened fire. Just as happened over a year later with the failure of the Easter Rising in Ireland, British troops quickly suppressed the Punjab uprising of February 1915. Sporadic armed resistance in India and the East Indies lasted until 1917. Throughout the entire time, German weapons never reached either group of revolutionists.

6

A Massive German Iceberg

UNBEKNOWNST TO THE AMERICAN government in general and the Bureau in particular, the Imperial War Department ordered Franz von Papen in the end of January 1915 to commence a sabotage campaign against "all kinds of factories for military supplies […]" in the United States:

> From the Acting General Staff of the Army, Section IIIB
>
> Berlin, January 24, 1915
>
> — Secret
>
> To the Foreign Office, Berlin.
>
> It is humbly requested that the following telegram is transmitted in code to the Imperial Embassy in Washington:
>
> 'For military attaché. To find suitable personnel for sabotage in the United States and Canada inquire with the following persons:
>
> 1) Joseph Mac Garrity [sic], 5412 Springfield Philadelphia, Pa.,
> 2) John P. Keating, Maryland Avenue Chicago,
> 3) Jeremia [sic] O'Leary, Park row [sic], New York.
>
> 1.
>
> No. 1 and 2 completely reliable and discreet, No. 3 reliable, not always discreet. Persons have been named by Sir Roger Casement.
>
> In the United States sabotage can cover all kinds of factories for military supplies; railroads, dams, bridges there cannot

be touched. Embassy can under no circumstances be compromised, neither can Irish-German propaganda.
Assistant chief of the General Staff
Nadolny[285]

While the order only was discovered many years later during the Mixed Claims Commission investigations in the 1920s, investigators on the ground in the US quickly realized that something was afoot. On February 4, 1915, the German government declared a war zone around the British Isles in which all shipping, including merchant ships of neutral powers, was subject to attack without prior warning.[286] The sabotage order and the declaration of unrestricted submarine warfare were two facets of the same campaign: end the flow of war materiel from the US to Germany's enemies, and loosen the stranglehold of the British sea blockade.

The first suspected German attack on a US factory was on the John A. Roebling's Sons Company in Trenton, New Jersey. Situated on an eight-acre compound with over a dozen factory buildings and worker housing, Roebling was the largest US manufacturer of any product having to do with cabling. Its steel cables held up the Brooklyn Bridge, provided rigging for ships, and secured airplane fuselages. Roebling telegraph wires crisscrossed the country. Roebling added a new product in 1915, that was in high demand in Europe: steel netting designed to secure entrances to British and French seaports against German submarines. Roebling's steel netting proved to be highly effective. Then, on the night of January 18, the entire factory complex burned to the ground in one of the largest fires Trenton, New Jersey had ever experienced. Over 300 workers escaped unharmed. Fire, police, and insurance investigators found that the fire alarm system in the entire complex had been disabled. The fires had started in multiple places, carefully set in trash heaps. While arson was the certified cause of the fire, the culprits escaped. As the fire happened before the official German sabotage order, it is possible that disaffected workers, many of them of German, Austrian, Czech, and Irish descent, took matters into their own hands. Considering that there were complex and coordinated arson incidents in multiple plants at the same time, this explanation seems unlikely.

In February, Werner Horn tried to blow up the Vanceboro bridge. Around the same time, the Bureau became aware of the *Annie Larsen* carrying German-owned arms and ammunition it believed to be destined for Mexico. The arms, as investigators found out in June, were headed to the Indian independence movement. As Bureau agents learned about other plots to fund Indian revolts, the Easter Rising of the Irish independence movement led investigators to German diplomats in the United States. It took the Bureau and local law enforcement agencies until mid-June 1915 to realize that German plots had changed from violating the neutrality laws to targeting domestic industry. To this day, most explosions and fires that occurred in the United States in 1915 and 1916 remain unsolved. And to be fair, hastily transformed production facilities that used to produce simple hardware and machinery now worked with explosives and incendiary chemicals to manufacture ammunition, artillery shells, and bombs.

It is reasonable to expect a fair share of accidents in these facilities, which all too easily were blamed on "foreign workers" and German saboteurs. The list of fires and explosions in 1915 is extensive, however; in June, Dupont's gunpowder manufacturing plant in Carney's Point, New Jersey, had three large fires. In addition, a barge laden with explosives blew up in Seattle harbor on May 25. This massive explosion indeed was the work of German saboteurs. Between June and December, five more Dupont powder factories erupted in flames. The Hopewell, Virginia facility of Dupont caused massive collateral damage as the entire part of the city where the plant was located burned to the ground. Bethlehem Steel burned on two occasions, Baldwin Locomotive Company, Packard Automobile Company and, yes, John A. Roebling's and Sons for a second time, burned, among dozens of other factories involved in lucrative business with the Allies. The Philadelphia Naval Yards also caught on fire, heavily damaging two destroyers in drydock. The cause of the conflagration was a dynamite bomb. No culprit was ever found. Investigators determined in a dozen of the factory fires that they resulted from arson, but the arsonists remained elusive.[287]

The torpedoing of the British ocean liner *Lusitania* only miles from the Irish coast on May 7, 1915, caused a tremendous international outcry and stern warnings from the United States for Germany to stop its submarine campaign. The German government heeded the warnings and ended the unrestricted commerce war on the high seas for a time. Yet, sabotage incidents in the US proper continued unabated. Most baffling were fires that erupted in cargo holds of ships destined for European harbors. On February 2, 1915, the *Grindon Hall* sailed from Havana on its voyage to London. Five days into the journey she pulled into Norfolk harbor ablaze. Two weeks later, the *Regina d'Itlalia* was scheduled to depart New York for Naples, Italy on February 17, when suddenly the cotton in her hold burst into flame. The conflagration spread quickly to the rest of the cargo, boxes of ammunition and tanks of oil. Ten days later, the *La Tourraine* left New York for Le Havre, France with a shipment of machine guns and other supplies. Shortly before arriving in France, she caught on fire.

It took the crew three days to gain control of the situation. The cargo was a total loss. On February 29, the *Knutsford* caught on fire dockside in New York. The burning cargo of sugar proved impossible to extinguish because of the intense heat the fire produced. The ship sank in its berth. In March another ship, the *San Guglielmo*, with a cargo of cotton sailing from Galveston via New York to Naples, caught on fire as it docked at its destination; 6,000 bales of cotton were destroyed. The *Devon City*, while docked in the New York harbor, burned at the end of April. In May, ten ships, all but one originating from New York, experienced fires in their holds. A clue finally emerged that helped the investigation into the ship fires.[288]

April 3, 1915, the day before Easter Sunday, was a drab day. Sinister clouds and high winds announced the arrival of a massive nor'easter, which for the next two days would dump over ten inches of snow on Manhattan and lash the city with sixty-mile gale force winds.[289] In the ominous calm before this record-setting storm a well-dressed man in his mid-thirties, clean shaven, about five-foot, seven inches tall, with blue eyes, and dark blond hair, disembarked from the Norwegian Line steamer, SS *Kristianiafjord*. He passed through the immigration barracks on Ellis Island, answering routine questions in perfect English, receiving a stamp into his Swiss passport under the name of Emile Victor Gasché, sales merchant, born in Solothurn, Switzerland, now living in Berlin, Germany.[290] After arriving in Manhattan on a ferry, he ordered the porters to take his trunk to a cab and headed for Grand Central Station.

Figure 29. Franz Rintelen, 1915
Source: Creative Commons

Maybe because of the weather there was no welcoming committee awaiting his arrival. More likely, there was never a plan to welcome him, a pattern that would repeat in the man's life. He neither was Swiss, nor a sales merchant. He did live in Berlin, however. The forged name in his passport was that of his sister Emilia, one of seven siblings, who had married a Victor Gasché from Switzerland.[291] His true identity was Lieutenant Commander of the Reserve Franz Dagobert Johannes Rintelen, sent from the Imperial War Department in Berlin to New York on a secret mission: to accelerate the German efforts to stop the shipment of arms and ammunition from the US to Germany's enemies.

Rintelen, who would recount his brief stay in the United States as the "Dark Invader" in two bestselling autobiographies in the years after the World War, came from a prominent family, albeit without a noble title.[292] His father had at one time represented the Catholic Party in the Reichstag and served as a director of the Disconto-Gesellschaft, one of the largest German banks of its time. Young Franz grew up in Cologne, and through his father navigated Berlin's high society. As an apprentice in his father's bank, he came to the US between 1905 and 1906 to learn about banking in America. His apprenticeship also took him to England, where he acquired not only a slight British accent but also the demeanor of upper-class British society.

Rintelen's immediate destination was Philadelphia, where he had scheduled Easter dinner with the family friend, James Francis Sullivan, who headed the Market Street National Bank in Philadelphia. Rintelen especially was looking forward to seeing Sullivan's daughter Lita, a love interest from a decade ago, before he married and had a daughter. While Lita had rejected young Franz's advances, he also maintained a longtime friendship with Lita's brother, R. Livingston Sullivan, who sponsored his admittance to the prestigious New York Yacht Club in 1906.[293] Rintelen was still a member and would entertain friends there in the months to come.

On April 5, Rintelen made his way to the German Club on 59th Street in Manhattan, where he would meet Karl Boy-Ed, his immediate superior, and Franz von Papen, who lived there. There is no record of the initial meeting, but the assumption is fair that the three men did not exactly harmonize. Rintelen related the message from the War Department that the Imperial government was not satisfied with the pace of the mission to prevent US supplies from arriving at the European battlefields. He accused von Papen of dabbling in ineffective schemes rather than making a significant impact. Rintelen wanted to sink ships, blow up the loading terminal of the Allies at Black Tom Island in the New York harbor, destroy factories, and personally convince President Wilson, after forcing his hand, to implement "true" neutrality. He had friends in high places (so he thought) and believed he could get an audience with the president at the White House. Von Bernstorff later proclaimed that Rintelen was delusional, a proper assessment at least with respect to meeting President Wilson and convincing him to change his war policies.

The idea that Rintelen could just come to New York, discount all the efforts of the German team to support the German war effort, and not even try to understand what the team had done up to this point, deeply offended von Papen. He fired off a furious wireless a few days later, defending his work and asking for a clear definition of Rintelen's mission. He did not get an answer. Boy-Ed, by nature of a calm and diplomatic demeanor, satisfied Rintelen's immediate demand for funding. Von Papen and Boy-Ed also described their efforts to their new colleague.

To Rintelen's surprise, and a clear sign that he had not paid any attention to what the New York team had achieved, von Papen, with Albert's help, had just closed on a deal. The had locked up the entire annual production of Dupont's smokeless powder, which would be stored in the German-owned Bridgeport Projectile Company warehouses. At the same time, Albert had also concluded a deal with the Spanish government to purchase the smokeless powder. Rintelen supposedly had the same idea and discussed it in Germany during meetings with American businessman Melvin A. Rice in January 1915 as one of the lowest hanging fruits in the effort to hamper American ammunition output.[294] To his great disappointment, he now had to find other venues to show his effectiveness to the impatient Imperial War Department.

Melvin Rice was President of the Donald MacLeod and Company, a linen and flax importing firm based in Manhattan. Rice had traveled to Berlin to negotiate the resumption of production of flax in a mill which his company owned in occupied Belgium. Clearly well-connected, Rice met with Chancellor von Bethmann-Hollweg and Admiral von Tirpitz, among others.[295] Rice encountered the boisterous Rintelen at these meetings, who freely ranted against the US support of the Allied war effort. Rice, at one point, suggested to his negotiation partners to "purchase as much ammunition as possible in the United States in order to prevent it from falling into the hands of the Allies."[296] Rice suggested sending Rintelen to the US, gave him his card, and promised to make available his wide-ranging connections, including President Woodrow Wilson. Rice was back in Europe when Rintelen arrived in early April. As the businessman returned to New York on April 24, at least one New York paper reported that "Melvin A. Rice, friend of President Wilson, returns from successful trip."[297] The factory in Belgium was allowed to resume production, and

Rintelen believed that Rice could indeed open the doors of the White House for him.

Rather than supporting the German efforts in the US or offering his connections, Rice reported on his negotiations in Germany, including the attitude of his negotiation partners, directly to his personal friend, President Wilson, even before Rintelen came to the US. Wilson informed his adviser, Colonel House, on March 1, "An intimate friend [who] just returned from Berlin[...] reports that the Germans[...] thoroughly despise America and Americans."[298]

Rice's direct line to the president did not set well with the State Department. The Ambassador to Germany, James W. Gerard, complained bitterly about Rice's meetings in Berlin, "making the situation there [Berlin] more difficult [for me]."[299] The president did not much care. Rice returned to Europe, including Germany, in March as Wilson's eyes and ears parallel to the State Department and to Edward House. Most significantly for the Rintelen mission to the US, the US president, Department of State, and presumably the Department of Justice knew that a German agent would be sent, knew his name, and just had to find out under what cover he would operate. Naïvely, Rintelen contacted Rice's office in the beginning of April, announcing his arrival. Rice clearly knew of Rintelen's attitude towards the US and at least about the commercial portion of his mission. It took until July 19, 1915, for Rice to finally meet the German agent at a mutual acquaintance's house. The meeting lasted only "one half or three quarters of an hour, during which conversation Rintelen scored [sic] the United States for permitting the shipments of munitions to the Allies."[300] By then, his cover had been blown and he was known to the Bureau.

Rintelen would later claim that from the start of his mission, Boy-Ed and von Papen were jealous and conspired to get rid of him. He was a reserve officer who had never commanded anything other than accounting ledgers. Boy-Ed was a seasoned naval commander. Von Papen was the scion of an aristocratic Prussian family. Rintelen, in his eyes, was an upstart. If the German agent indeed introduced himself with the "von" title, that would certainly have exacerbated von Papen's feelings. Rintelen also claimed that he had made enemies in the Admiralty because of his outspoken opposition to unrestricted submarine warfare.[301] There is no record supporting this claim and, in view of Rintelen's documented hatred for the US economic support of the Allied war effort and his membership in the Flottenverein, Tirpitz's organization to promote German naval supremacy, it seems contrived.[302] Given the agent's brash and undiplomatic manner, however, it is likely that he had made plenty of enemies in Germany, as he now proceeded to do in the US. As von Papen's complaint to the War Department showed, Rintelen was insubordinate. That would be his downfall.

Within a few days, Albert transferred $500,000 from Boy-Ed's account to a new account at the Transatlantic Trust Company. While Rintelen claimed in his books that he had "unlimited funds," and told associates such as Walter Scheele that he received "$30 million" for his mission, his total funds amounted to $508,000 - $500,000 from Boy-Ed and $8,000 which he transferred from Germany before his arrival.[303] Scores of historians, including Barbara Tuchman, took his claims of funding as fact, and included wild schemes of money transfers from Berlin to Rintelen via Havana and South America.[304] To emphasize how unrealistic these claims are, the entire amount of funding of the Albert office in New York from 1914 to 1917, which included propaganda, supporting the interned commercial fleet, supplying the remnants of the German naval fleet, purchasing of supplies (for storage or blockade running efforts), sabotage, and cornering US industries amounted to $26 million. The $500,000 Rintelen received for his mission was the remainder of Boy-Ed's funds for supplying the remnants of the German navy in the fall of 1914.[305] Rintelen's old banking friend George Plochmann, with whom he had worked in England a decade earlier, was now vice president and treasurer of the Transatlantic Trust Co. Plochmann took the funds and helped set up a network of accounts for Rintelen's clandestine work. The German agent also registered a business, the E. V. Gibbons Co., and rented an office under that name at 43 Cedar Street, room 803, in the bank building. He took the alias of Frederick Hansen. His phone lines connected through the Transatlantic Trust's switchboard.

The first project Boy-Ed and von Papen handed over to Rintelen was a bomb-making scheme. Dr. Walter Theodor Scheele, who had worked for the German-owned Bayer Corporation as a chemist, had started his own drugstore on the corner of Harmon and Cypress Streets in Brooklyn. Dr. Scheele had been a sleeper agent since 1893 of the Imperial War Department on an annual retainer of $1,500.[306] Before moving to the US, he had served in an artillery unit and was a major in the German reserve.[307] Under cover as a chemist, Scheele designed explosives and artillery charges for the Imperial army before the war. He also provided the War Department with intelligence on American industry. While on standby for active service, he approached Heinrich Albert and Franz von Papen in January 1915 with several proposals to support the German war effort. Von Papen activated him in February 1915.[308]

Scheele was, at the same time, a brilliant and devious inventor and a bombmaker. One of his inventions was to hide strategic materials such as rubber and oil within cover products. The chemist had found a way to solidify oil, rubber through chemical processes, and turn them into unassuming pellets and powders filled into boxes and bags designated as "fertilizer." The brand name Scheele chose for his "fertilizer" was "Americana," which contained fifty percent "lubricating oil mixed with carbonate of Magnesia." The remaining fifty percent was oil, rubber, or copper depending on the composition.[309] Once in Germany, the pellets could be liquified and stratified into the original compounds. The company doing the conversion was the Anglo-Continental Guano Works in Duesseldorf, where his brother, Dr. Oswald T. Scheele, was the lead chemist.[310] Albert agreed to Scheele's proposal to produce the contraband on a large scale and paid him $1,000 in earnest money.[311] In February, on orders from von Papen, Scheele sold his drugstore in Brooklyn and bought a house at 1229 Park Avenue in Hoboken, New Jersey. He reported to the military attaché, who was designated to supervise the plot on March 1, 1915.[312] Three days later, von Papen financed the establishment of a "fertilizer" plant at 1133 Clinton Street in Hoboken for Scheele, granting him $10,000 in seed money.[313]

Figure 30. Portrait of Walter T. Scheele, April 13, 1916
Source: New York World
British Archives

Scheele had shown von Papen several of his other inventions. One of these stood out. Besides air propelled mortars and new kinds of explosives, Dr. Scheele had designed an ingenious timed incendiary device. Scheele described his "pencil" or "cigar" bombs as follows:

> "Urotropin[e] one-third; peroxide of soda two-thirds. In the upper part there is a tube about four inches high [filled with these chemicals]. The lower part is separated, about three inches, and the inch above is for sulphuric [sic] acid and [a] tin plate."[314] The Czech spymaster in New York, Emmanuel Voska, one of Germany's biggest nemeses in the World War, described Scheele's design in his memoirs, "The device was so simple that one cannot even call it ingenious. The literature of the First World War has named these infernal machines indifferently 'pencil bombs,' and 'cigar bombs.' They looked externally like a cross between the two. Inside a copper disk bisected the bomb vertically. A chemical which has a rapid corrosive effect on copper filled the upper compartment. When it had eaten through the disk it came into contact with the chemical in the lower compartment. The combination produced instantly a flame as hot as a tiny fragment of the sun. The acid did not begin to work on the copper until one broke off a little knob at the upper end. Then it became a time bomb, the time—from two days to a week—being regulated by the thickness or thinness of the copper disk."[315]

Scheele had solved the issue of size (as traditional time bombs would be large with some sort of clock attached to the firing mechanism), and changed the target from a hard-to-destroy steel hull of a freighter to setting its cargo on fire. Thus, he relegated the complicated timing and firing mechanisms of yesteryear to the heap of outdated bomb-building technology. The little bombs burnt so hot that their lead hulls melted completely. Even the use of lead screws ensured that the incendiary devices left virtually no trace. Workers could easily hide the seven-inch "cigars" in their clothes and casually drop them within the cargo they were stacking.[316] The firebombs worked especially well with cargoes of sugar, which, when ignited, developed such intense heat that it became very difficult to extinguish the resulting fire.

Von Papen accepted Scheele's proposal to produce the firebombs after seeing several samples on April 10, 1915. Scheele received $2,500 to get started.

On April 14, he purchased lead piping and the required chemicals. The doctor was in charge of production but would have little to do with the distribution and placement of the bombs. Von Papen detailed for that part of the scheme two German merchant marine captains and a sabotage agent to the project. One of the captains was Eno Bode, a superintendent of the Hamburg-America Line. The second captain was Otto Wolpert, pier superintendent of the Atlas Line, a subsidiary of HAPAG. Erich von Steinmetz alias Sternberg, Stern, and Rasmussen, was a German sabotage agent who had come to the US in January 1915 via Russia "disguised as a woman."[317] He had carried with him glanders cultures designed to poison horses.[318]

The Scheele projects took longer than anticipated. By the middle of April, Scheele had not yet shipped the first bag of "fertilizer," and Albert feared that the chemist was pocketing the funds he had furnished. In April, the first bombs made their way into the holds of several merchant ships, but many did not explode, causing Bode and Wolpert, responsible for distributing the bombs, to get into arguments with the doctor. Also, around that time, von Steinmetz brought a suitcase of glanders cultures to Scheele's laboratory. The ill-tempered doctor went crazy when he saw the vials and catapulted Steinmetz out of his lab in a fistfight. The sabotage agent henceforth was barred from the premises.[319] As another lab found out a few weeks later, von Steinmetz's germs had not survived the long trip from Europe. While von Papen later claimed that he

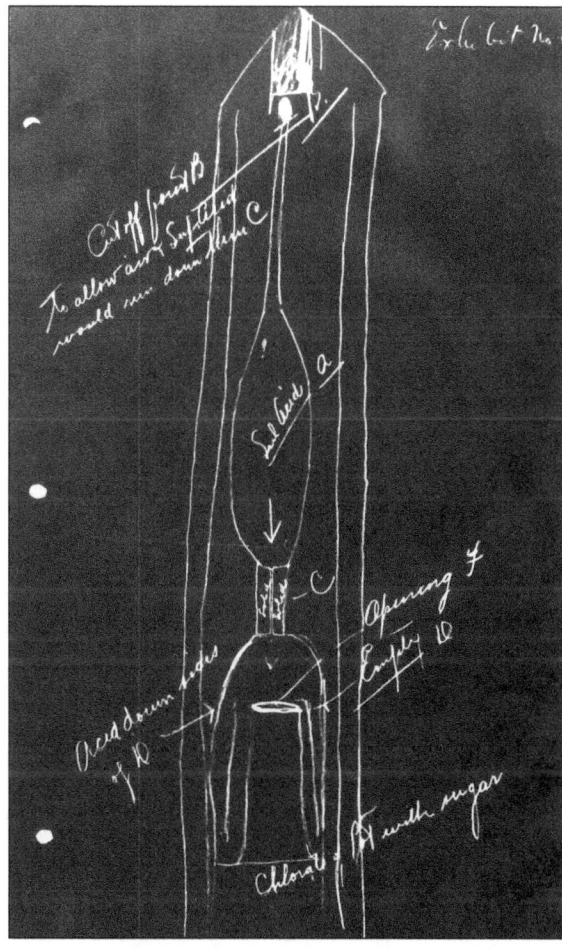

Figure 31. Herrmann, drawing of cigar bomb
Source: Mixed Claims Commission Box 7

gave the firebomb project to Rintelen only grudgingly, the opposite was likely true. Only too glad to rid himself of responsibility for Scheele and his unruly team, he acted without delay.

Von Papen turned the Scheele project over to Rintelen in the second week of April 1915. Whether Scheele did not want to have the bomb production located on his premises, or, more likely, Rintelen decided that the chemist lacked the expertise and resources for scaling up the production, the manufacturing of the bombs moved to the interned German liner, SS *Friedrich der Grosse*, in the nearby North German Lloyd docks. Rintelen paid Scheele to put together a shop with a group of four machinists and a supervising officer, and start production of the lead cylinders under Scheele's supervision. Deliveries of lead piping material attest to production ramping up rapidly. The machinists cut the pipes into the desired lengths, soldered the caps, drilled and threaded the fill holes. Scheele's plant manager or the chief engineer of the *Friedrich der Grosse* then picked the cylinders up and took them to the lab.

There, Scheele checked the quality, inserted the timing discs and an activator (a small disc which when pulled out would allow contact of the sulfuric acid with the timing disc), filled the two halves with the incendiary compounds, and sealed the holes with lead screws. The entire design, including the lead screws, guaranteed that upon activation the bombs would completely burn up, not leaving a trace. Once filled and sealed, the three German merchant marine captains took the bombs and distributed them among the lighter captains and their stevedores. As production expanded, these little bombs also found their way to workers of German, Austrian or Irish descent to set factories on fire.

The ship bombing campaign not only covered Allied loading docks in New York and New Jersey. Von Steinmetz, still trying to deploy his germs against horses that were mainly transported from New Orleans, traveled there in the middle of April. On the orders of Rintelen, Dr. Scheele and Captain Bode joined him as they were supposed to establish a distribution network similar to that in New York harbor. Bode took Maurice D. Conners, a shady businessman, into his confidence and offered him a job as the main contact and organizer for the firebombing project. Captain Bode described Conners as a man in his mid-forties, "five feet ten, weight about one hundred sixty-five, reddish hair, mark drooped under-lid right eye, giving appearance torn at lower corner."[320]

When Bode and Steinmetz told Conners of the money available from the German government for this project, his interest piqued. The negotiations seemed to be on a good footing. Conners introduced his associate and chauffeur Edward John Reilly, alias John Riley, also one of the usual suspects of crooked business dealings in New Orleans, as well as a pro-German Irishman, Michael O'Leary, alias Norton O'Leary, to the group.³²¹ Reilly, also of Irish descent, was in his late 20s, had a dark mustache, and impressed Scheele as "a very strong man."³²² Scheele who had brought "three or four" firebombs with him, showed the new hires how to handle and activate them.³²³ Conners, who used various first names such as Maurice D., Wilhelm J., or James E., ran an automobile dealership in the city with Reilly as his partner.

Unbeknownst to the German conspirators, Conners was also a valuable Bureau informant. He had assisted Agent in Charge Billups Harris as his principal informant in New Orleans in 1913.³²⁴ As Harris's successor, Agent in Charge Forrest Pendleton attested in June 1916, "I feel confident that Conners will give us the benefit of any information he can get, because he has proven many times his loyalty to this office."³²⁵ While peddling cars in 1915, Conners and Reilly also worked on sourcing and smuggling arms for the Mexican consul in the city.³²⁶ Predictably, Conners, now in the know of what the Germans were planning to do, demanded $50,000 ($1 million in today's value) as a retainer plus a $5,000 bonus for each ship that experienced a fire.³²⁷ Scheele sent a dispatch with Conners's demands to Rintelen in New York and returned to Hoboken.

Figure 32. Forrest Currier Pendleton, 1920

Rintelen met Scheele in the Great Northern Hotel in New York, where he was staying, the following week. Fearing to be followed by British agents, as probably they were, the two men took a stroll through Central Park. Scheele told Rintelen that Conners had threatened that "he would do something which would be disagreeable for the whole gang," if the money were not forthcoming.³²⁸ Rintelen sent Scheele back to New Orleans on April 27 to attempt to defuse the situation and close a better deal with Conners. The negotiations were successful. Conners relented and agreed to a tenth of his original demands. The doctor transmitted a new "understanding" to Rintelen that allowed a $5,000 retainer and a $20,000 success premium.[329] Rintelen agreed.

A few weeks later, the three men indeed came to the East Coast. Conners met Rintelen in New York, who gave him a $5,000 check, while Reilly and O'Leary stopped by the lab in Hoboken and picked up two suitcases with "80 to 90" cigar bombs.[330] According to Conners's statement after his arrest in 1918, the 'cigars' were never deployed. Instead, he sold the firebombs to a "junk dealer."[331] Scheele, on the other hand, claimed that he gave Conners firebombs which Reilly filled and activated, damaging nine ships.[332] Conners and Reilly were convicted of these charges in 1918.

Despite Scheele's successful mission to New Orleans to keep the firebombing project on track, Rintelen suspected that it was not Conners but Scheele who tried to shake him down. He already suspected that Scheele had defrauded him on earlier payments. In a meeting with Boy-Ed and von Papen, Rintelen accused Scheele of trying to blackmail him. The only way out, so Rintelen said, was to assassinate the good doctor. The plan he presented was to get Scheele drunk, which considering Scheele's preference of good German beer seemed an achievable goal, and then dump him into the Hudson. According to Rintelen, the two attachés refused to authorize the plan "because they were in too deep."[333] Indeed, they were and so was he.

Independent of Scheele, Rintelen also established a connection with the North German Lloyd offices in Baltimore. Paul Gerhard Hilken, whose father was a prominent German-American businessman in the city, owned A. Schumacher and Co. located in the Hansa Haus in Baltimore, happened to be in New York on business at the beginning of May. Through a mutual friend in the North German Lloyd management, Rintelen met Hilken in the Hotel Astor on Times Square. The two men, both young, energetic, social, and well-traveled, immediately liked each other and vowed to work together. Following the initial meeting, Rintelen went to Baltimore several times. There he also met Captain Friedrich Carl Hinsch, a merchant fleet captain who brought the cargo ship, SS *Neckar*, into internment at Baltimore when the war started. Both Hinsch and Hilken worked for *Abteilung* IIIb, the Imperial General Staff's intelligence service, and eagerly took on the firebomb mission. While no firebombed ships from Baltimore harbor are documented, the sabotage cell around Hilken and Hinsch in July 1916 blew up the Black Tom Island Allied loading terminal, the largest sabotage attack on the United States of the entire war. This all happened under the nose of Agent Billups Harris, formerly in charge of the New Orleans field office.

Thomas Tunney, the head of the New York bomb squad formed in August 1914 in response to the outbreak of war in Europe, led the investigations into the mysterious ship fires.[334] On May 20, French authorities in Marseille notified Tunney that they had recovered four mysterious lead cylinders filled with chemicals from the hold of the SS *Kirkoswald*, which had sailed from New York on May 2. The *Kirkoswald* was not the only ship where French authorities found the suspicious pipes. Three ships that left New York between April 29 and May 1, arrived in Le Havre, France, having experienced fires on the journey. In all three cases, French authorities recovered the mysterious lead cylinders, which turned out to be unexploded timed firebombs. Tunney now had a description of the bombs, and he had reasonable evidence that the sabotage occurred in the New York harbor.

Tunney suspected the personnel on lighters, the freight transfer boats used in the harbor to move freight from warehouses to ships, of placing the bombs into certain freight. Upon investigation, Tunney's team found that the fires originated in sugar or highly flammable materials such as cotton, hay, or clothing.[335] The investigators determined that the freight in the harbor, including on ships, docks, and in warehouses, was heavily guarded by all kinds of security staff. During the time when the freight was transferred from the warehouses to the shipping docks or freighters, it was unguarded. In addition, several of the lighter captains had German-sounding names.

In the process of investigating the origin of the firebombs, Tunney's men canvassed outlets of explosives and chemicals. One of the detectives came across a promising lead: An unlikely shopper, Herbert O. Kienzle, owner of a German clock factory outlet in Manhattan, sought to purchase TNT and various other chemicals. The combination of clocks and TNT, as the men were searching for makers of timebombs, understandably triggered a major police investigation. Over the next months, Tunney's detectives followed the clock dealer, and identified a wooded property in Grantwood, New Jersey, near Weehawken, where bombs were being built and tested.

The bomb squad arrested four men in short order. The main suspect was a man named Robert Fay, a lieutenant in the German army, who had worked in Boston before the war as an engineer. He spoke English fluently and his sister and brother-in-law lived in New Jersey. At the beginning of 1915, Fay had shown a timed rudder bomb design to his military superiors in Germany. They gave him $4,000 and an English passport with a false name, and sent him to the US, where he arrived on April 23, 1915. As Tunney had surmised, Fay indeed had worked on building a timed explosive device to be attached to ship rudders using clocks and explosives.

Luckily, the bomb design never left the experimental stage. Local police and Tunney's men arrested Fay with several of his co-conspirators in Grantwood on October 24, 1915. There seems to be evidence of US Secret Service involvement in Fay's arrest.[336] While up to October 22, Secret Service Agent Frank Burke worked on a counterfeit investigation, Agents Burke, Savage, and Howell were detailed to a "special investigation by direction of Chief" on October 23 that lasted into the end of November.[337] Agent Kavanaugh reported on October 24, that he brought an overcoat to Agent Burke near Weehawken, New Jersey, where the arrest occurred later that day. Fay was held at the local police station to be released to the custody of New York City police. Agent Burke reported on October 26 that he "paid for dinners prisoners Walter Scholz and Robert Fay."[338] In the press, USSS Chief Flynn claimed that the US Secret Service had followed and arrested Fay. From the agents' daily reports, it is clear that USSS agents did not follow Fay before his arrest. Captain Tunney and his men clearly deserve the credit.

Figure 33. Robert Fay, c. 1917-1918
Source: US National Archives and Records Administration

Perhaps the US Secret Service involvement may be related to customs inspectors (also part of the Treasury Department) who had been involved in the investigation of Fay and his associates. Dudley Field Malone, the New York Collector of Customs, had organized an eighty-man-strong "Customs Neutrality Squad" in 1914. Malone's men had noticed Fay and his associates milling around the harbor and reported those observations to the New York police, but may also have involved Chief Flynn in their investigation.[339]

Under arrest, Fay quickly confessed and gave a detailed statement to Captain Thomas Tunney, Sergeant George Barnitz (Tunney's second in command), and Deputy Police Commissioner (and former Bureau Special Agent) Guy Scull on October 24, 1915.[340] No Secret Service agent was present for the interrogation. Although Fay retracted his confession to save his family members, a federal grand jury handed down indictments for all five conspirators. Fay was sentenced to eight years of hard time in April 1916, and entered Atlanta penitentiary in June 1916.[341] A few months after Fay began his prison sentence, he managed to escape, in September 1916.

While up to that point the Bureau had had no involvement in the Fay case, apprehending Fay now became a priority.[342] Chief Bielaski started a major manhunt, conducted all along the Eastern seaboard.[343] Fay, who received money and safehouses from the German military attaché, hid out in Baltimore under the not-so-watchful eyes of Agent Billups Harris. Although a second escapee was captured, Fay managed to slip away to Spain. In August 1918, Spanish authorities captured and unceremoniously deported him to the US as Fay had waived formal extradition proceedings.[344] He served his remaining sentence until October 1922, when President Warren G. Harding pardoned him, and he returned to Germany.[345]

The Fay investigation in June and July of 1915 did not yield the makers of the firebombs for whom Tunney was looking, but a curious set of reports in the Bureau file on the chemist in July 1915 reveal a separate avenue of investigation into the Scheele factory and laboratory. While Tunney fretted over who was making and distributing the bombs, British intelligence had infiltrated Scheele's operation in the beginning of July. The targeting of Scheele was the result of British agents following Rintelen's every move. One of the meetings between Scheele and Rintelen put the chemist on Naval Attaché Guy Gaunt's radar. Surveilling Scheele between July 12 and 28, 1915, operatives of the Mooney and Boland Detective Agency working for Gaunt staked out Scheele's house and the chemical factory in Hoboken.[346]

One of the detectives identified the plant manager of the factory as Charles von Kleist.[347] Captain Thomas Tunney would later describe him as a "funny little man who looked like a cartoon of the late Prussian eagle."[348] Indeed, the five-foot, seven-inch tall, proud Germanic-looking veteran of the Franco-Prussian war of 1870 to 1871, with a well-kempt chin beard, spectacles and bowler hat, did not quite blend into the New York crowds as one would expect from a secret agent. The sixty-seven-year-old Hermann Ewald Carl von

Kleist was the black sheep of a very renowned, old noble family in Germany. His brother was a famous field marshal. Rather than follow in the prescribed footsteps of his ancestors as military men, university professors, poets, and clergy, von Kleist decided to join the merchant marine and follow that career to retirement.[349]

"Before the war, von Kleist was in the command of the freighter *Haulloway*, owned by Church Bros. of Tiffany, R. I."[350] At the outbreak of the war, von Kleist lived in a small house at 1121 Garden Street in Hoboken, New Jersey, with his wife Mary, a former opera singer. Possibly out of boredom or feeling the call of patriotic duty, the retired merchant marine captain decided to support the Kaiser and Fatherland. He took a job as superintendent of Walter Scheele's "fertilizer" plant.

Figure 34. Franz Rintelen, c. World War II
Source: File KV2 British National Archives

Over the next weeks, one of the Mooney and Boland detectives, who befriended von Kleist's son, William, gained the confidence of the gullible nobleman.[351] Believing that the detective was in desperate need of a job, von Kleist hired the man, who only stayed employed for three days. That was enough to get a good look around the facility:

> There are three doors to be passed before entering the works, and an electric contact bell rings when the doors are being opened. On the ground floor are a number of bags, which are said to contain manure. In the rear [,] are two large hogsheads, one of which is empty, and the other, apparently, full, said to contain a chemical which is used for the manufacture of artificial rubber. There are six barrels of naphtha and smoking is

prohibited. There were about four live chickens in the yard. On the upper floor (one flight up) Kleist has a small live alligator in a small aquarium. On the upper floor, which is divided into three compartments are located what appear to be laboratories [...]. These compartments are extremely hot [...].[352]

The detective did not look for or find evidence of explosives.

On August 27, 1915, three months from the discovery of the bombs in Marseille, the New York bomb squad arrested the lighter captains.[353] Captains Mike Matzet, Ferdinand Hahn, Richard Meyerhofer, and Jene Storms all turned out to be German citizens. The lead Mooney and Boland detective mentioned in his report that he worked in tandem with a certain detective Ryan. While there was no employee of the bomb squad under that name, a US Secret Service daily report dated September 3, 1915, mentions a Detective Ryan of the "3rd Branch Detective Bureau," formerly an employee of the Burns Detective Agency.[354] Ryan may be the informant who identified the Scheele factory as a target for the New York bomb squad in September.

Tunney's men decided to raid the Scheele factory in the middle of September 1915. Local police Detective Sergeant Daniel J. Kiely, Detectives George Busby and James Sterett, as well as a chemist working for the bomb squad, named Liebermann, entered the premises.[355] They found nine employees hard at work.[356] With respect to finding a bomb factory, the raid was a bust. The detectives found some bags of guano and chemicals associated with the production of fertilizer.

While the flow of information on the police raid of Scheele's premises is not documented, Tunney likely reported the raid to the Bureau. The bulk of intelligence that is found in the Bureau files about Scheele, however, came from British intelligence. Around September 20, Bielaski received case files of the Mooney and Boland detectives from Gaunt. Bielaski referred to "the special data" in a letter to New York Division Superintendent William Offley, urging him to keep investigating the "fertilizer," as there may be "some element in the fertilizer that can be used for other purposes." Bielaski's letter also referred to a man at 31 Water Street in Brooklyn who was the freight forwarder, data that came from the Mooney and Boland reports.[357] The Chief added other British intelligence to the list of items he wanted Offley to investigate: a ship Heinrich Albert was about to sell, and a line captain with the name Bode who required some scrutiny.[358] Bielaski again urged Offley on October 7, 1915, to stay on the "fertilizer" case, using the "special data" at his disposal.[359]

Guy Gaunt's intelligence proved to be extremely valuable and triggered the end of Scheele's projects. New York Bureau Special Agents Henry Dotzert and Charles Scully spoke to the shipper of the fertilizer, Frederick Henjes of Oelrichs and Co. at 31 Water Street in Brooklyn. This was the company at the center of the earlier von Wedell passport fraud investigation. Henjes, likely not keen on following his colleague, Carl Ruroede, to prison, spilled the beans on the mysterious fertilizer. He confirmed that the plant was a German operation, and he described that the fertilizer was mostly oil that had been solidified.[360] He testified that upon reaching Germany, the oil could be separated through a chemical process.

The investigation showed that in May the first shipment, 1,000 bags of fertilizer, left the plant consigned to Sweden on the SS *Riga*. From Sweden, the cargo would eventually be transferred to Germany.[361] Another shipment crossed the Atlantic to Gothenburg in July 1915 on the SS *Seaconnet*.[362] A consignment of fertilizer with a bill of lading dated August 7, 1915, which Henjes sent in the middle of October on the Danish flagged SS *Esrom*, ended the fertilizer ruse.[363] British inspectors seized the ship, and impounded the "fertilizer." Using the Mooney and Boland detective reports, in which von Kleist had detailed to the operatives how the fertilizer could be reconstituted into the original ingredients, British investigators proved that the powders and pellets were indeed contraband.

After concluding their investigation, British authorities notified US Ambassador Walter Hines Page of the innovative smuggling attempt.[364] The State Department asked the Justice Department for information on the seized ship, and to investigate a potential violation of US neutrality laws.[365] William Offley assigned Agent Scully in New York to determine when the ship had left, and find a copy of the bill of lading with information about the "fertilizer." He reported back to Chief Bielaski on November 20.[366] In response to Lansing's request to investigate Scheele's company, Attorney General Gregory asked the State Department on January 17, 1916, to intervene with the British government, and send the results of their investigation into the "fertilizer" to the Bureau.[367]

While the British used official channels to bust the Scheele cell, Bureau files show that sometime in December 1915, a mysterious man named Oswald Scheidemann, supposedly the son of a friend of Kleist's sister, Olga, who lived in Germany, contacted him. A month later, with the help of the gullible von Kleist who paid his train fare, he showed up in Hoboken.[368] Almost simultaneously a letter from his sister arrived asking him to help the young man. Von Kleist complied. The interesting part about this "family friend" is that he is not listed in the Bureau files among the persons associated with the Scheele case.[369]

The kind, but gullible nobleman, took the young man in and let him stay with the family. Von Kleist even briefly employed the man in the factory, and over the next weeks told him all about Scheele's work and the dark purpose of the facility besides producing contraband: the production of firebombs.[370] In addition, Scheidemann learned that the bombs were produced on the interned German liner *Friedrich der Grosse*, which explained why the raid in September had yielded no results.

Von Kleist had meanwhile fallen out with Scheele who owed him paychecks amounting to $235. He was disgruntled. Scheidemann promised to help his benefactor contact Wolf von Igel, the German military attaché, who was Scheele's superior, and settle the matter. At Scheidemann's urging, von Kleist drafted a letter to von Igel, describing the issue and asking for help. Not "knowing" von Igel's office address, Scheidemann went to the German consulate general to find out where von Igel's office was. The consulate staff declined to give out the information, but supposedly took the letter. A copy of the letter also turned up at Captain Tunney's office. A few days later, Scheidemann reported to von Kleist that he had made contact with von Igel's secretary, and arranged for a meeting at Haan's restaurant in the St. Regis Hotel on 5th Avenue in Manhattan. There he introduced von Kleist to a Mr. Moeller, supposedly von Igel's secretary, who strangely did not speak German.[371] Moeller was Detective Henry Barth of the New York bomb squad. He promised to help. The next day, when the men met at the same café, Moeller and Scheidemann brought with them

Figure 35. Captain Charles von Kleist, 1916
Source: Library of Congress Prints and Photographs Division

another supposed employee of von Igel. That person aroused von Kleist's suspicions as he looked to him like a cop. He was. Detectives George Busby and Henry Barth invited von Kleist and Scheidemann on a car ride into Manhattan. There was no use in refusing. According to Detective Barth, von Kleist knew "the jig was up."[372]

In Manhattan, Barth and Busby took von Kleist and Scheidemann to police headquarters and placed them under arrest. Captain Tunney interviewed von Kleist and, the next day, confronted him with the freshly arrested Captains Bode and Wolpert. After the stories of the three suspects were corroborated, Tunney turned them over to the Bureau.[373] Curiously, after initially being booked together with von Kleist, Scheidemann was never interviewed or heard of again. He slipped away, unrecognized by the German officials and unidentified in the court documents. Von Kleist complained in a letter to his sister, who had recommended he take care of Scheidemann, that he had betrayed him. "He went to the police and told them that if they would give him two thousand dollars, he would tell them about a German bomb society of which I was one of the leading men."[374] It is highly unlikely that an informant, to whom the Bureau paid $2 to $3 a day, would receive $2,000 for a tip. And, according to von Kleist, clearly embittered by the situation, he wrote to his sister that he didn't: "P.S. Of course the dirty Jew did not get the 2000 dollars from the Police [...]. God willing, the miserable Jew will get his sentence if he goes back to Germany [...]. Don't take it to heart that the miserable dog, as it were, came to my house through your agency [...]. If my son ever lays hands on him, it might go ill with him."[375] US immigration records, as well as census data, city directories, and other archives covering the period do not contain an Oswald Scheidemann. He could have been the traitor von Kleist believed him to be, using a false name. However, more likely is the possibility that British intelligence contacted von Kleist's sister as a ruse, thus infiltrating one of their agents into the von Kleist household.

Between April 5 and 21, 1916, close to a year after the first bombs went off, Bureau agents and New York police arrested the conspirators, including Charles von Kleist, Otto Wolpert, Eno Bode, the chief engineer of the *Friedrich der Grosse*, Carl Schmidt, and the engineers Wilhelm Paradies, George Praedel, Ernst Friedrich Garbade, and Ernst Becker.[376] The suspects were arraigned at the New York federal building before District Judge Howe.[377] All pleaded, "not guilty." The commissioner set the bail at $25,000 for Wolpert and Bode, $10,000 for Schmidt, and $5,000 for the others.[378] After the arraignment,

Agent Underhill interrogated the suspects with Agent Grgurevich interpreting.[379] Transcripts of the prisoners' statements went to Superintendent Offley and Chief Bielaski.[380]

On April 17, Bureau Assistant Division Superintendent Baker, together with Agents Dotzert and Grgurevich, attempted to seize Scheele at his house in Hoboken.[381] However, in this case P. K. had been one step ahead. The German agent had learned of the arrest warrants being prepared. German military attaché von Igel forwarded P. K.'s tip to the doctor a few days before the arrests. On April 1, 1916, Scheele skipped town at the last moment.[382] At the subsequent trial, the eight German conspirators, including von Kleist, received sentences ranging from six months and two years in a federal penitentiary and fines ranging from $500 to $5,000.[383]

Officials believed Scheele, who claimed that he did not produce any bombs after April 1915. Lead pipe deliveries in January and February of 1916 prove the opposite. The government believed that the bombing campaign damaged thirty-five ships and caused damages in excess of $10 million.[384] Closer scrutiny reveals that at least seventy-four ships burned; some even sank. In addition, an estimated $12 million in damages was the result of factory attacks.[385] Von Kleist died in the Atlanta penitentiary in 1919 of influenza while serving together with Rintelen. Rintelen later honored the old sailor by creating the pseudonym, Captain Franz Rintelen von Kleist, as author of his autobiographies.[386]

In his autobiography, *Throttled!*, Captain Tunney claimed that when raids occurred outside the New York police's jurisdiction, he asked US Secret Service Chief Flynn for help.[387] Bureau files indicate, however, that special agents of the Bureau—not US Secret Service agents—accompanied Tunney's men and conducted investigations in concert with the bomb squad and local police. When the Bureau raided Scheele's factory on April 21, 1916, Agent Dotzert reported:

> Pursuant to instructions of Asst. Div. Supt. Baker, I proceeded to Captain Tunney's office, Police Headquarters, for the purpose of accompanying Detective Sergeant Geo. Busby and two other detectives to the New Jersey Agricultural Chemical Company, 1113 Clinton Ave., Hoboken, N.J. at which place Dr. Scheele had his laboratory [...]. On our way over we stopped at Police Headquarters, Hoboken, N.J. for Detective Sergeant Dan Keily [sic] [...].[388]

There is no other evidence of Secret Service involvement in this investigation. Tunney may have embellished his recollection later as Flynn, the former Chief of the US Secret Service and a celebrity in New York, published his adventures as a German spy hunter in the war.

Agents of the Bureau hunted down any lead they could find on Dr. Scheele, receiving the following description: "50 years; five foot eight; 190 pounds; stocky; deep chested; heavy gray mustache; light hair, mixed with gray; prominent scar on right cheek, probably sabre cut; neat dresser; wears alpine hat; inveterate cigar smoker; drinks considerably and wears pearl handle gun on belt."[389]

By April 20, 1916, agents had tracked him to Richmond, Virginia, Jacksonville, Florida, Daytona, Florida, and finally Havana, Cuba.[390] Scheele had actually gone to Jacksonville to meet a contact from the German embassy, who gave him identification documents. Scheele's alias was Walter Theodor Rheinfelder, representative of the German language Jacksonville *Staats Zeitung*, not the most sophisticated cover for the Bureau's most-wanted. Told to wait for instructions, Scheele stayed at a friend's house in Daytona for over a week. As the dragnet tightened around him, Scheele decided to go to Washington, DC, and meet with Prinz Hatzfeld of the German embassy. Hatzfeld instructed him to go to Havana and go into hiding. The local German consul would be instructed to pay his expenses. The embassy would also take care of Scheele's wife. The German agent took a train to Charleston, South Carolina, on April 12, and from there via Key West to Havana.[391]

Bielaski knew from the case of Dr. Felipe Dusart Quintana, which will be discussed later in the book, that extradition proceedings from Cuba could take years. He, therefore, tried to coax Agent Louis Means Cantrell, already operating in Havana under cover shadowing Dusart and other Mexican expatriates, into bribing Cuban officials to allow kidnapping Scheele and bringing him back to the US. Bielaski sent a coded telegram to Cantrell at 11:00 a.m. on April 21: "Prefer if practicable you arrange confidentially to have party placed on steamship bound for United States *without any proceedings* [emphasis added]. Authorized expend reasonable amount to perfect arrangements drawing on me for necessary funds. Secure all documentary evidence. Answer."[392]

Cantrell did not hesitate with his answer. At 1:00 p.m. he responded: "Telegram received fourteen [Cuban] secret service operatives searching. Registered Hotel Luz eighteenth left nineteenth police sure can locate today. Doubt under conditions your plan. Will make every effort and report."[393] Cantrell indeed made every effort as the following days would show. On May 1, 1916, when Cantrell reported to the Chief that he had located Scheele in

Havana, Bielaski ordered him to arrest the fugitive and wait for instructions.[394] Cantrell, of course, did not have authority to arrest anyone in Cuba.

Bielaski conferred with the State Department in the hope of getting Scheele deported for using a false identity. Secretary Lansing instructed the American minister to appeal to the Cuban government. Cantrell patiently waited most of May 3. When he learned that the minister was playing golf rather than working on his case, he took matters into his own hands. He went to the Cuban foreign secretary, who went to President Mario García Menocal on his behalf. The Cuban president agreed to expel Scheele "quietly" on the following day.[395] Cantrell reported on his negotiations to Bielaski, who in turn informed Lansing. Lansing notified Attorney General Gregory on May 4, that "American Legation Havanna reports Walter Scheele will be expelled from Cuba to Key West probably today," making it sound as if it had been the American minister who had made the arrangements.[396] Expecting the immediate expulsion of Scheele, Bielaski asked the deputy US marshal in Key West, under strict secrecy to be ready to receive the suspect and bring him to New York. At the same time, Superintendent Offley sent the indictment and warrant from New York.[397] In the meantime, Cantrell conferred with the chief of Cuba's National Secret Police, Rafael Muñoz, on the details of Scheele's arrest and expulsion.[398]

While Bielaski laid the groundwork for the deputy marshal in Key West to receive Scheele, Cantrell developed a different plan that would circumvent the untrustworthy Cuban government (which indeed withdrew support) and the disinterested American legation.[399] He described his plan to the Chief on May 4 in a coded cable. Cantrell wanted to kidnap Scheele with the help of Muñoz's secret police, and bring him aboard a US-flagged United Fruit steamer, which would bring the suspect straight to New York.[400] Bielaski immediately cabled back, "Arrangement highly satisfactory."[401]

Neither the official nor Cantrell's plan came to fruition. Scheele apparently had bribed the Cuban police authorities, who suddenly claimed to Cantrell that they could not lay a hand on the suspect who was staying on the interned Austrian steamer, *Virginia*.[402] The Cuban police went to the ship without telling Cantrell and supposedly could not find Scheele. Cantrell reported to Bielaski, "Agent hasn't the slightest doubt but that there is something absolutely crooked about this sudden action."[403] Furious, Cantrell went all the way to the Cuban president to complain. The president stated that he trusted his Chief of Police.[404]

Apparently, in this spat Cantrell was accused of being a spy by Cuban officials, an accusation he addressed to the American minister in an eighteen-page statement dated May 8. "I am commissioned by the Attorney General as a Special Agent of the United States Department of Justice and belong to what is known officially as the Bureau of Investigation. This Bureau is in no way connected with the Secret Service of the United States nor am I in any sense [...] a 'DETECTIVE' [all caps in the original]."[405] In a coded telegram, Chief Bielaski described to Agent Richmond M. Levering in 1917 that Scheele had indeed been "located there [Cuba] April last year but [Cuban] police double-crossed agent and fugitive escaped."[406]

Having given up on the kidnapping idea, Bielaski now asked the State Department to work on an official extradition request for Scheele.[407] Agent Cantrell in Havana, despite the sore feelings towards the Cuban police, monitored their investigation. He also closely watched steamers leaving Cuba, interviewed the pursers, and reviewed the passenger lists to ensure that Scheele did not leave.[408] Despite rumors that the doctor was headed to the Dutch West Indies, he remained in hiding on interned German ships. Bureau agents opened Scheele's wife's mail for the next year, as well as the mail of known family friends and neighbors whom Scheele used to correspond with his wife.[409] Bielaski authorized Offley in mid-June to infiltrate the Scheele household and gain the confidence of Mrs. Scheele using "a man or a woman" under cover to find out where the doctor was hiding.[410] Offley did not like the idea as Mrs. Scheele was "suspicious" of anyone asking probing questions.[411] Still, he detailed Agent Nils Chalmers to chat with Mrs. Scheele under cover as someone interested in buying her house.[412] To the agent's great surprise, she was very cordial, invited him inside, offered refreshments, and maintained that she did not know where her husband was. Chalmers believed that she

Figure 36. Richmond Mortimer Levering
Source: Courtesy Bobby Kelley

was telling the truth.⁴¹³ Field offices from San Antonio to New Orleans were on the lookout for any information.⁴¹⁴ Scheele had disappeared.

As Bielaski had feared, the official extradition process moved at a snail's pace. The mastermind and bombmaker of the German sabotage campaign was finally arrested by Cuban authorities and extradited in March 1918. The arrest was just a formality, as records show that Scheele had not been supported financially by the German consul in Cuba. After complaints, which Franz Rintelen in an interview in 1918 described as Scheele attempting to blackmail the German consul, Scheele offered to surrender to US authorities.⁴¹⁵ He returned to Florida in the company of Agent Richmond M. Levering, who also conducted the initial debriefing and wrote an extensive report on Scheele's activities and culpability.⁴¹⁶

Scheele, fearing that he would be court martialed and executed, offered full cooperation and his services. The deal was sealed when chemists of Thomas Edison's laboratories debriefed the doctor and field tested several of his inventions, including the pencil bombs.⁴¹⁷ They could not believe their eyes and ears when the German agent showed his notes and designs while he told all he knew.⁴¹⁸ Not all his inventions were deadly. Smiling deviously, Scheele recounted having produced little wheat-size grains in the spring of 1916. The grains found their way into wheat bags in nineteen carloads of grain in New Orleans between February and March 1916, all destined for the Allies. Once in Europe, the grain was milled and distributed to bakeries. As soon as the bakers mixed the flour with water, Scheele's grains turned the dough blue.⁴¹⁹ It was a harmless blue dye. Still, the bakers discarded the discolored loaves. It is unknown how many thousands of pounds of bread Scheele's grains thus ruined.

Abandoned by the German government and branded a traitor, the "brain of the [firebomb] conspiracies" became an American agent.⁴²⁰ He worked with the US military at the Jones Point Experimental Laboratory until the end of the war on multiple bomb designs, air propelled artillery shells, and a host of other inventions he had in his repertoire. Agent Levering stayed in close contact with Scheele and his wife, convinced of Scheele's loyalty and value for the war effort.⁴²¹

Bringing Scheele into the fold as an American agent was not without problems. In November 1918, a few months after his arrival in the United States and still in the custody of the Bureau, Scheele developed acute appendicitis and underwent an operation. Presented with the $938.37 bill, Bielaski balked. Grudgingly, after several months of back and forth, he paid.⁴²²

Scheele settled in Hackensack, New Jersey, after the war, adopting "Smith" as his new family name.⁴²³ To settle the legal case against him, Scheele pled guilty to "manufacturing firebombs and [sic] be placed in ships going to the Allied Powers" on February 26, 1921. He was sentenced to one day in custody of a US marshal.[424] Franz Rintelen would not be so lucky.

7

Huerta Comeback

Just ten days after Franz Rintelen walked off the gangway of the SS *Kristianiafjord*, Victoriano Huerta, the former dictator of Mexico, arrived in New York from Barcelona, Spain. The arrival of Huerta days after that of Rintelen spurred many a rumor in the press and in histories of the era: Was this mere coincidence? General Huerta had settled in Barcelona with his family, but his exile from Mexico lasted little more than seven months. Although he was down, he was not entirely out. Huerta kept a close eye on developments in Mexico, and he felt that the vicious fighting among the victorious Constitutionalists afforded an opportunity to make a comeback in a country desperate for a leader strong enough to restore stability. Huerta began organizing his adherents in Europe, in the United States, and in Havana.

New York became a major hub of *huertista* activity. A person of increasing interest was José B. Ratner, of the *Tampico News Agency*, who had made a fortune purchasing munitions, including fifty machine guns and 3,000,000 cartridges, for Huerta in 1913-1914.[425] Ratner was a Russian "about 42 years of age, 5' 6", 150 pounds, dark hair, small dark mustache, said to have some defect in one eye." The State Department was concerned Ratner might be involved in yet another Mexican affair, and requested that the Department of Justice investigate him. Chief Bielaski instructed Superintendent Offley to give the Ratner matter "prompt and careful attention," place Ratner under surveillance, and send the State Department copies of Bureau agents' reports.[426]

Offley informed Bielaski that his agents said it would be very difficult to secure any reliable information without the assistance of someone familiar with Mexican conditions and with Spanish. When it came to informants, a new arrow in the Bureau's quiver in New York was Harry Berliner. He was an "old Mexico hand," having been a businessman in Mexico City for years. Berliner had remained in Mexico until July 22, 1915, when First Chief Carranza expelled him from Veracruz. Berliner, ostensibly working for general manager

W. A. Parker selling Oliver typewriters and adding machines in Mexico, supposedly called Carranza "a darn fool."[427] He did not deny the charge, telling reporters, "If Carranza is going to deport every man who curses his administration, he'll have to deport nine tenths of the Mexican population."[428] Carranza refused to permit American Consul John R. Silliman to intervene on Berliner's behalf and charged the American with being a Huerta sympathizer. Berliner strongly rejected the accusation.[429] The steamer *Morro Castle* took him to New York City. In the meantime, the members of the American business community in Veracruz and Mexico City vehemently protested his expulsion. According to the press, "Carranza money declined here to the lowest it has ever been, selling at 32 Pesos for one American dollar" as a result of the scandal.[430] In New York, Berliner sold typewriters for the Oliver Typewriter Company and kept up his network of acquaintances, many of them prominent Conservative exiles. And not just Mexicans—Berliner called on the *huertista* Ratner brothers and had a long talk with José B. Ratner.

Figure 37. Venustiano Carranza, 1913
Source: Library of Congress Prints and Photographs Division

Berliner was classified as a Bureau special employee, and he had one of the more enviable jobs around. His modus operandi was to make daily rounds of the leading hotels and to call at the offices of his many friends and acquaintances. He often invited those with whom he chatted to have a cigar or a "refreshment," as he put it in his reports, at the bar. When he thought he was on to something important, he would take the individual to dinner. Berliner seemingly had a pleasant life. He reported a mixture of gossip and hard information. The Bureau got its money's worth from its special employee, who charged his expenses to Oliver Typewriter.⁴³¹

Besides Berliner, Chief Bielaski reluctantly authorized the employment of Sherburne Hopkins's former assistant Harvey Phillips. Phillips had visited the New York field office several times seeking employment. Although Phillips's Spanish was less than fluent, through his work with one of the most influential lobbyists and lawyers when it came to revolutions in Mexico and Central America, he knew a number of those involved in revolutionary matters. Offley suggested him as a possibility. But because of Phillips's checkered past, including a conviction for neutrality laws violation, Bielaski was not enthusiastic, wiring "Do not desire employ Phillips unless no one else available." No one was, and Offley hired Phillips on a temporary basis as a special employee at $4 per day.⁴³² Offley briefed Phillips, who began his work on February 13, sounding out his acquaintances regarding Mexican affairs. Phillips also approached José Ratner using the ploy of being an arms broker with weapons to sell. Ratner did not take the bait, informing Phillips that he was no longer interested in munitions. Perhaps because of financial stringency, Offley dismissed Phillips on March 7, but Phillips continued to provide information to the Bureau.⁴³³ Meanwhile, Bureau agents learned that Ratner had an office with an unlisted telephone number at room 822, 130 Fulton Street. They also placed a cover on Ratner's mail.⁴³⁴

Figure 38. *Harry Berliner (second from right) at the border*
Source: *Courtesy Kristin Rounds*

The situation changed dramatically, when on April 12, 1915, General Victoriano Huerta arrived in New York City from Barcelona. The exiled strongman passed through customs "as a transient alien after having declared under oath that he would do nothing to violate the neutrality laws."[435] Ratner arranged for a suite for Huerta at the luxurious Hotel Ansonia. The hotel staff readily gave the Bureau carte blanche to monitor Huerta's activities. This included listing those who called on Huerta, telephone calls from Huerta's suite, and telegrams delivered, as well as making envelope tracings of the general's correspondence. In addition, a Bureau forensic accountant began auditing the bank accounts of the Ratner brothers. Huerta's entourage included Abraham Z. Ratner, José's brother and partner in the *Tampico News* Co., who described himself to the press as an importer and a resident of New York.

The gatekeeper to Huerta's suite was twenty-six-year-old Lt. Colonel Rafael Pimienta, who had an interesting background. In 1913, Pimienta was a corporal and was part of the military detail taking President Francisco I. Madero and Vice President José María Pino Suárez to the penitentiary in Mexico City when they executed the deposed pair. Reportedly it was Pimienta who shot the vice president.[436] Pimienta received a series of promotions, and he remained a staunch *huertista*. Among those cleared to enter Huerta's hotel suite was Leon Rasst of *Ypiranga* fame. More importantly, another visitor was General Pascual Orozco, Huerta's former subordinate and, like Huerta, a proven loser. Huerta had a succession of visitors and rarely left his suite except on Sundays, when he relaxed by, among other things, attending a baseball game. He did announce that he planned to lease a house on Long Island for himself and his family, who were coming from Barcelona.[437]

Agent H. H. Childers, who had been monitoring Huerta at the Hotel Ansonia, reported that on May 15, Huerta had left the hotel accompanied by his secretary General José Delgado and his son-in-law Alberto Quiroz. Abraham Ratner remained in the Huerta suite. Childers stated:

> In concluding my report, I am inclined to think that in view of Huerta's having leased a home on Long Island, at Forest Hills, for a term of months, it would not seem that he contemplates taking any immediate steps that might be construed into any violation of the neutrality act. I say this after visiting his headquarters for more than two weeks and observing the movement of those who have called to see him.[438]

HUERTA COMEBACK

Figure 39. Left to right: José C. Delgado, Victoriano Huerta, Abraham Z. Ratner, c. 1906-1916
Source: George Grantham Bain Collection
Library of Congress Prints and Photographs Division

The agent then covered himself by adding, "Of course it is unlikely [sic —likely] that if he did contemplate making any important move, he might be acting with such consummate secrecy that the conspiracy might not be readily detected."[439]

Superintendent Offley was worried about the second possibility, informing Chief Bielaski that Huerta's move to the large summer residence he had rented at Forest Hills was disquieting:

> Forest Hills is a small and fashionable suburb of New York City, and President Huerta will occupy the cottage [In this connection, "cottage" was a euphemism for "mansion."] with his family and servants, comprising upward of twenty persons in all. Under these circumstances it will be extremely difficult to secure any reliable information concerning his movements or visitors unless we expend considerable time and money in the effort, there being only one hotel in the place, and that is not very near the Huerta cottage, and for this reason it would be almost impossible to maintain any efficient observation of the man unless one or more agents would take up their residence in the neighborhood and spend most of the time thereabouts. Please advise me of your wishes in [sic] the premises.[440]

Bielaski instructed Offley to make an immediate investigation. Offley wrote him on May 27 reiterating the difficulties:

> Replying to yours of May 20 relative to the possible activities of Huerta, I have to advise you that owing to the scarcity of available agents and the pressure of work upon this office and considering the character of your previous letter, no action was taken until last night, when Agent [Lewis M.] Cantrell was instructed to proceed this morning to Forest Hills, Long Island, and after looking over the ground, see what, if any, arrangements can be made through the Postmaster or otherwise to keep track of the situation.[441] As I have heretofore explained, Forest Hills is a small and rather fashionable suburb of the city, the houses being detached, and there being but one hotel. Huerta has rented quite a large house, and his family and retinue of servants aggregate a large number of persons. The situation is such that it would be a rather difficult matter

to secure any reliable information without arousing suspicion unless we either have an agent take up his residence in the hotel or rely upon the carrier [postman] to some extent.[442]

Offley briefed Cantrell and dispatched him to Forest Hills. Cantrell's report was not encouraging. He learned that Huerta occupied an isolated residence at 129 Seminole Avenue. Cantrell spotted no telephone wire running to the house, and there was no vantage point from which the house could be watched. The agent spoke with the postmaster and the mailman whose route included Huerta's house. The postman, who promised to report everything, stated that the house had been leased fully furnished until October 1. Some thirty-five people had been living there, but the owner had objected to so many occupants, and two Huerta families had moved elsewhere. The postman delivered considerable mail to the house daily. He believed Huerta conducted business with the Corn Exchange Bank of New York, having recently delivered a registered package from that bank. Huerta bought all the groceries, including a lot of liquor. Alberto Quiroz lived with Huerta, as did Colonel Venegas, probably a bodyguard. Huerta had an automobile which he kept in the garage, and he was driven daily into New York City. Cantrell arranged for tracings of Huerta's mail until further instructed, and he "arranged to call back from time to time as might be deemed advisable."[443]

Cantrell continued to make periodic visits to Forest Hills. The postmaster had no new developments, but continued to send tracings of all mail going to Huerta. These included a telephone bill, so Cantrell slipped around near the back of Huerta's house, finding a telephone wire. The agent returned to the post office, where the postman informed him that Huerta went out in his automobile almost every day with Colonel Venegas, and that the barber and other tradesmen who went to the house always found Venegas in the room with Huerta, who never went anywhere except with Venegas. It turned out that Huerta had two Chalmers vehicles, a touring car and a limousine. Interestingly, Cantrell learned that several *carrancistas* had tried to rent a house in Forest Hills.[444]

While Huerta formulated his plans, his partisans in San Antonio were busy. The Bureau's efforts to keep track of them were materially assisted by information from factions opposed to Huerta. Both *villistas* and *carrancistas* were eager to help. Especially noteworthy was informant DELAG, who reported frequently at the Bureau office. He was an upper-class Mexican who seemed to know everybody worth knowing. The Bureau had given him the cover name DELAG as an extra security measure. DELAG's residence was at 310 Monterrey Street. This was the residence of A. [Salvador?] Fuentes, who had an office in room 222 of the Gunter Building. Informant DELAG lived with one Fernando Guerra. DELAG was a *villista* agent. When Agent Frederick Guy called on Fernando Padilla, Pancho Villa's consul in San Antonio, Padilla allowed Guy to examine DELAG's reports to Padilla for the previous three months because they might be of assistance in the Huerta case. Guy then called on DELAG at his residence to learn about *huertista* recruitment efforts. DELAG stated that this would be rather difficult because Huerta, whom he knew personally, was very shrewd. The general had instructed his agents not to use telegraph companies or the mail, or at least to the smallest degree possible. Huerta used special couriers between himself and his trusted lieutenants. And among those in his confidence was Rafael Pimienta, who had arrived a few days earlier from New York with a sealed envelope of instructions and who had proceeded to El Paso for further instructions. According to DELAG, another trusted *huertista* agent was General Eduardo M. Cauz, who had received by special courier money from Huerta to finance the new movement. But DELAG doubted whether any bank in San Antonio could furnish any evidence along those lines.[445] He did say that one Luis Hernández was recruiting former Huerta officers. Agent in charge of the San Antonio field office Robert Lee Barnes asked DELAG "to cover the matter very closely and notify me as soon as these persons leave. DELAG will accompany them to the depot. Similar information has been secured from Fernando Padilla."[446]

DELAG subsequently told agent Guy that General José Delgado, Huerta's secretary, was in town, stopping at the St. Anthony Hotel and conferring with Generals Enrique Gorostieta and Luís Medina Barrón as well as and other prominent local Huerta supporters. Of particular interest, DELAG said Pascual Orozco had left San Antonio by auto for El Paso. The invaluable DELAG reported that after spending several days in San Antonio, General Delgado had returned to New York, accompanied by Generals Ignacio R. Bravo and Eduardo M. Cauz, presumably to confer with Huerta about setting on foot a military expedition. DELAG then called at the Bureau office to say that General Cauz had reportedly returned to San Antonio with $25,000 to purchase horses for the new movement. DELAG identified several individuals involved in purchasing horses.[447] Agent Guy made several more visits to the office of *villista* consul Padilla. During one of these, Padilla received a telephone message from DELAG that Orozco had just arrived from El Paso and was now at 16 East Elmira Street. Orozco was spending considerable time with Rodolfo Reyes, son of the late General Bernardo Reyes. The informant also mentioned a recent meeting attended by Pascual Orozco and Dr. Aureliano Urrutia, formerly Huerta's powerful Minister of *Gobernación* (Interior.) He stated that

General Eduardo Cauz, living at 817 South Presa Street, was the leader of ex-Federal activities in San Antonio. A subsequent report was that Orozco was receiving mail at 105 West Elmira Street using the alias of "P. O. Vázquez." Since the Bureau was trying to cover Orozco's movements, Padilla helpfully pointed out that Orozco and a woman companion had not entered the United States through a regular port of entry, and might thus be subject to immigration deportation proceedings.[448]

While not as valuable as informant DELAG, the Bureau at San Antonio was also receiving information from Constitutionalist (*carrancista*) sources. Agent Guy met with long-time informant Charles Stevens, the former Bexar County deputy sheriff and future Texas Ranger captain, who was currently working for the Carranza faction. Stevens stated that Huerta's revolution had started, and that Huerta's San Antonio representative was Dr. Aureliano Urrutia, formerly Huerta's Secretary of Interior. He described Urrutia as an able man whose methods were very subtle. Stevens promised to provide the names of ex-Federal officers now supporting Huerta. Guy promptly arranged for a mail cover on Urrutia.[449] The Constitutionalist consul, Teódulo R. Beltrán, was a highly prized source. Agent Barnes writing in July 1914, stated, "I have known Mr. Beltrán for about two years, and he is one of the most reliable Mexicans to secure information that I have ever known."[450] Beltrán said that General Eduardo Cauz paid the rail fare to El Paso for several of his ex-Huerta general colleagues. Another *carrancista* source alleged that Indalecio Ballesteros, the onetime Bureau informant, had been very close to Pascual Orozco while the latter was in San Antonio.[451]

Further light on Huerta's activities came from Randolph Robertson, deputy clerk of the federal court in Laredo. He forwarded to the San Antonio office a number of documents belonging to General Enrique Gorostieta, several of which bore on clandestine matters, such as a substitution cipher in which Orozco was "King," and Huerta's son-in-law, Alberto Quiroz, was "Alberto," and a letter to Gorostieta from Ricardo Gomez Robelo at 120 Mill Street, San Antonio, stating that Orozco was counting on Gorostieta.[452]

Yet, it was El Paso where the critical situation developed. Intrigue reached a new intensity there by May, where conditions compelled the Secretary of State to write to the Attorney General. Chief Bielaski received the communication and instructed Agent Beckham to investigate and furnish copies of his reports to the US attorney.[453] Agent Pinckney reported on the situation in El Paso and vicinity:

> The border is in more turmoil at present than it has been since the Mexican revolution began. Every faction that now exists or has existed in the past is pretty well represented in El Paso, each faction having scores of informants and detectives keeping tab on the others, and there is more <u>double crossing</u> [underlined in original] and crooked dealing going on than any other place on the globe. The juntas of the various factions hold their meetings in El Paso and direct their operations from this side; the town is at present full of soldiers of fortune, etc. and decided developments are hourly expected.[454]

The El Paso office requested and received authorization to employ two Anglo informants, at $3 per day. But these informants proved useless and were soon fired.[455] Pancho Villa's representative in Washington, DC, Enrique Llorente, protested vigorously to the State Department that the neutrality laws were being violated. (Llorente was quite familiar with these laws, having violated them repeatedly in 1912 when he was the *maderista* consul in El Paso).[456]

Beckham worked closely with the provost marshal at Fort Bliss, who ran informants of his own. Villa's intelligence chief, Hector Ramos, had a much better grasp of the situation than did the Bureau or the provost marshal. Ramos claimed to have a dozen agents, among them former Bureau Agent in Charge at San Antonio H. A. Thompson, former manager of the Thiel Detective Service Henry Kramp, and former Constitutionalist agent Powell Roberts.[457] When Pinckney approached Ramos for information, Ramos

> said he knew all about this *Científico* movement; that they had the business well organized and equipped; that they had arms and ammunition, grenades and dynamite right in El Paso; that they had rented houses along the river front and stationed their men in them, and that the attack on Juárez was to be made from the American side of the river; that the officers knew that these things existed and still they would not take any action; that they ought to go out and arrest all these men and seize the ammunition, put the men in jail, etc. Ramos was explained to that this was the United States and that we did not do things here as they did in Mexico, and that we would not put people in jail, break into houses etc. without cause, etc. He was given to understand that we were at all times ready to punish violators

of the law and would appreciate any information furnished us, and would go the limit in running the men down, but that we would first have to get the evidence, etc.[458]

Against the possibility of an attack on Ciudad Juárez, the commander of the El Paso Patrol District, General John J. Pershing, traveled incognito accompanied by Beckham to reconnoiter Hispanic south El Paso and the riverbank across from Juárez.[459]

Huerta's partisans in El Paso were busy, and it was the *villistas* who continued to feed the Bureau information in the form of daily memoranda. Henry Kramp called at the field office and described the *huertista* system of compartmentalization. Recruits would not be told who else was being enlisted. A lieutenant headed each group but knew nothing about the other groups. Thus, if a cell were discovered, the entire network would not be rolled up.[460] Ramos named individuals involved in the Huerta movement, persons such as brothers Frank and Ike Alderete, whose real estate office was at 183 Mesa Avenue. Besides whatever belief they might have in the cause, the Alderetes had a very practical reason for supporting the movement—they had enjoyed a lucrative gambling

Figure 40. *Brigadier General John J. Pershing and 10th US Cavalry Staff, 1916*
Source: Buffalo Soldiers Greater Washington DC Chapter 9th and 10th (Horse) Cavalry Association

concession in Ciudad Juárez which Villa had ended when he seized the town. They hoped to get the concession back.[461] Ramos further informed the Bureau that the Alderetes were acquiring munitions, including pipe bombs to be used as hand grenades. Some of the ammunition, though, was of dubious quality; 200,000 30-30 cartridges had been salvaged from a sunken vessel, polished by young women at the El Paso smelter, and sold to the Alderetes.[462] Things did not always go smoothly for the brothers. They hired a notorious character as watchman over a cache of munitions they were stockpiling in a house near the river, but he stole the munitions and sold the whole lot— 500 hand grenades, 156 rifles, and 60,000 cartridges—to the Villa authorities in Juárez.

Although some of the intelligence Ramos was providing proved to be accurate, such as the information about the Alderetes, Agent Beckham complained that, "Feeling the information I was getting through the Villa Agency, while helpful, was too vague, indefinite, and generally without corroboration, and that I could to advantage use a capable Spanish-speaking informant at $5 a day for general work in connection with investigation of neutrality violations." Chief Bielaski authorized hiring such an informant for thirty days, subject to renewal if necessary. Beckham's Mexican informant reported that prominent businessman José Zozaya was the principal financial agent of the new movement in El Paso. Furthermore, there were many strange Mexicans in town. They were restless, as though expecting something to happen.[463]

In the investigations to prosecute the German intelligence agent and representative of Friedrich Krupp AG in the United States, Hans Tauscher, Felix A. Sommerfeld's name appeared in his business logs as a buyer of arms for Pancho Villa. The Bureau began to suspect that Sommerfeld, a highly sophisticated German naval intelligence agent and official representative of Pancho Villa in the United States, led the German war strategy vis-a-vis Mexico. Indeed, he did. When Sommerfeld's previous intelligence handler, the German minister to Mexico, Paul von Hintze, left for his wartime assignment in China, Sommerfeld moved to New York in the summer of 1914, and reported for war duty to Naval Attaché Karl Boy-Ed.[464]

Sommerfeld, who occupied a lavish suite in the Hotel Astor on Times Square, officially acted as Villa's US representative and chief munitions buyer. Since the *Lusitania* sinking, Sommerfeld's principal intelligence mission was to create a US military intervention in Mexico. With the waning fortunes of Pancho Villa in April and May 1915, after he had lost major engagements against the *carrancista* general Álvaro Obregón and financial backing as a result, Sommerfeld had convinced Heinrich Albert to finance Villa's munitions purchases. Rather than being defeated, Villa would keep up the pressure on the

Figure 41. Hotel Astor, New York, c. 1900-1910
Source: Wm. C. Muschenheim

carrancistas. Sommerfeld had witnessed firsthand, and helped negotiate, a settlement between the US government and Pancho Villa, whom he represented, in the Naco, Sonora standoff in the fall of 1914.

The battle of Naco, a standoff between the forces of Sonora governor José María Maytorena, who sided with the Villa faction at the time, and the *carrancista* forces of Plutarco Elías Calles. Intense shelling of the fortified *carrancista* positions resulted in bullets and shrapnel to rain down on the Arizona side of the border. The US army chief of staff, General Hugh Lenox Scott, negotiated for an end to the standoff, with Sommerfeld mediating between Pancho Villa and the US government. He explained to Bernhard Dernburg, who related Sommerfeld's thoughts to Admiral Henning von Holtzendorff, that he could have easily precipitated a US military intervention at the time (December 1914 to January 1915), but was "unsure of German strategic interests." Sommerfeld proposed on May 10, 1915, that he was willing to provoke such a situation if he received such orders. Von Holtzendorff consulted with German Chancellor von Bethmann-Hollweg, who sent his approval of Sommerfeld's proposal via Foreign Secretary von Jagow a week later.⁴⁶⁵

As Sommerfeld, Boy-Ed, and Albert were working, the German general staff sent Rintelen to the US. Not satisfied to concentrate on his mission—the interruption of war supplies from the US—Rintelen now threatened to involve himself in the Mexican situation. Von Papen and Boy-Ed steadfastly refused to meet with Huerta while he was in New York. Rintelen, on the other hand, gladly offered to meet with Huerta. While his entreaties to Huerta are documented, it is unlikely that Rintelen personally met the general, as the German agent claimed in his autobiography. Instead, Huerta delegated the task of meeting with Rintelen to General Pascual Orozco, who visited him in New York in the beginning of June.

Figure 42. Heinrich Albert at his Desk
Source: Albert Papers RG 65
US National Archives and Records Administration

Sommerfeld and Orozco had a long history together. One of Sommerfeld's first assignments as an intelligence agent for Germany was to imbed in 1911 with the future Mexican president, Francisco Madero. Under cover as an Associated Press stringer, Sommerfeld knew Orozco, the principal Madero general, well. In 1912, Orozco became a traitor to the Mexican government and staged a serious revolt against President Madero. Sommerfeld, who at the time headed the Mexican secret service, was instrumental in the Mexican federal army (headed by Victoriano Huerta at the time) defeating the rebels. Only a few months later, in February 1913, Huerta staged his own rebellion and deposed President Madero, who was executed, reportedly on Huerta's orders. Sommerfeld barely escaped the usurper's execution squads. Orozco, who had supported the coup, became a general in Huerta's federal army. Sommerfeld once again hounded Orozco and, once again, this time as the principal munitions' buyer for the Constitutionalists (particularly for Pancho Villa), was instrumental in Orozco's defeat. Unsurprisingly, there was not much love lost between the two men.

Sommerfeld verified the rumors of Rintelen conducting negotiations with Huerta through Pascual Orozco in late April 1915, which Rintelen had initiated through a letter of introduction from Sommerfeld's former intelligence handler, Peter Bruchhausen.[466] Sommerfeld tried to convince Rintelen that supporting Huerta against Carranza and Villa was bound to fail. Most disconcerted, Rintelen complained to Boy-Ed, with whom he had dinner at the New York Yacht Club on May 15.[467] Rintelen's further engagement with Huerta activities suggest that he refused to subordinate himself to Boy-Ed's authority. Sommerfeld, likely with Boy-Ed's approval, decided to blow Rintelen's

Figure 43. Francisco "Pancho" Villa, Possibly Battle of Ojinaga, January 1914
Source: Bain News Service Collection
Library of Congress Prints and Photographs Division

cover. Two days after the dinner meeting with Rintelen, Sommerfeld contacted a close friend, the editor of *The New York Herald*, William Willis, who put him in touch with James F. McElhone, a Herald contributor and religion author.[468] Sommerfeld told McElhone that a certain Mr. Hansen, located in the Transatlantic Trust building, and who was purchasing war supplies, was a German secret agent. McElhone ran with the information not only to the press, but to William Flynn of the Secret Service, who in turn informed the Bureau.[469]

William Offley reported on McElhone's intelligence on May 26, "Hansen, the incognito of a German official representative, evidently of high rank, unlimited powers and in command of unlimited funds, appeared in the U.S. several weeks ago. He brought to Summerfeld [sic] a note of introduction from Brueckhausen [sic—Peter Bruchhausen] [...] Summerfeld told me [McElhone] Sunday night last that Hansen had the 'powers of a chancellor and millions to spend if needed.' [...] I am going to let him [Sommerfeld] go as far as he likes with a view to getting a really valuable newspaper story for the Herald."[470] *The Sun* beat the *Herald* to the story. The same day, Offley reported his findings to the Chief, *The New York Sun* ran an article under the heading "New Evidence Found Here the Food Was Taken to Germany."[471] In the article, the paper cited a mysterious "Mr. Hansen" working out of the Transatlantic Trust offices as a German agent responsible for shipping contraband via Gothenburg to Germany. According to the article, Mr. Hansen could not be found, and the Transatlantic Trust Company claimed never to have heard of him.[472] Furthermore, a publicist, "Jack" John C. Hammond, who gave the lead of this mysterious agent to the newspapers, was quoted as having been approached by Mr. Hansen, but refused to be engaged.

The truth was that Hammond indeed received an offer to work on propaganda against the Allies in the latter part of April, and had accepted $10,000 from Mr. Hansen. After having learned all he could about the German agent's activities, he informed his personal friend, President Woodrow Wilson, via Chief of Staff Joseph Tumulty.[473] Hammond had worked on Wilson's presidential campaign in 1912 as a publicist.[474] In his letter to the White House, Hammond disclosed Rintelen's real name, arrival date, his office address, where he was living, also that he was "a member of the Kaiser's household," and that he had a $20,000,000 credit "with power to secure more money." Clearly, Rintelen had fed Hammond all this information. Rintelen apparently also told the publicity agent that he had made "three tentative appointments with President Wilson."[475]

Rintelen wanted to use Hammond to upstage the propaganda efforts of Bernhard Dernburg, who had gotten himself in trouble by publicly defending the sinking of the *Lusitania*. The scandal prompted the State Department to ask Dernburg to leave the country. It was not Dernburg's fault that German propaganda collapsed in the wake of the liner's demise. American public opinion, fueled by British propaganda, turned sharply against Germany.

Rintelen's plan to use Hammond to revive public sympathy for Germany was ludicrous. Rintelen also once again miscalculated badly by confiding in Hammond after already having missed that Melvin Rice also was a friend of President Wilson. Hammond, who meanwhile supplied the Bureau with information about Huerta, also knew Rintelen's true identity but did not divulge it to Bureau agents.[476] The Bureau learned of the information Hammond had given to the President on July 10, when Assistant Attorney General Charles Warren forwarded the publicist's information to Assistant Chief Horn. The President obviously wanted to protect Hammond's identity. The informant in Warren's memorandum is referred to as "X."[477]

Figure 44. Bernhard Dernburg, 1931
Source: Wikimedia Commons

Bureau agents and journalists alike were asking themselves after the *Sun* article who the mysterious Mr. Hansen was. Superintendent Offley had assigned Agent Cantrell to interview Hammond at the latter's office in the Hardridge Building. Cantrell reported that

> Hammond said he's connected with several newspapers and advertising agencies; had considerable political press work experience and had been approached by some six different factions of Mexico to do publicity work in behalf of each,

including Huerta crowd; that he has had two interviews with Huerta at the Ansonia Hotel and one at Forest Hills, at one of which Huerta offered him $20,000 to conduct a publicity campaign educating the American public [...] This statement of Mr. Hammond was so full that in order to make himself more clear, Hammond consented to meet agent at 2:30 p.m. and dictate a statement in detail to his stenographer in the presence of this Agent, which was done, and this statement was this day turned over to Offley, which is referred to and made a part of this report. He says he'll help government in any way, both in New York or elsewhere.[478]

Offley wrote a "PERSONAL AND CONFIDENTIAL" letter to Assistant Bureau Chief Raymond G. Horn, on July 23, 1915, informing him that Hammond had advised Offley confidentially that Leon Canova, Chief, Division of Mexican Affairs, and Samuel Miller Breckinridge Long had access to sensitive files in the State Department relating to Mexican matters.[479] Offley wrote that they

make it a practice to repeat the purport of confidential reports and messages bearing upon this situation, to outside sources; that at times this information is so conveyed prior to or certainly as soon as it shall have reached the President and Secretary [of State Robert] Lansing; that at times these men have withdrawn confidential papers from the files and taken them from the Department for the purpose of exhibiting them to outsiders. Mr. Hammond was positive in his assertions and stated further that yesterday he was told by three different persons of facts from which he considers himself fully justified in believing that the Huerta faction, if not General Huerta himself, is aware that he, Hammond, has informed this Bureau of his knowledge of the operations and aims of Huerta.[480]

Jack Hammond, though, was unwilling to name his informants, McElhone certainly being one of them, Sommerfeld and Llorente, most likely the others. Offley recalled

that in one of the reports of former Special Employee Harvey Phillips he made the statement that while associated with

Sherburne Hopkins, the latter made the statement upon several occasions that he had an underground channel through which he was kept informed of the plans of the Department of Justice; that this channel led to the State Department, and that Phillips knew of certain reports or papers of which copies had reached Hopkins, but that he, Phillips, was never able to locate the source of the information, although he suspected a certain person.[481]

In order to determine the truth of Hammond's allegations, Offley suggested that Horn authorize a report purportedly containing important information about Huerta: "[T]ell nothing to Hammond of the nature of the same, allow it to reach the State Department in the regular way, inform Hammond of what we have done, and then ask him to ascertain from his friends and inform us of the substance of the report." Offley believed Hammond would go along, and if the scheme produced evidence, appropriate action could be taken. "It would be necessary of course that the plan be unknown to anyone except the higher officials of the Department."[482] Whether this plan was implemented is not known, but Hammond continued to provide the Bureau with information.[483]

While the May 26 article in *The Sun* contained few correct details about Rintelen's true business activities, the revelation of his cover name and location of his office was sufficient to throw him into a panic. Confiding for the second time in a personal friend of the president of the United States would not be the last time Rintelen blundered in this respect. In the weeks after *The Sun* exposé, Rintelen invited Anne Leddell Sewell, the niece of former US Secretary of State William Seward, out on several dates in New York and took her on a trip to Kennebunkport, Maine. He had met the young schoolteacher in Berlin before the war. Sewell now taught at the Hartridge School in Plainfield, New Jersey.[484] As a consequence of meeting Rintelen in Berlin, she knew his real identity. Naïvely, or perhaps completely ignorant of the possible consequences, Rintelen told Sewell and other dinner guests at the Holland House that he was on a secret mission from Berlin and had unlimited funds to stop US war supplies from reaching the Allies. On another occasion, at Delmonico's restaurant, he loudly criticized President Wilson and his policies towards Germany.[485] On a date at Kennebunkport, he went even further and claimed that he had "planned the destruction of the *Lusitania*."[486] Sewell, alarmed by what she learned, promptly sent a letter to President Wilson on July 1, describing the encounter with a German secret agent named Franz Rintelen.[487]

The "Dark Invader" of course did not realize yet how thoroughly he had compromised his mission. All he knew after the May 26 article in The Sun was that Hammond was not on his side, and that he needed to change offices immediately. An opportunity offered itself literally on the other side of the Transatlantic Trust building at 43 Cedar Street, where he had rented room 803. The same building had entrances at 55 Liberty Street, where the German-Mexican Frederico Stallforth sought to sublet office space for his friend and business partner, Andrew Meloy, who was on an extended trip to Europe. Stallforth had worked under Felix Sommerfeld as a German intelligence agent in Chihuahua, then moved to New York working for the family of the assassinated President Francisco Madero selling real estate. He finally wound up working for Albert as a financial agent. Stallforth, at the time, worked with Heinrich Albert on selling German war bonds and manipulating the Dollar-Reichsmark exchange rate.

Rintelen agreed to rent an office from Stallforth. Sommerfeld, who worked closely with Stallforth, came into Rintelen's orbit as an "adviser" on all things Mexican.[488] When The Sun article broke, Rintelen "in his fright went to Summerfeld [sic] for advice, knowing that he [Sommerfeld] knows America and American newspapers better than any of the German circle.[489] Sommerfeld had succeeded in controlling the "Dark Invader."[490]

At the beginning of June 1915, Sommerfeld and Orozco, who had not seen each other since 1911, almost came face-to-face in the new office. Orozco had agreed to a meeting with Rintelen to discuss financing Huerta's planned return to Mexico at the head of a reactionary army. According to Stallforth, he had shepherded Sommerfeld, who had come unannounced into the office, into a separate area of the offices and barely prevented the two men from running into each other.[491]

Some historians have taken Rintelen's unauthorized approach as proof of Germany supporting Huerta's comeback attempt, even providing gigantic sums of up to $12,000,000.[492] Barbara Tuchman quoted newspaper sources for her claim that "Eight million rounds of ammunition were purchased in St. Louis [...] and a preliminary sum of $800,000 deposited to Huerta's account in the Deutsche Bank in Havana as well as $95,000 in a Mexican account."[493] Tuchman and others have also alleged meetings between the German naval attaché Boy-Ed and Huerta, giving further credence to a German conspiracy to bring Huerta back. The source for these meetings was John R. Rathom, editor of The Providence Journal and British propagandist. Under pressure from the Justice Department, Rathom had to admit publicly in February 1918 that many of his reports during the previous years had been lies. Among other admissions Rathom wrote, "The suggested interview between Captain Boy-Ed and General Huerta in a New York hotel was printed by us in good faith, the entire material having been supplied to us from a source which we considered trustworthy [most likely agents of the British Naval Intelligence]. We have since ascertained, however, by conference with officials of the Department of Justice, that it is doubtful if such a meeting was ever held [...]."[494]

Scores of historians have since accepted these claims that were essentially British propaganda, such as the British-owned *Providence Journal* and Franz Rintelen's own accounts published while he lived in England.[495] The discovery in the 1990s of the financial records of the German embassy shed new light on the matter. They clearly showed that the German government had not provided any substantial financial support to Huerta. That left open the question of where Huerta's funds had originated.[496]

The Bureau solved this mystery on July 7, 1915: Huerta's funds came from the ex-president himself.[497] Huerta had cashed several hundred thousand dollars of his own securities, as Felix Sommerfeld had explained to Agent Cantrell a few days earlier.[498] According to Sommerfeld, this money came from Mexican bonds Huerta had on deposit in New York. Agents of the Bureau confirmed Sommerfeld's allegations, namely that Huerta sold Mexican bonds to finance his conspiracy. According to the captain of the German warship that took Huerta into exile in 1914, "Huerta and General Blanquet were well supplied with travelling money, and the women similarly with jewelry. Huerta had roughly half a million marks in gold with him. In addition, he had a much greater amount in checks and other paper [i.e. treasury bonds]."[499] Division Superintendent Offley later interviewed Rudolph Otto, who had been German consul in Jamaica in 1914. When Huerta left Mexico for Spain, he was Otto's guest for five weeks, at which time Huerta turned over to Otto for safekeeping four valises containing $400,000. Otto kept the receipt as a memento.[500] José Vasconcelos, Mexican lawyer and member of the Madero and Gutiérrez administrations, testified: "When he [Huerta] left Mexico it was estimated that he took out with him around five million [pesos in] gold."[501] In short, Sommerfeld and Vasconcelos both estimated that Huerta had access to millions of dollars of "his" own money while in New York, an estimation matching the observations of Captain Köhler of the German cruiser *Dresden* that whisked Huerta into exile.

Emeterio de la Garza, attorney and former congressman from Coahuila who was a *huertista*, corroborated that Huerta did not have German backing or promises, and did not get cash from them. De la Garza said he had personally gone to the American Bank Note Company to have Huerta fiat money printed.

He had ordered the plates and was ready to have 300 million pesos in bills struck off. (The American Bank Note Company declined the order.) He also mentioned that Pascual Orozco had gone there with him at the time.[502] There was a reason why the German government did not finance the Huerta conspiracy. Felix Sommerfeld had orders to create a military intervention of the United States in Mexico. The German money was on Villa and Carranza with Huerta quickly becoming a distraction.

In El Paso, Agent Beckham, who initially reported the movement as being "the old Científico bunch" now reported that the "New Movement" was actually for Victoriano Huerta, and that his co-conspirator, Pascual Orozco, was in town rallying his old Red Flagger associates.[503] Beckham remained skeptical about the quality of the intelligence the *villistas* were providing, writing on June 4, "Kramp brought me memoranda for May 27, 28, 29, and 31, but they disclose nothing of value not heretofore set out in my reports, the sources of the information given not being divulged and a large proportion thereof being conclusions on the part of the writer of the memoranda."[504] The El Paso rumor mill was in high gear by late June, and Beckham was trying to sort out facts from all the reports of munitions, money, and suspicious characters flooding into town.

Chief Bielaski sent a coded telegram on June 26 to Barnes in San Antonio that he had received a report that General Huerta, his staff, and personal friends in San Antonio were leaving that day for El Paso, and that Orozco was busily engaged preparing an attack on Ojinaga in the Big Bend. Bielaski instructed that these persons be fully covered both in San Antonio and in El Paso.[505]

The New York Bureau field office was also jolted into action. Superintendent Offley dispatched Cantrell back to Forest Hills to check for any unusual activity, it having been reported that numerous conferences were being held at Huerta's home. Cantrell consulted the postman, who said he passed Huerta's house four times daily and had seen nothing unusual, but had not seen Huerta or Colonel Venegas in two or three days. Upon returning to the office, Cantrell learned from Offley that he had just received word from Washington about a rumor that Huerta had left Forest Hills and was on his way to Mexico. Cantrell immediately returned to Forest Hills, went to Huerta's residence, found both of Huerta's cars there, and spoke with someone who informed him in Spanish that Huerta was not at home and would be away for some time, suggesting that the agent telephone the office of Abraham Ratner for information. Cantrell did so. The person who answered, evidently a cleaning lady, stated that there was no one present who knew anything about Huerta. Offley sent Agent Jentzer to Ratner's office at 61 Broadway, where Huerta had been having frequent meetings. The cleaning lady there said Huerta had indeed been there several days earlier.[506]

The Bureau had lost track of Huerta.

At least the Bureau had a line on Huerta's generals. Corroborating the report of Huerta's followers in San Antonio leaving for El Paso enroute to Mexico, the villista representative in San Antonio, Fernando Padilla, informed Agent Guy that ten former Huerta generals had indeed left for the border city. Barnes immediately telegraphed Beckham to detain the generals by filing some suitable criminal complaint, if necessary, but in any event to prevent their crossing to Mexico until the full facts could be ascertained and further instructions received. Guy was at all costs to prevent the generals from crossing the border. Barnes also instructed Agent Stephen L. Pinckney at Naco to proceed immediately to El Paso to assist Beckham.[507]

It turned out that Huerta had left New York by rail on June 24 and had later stated to the press that he was traveling to California to attend the Panama Pacific International Exposition. Zach Lamar Cobb, the El Paso Collector of Customs, however, received from friendly journalists some disturbing news about Huerta's intentions. As a collector of customs, Cobb was an employee of the Treasury Department. Few people knew that he was also an agent of the State Department's Bureau of Secret Intelligence. Cobb went to the Bureau office on June 26, and informed Beckham that he had sent the State Department a telegram stating that he had been told that instead of going to California, Huerta had left Kansas City and would arrive in El Paso on June 27.

Figure 45. Zach Lamar Cobb, 1916
Source: Bain News Service Collection
Library of Congress Prints and Photographs Division

The State Department instructed Cobb to cooperate with the El Paso Bureau field office. Beckham was uneasy about detaining Huerta. He had received no instructions to do so, and Huerta had been living peacefully in the United States.[508] Cobb informed Beckham in the early hours of June 27 that he had received a wire from the conductor of the train on which Huerta was traveling that the former strongman intended to get off at Newman, New Mexico, just across the Texas state line.[509] Adding to Beckham's stress, five autos full of Huerta supporters were supposed to meet him at Newman. Beckham wired Barnes asking for instructions and boldly proceeded to act, instructions or no instructions.

He was able to contact the assistant US attorney, who authorized him to file complaints against Huerta, Orozco, and José Zozaya for conspiracy to violate the neutrality laws. The US Commissioner issued arrest warrants. Since numerous *huertistas* would reportedly await Huerta's arrival at Newman, Beckham felt he needed backup. The provost marshal declined to participate, but Beckham persuaded the colonel commanding the 16th US Cavalry at Fort Bliss to accompany him and Cobb to Newman with fifteen troopers in autos Cobb provided, and to send ten more troopers on horseback. The military's role merely was to be available in case of trouble. With little time to spare, Beckham and Cobb picked up the soldiers and two deputy US marshals and raced to Newman. Enroute, a relieved Beckham telephoned his office and learned that permission to detain the Huerta party had just been received. Upon reaching Newman, however, the deputy marshals informed an astonished Beckham that they had no jurisdiction in New Mexico. With the operation unraveling, it was again Cobb who saved the day. He wired his personal friend the superintendent of the railroad to have the train stopped just across the line in Texas.

Beckham entered Huerta's Pullman drawing room, introduced himself and the marshals, and informed Huerta that he had to accompany them to the federal building in El Paso for questioning. Beckham also detained General Pascual Orozco, who was waiting to meet Huerta. Orozco, by the way, was observed frantically tossing his checkbook, pistol, and cartridge belt into the bushes. As it happened, the army detachment was not needed, as there were not five carloads of Huerta supporters at the scene.

The Mexican generals were escorted to the federal building in El Paso in a grumpy mood even though they were served refreshments at the country club on the way.[510] The attorney who arrived at the federal building to represent Huerta and Orozco was none other than Tom Lea, the recently elected mayor of El Paso. The US Commissioner set their bonds at $15,000 for Huerta and $7,500 for Orozco, which Huerta provided.[511] The two generals left the building into a frenzy of press coverage.

The next day, June 28, Bielaski instructed Barnes to "Wire full report immediately all details Huerta matter." Bielaski also telegraphed Beckham, "Understand from press reports parties released on bond. Cover carefully and employ all assistance necessary to prevent crossing Mexico. Apply court for increase in amount bond. keep in touch military authorities."[512]

Huerta held a press conference, explaining that he had come to El Paso to visit his daughter and son-in-law, Alberto Quiroz, who had been living at the fashionable Georgette Apartments for the last three weeks. The general joined them there. The rest of the family gave up their Forest Hills residence in July, and with sixty pieces of luggage, joined Huerta in El Paso.[513]

The villistas had been following Huerta closely, of course. Villa's military governor in Chihuahua promptly contacted the governor of Texas requesting Huerta's extradition under the 1899 treaty. Venustiano Carranza also requested Huerta's extradition. The Wilson administration, however, was unwilling to send Huerta to face a firing squad. As one observer cynically noted, Huerta was lucky—if he had crossed the border, he would have been executed by either the Villa or the Carranza faction.[514]

Agent Pinckney arranged with the provost marshal to have Huerta guarded day and night and accompanied by his guards wherever he went, such as when he was invited to dinner at Fort Bliss. Beckham's relief at having Huerta under control was tempered by the fact that Huerta conferred with twelve of his former generals, who claimed they had gone to the Georgette Apartments just to pay their respects. They, together with José B. Ratner, were currently

Figure 46. Stephen Lee Pinckney, 1912
Source: University of Texas

stopping at the best hotel in town, the Paso del Norte. Offsetting this disturbing development, Beckham had Huerta's local financial agent, José Zozaya, arrested for conspiracy.

The newly arrived Agent Stephen Lee Pinckney disapproved of the way his colleague Beckham had handled the situation. Pinckney, an ambitious twenty-eight-year-old lawyer born in Austin, wired Chief Bielaski:

> Initial steps taken few hours prior my arrival this city not in accord my best judgment that Huerta had more of unquestioned entry of here than arrest of prisoner due to steps of over breaches of diplomacy which now attempting to overcome by quieter, firmer procedure. Guard now maintained continuously over Huerta upon whom agent called this morning stating clearly that account to be taken of his every move. Careful observation to date brings me this conclusion that he will not attempt enter Mexico at this time but here for purpose of counseling leaders third party in Mexico and entry after first strike made. Immigration contemplates no action, say regularly admitted New York. Huerta sentiment El Paso strong particularly in financial circles. Military ready orders but invite Huerta to Ft. Bliss tonight for dinner. These conditions, together with fact Tom Lea, Mayor El Paso counsel for him, makes matters difficult to handle conditions across border restless.[515]

Bielaski, however, said he had nothing indicating poor judgment on Beckham's part.[516] With regard to Tom Lea, he was not only mayor of El Paso and Huerta's attorney, but he was deeply implicated in the New Movement, his ranch being used to assemble a *huertista* military expedition.

Astoundingly, as for Pascual Orozco's whereabouts, the Bureau had no clue. Pinckney had to ask Huerta for Orozco's home address on Montana Street. Pinckney, accompanied by two provost guards and a deputy US marshal, went there, but Orozco's wife said he was not at home and suggested they try her husband's headquarters, 604 Myrtle Avenue. (Not until months later did the Bureau learn, from his landlady, the details about Orozco having rented a room from her in June and using it as his headquarters).[517] A frustrated Pinckney reported that "none of his force would tell us where he was, stating that he had not been there during the day. It was apparent that they did not desire to give the information." One of them finally suggested that the officers try a house at 1024 Myrtle. There, the occupants reluctantly produced Orozco. The Bureau agent "told him substantially what I had told Huerta, but even more emphatically."

But while Pinckney was assigning the provost guards their shifts in front of the house, Orozco disappeared. Panic ensued, and the officers "searched the premises, which we found to be an unending confusion of several houses joined together, with all manner of avenues of escape, closets, etc." One of the guards spotted Orozco a short distance away strolling toward downtown. He was escorted back in a sullen mood.

Orozco's mood improved markedly, for on the night of July 2, he escaped. An embarrassed Beckham had to wire Chief Bielaski on July 3 that "Deputy marshal reports Orozco escaped last night; every effort being made to prevent crossing border; military immigration and customs service assisting Department of Justice to arrest." The front of the house had been guarded, but at about midnight Orozco had jumped out of a side window and had disappeared. Pinckney blamed the provost guard: "I believe that the guards simply were asleep on the job, as there was an ample number of men, six in number, to guard the place." A frantic search ensued. While the provost guard deployed to check Orozco's reputed haunts, Pinckney led raids on the premises of Huerta-Orozco sympathizers. At the Alderete brothers' Alcazar Theater, for instance, officers seized three Colt machine guns. Frank Alderete protested vehemently, saying there was no law against selling munitions to the New Movement.

To forestall any further embarrassment, the Bureau filed complaints against Victoriano Huerta and eleven others, including Orozco.[518] Huerta and five of his associates were quickly arrested. Their bonds were set at $15,000 each. All the defendants, except Huerta and the fugitive Orozco, eventually posted bond and were released. Huerta was a major problem, not only in terms of preventing his escape, but also in terms of preventing his assassination, for it was no secret that the *villistas* wanted him dead. Huerta's attorney, Tom Lea, and the assistant US attorney worked out an agreement for Huerta to appear before the US Commissioner and waive his examining trial and bond. Huerta was then transferred to Fort Bliss for safekeeping.

The Huerta matter was of such importance that Chief Bielaski left his assistant, Raymond G. Horn, in charge at headquarters in Washington and traveled to El Paso, arriving on July 9 to direct operations. For example, Bielaski and Pinckney went to the Valley Inn, located between El Paso and its suburb, Ysleta, and searched a party of five Mexicans suspected of recruiting, but found nothing incriminating.[519] Besides Agents Beckham and Pinckney, Special Employee Edward B. Stone was brought in from his home station at

Muskogee, Oklahoma. Stone operated under cover and was one of the few agents who spoke Spanish. At his room in the McCoy Hotel, Stone conferred with Bielaski, Beckham, and Pinckney. Bielaski continued on to Tucson on July 13. During his return trip to Washington, the Chief spent time with Agent in Charge Barnes in San Antonio.

Just before leaving for El Paso, Agent Stone had held a most fruitful interview in the San Antonio jail with Ricardo Gomez Robelo, the onetime Vázquez Gomez sympathizer. Gomez Robelo had spent several months with Huerta in Barcelona defending him from attacks in the press. Returning to New York, Gomez Robelo had been met by his friend, Pascual Orozco. Gomez Robelo, who spoke English fluently, laid out what had been the New Movement's strategy:

> 1. He and Orozco had gone to Washington to sound out some high government officials regarding the attitude of the United States; [To help in the effort of recruiting, the *huertistas* claimed that the United States government approved of the New Movement.]
> 2. And, to finance the New Movement, they had approached the American Bank Note Company in May 1915, to print 5,000,000 worth of pesos in denominations of one, two, three, ten, twenty, fifty, and one hundred. The firm's president, Warren L. Green, said that they would not print currency for any country that did not have a recognized, or properly elected head. Ratner assured him that Huerta did not intend to have the printing done until he had become the regularly elected president of Mexico. Ratner made a second visit to the company, paying $5,000 on account. But Green kept abreast of Huerta's fortunes and decided that his chances of being elected president were nil. Ratner's order was cancelled.[520]
> 3. The most important step of all was forming an army strong enough to topple both Villa and Carranza. This was to have been accomplished not so much by recruiting as by suborning *villista* and *carrancista* commanders, who would turn their coats and bring their troops with them. Gomez Robelo asserted that Orozco had received many letters from ranking officers promising their support when he entered Mexico. It was anticipated that when a manifesto was issued and the call to arms was made, such an army would rally in support of the New

Movement. As for Huerta, it had been decided that if Mexicans called for him to cross the border and head this army he would do so; otherwise, he would remain in El Paso and Orozco would lead the rebellion.[521] At Gomez Robelo's hearing before the US Commissioner, he was represented by the former US attorney in Brownsville, was bound over to await the action of the grand jury, and his bond was set at $2,500.[522]

The Bureau was developing a strong case for the forthcoming trials of Huerta and his associates. Bureau agents on the border and at places such as San Francisco, Los Angeles, New Orleans, Boston, and New York spent considerable time trying to locate *huertistas* and to follow the money, all this with as little publicity as possible. And, of course, the *villistas* and *carrancistas* were eager to help. Felix Sommerfeld, for instance, informed Cantrell in New York that a certain C. A. Eron, proprietor of a small bookstore at 50 John Street, had been acquiring munitions for the *huertistas*. *Carrancista* consul T. R. Beltrán alerted the San Antonio office to the arrival of suspicious persons, and *carrancista* secret agent H. N. Gray provided information on munitions purchases. Bureau agents conducted a series of raids in El Paso searching for munitions. They also received the pistol and documents Orozco had tried to hide at Newman, New Mexico when he met Huerta. Children playing in the vicinity had found them, and their fathers sent them to the Bureau.[523] Furthermore, agents used the subpoena duces tecum to great effect in El Paso and San Antonio, producing a mass of incriminating telegrams. On another front, the Bureau continued to examine the bank accounts of the Ratners.[524]

Agents Stone and Beckham interviewed Huerta, interned at Fort Bliss. Stone conducted the interview in Spanish and later translated it for Beckham. As Stone reported:

> Delegation of fifteen prominent Mexicans came to post to confer with Huerta in our presence. One read document in Spanish rapidly in hopes we wouldn't be able to grasp its meaning. All, including Huerta, signified approval of its contents. Huerta signed same. They then conferred together confidentially at the table concerning the business of the meeting, etc. Beckham and I decided we'd best have the original of the document read, to make a true copy. Some objected. Huerta finally insisted that they hand it over. We took [the] document to post headquarters and made a true copy. Then we returned

with the copies and obtained Huerta's signature to same. Document purports to be a letter written at Fort Bliss on July 11 by Huerta to his wife in New York City, with comments thereon by members of the press present. It's contained in full on pp. 3-7 [of Stone's report]; also, a list of those present at this conference: pp. 8-13. Yesterday several Mexican newspaper men visited General Huerta in his prison at Fort Bliss. They had obtained passes from the [Provost] Marshal and with them it was a very easy matter to gain admittance to the building where, attended by ten guards, the ex-President of Mexico is passing the summer against his will [...] Several of the above remained in close conference with Huerta for several hours after the reading of the document previously referred to. In commenting on this conference held with Huerta by his followers and advisers, would respectfully suggest that I believe this letter which Huerta pretends to write to his wife contains an expression of his wishes with respect to future movements, etc. and may be [in] the form of a manifesto his party have issued to take some action. It is strange to say the least that all these persons would have gathered about Huerta simply for the purpose of hearing a letter he had written to his wife a few days ago [...].[525]

During the evening, another conference was held by the majority of these same persons in a room at the Paso del Norte Hotel in El Paso.[526] Beckham wrote that he was "trying to substantiate [sic] a conference between Stone, Pinckney, and me to elicit from her [Mrs. Huerta] information to show conclusively that the letter purported to be from Huerta to his wife was not such, in fact, but in the guise of such, really an address or manifesto, his country being for the purposes of that document, his wife."[527]

A despondent Huerta railed against the Bureau of Investigation. He appealed to the German ambassador: [Translation] "I am at Fort Bliss and my family which consists of thirty or thirty-five persons who are in the city of El Paso, have no guarantees of any kind. I would like to know if the government of his Imperial Majesty that is so worthily represented by yourself in Washington can do me the favor of sheltering my wife and children, for the representatives of American Federal Justice do not permit them in the city either to sleep or to eat and they break into my home whenever they desire. I respectfully beg for an answer."[528]

Apparently, the German government could not help Huerta out. Neither could the Chief Justice of the Supreme Court, to whom Huerta sent the same letter, mentioning that this was the second time he had appealed to that personage, adding that "the agents of the American federal justice violate my home without scruple, and I wish to know if my family can live in this country with protection that the law extends to everybody." For good measure, Huerta sent the same letter to the Associated Press, again without result.[529] The Mexican general was further depressed by a telegram he received from Abraham Z. Ratner: [Translation]: "It is not possible for me at present to remit you the amount desired. Regards."[530]

Agent Beckham, for one, had little use for Huerta, who had also complained to the Attorney General:

> Deputy Marshal Dubose said Huerta requests privilege of visiting family in their new El Paso home. Family visit him almost daily at Fort Bliss. Desire of Department is to keep him as well contented as possible so that he would not ask for bond. [Assistant US Attorney R. E.] Crawford and [US Commissioner George B.] Oliver had no objection to Huerta making a visit to his family. For a narrative of the visit see Stone's report for July 26, which I adopt as my own. I might add, parenthetically, that at the foot of the long flight of steps leading from the house down to the sidewalk Huerta stumbled and was falling when Gil and I caught him—when he thinks of it, he may incorporate this incident in another complaint to the Chief Justice of the US Supreme Court or to the Attorney General as an unwarranted interference on my part with his inalienable right to fall downstairs. Judge Crawford on July 27 exhibited a telegram from [the] Attorney General directing him to ascertain from Huerta and from [Agent] Stone any myself the facts on which Huerta had based a telegram to him to the effect that his home had been violated 'by special Agents without scruple.'[531]

Stone shed additional light on the Huerta visit. He and Beckham had gone to the Huerta family's residence prior to the visit to familiarize themselves with the house and the thirty-odd family and servants. The agents were joined by Huerta, escorted to the house by a deputy marshal and four provost guards. Huerta not only enjoyed his family but was a genial host, offering the Bureau agents refreshments and cigars. He produced a tray of small glasses filled with liquor, but fearing the liquor might be doped, the agents and the others refused to drink. Huerta's visit lasted more than an hour, after which he was escorted back to Fort Bliss.[532]

Huerta might be safely interned, but Orozco was still at large, and the Bureau was frantically following leads placing him as far away as California. Barnes recommended that a reward of $25 be offered for Orozco's arrest; the request was approved.[533] As matters developed, the reward was not needed. The El Paso rumor mill had been going full blast since Orozco's escape, and the bitter rivals, El Paso Morning Times and El Paso Herald newspapers, published stories alleging Orozco was still in town using a disguise, was heading for Mexico, or was already in Mexico. As Agent Beckham put it—in capital letters—"AMONG DEPARTMENT OF JUSTICE OFFICERS THE CONSENSUS IS THAT BOTH STORIES ARE 'FAKES;' IT IS CUSTOMARY FOR EACH OF THE EL PASO PAPERS TO DENY PRACTICALLY ANY AND EVERYTHING PUBLISHED BY THE OTHER."[534] According to Mrs. Orozco, her husband had hidden out at their residence and had slipped out of town on horseback during the night of August 24.

Figure 47. Pascual Orozco, c. 1910-1915
Source: Bain News Service Collection

The fugitive general reappeared on August 29. He had joined four of his closest associates, and they were making their way on horseback to the Rio Grande. When they reached Dick Love's ranch near Sierra Blanca, Texas, they forced the ranch hands to prepare breakfast for them and to shoe a horse. When Love and several companions followed them, the Mexicans opened fire.

A quickly organized posse took up their trail. On August 30, the posse located them encamped in a canyon about thirty miles south of Sierra Blanca. The posse unceremoniously shot them down, alleging they were rustlers. Beckham traveled to nearby Van Horn to identify the bodies, which were laid out in a courtroom.[535] To resolve any legal consequences, the sheriff insisted that he and the rest of the posse be indicted for murder. They were, and the jury quickly acquitted them. Some three thousand mourners paid their respects at Orozco's funeral in El Paso. Huerta sent a wreath.

With Orozco dead and Huerta under guard, the "New Movement" collapsed. Once again, the United States government had influenced the course of the Mexican Revolution.

There was now a glut of Huerta munitions on the open market. At El Paso, Collector of Customs Cobb declared that he could use fifty men to watch all the caches of munitions hidden around the city. The *carrancista* consul, Andrés García, was buying all the armament he could find in order to keep the *villistas* from acquiring it. The Alderete brothers were trying to dispose of the weaponry they had amassed, prompting Agent Frederick Guy to comment that "it may be assumed that inasmuch as the Huerta movement has collapsed, the business instinct of the Alderetes in all probability prevails over partisan feelings; that the goods if they are to be sold at all, will be sold here; that Juárez is the nearest Mexican point which is a Villa stronghold; the ammunition is intended for the *villistas*."[536] Even Orozco's widow was trying to sell her late husband's weapons, as she had been left destitute.[537] In New York, the Ratner brothers had sixty-seven Colt machine guns and 1,000,000 7-millimeter rounds for sale.[538]

The El Paso Bureau office acquired a new informer: Antonio Garibay, a graduate of the Chapultepec Military Academy, the Mexican equivalent of West Point. Garibay was among a twenty-four-man *huertista* filibustering expedition the United States army had captured in August near Fort Hancock, downriver from El Paso.[539] He was released on his own recognizance, and readily agreed to become an informant. Agent Stone enlisted him at $3 per day.[540] Garibay proved to be valuable, alerting the Bureau to a proposed uprising in El Paso in favor of Orozco.[541] On occasion, the Bureau decided not to file a complaint against a suspect or produce documentary evidence which Garibay had procured in order not to blow his cover.[542] But his cover was rather thin, for as Agent Stone reported, "It was suggested that Garibay not come to the Bureau office in the future with his information, account the danger [of] his being seen and tipped off, so it has been arranged that he report to me direct in my room at the McCoy Hotel."[543] Through December, Garibay provided information about the Huerta conspiracy. His credibility plummeted, however, when he positively identified the fugitive *huertista* Colonel Rafael Pimienta, who had just been arrested. The individual turned out to be a certain Filemón Lepe, a grocery store deliveryman.[544]

Bureau agents, usually working with interpreters, took lengthy statements concerning the Huerta-Orozco machinations from *huertistas* who were either in jail or who were brought to a field office to assist the agents in their inquiries. The mass of detail produced gave a much fuller account of the affair, and the agents spent considerable time organizing their files in preparation for trial. By December 15, the El Paso field office had prepared its voluminous Huerta file, which had initially been entitled "in re Científico Movement."[545] The assistant US attorney was delighted, saying there was now a "perfect case" against Huerta.[546]

Still, agents kept investigating. As late as April 1916, Agent Guy at El Paso reported that José Orozco, Pascual's cousin and currently a prisoner in the county jail, convicted of violating the neutrality laws in the 1914 Columbus expedition, was brought to the Bureau office and interrogated about his knowledge of the Huerta movement. He said he was willing to make a voluntary and full statement of the facts of this conspiracy. With Deputy US Marshal Ed Bryant acting as interpreter and Guy as stenographer, Orozco said that "a few days after Huerta arrived here, he sent word to me by Cristoforo Caballero that he wanted to see me. I went to Huerta's house on North Stanton St. where he talked with me and asked if I wanted to help him in a movement that was going to start; that he had everything arranged and that the President of the US had authorized this moment. I told him that if that was the kind of movement he had in mind I was ready to help him. There were present during this conversation Alberto Quiroz and Nicolás Chavarría. After this conversation Alberto Quiroz was ordered by Huerta to give me $300 to assist in getting ready for this."[547] (Chavarría participated in a revolt in Juárez against Carranza in April 1916. He and two companions were executed.)

Shifting loyalties of many of those involved in the Mexican Revolution allowed the Bureau to keep track of conspiratorial activities. Through an informant the Bureau learned of a meeting at the Gunter Hotel in San Antonio. Present were Francisco Chavez, formerly chief of Huerta's secret police in Mexico City, Huerta's attorney Tom Lea, and H. A. Thompson. It was believed they were planning to assist Huerta at his forthcoming trial in January 1916.[548] Thompson, onetime Agent in Charge of the Bureau office in San Antonio, had resigned in 1913 to become a secret agent for the Constitutionalists. After the

Carranza-Villa split he became a secret agent under Villa's spy chief Hector Ramos. Now he was evidently working on behalf of Huerta.

The government planned to present the case of Victoriano Huerta et al. to the grand jury in San Antonio during the first week in January 1916. Barnes was worried: "There have recently arrived in San Antonio a number of Mexicans believed to be associated with Huerta who have probably come here for the purpose of tampering with the Government's witnesses." To counter this threat, he requested that Bielaski authorize employing two Spanish-speaking informants at $5 per day for ten days.[549] The government's witness list for the grand jury included the Ratners, José Z. Zozaya, Felix Sommerfeld, Ricardo Gómez Robelo, Emilio Kosterlitzky, Charles A. Eron, and Antonio Garibay.[550] The grand jury indicted Victoriano Huerta and sixteen co-conspirators for conspiring to set on foot a military expedition.[551] Bonds, except for those already under bond, were $2,500 each.[552]

Huerta's appearance at trial became problematic. He was an alcoholic, and his health had been declining. On November 5, the attorney general authorized for Huerta be transferred from Fort Bliss to his family's home. He remained there for about a month, but the US marshal had him returned to the fort. He remained bedridden, and at the end of December, army doctors decided that he was probably terminally ill. Huerta was once again taken to his family's home in early January 1916. He underwent two operations and died on January 13, 1916, from cirrhosis of the liver.[553] Perhaps no one enjoyed this news more than Pancho Villa, who hated Huerta with a passion.

With the two principals in the case deceased, as well as José C. Delgado, killed along with Orozco, the Bureau concentrated on tracking down Huerta's associates under indictment, especially Rafael Pimienta, Francisco Escandón, and Alberto Quiroz. Quiroz hid out in El Paso for a time, made his way to New York and then to Havana. Escandón was apprehended at Nogales.[554]

In San Antonio, Bureau informant Charles Stevens supplied the names of prominent *huertistas* known to be in town.[555] In Los Angeles, Bureau informant Emilio Kosterlitzky located *huertista* Francisco Escandón. Kosterlitzky had been a commander of the Sonoran Rurales (rural police forces) and a colonel in the federal army under Porfirio Díaz. Kosterlitzky, nicknamed the "Mexican Kossak" [sic], as he fought against the overwhelming forces of the Mexican revolutionaries under General Obregón. He surrendered to US authorities after losing the Battle of Nogales in March 1913, spending the following year in internment. A polyglot—Kosterlitzky spoke German, English, French, and Russian—the retired colonel caught the attention of journalists who reported on his real and exaggerated adventures in Mexico. Eventually,

Kosterlitzky became an informer for the Bureau as a result of his personal knowledge of many of the key players of the Mexican Revolution, and because of his language abilities. While Kosterlitzky claimed to have descended from a Russian family, with his father having served in the Czarist navy, his birth certificate shows that his family came from Poland and that his father was a shoemaker.[556] The Bureau never questioned his claimed country of origin and inadvertently hired an informant who likely was still both a Mexican and a German citizen.[557]

Kosterlitzky related a delightful tale of treachery to the Bureau. Escandón reportedly got $50,000 from Huerta and Orozco in El Paso to buy weapons and ammunition for the proposed Huerta invasion. He did buy some munitions, but sold them to Villa agents in Juárez and absconded to Los Angeles with the proceeds and the balance of the $50,000. Kosterlitzky had contempt for Escandón, whom he said was "treacherous to the last degree" and would betray his own mother for a price.[558]

Bureau agents tried to locate Pimienta and Quiroz, who were reported to be in New York, New Orleans, Toronto, and Havana, but that investigation was soon on the back burner. The Bureau was now much more interested in German machinations than in tying up the loose ends of the Huerta case.[559] On a motion by the US attorney, the Huerta case was dismissed in January 1919.[560]

As a result of his own doing, and Sommerfeld and Boy-Ed lending a helping hand, Franz Rintelen's cover was thoroughly compromised by the time Huerta was arrested near El Paso. Boy-Ed notified his superiors in Berlin of the situation and suggested they recall Rintelen as quickly as possible, as "he was in danger" of being arrested.[561] Rintelen's dabbling in Boy-Ed and Sommerfeld's Mexican strategy that had been approved by the highest echelons of the German government marked him a rogue agent to be neutralized. The American public, however, would soon learn of an even more daring and reckless project Rintelen had undertaken while everyone was focused on the unfolding Huerta conspiracy.

8

THE WOLF AND THE TIGER

AFTER HIS COVER NAME appeared in The New York Sun on May 26, Rintelen moved into his new office with Frederico Stallforth and Andrew Meloy in the first week of June 1915. E.V. Gibbons Company and Frederick Hansen now became Edward V[ictor]. Gates, wine merchants of Millersville, Pennsylvania.[562] As Rintelen carried on his various conspiratorial plots, Stallforth got to know his new office mate better by the day. He saw in Rintelen a man with big ambitions and big money, always attractive for someone who had lost his family business in Mexico and struggled to get back on his financial feet. The beckoning call of "unlimited funds" had caused Stallforth to offer his services to Heinrich Albert in the fall of 1914. Now another source, and a very naïve one at that, of "unlimited funds" had taken up the office beside him. Rintelen confided in Stallforth that he wanted to infiltrate the American peace and labor movements, which were opposed to the US entering the war on the side of the Allies. On August 9, 1914, the leading proponent of absolute American neutrality, William Jennings Bryan, had decried American funding of French, British, and Russian purchases of war materiel as the real "contraband" in the war in a letter to President Woodrow Wilson.[563] In a spat over President Wilson's Lusitania notes to the German government, which Bryan considered too harsh, he resigned in protest as Secretary of State on June 9, 1915.

Rintelen was fascinated. Would it be possible to manipulate the labor movement into strikes on behalf of world peace? Or use the peace movement to promote a boycott of munitions exports? At a lecture of the American Truth Society in the Hotel Astor in New York on April 28, 1915, which Rintelen sponsored and likely attended, Professor Thomas C. Hall, a seminarian, avowed socialist, and powerful voice gave a speech denouncing British "warmongering" propaganda.[564] Hall had co-authored the monograph, Germany's Just Cause, with George Sylvester Viereck and Bernhard Dernburg in 1914. He also had regularly contributed articles in Viereck's weekly *Fatherland*, defending Germany and denouncing British propaganda in the US.[565] The two men met at the New York Yacht Club on May 17.[566] Rintelen asked Hall how to organize American labor effectively to agitate for peace and push for a munitions boycott. Hall suggested that Rintelen associate with someone of important political influence, as in owning politicians and having connections to the labor movement. The person Hall had in mind was the infamous "Wolf of Wall Street," David Lamar.

David M. Levy, aka David Lamar, a law office clerk, had moved from Omaha, Nebraska, to New York in 1899 at the age of 35. A gifted promoter without scruples, Lamar quickly caught the attention of Wall Street insiders. Targeting J. P. Morgan's U.S. Steel Corporation in an attempt to break railroad and steel monopolies endeared him to many lower-level investors. In the next decade he testified in Congress against Morgan, lobbied for trust-busting legislation through his brainchild, the Anti-Trust League, and rose to Wall Street fame with his specialty of promoting undervalued company stocks in his infamous bear raids.[567] In 1913, *The New York Tribune*, *New York Evening World*, and *The Sun* crowned Lamar as a "Wolf of Wall Street," a creature instilling both awe and fear into investors.[568]

Figure 48. David Lamar, c. 1917-1918
Source: New York Herald
US National Archives and Records Administration

In the spring of 1915, however, the Wolf was not doing too well. He had been convicted in a highly publicized trial for impersonating progressive Democratic House member and future Attorney General, A. Mitchell Palmer. Lamar first eluded capture but was finally arrested in November 1914. He posted bond and filed an appeal which was currently pending. His luck on Wall Street had run out, and the expensive trial had drained his assets. Lamar was broke and desperate by June 1915. Rintelen either appreciated Lamar's predicament as fertile soil for dedication to a new, profitable cause, or, more likely, he never bothered to check Lamar's recent background.[569]

Hall offered to introduce Lamar to Rintelen, and the two met in the first week of June. The German agent was "on fire with passion that blinded him to the consequences and who flourished before the eyes of the famished Wolf a half million dollars. He [Rintelen] was manna [to Lamar] fallen from heaven."[570] George Plochmann, who described the relationship between Rintelen and Lamar to the Bureau a year later, tried to save his friend: "I said to him that he [Lamar] was the last person I would have anything to do with."[571] To no avail. Rintelen believed that Lamar was the man with whom to partner. The "Wolf of Wall Street" aligned with the "Tiger of Berlin."[572]

The Wolf wanted to revive the defunct Anti-Trust League, which he had spearheaded as a political tool to defeat Morgan. He also proposed to create a labor union, the Labor's National Peace Council, and attract membership from the peace-loving, internationalist wings of existing labor unions. The leaders of this new union would be nationally recognized political leaders with a large labor following. At the same time, Lamar would bring politicians whom he had in his pocket to lobby Congress for an arms embargo against the Allies. He envisioned this union to create the seed for a movement that would force the Wilson administration to accede to the demands for peace and neutrality. All Rintelen had to do was to stay in the background and pay.

In Lamar's defense, he did not pocket Rintelen's money and disappear back into the shadows. The Labor's National Peace Council organized within days. Lamar created a labor lobby dream team to head the new union that included: Representative Frank Buchanan of Illinois and former president of the International Union of Iron Workers; former Congressman H. Robert Fowler of Illinois; former US Ambassador to Spain and law professor Hannis Taylor; Henry B. Martin, a labor lobbyist and former secretary of the Anti-Trust League, who had been expelled from the American Federation of Labor (AFL) as a result; the president of the Cigarmaker's Union Jacob C. Taylor; Herman J. Schultheis and Frank Monett, prominent lawyers; Milton Snelling, and Ernest Bohm of the Central Federated Union. Of course, all of these men were in Lamar's pocket or at least owed him favors.

New York papers on June 12 announced a meeting at Carnegie Hall, organized by the "National Labor Union" and "Socialists." The organizers were Buchanan and Bohm, who called Bryan the "Anti-War Napoleon," and a hero for having resigned as Secretary of State.⁵⁷³ The lobbying effort worked. The Carnegie Hall rally on June 19 featured none other than former Secretary William J. Bryan as the main speaker.⁵⁷⁴ A private citizen unleashed from his government job, Bryan now loudly voiced his support for "peace at any price."⁵⁷⁵ Other rallies followed in short order. The organizers of the new union promised a national platform for promoting world peace, establishing a forty-hour workweek, and forcing the Wilson administration to establish an arms embargo against all warring nations.

The second arm of Lamar's strategy also immediately manifested. Funneling money into the unions at a time when the American war industry boomed, had the same effect as throwing a match into a tinder box. Union leaders in Bridgeport, Connecticut, announced on June 16 that they would call for a walkout if demands for eight-hour workdays and a minimum wage were not met. Factory managers denounced the workers as being financed by German money.⁵⁷⁶ On June 19, 800 workers walked out of the Remington Arms factory in Bridgeport, Connecticut, starting what would become known as the Great Bridgeport Strike. Two days later, another 1,200 workers joined the picket lines.⁵⁷⁷ The strikes now also spilled over to other factories in Bridgeport, such as the Gaynor Manufacturing Company and the Bridgeport Manufacturing Company.⁵⁷⁸

Figure 49. Labor's National Peace Council Meeting, c. 1915
Source: File 8000-174 Franz von Rintelen, RG65, Bureau of Investigation Case Files
US National Archives and Records Administration

The AFL president, Samuel Gompers, smelled a rat when he heard that workers were being paid liberal sums for striking. The strike money, Gompers noted to the press, did not come from his coffers. He seconded the suspicions of Remington's management that German money was behind this strike, as well as simultaneous efforts to entice the longshoremen's and seamen's unions with large slush funds to paralyze harbor operations all along the East Coast.[579] Ernest Bohm, in the newspaper quoted as Ernest Helm, the treasurer of the Labor's National Peace Council, denied the charges on June 19.[580] No matter the denials, the scent of German money pervaded the activities of the new union.

It did not matter. The strikes took on their own momentum. Gompers called on Bridgeport labor leaders to meet in Washington and settle the strikes. They refused and called for a general strike, instead.[581] The AFL president decided to come to Bridgeport on June 22, but was unable to negotiate any solution. By the end of July, union members across the rustbelt threatened walkouts in 500 munitions factories involving over 600,000 workers. The main demands were not for peace or a munitions boycott, but rather an eight-hour workday and higher pay. Lamar was worth every penny Rintelen had paid him.

The question of who was behind the strikes loomed large, especially for Great Britain. While the unrest potentially threatened the American economy, the Bureau seemed wholly uninterested in inserting itself into this labor dispute, at least at the onset. It was Britain that worried most, as it was dependent on US arms and munitions exports. Around July 12, Guy Gaunt once again hired the Mooney and Boland Detective Agency. Gaunt's manifest fear was that German agents had infiltrated and manipulated the labor and peace movements of the United States with the goal of impeding production and shipping of war materials to the Allies. The Mooney and Boland Agency was the perfect choice for this type of investigation. While other private investigation agencies, such as Thiel, Pinkerton, and Burns, had long engaged in strike-breaking for large US corporations, Mooney and Boland's core competency was the collection of "labor intelligence." Mooney operatives had infiltrated most unions on the East Coast and in the Midwest, and counted many of the labor leaders among their informants. German Naval Attaché Karl Boy-Ed, without an inkling that his British counterpart had hired Mooney and Boland detectives, asked the private eyes to follow Lamar and the people with whom he associated.[582] In effect, Mooney and Boland doubled their money selling intelligence on union leaders to both sides.

The most powerful union leader in the United States was Samuel Gompers, President of the American Federation of Labor. The Mooney and

Boland Detective Agency, as well as operatives of the Burns Detective Agency, shadowed Gompers meticulously. Lacking the investigative reports, it remains unclear who Burns worked for in this case. In general, Burns worked at the same time for British and German intelligence during the neutrality years. Gompers "appears to be about 55 years of age, 5 ft, 3 in. in height, 190 lbs. in weight, brown hair turning grey, full round smooth-shaven face, dark complexion. He wore spectacles and was dressed in a grey suit and Panama hat."⁵⁸³ Gompers had publicly declared his opposition to the Bridgeport strike and had reported on his suspicions of German backing to the Bureau. On July 16, a Mooney and Boland detective following Gompers reported that the union boss had left New York for Washington, DC. Arrangements were made to keep him under surveillance to ascertain his connections.⁵⁸⁴ Detectives followed his every step in Washington; from getting up, to entering and leaving his office in the Ouray Building at 805 G Street, to having dinner at McGuire's Café late at night.⁵⁸⁵

Figure 50. *Samuel Gompers, c. 1908*
Source: The Chicago Historical Society

The detectives also watched David Lamar. He was traveling the Midwest with Buchanan and Martin to round up as many delegates as possible for a planned Washington, DC, rally at the end of July. The New York office of Mooney and Boland contacted the head of the Chicago bureau of the agency on July 17, W. J. Sutherland, to assist in locating and shadowing Lamar and his cohorts.

The request mentions the "Labor Peace Council," as well as Representatives Buchanan and Fowler as subjects of investigation. Lamar is described as "a man, about fifty years old, five foot ten and one half, well proportioned, very dark complexion, black hair, jet black, heavy mustache, usually fashionably attired and walked with more or less if [sic] a swagger. He is doubtless stopping at one of the prominent hotels where his identity can be established."[586]

Over the next weeks, Mooney and Boland operatives did not find any connection between Lamar and Gompers. A detective overheard Gompers discussing the war, proclaiming that "we are strictly neutral. We do not care who licks the Kaiser."[587] The private eyes also focused on the people around Lamar, Martin, and Schultheis, who the reports identified as his "lieutenants."[588] Sounding surprised, one report stated, "We are advised that the Department of Justice has made no investigation of the Labor Peace Party and manifests no interest in it. So far, its operation seems to be public, and any subterranean operations have not yet developed such a phase as would call for governmental action [...]."[589] The statement seems to indicate that Gaunt had conferred with either Offley or Bielaski, and was told to produce more evidence before the Bureau would get involved. Bielaski may have been reluctant to get embroiled in what could only be described as a political minefield. The private investigation continued.

Between July 21 and 25, detectives of the agency canvassed the Bridgeport strike. In their subsequent report, they identified "outside influence" as the cause of the strikes. A man named John Gill of the Bricklayers' Union is reported to have come two weeks earlier from New York with "a large amount of money." He was the "instigator of the original trouble recently in Bridgeport, where it was merely considered a local disturbance." The report also states that local union leaders (of the AFL) ran "him out of the town." There is no mention whether he left the money he brought.[590] The strikes continued, and because newspapers picked up the statement from Gompers, the report contained suspicions of German influence behind the strikes. The leader of the local Iron Workers Union took advantage of the publicity to demand eight-hour workdays and higher pay. The former president of the Iron Workers, Representative Buchanan, of course, was on the payroll of the Labor's National Peace Council. Lamar later claimed that he bought his influence for a mere $12,500, the same he claimed the British were paying Gompers to stay out of it.[591] The report also concludes with a new development: "It was further learned that the Federal Government has started a thorough and rigorous investigation to ascertain the true status of the labor situation[...] and the identity of the people engaged in fomenting the trouble."[592]

The Mooney and Boland investigation abruptly ended on July 25. There is no evidence that the Bureau indeed picked up the pace, at least not for two weeks, when Guy Gaunt turned his records over to Bielaski in the middle of August. The organizers of the Labor's National Peace Council announced that a large peace conference with labor representatives from all over the country would be held in Washington, DC on July 31 and August 1. Lamar, Martin, Buchanan and Fowler had traveled for weeks to union meetings from Baltimore to Chicago looking for delegates to the peace conference in Washington—all expenses paid. Rintelen, who was known only as "the big man in New York," seemed to have not withstood the urge to attend some of the meetings. A participant in a union meeting on July 14, testified a year later that he saw a man in the background, who did not participate, and to whom he was not introduced. He was sure that he recognized Rintelen from the photograph Agent Benham showed him.[593]

Rather than hundreds of delegates, a disappointing three dozen labor representatives streamed into Washington on July 31 from all over the country, courtesy the "big man in New York." During the conference at the Willard Hotel, Representative Buchanan demanded a meeting with President Wilson on August 1. This may have been the only and faint chance for Rintelen to come before the President.[594] Wilson wisely sent his regrets through Secretary Tumulty. The papers branded Buchanan the next day as working for the "Germans."[595]

Rintelen, his cover blown and Boy-Ed demanding his recall, received orders from the Imperial Navy Department to leave the country in the beginning of July. He applied for a passport on July 29, under the name Edward V. Gates, born in Millersville, PA. Andrew Meloy, who had returned from Europe a few weeks earlier, asked Melville C. Barnard, a salesman who just happened to be in the office, to go to the passport office and witness Rintelen's application.[596] Meloy offered to join Rintelen on his trip to Berlin, hoping to further promote his idea of an exile force to capture power in Mexico. Andrew D. Meloy was a promoter and investor. His principal investment was in a railroad project in Durango, the Mexico Western Railway, which on account of the ongoing Mexican civil war was a financial disaster. With his can-do attitude, Meloy sincerely believed he could settle the Mexican Revolution with German and Wall Street money and a coalition of Mexican leaders fallen from power, including Victoriano Huerta, Pascual Orozco, Manuel Mondragón, Aureliano Blanquet, Félix Díaz, and Pancho Villa. Deaf, and conversing with a giant ear trumpet, the shrewd promoter tirelessly shuttled between Berlin, Paris, and Barcelona to pull together his improbable plan. Rintelen promised Meloy to access his banking and government connections in Berlin. Therefore, once again, after just having returned from Europe, Meloy, his wife, his secretary Ms. Hatty E. Brophy, and Rintelen booked passage on the SS *Noordam* for August 3.

The travel day approached, but Rintelen had yet to receive his passport. Finally, on August 2, the State Department declined to hand out the passport without Mr. Gates personally appearing in the passport office.[597] Panicked that his arrest would be imminent, he rebooked his reservation under the passport name with which he had arrived on April 3, Emile Victor Gasché. The new passport would not have changed the situation. British intelligence had followed Rintelen's every step. George S. Dougherty, a private detective working for the British consulate, appeared at the passport office the day after the *Noordam* had sailed. The passport employee, Mr. Roosa, told the detective that the Holland-American Line agent had phoned him on the day before the *Noordam* sailed. The mysterious Mr. Gates had cancelled his reservation, but inexplicably booked a new passage immediately, now telling the same agent that he was Swiss citizen Gasché.[598] When Agent Cantrell later contacted Doughterty, he showed him three photographs and three signatures of the mysterious Mr. Gates.[599]

Rintelen obviously still believed, even after the disastrous failure of Huerta's attempted return to power, that Berlin would commit to financial support of yet another offensive against Carranza. While aboard the SS *Noordam*, he wrote General Manuel Mondragón, who had conspired with Huerta on his planned uprising, but wisely had refused to actively participate. In the August 9 letter, Gasché was "anxious to get back to New York for the final settlement as to Mexico's problems. [He] will leave for New York about September 1st [...]."[600] Another letter of Rintelen, dated August 8, shows how deeply he had involved himself in the Mexican situation. The recipient of the letter was Charles Douglas, a prominent lawyer who represented the interests of Venustiano Carranza in the United States. Douglas was well acquainted with Meloy, who likely made the connection between the two men. The German agent wrote that he wanted to see Douglas in Washington upon his return in the "second half of September [...] to discuss the reorganization of Mexico's finances [...]."[601] If he really believed what he was writing, one could assume that Rintelen had lost his mind.

The *Noordam* was intercepted by a British patrol in the English Channel on August 13. The port control officers boarded the ship and called for a Mr. Rintelen to identify himself. No one followed the call. However, when the British soldiers searched the cabins, a satchel in Andrew Meloy's stateroom contained correspondence of Franz Rintelen. Other passengers quickly identified a Swiss man who had been seen in company with Meloy. Both men were taken off the ship and transported to Ramsgate harbor. There Meloy and Gasché were arrested and booked into the local jail. Meloy, an American citizen, immediately protested his arrest to the American embassy, and mentioned Charles Douglas as his lawyer.[602] He was promptly freed on August 17, rearrested on the suspicion of being a German, then released for good on August 18.[603] Meloy claimed that he had received the satchel with incriminating letters in New York from his banking colleague, Frederico Stallforth. He knew nothing about the contents, and believed the papers were to be handed to the Deutsche Bank in Berlin.

Scotland Yard transferred Rintelen to Donington Hall in London, were Admiral Reginald "Blinker" Hall interrogated him.[604] Rintelen confessed to his true identity and became a prisoner of war. British authorities recognized him as an officer and arranged that he be "paid as such from the date of his internment."[605] Through the good offices of the American embassy in Berlin, Rintelen received his Lieutenant Commander's uniform to wear while in detention.[606] Admiral Hall also wanted to identify Rintelen positively. Livingston Sullivan, his friend from Philadelphia, happened to be in the UK. Admiral Hall saw his name mentioned in the captured documents that belonged to Rintelen. Hall summoned Sullivan to Donington Hall on August 30, 1915, to make a positive identification.[607] Frederico Stallforth back in New York, who held $80,000 of Rintelen's funds, paid a retainer of $10,000 to the law firm Wherry and Mygatt of New York to represent Rintelen.[608]

It was the reports of Franz Rintelen's arrest in England that finally spurned the Bureau into action. Guy Gaunt forwarded the Mooney and Boland reports to Bielaski around the middle of August. Felix Sommerfeld visited William Offley on August 24 to inquire about why the Bureau was investigating his bank accounts. Offley showed Sommerfeld several investigative reports, one of them containing a photograph of a certain Edward V. Gates. Sommerfeld "immediately recognized the latter as a photograph of Hansen [the known alias for Rintelen]."[609] William Flynn, Chief of the US Secret Service, copied Bielaski on August 26 to a separate Treasury investigation into union activities, especially those of the International Longshoremen's Union. His report showed that Secret Service operatives had investigated the harbors of New York, Philadelphia, and Boston since May 7, shadowing union leaders. Activities of the president of the Longshoreman, Thomas Ventry O'Connor, and a certain Matthew Cummings occupied most of the report. O'Connor, a labor powerhouse, had led the Longshoremen since 1908.

The investigation did not establish definite links between German money and union activities, but mentioned the "big man in New York," a reference to Rintelen, as well as contacts between George Sylvester Viereck and Cummings.[610] Flynn did not mention the Labor's National Peace Council, with which T. V. O'Connor was connected. Under what authority he conducted this investigation is questionable. It is possible that Flynn did not have the same sense as Bielaski in deciding to stay out of labor politics. Wilson's papers for this period do not contain any directives to either Secretary Gregory or McAdoo to determine details on labor unions or the Bridgeport strike.

Spurred by British leads, the Bureau pursued all avenues of Rintelen's misdeeds. In the middle of September, the US Attorney for the Southern District of New York, H. Snowden Marshall, constituted a grand jury. Agents Cantrell, Dotzert, and Underhill had the unenviable task of collecting the evidence to prosecute dozens of suspects. Cantrell and Offley interviewed Meloy's office manager on August 20, and confirmed that Rintelen and Stallforth shared offices with Meloy.[611] William Offley interviewed Anne Sewell by phone on September 29. She confirmed that she had known Rintelen in Berlin in 1914. In the July crisis, which precipitated the start of the war, Rintelen had helped her, and her mother convert their funds into gold, and secured their safe passage back to the United States.[612]

Agent Cantrell tried to contact Frederico Stallforth, who for the next month was nowhere to be found.[613] Finally, on September 29, he was able to interview him. Stallforth freely admitted knowing Rintelen but not his business dealings. He did mention his close working relationship with Felix Sommerfeld and how he kept Orozco and Sommerfeld from killing each other a few weeks prior. Stallforth lied about the papers he had given to Meloy to carry. Cantrell was not impressed: "Mr. Stallforth's attitude was very backward about giving any information as he stated he did not desire to get Mr. Meloy in any way into trouble... Mr. Stallforth's attitude and point of view appeared to Agent to be typical German, absolutely disregarding the laws of the United States."[614] A few hours later, Agent Klawans served him with a Grand Jury subpoena.[615] Stallforth protested the subpoena through his lawyer and received a contempt of court charge as a result.

Meloy returned from Europe on the SS *Niew Amsterdam* on September 29. Agent Scully and two colleagues hitched a ride on a revenue cutter set to intercept the liner before docking, but she was a day late.[616] The next day, Agents Cantrell, Underhill, and Dotzert boarded the ship and duly arrested Meloy on the suspicion of having committed passport fraud.[617] That same day, Sommerfeld, Plochmann, Brophy, Hammond, Mondragón, and a host of others received subpoenas to appear before the grand jury.[618]

The investigation into the Labor's National Peace Council proved to be the political minefield Bielaski had initially feared. Lamar, Martin, Monett, Buchanan, Taylor, Schultheis, Fowler, and Rintelen in absentia were indicted in

December 1915 for violating the Sherman Anti-Trust Act. The accusation was that the men had conspired to "restrain, hinder and prevent the transportation of munitions of war manufactured in the United States [...]."[619]

Missing from the list of indictments were Stallforth and Meloy. Meloy was an old man, whose intention to carry incriminating papers for Stallforth and Rintelen could not be proven beyond a reasonable doubt. He may have just been naïve enough to not suspect any foul play. The passport fraud charge also was hard to prosecute, since the hapless salesperson, Melville C. Barnard, committed the fraud when he happened to be in Meloy's office and volunteered to sign an affidavit for Rintelen.[620]

Assistant Expert Bank Accountant L. G. Munson, one of the Bureau's expert financial investigators, took apart Stallforth's company books in December 1915 and January 1916. Munson found nothing ostensibly incriminating. Stallforth had kept his company records squeaky clean.[621] Despite Stallforth refusing to testify before a grand jury, US District Attorney Marshall decided in January 1916 to stay the case and not press charges pending Rintelen's return to the US through extradition proceedings.[622] Bielaski seemed to have considered Stallforth a minor player, and turned the case over to the newly created Bureau of Secret Intelligence within the State Department.

Yet, there were many indications that Stallforth was a major player. In October, Agent William Benham received the guest register for Franz Rintelen's visits to the New York Yacht Club. It showed that Rintelen had freely entertained guests, including Karl Boy-Ed, Franz von Papen, and Frederico Stallforth between May and July 1915.[623] Frank Polk, Counselor to the State Department and now in charge of the Stallforth matter, interviewed Stallforth in March 1916 at his Washington, DC, office. Despite receiving intelligence concerning Mexico, Horst von der Goltz, Rintelen, Meloy, and others, Polk did not appear to have forwarded a report to the Bureau.[624] Instead, satisfied with Stallforth's cooperation, Polk supported a motion to dismiss the contempt charge against the smooth-talking German agent. In a letter from US District Judge Wolverton on May 12, 1916, the German agent was informed that the contempt charge against him was dropped, and his lawyer (whom Stallforth had also hired to represent Franz Rintelen) assured his client that he would be "free of any danger of prosecution."[625] Failing to keep up with Stallforth's activities both by the State Department and the Bureau proved to be a massive blunder.

In the fall of 1915 and all the way into 1917, Stallforth became the person entrusted with distributing funds from Albert's office to German sabotage agents. The most significant sabotage cell existed around Paul Hilken and Friedrich Hinsch in Baltimore. Operating under the not-so-watchful eyes of Agent Billups Harris, the group was plotting virtually in plain sight the destruction of Black Tom Island. Hilken had founded the Eastern Forwarding Company in the spring of 1916, ostensibly handling the operations of a new class of large North German Lloyd cargo submarines, able to transport 1,000 tons of freight per voyage between Germany and the United States past the Royal Navy. U-*Deutschland* departed Bremerhaven on June 23, 1916, and arrived in Baltimore on July 9 to great public excitement. Captain Paul Koenig (not to be confused with intelligence agent P. K.), standing next to Hilken and Hinsch crowned the front pages of several US dailies.[626] The freighter carried dye and pharmaceutical chemicals, German government mail, and the sabotage agent Hans Boehm, who slipped away unseen.

During the spring of 1916, Hilken and Hinsch traveled extensively between New London, Connecticut (where they prepared a second landing site for the submarine freighters), New York, and Baltimore. Their activities aroused no attention. Hilken regularly met Stallforth in New York and Baltimore, where he received funds for his clandestine work. While ostensibly planning the landing of the U-*Deutschland*, Hilken and Hinsch conducted sabotage operations. With the help of German military intelligence agent Dr. Anton Dilger, a veterinarian from Front Royal, Virginia with a laboratory in Baltimore, Hinsch organized the inoculation with glanders, an infectious bacterial disease, of horses destined for Europe. Hilken personally drove to Norfolk with Dilger on at least one of these historic biological warfare missions.[627] Hinsch also received a new type of timed firebomb from German intelligence headquarters which his agents allegedly placed on ships and in factories. It is unknown, but likely, that the U-*Deutschland* carried a good number of these bombs.[628]

While the U-*Deutschland* rested in her closely guarded berth in Baltimore harbor on July 30, 1916, the Allied loading terminals on Black Tom Island in the New York harbor exploded with such force that most windows in lower Manhattan shattered, Ellis Island had to be evacuated, and Lady Liberty barely held up her torch, structurally damaged and peppered with shrapnel. It took days for New York and New Jersey fire departments to be able even to approach the site. Fire department and insurance investigators determined that the conflagration had resulted from several guards having lit oil barrels at the docks to keep away mosquitoes. Somehow, without witnesses, these barrels set fire to a parked railroad car, which in turn, ignited the entire complex in a chain reaction.[629] Had the Bureau kept up with Stallforth, and had Agent Billups Harris looked behind the curtain of the Hilken and Hinsch smokescreen, this largest attack on US soil during the war may have been averted, or at least investigated from the onset as a German attack.

Stallforth, despite his case being stayed until Rintelen came back to the United States, was never indicted. He voluntarily submitted to the interview with Counselor Frank Polk on March 15 to 16, 1916.[630] On the day of the US Declaration of War on April 6, 1917, Stallforth was arrested again. This time, he did not face a well-meaning State Department counselor casually asking softball questions. During several days of interrogations, which Chief Bielaski and Superintendent Offley personally conducted, he caved under intense questioning.[631] He told all that he knew, helped decipher coded German reports, and filled holes in pending investigations. Chief Bielaski seemed satisfied as Stallforth painstakingly deciphered German coded messages and aliases used in the captured documents, gave background on the German sabotage and biological campaigns, and verified payments to German operatives.

Bielaski confronted the German agent with a captured letter Stallforth had written to Rintelen in August 1915, before he knew of his arrest in England. How and when this document came into the possession of the Bureau is unknown. It is neither cited in the Mixed Claims Commission files of the 1920s and 30s, nor used in histories of the German sabotage campaign of 1915 to 1917. Stallforth confirmed it was authentic when Bielaski interrogated him. The thirteen-page letter presents the clearest overview yet of German strategy

Figure 51. U-Deutschland, 1916
Source: Mixed Claims Commission
US National Archives and Records Administration

during the sabotage campaign of 1915, while it delineates mission goals and achievements.

Stallforth wrote to Rintelen "how well everything is going here [...]" and was happy to hear from Mooney and Boland detectives (yes, the same company working for Captain Gaunt at the same time) that "the boat [carrying Rintelen] is safe in Rotterdam and you have also arrived there in the conduct of your great gigantic business on European shores." He described the sabotage campaign as a great success: "Every chest which is transported to-day from here to England must be held up at the dock and searched over. This makes an enormous cost, and in addition extra policemen and watchmen have been installed, and this costs the Allies a great sum." He continued, "Here in Yonkers during the past few weeks over a thousand horses must have fallen to the ground," referring to the glanders infections.[632] "[...] more money must be placed on call here for the undertakings with the Captains [firebombing campaign] and Baltimore if that [Black Tom explosion] is to be done and to sustain over other very important undertakings." Finally, in a reference to Germany's orders to create a US military intervention in Mexico, he wrote, "In Mexico, the thing is working quietly here [...] The President [Wilson with his threat of intervention in the summer of 1915] has run ahead so firmly that nothing more remains to be done, either fight, or the people will blame him horribly." Referring to the peace movement and labor unrest, Stallforth predicted that "the majority in the Senate and Congress [sic] would speak against the exportation of weapons and munitions in order to simply protect itself. I am very optimistic about the matter, as are all our fellow workers."[633] In this single document, all dimensions of German attacks against the US in 1915 are clearly laid out—yet, for unknown reasons, it was stowed away in a dusty bin within Frederico Stallforth's case file.

As a result of Stallforth's full cooperation, the Chief supported the agent's release on parole, rather than recommending internment or arrest. The next day, on April 22, Stallforth in the presence of his brother, Alberto, gave a full statement comprising forty-two pages to Assistant District Attorney Sarfaty.[634] Curiously, the "official" statement did not contain the highly explosive letter Stallforth had written to Rintelen in 1915. Division Superintendent William Offley contended that "nothing has been found to indicate that he [Stallforth] took part in any so called 'strong arm' operations or that he had been active since the severance of relations between this country and Germany."[635] Stallforth had assisted in the trial of Rintelen and Lamar, as well as aiding in other investigations of German agents. He may also have gotten a personal hardship break from Chief Bielaski. The love of his life and mother of two underaged daughters, Anita Risse Stallforth had just passed away on January 25, 1917.⁶³⁶ He was allowed to return home and take care of his family after posting a $500 bond on April 28.⁶³⁷

Stallforth once again came forward in the 1930s after the statute of limitations had expired for his prosecution, and explained his responsibility as a bagman between the Baltimore cell and Heinrich Albert. As the lawyer representing the US in the Mixed Claims Commission, Herold H. Martin, noted, Stallforth's fingerprints were all over the Bureau investigative files. The files established that Stallforth paid Hilken to conduct his sabotage activities.⁶³⁸ Hilken's extensive diaries, which the Mixed Claims Commission received after the war, showed that neither Stallforth nor Hilken made any attempts to hide their activities.⁶³⁹ They partied frequently, drove all over the East Coast in their cars, attended theater performances and concerts, and met in known hangouts, such as the "Kaiserkeller" in Hoboken, the Hotel Astor roof garden, Delmonico's steak house, and the German Club in New York.⁶⁴⁰ They openly consorted with other Germans under surveillance, such as Count Bernstorff, Heinrich Albert, Eno Bode, P. K., and Andrew Meloy, meeting in public spaces, and even invited them to their houses.⁶⁴¹ An entry in Stallforth's guest book on May 23, 1915, is signed by "the lofty character, Hansen," Rintelen's alias at the time.⁶⁴² Both agents visited Baltimore, where Hilken entertained Rintelen at least on one occasion in the Baltimore Country Club. On several occasions, Hilken also stayed in the Astor Hotel at Times Square, where Heinrich Albert took up residence after August 1915, and where the Bureau knew German agents to congregate in New York. Hilken

Figure 52. Frederico Stallforth with Daughters, c. 1925
Source: Stallforth Papers, Courtesy Mary Prevo

and Hinsch are documented to have met with Captain Bode, whom the Bureau investigated as part of the Scheele affair, and Carl Heynen, Albert's secretary and manager of the German sham business, the Bridgeport Projectile Company.[643] Anton Dilger, the German agent tasked with infecting horses with glanders, and Fred Herrmann, the person later accused of setting fire to the Black Tom loading terminals, also appear in Hilken diaries.[644]

There is no doubt that even a casual observation of Stallforth and Hilken's activities in the fall of 1915 and the first half of 1916 in New York and Baltimore would have yielded actionable intelligence about the plots both agents were hatching. Once the Black Tom explosion had occurred in July 1916, the Bureau again missed the opportunity to investigate the sabotage cell in Baltimore and arrest the most dangerous German agents active in the United States: Hans Boehm, Friedrich Hinsch, Paul Hilken, Anton Dilger, Felix Sommerfeld, Fred Herrmann, Kurt Jahnke, and Frederico Stallforth. When Stallforth was briefly held in April 1917, all leading German agents, save for Felix Sommerfeld, had left for Mexico. The "full cooperation" of Stallforth with the Bureau had only helped the legal cases against Rintelen and Lamar. The German saboteurs freely plotted new attacks from south of the border. Eventually, Stallforth and Sommerfeld were detained in 1918 and spent a year in Fort Oglethorpe, Georgia as dangerous enemy aliens. The Bureau and the State Department's Bureau of Secret Intelligence had missed the single largest sabotage operation during the war, a monumental blunder.

The prosecution of Lamar, Martin, Monett, Schulteis, Fowler, Bohm, Taylor, and Buchanan in the fall of 1915 proved to be a huge headache. Politically well connected, Martin, Bohm, and Taylor attacked the District Attorney for the Southern District of New York, Hudson Snowden Marshall. They accused Marshall of "bribery, forgery and intimidation," tried to have him removed from the case, and impeached.[645] The threats became so violent that William Offley dispatched Agents Jentzer and Timney to provide security for the embattled district attorney.[646] The plot to decapitate the prosecution almost succeeded. In an emergency move, the Justice Department brought William Sarfaty from Chicago as the lead prosecutor, effectively replacing Marshall on this case. William Offley cabled Agent Clabaugh in Chicago, "Please advise me promptly when Sarfaty will reach New York. This [is] important and enquiry at request U.S. Attorney."[647] A. Bruce Bielaski also became a target. Fowler accused the Chief of having burgled his offices and stolen a "book." What the book contained he did not describe.[648]

One of the main witnesses against the Labor's National Peace Council was Samuel Gompers, the AFL president. Gompers had approached the Bureau early in July 1915 with his suspicions that German money was financing the new union. He also reported that Buchanan had offered him $50,000 to publicly support the "Peace Council."[649] Gompers wisely declined. The union chief subsequently cooperated closely with William Offley in the investigation of Labor's National Peace Council and in preparation of his grand jury testimony, which took place on December 20, 1915. Security was tight. Two Bureau agents accompanied Gompers to the federal building "for the purpose of affording such protection as might be necessary."[650] He testified to his suspicions and stated that he "refused to entertain negotiations with them [the accused Labor's Peace Council organizers]."[651]

Around the time of Gompers's grand jury testimony, the Bureau finally caught up with David Lamar who had eluded agents for months. He absolutely refused to cooperate. Together with Henry Martin he sued the United States in the Circuit Court of Appeals for the Second Circuit—and won. His final trial took place in November 1918 and resulted in his case being dismissed.[652]

Rintelen's criminal prosecution in 1915 could only proceed with the German agent in absentia. As a prisoner of war in Great Britain, he was out of reach for the time being. However, Ambassador Count Bernstorff, under pressure from Robert Lansing, disavowed Rintelen as a German agent in December 1915.[653] As a result, the State Department challenged Rintelen's status as a prisoner of war and demanded his extradition to the US for prosecution as a civilian.

In April 1917, British authorities revoked Franz Rintelen's status and returned him to the United States to be tried as a civilian, while promising him to return to England after the trial as a prisoner of war.[654] The trial against Rintelen and his cohorts from the Labor's National Peace Council proceeded swiftly. The Bureau had built an airtight case. "Out of the investigations of the Government rose a card index of every man that Rintelen and Lamar had seen during the four months from April 3 to August 3, 1915, of every hotel they had visited, of practically every telephone call they had made, and telegram sent or received, of nearly every dollar they had had and spent. Thousands upon thousands of these cards were made and filed."[655] Of the accused, Frank Monett, a former attorney general of Ohio, was acquitted. The cases against US representative Frank Buchanan, former congressman H. Robert Fowler, labor lawyer Herman Schulteis, and former ambassador Hannis Taylor ended in a mistrial because of a hung jury.[656] In a retrial, the men, including Rintelen, Martin, and Lamar, received twelve to eighteen-month sentences.[657] Lamar and Martin kept fighting until their case was finally dismissed in 1918.

Rintelen did not cooperate with prosecutors, citing his military honor code as the reason; he also did not appeal his sentence. While his code of honor claims sound noble, even self-sacrificing, the real reason for Rintelen's lack of cooperation more likely stemmed from his hope to return to England as a prisoner of war after the trial. He knew that he had gone rogue and had been disavowed by his own government for that reason. In New York, Felix Sommerfeld and Frederico Stallforth were still around in the summer of 1917, and available as possible witnesses for the prosecution. Rintelen did not want any evidence to be introduced that would further erode his status as an official agent of the German government. He miscalculated. Instead of returning to England, he served a twelve-month sentence in the Atlanta penitentiary for fomenting strikes.[658] In a second trial in March 1918, he faced fifteen indictments, from perjury in the Edward V. Gates passport matter to conspiracy to place incendiary bombs on thirty-five ships. The second conviction added another twelve months for passport fraud, and eighteen months and a $2,000 fine for fire-bombing thirty-five ships to his previous sentence, to be served consecutively.[659] As the author [likely Chief Bielaski himself] of a 1918 "Memorandum re.: Franz Rintelen" wrote, "The Tiger of Berlin is securely caged, and not likely soon to be at large."[660] Rintelen was released in 1922 and returned to a different Germany. He arrived without fanfare or acknowledgement by the Weimar government. He had been utterly forgotten.[661]

The FBI and American Neutrality, 1914-1917

9

The Great Cover-Up

ARGUABLY THE MOST PUBLICIZED counterintelligence coup of World War I occurred in mid-August 1915, when the contents of German Commercial Attaché Heinrich F. Albert's stolen briefcase found their way into the editing rooms of the New York World.[662] A sensational exposé of German intrigue in the neutral United States ran from August 15 to 18, pushing from the front pages the landfall of a devastating category 5 hurricane at Galveston, Texas. Headlines in all caps screamed at the American public: "HOW GERMANY HAS WORKED IN U.S. TO SHAPE OPINION, BLOCK THE ALLIES AND GET MUNITIONS FOR HERSELF, TOLD IN SECRET AGENTS' LETTERS" (August 15); "NO DENIAL OF WORLD EXPOSURES BY AGENTS OF GERMANY" (August 16); "NATION-WIDE SENSATION OVER SECRET ACTIVITY OF GERMANY" (August 16); "OFFICIAL INQUIRY IS FORECAST" (August 16); "GERMANY, WHILE SEEKING EMBARGO TO BALK ALLIES, SECRETLY ARRANGES TO GET AMERICAN ARMS AND SUPPLIES" (August 17); "EDISON SUPPLY OF ACID TAKEN UNDER AN IMPERIAL GUARANTEE" (August 17); "BRIDGEPORT PROJECTILE CO. BACKED BY HOADLEYS TO GET SMOKELESS POWDER SUPPLY" (August 18).[663]

Years later the former US Secret Service Chief William J. Flynn and his former boss, Treasury Secretary William Gibbs McAdoo, credited US Secret Service Agent Frank Burke with the daring feat, billed as the most successful US counterintelligence operation of the Great War.[664] Upon thorough scrutiny of all available archival documentation, the story of Albert's briefcase theft was not a "counterintelligence" coup, at least not one to be credited to US intelligence organizations. It rather appears to have been one of the most successful, long-lasting, and elaborate cover-ups of a British propaganda plot that played into a scheme by members of the Wilson administration to silence the anti-war movement headed by the former Secretary of State William J. Bryan and

Senator Hoke Smith. Both publicly decried the Wilson foreign policy at the time and called for moderation in dealing with Germany after the sinking of the *Lusitania*. In a letter to President Wilson the week before the *New York World* exposé, presidential advisor and confidante Edward Mandell House wrote: "McAdoo [...] has done fine work. The publication will cause excitement and deep feeling. It may, in my opinion, even lead us into war, but I think the publication should go ahead. It will strengthen our hands tremendously [...] and [...] weaken such agitators as Mr. [William Jennings] Bryan and Hoke Smith."[665] Secretary Bryan had resigned on June 9, 1915, in protest to the severity of the second *Lusitania* note, fearing that the US might be forced to join the war on the side of the Allies. That was, of course, Great Britain's greatest desire, and the motivation for getting the Albert papers into the American public's hands.

The theft of Albert's papers and the sensationalist revelations had far-reaching immediate, medium, and longer-term effects. When Albert noticed his briefcase missing on Saturday, July 24, 1915, around 4:00 p.m., the German commercial attaché and his colleagues scrambled to find the culprit and try to get it back. At the time he did not know who had taken it. P. K. of the German secret service investigated. A "former British detective," possibly a member of the Burns agency, told P. K. within a week of the theft, that a certain "independent newspaper writer" named George Calvert had proffered a selection of the papers to the *New York World* editor, Timothy Walsh, on August 2.[666] According to P. K.'s source, Calvert had shadowed Albert for several weeks, indicating that he may not have been a mere reporter.[667]

While a small chance existed that a common thief had just been looking for valuables and might have discarded the "worthless" papers, it was unlikely. Still, on Monday, July 27, König placed an ad in the *New York Tribune*: "Lost on Saturday. On 3:30 Harlem Elevated Train, at 50th St. Station, Brown Leather Bag, Containing Documents. Deliver to G. H. Hoffman, 5 E. 47th St., Against $20 Reward."[668] Hoffman was Albert's servant. The briefcase did not turn up.

Not getting a hold of the briefcase and the compromising papers contained therein, and with König having accurately traced the papers to the editing rooms of the *New York World*, Ambassador Count Bernstorff, Albert himself, German Naval Attaché Karl Boy-Ed, and Military Attaché Franz von Papen went into overdrive to identify the contents and assess the potential damage the disclosures would cause. The group concluded that most of the information was of a financial nature, embarrassing, yes, but not necessarily illegal. The papers revealed the German ownership of the Bridgeport Projectile Company, the purchase and storage of arms and munitions, industrial market-cornering efforts, financing of labor unrest, investments in newspapers, most notably the New York Evening News, which Albert had purchased in the spring of 1915, bribes to American politicians, links of the Deutsche Bank to the German clandestine operations, and payments of the German government to a wide range of editors, most notably to George Sylvester Viereck and his English language weekly, the Fatherland. Nonetheless, the publication of the Albert papers would be disastrous, both with respect to the American public's perception of Germany, and to ongoing clandestine activities. The group decided to try to convince the US government to intervene and stop the publication.

As soon as P. K. had traced the papers to the New York World on August 2, Count Bernstorff sent the prominent New York lawyer, Samuel Untermeyer, to intercede on his behalf with the New York World's editor-in-chief, Frank Cobb, to prevent the publication. The fifty-seven-year-old, tall, mustached Untermeyer had worked with Albert on several legal cases emanating from Albert's attempts to circumvent the British blockade and the purchase of the New York Evening News.[669] The emergency meeting with Cobb on August 2 yielded no results.[670]

Figure 53. Frank I. Cobb
Source: Creative Commons

Untermeyer also worked as an official advisor to the US Treasury Department at the time. Count Bernstorff decided to use the lawyer's connections to Treasury Secretary William McAdoo and attempt to speak directly with President Wilson the next day. The Treasury Secretary was Wilson's son-in-law, who, according to the President, had "a very warm feeling of friendship" for Untermeyer. McAdoo indeed organized a meeting the next day, August 3.[671] A letter to the President's fiancée, Edith Bolling Galt, about the meeting suggests that neither Wilson nor McAdoo had any knowledge of the briefcase and its contents.⁶⁷² The President seemed favorably inclined to look into the issue. It is at this juncture, that McAdoo likely asked his Secret Service Chief William Flynn to procure the papers from the New York World.⁶⁷³

President Wilson delegated the matter to his confidante, Colonel Edward M. House. House, together with McAdoo and Secretary of State Robert Lansing, but without including Attorney General Thomas Watt Gregory, reviewed the contents of the briefcase after Flynn had secured them in the week following Untermeyer's entreaty.⁶⁷⁴ The daily report of Agent in Charge John McHenry of the New York office of the US Secret Service on August 5 noted that Agents Frank C. Burke and Miles C. McCahill worked on a "special investigation" directed by Chief Flynn.⁶⁷⁵ They may have been sent to recover the Albert papers from the World that day.

Figure 54. Samuel Untermeyer, c. 1915
Source: Library of Congress Prints and Photographs Division

The New York Tribune, in a well-researched exposé in November 1918, spoke to the fact that the Attorney General was not involved in the efforts to locate the papers or in the decision-making process of what to do with them: "...it was perfectly possible—even one might imagine, advisable—for Secretaries Lansing and McAdoo to inform the Attorney General. Yet, as a matter of fact, a representative of the Department of Justice was sent to the 'New York World' to say that the Albert documents seemed too serious and important to remain in private hands, and to request the paper to turn its 'discoveries' over to the Attorney General."⁶⁷⁶ If the Tribune's reporting is accurate, the Bureau independently tried to prevent the publication of Albert's papers around the same time that Untermeyer made his request to Frank Cobb.⁶⁷⁷ In

THE GREAT COVER-UP

the Bureau of Investigation case files Bureau Agents Cantrell and Baker and the New York World were in contact between July 28 and August 4, 1915. The Bureau was investigating a wanted ad for a film covering military fortifications in New York. The ad turned out to be a hoax.[678] The investigation ended just as the Albert papers reached the World. There is no surviving report as to the agents learning about the Albert papers. They may have missed the chance by just a few days.

However, the theory that the Justice Department would have sought to prevent the publication makes perfect sense: There were dozens of active investigations under way in July and August 1915, from the prosecution of the HAPAG managers, to the attacks on the Vanceboro bridge and the Welland Canal, to the discovery of the *Annie Larsen*. Franz Rintelen fled the country on August 3, 1915, with Bureau agents closing in on his incitements of labor unrest, suspected attempts to finance Victoriano Huerta's return to Mexico, and firebombing of merchant ships. Without analyzing the Albert papers, and the chance to withhold information that might affect these and other active investigations, the work of the Bureau could be severely damaged, and arguably it was, as the Albert organization quickly ceased propaganda and industry-cornering efforts. Frank Cobb not only refused the German entreaties but also must have denied the request of the Bureau if it was ever made.

Figure 55. *Vanceboro Bridge, 1915*
Source: *Creative Commons*

House notified President Wilson on August 10 that the group recommended not to intercede on behalf of the German government and to let the New York World proceed. House also reported in the same letter that two editors of the *Providence Journal* had lunched with him: "You know, of course the work they are doing," indicating that the President was aware of known British propagandists in close contact with his confidante during the deliberations.[679] It also implies Wilson's tacit approval of such contacts.

The New York World officially notified Albert and House on August 13, that the papers in their possession would be published shortly.[680] In a last-minute effort, the German embassy sent Untermeyer and the sixty-six-year-old Second Counselor of the German Embassy in Washington, a member of the royal aristocracy of Prussia and former member of the German parliament, Hermann Prinz Hatzfeld zu Trachenberg, to speak with Secretary of State Robert Lansing.[681] The Secretary was unwilling to help the German delegation.

The revelations appeared between August 15 and August 18, 1915, in the New York World and, as expected, were devastating for the German war strategy in the US. Using American strawmen, Albert had indeed succeeded in securing contracts from Dupont's Aetna division to buy one year's worth of smokeless powder, severely hampering production of munitions. The monthly deliveries were stored in the Bridgeport factory, and subsequently sold off to the Spanish government.[682] The Thomas A. Edison Corporation had also agreed with the CEO of Bayer in the United States (and German military intelligence agent), Dr. Hugo Schweitzer, to sell the entire annual phenol production to the German concern. Phenol was vital in the production of aspirin, but also the main ingredient in picric acid, a compound used for explosives. These contracts now came under public scrutiny and, in the case of Edison, abruptly ended. Other companies, such as hydraulic press manufacturers, who sold their production capacities of vital presses to produce cartridges and artillery shells to Albert's strawmen, now realized whom they were really dealing with and cancelled their contracts. Not only were German propaganda efforts already in shambles after the *Lusitania* sinking on May 7, 1915, but the clandestine German ownership of the New York Evening News was now revealed. Readership caved and the paper was sold at a huge loss a few months later.

Albert personally suffered the consequences of his carelessness. Not only should he not have carried such sensitive and classified documents with him. He also would have done well to have stayed awake on the train that fateful Saturday afternoon. A New York paper called Albert's briefcase theft a case of "bovine stupidity," a description Albert admitted to his wife a few months later was "not so entirely unjustified [...]."[683]

THE GREAT COVER-UP

Earlier in June, worried about potential criminal liability for Albert, Ambassador Count Bernstorff had elevated Albert's status from financial advisor to commercial attaché without the approval of the Imperial Foreign Service.[684] As a result of the briefcase scandal in August, the German chancellor personally demanded Albert's recall.[685] Albert was not opposed to returning to Germany and defend himself personally (and, according to a letter to his superior, he wanted to return home to his family after two years on the US assignment).[686] However, Count Bernstorff's blunder of giving Albert diplomatic status without registering with the German Foreign Service prompted the British government to refuse safe passage for the German attaché. Without an alternative, Albert stayed in the US. The public embarrassment faded over the next few years. The new German chancellor even supported a defamation lawsuit against Albert's detractors in 1917 (which he won in 1918),[687] and his career propelled him all the way to Secretary of Treasury in 1922, albeit being publicly ridiculed as "Minister without Portfolio." Thus, in a historical irony, the British government had salvaged Albert's job in 1915 and promoted his career.

Just who stole the papers remained shrouded in mystery until 1918, when the former Chief of the US Secret Service, William J. Flynn, published a "novelized" autobiography of his exploits during the Great War, which became a movie a year later.[688] In it, he intimated that one of his agents (not the experienced career agent Frank Burke who was later credited, but rather unflatteringly an amateurish skinny boy named "Jimmy") had snatched the satchel.[689] To support his claim, Flynn included a photograph of the purported briefcase with an USSS evidence tag

Figure 56. William J. Flynn, 1919
Source: Harris & Ewing Collection
Library of Congress Prints and Photographs Division

159

attached, albeit looking black rather than tan as the text claims. The evidence tag read: "Portfolio taken from H.F. Albert July 24, 1915, at 5:30 p.m., containing documents relating to German intrigue [illegible], W.J. Flynn."[690] Flynn claimed until his death in 1928 to have the briefcase in his possession.

By 1917 Attorney General Thomas Gregory could no longer stomach Flynn's public grandstanding and interference with Bureau investigations in New York. As a result of the Attorney General's pressure Flynn was forced out of the Secret Service for his rogue behavior. To supplement his income and feed his ego, he started to write adventure, detective, and spy stories that were widely published in New York papers. Within a year, Flynn had completed a novelized memoir, *The Eagle's Eye: A True Story of the Imperial German Government's Spies and Intrigues in America from Facts Furnished by William J. Flynn, Recently Retired Chief of the U.S. Secret Service*, and was promoting it. The book became successful enough to be adapted into a movie in 1919.[691] Likely as part of Flynn's publicity campaign, Frank Burke was first named in New York newspapers in November 1918 as the agent who had pulled off the Albert briefcase feat.[692] Burke and Flynn's careers continued to blossom when Attorney General Harry Dougherty appointed Flynn Chief of the Bureau of Investigation in 1920. Flynn took Burke, now a fellow counterintelligence legend, with him to become Assistant Chief. Former Treasury Secretary William G. McAdoo's autobiography, *Crowded Years*,

Figure 57. US Attorney General Thomas Watt Gregory, 1917
Source: Harris & Ewing Collection
Library of Congress Prints and Photographs Division

which appeared in 1931, cemented the Flynn and Burke story to become the official and authoritative version of what happened. According to the memoirs, McAdoo received authorization to surveil German diplomats from President Wilson on May 14, 1915, one week after the tragic sinking of the ocean liner *Lusitania*, in the form of an executive order. In his book, McAdoo then quoted a statement from USSS Agent Frank Burke as to exactly what happened.

Burke described that he and USSS Agent William Houghton shadowed the German-American propagandist George Sylvester Viereck and Heinrich F. Albert on the 6th Avenue elevated train going uptown on the afternoon of July 24, 1915. Houghton exited the train staying with Viereck after a few stops. Burke remained on the train, seated behind the German commercial attaché. Albert fell asleep, woke up in a panic when the train stopped, and left the train forgetting his satchel. Burke saw an opportunity, grabbed the portfolio, and evaded an irate Albert. According to Burke, Albert had noticed him and pursued him down the platform. Burke jumped on a streetcar and told the conductor to speed up as a crazy person was after him. At a stop a few streets later, Burke phoned Flynn who "came up in his machine [automobile] and we drove to the office."693 After looking through the contents of the briefcase with Burke, Flynn took the papers to McAdoo's vacation home in Maine the next day. The Treasury Secretary then claimed that he unilaterally decided to give the papers to the *New York World* for publication.694

Figure 58. William Gibbs McAdoo, c. 1914
Source: Harris & Ewing Collection
Library of Congress Prints and Photographs Division

Burke received widely reported recognition for his daring counter-intelligence success upon retirement in 1942.695 Assistant USSS Chief Joseph

E. Murphy honored Burke's famous achievement, Treasury Secretary Henry Morgenthau praised his "faithful and intelligent service" in a signed letter, and President Roosevelt gave him a signed photograph, "To my friend, Frank Burke, Franklin D. Roosevelt."[696] Numerous historians, including Barbara Tuchman and Arthur S. Link, have adopted this "official" version at face value.[697]

Historian Rhodri Jeffreys-Jones in *American Espionage: From Secret Service to CIA* is one of those who has accepted the US Secret Service version of the Albert briefcase affair, adding: "Yet in spite of all this the Germans remained ignorant of Burke because American sources managed to convey the impression that British intelligence had brought off the coup." [698]

Figure 59. Agent Frank Burke upon retirement
Source: Personnel file

But Jeffreys-Jones has gone much further, postulating an intelligence partnership between the Secret Service and the State Department, asserting: "In the post-Bryan era, MID [Military Intelligence Division], ONI [Office of Naval Intelligence], and the Bureau of Investigation had increased in size and extended their activities. The State Department coordinated their efforts and those of the Secret Service, already a going concern, with its own requirements."[699] "The partnership between State Department and Secret Service produced good intelligence. For example, by the fall of 1915, State had been made aware of German strategic thinking through its surveillance of von Bernstorff's agents. The Secret Service kept a particular watch of Captain Hans Tauscher, because Flynn at first mistook him for the head of the German espionage system in this country."[700] "Paul Fuller [...] supervised Secret Service operations in Cuba."[701] "It is as certain that the Pinkerton Agency was discredited as it is that the Secret Service was directed from the State Department."[702] "Since the British were listening in on and decoding his wireless and telegraph messages and the Secret Service was transcribing his telephone calls, the German ambassador kept very few secrets."[703] "In December 1915, the State Department allowed the Secret Service to make a further arrest but, having thereby obtained its intelligence goal in the form of confiscated papers, refrained from pushing its case in the courts."[704] "The Secret Service served the State Department well during the period of America's neutrality. Its agents made swoop after swoop, yet never fully alerted the Germans to the methods being employed against them."[705] "American intelligence was good in World War I, and won the reputation of being even better. Efficacious through the State Department-Secret Service combination was, it did not entirely meet the requirements of the Wilson administration."[706]

Remarkably, Jeffreys-Jones has completely misinterpreted the Secret Service's intelligence role. The partnership he describes between the State Department and the Secret Service simply did not exist. The partnership that *did* exist was between the State Department and the Bureau of Investigation, an agency to which Jeffreys-Jones refers as: "Outstanding in the second rank of intelligence organizations were two additional national bodies, the Justice Department's Bureau of Investigation and The Inquiry."[707] In the above-mentioned excerpts the exploits attributed to the US Secret Service actually pertain to the Bureau of Investigation.

The State Department during the war crisis with Mexico in June 1916 furnished the Bureau with funds to hire special employees to be stationed along the border and in Mexico to gather intelligence.[708] And Chief Bielaski testified that as of July 1, 1916 at the Bureau's request, "the appropriation which provides the money for the Bureau of Investigation was amended so as to make it possible to make investigations of matters in which the State Department was interested, at the request of the Secretary of State, and with the approval of the Attorney General, even though those matters did not amount to violations of law."[709] Furthermore, the archives provide ample evidence of the close cooperation between Bielaski and Leland Harrison of the State Department's Office of the Counselor who frequently shared intelligence reports.

Despite the by-then declassified FBI files being open to the public, Jeffreys-Jones presents the same flawed interpretation in his 2007 book, The FBI: A History. In it he describes the efforts of Robert Lansing to establish a "central intelligence agency" in 1915 resulting from the alleged rivalry between the US Secret Service and the Bureau.[710] The envisioned State Department agency was to function as a clearing house for intelligence gathered by the Bureau, State, ONI, and MID. Jeffreys-Jones failed to mention in his monograph that the Wilson administration roundly rejected Lansing's plan and in 1916 increased funding for the Bureau instead. He also ignores that the US Secret Service was not part of Lansing's plan, a detail that derails his entire thesis and attests to the fact that in the neutrality years of World War I the Secret Service had no counterintelligence funding or mission.[711]

As a result of the publications by Flynn and McAdoo taking credit for stealing the briefcase, and the subsequent adoption of their version of the Albert affair by historians, the official website of the US Secret Service not only recounts this World War I feat by one of their own, but it also bases the birth of the USSS counterintelligence mission on the Albert briefcase affair.[712] Yet, the story told in Flynn's books and McAdoo's memoirs, quoting Burke's recall of the event, likely never happened.

One of the foundational claims for the US Secret Service (USSS) having captured Heinrich Albert's documents is the supposed existence of an executive order, dated May 14, 1915, which authorized the Treasury agents to shadow German

Figure 60. Heinrich Friedrich Albert
Source: Albert Papers
US National Archives and Records Administration

diplomats.⁷¹³ This order is crucial since the mission of the USSS since May 1908 consisted only of presidential protection and counterfeiting investigations.⁷¹⁴ In contrast, the mission of the Bureau of Investigation was to enforce federal laws on a national level. Since 1908, Bureau special agents had investigated land fraud cases, White Slave Act violations, and enforced the Neutrality Laws of the United States. German intrigue, such as supplying the German fleet from US harbors using false manifests, sending reservists with false passports to Germany, and mounting attacks on Canada from US soil clearly fell under potential violations of the neutrality laws. As a consequence, and despite Chief Flynn's frequent and public claims to the contrary, the US Secret Service had no authorized role in these investigations between 1914 and 1917.⁷¹⁵ The presidential authorization of sweeping investigative powers for the USSS in May 1915 would have marked not only a surprising departure from previous departmental separation of responsibilities. It also would have likely triggered congressional scrutiny as the founding of the Bureau was the result of an express congressional ban on using US Secret Service agents in the enforcement of federal law other than counterfeiting.

The literature covering the briefcase affair includes the current official websites of the US Secret Service, FBI, and Homeland Security and encompasses well over a hundred books and peer reviewed articles.⁷¹⁶ The main justification, also listed on the US Secret Service official website as the historical beginning of that agency's counterintelligence mission, is that President Wilson issued an Executive Order on May 14: "Before President Wilson signed an Executive Order on 14 May 1915, authorizing surveillance of German Embassy personnel in the United States, the Secret Service was limited to watching clerks, technicians and errand boys for the Germans."⁷¹⁷ According to the Secret Service, "President Wilson directed the Secretary of the Treasury to have the Secret Service investigate foreign espionage in the United States."⁷¹⁸ And "During World War I, President Woodrow Wilson directed the Secretary of the Treasury to have the Secret Service investigate possible espionage inside the United States. He wanted the Service to uncover and disrupt a German sabotage network that was believed to be plotting against France, England and the United States. To do this, an eleven-man counterespionage unit was established in New York City. Their most publicized investigation concerned the activities of Dr. Heinrich Albert and his infamous briefcase."⁷¹⁹ According to the website, Agent Burke was the leader of this unit.

The reason there never was a Congressional inquiry or investigation into the use of the Secret Service for counterespionage during World War I is that there was neither an executive order from the president on May 14,

1915, nor a Secret Service counterintelligence unit in New York under Burke's leadership.

President Wilson issued forty executive orders in 1915, two of them in May pertaining to vessel registrations (May 15) and the Panama Canal (May 25). He did not issue a numbered and registered executive order on May 14, 1915. None of the known forty executive orders in 1915 pertains to the US Secret Service or investigation of German subjects in the US.

However, a registered executive order does not account for all presidential directives. A president can also issue a memorandum, directive, or sign a departmental memorandum thus authorizing its content. A thorough scan of the papers of Woodrow Wilson, Robert Lansing, William J. Bryan, Edward M. House, and William G. McAdoo reveal no such memorandum, directive, or authorization. Most importantly, President Wilson's papers do not contain any written interaction with Secretary McAdoo between May 7 (*Lusitania* sinking) and August 3 (when McAdoo and Untermeyer informed the president).[720] Could President Wilson have given an oral directive to McAdoo without any documentation, counsel of other cabinet members, or legal advice which counteracted a 1908 Congressional law? It does not seem plausible.

While the US Secret Service was not authorized, the ambitious Chief Flynn and Secretary McAdoo could have taken the liberty to mount a rogue operation against German agents in the summer of 1915. However, Secret Service agents' daily reports shed a light on the purported existence of a counterintelligence unit in New York and the weeks or months of alleged shadowing of German agents and diplomats.

The complexity and necessary resources of such shadowing operations are well documented in the declassified files of the Bureau of Investigation.[721] In the case of the passport forgers Hans Adam von Wedell and Carl Ruroede, Sr. in January 1915, a dozen Bureau agents were required to keep track of the suspects. While the Bureau employed 219 agents in a dozen field offices in 1915,[722] not including special employees and informants, the US Secret Service staff in 1915 amounted to fifty men, including the presidential protection detail and counterfeiting investigators on a national scale.[723] In New York in July 1915, the US Secret Service employed twelve agents, one of whom was permanently detailed to Boston, MA, another to Buffalo, NY, and a third to presidential protection in Cornish, NH, President Wilson's summer retreat.[724] Agent William Houghton, whom Burke mentioned as his Secret Service companion on July 24, was not attached to the New York field office. He was a member of the presidential protection detail in Washington, DC, and was not in New York in July 1915. With only a handful agents available, it is inconceivable that there was any organized and regular surveillance of German and Austrian diplomats and officials in New York. Agents would have had to shadow Count Bernstorff (who frequently stayed at his vacation home on Long Island or at the Ritz-Carlton at Central Park in New York), Count Dumba, Consuls von Nuber and Hossenfelder, Attachés Albert, Boy-Ed, and von Papen. Also in New York were propagandists Karl Fuehr and George Sylvester Viereck. And these were just the top tier of the German organization. There were certainly more potential German targets than Secret Service agents.

The remaining nine US Secret Service agents in New York during the time of Albert's briefcase theft also did not dedicate all their time to shadowing Germans. All agents worked on non-connected cases. Agent Burke, rather than shadowing Germans in the week before the briefcase theft, worked in Boston, MA, on a counterfeiting investigation.[725] He briefly returned to New York to investigate a case in Albany, NY, on July 19.[726] Agent Rubano also worked on a counterfeiting investigation in Bradley Beach, NJ, between July 20 and 24.[727] A letter threatening the president arrived on July 18, and three agents of the New York office were working on investigating this threat.[728] On July 23, the day before Burke allegedly snatched the briefcase, he worked on a counterfeiting case on "special assignment" from Chief Flynn. The investigation took him to Ashbury Park, Ocean Grove, and Allenhurst, NJ, where he tried to locate a certain M.E. Johnson. Burke returned to New York from Allenhurst, NJ, at 6:00 p.m., July 23, and went home.[729]

Figure 61. George Sylvester Viereck, 1922
Source: Underwood and Underwood
Library of Congress Prints and Photographs Division

On July 24, the New York office's daily reports show activity in several counterfeiting investigations. Agent Burke reported, "At the office at 9 am and balance of the day I was engaged on special investigation under directions of the Chief." This special investigation likely referred to the case he had investigated the day before. His expense report for the day lists "car fares .10."⁷³⁰ A single ride on the elevated train, on a trolley, or bus in 1915 was 5 cents, accounting for two rides on July 24. According to Burke's account in McAdoo's memoirs, the agent had planned to take the afternoon off after a long week on the road.⁷³¹

According to the ad König placed in the papers, Albert's briefcase disappeared on the 3:30 train on the afternoon of July 24. Agent in Charge John Henry, Burke's direct superior and present in the office when Burke and Flynn supposedly arrived with the briefcase, went home at 5:00 p.m., only to be roused at 6:00 p.m., when the New York customs house reported the arrest of a counterfeit suspect. Henry then asked Agent Rubano to search an apartment related to the suspect. No "contraband" was found. Had Burke and Flynn brought the Albert briefcase to the field office as Burke claimed, it does not seem plausible that the agent in charge went home and later preoccupied himself with a counterfeit investigation. A further open question is where Chief Flynn was on that day. In the agents' daily reports for that week, messages to Chief Flynn are addressed to Washington, DC.⁷³² He may not even have been in New York at the time.

On July 25, Sunday, Burke came into the office at 10:00 am and left at 2:00 p.m. He was working on an unspecified special investigation under the direction of Chief Flynn. The "special investigation" continued through August 5, when Agent McCahill joined Burke.⁷³³ On August 17, Agent Howell joined Burke's special investigation. The investigation may have come to a close that day, because Burke and the other agents worked at the office on August 18 without specifying a "special investigation." August 18 also contains the first mention of Agent Houghton, who met Agent Savage at Grand Central Station at 7:00 a.m.⁷³⁴ In September, Agent Burke once more is detailed to a "special investigation."⁷³⁵ Agent Houghton, who only briefly appears in the agents' daily reports in August, is mentioned in the *Sunday Telegram* on October 24, 1915, as a member of a party arresting a counterfeiting ring in Washington, DC, led by Chief Flynn. He was then still assigned to the DC office.⁷³⁶

The sporadic assignments of Secret Service agents to special investigations seem to have consisted of investigations in jurisdictions other than the New York field office, for example Burke's trips to Boston and Allenhurst, NJ, in the week before the briefcase affair. They also included investigations where the agents reported directly to Chief Flynn and not to the agent in charge of the field office. However, the sporadic nature and the lack of assigned resources does support the assumption that Burke and his colleagues worked on counterfeiting investigations, as well as investigating threats to the president, rather than shadow German subjects. Burke, for instance, worked on counterfeiting cases in the months and weeks before the Albert affair, and also in the weeks and months after. There is no evidence in the daily reports that a counterespionage task force existed, or that William Houghton and Frank Burke shadowed George Sylvester Viereck and Heinrich Albert on July 24, or that indeed Burke stole Albert's briefcase.

The collection of declassified Bureau of Investigation files shows that the Bureau had nothing to do with the theft of Albert's briefcase. And if the US Secret Service did not have the manpower or authority to follow German officials in New York in 1915, who did?

In the fall of 1914, the British naval attaché Guy Gaunt had received an offer from the leader of the Bohemian National Alliance, Victor Emanual Voska, to provide intelligence and manpower to the British government. Gaunt lovingly referred to Voska's organization as the Alliance of the "Little People."[737] Most interestingly for Gaunt was the ability of Voska's people, many of them working class, to infiltrate German and Austro-Hungarian consulates and businesses. For example, the first Czech consul in the US after World War I was Francis Kopecky, one of four of Voska's key men in the Austro-Hungarian Consulate in New York during the war.[738]

Revelations of Austrian efforts to foment strikes, falsify passports, and hamper US munitions factories led to the expulsion of the Austrian ambassador Count Konstantin Dumba on September 9, 1915. The most devastating information on the Austrian plots came from Voska's discovery of

Figure 62. James Francis Jewell Archibald, c. 1915
Source: Creative Commons

an American journalist, James Archibald, carrying papers for Franz von Papen to Berlin. The journalist was arrested at Falmouth, England, in August 1915, and the papers seized. Once again, the British government turned the documents over to the *New York World*.⁷³⁹ The resulting scandal at the beginning of September rivaled that of the Albert exposé. Among the discovered letters was one von Papen had written to his wife, referring to Americans as "idiotic Yankees."⁷⁴⁰ It was a propaganda bloodbath. When the Count Dumba left the US in disgrace in October, British intelligence could celebrate one of their biggest propaganda successes of the war to date.

Figure 63. "Those Idiotic Yankees," September 24, 1915
Source: *The New York Herald*
Library of Congress Prints and Photographs Division

Compared to the resources of the Bureau and the USSS, Voska had a virtual army of agents in New York, eighty-four men and women.⁷⁴¹ These volunteers had been carefully selected from the Slavic organizations that existed in many of the Eastern and Midwestern states. Altogether, Voska claimed to have had 320,000 members nationwide in 1917.⁷⁴²

Voska not only provided information to British Naval Intelligence, but he also had direct contact with A. Bruce Bielaski. In 1918, Bielaski credited the Czech agent with having "rendered the Allies and this Government considerable assistance."⁷⁴³ John R. Rathom of the *Providence Journal* became Guy Gaunt's main propaganda agent in September 1914, and was paid by the Admiralty for his services.⁷⁴⁴ For the next two years, in a propaganda "triangle" Voska and his organization retrieved intelligence from their various sources, submitted them to Gaunt for analysis, who then released selected parts to Rathom for publication. Rathom, with frequent first scoops on German scandals also contacted the *New York Times* and *New York World* with information. These papers prefaced

THE GREAT COVER-UP

their reports with "the Providence Journal will say to-morrow morning..." and published British propaganda unchecked.[745] Rathom also had frequent contact with A. Bruce Bielaski, who for the most part appreciated the leads for his investigations, although several leads proved to be unreliable.[746] Not being allowed to divulge the existence of his sources, Rathom claimed that he ran his own intelligence network. This and many falsehoods he published over the years became exposed in February 1918, when Attorney General Gregory forced the editor to issue a sworn statement as to his being an utter fraud.[747]

One of the curious claims Voska made in his memoirs is that his daughter Villa worked in the Albert office in the summer of 1915 as a stenographer and "rummaged discreetly in his files."[748] She would certainly have known what Albert carried in his briefcase. Voska wrote in his book that she was discovered and fired on May 31, 1915.[749] Voska's claim that Villa worked for Albert cannot be verified independently since Albert's accounts do not list the names of his administrative staff other than that of his servant Hoffman. However, the claim is not unrealistic. The stunningly beautiful Villa Voska knew how to type and spoke German fluently. Whether Voska had his daughter placed into Albert's office or just had him closely watched, it was not far-fetched to think that the German attaché's bulging briefcase that accompanied him home every night might be of interest.

Voska's story of how the briefcase came into his hands seems embellished. Supposedly, his man had an identical portfolio made, with Albert's inscription "HA" on the lock.[750] This, of course, does not match the Flynn photograph. The Voska shadow then followed Albert and switched the briefcase when he was dozing off.[751] According to Voska, Albert had not noticed the switch and went home with a briefcase full of newspapers. Upon realizing that his

Figure 64. Villa Voska, 1920

171

papers were missing, Albert, according to Voska, called the police. There is no record showing that Albert called the police, and it would be a highly unlikely move. How would he explain the contents of his satchel?

However embellished Voska's story appears, he had the resources, motivation, and connections to steal the briefcase and make it available to British intelligence. The theft occurred on July 24, and the papers arrived at the New York World on August 2. In a week's time, Gaunt and his superiors could easily analyze the contents, translate the parts they wanted to be published, and prepare one of the greatest propaganda coups of the World War. With Untermeyer alerting the US government to the existence of the papers, Gaunt did not even have to hand the documents to the Wilson administration. Not knowing where they had come from and obviously assuming the veracity and completeness of the information, Wilson, House, McAdoo, and Lansing went along with the British coup, hoping to inflict damage on William J. Bryan and the peace movement.

Figure 65. Sir Guy Reginald Archer Gaunt
Source: The Yield of the Years

Other than Voska, who else believed that British agents were responsible for the briefcase theft? Albert, von Papen, and P. K. all believed British intelligence to have been responsible. Guy Gaunt, somewhat sheepishly, wrote in his memoirs, "Suggestions appeared in the pro-German press that agents of mine had robbed him. Quite untrue, however; the Doktor's papers were in the possession of the secret police and my friend, Captain Flynn, kindly returned them to their owner—after they had been carefully photographed."[752] As a spook, Gaunt's explanation is quite telling. It is true that "his agents" had not robbed Albert. The Czechs were unpaid and technically not "his agents." The papers also were in the possession of the US Secret Service at some point. The more interesting part would, of course, be how and when "his friend, Captain Flynn" came into possession of the papers. He did not elaborate on that point. That the papers were dutifully returned is not true. Neither the British National Archives, nor the collection called "Albert Papers" in the US National Archives, captured in 1917 by the Bureau, contain the contents of the briefcase.

It was not only the German-friendly press who suspected the British behind the theft. Most US papers agreed with the suspicion, at least until 1918.[753] Most telling, however, is a comment in a collection of Major General Ralph H. Van Deman's papers, *The Final Memoranda*, which he wrote on June 5, 1950, long after the Burke and Flynn stories dominated the historiography. Van Deman, the "Father of U.S. Military Intelligence," was working closely with the Bureau to identify German intelligence operations in 1915. Voska cooperated with Van Deman just as he did with the Bureau during the neutrality years and became a MID agent in 1917. The two men had a close relationship. In his recall of events during the World War, Van Deman wrote: "He [Voska] worked for the British Intelligence in 1914-15 and 16 and did some exceedingly clever work[...]. It was Voska who got the handbag from Dr. Albert."[754] He should have known.

Figure 66. Ralph Van Deman
Source: US Army

The revelation of the Albert papers in the *New York World* and other dailies in the summer of 1915 coincided with a massive effort of the British Government to capitalize on the American public's outcry over the sinking of the *Lusitania*. A thorough reading of the *World* front pages showcasing the contents of Albert's briefcase reveal a clever sprinkling of more scandalous — and untrue — news on the same pages: "EVIDENCE IS GIVEN TO DANIELS

ABOUT GERMANY'S SPYING: Providence, R.I., Aug 17.—The *Providence Journal* will say to-morrow morning [...]." Also, GERMANY CHARGED WITH HAVING SPIES IN OFFICES OF U.S.: The *Providence Journal* in its issue to-morrow will make the following charges [...]."[755]

The British propaganda campaign did not rest there. In September 1915, the publication of the Archibald papers continued the pressure on the American public to side with the Allies. The campaign yielded great success: Bernhard Dernburg, head of German propaganda had to leave the country at the end of May. Ambassador Dumba was expelled in September. The two German attachés, von Papen and Boy-Ed, followed in December. Albert remained the lone, accredited attaché in New York. None of the revelations showed "sufficient criminal evidence" on his part, and Secretary of State Lansing thought Albert too important for trade than to send him packing. President Wilson admitted to Secretary Lansing, "Albert has been able, and willing, to tender our trade in many particulars."[756] However, after the scandal the discredited attaché sequestered himself in a suite at the Astor Hotel and rarely ventured out in public. His work lay in shambles. The German propaganda operation, blockade running, and efforts to find a modus vivendi with the Wilson administration faded. Instead, a lower cadre of German operatives,

Figure 67. *Constantin Dumba, c. 1910-1915*
Source: Bain News Service Collection
Library of Congress Prints and Photographs Division

some of whom named in Albert's and Archibald's documents, took charge of clandestine efforts and concentrated on new and deadly ways to stop the US support of the Allies.

In the aftermath of the Lusitania sinking and the tremendous outcry it produced, a member of this "lower cadre" of German agents proposed one of the most ambitious clandestine missions to the German government. Felix A. Sommerfeld, naval intelligence agent and in charge of German strategy towards Mexico proposed to Bernhard Dernburg on May 15, 1915, that he could produce a US military intervention in Mexico. The conflict would tie up the US army along the border and in Mexico, remove military supplies from the US market as the military would arm and supply itself, and remove the possibility that the US would militarily engage with the Allies in Europe. Dernburg passed this proposal on to Admiral Henning von Holtzendorff, head of the Imperial Admiralty, asking for a green light for Sommerfeld. Von Holtzendorff, an adamant supporter of unrestricted submarine warfare brought Sommerfeld's idea to the attention of Chancellor von Bethmann-Hollweg. If the US was militarily embroiled with Mexico, von Holtzendorff convinced von Bethmann-Hollweg, the submarine war could finally be resumed without bringing the US military into the war. The Chancellor gave his approval a few days after the May 15 transmission. Sommerfeld, who was the main ammunitions buyer for the Villa faction in the US, went to work.

Figure 68. Sinking of the "Lusitania", May 1915
Source: Norman Wilkinson engraving
The Illustrated London News

The FBI and American Neutrality, 1914-1917

10

From Friend to Foe

General Pancho Villa seemed unstoppable at the beginning of 1915. As "Commander in Chief" of the Convention government, his Division of the North triumphed in engagement after engagement against the *carrancistas*. Villa and Zapata had even occupied Mexico City in November 1914. Villa, with Felix Sommerfeld as intermediary, brokered a deal in January between the governor of Sonora, José María Maytorena, and US Army Chief of Staff Hugh L. Scott to end the standoff between the governor and *carrancista* forces under Plutarco Elías Calles in Naco, Sonora.[757] Maytorena then proceeded to secure the Arizona border. He was reportedly recruiting in Los Angeles, with recruits being sent by rail to Nogales.[758] In January, the *villistas* captured Monterrey. They occupied Guadalajara in February. Carranza had been driven back to Veracruz, and his prospects seemed dim.

Perhaps reflecting the prevailing view of Villa's ultimate triumph, some enterprising Americans tried to sell him a submarine. Former El Paso consul Enrique Llorente, now Villa's representative in Washington, notified the general in February that they had been offered a submarine, property of one of the best shipyards in the US, for a mere $340,000 (batteries included.) The submarine had been built for the Russian government, but the United States had prohibited its sale as a violation of neutrality. The prospective sellers outlined a scheme to circumvent the neutrality laws.[759] Lacking sufficient depth for operation in the Rio Grande, Villa did not purchase the sub.

Villa's forces were also battling *carrancistas* for control of the lower Rio Grande border. Very little recruiting was going on at Laredo, but General R. K. Evans, commanding the garrison at Fort McIntosh, believed that even if there was recruiting, it would be a most difficult thing to prove, since "heretofore a conviction on a charge of the violation of the neutrality laws has been impossible."[760] But *villistas* were actively recruiting elsewhere on the Rio Grande. At

Sanderson, scene of the Bureau's 1911 sting operation, the sheriff jailed one Pedro Alvarado, and requested that a Bureau agent investigate. Agent F. J. McDevitt reported that the sheriff's assistant and jailer, former county attorney A. T. Folsom, was the brother of A. T. S. Folsom, Carranza's attorney in El Paso, and had telegraphed him in code. With A. T. Folsom interpreting, McDevitt interrogated Alvarado, who claimed to be a *zapatista* but whose *villista* affiliation the Bureau subsequently established.[761] *Villistas* repeatedly launched military expeditions across the river against Carranza garrisons in the lower Rio Grande valley, where support for Villa was strong. McDevitt investigated in Brownsville, and the Carranza consul was only too happy to help.[762] Likewise, the Carranza consul in San Antonio informed Agent Barnes that his colleague at Roma had reported *villista* recruitment in that vicinity in order to attack Piedras Negras.[763] There were also reports of *villistas* organizing to attack Nuevo Laredo.[764]

Prominent in these endeavors was Dr. Andrés Villarreal, a wealthy physician from Monterrey who had been Pancho Villa's chief medical officer and who was, at present, the principal *villista* representative in the area. Villarreal lived in McAllen and received noteworthy assistance in advancing the *villista* cause from Deodoro Guerra, the leading merchant and the political boss of Hidalgo County, as well as support from the McAllen city marshal and the Hidalgo County sheriff.[765] Both Villarreal and Guerra were busily involved in recruiting, organizing, and dispatching expeditions across the river. A contingent of some 175 men managed to elude army patrols and cross in January, their objective being the town of Reynosa, which had only a small *carrancista* garrison. A further incentive was that *carrancista* officers had been charging an outrageous duty on cattle being exported to Texas. *Villistas* would reduce the export duty if they could capture Reynosa, but they failed to capture the significantly reinforced town.[766]

American troops apprehended some militants as they headed toward the Rio Grande.[767] When the prisoners were taken to Brownsville, the grand jury indicted the entire filibustering party. The Bureau's efforts to build a solid case suffered a setback, though, when one of their witnesses was indicted for bank robbery.[768] The six rank-and-file members of the expedition pled guilty and were sentenced to sixty days in the county jail. The presiding judge, Waller T. Burns, explained the light sentence by stating that they were perhaps ignorant of the law, had been deserted by their officers, and had promised not to violate the law again.[769] This did not set well with Barnes, who informed the Chief that "it would appear in view of the difficulty which the government is encountering in efforts to enforce the neutrality laws along the border, that in a case of this kind where the evidence is so conclusive, the sentence should have been for a longer period of time than these men received."[770]

One of the organizers of the expedition, Major Arturo Margaín, was currently in jail at Brownsville. Agent Breniman described him as "an old offender against neutrality in this section. If I am reliably informed, he forfeited his bond during the Reyes revolution and was before the Court in this District at some time within the last two years on a similar offence and secured a light sentence on his promise that he would not again violate neutrality laws."[771] Breniman interviewed Margaín in jail through an interpreter. The suspect stoutly refused to implicate any prominent Mexicans who were behind the movement, and claimed he had acted alone. He was indicted in December 1914. Facing probable conviction, he jumped bond and fled to Baja California. There, Governor Esteban Cantú jailed him on suspicion of being a Carranza spy, but Margaín soon enjoyed the governor's favor. This happy situation came about because Margaín's sister was married to H. A. Houser, who had paid Cantú thousands of dollars for a gambling and racetrack concession at Tijuana. Cantú used the money to purchase arms. The Bureau did manage to locate several of Margaín's co-defendants in El Paso and had them arrested.[772] And in 1916, the Bureau arranged for Margaín to return to California and surrender himself, under a reduced bond of $750. He waived extradition to Texas and was quickly taken to Brownsville to stand trial. The Bureau hoped to use him as a witness against Dr. Villarreal.[773]

El Paso remained Villa's lifeline, as it had been for Madero in 1911, Orozco in 1912, and Villa in 1913-1914. Villa was, for example, receiving a steady flow of munitions from the firm of Cal Hirsch & Sons Iron & Metal Company in St. Louis, Missouri. In 1914, the US government contracted with Hirsch to sell them 50,000 Krag Jorgensen rifles at $4 each, and 4,000,000 cartridges at $20 per thousand. The Hirsch firm bound itself not to sell to Mexico or make deliveries at an American port, furnishing a $50,000 bond as guarantee of good faith. But they continuously sold both to the Huerta and Villa factions, on one occasion shipping 1,000 rifles to Hamburg, Germany and reshipping them through the United States to Mexico. The principal point of delivery for Hirsch was El Paso; shipments by rail being billed as "machinery," etc. The government laid claim to the $50,000 bond for breach of contract.[774]

The Bureau tried to keep abreast of *villista* activities, being aided by the army's "Weekly report of general conditions along the Mexican border, based on weekly reports [...] from the local military commanding officers upon information received from all sources to date."[775] In El Paso, Collector of Customs Cobb sent the Bureau copies of his State Department reports about the activities of Felix Sommerfeld's man, the soldier of fortune, Sam Dreben, acquiring ammunition. Carranza agent Henry N. Gray continued to provide information, as did the attorney for the *carrancistas*, C. S. T. Folsom.[776]

Villa had in El Paso a most effective spymaster, Hector Ramos, "former head of the Thiel Detective Agency's office in Mexico City during Madero's presidency."[777] Ramos, in fact, wanted to build an intelligence network spanning the entire border.[778] He provided considerable information to the Bureau, which reciprocated in a most unusual way—delivering an urgent coded message to Villa's brother, Colonel Hipólito Villa, in Juárez. Agent in Charge Barnes in San Antonio telegraphed Agent Frederick Guy in El Paso in January instructing him immediately to transmit a coded telegram from H. A. Thompson, the former Bureau special agent: "Utmost importance you communicate with Gen. Villa that plot had been formed with its head in New York to assassinate him at Monterrey." Barnes instructed Guy to translate and deliver the message, but to be sure not to use any of the Bureau's code words. Guy met with Ramos, who accompanied him to Juárez and introduced him to Hipólito Villa, to whom Guy delivered the message, stipulating that the Bureau knew nothing about the truthfulness of the report.[779] Presumably, Hipólito warned his brother, but whether there was in fact a plot is unknown.

The incident does illustrate the close cooperation between the Bureau and the *villistas*. But some of the information Ramos was providing was of little use. Agent Beckham pointed out to Ramos's subordinate, Kramp, the former manager of the Thiel Detective Agency, "wherein and how the 'memoranda' he was furnishing us might be made of real value instead of consisting of glittering generalities and allegations impossible of corroboration, which suggestions Kramp approved."[780] Agent Pinckney dealt with another *villista* agent, Powell Roberts, a former *maderista* and *carrancista*.[781]

Hy A. Thompson, who brought the plot to the Bureau's attention, had left the Bureau in 1913 and joined the Mexican Secret Service under Felix Sommerfeld. Thus, the apparent sympathies for General Villa. After leaving the Mexican Secret Service, he was based in northern San Antonio at 301 Arden Grove Street and remained there throughout World War I (as he was too old to be considered for service in the war).[782] His former Bureau colleague, Fred Lancaster, who periodically provided information to the Bureau, served as Chief of Police during that period. Thompson may have assisted him in criminal investigations. The *El Paso Herald* mistook Hy A. Thompson for Eck Thompson, a lawyer, who was killed in the Houston race riots of 1917, and prematurely announced his passing.[783] By 1921, Hy Thompson returned to

Sapulpa, Oklahoma, where he once again worked as a special agent for the railroads.[784] He died in Kingfisher, Oklahoma on March 2, 1922.[785]

Villa had a well-organized supply system under the financial auspices of his purchasing agent Lázaro de la Garza and the Madero Brothers Company in New York.[786] Munitions and supplies from the Eastern and Midwestern United States flowed through El Paso to the Villa Agency in Ciudad Juárez, headed by Villa's brother, Colonel Hipólito Villa. Much of Villa's ammunition passed through the Shelton-Payne hardware company. The Rio Grande Bank & Trust Company in El Paso handled most of the *villistas'* finances. Felix Sommerfeld was Villa's main purchasing agent for munitions, operating primarily out of the Astor Hotel in New York. In February 1915, he contracted with Western Cartridge Company for 12,000,000 7-millimeter

Figure 69. Stephen Pinckney, 1912
Source: University of Texas Yearbook

cartridges.[787] Between April and June, more than 8,000,000 cartridges and some 4,400 rifles passed through El Paso, besides an impressive quantity of uniforms, shoes, and other supplies for Villa's troops.[788] In addition, freelancers provided some munitions—Amador Sánchez, the unsavory former sheriff in Laredo, sold 10,000 rounds to *villistas*.[789] *Villista* ammunition supply also occurred at a retail level. Soldiers in Juárez, whose pay was usually in arrears, gave cartridges to their women, who smuggled them across on the streetcars to El Paso. There they sold them to petty dealers who transported the cartridges back to Juárez on the streetcars.[790] What kept Villa going financially was his commercial operation in El Paso marketing loot the villistas had liberated.

The Western Cartridge Company in Alton, Illinois had become Villa's largest source of ammunition. Founded and owned by Franklin Walter Olin, the company before 1914 mainly produced cartridges for hunting and sports uses, as well as dynamite for mining. Olin's sons, Franklin Jr. and John, were starting to take over their father's business and had ambition. They wanted to build a large brass mill for cartridge cup production in Alton to expand the business. The brothers met Felix Sommerfeld in the spring of 1914, after Villa gave him the sole concession for dynamite imports into Chihuahua. The Equitable Powder Manufacturing Company in Alton, also owned by Olin, was one of the main suppliers. Sommerfeld and the Olin family became friends. The outbreak of World War I in August and the subsequent buying spree by Allied purchasing agents in the US created the opportunity for which Franklin Olin Sr. had waited. Sommerfeld needed substantial amounts of 7-millimeter cartridges for Villa's Division of the North, since European armies for the most part used 30-06/7.62-57 cartridges. Of the major manufacturers in the US, only Remington produced small amounts of this caliber. As a result, there was a continual shortage of 7-millimeter cartridges on the US market. Rather than following the big munitions manufacturers in the US—Remington, Winchester, Savage, and United States Cartridge—Olin made a smart decision in 1915: He built new production capacities for 7-millimeter-style Mauser cartridges in Alton underwritten by a deal with Sommerfeld.

Sommerfeld's deal with Olin was simple: The German agent guaranteed Olin exclusive supply for Villa's army, if he refrained from producing any munitions for the Allies. Sommerfeld thus implemented the German strategy of cornering the munitions market, and secured ever increasing amounts of munitions for Pancho Villa. Olin signed on. Sommerfeld's orders increased to the point that Western Cartridge had orders for its entire production (1 million cartridges per week) to go to the border.[791] A quid pro quo arrangement between Olin and Sommerfeld kept the price for 7-millimeter cartridges steady, while inflation as a result of the war sent prices anywhere else through the roof, a fact that even surprised Chief Bielaski.[792] The price per thousand cartridges was an astonishingly low $35, while Remington and Winchester charged $50 for the same product, and Peters Cartridge Company between $55 and $60.[793]

Sommerfeld arranged that Olin received the necessary hydraulic presses for his new brass mill from the German agent, Carl Heynen, while no one in the US market could find such presses. In return, Sommerfeld received 7-millimeter cartridges for $32 to $35 per thousand (market price was $48 per thousand). The balance, which eventually amounted to over $400,000 (over $8 million in today's value), paid for the presses. The Albert office had bought a year's supply early in 1915 and stored the equipment at its own Bridgeport Projectile Company. After the US entry into the war, Olin's production went to the Allies. The Western Cartridge company came out of the World War so strong and profitable that the Olin family was not only rich, but was able to expand market share eventually to purchase its much larger competitor, Winchester Repeating Arms Company, in 1931. In no small part as a result of his business relationship with Sommerfeld and the German government, Franklin Olin became a multi-millionaire, philanthropist, and defense industry powerhouse.[794]

With Villa firmly in control of Ciudad Juárez, the Bureau gave increased attention to other sections of the border. This included monitoring shipments of men and munitions from El Paso to Nogales for Villa's ally Maytorena, the titular governor of Sonora, who now used the title of "General."[795]

Despite its bright beginning, 1915 turned into a disaster for Villa, who suffered a series of costly defeats in central Mexico. Villa tried to open a second front by capitalizing on the situation in the southern State of Chiapas. There, conservative landowners rebelled against Carranza's authority, and since Pancho Villa was also fighting against Carranza's authority, they declared themselves to be "villistas."[796] Villa used neighboring Guatemala as a base from which his supporters could fan the flames in Chiapas.[797] Guatemala was a base because the dictator of Guatemala, Manuel Estrada Cabrera, despised Carranza and did what he could to support any anti-Carranza movement. Carranza returned the compliment by supporting anti-Cabrera Guatemalan exiles.

Villa commissioned a brigadier general to lead the grandiloquently named "Division of the Southwest Francisco I. Madero." He was Manuel Centurión, a noted sculptor, whose military experience was quite limited.[798] This did not really matter, for the "Division of the Southwest" barely existed. Not only that, but José Santos Chocano, reportedly an accredited agent of President Estrada Cabrera of Guatemala, as well as a *villista* agent, together with Rosendo Márquez, a known Villa agent, had contracted on June 2, 1914, with Charles E. Jones, a New Orleans arms dealer, for $124,000 worth of munitions for an expedition against Chiapas. The deal fell through, however, because the *villistas* were unable to come up with the money.[799]

Villistas tried to resuscitate their declining cause by funneling munitions through New Orleans and several Florida seaports. The Bureau devoted considerable attention to these matters, which constituted one of its more interesting investigations and illustrated the complexity involved in them.

Agent Forrest C. Pendleton wrote from New Orleans in July 1915, "I am in touch with both the Carranza and the Villa consuls here, and each of them have agents who keep close watch on each other as well as the [Félix] Díaz and Huerta sympathizers, and they have in the past given me a great deal of information regarding their work."[800] Pendleton was an outstanding agent, although he did not speak Spanish and relied on William Ibs to interpret. Ibs, who was tall, slender, and blue-eyed, was born in 1877 in Hamburg. His family moved to New Orleans when he was twelve, but he retained his German citizenship. Holding down a variety of jobs, including being an interpreter and translator, he traveled extensively in Central America and the Caribbean. Several sources had advised Pendleton that Ibs "is a very irresponsible person and, as a general proposition, is not to be relied on."[801]

Nevertheless, Ibs was valuable because he knew his way around the arms dealing community, working with the broker Charles E. Jones, about whom there is more to come. Pendleton located and took to his office General Rosendo Márquez, whom Jones claimed was "an unprincipled scoundrel and as crooked as he can be." With Ibs translating, Márquez related that he was currently a broker for the Villa faction. He had been in town for two months and had dealt with a certain Pedro Serrano, a Spaniard based in San Antonio who was a businessman selling to any faction that had the money. Special Employee Harry Berliner in New York would round out the picture by stating that his sources alleged that Márquez lived there with the notorious Peruvian poet and arms dealer José Santos Chocano. The pair had been active in procuring armament, but with Huerta's arrest had abruptly ceased their activities. They were currently trying to peddle counterfeit Carranza fiat currency.[802]

Pendleton reported that Villa consul Manuel Garza's office was room 402 Interstate Bank Building, the former office of Constitutionalist consul Alberto Méndez prior to the Carranza-Villa split.

> I have had occasion to visit these offices a number of times. These rooms are fitted up with desks, etc., the outer room being used by his various agents and informants, and there are always from two to six Mexicans hanging around in this outer office. Garza has always been, apparently, very willing to give me any information. He appears to be a high-class man, compared to some other Mexican officials whom I have had occasion to observe. I went to Garza's office today and casually asked about arms shipments. He unhesitatingly told me that while he had not succeeded in obtaining any large amount of war supplies, he had a few days ago shipped to Pensacola some rifles and small arms

ammunition. In his private office, Garza introduced me to one [Tomás] Cárdenas [According to one report, his real name was Luís G. Suzán.] saying he held the rank of colonel in the Villa army but was now an agent in the interest of [the] Villa faction and was trying to get munitions for shipment to Villa.[803]

With consul Garza translating, Cárdenas showed Pendleton a bill of lading for munitions he had bought from A. Baldwin & Company, and said he was shipping them to Pensacola, where he planned to take stockpiled munitions out on his schooner, *Isidoro*. Pendleton suggested that the Bureau's local White Slave Officer Arthur W. Davis at Pensacola monitor the situation there, for while it was probable that Garza was giving him the true facts as far as he knew them, it might be that Cárdenas was working at cross purposes with Garza, as it would not be unusual for a Mexican agent to double cross his superior and support some other faction.[804]

Cárdenas's ostensible mission was to use the *Isidoro*, which *villistas* had seized from *carrancistas*. Self-proclaimed governor of Yucatán, General Abel Ortiz Argumedo, had fled on the *Isidoro* from advancing *carrancista* forces, taking along $472,305. He reached Havana, where he left the *Isidoro* and proceeded to New York with his loot. There, as Harry Berliner learned, Ortiz Argumedo kept the money in a safety deposit box. Ortiz Argumedo had simply abandoned the *Isidoro* at the dock, whereupon the *carrancista* consul in Havana claimed her as property stolen from his government and placed a watchman on it. *Villistas* seized the vessel from the watchman, and Cárdenas sailed the schooner to Pensacola. Cárdenas now proposed using the *Isidoro* to transport nine officers and 200 rifles to Chiapas as part of the "Division of the Southwest" to operate against Carranza forces.[805] This matter was considered important enough for the assistant US attorney at Pensacola to instruct Agent Donald D. Hawkins to stay at the same hotel as the Mexicans and keep them and the *Isidoro* under surveillance. Hawkins reported by coded telegrams directly to Chief Bielaski and the attorney general. Local Officer Davis also reported directly to Bielaski.

The *villistas* had received their clearance papers and were trying to get the *Isidoro* out to sea before the US marshal could seize it. The Carranza consul in New Orleans, Francisco R. Villavicencio, arrived in Pensacola to institute legal proceedings to recover the *Isidoro*. The Villa consul in New Orleans, Manuel Garza, arrived to institute legal proceedings to retain the schooner. The authorities held the vessel until the legal dispute was resolved. And since the *villistas* would have to post a $15,000 bond to secure the schooner, the US attorney advised that no further investigation was needed and released Hawkins.[806]

The sequel to this affair was that on September 4, a railroad freight agent at New Orleans notified Pendleton that two Mexicans had attempted to ship seven chests marked as merchandise to T. Cárdenas at Pensacola. One of the clerks had opened a chest and discovered that it contained Mexican currency. Pendleton went to the freight office, examined the chests, and found that two contained miscellaneous army supplies and five contained Villa fiat currency. According to the Villa consul, its value was about $2,000. Since this currency was currently worth one cent on the dollar, Pendleton estimated that some 200,000 pesos' worth was involved. It developed that Tomás Cárdenas had tried to ship the trunks to himself at Pensacola but was unaware that currency could not be shipped by freight. He subsequently shipped it by express. Moreover, Cárdenas purchased dynamite, nitroglycerine, and electric fuses from A. Baldwin & Company for shipment to Pensacola. Instead of using the *Isidoro*, Cárdenas had chartered the auxiliary schooner, *Lucy H*.[807]

Further light on the Chiapas matter came from the munitions broker, Charles Eugene Jones, a fascinating character who lived in a world of intrigue and became the gold standard of Bureau informants, in effect writing his own ticket. The second son of the Reverend Charles Octavius Jones, Charles E. Jones was born on April 10, 1876, in St. Michel, Missouri. He settled in New Orleans. Physically, Jones was unprepossessing—of medium height, stout, gray eyes and brown hair. As of 1912, he was vice president of Yochim Brothers Co., Ltd. A journalist by profession, Jones was the manager of the Newspaper Service Company as of July 1915, room 738 Audubon Building in New Orleans. He was also the manager of the National Arms Company, according to its letterhead, headquartered in the same office.[808] In reality, the company was never registered and only existed by virtue of its letterhead.[809] Jones *was* the National Arms Company, a Bureau of Investigation front with the singular purpose of gathering intelligence on the firearms and munitions markets in North and Central America during the World War.

There were several companies with that name in the US, a common brand of a Brooklyn, New York, manufacturer that merged with Colt in the 1870s. Jones's National Arms Company claimed to have customers in Mexico and Central America, although there is no evidence of the brokerage ever delivering a single cartridge or gun to anyone. On occasion, Jones went beyond just quoting. In the fall of 1917, he took a down payment of $5,000 from Máximo Rosales Betancourt. Rosales, a former president of Honduras (February 1 to February 18, 1903), was now involved in a plot to overthrow his home country's government with a military force assembling in neighboring Costa Rica. Not knowing that Jones operated as a secret agent for the Bureau, Rosales bitterly complained to the "Secretary of State of the Justice Department" in February of the following year, appealing for help to recover the "stolen" money.[810] Bielaski seemed to let Jones, who worked for the Justice Department without compensation, keep the money, a quid-pro-quo for Jones's work.[811] Through this construct, Jones—and the Bureau—gathered vital intelligence on who was buying, and smuggling, what from whom, and for how much.[812] A complication for the Bureau was that more often than not, the same weaponry was offered by multiple traders, and the Bureau had to unravel that it was the same lot of munitions.

Jones was a unique informer. He had been a reliable informant for Agent Pendleton and reported to the Bureau through the New Orleans agent in charge. But sometimes Jones reported directly to Chief Bielaski, sending him lengthy written communications. And on occasion, Jones conferred personally with Bielaski in Washington.[813]

Jones testified extensively before a Senate subcommittee in 1920.[814] He described himself as a newspaper man living in New York, who, since 1915, had been cooperating with the Bureau of Investigation, sending them almost daily reports. Agent Pendleton was a personal friend of Jones's and, knowing of Jones's familiarity with conditions in Central America, had tried to recruit him as a Bureau agent. Jones testified:

> [A]s the revolutionary movement on foot in Honduras at that particular time was most active, and due to certain connections I had in Honduras, I was in a position to get the inside facts. The Bureau of Investigation at that time probably only had 250 or 300 men and a very limited appropriation for the financial support of the Bureau. Pendleton's hands were absolutely tied as far as being able to get the information he wanted was concerned; therefore, knowing that probably I might be able to get it, he came to me to get me to do it. [I] told him that due to their remuneration and my own business affairs that it would be impossible to consider a proposition of that kind, but that I would agree to help them out, providing it would be absolutely at all times kept thoroughly confidential. So, with that understanding I became connected with them, always in an inside capacity [...]. When I first started in with the Department of Justice it was thoroughly understood between Mr. Bielaski and myself that under no circumstances would I accept any remuneration, nor was I

ever sworn in to the Department of Justice service, although they were anxious to have same done [...]. About two weeks after that Mr. Bielaski came to New Orleans where I was at that time, to see me, and asked me if I would continue to cooperate with them. So, I agreed with him to do so, provided, as I have stated, it would be kept entirely confidential, and that my hands would not be tied, as far as information or anything of that kind that I might secure was concerned, if at any time I wanted to use it. So, in that way we started [...]. For a period of a year and a half or probably two years I even paid all of my own expenses, although they repeatedly insisted upon me rendering accounts, which I refused to do. At the time Mr. Bielaski entered into this agreement with me I told him that eventually I expected to utilize in a newspaper way at any time any stuff I might get. So, it was thoroughly understood and agreed between he [sic] and myself that if at any time I wanted to use the stuff I had a perfect right to do so. [Jones acquired information primarily for newspaper work,] but at the request of Chief Bielaski, Mr. Pendleton, or others, I had to choke 95 percent of it to death, because if I had published the information. I secured it would have, 9 times out of 10, interfered with the plans and future efforts of the Bureau of Investigation. So, in the end my connection and association with the Bureau was decidedly a very undesirable connection for me." Jones claimed he lost money because he lost scoops.[815]

Chief Bielaski himself assigned Jones the cover name, CRESSE, "because there were in the State Department innumerable leaks which went directly back to various Mexican factions."[816] We will see in a later chapter that Jones was also well connected politically and among the press. His sources included his brother, Clarence Winfield Jones, who was a well-known newspaperman in Washington, DC.[817]

Jones suggested to Bielaski:

It occurs to me that it would be an excellent idea whenever your office received information that certain parties are buying ammunition or securing prices on same that you immediately forward through your New Orleans office me names and addresses of these parties and I will write or wire them in the name of the National Arms Company offering them goods they want, and at a price that if they really want to do business will bring their order. In this way the matter then will always be in our hands, and we will know exactly what these people are doing, likewise the class and quantity of arms and ammunition they are paying for and just exactly where it is to be shipped and the shipping dates of same.[818]

Charles E. Jones, aka CRESSE, was Agent in Charge Pendleton's principal informant, but the agent never entirely trusted him:

I would say also that Jones has often expressed to me his friendship for the Guatemalan Government, and his belief that the consul, Saenz, in New Orleans, is a splendid man and is very reliable and, therefore, with all this in mind I was very careful in talking to Jones not to indicate that I had any information which would lead him to believe that the [Estrada] Cabrera Government would aid any movement against Carranza, and the information Jones gave was volunteered, without any suggestion on my part.

And William Ibs, who interpreted for Jones as well as for Pendleton, was suspected of being a secret agent of the Guatemalan government. Jones was involved not just with Mexico and Guatemala. Pendleton continued:

[He] is extremely friendly to General Máximo B. Rosales, the party who is hoping, through the shaping of public opinion, to become the next President of Honduras, and Jones is very anxious that Rosales will succeed in having his ambitions realized. [Still, Pendleton reported,] Jones has requested me to say that he will give the Department the benefit of any information he has at any time but says that if his name is mentioned to prospective purchasers as having given the information it would probably hurt his sales and tend to destroy his usefulness as an informant on these matters.[819]

Pendleton telegraphed Bielaski on October 12, forwarding CRESSE's report on the activities of a certain Dr. Felipe Dusart Quintana, described as being short and very fat, about five-foot, two inches, 180 pounds, iron gray hair, black and white mustache, dark glasses, between thirty-five and forty, who generally wore a Prince Albert coat and carried a cane. He was a heavy drinker.[820] It seems Pancho Villa still labored under the delusion that a campaign in Chiapas against Carranza was viable. In February 1915, he had appointed Flavio Guillén as "Military Governor of Chiapas," but six months later, Guillén still remained safely in Guatemala. Therefore, Villa on August 19, 1915, appointed Dr. Felipe Dusart as the "General Commander in Chief of Operations in the State of Chiapas" with General Arturo Santibáñez as his second in command. Santibáñez also proved to be a reluctant warrior. Dusart sent him to San Francisco to arrange shipments down the Pacific coast of Mexico for the Chiapas expedition, but Santibáñez did nothing, and Dusart dismissed him.[821]

Pudgy Doctor and General Felipe Dusart Quintana, who sometimes used the name "Felipe D. Quintana," seemed determined to do his duty. Jones reported that Villa consul Garza helped Dusart purchase through Jones from the W. Stokes Kirk Company of Philadelphia 545 rifles and 50,000 rounds, which were enroute to New Orleans. Bielaski forwarded the report to Leon Canova at the State Department. Jones further advised that Dusart planned to move the 545 rifles and 50,000 rounds from New Orleans to Key West, ship them out on a boat he had recently purchased, and continue the mission of opening the second

Figure 70. Charles E. Jones (top right), mother and father (bottom left), and older brother Winfield (top center)
Source: Jones Family Tree
Ancestry.com

villista front.⁸²² But with Villa's fortunes declining, Consul Garza was at a loss regarding the munitions. He asked the Convention's [really Villa's] Minister of Foreign Affairs for permission to sell another 14,000 cartridges that Dusart had bought and for instruction as to what to do with the proceeds.⁸²³

The United States dealt Villa a devastating blow on October 19, 1915, by extending diplomatic recognition to Carranza as the head of the de facto government of Mexico. This meant, of course, that any other faction was now prohibited from importing munitions legally. In desperation, Tomás Cárdenas slipped the Lucy H out of Key West on the night of October 19 without clearance papers.⁸²⁴ A revenue cutter gave chase but lost her. The schooner sailed to a point near Tuxpan in the Gulf coast of Mexico, contacted *villistas*, and unloaded her cargo of fifty cases of ammunition and 200 surplus American army rifles with bayonets, using a float made of empty gasoline drums. On November 1, the Lucy H arrived back at Pensacola. Local businessman I. J. Díaz, who had purchased the schooner, paid off the crew, minus two who had been stranded ashore, arrested by Carranza soldiers, and taken to Veracruz for trial. I. J. Díaz was the son of the Mexican consul in Porfirio Díaz's administration, and was the partner in a lumber business, the German-American Company, with M. [E.?] Lutz, a wealthy German. The Bureau placed a mail cover on Lutz and brought in a forensic accountant to examine his finances.⁸²⁵ Bielaski instructed Agent Chastain at Pensacola to learn everything possible about the Isidoro and the Lucy H and the shady characters connected with them. Agent Lewis J. Baley followed up a lead at Key West and received considerable information from the collector of customs.⁸²⁶

The munitions—545 rifles and 50,000 rounds—Dusart had purchased for the Lucy H to transport were still in New Orleans. Dusart himself went to Key West, leaving the bill of lading for these supplies with a New Orleans bank. Upon reflection, Dusart realized he would be in serious trouble if he tried to smuggle these munitions out of the United States, so he wanted Charles E. Jones to sell them for him. Pancho Villa's brother, Hipólito, who headed the Villa Agency in Ciudad Juárez, had supplied the money to purchase them, but Dusart planned to keep the proceeds. He was desperate to have the munitions sold immediately, before the New Orleans bank holding the bill of lading or the Villa consul could act.⁸²⁷

Illustrating the uncertainties under which Pendleton operated, there were also in New Orleans exiles from Guatemala planning a military expedition against that government. Pendleton asked Bielaski whether there was any evidence of Dusart working on their behalf, and whether Dr. Dusart and a

General Dusart mentioned in a report from Agent Beckham were the same person. They were.[828]

Villa Consul Manuel Garza, who resigned as soon as Carranza was recognized, shed further light on Dusart. Pendleton met with Garza at Charles Jones's office and asked Garza about his former associate, Dusart. Garza said Dusart was a crook and that he had broken faith with him, and Garza would be glad to see him punished. Pendleton tried to get Garza to tell him about the expedition to Chiapas, but Garza asked Pendleton to excuse him from talking about this until he had gotten advice from other parties. Garza said he knew all about the matter, but that when he was interested in the proposed expedition there was no violation of neutrality laws, and he had been very careful to see that these parties kept within the law. He said he might give Pendleton further information on the matter after he had seen his advisers. Garza did give Pendleton letters and telegrams between himself and Dusart. These communications had to do with the disposal of the munitions Dusart wanted Jones to sell for him.[829] A valuable supplement to all this was the Carranza consul in New Orleans, Francisco R. Villavicencio, who provided Pendleton with items such as photographs of documents, among them Dusart's commission as Chief of Operations in Chiapas, letters signed by Dusart, and the names of parties who could testify about Dusart's role in the conspiracy to violate the neutrality laws.[830]

Dusart, meanwhile, had been busy. He made a quick trip to Havana and left for Key West on November 8 to acquire the steam yacht, *Ventura*. Its owner had sold the yacht in New York a few months earlier to a Carranza agent to be delivered in Havana, but enroute the *Ventura* put in at Key West and was left there. The captain sold his claim for wages to a local firm, W. Curry Sons, using the boat's papers as collateral. After *villistas* in the *Lucy H* tried to steal her, Curry sued and embargoed the vessel for the amount of the indebtedness.[831] Dusart, going under the alias of F. D. Quintana, bought her from the US marshal at auction for $1,540. Through an interpreter, Agent Chastain interviewed Dusart regarding the purchase, the use he intended for the *Ventura*, and any connection he had with the Mexican military. Dusart became furious, informed the agent that he was Doctor Felipe Dusart of New Orleans, was tired of being chased by American police, was an important and prominent man in Mexico, and expected to be the next president. He then stormed out, but returned with his attorney, "a domineering self-important sort of man who apparently has only ordinary ability."

Chastain told the attorney that if Dusart, as he contended, had no connection with any effort to violate the neutrality laws he had no reason to object to being questioned. The attorney asserted that Dusart was buying the *Ventura* for his personal use, that he now had no connection with the Mexican military, and certainly had no intention of violating the neutrality laws. Moreover, he would not consent for his client to make any further statement or answer any material questions regarding Mexican military operations because he felt he should not permit his client to make any statement that might incriminate him. Chastain informed Bielaski, stating that the evidence seemed insufficient to warrant arresting Dusart. Bielaski agreed. Chastain learned that Dusart had left for New Orleans.[832]

At New Orleans, the Carranza consul persuaded an attorney from Chiapas, José de las Muñecas Zimavilla, to tell Pendleton what he knew of Dusart's operations. He knew quite a bit, having been associated with Dusart up to November 15. He said that in August, M. Robelo Argüello, who was now in Chiapas, Teófilo Castillo Corzo, now in Guatemala, Adeodato Flores, whereabouts unknown, Arturo Santibáñez, who had finally made it to Guatemala, Angel Pérez Figueroa, now in Chihuahua, Diógenes Pastrana, now in Chihuahua, Dusart, and himself had met in El Paso [sic—Ciudad Juárez] with other officers of Villa's staff to organize the Chiapas expedition. The plan was to acquire the necessary munitions and a boat in the United States. Villa had appointed Dusart as Chief of Operations. Dusart appointed Muñecas Zimavilla as brigadier general to command the troops in Chiapas and also gave Adeodato Flores an appointment. Muñecas Zimavilla and Dusart proceeded to New Orleans, where Dusart purchased the munitions from Charles E. Jones. Dusart then went to Pensacola and Key West to acquire a boat.

Muñecas Zimavilla said that after Carranza was recognized by the US, he saw Dusart in Havana. Dusart said he was going ahead with the plan and asked Muñecas Zimavilla's help. The latter returned to the United States, but Dusart never sent him any money, and he alleged that Dusart was such a crook that he decided to inform the Carranza consul, and later had been persuaded to give Pendleton the information. Muñecas Zimavilla said that in return for immunity, he would give all the information he had, and testify against Dusart. He would, for example, testify that Dusart had shipped to Pensacola fifty rifles to be part of the cargo of the *Ventura*. Pendleton wired Bielaski that Dusart's purchase of the *Ventura* and shipping of the rifles constituted an overt act violating the neutrality laws. Muñecas Zimavilla said Dusart was back in New Orleans, but was about to leave for El Paso to peddle the Villa fiat currency the Bureau had seized there. Pendleton consulted with the assistant US attorney, who said he might recommend immunity for Muñecas Zimavilla and advised that Dusart be apprehended. Pendleton and other agents followed Dusart, and at Pendleton's request, the New Orleans police arrested him. He was held on a stiff $15,000 bond, which he was unable to post. Pendleton tried to interrogate Dusart, who maintained that he did not understand English. In yet another twist in the Dusart saga, Muñecas Zimavilla stated that "Felipe Dusart" was an alias—the man's real name was Felipe Dávalos, a pickpocket and all-around crook in Mexico City before he became associated with the villistas.

Pendleton was finally able to interview Dusart using an interpreter. The Mexican maintained that he had purchased the Ventura merely as a speculation, planning to sell the yacht later. He did admit that Villa had commissioned him Chief of Operations in Chiapas, but insisted that it was necessary to get this appointment to come to the United States without being shot, and that he hated the Villa faction and would do anything to injure them. Dusart admitted that he was a general in Villa's army and that one Adeodato Flores was a major under his command. He thought that Flores was now somewhere in Louisiana, working on an oyster lugger. Dusart alleged that he was formerly a general under Carranza, but was with Villa only a few months. He said he bought 500 rifles and 50,000 rounds from Charles E. Jones, and that Lin Dinkins, president of the Interstate Bank & Trust Company, was the intermediary in this sale. He said he bought them for speculative purposes and had no connection with the Villa faction at that time. Furthermore, he added that he sent two trunks and a box of Villa currency to the Rio Grande Bank & Trust Company at El Paso, and that this bank had agreed to pay him 75 cents on every 1,000 pesos' worth, and that the total amount which he would realize would be about $750.[833] Bureau agents in El Paso located the trunks and box Dusart had sent there by express. The Rio Grande Valley Bank refused to accept them and rejected Dusart's request to find a buyer for 1,000,000 pesos' worth of Villa currency.[834]

Dusart later admitted shipping the fifty rifles to Pensacola, claiming he had simply sent them there to see if he could sell them. Pendleton observed that "This man is very shrewd and was clearly lying all the way through, as he made several conflicting statements. He denied, absolutely, that he had ever had any idea of going to Chiapas or of assisting in any way the Villa faction."[835] Pendleton filed a criminal complaint against Dusart and Muñecas Zimavilla for conspiracy to violate the neutrality laws. A warrant was served on Dusart and one on Muñecas Zimavilla because Pendleton believed he was much more involved than he let on. And in fact, William Ibs translated a letter Muñecas Zimavilla had written on November 3, 1915 [after Carranza's recognition] to General Arturo Santibáñez at Guatemala detailing his own role in the continuing conspiracy.[836]

Agents at New Orleans and Pensacola continued to build the case against Dusart and his associates. Chief Bielaski suggested that as a last resort,

Pendleton and the US attorney consider naming former Villa consul Garza as co-defendant with Dusart to induce Garza to give information he was withholding.[837] The federal grand jury in Gainesville on December 16, 1915, indicted T. Cárdenas, I. J. Díaz, Felipe Dusart, Adrián Rodríguez, B. Schone, and H. B. Snell for conspiracy to set on foot a military expedition in the Lucy H affair.[838] Two of Dusart's associates plead guilty in May 1916: I. J. Díaz was fined $200, and H. B. Snell was fined $50.[839]

Bielaski wrote to Pendleton:

> I think Dusart should be proceeded against in the district where evidence and likelihood of a substantial sentence are strongest. Please prepare for me as soon as possible a brief synopsis of the evidence you have, and the important testimony adduced before the grand jury in the case at New Orleans so Department may consider the relative strengths of the case against Dusart there and that which is pending against him in Pensacola. If the case at New Orleans is sufficiently strong to sustain a prosecution, Department will also want to consider the advisability of proceeding first with the case there and then giving Dusart his choice of appearing as a defendant or witness in the Pensacola trial.[840]

In his synopsis, Pendleton stated that defendant Muñecas Zimavilla was anxious to testify, plead guilty, and throw himself on the mercy of the court. He would make a splendid witness because he was very convincing in his manner of speaking, had a very pleasing personality, and was very frank in his manner. Ex-Villa Consul Manuel Garza and Charles E. Jones would also testify. And the government had evidence, such as the copy of Dusart's commission, the records of Western Union and railroad freight offices, as well as the evidence in the US marshal's office. Not surprisingly, the Carranza administration was eager to help, retaining an attorney to assist in the prosecution of Dusart. And the Carranza consul filed a civil suit for the arms, ammunition, and boat. The consul would win by default if Dusart did not appear and defend the suit.[841]

The Dusart case was set for trial in New Orleans on February 23, 1916. Agent Pendleton assisted the US attorney in rehearsing the government witnesses' testimony and in compiling evidence. The defense moved for a directed verdict of "not guilty" and was overruled. The trial was postponed because the US attorney was ill, whereupon the judge released Dusart on his own recognizance. Pendleton related that Judge Foster told him he did not think there was any harm in releasing Dusart on his own recognizance because there was no chance of convicting him. This upset Pendleton, who felt the case against Dusart was an exceedingly strong one, and he could not understand why the judge would make such a remark. An attorney representing the Carranza consul, and Assistant US attorney Joseph W. Montgomery, who was prosecuting the case, believed the case had been proven beyond a doubt. Judge Foster's attitude throughout the trial, however, had indicated that he did not think much of the case, and after he had overruled the motion of the defense attorney, he was said to have remarked to [defense] attorney Beattie that the jury would take care of the case. Montgomery inferred from the judge's tone that the jury would return a verdict of "not guilty."[842]

Furthermore, Pendleton noted:

> A surprising incident in connection with the trial of this case today was the fact that Judge Foster allowed the defense to introduce the carbon copies of several letters which the defendant testified that he had written to various parties showing his intention to sell the arms and ammunition as soon as the embargo was proclaimed. The copies of the alleged letters, as stated, were permitted to go in as evidence without any evidence except Dusart's testimony that he had written them; no evidence, except his, that they had been sent, and while it may have been possible that he sent such letters before his arrest, as he testified, it is my firm belief that these letters, which were purely self-serving declarations, and under no circumstances should have been permitted in evidence, were written after he was placed in jail.[843]

The jury was unable to reach an agreement, and a mistrial was declared on March 2, 1916. Pendleton continued, "As near as I could find out, the jury were about evenly divided on the question of the guilt of the accused. The jury's report, while far from being what the government desired, was surely a great disappointment to the defense, who were confident that Dusart would be acquitted. The case, however, appeared to me to be thoroughly established, and I have never seen a stronger conspiracy case shown."[844]

Despite this disappointing result, the Bureau continued its investigation of Dusart, hoping to present an even stronger case in the event of a new trial. Agent Stone in El Paso located a refugee, former Mexico City police chief, Antonio Villavicencio. Stone interviewed Villavicencio, who said, "he knew Dusart personally as a man of base character, a thief and a reprobate and would sell his honor for any consideration; that he was no good to himself or to his country. For this reason, the police chief said, he would be glad to furnish our Department with all the information he can concerning Dusart et al." Villavicencio prepared for Stone a memorandum setting forth everything he knew about Dusart and the Chiapas expedition. It was a lot. Felipe Dusart's real name was Enrique G. Dávalos. During the Porfirio Díaz administration, he was indicted as a known pickpocket. He later organized a band of pickpockets who robbed on trains. Dávalos was arrested in Monterrey and Querétaro. He later went to the city of Silao and opened an office in a hotel, with the object of stealing packages. He was sentenced to two years in the Silao jail for robbery. He later appeared in Mérida, Yucatán, as a Cuban general named Larquete, trying to defraud a bank in a cattle swindle. His friend, Manuel Gómez Farias, was employed at the bank, but he denounced Dávalos, who had to flee.

During Madero's administration, Dávalos appeared in Salina Cruz operating a drug store and calling himself Doctor Felipe Dusart. He participated in the Carranza revolution, serving under Villa. For a few days he was governor of the State of Guanajuato, reaching the rank of general so as to steal all he could. He burned records at jails and police stations where he had been imprisoned as a thief. Dusart was a dexterous and clever man, imitating a Cuban accent very well. He frequently posed as a Cuban. At El Paso, he was frequently in the company of the Peruvian poet and filibuster José Santos Chocano and men from Chiapas—Teófilo del Castillo Corzo and attorney Muñecas Zimavilla. Castillo Corzo had come from Chiapas hoping that Villa would furnish him with arms and money to operate in Chiapas, being helped by Santos Chocano. Castillo Corzo was related by marriage to President Estrada Cabrera of Guatemala. Muñecas Zimavilla was a noted villista; he and Castillo Corzo were in sympathy with revolution in Chiapas. Muñecas Zimavilla conferred with Villa, who wanted Felipe Dusart to be commander in Chiapas, and he gave Dusart money to go to New Orleans to purchase arms. Santos Chocano was a filibuster, well known for his bad record. Attorney Muñecas Zimavilla was without scruples and was dishonorable.[845]

Dusart was under indictment in the Northern District of Florida for conspiracy to violate the neutrality laws by beginning and setting on foot and providing the means for a military expedition. That trial was set for May 1, 1916, at Pensacola, but Dusart slipped out of New Orleans on April 14 and fled to Havana, taking up residence at a rooming house at No. 9 O'Reilly Street. Charles E. Jones showed Pendleton a letter Dusart had written him from there on October 23 informing Jones that he had left the bill of lading for the supplies he had in New Orleans with the president of the Interstate Bank & Trust Company. He wanted the bank to be the depository for the supplies.[846]

The State Department wired the American Minister in Havana to approach the Cuban government about returning Dusart to Pensacola. The Bureau was most anxious to have Dusart returned to the United States for trial. And the Bureau had a presence in Cuba. Havana was a hotbed of Mexican intrigue because plotting could be carried on there without having to worry about the US neutrality laws. Acting Chief Horn in January 1916 instructed Agent Lewis M. Cantrell, then at Jacksonville, Florida, to drop everything and proceed to Havana for special work there.[847] Cantrell was in Cuba under commercial cover monitoring Mexican revolutionary activity, as well as keeping an eye out for Walter Scheele, the German bombmaker who had fled the United States in April 1916. The Chief instructed Cantrell to try to arrange with the Cuban authorities to deport Dusart back to Florida for trial.[848]

The American Minister was instructed to cooperate fully with Cantrell in the Dusart matter. Cantrell, operating at a disadvantage because he could not speak Spanish, reported that he received little cooperation from the US Legation. To carry out his assignment, Cantrell not only made the rounds of places in Havana where Dusart might appear, but he also established close ties with the *Policía Judicial*, whom he termed the 'secret police,' in Havana and enlisted that agency's aid. And indeed, the police located Dusart and kept him under surveillance, but would not arrest him without instructions from the Cuban government. Bielaski sent Cantrell a cable containing Dusart's criminal record, so the agent could present it to the Cuban government as an inducement to deport Dusart. But when Cantrell spoke with the Cuban undersecretary of state, that official declared that Dusart's deportation was doubtful.[849] A complication was the arrival of Francisco R. Villavicencio, the New Orleans consul for Carranza, who located and met with Dusart. Villavicencio persuaded Dusart to convey to him the title to the arms and ammunition and the *Ventura*, which the US government had seized. The consul had the document notarized and immediately returned to New Orleans.[850]

The upshot of the Dusart affair was that the Cuban government demanded that the American Minister make a formal request for Dusart's deportation, and the Minister refused, as he had already made an informal request and thought it might violate some diplomatic propriety. A disgusted Cantrell wrote, "The method, etc. of the request seemed to be the big thing between them rather than the fact that he was wanted, and that all-important time was being lost while they discussed and wrangled over flimsy technicalities, and in the meantime Dusart has in all probability leisurely left Havana for parts unknown, said and believed by some to be to Guatemala."⁸⁵¹ On June 15, 1916, the Cuban government informed the American legation that Dusart had left Cuba on a United Fruit Company steamer for some Central or South American port. Muñecas Zimavilla said that he had information that Dusart and his family were in Puerto Cortés, Honduras. Dusart appeared to have plenty of money, given him by Consul Villavicencio when Villavicencio went to Havana and secured from Dusart a waiver of the latter's claim to the *Ventura*.⁸⁵² By then, Pancho Villa could not have cared less about Dusart.

American authorities were gaining knowledge about Villa's logistical system through an unusual instance of cooperation between the US Secret Service and the Bureau at the agent level. In San Francisco, Agent Allen shared information about munitions with Agent Tidwell of the Treasury Department's Secret Service Division regarding information already furnished the Bureau through informants, and he found that through a different source, Tidwell had obtained practically the same information. The Treasury agent's office was keeping a record of the arms and ammunition procured or sought for together with the names of those who were active in this work, for future reference in case an embargo might be placed on munitions to Mexico. In a notable development, the San Francisco office of the Secret Service turned an informant over to Allen.⁸⁵³

There was closer cooperation between the military and the Bureau, evidenced by a CONFIDENTIAL report from Second Cavalry Brigade headquarters at Douglas to the Intelligence officer at Fort Sam Houston regarding the activities of *villista* General Maytorena in Sonora. The army promptly forwarded a copy of the report to the Bureau.⁸⁵⁴ To investigate Maytorena's intrigues on the Arizona border, the overstretched Bureau once again supplemented its special agents with a local White Slave Officer, Fred Kain, based at Tucson. He reported from Nogales, Arizona on the condition of Maytorena's troops at Nogales, Sonora across the street.

> Many rumors circulated. Maytorena's troops across the line are well supplied with ammunition but with nothing else. Their food supply and their clothing is [sic] very meager. Filth and dirt are about all they are supplied with. Children (boys) ranging from 12 years up are enlisted as soldiers. Each soldier has two belts of cartridges containing 100 in each belt, strapped around his body. Most of these boys are barefooted and have no hats. The meat that they have to eat is strung on lines covered with flies. They have an airplane manned by an

Englishman and, I think, a Spaniard, and they have two kinds of bombs. In my opinion, if conditions are not improved across the line at Nogales an epidemic of some sort will break out, owing to the filth.[855]

Not only was Maytorena bottled up in Nogales by the increasingly confident *carrancista* General Plutarco Elías Calles, but Maytorena was increasingly fearful for his life. The *carrancista* consul in Nogales, Arizona, had been waging an aggressive campaign against Maytorena, up to and including instigating a plot to assassinate him.[856]

Villista activity on the Arizona border was of secondary importance. Bureau agents in El Paso became increasingly concerned with a flood of munitions showing up consigned to Villa's forces. To give some idea of the scale of the ammunition traffic, between August 24 and September 28, 1915, 2,649,392 7-millimeter cartridges went by Wells Fargo express to El Paso consigned to the Rio Grande Valley Bank & Trust Company, which handled most of Villa's finances. Another 1,000,896 7-millimeter cartridges went on September 21, 1915, consigned to James Manoil, 60 Broadway, New York City, care of the Mississippi Valley Trust Company of St. Louis.[857]

James Manoil was a twenty-seven-year-old Russian-Rumanian immigrant who occupied a suite at 60 Broadway in New York. James Manoil and Company produced a "manophone and other musical instruments."[858] It should have baffled agents of the Bureau who discovered Manoil's name on massive munitions shipments starting in June 1915 that they had never heard of a prominent arms dealer of that name, who purchased millions of cartridges every month between June and October 1915. The assistant treasurer of the Guaranty Trust Company that transferred payments to the Mississippi Trust Company of St. Louis stated to investigators, "concerning Mr. James Manoil [...] we have known him for some time and have extended him accommodation in small amounts on notes [...] We have never had a statement of his financial affairs, but we are inclined to think his means are moderate."[859] The American military attaché in Mexico, investigating Manoil's whereabouts in 1918, described him to be "very shrewd, intelligent, not well educated [...] of a rather aggressive character."[860] What all investigators seemed to have missed was the suspicious coincidence that Manoil's address matched that of the German military attaché's office in New York. The potential connection between Franz von Papen's successor Wolf von Igel and Manoil received no attention from the authorities.

The main person in Albert's organization in charge of cornering the US munitions market was Carl Heynen, the former HAPAG agent in Mexico, whose office was near that of Manoil at 45 Broadway. Most importantly, the accounts at the Guaranty Trust Company of New York that Manoil used for paying the purchases belonged to Heinrich Albert, the head of the German clandestine organization in the US. It follows that Manoil was a front for the German government.[861]

Agents of the Bureau came within reach of figuring out the story behind the mysterious Manoil. As massive shipments of cartridges for Villa arrived on the border, they identified the Western Cartridge Company in Alton, Illinois as the source. Agent Webster in Los Angeles interviewed the *carrancista* arms buyer R. L. Hall in September who confirmed that he was in the process of buying three million rounds of 7-millimeter cartridges from James Manoil.[862] Hall confirmed that the original order for the cartridges came from Villa's main buyer, Felix Sommerfeld. Somehow, according to the informant, Lázaro de la Garza at 115 Broadway, who handled the logistics of shipping Villa's supplies, diverted the cartridges to Carranza's faction. In what can only be seen as a major intelligence blunder, the Bureau did not follow up on the leads that could have linked James Manoil and the German military attaché, Wolf von Igel, Heinrich Albert, Carl Heynen, and Felix Sommerfeld with Pancho Villa until a year later, when the US and Mexico stood at the brink of war.

During the late spring and summer of 1915, major battles were being fought in central Mexico. There, Villa's nemesis was General Álvaro Obregón, at this time a Carranza loyalist and usually considered the best general the Mexican Revolution produced. Beginning in April, Obregón inflicted a series of crushing defeats on Villa in the Bajío region northwest of Mexico City, shattering the Division of the North's image of invincibility. Obregón's strategy was to prepare fortified positions and in effect dare Villa to attack, which he did, sending massed charges against Obregón's entrenchments. The *villistas* were slaughtered. Lacking sufficient reserves to mount counterattacks, they fled in disorganized retreat. (But putting Villa's disastrous tactics in perspective, some of the leading military minds in Europe were launching daylight mass attacks over open ground against fortified positions, with equally disastrous results.) As for Obregón, he was lucky to be alive. During the battle for the city of León, on June 3, shrapnel shattered his right arm. Crazed with pain, he tried to blow his brains out, but was restrained by his staff. Subordinate generals completed the victory, capturing the city of León.[863] Obregón's arm, incidentally, was amputated, and it was preserved in a jar of formaldehyde in a marble monument in Mexico City.

Obregón's juggernaut pressed on. Logistics and supply were the most pressing issues for both the attacking Obregón and the retreating Villa. German documents from the Heinrich Albert office as well as the papers of Lázaro de la Garza show that in the spring of 1915, Sommerfeld had contracted a staggering 27 million 7-millimeter cartridges with the Western Cartridge Company for delivery to Pancho Villa.[864] W. H. Shelton of Shelton Payne, the main dealer through which the munitions came, gave a talk in 1916 entitled, "Villa as a Customer." He recalled that he met with Villa and "contracted to sell him enough ammunition to kill all the revolutionists in Mexico if it had been judiciously used."[865]

Increasingly on the defensive by the summer, Villa began retreating up the central rail line toward Ciudad Juárez.[866] As his military fortunes declined, so did the value of his fiat currency, making it increasingly difficult to pay for desperately needed munitions. Sommerfeld testified later that in the summer of 1915 "he [Villa] stopped sending money..."[867] This is the point at which James Manoil entered the picture. Between June and September, Carl Heynen, through Manoil, transferred $381,000 [approximately $8 million in today's value] to the Western Cartridge Company to pay for Sommerfeld's shipments.[868]

It became clear by September that Villa would not regain his military superiority in Mexico. As a consequence, Carl Heynen decided to contact the *carrancista* purchasing agent, Arturo González, through a broker Sommerfeld knew well, R. L. Hall of Los Angeles.[869] Using de la Garza as the middleman, deliveries now reached the forces of Álvaro Obregón, albeit at a thirty percent higher price, $48 per thousand, giving Heynen a welcome windfall profit. After only two months, however, Obregón stopped the order, ostensibly because he considered the cost "excessive;" maybe, in reality, because by then Villa was defeated.[870] With the German government unwilling to fund any more munitions for Villa, de la Garza sold the remainder of the contract to the French government. Since the specification allowed only Spanish-type Mausers to use this cartridge, the French realized not too long after paying for the contract, that the cartridges were unusable. In the end, de la Garza made off with the $65,000 of the original deposit on the contract, and $119,000 in French commissions (approximately $3.8 million in today's value).

By the end of 1915, *villista* currency was being sold in curio shops. In July, Lázaro de la Garza, whose financial expertise had kept the Division of the North supplied, was forced out of the Villa Agency in Juárez by the jealousy of Villa's brother, Hipólito. De la Garza abandoned the sinking ship and moved to Los Angeles. The Carranza consul there, Adolfo Carrillo, told Agent Webster that de la Garza, "former Secretary and Treasurer" of Villa, was now living in his $100,000 (approximately $2 million in today's value) mansion at 357 Occidental Boulevard, and that he had been entertaining prominent Mexicans.[871]

As Carranza's forces continued their advance up the central rail line toward Juárez, Villa's dominance in Chihuahua crumbled, and he retreated across the Sierra Madre into Sonora, trying to make a comeback along the Arizona border, only to suffer another series of crushing defeats. Villa retreated back across the Sierra Madre into Chihuahua with the remnants of his forces.[872]

Pancho Villa had been reduced from the most powerful general in Mexico to leader of a regional guerrilla movement.[873] By the fall, more and more prominent *villistas* were deserting the losing cause and taking refuge in the United States. They included Villa's ally Maytorena, who fled to Los Angeles, intelligence chief Hector Ramos, General Tomás Ornelas, who commanded the Juárez garrison, and even Hipólito Villa. On December 20, 1915, a group of senior *villista* officers went to the Mexican consulate in El Paso to deliver Ciudad Juárez and receive amnesty from Carranza.[874]

11

THE CHIEF MANIPULATOR

As VILLA AND CARRANZA BATTLED for control of Mexico in 1915, the Bureau went to extraordinary lengths to secure firsthand information on conditions, as evidenced by the report on June 9 by Agent Frank L. Garbarino: "I today prepared and submitted to the Chief a special report covering observations made by me while in Tampico and Veracruz with respect to the conditions of the natives. Was requested to do so by the Chief in New York on Sunday last after having recited to him my experiences while in Mexico. Many are starving. In Tampico, reportedly a poor ragged soldier offered to sell his ammunition and gun to J. C. Lecardis for a small sum that he might be able to purchase food. Famine also in interior."[875] Still, most of the Bureau's intelligence came from sources within the United States, especially along the border.

Villistas and carrancistas were battling for control of the Arizona border; Carranza generals Benjamin Hill and Plutarco Elías Calles fought villista general José María Maytorena at the ports of entry: Naco, Nogales, and Agua Prieta. Besides what transpired on the battlefield, carrancistas continued to operate from American soil, as Bureau investigations brought to light.

There was, for example, the Sonora War Tax Commission, operating quietly from an office in the post office building in Douglas. It was common knowledge that the Commission collected large sums, either voluntarily or by extortion, from those who had property in Sonora. Originally, Carranza consul Francisco "Pancho" S. Elías was the moving figure in the Commission, but he was transferred to New York City as the Carranza consul general. He was succeeded in the War Tax Commission by C. G. Soriano and then by Ives G. Lelevier, the current consul. Associated with the Commission was W. H. Fisher, formerly a member of the Douglas Hardware Company, who had been indicted in 1913 for smuggling munitions. The Commission bought impressive amounts of ammunition and supplies from local merchants. It also helped to finance the forces of *carrancista* general Plutarco Elías Calles in Sonora.[876]

Part of Calles's success was his control of the railroad between Agua Prieta and Nacozari. But as a commentary on the travails of a company trying to remain in business in the midst of revolution, the Maytorena consul at Douglas was holding the railroad officials responsible for Calles's success and openly announced that the railroad would be destroyed by bridge burners. He was carrying on an active campaign, securing information and telephoning it to Maytorena as well as meeting Maytorena personally at Nogales. This CONFIDENTIAL intelligence report came from headquarters of the Second Cavalry Brigade at Douglas to the Intelligence officer at Fort Sam Houston, who forwarded the report to the Bureau. Agent Barnes believed "that such actions are in violation of the neutrality laws and should be made a matter of investigation. I will make as close an investigation as I can with the means at hand and report without delay."[877]

Agent Pinckney went to Nogales, Arizona in August at the army's request to investigate *carrancista* consul Gustavo Padrés's violations of neutrality. Pinckney conferred with Consul Simpich and army officers who stated that *carrancista* general Calles had *villista* general Maytorena trapped in Nogales, Sonora and was steadily advancing. In this critical situation, Consul Gustavo Padrés was doing all he could to bring about the fall of the Sonoran town, including fomenting a plot to have Maytorena assassinated. Consul Simpich provided Pinckney with certified copies of the confessions of three Maytorena captains recently executed for attempting his assassination. Pinckney reported that besides plotting assassination, Consul Padrés was outspokenly anti-American and had made himself so unpopular by threatening Consul Simpich and American businessmen that an anti-Mexican riot had resulted.[878] Padrés, it will be remembered, had engineered the sale in El Paso of 448,000 cartridges in 1913 for the Constitutionalists.

Carranza recruiters were busy feeding fresh recruits into the Arizona campaign while denouncing Villa recruiters who were also violating the neutrality laws.[879] But recruiting cases were sometimes tricky, such as in that of *carrancistas* Joaquín Esquer and Alfonso Coronado. The Bureau developed little documentary evidence against the pair, relying instead on recruit testimony. But the alleged recruits testified before the grand jury that they were employed by the Carranza faction and had no real intention of crossing into Mexico. Nevertheless, Esquer and Coronado were indicted. Esquer was apprehended, arraigned, plead "not guilty," and was released on his own recognizance; Coronado was never apprehended. Agent Barnes wanted Esquer to be vigorously prosecuted, for he had been violating the neutrality laws for the last four years. Although Esquer's case was set for trial, US Attorney Thomas A. Flynn decided that the case was too weak to merit further investigation.[880]

Long-time revolutionist Victor Ochoa was assisting *carrancista* recruiting efforts in El Paso. He was under indictment and scheduled for trial, but Barnes was worried. He wrote to Agent Pinckney that "owing to the difficulty in keeping the Government's witnesses together and away from the influence of this defendant, [it is] very important that this case be tried at this term of Court. I therefore beg to suggest that you confer with the US attorney along these lines, and in the event that there are any developments which indicate that this course cannot be followed, I would thank you to telegraph me immediately."[881]

Andrés García, the capable Carranza consul in El Paso, busily dispatched men by rail to bolster General Hills's defense of Naco. As was to be expected, Villa's intelligence chief Hector Ramos eagerly supplied the Bureau with information about this activity. At Ramos's suggestion, Agent Guy interviewed the ticket agent at the depot regarding Mexicans leaving ostensibly for Columbus.[882] And acting on Ramos's information about a *carrancista* recruiter carrying an incriminating document, Guy, John Wren, and Villa operative Henry Kramp boarded a westbound train to interrogate suspected Carranza recruits and if possible secure the document. Guy said he informed Ramos he would do what he could to obtain this document but he was not sure he had the right to search since no warrant had been issued for that purpose and as yet there was no evidence to justify

Figure 71. John Killian Wren
Source: Wren Family Tree

such a search. As matters developed, the *carrancista* recruiter eluded them, but Guy took the recruiter's suitcase off to the Bureau office and examined its contents.[883] On a subsequent occasion, Agent Beckham wrote that "Fred Delgado, former city detective, also works for Hector Ramos and will be at the depot. I deprecated the use of Mr. Delgado on account of his reputation and on account of his connection with the Villa Agency, but there was available at the time no other interpreter."[884]

The El Paso office of the Bureau continued to work closely with Hector Ramos, and with informant DELAG, to monitor *carrancista* recruiting. Agent in Charge Pinckney planned to travel with *villista* operatives on the same train to shadow recruits. Agents Pinckney and Breniman went to Ramos's office to have him translate a seized letter to General Calles at Agua Prieta suggesting that recruits in El Paso use the pretext of seeking work on a Sonoran railroad. With Ramos's assistance, several recruits were returned to El Paso, where each was "rigidly examined" by Pinckney and Breniman. Pinckney conferred with the US attorney and filed a complaint charging all involved with conspiring to recruit. Warrants were issued, including one for General Calles, who was to be detained should he cross into the United States.[885]

Besides investigating recruiting violations, another Bureau priority was keeping track of *carrancista* purchases of munitions and supplies. Since no embargo was in effect, ammunition could be shipped as merchandise unless it was part of a military expedition organized in the United States.[886] In their battle to the death, Carranza had an enormous advantage over Villa. While Villa remained dependent for supplies on the rail line from El Paso, Carranza controlled the seacoasts, generated revenues from exports through the Gulf of petroleum and from exports of sisal, much in demand for binding twine in the US, from Yucatán. He could pay for munitions in substantial quantities.

A few examples were Remington supplying 750,000 7-millimeter cartridges to Veracruz in a single shipment. On the Pacific coast, the steamer *Prince Albert* of the Southwestern Steamship Company of San Francisco transported 308,000 30-30 rounds and fifty-four cases of rifles to Mazatlán. A subsequent shipment was for 450,000 cartridges. The American steamship *Coaster* carried twenty cases (200,000 cartridges) to that port. And Arturo González, a *carrancista* purchasing agent, arrived in Los Angeles from Mazatlán to procure 700,000 30-30 and 500,000 7-millimeter cartridges. González dealt with the prominent broker—and Bureau informant—R. L. Hall, who was also sending to Douglas 1,000,000 cartridges for General Calles. Most of this ammunition, incidentally, had been obtained from Villa agents now looking for new customers.[887]

Carrancistas were also purchasing vessels. In San Francisco, they acquired the *Manila*, a former Spanish prison ship the US had captured in the Spanish-American War. Agent Arthur M. Allen learned that the government had sold the steamer at auction to a certain John A. McDonald. When he began refitting her by tearing out the cells, the hull was damaged, and the boat sank. She was raised and taken to the Union Iron Works for repair. As it happened, McDonald was president of the Union Iron Works, and he was negotiating her sale to the *carrancistas*, who planned to outfit the *Manila* with four Hotchkiss guns as soon as she cleared United States waters.[888]

Also in San Francisco, the *carrancistas* had to play defense on naval matters. Agent Allen called on Ramón P. DeNegri, Carranza consul at 519 California Street. DeNegri said Captain I. Arenas, formerly captain of the gunboat *Guerrero* under Huerta left on July 6 for El Paso; registering at the Hotel McCoy. His purpose was to seek funds to purchase and outfit a vessel to harass the Pacific coast of Mexico. DeNegri stated that his confidential information disclosed the fact that the Villa people did not trust Alberto Méndez Acerto, their consul in San Francisco, and hence employed an American named W. Parker of doubtful reputation to stir up dissention on west coast of Mexico. A part of his work was to secure control of gunboat *Guerrero* by instigating a mutiny among the crew. Before Parker had accomplished anything, the Carranza interests brought Parker over by giving him more money, and he was now drawing money from each faction, neither feeling sure of him but each being afraid to let him go. At this juncture, Lt. Paramoro [sic] who had that rank on the *Guerrero* and who was now in the secret service

Figure 72. Ramón P. DeNegri
Source: Harris & Ewing Collection
Library of Congress Prints and Photographs Division

of the Villa faction, hunted up Captain Arenas and sent him to Chihuahua to confer with Villa's brother Hipólito to plan a mutiny on the Guerrero to seize the gunboat.[889]

At Baltimore, carrancistas purchased the steamer Atlanta. An American crew of twenty sailed her to Veracruz, delivered her to Carranza representatives, and returned to the United States. Acting Chief Horn instructed that the crew be interviewed to secure all possible information as to the ship's cargo and other details. Agent John J. Grgurevich at Baltimore contacted the crew by mail.[890]

Carrancistas in New Orleans acquired the steamer, Maclovio Herrera, formerly the Spanish gunboat, Alvarado, captured by the United States in the Spanish American War and sold to residents of New Orleans, who in turn sold it to the Carranza government for use as a revenue cutter and troop transport. The Bureau kept the vessel under surveillance for weeks. The steamer was repaired and loaded with 60,000 rounds of rifle ammunition, but the ammunition was transferred to a Wolvin Line ship for quicker transportation to Veracruz. The Bureau took no further action on these efforts to build a Carranza navy.[891]

Division Superintendent Offley in New York was particularly interested in the activities of Francisco S. Elías, the Carranza consul general who had formerly headed the Sonora War Tax Commission and whose offices were rooms 3015 and 3017 in the Equitable Building, 120 Broadway. Elías used the Ward Line exclusively to ship munitions from New York to Veracruz.[892] Offley assigned Agent Scully and Special Employee Harvey Phillips to investigate these shipments. In February, Elías had dispatched by the Morro Castle a huge consignment of Winchester arms and ammunition. The Ward Line people said it was the biggest munitions shipment they had ever made.

Figure 73. William M. Offley, c. 1912-1919
Source: FBI Media

The consignment also included large quantities of shoes, shirts, and other items of clothing. Although Ward Line officials were most reluctant to permit the Bureau to examine their records, Customs provided the vessel's manifest.[893] Elías also signed a contract with the Remington Arms Company for 8,000,000 7-millimeter cartridges, 3,000,000 of which had been shipped as of July 1915 and another 250,000 in August.[894]

Assisting Elías was Jorge Orozco, the onetime *carrancista* consul in El Paso who had been indicted for neutrality violation for financing the unsuccessful 1914 expedition to Columbus. Superintendent Offley assigned Agents Scully and Adams to apprehend him. They learned the name of Orozco's closest friend, went to the post office where they prepared and arranged for the delivery of a decoy registered letter purporting to have been sent by Orozco's friend and delivered to Orozco's address. The agents accompanied the postman and apprehended Orozco when he signed for the letter. At the field office, Offley interviewed Orozco, who readily admitted his identity and having purchased arms and ammunition for the Carranza faction. Orozco was turned over to a deputy US marshal. At his arraignment before the US Commissioner, his bond was fixed at $2,500, which was subsequently furnished.[895]

There was no lack of brokers eager to do business with Elías.[896] Randolph Robertson, the former deputy clerk of the US district court in Laredo who was now vice consul in Monterrey—and a continuing valuable Bureau informant- supplied copies of telegrams he had obtained "confidentially" in which Abraham and Company of Laredo offered to sell to Elías 60,000,000 7-millimeter cartridges, in installments. Elías replied: "Your wire would like deal with you personally as matter is very important." Robertson suggested that an agent from the San Antonio field office be sent to investigate. Agent in Charge Barnes readily agreed.[897] Agent A. L. Barkey spoke with Robertson, who explained that he had obtained the telegrams from a clerk in the local Western Union office. Robertson asked that before any action was taken on the Abraham matter, that Barkey obtain the telegrams directly from Western Union in order to protect Robertson's informant.[898]

Assuming that negotiations between Pedro Abraham and Elías would be by mail, Barkey arranged for a cover on Abraham's mail. But Barkey was recalled to San Antonio because Abraham had recently gone there. He located Abraham at the St. Anthony Hotel and shadowed him for hours. Disappointingly, Abraham only spoke with a prostitute. Barkey then had Abraham come to the field office for an interview, which Agent Barnes conducted. Abraham stated that the was a moneychanger and commission man in Laredo, and in this capacity had dealings with the broker Pedro Serrano of

San Antonio, whom we have encountered before. Serrano told Abraham he had at his disposal 60,000,000 cartridges which were surplus to the Spanish government. Abraham had immediately contacted the Carranza consul in Laredo, Melquíades García, who told him he had to negotiate with Francisco Elías. Pedro Serrano was then interviewed and stated that L. Márquez, De Soto Hotel, New Orleans, had advised him that he had the 60,000,000 cartridges for sale. Serrano had then contacted Abraham to find a buyer.[899]

In response to a telegram from Barnes, Agent Pendleton talked with New Orleans munitions broker Charles E. Jones,[900] who advised that the 60,000,000 cartridges Pedro Serrano was trying to peddle were in the warehouse of Hibbard Spencer & Bartlett Company of Chicago and had been sold to the Empire Trust Company of New York City.[901]

A major *carrancista* munitions pipeline was from New York through Laredo and Brownsville. In Laredo, Deutz Bros. Hardware Company was the conduit. In Brownsville, the key figures were brothers George F. and H. B. Walker, owners of Walker Brothers-Hancock Company. They also did business as Walker Bros. Wholesale Hardware Co., Walker Bros. Hardware Co., and Walker Bros. Frontier Hardware Company. The firm supplied Carranza with quantities of ammunition and eleven machine guns. George F. Walker stated that he had solicited business only with the *carrancistas*. He had sold to other factions but felt obliged to notify the Carranza faction first, and he consistently had refused to sell to the *villistas*. Walker usually refused to cooperate with the Bureau in order to protect his customers' confidentiality. Barnes authorized Agent Guy to remain in Laredo as long as necessary to investigate.[902]

Guy enlisted *villista* help to maintain surveillance on *carrancista* activities, which according to Randolph Robertson were the subject of common talk among the Mexicans, many of whom believed that Carranza was allowed to do this because of some special privilege granted by the US. The Bureau agent also conferred with the local head of Customs, who said that only the day before some 300,000 rounds went across the bridge to Carranza. Guy also learned that local hardware dealer Deutz was negotiating a substantial ammunition transaction with Melquíades García, the Carranza consul. The local Villa consul, Manuel de Icaza, claimed that Francisco Elías in New York had ordered 10,000,000 rounds; the first shipment had already crossed over to Nuevo Laredo.[903]

Agent Pendleton received information from munitions broker and Bureau informant Maurice Conners, who advised that Carranza Consul Francisco R. Villavicencio said he had been ordered to purchase at once all available .30-caliber ammunition and rush it to Mexico in case the United States decided to intervene in Mexico or imposed another arms embargo.

Conners stated that approximately 4,000,000 cartridges were involved, and he had accepted the contract with Villavicencio. But he would ensure that all the ammunition came through New Orleans and would be in a position to delay shipment and notify the Bureau of the ammunition's location in case of an embargo. Pendleton was cautious: "Conners is a speculator, and it seems clear from his statements he would not hesitate to double cross these Mexicans. However, I have always found him to be reliable in any information he has given to this office."[904] The Chief was also cautious, instructing Pendleton: "Referring your telegram proposed purchase ammunition Mexico desired you give no advice to Conners but watch situation and keep me advised developments."[905] Pendleton also had to be cautious in his dealings with the assistant US attorney in New Orleans, Joseph W. Montgomery—he was the legal adviser to Carranza Consul Villavicencio, who complained that he had to pay Montgomery double what other attorneys would charge.[906]

Bielaski instructed Pendleton to secure all information possible about munitions and report promptly by telegraph. The agent went to the office of Villavicencio, and the consul readily supplied the data on his shipments because he wanted no trouble with the government. The shipments were 7,700,000 30-30 cartridges bought from A. Baldwin and Company, sent to Veracruz on the Wolvin Line, *City of Tampico*, and 125,000 30-30s purchased from Walker Brothers in Brownsville and sent to Douglas for General Calles. Villavicencio was negotiating with broker Charles E. Jones for another 250,000 30-30s.[907]

Besides munitions, Carranza was in the process of acquiring an air force. Agent J. F. Kropidlowski in New York interviewed Henry Woodhouse of the Aero Club of America in July 1915. Woodhouse was concerned that both Villa and Carranza had recently purchased airplanes, and he had tried to bring this to the US government's attention by having an article published in the *New York Herald* in hopes that the government would take some action. The article passed unnoticed, and the aircraft were duly delivered. Now the Bureau was investigating. Woodhouse related that a nephew of Carranza's, Captain Alberto Salinas, had recruited American aviators W. Leonard Bonney and Lawrence M. Brown. Superintendent Offley was instructed to determine if the fliers had returned to the US and if so to interview them to learn if their enlistment came within the provisions of Section 10 of the Federal Criminal Code. Kropidlowski interviewed Bonney's wife, who was reluctant to divulge all she knew but said Captain Salinas had telegraphed the Aero Club seeking expert pilots. Salinas had visited the Bonney home in New York and had recruited her husband in February. She inferred that Bonney was the only aviator recruited but that Salinas had also hired several American mechanics to assemble aircraft and perform repairs.

Bonney had returned to New York a month earlier because he had contracted fever in Mexico but had returned there recently. She said Bonney was disgusted with the American government because it showed no interest in American aviators and would not consider his services, and this had impelled him to enlist with the *carrancistas*, who paid him a handsome salary. Mrs. Bonney stated that she would be glad to advise the Bureau of his return so he could be interviewed. He would probably report to the Aero Club. If he did so, Woodhouse agreed to advise the Bureau. Woodhouse also mentioned to Kropidlowski that an American aviator named Charles F. Niles had been in Mexico about the time Bonney enlisted but became dissatisfied with conditions in Mexico and returned to the US after a short stay. His present whereabouts were unknown, but Woodhouse would report on him if located, as he would for other aviators in whom the Bureau might be interested.[908]

Carrancistas were also busy on the Texas border. The year 1915 was notable because on May 13, 1915, a federal grand jury in Brownsville indicted nine individuals for conspiring "to steal certain property of the United States of America, contrary to the authority thereof, to wit, the states of Texas, Oklahoma, New Mexico, Arizona, Colorado and California [...]."[909] Back in January 1915, there had come to light the so-called Plan de San Diego, a manifesto supposedly written at the small South Texas town of San Diego.[910] On its face the manifesto was risible. It called for a rebellion by Hispanics to establish an independent republic encompassing the American Southwest, a republic which might request annexation by Mexico. There was no place in this proposed republic for blacks—they would be granted six adjoining states to form their own republic, and they would be permitted to select their own flag. All this was to be accomplished by a revolutionary congress guiding the "Liberating Army of Races and Peoples." All Anglo males over the age of sixteen were to be killed. As the army of liberation seized each state capital, a provisional government would be formed. The Plan bore all the hallmarks of yet another wildly improbable *magonista* undertaking which did not have a prayer of succeeding.

The Plan came to light when one Basilio Ramos was arrested with a copy of the document.[911] He claimed it was a *huertista* scheme, and some historians have accepted this just because Ramos said it was.[912] However, captured secret agents have been known to lie. The *carrancistas* seized on the ridiculous *magonista* Plan and secretly supported it as a way to exert pressure on the United States for diplomatic recognition, crucial to their success. *Carrancistas* had gained control of the lower Rio Grande border, and they used the Plan to sponsor incursions into South Texas. The only times the Plan mattered was when it had support from Mexico, and the only times it had support from Mexico was when it suited the Carranza faction. Plan insurgents became pawns of the *carrancistas*, who used them to create turmoil, with Carranza informing the United States that if he received recognition, he would promptly put an end to the unrest on the border.

The most prominent of the *sediciosos* (Plan militants engaged in sedition) were Agustín S. Garza, the leader of the movement, who used the alias of "León Caballo," guerrilla chieftains Luís de la Rosa and Aniceto Pizaña, a confirmed *magonista*. Texas authorities announced a $1,000 reward for De la Rosa and Pizaña dead or alive. *Carrancista* forces provided logistical support to the militants and on occasion soldiers in mufti who participated in the raids. These incursions became serious by the late summer of 1915, reaching as far into Texas as seventy miles north of Brownsville.

Besides their own investigations, Bureau agents received intelligence about the Plan de San Diego movement from a number of sources. *Villistas* were of course eager to provide information about *carrancista* machinations. Information also came from subpoenas duces tecum and from confidential informants in Texas and in northern Mexico. An important informant in Mexico was Randolph Robertson, vice consul in Monterrey. And in an unusual arrangement, because the State Department refused to send someone under cover into Mexico to report on *sedicioso* activities, Bureau Agent J. B. Rogers was detailed for this mission.[913] Chief Bielaski approved, provided the assignment was not too dangerous. Rogers traveled to Monterrey, gathering intelligence on the Plan and on the German consul, who was reportedly assisting the *sediciosos*. Rogers then traveled to Ciudad Victoria, Tamaulipas, to investigate Plan recruiting. Another agent, E. B. Stone, was not averse to having De la Rosa and Pizaña eliminated by treachery, reporting a plot to have their bodyguards kill them for the reward and deliver their heads in a sack on the Texas bank of the Rio Grande. Stone carefully covered himself with his superiors, though, stressing that he was merely reporting and had neither agreed to nor had sanctioned anything with the parties involved. The US attorney was horrified, and the matter was dropped.

The Bureau experienced frustration at several levels. Texas authorities, from the adjutant general on down, were reluctant to cooperate, as illustrated by the Morin affair. General José Morin was an important Plan recruiter, but he was betrayed by an associate. Agent Howard P. Wright helped to shadow Morin and arrest him when he traveled to Kingsville to confer with a subordinate,

Victoriano Ponce. Wright interrogated the pair and participated in rolling up the *sedicioso* network in Kingsville. At the suggestion of Agent in Charge Barnes, Wright had Morin and Ponce kept in the Kingsville jail while he prepared to present their cases to a federal grand jury in San Antonio. But the pair vanished while in the custody of the Texas Rangers. A distressed Wright investigated, only to be thwarted by Texas Adjutant General Henry Hutchings, who commanded the Rangers. Through a fluke, Wright obtained the Rangers' official report stating that the pair had escaped, but what evidently happened was that the Rangers shot them, disposed of the bodies, and announced that Morin and Ponce had indeed escaped, and they had no idea where they might be. Secretary of War Lindley Garrison later suggested that in the future, federal prisoners in Texas be turned over to the army rather than to the civil authorities to prevent their being killed before they could be brought to trial.

The leaders of the Plan de San Diego were never brought to trial. A strong case against them had been developed, with a federal grand jury hearing testimony corroborating the evidence the Bureau agents had amassed, but an order from the court abruptly terminated the grand jury's investigation. Judge Waller T. Burns, of the 1911 *reyista* trials fame, ruled that the federal government was without jurisdiction to prosecute the case because federal law had not been violated—*sediciosos* should be prosecuted under Texas law.[914]

President Wilson issued an ultimatum on June 2, 1915, to the various Mexican factions to come to an agreement or the U.S. would intervene militarily.[915] A flurry of action started within the State Department as a result. William Jennings Bryan resigned as Secretary of State on June 9 over his frustration with Wilson's foreign policy towards Germany, which he believed would eventually drag the United States into the conflict. Robert Lansing, the Counselor of the State Department who had advised the President on a stricter course towards Germany, succeed Bryan. However, Lansing also believed that the continuation of the Mexican Revolution posed a national security risk and undercut the US's ability to join the Allies in Europe if needed.[916] All factions except the *carrancistas* proposed candidates within the framework of the Pan-American Conference to form a "unity government," President Wilson's key demand as a prerequisite for peace in Mexico. Carranza refused to participate officially because he considered himself the winner of the civil war with Villa, and thus the only rightful and logical candidate for the presidency. Ultimately his assessment of the situation proved to be convincing. He did send his chief of secret service as an "observer," while his attorney Charles Douglas kept the lines open with Secretary Lansing.

By the end of July, Wilson's effort to promote a unity government started to take shape. He sent special envoys to *carrancista* generals Álvaro Obregón and Pablo González to determine if they would support a candidate other than Carranza. They remained ambiguous.⁹¹⁷ In order to put pressure on the *villista* faction, Wilson dispatched Army Chief of Staff Hugh Lenox Scott in early August to confer with Pancho Villa (who had declared that he personally had no interest in the Mexican presidency). According to Villa, Scott informed him that if he released confiscated American property in Mexico, the US government would guarantee not to recognize Carranza as de facto president.⁹¹⁸ In his memoirs, Scott denied having proposed this quid pro quo. Scott's papers housed in the Library of Congress are inconclusive, but clearly some promises must have been made.⁹¹⁹ Scott later wrote in his memoirs, "In all, there was more than six million dollars [Villa returned to American businesses] for which I had no equivalent to offer to Villa or promises to make, and he gave them up because I asked him; no more and no less."⁹²⁰ To be fair, what Villa conceded to Scott was the expected revenue of some American-owned mines and a much lower value of confiscated merchandise in Chihuahua. Yet, with his fiat money devalued and his area of control shrinking by the day, Villa's concessions did constitute a major sacrifice on his part.⁹²¹

With the two leading *carrancista* generals at least open to a president other than Carranza, Villa was willing to submit to the decisions of the Pan-American Conference, and even Emiliano Zapata made the same commitment.⁹²² The conference was to meet in September to tie the knot around an agreeable Mexican unity government.⁹²³ Only Carranza remained staunchly opposed. Instead of cooperating, he dusted off the Plan de San Diego and put pressure on the US government with renewed raids. Carranza wanted to make clear that he was the only law and order option.

President Wilson spent the summer at Cornish, New Hampshire, from the end of July until August 4, ostensibly to relax but also to contemplate a solution to the "Mexican problem." It appeared to most observers that he sincerely tried to look at all options. He conferred periodically with his new Secretary of State, Robert Lansing. While at Cornish, and likely under the influence of Lansing's opinion that Carranza was the only realistic option for a stable Mexican government, Wilson abandoned his earlier requirement of a unity government in Mexico as a prerequisite for diplomatic recognition. Lansing wrote in his diary on July 11, 1915 "[...] it will be necessary to recognize Carranza's faction which seems to be stronger."⁹²⁴ Wilson adopted the pragmatic strategy Lansing promoted, namely that the militarily dominant Carranza would have to be recognized, mainly create political stability and stave off German attempts to weaponize the border against the US. Although he reached this decision while at his summer retreat, he told no one, maybe excluding his Secretary of State, who later maintained that he did not know either.

The *carrancista* use of the Plan de San Diego succeeded brilliantly. The United States remained reluctant to extend diplomatic recognition to Carranza as late as August 7, 1915, when President Wilson inquired of Secretary of State Robert Lansing why "you think it wise to put [Pancho] Villa in the way of getting money [through cattle exports] just at the moment when he is apparently weakened and on the verge of collapse?" Lansing replied: "The reason for furnishing Villa with an opportunity to obtain funds is this: We do not wish the Carranza faction to be the only one to deal with in Mexico. Carranza seems so impossible that an appearance, at least, of opposition to him will give us an opportunity to invite a compromise of factions. I think, therefore, it is politic, for the time, to allow Villa to obtain sufficient financial resources to allow his faction to remain in arms until a compromise can be effected."[925]

A unity government for Mexico remained the stated foreign policy goal as the Pan-American Conference met later in August. Wilson also made no effort to stop a multitude of interest groups lobbying his administration. In the end, all of them felt deceived, most notably Pancho Villa and the people that had supported him. The Pan-American Conference rubber-stamped the new US foreign policy and recommended Carranza be the de facto president of Mexico.

On October 19, 1915, Carranza received de facto US diplomatic recognition as head of the faction that was winning on the battlefield.[926] His assurance that if recognized he would end the turmoil on the border helped change Washington's mind. Carranza's use of the Plan de San Diego as a political pressure strategy had come to fruition. Within a week of his diplomatic recognition the raids into Texas stopped. To the Wilson administration, the de facto Mexican president expressed his intention to cooperate in bringing to justice those who had committed crimes against the laws of the United States, prevent a recurrence of the border troubles, and restore order and good feeling between Anglos and Hispanics.[927] The leaders of the Plan de San Diego had no alternative but to remain in Mexico at Carranza's pleasure, for if they returned to Texas, they were dead men. Carranza kept them on a short leash, just in case they might be needed again.

Carranza received several immediate benefits from recognition. The Department of State granted the de facto government of Mexico permission to transport between 4,000 and 5,000 troops from Eagle Pass and Laredo to Agua Prieta via United States railroads unarmed, their arms and ammunition being sent as baggage.[928] These troop reinforcements were crucial in enabling the *carrancistas* to repel a determined *villista* attack on Agua Prieta. Second, President Wilson issued an arms embargo favoring Carranza. As Chief Bielaski informed his agents: The "President has issued embargo proclamation effective today prohibiting shipment munitions of war into Mexico in precise language of previous proclamation of 1912. President has also limited operation so as to exempt from the prohibition munitions consigned for use of recognized Carranza Government or for industrial or commercial uses except in Chihuahua, Sonora and Lower California. As to these States and territory embargo is complete [because Villa still operated in Chihuahua and Sonora and Colonel Esteban Cantú's situation in Lower California was unclear]. You are directed to take prompt and vigorous measures to enforce [the] law under this proclamation."[929] The State Department had requested the Treasury Department to instruct all collectors of customs at border towns to detain munitions intended for use in Mexico until further notice.[930] This put rival factions such as the *villistas* at an enormous disadvantage, for they were now reduced to smuggling.[931]

Sommerfeld, who had taken the pulse of the US administration for Villa, as well as Villa's negotiators at the conference, pushed the idea that something untoward must have happened. Even Scott noted in his memoirs that the decision "surprised him." Villa became convinced that Carranza had sold out Mexican sovereignty to the United States.

His suspicions were not unfounded. American envoy Silliman had approached him earlier in 1915 to request a commitment for leasing Magdalena Bay to the American navy in return for recognition.[932] A messenger from the head of the Mexican desk at the State Department, Leon Canova, even proposed to Villa in September 1915, that the US would require the right to name a *villista* cabinet in return for recognition.[933] The messenger turned out to be a German agent.[934] The reports Villa now received from his envoys contained no other plausible explanation for Wilson's abrupt change of foreign policy than a secret pact.[935]

Historian Friedrich Katz, the preeminent biographer of Pancho Villa, researched the existence of this secret agreement thoroughly. He found evidence that Carranza agreed to examine US claims for damages and that Speyer and Company had offered to support a new Mexican government with $500 million. Surprisingly, Katz still concluded, "There is no evidence that Carranza ever signed such a pact."[936] As a matter of fact, Carranza satisfied several more of the key concessions within months of recognition, allowing the conjecture that, albeit not in written form, a substantial understanding between Carranza and the Wilson administration had been reached before the formal recognition.[937] The embargo and a disastrous military campaign in Sonora in October provided the death knell for Villa's army. Villa disbanded the shattered Division of the North in November 1915 and retreated into the sierras, vowing revenge on the United States.

Now that the United States had recognized the Carranza regime the Bureau was again, as it had been with Díaz in 1911 and Madero in 1912, tasked with enforcing neutrality against the enemies of the Mexican government, only this time also keeping alert for any signs of Mexican-German cooperation. Most of what the Bureau did was to monitor what had become a torrent of munitions from the United States pouring into Mexico for the *carrancistas*.[938] The Bureau also paid greater attention to Carranza's efforts to become less dependent on the United States for munitions by acquiring the machinery for manufacturing rifles, cartridges and artillery shells.[939]

Broker Charles E. Jones, CRESSE, of New Orleans played a major role in this arms traffic, also handling the purchase of three airplanes from Glenn Martin for Carranza.[940] But Jones's ethics allegedly left something to be desired. The Carranza consul in New Orleans, Francisco R. Villavicencio, transacted considerable business with Jones, who intimated to him that he had influence with Agent Pendleton and had "fixed" matters for the Carranza government with the Bureau of Investigation. Villavicencio did not trust Jones, alleging that he used underhand methods to get business and had double-crossed Villavicencio on several occasions. The consul laid out his woes to Pendleton, who wrote to Chief Bielaski, "I desire to state that Jones has always been very courteous to me and seemed at all times willing to give me any information in his possession, although I have never felt that he was a man of much character. However, this is the first intimation that I have had that he has been using my name, and while I do not attach much importance to this matter, I thought it best to bring same to your attention at once, for your information."[941]

Not only were munitions pouring in for Carranza, but Villa's followers were pouring out of his sinking ship. Agent Stone at El Paso reported, "H. N. Gray, secret agent for Carranza consul at El Paso, called at office and reported that through efforts of himself and other Carranza agents, about 30 Villa officers at Juárez and Chihuahua had been paid about $1,500 each to switch from Villa to Carranza; that in view of the danger attached to their living in Juárez and Chihuahua after so switching, it was believed that these officers would come to the American side until such time as Carranza forces had obtained possession of territory in which they formerly served under Villa."[942]

American recognition of Carranza had broken the back of the declining *villista* movement.

12

War Crisis

During the spring of 1916, the Bureau engaged in assisting the de facto Carranza regime by interdicting munitions smuggling for Pancho Villa, who still held out in Sonora and especially Chihuahua. There Villa had convened a war council on December 23, 1915, at the Hacienda de Bustillos.[943] The fighting in Chihuahua resulted from the resistance of the villistas combined with the incompetence and corruption of the carrancista forces opposing them. And in yet another instance of the political "outs" combining, Villa wrote to General Emiliano Zapata on January 8, 1916, inviting him to bring his forces to Chihuahua so that within six months they could jointly attack the United States.[944] Operating from his base in the landlocked State of Morelos adjoining the Federal District, Zapata had been waging his own war against Carranza, as he had against Díaz, Madero, and Huerta. Villa's invitation begged the question of just how Zapata was supposed to march his peasant army across a thousand miles of largely Carranza-controlled territory to join him.

Villa hated the United States for having recognized Carranza, and he hated Carranza because he believed Carranza had sold out Mexico's national interests in order to secure recognition. Evidencing villista antipathy toward Americans, one of Villa's subordinates stopped a train in Chihuahua on January 10, 1916, and massacred eighteen American mining personnel. Villa himself thought about attacking El Paso, but some of his generals dissuaded him from such a foolhardy course. Instead, Villa attacked the New Mexico border hamlet of Columbus, thereby setting off a series of events that brought the United States and Mexico to the brink of war.

Columbus was the headquarters of the 13th US Cavalry, charged with protecting the New Mexico border. The raid was a kind of poor man's Pearl Harbor, much smaller in scale, but it was a complete surprise. It need not have been, for there were reports that Villa was approaching. Special Employee Harry Berliner later learned from W. W. Turney, a friend who was an official of the Mexico Northwestern Railway, that Turney had received word of the impending raid two days before it happened. Turney had immediately informed Zach Cobb, the collector of customs in El Paso, who notified the State Department that Villa, with some 400 men, was approaching Columbus. The *carrancista* commander in Ciudad Juárez, General Gabriel Gavira, warned that Villa was headed for the border and requested that the United States army be on alert for him.[945] And George L. Seese, an *Associated Press* correspondent, arrived in Columbus two days before the raid and informed the American commander, Colonel Herbert Slocum, that Villa was only ten miles from Columbus, and that he understood Villa was coming to present his case later to the government in Washington. Seese said Slocum laughed at him and asserted that his information was that Villa was at least forty-five miles from the border.

Much has been written about the Columbus raid, which occurred in the predawn hours of March 9, 1916, with Pancho Villa personally supervising the surprise attack which resulted in part of the town being burned, and ten cavalrymen and eight civilians being killed.[946] The 13th Cavalry quickly rallied, repelled the attack, pursued the raiders into Mexico, and inflicted an estimated one hundred casualties on the *villistas*.[947]

The Bureau immediately sprang into action. General Pershing notified Agent Stone in El Paso of the attack. Stone, in turn, asked Agent in Charge Barnes in San Antonio for instructions. Barnes wired Stone to "Proceed next train to Columbus." From there, Stone reported on March 10 that he was preparing to file criminal complaints against the six wounded *villistas* taken captive. One was a twelve-year-old-boy, whom he planned to use as a witness against the others.[948] He interviewed several American captives of Villa, who swore that Villa himself had supervised the raid. And he examined the valuable documents from the two large saddle bags recovered from the body of a dead *villista* officer. One was Villa's private bag and contained his official records and correspondence, including the letter to Zapata.[949]

Within days after the Columbus raid, Bielaski wired Superintendent Offley in New York on March 14: "Legal representative Carranza Government [Charles A. Douglas, Carranza's attorney] wires Felix Sommerfeld assisting Villa and suggest he be shadowed, and [his] effects examined for incriminating evidence. Please give Sommerfeld activities immediate attention and make best possible effort to see what he is doing." Offley stated that an effort would be made to secure the information desired by installing a Bureau agent in the Hotel Astor, where Sommerfeld maintained a lavish suite.[950] This effort by

Carranza's attorney to point the Bureau at Sommerfeld raises the possibility that the Bureau was being manipulated.

The Bureau did investigate Sommerfeld's connection with Villa by sending Agent Richard B. Spencer on April 10 to Alton, Illinois, to obtain the records of the Western Cartridge Company, which had been Villa's principal supplier of ammunition. What Spencer learned was that the last reference to Sommerfeld had been in August 1915.[951] Several Bureau field offices tried to locate Sommerfeld, but found no suspicious activity. As Agent Schmid asked, why did the Bureau not just interview Sommerfeld? It was not until May 5 that Offley reported to Bielaski that Sommerfeld was in the Hotel Astor.[952]

Perhaps the Bureau's seeming lack of interest in Sommerfeld's connection with Villa and Columbus was because the agency was enlisting Sommerfeld's help in something else—protecting President Wilson's image. Bielaski on March 18 informed Superintendent Offley in New York that he had just received information through Felix Sommerfeld that Francisco Bulnes, formerly a Mexican newspaper correspondent, had written a libelous book attacking President Wilson's Mexico policy.[953] The book was to be published in New York. Bielaski believed Sommerfeld could furnish more definite information, and he instructed Offley to interview Sommerfeld and make further inquiry as to whether the book violated Section 211 of the Federal Penal Code, as amended.[954]

Offley sent Special Employee Underhill to interview Sommerfeld at the Hotel Astor. Sommerfeld stated he had been told the book was to be published, and that an arrangement had been made with the Republican Party to use it for campaign purposes in the forthcoming presidential campaign, pitting Charles Evans Hughes against Woodrow Wilson seeking reelection. Sommerfeld added that he had recently learned that the book's English translation had been completed, and that the book was being printed in New York, but he did not know where. He did know, though, that the author's son, Mario Bulnes, had just arrived to handle the publication. Underhill reported that Sommerfeld thought he could get Mario's address for the Bureau, and in that way the Bureau could learn where the printing was being done.[955]

Underhill kept in touch with Sommerfeld. The latter said the book had not yet been in the hands of a printer, and he had devised a plan to get a look at the manuscript. Sommerfeld had located a friend of Bulnes's and had told the friend that he would gladly pay the cost of publication if the book were of value. The friend would discuss this proposition with Mario Bulnes. Sommerfeld was confident that in this way he would obtain temporary possession of the manuscript. He would keep the Bureau informed.

The next development was when Underhill took Sommerfeld to lunch at the Astor. Sommerfeld said he had seen part of the manuscript but had been unable to gain possession of it. Underhill perked up when Sommerfeld said he would mail him a copy of the table of contents and the index of that portion of the book dealing with Wilson's handling of the Mexican problem. According to Sommerfeld, the work would contain nothing libelous but would be a strong attack on the Wilson administration. Interestingly, Sommerfeld said that Theodore Roosevelt would give an answer within days as to whether he would write an introduction to the book, and even if he did not, he had promised to call attention to the book with a glowing review of it. Sommerfeld said he understood that the book was to be used chiefly for campaign purposes; the first 10,000 or 12,000 copies to be mailed to all congressmen, governors, and state legislators. In addition, a Catholic group headed by Fathers Kelley and Tierney would purchase a large number for distribution. To date, the only publisher approached was Appleton, and they had quoted a price of $3,500 for the first 10,000 copies, and $2,800 for every 10,000 copies thereafter. Sommerfeld ended his discourse by describing Bulnes as the most brilliant of Mexican writers and mentioning that he was now in Havana. The German did send by special messenger to Underhill the papers he promised, and Underhill turned them over to Offley.[956] Offley sent Bielaski a PERSONAL AND CONFIDENTIAL letter enclosing a copy of the book's index and table of contents in Spanish, furnished by Sommerfeld, who said Mario Bulnes was trying to conclude the arrangements for publication.[957]

The Superintendent instructed Underhill to maintain contact with Sommerfeld. The Bulnes matter went up to Attorney General Gregory, and that official instructed Bielaski to prepare a letter to the State Department about Bulnes and summarize what the Bureau had learned about Bulnes and his operation.[958]

Sommerfeld continued to provide information, saying that Bulnes was still in Havana, but little seemed to be known about him there. Moreover, Sommerfeld said he had proposed to Mario Bulnes that he might pay the cost of publication if the manuscript were reduced to pamphlet size. The German said he did this as a ploy to delay the publication.[959] The assistant Attorney General sent to Frank L. Polk, the Counselor of the State Department, the information about the book and its contents furnished by Sommerfeld.[960]

Bielaski wrote to Offley on May 22, referring to his letter of March 18 informing Offley about Sommerfeld and the book and instructing him to investigate. "I beg to advise you that I am unable to locate in the files of this office any report from you on this matter other than your acknowledgment of March 20. Please advise me what, if anything, has been done in the premises."[961] The Acting Chief of the Bureau wrote to Offley on May 23, regarding Offley's report of May 16 and accompanying enclosures about Francisco Bulnes. "Please endeavor to get a line on this man in the nature and extent of his recent activities as they affect the neutrality situation."[962] Underhill encountered Sommerfeld at the Astor in September 1916. Sommerfeld told him that a printing firm named Trow was engaged in printing the Bulnes book.[963]

The book was indeed published in 1916, titled: *The Whole Truth About Mexico: President Wilson's Responsibility*. The publisher in New York was "M. Bulnes Book Co." This raises the question of who financed the publication.

So, instead of locating and interrogating Sommerfeld about Villa and the Columbus raid, the Bureau focused on Sommerfeld and the Bulnes book. Not only was this a case of the Bureau acting for political purposes, protecting the Wilson administration, but it raises the question as to why. Perhaps the word had come down from a member of Wilson's cabinet—Sommerfeld had close relations with the secretaries of war and interior—to go easy on Sommerfeld, and Bielaski could cover himself by citing his March 18 instruction to Offley.

Columbus continued to be in the news. In response to the raid, the Wilson administration dispatched into Mexico the Punitive Expedition commanded by Brigadier General John J. Pershing. On March 10, the day following the raid, Major General Tasker H. Bliss sent the adjutant general a memorandum stating: "The President has directed that an armed force be sent into Mexico with the sole object of *capturing* [italics added] Villa and preventing further raids by his band, and with scrupulous regard to the sovereignty of Mexico."[964] The Expedition, which eventually numbered between 8,000 and 12,000 regulars, crossed into the State of Chihuahua on March 15. It had occurred to someone that if the Expedition was unable to capture Villa, the mission, by definition, would be a failure, so the order was amended to scattering Villa's guerrilla band and safeguarding the border. The presence of thousands of American troops on Mexican soil did call into question the "scrupulous regard to the sovereignty of Mexico."[965]

The Expedition, however, was based on a false premise: since Villa was the enemy of both Carranza and the United States, presumably Carranza would welcome American assistance against Villa. What the Wilson administration naïvely failed to grasp was that Carranza was an ultranationalist. He denounced the Expedition as an invasion of Mexico and demanded its withdrawal. He forbade American troops to use Mexican railroads or to enter Mexican towns. This disrupted the original plan for the Punitive Expedition:

to be based at Fort Bliss in El Paso, and to supply itself by using the Mexico Northwestern and Mexican National railroads. So, instead of El Paso being the base, the Expedition, of necessity, was based in Columbus and supplied by truck convoys. Since the army had few trucks, there occurred a crash program to acquire hundreds of trucks, manned by civilian drivers. As the army reoriented the Expedition, Bureau informant Kosterlitzky translated and furnished information about the Mexican attitude toward the American incursion.[966]

While the army was trying to get its act together, the Bureau was anxious to locate and interview people who had been on the ground during the raid, such as reporter George L. Seese.[967] The Bureau was also anxious to interview one Morris Nordhaus. Collector Cobb notified Bielaski that Nordhaus, a businessman from nearby Deming, had collected a quantity of souvenirs from the battlefield and planned to display them either in Chicago or Kansas City. The Bureau immediately launched a search for Nordhaus, seeking to interview him and examine the items for any possible intelligence value. Nordhaus was tracked down in Kansas City and interrogated. His souvenirs were impounded, and he did not recover them until 1917.[968]

In the aftermath of Columbus, the attorney general's office instructed Bielaski to have his agents cooperate fully with General Frederick Funston, commander of the Southern Department, and carry out anything he wanted. Barnes conferred with the general at Fort Sam Houston in San Antonio not just about Columbus, but also about the loyalty of Mexican refugees and native-born Hispanics.[969] Barnes then traveled to El Paso to direct operations in person. He conferred with the assistant US attorney, Mayor Tom Lea, and General George Bell, who had relieved Pershing at El Paso. Barnes also met with officials of Customs, Immigration, police, and the sheriff's departments. Not surprisingly, there was a roundup of known *villistas* in El Paso, many of them run out of town under the threat of arrest for vagrancy. General Bell was especially anxious to rid the town of Juan Medina, a former Federal officer who later became Villa's chief of staff and whom Villa had sent on a mission to Japan to negotiate an arms deal. Medina had traveled there with his longtime mistress, and General Bell demanded that Agent Pinckney file a white slave charge against him, which Pinckney was reluctant to do. The matter was resolved when Pinckney persuaded Medina's lawyer to have his client leave town voluntarily. Nevertheless, the US attorney authorized a complaint against Medina, and Pinckney was instructed to arrest him.[970]

Barnes reported to Bielaski that "if conditions do not continue to improve and the situation takes a turn for the worse, I anticipate that there will be in the United States along the border a large number of Mexicans who will be dangerous to the community and against whom there will be neither evidence on which to base a prosecution nor to cause their deportation. It has occurred to me that probably the only way they could be handled would be for the military authorities to hold them as a war measure. I have discussed this matter briefly with General Bell commanding the forces here and he expresses a dislike to be bothered with prisoners."[971]

Bielaski instructed his agents that, because of the delicate situation with Mexico, persons furnishing or attempting to furnish munitions, money, or aid of any kind to Villa should be arrested if evidence of probable guilt had been secured, without waiting to obtain evidence in complete form as under usual circumstances.[972]

Given Carranza's hostility toward the Punitive Expedition, the government also began taking precautions regarding the Carranza regime's military capability. Barnes telegraphed Agent H. P. Wright in Del Rio on March 23: "Desire prevent all shipments arms ammunition to persons in Mexico other than de facto government; shipment to de facto government should with assistance freight agents be delayed. These instructions *extremely confidential* [italics added]. Information indicates Thomas Hardware Company, Del Rio and Eagle Pass making effort secure large amounts arms ammunition."[973]

Even more important was preventing Carranza from acquiring the machinery to manufacture munitions. The secretary of state sent the secretary of war and the Department of Justice a CONFIDENTIAL letter on April 18 regarding a cartridge manufacturing plant being exported to the Carranza government. In 1915, the Bureau had learned that Consolidated Rolling Mills Company was selling to the Carranza government the components for a cartridge factory.[974] At the time, this was not particularly alarming. Now, with US-Mexican relations tense, the Bureau focused on Consolidated. Unfortunately, all but five machines had already been shipped. The State Department asked that the shipment of these five machines be delayed as much as possible.[975] The shipment was held up in New York City, and the Ward Line, which was going to transport the machines to Mexico, announced that it intended to return them to the consignors. The goods were stored in a warehouse in New York.[976]

The Bureau learned in May that General Salvador Alvarado, Carranza's governor of Yucatán, had ordered a large quantity of rifles and ammunition in New York. Bielaski wired Offley that Alvarado was rabidly anti-American and had tried to stir up anti-American sentiment in Yucatán and Chiapas. The Chief ordered Offley to "Take every precaution prevent shipment."[977] In June, the American representative in Mexico City sent a CONFIDENTIAL message to the secretary of state that the Carranza government had ordered from New York through a Spanish firm 35,000 kilos of potassium nitrate, and one hundred kilos of camphor to be used at the Santa Fe munitions plant in the capital.[978] Moreover, Western Cartridge Company of Alton, Illinois, which had been Villa's principal supplier of ammunition until his decline, had begun dealing with Carranza.

The Western Cartridge Company in June had contracted with the *carrancistas* for 5,000,000 cartridges. Because of the strained relations with Mexico, Western Cartridge cancelled the contract and returned the down payment.[979] Bielaski instructed Agent Breniman at Tucson to confer with the army and arrange to detain a shipment of 3,000 uniforms for Carranza. The uniforms were detained at Nogales, and customs would not release them without a direct order from Washington. The Chief also ordered that an investigation be made into all of Carranza's purchases of uniforms, canteens, blankets, etc., and how these purchases were financed.[980]

A disquieting letter the Bureau obtained was from J. H. S. [Siebert] to Hans Tauscher, 520 Broadway, New York City. "Enclosed please find photographs of all the Gun Making Machinery quoted you. The photographs for Cartridge Machinery will be forthcoming within a few days. When can you give me the particulars of the lathes, so then I can get quotation for you?"[981]

The Bureau thwarted yet another attempt by the Carranza regime to acquire munitions. A Burns Detective Agency operative notified Offley that the Mexican ambassador had hired Burns to locate the munitions the American army had seized during the occupation of Veracruz in 1914, with an eye to claiming them as Mexican government property. Through a confidential informant, the operative had located the munitions at the Brooklyn Navy Yard, and had so reported to his superiors. They instructed him to contact the Bureau and determine whether there was any objection to the ambassador being notified. If so, Burns would simply report to him that the munitions had not been located. This was done.[982]

In a quest to find out more about the mysterious cache of arms, Agent Cantrell contacted Felix Sommerfeld. The German agent related the history of two large caches of arms and ammunition. One, the Mexican government had supposedly bought in 1913. Huerta, through the Ratner brothers (his supply agents in New York) and the Russian-Jewish-Mexican merchant, Leon Rasst, had laid his hands on these supplies and shipped them to the border. The second cache passed through New York harbor in April 1915 on the SS *Monterrey*.[983] Based on a tip, customs officials impounded a large load of rifles, machine guns and ammunition, and stored them in the New York Navy Yard. According to

Sommerfeld, it was this cache that had been stored in the Navy Yard ever since Huerta's demise and belonged to the Mexican government. Sommerfeld also said that Leon Rasst tried to have the impounded shipment released. However, US authorities determined that the true owner was Abraham Ratner, who subsequently received the title to the arms.[984] Officials in El Paso tried to find out on May 12, 1915, who had received eight carloads of munitions, approximately matching the size of Ratner's cache. The *villista* secret service further confirmed that the consignment was not theirs.[985]

Like a bad dream, Leon Rasst once more crossed the radar of busy Bureau agents trying to discern who bought weapons and munitions for which faction in 1915. Apparently, Felix Sommerfeld, the munitions buyer for Villa, had contracted Rasst in April 1915 to handle orders for Villa with Remington Arms. Agent Cantrell reported in November that, unsurprisingly, a legal dispute had erupted between Sommerfeld and Rasst. Sommerfeld had apparently agreed to purchase 7-millimeter cartridges from a contract Rasst claimed belonged to the Russian government, and to which he had access. Sommerfeld made a substantial down payment. The ammunition Rasst delivered was not 7-millimeter Mauser but the much more widely available Remington 30-30 cartridges, a fact Cantrell confirmed with Remington's sales manager.[986] Sommerfeld, still cooperative and friendly at this juncture in the deal, managed to find a customer for the 30-30 ammunition and credited Rasst with the balance of the sale. That was his mistake. Rasst made off with Sommerfeld's down payment of more than $17,000 (approximately $357,000 in today's value).[987] The ensuing legal dispute lasted until 1918, ending with Sommerfeld failing to recover the $17,000.[988]

Rasst made Baltimore his permanent home in exile, buying a house where he lived with his wife and two children. But it did not take long for him to engage in new criminal enterprises. The press reported that Leon Rasst, representative of Russia, was present when the "Spanish-American Trading Syndicate" announced plans for manufacturing an airplane "with two six-cylinder sixty horsepower engines, which will give it enormous speed."[989] On August 10, the German-language paper *Der Deutsche Korrespondent*, reported that Leon Rasst, who for "28 years has been Russian consul in Pueblo [sic]," is planning to "build a factory to manufacture gun cotton, cartridges and other ammunition. The company, which he is running, is called the 'Spanish-American Trading Co.', and is incorporated in Delaware."[990] *Der Deutsche Korrespondent* found it "doubly regretful" in September that Rasst was not only building a munitions factory, but committed the high crime of converting an old brewery for this purpose.[991]

How did Rasst acquire the Mount Vernon brewery? A subsequent lawsuit brought by a certain Abbott Morris showed that Rasst had paid for the venerable building with worthless Carranza fiat money. Morris lost the claim in 1916, blamed by the judge for his lack of judgment when he accepted Mexican fiat money. The Maryland appellate court in 1918 found that because Rasst explicitly was not obliged in the contract to guarantee the value of the currency, Rasst legally owned the property with a lien to be paid sometime in the future. The judgment was upheld in the Maryland Supreme Court in 1922.[992]

Rasst shipped 636 cases (1,000 each) of 7-milllimeter cartridges to Galveston c/o the French consul in March 1916. According to informant Jorge Orozco, the shipment was destined for Félix Díaz.[993] The French consul claimed not to have any idea why he would be named in the consignment. He "knew Rasst only slightly [...] when [...] [he] introduced himself as the Russian consul and then explained that while he was not yet Russian consul here [Galveston], he would be in a short time."[994] Orozco understood the way Rasst conducted business. He informed Bureau Assistant Superintendent Baker, "I can compel Rasst to sell them to us for $46. Tell me if I can buy." Agent Chalmers explained, "Orozco is convinced that Leon Rasst sells ammunition to highest bidder [...]."[995]

Bureau agents hovered over the shipment after it had arrived in Galveston and sat on the Mallory Line docks. The new count was for only 500 cases. Rasst arrived in Galveston a few days later and the Bureau agents followed his every move. The investigation was so important to the Bureau that Superintendent Offley traveled to Galveston to direct operations.[996] Orozco's assessment was right on the money, as Rasst seemed to work on finding the highest bidder for his cartridges. Obviously, Sommerfeld was not one of them; neither were the Mexican consuls.[997] In the meantime, Bureau agents in Baltimore found out that Rasst had not only passed Carranza fiat money to the naïve Mr. Morris for his brewery, but that the money was counterfeit. The Bureau now consulted with the US Secret Service, who knew all about Rasst. US Secret Service Agent Captain Wright, who had arrested Rasst a month earlier, confirmed that Rasst had paid 299,000 pesos of counterfeit money to Morris for the brewery.[998]

Rasst seemed to have failed to find a way to smuggle the cartridges into Mexico. Bielaski alerted Agent Frank Garbarino in Philadelphia, on May 16, 1916, that Rasst's 500,000 cartridges were on their way there.[999] They arrived in June. Mysteriously, the additional 135 cases that had disappeared also appeared in the Pennsylvania Warehouse and Safe Deposit Co.[1000] This time, Rasst's shenanigans seemed to have caught up with him. In the process of moving the cartridges to Philadelphia, the boxes "had been damaged by water," and Rasst had neglected to insure them. He filed suit but lost.[1001]

After the Bureau thwarted the shipment of the 5,000,000 cartridges in 1916, Rasst did not occupy more investigative time for the Bureau. He applied for American citizenship in 1917, which was denied. In 1918 and 1919, Rasst appeared one last time in the Bureau's files. He informed the Bureau on "Bolshevists" having allegedly infiltrated his Russian Orthodox church community in Baltimore. The motivation behind Rasst's denunciations was a dispute between him and the orthodox priest.[1002] Rasst's wife, Elisa, died in 1919 and, despite claiming that he begged the Mexican government to return to his beloved second home, he remained firmly established in Baltimore until his death in 1923.

The Bureau cooperated with the Office of Naval Intelligence and with the Military Intelligence Department by the routine exchange of communications. And despite the legal prohibition against the military enforcing civilian law, the army on occasion made undercover personnel available to the Bureau to surveille suspected arms shipments. Another area where the Bureau cooperated with the army was with regard to codes.[1003] The army tapped *carrancista* telegraph lines in northern Mexico, even preparing a "Special Report on Tapping Telegraph Wires."[1004]

Intercepting telegraphic traffic was one thing; reading it was another. The army relied heavily on its few cryptanalysts, such as the overworked Captain Parker Hitt of the 19th Infantry, who besides commanding a company at Del Rio, spent many evenings deciphering Carranza codes.[1005] Fortunately, a wealthy businessman, George Fabyan, had at his estate at Geneva, Illinois, the Riverbank Laboratories, facilities to conduct research in subjects that interested him, such as chemistry, genetics, and cryptology. Among Fabyan's staff was William Friedman, who with his wife, would form the most distinguished team in the history of cryptology. Fabyan patriotically put the Riverbank Laboratories' code-breaking skills at the disposal of a grateful government.[1006]

The Bureau also had expertise in this area. Special Employee Victor Weiskopf, based at Presidio, proved to be an outstanding cryptanalyst. Weiskopf was "a short, stocky man with a crew cut and a pince-nez. He had immigrated from Bavaria when he was sixteen and had gone to Mexico. There he sold stamps, showed motion pictures from town to town, lost a valuable lead mine in the Mexican Revolution, and, after narrowly missing death when a sniper's bullet was deflected by a trolly wire, joined the Department of Justice as an agent in the Southwest. He solved a number of Mexican ciphers and, when war broke out, began working for MI-8."[1007] The assistant attorney general sent the secretary of war copies on June 9 of all the codes used by the various Mexican factions which the Bureau had obtained.[1008]

Relations between the United States and Mexico worsened because on May 5, raiders from across the Rio Grande attacked the isolated settlement of Glenn Springs in the Big Bend region of Texas. American troops pursued them for a time, in what became a little Punitive Expedition. And on May 9, not only were three additional regiments

Figure 74. *Victor and Bessie Weiskopf, June 1921*
Source: *Department of State*

of regulars ordered to the border, but the army cancelled its service schools and sent the students to the border. In another major development, the National Guard of Arizona, New Mexico, and Texas was called up for border duty and ordered to recruit up to wartime strength.

The Bureau's intelligence role was becoming more urgent. The army looked to the Bureau for assistance in acquiring intelligence about Mexican troop dispositions because the agency had experience in running undercover operations in Mexico, such as during the Plan de San Diego. Bielaski sent a circular letter on May 16 to all his agents: "The Treasury Department, under date of May 11, 1916, instructed collectors of Customs throughout the country to hold for the present all shipments, without exception, of munitions of war, including explosives, for Mexico, until authority for exportation is obtained from the Treasury Department. In view of the terms of the embargo on arms and ammunition now in force, which prohibits all shipments of munitions of war, including explosives, into Mexico unless excepted by the President, you will endeavor to keep advised of all shipments of this sort, with a view not only to preventing the crossing into Mexico of such commodities but to the end that all persons who succeed in doing so shall be vigorously prosecuted."[1009]

In accordance with the Attorney General's verbal instructions, Bielaski left Washington on May 17 for a tour of the border to confer with his agents and with the military "to ascertain what investigative work should be undertaken in addition to that which our limited force available for duty in Louisiana, Texas, Arizona, and New Mexico had been able to undertake."[1010] He submitted a comprehensive report on his trip to the attorney general on June 8.

Significantly, before Bielaski left Washington, Assistant Attorney General Charles Warren informed him that the secretary of state wished that while Bielaski was on the ground he would arrange to employ "such additional assistance as might be necessary to adequately handle the situation." Bielaski "was advised that any necessary funds therefore would be promptly furnished by the Secretary of State either in lump sum in advance or by transfer after the accounts involved had been paid by this Department [BI] as might be desired."[1011] State Department funding would make all the difference.

Bielaski arrived in San Antonio on May 19, and immediately conferred with Agent in Charge Barnes and the other agents there as to what points on the border needed to be covered constantly, "if the best results were to be obtained in the matter of learning of the activities of Mexicans on both sides of the border with respect to contemplated raids, violations of the neutrality statutes, uprisings of Mexicans in this country, military movements of importance in Mexico, etc."[1012] The following day, Bielaski conferred at length with General Funston and his intelligence officers, learning where along the border they thought special efforts should be made to secure information, what kind of information was desired regarding troop movements in Mexico, and where in Mexico they were particularly interested. Bielaski "found that the ideas of General Funston and his aides as to the points to be covered were almost identical with the views of our agents who have been engaged in this class of work."[1013] The areas of greatest interest were in the vicinity of Brownsville, where there were rumblings of renewed Plan de San Diego activity, and along the Arizona border.

Bielaski took with him to Texas from the Bureau's files a number of applications from those wanting to become special agents, who had investigative experience, and who were familiar with the border. He tried to vet the candidates to ensure that only those whose character, reputation, and qualifications especially fitted them for the work required were considered. In vetting the candidates, Bielaski conferred with the US Attorney and an assistant, the postmaster, the US marshal and a deputy, "and also made inquiries of various other government officials and representative citizens in San Antonio and vicinity."[1014]

The result was the hurried hiring of informants and special employees, some of them "old Mexico hands," to reinforce the special agents already on the scene. The following gives some idea of how the Bureau was deployed and the Bureau's comments about the special employees:[1015]

> San Francisco
>   Agent Don Rathbun
>   Agent Arthur M. Allen
>
> Los Angeles
>   Agent E. M. Blanford
>   Agent F. P. Webster
>
> San Diego
>   Local Officer Dave Gershon
>
> Tucson
>   AIC Charles E. Breniman (in charge of Arizona)
>   Special Employee William W. Neunhoffer
>   Texan
>   Spoke Spanish and German
>   Had attended the University of Texas for two years.
>
> Douglas
>   Position was being filled.
>
> Nogales
>   Position was being filled.
>
> Bisbee
>   Special Employee Arthur A. Hopkins. Was hired at $2.5 a day plus expenses.
>   39
>   Lived in Warren, a suburb of Bisbee
>   Spoke, read, and wrote Spanish fluently.
>   Served in US Volunteers during Spanish American War,
>   US Volunteers in Philippines.
>   Served five years in Arizona Rangers
>   Five years as a deputy sheriff
>   Had been a deputy US marshal

"Has assisted agents of this Department in a number of
  investigations."
"At present, a peace officer [deputy sheriff] at Bisbee
  but is able to devote a very large part of his time to
  the service of the Department."
Covered Bisbee and Naco.

El Paso
  AIC Steve Pinckney
  Agent Gustave T. (Buster) Jones
  Special Employee Edward B. Stone
  Local Officer Lloyd Fletcher (transferred from Amarillo)
  Special Employee C. E. Minck. Was hired at $4 a day.
    46
    Peruvian
    Spoke, read, and wrote Spanish and German
    Had worked in a Mexico City newspaper
    Bureau had employed him from time to time in Los
    Angeles in neutrality work among Germans and Mexicans.
    "Has rendered very satisfactory service."

  Special Employee Edgar W. Mebus. Was hired @ $3 a day
    39
    Spoke Spanish
    Over last 14 years was deputy sheriff, policeman,
      city detective in El Paso
    Had been a Bureau informant
    Was strongly recommended by assistant US attorney in
      El Paso
    Covered El Paso, Fabens, Clint, Fort Hancock, Sierra
      Blanca

Presidio
  Special Employee Victor Weiskopf. Was hired @ $4 a day
    Spoke Spanish and German
    Had lived and worked for many years in Mexico; had
      lived in Monterrey
    "If necessary, could go into Mexico and pass as a
      German." [since he *was* a German.]

Was a codebreaker; worked closely with the military
Covered the Big Bend

Sanderson, Alpine, Marathon, Marfa (on Southern Pacific Railway)
Special Employee C. A. Pederson. Was hired at @ $100 a month ($3 a day)
41
Languages: Spanish, Norwegian, Swedish, Danish, and some German
Served for years in US Coast Artillery
Operated a hotel
Worked in Mexico for years as a railroad employee

San Antonio
AIC Robert L. Barnes (in charge of Texas Division)
Agent Clifford G. Beckham
Agent Calvin S. Weakley
Agent Hyman Harris
Agent Willard Utley
Special Employee T. F. Weiss (transferred from Oklahoma City to El Paso)
NOTE: The San Antonio office had a translator, a Miss Lafon.

Del Rio
Special Employee John Jay Lawrence. Was hired @ $3.50 a day
40
City detective in San Antonio
$4\frac{1}{2}$ years Chief of Detectives in San Antonio
4 years deputy sheriff
Worked on and managed a stock farm
General merchandise business
Investigator for San Antonio Traction Company
"Seems to be an intelligent, trained man, and should be able to render satisfactory service."

Eagle Pass

Special Employee John Henry Lege. Hired @ $3.50 a day
38
Speaks Spanish
Worked in Mexico and Brazil
For four years investigator at San Antonio for attorneys
Knows many men working on trains in Mexico
Works more or less OPENLY

Special Employee William Adolf Wiseman - Lege's Assistant. Hired @ $2 a day
Had been employed by the army in Eagle Pass
Fluent in Spanish
Went to school in Mexico
Salesman
NOTE: Had been a special agent in Madero's "information service" [i. e. had worked for Sommerfeld]
At present—auto repair
Can't work full time but can get information on both sides of Rio Grande
Works UNDERCOVER

Rio Grande City
Special Employee Fred E. Marks. Hired @ $3 a day plus expenses while away
Druggist
Fluent in Spanish
Works UNDERCOVER
Was issued a badge and code book
Recommended by Special Agent Rogers
Covered Rio Grande City and vicinity

Laredo
Special Employee Thomas M. Ross
44
Speaks, reads, and writes Spanish with great fluency
Former Texas Ranger captain
Deputy sheriff
City marshal

Customs inspector
Recommended by US Attorney Green
Worked more or less OPENLY in connection with military and other federal officers.
Covered Laredo and vicinity
[Was fired for drunkenness]

Informant Clemente Nicasio Idar. Was hired @ $4 a day plus expenses
    32
    US citizen
    Speaks Spanish fluently.
    Can, if necessary, pass as a Mexican
    Had worked in Mexico City and elsewhere in Mexico as railroad employee.
    Debriefed passengers arriving by rail from Mexico
    Worked UNDERCOVER
    Deputy clerk
    Court interpreter
    Had brother working as brakeman on train between Laredo and Monterrey.
    Had brother working on train between Monterrey and Saltillo.
    Thus, can get information on troop movements, etc.

Brownsville
    Agent J. B. Rogers
        Covered Brownsville and Hidalgo on both sides of Rio Grande
    Special Employee William C. Chamberlain. Hired @ $3 a day, $3 a day for expenses
        Fluent in Spanish
        Member of Mexican Masonic fraternity [Stallforth and Madero were also members] whose head is Arnoldo Krum Heller
        Deputy marshal
        Army scout
        Formerly in Consular Service, in Mexico
        Deputy Collector of Customs

>   Bureau informant in Reyes conspiracy ("Proved to be very valuable in securing evidence when formerly employed by this Bureau.")
>
>   Was issued a badge and code book
>
>   Worked UNDERCOVER
>
>   Currently a Customs officer
>
>   Was able to work in Mexico as well as on this side of the border.
>
> Special Employee J. P. S. Mennet
>
>   Fluent in Spanish
>
>   Stenographer and interpreter
>
>   Read law for four years
>
>   Worked in Mexico for ASARCO
>
>   Still retained by ASARCO — excellent UNDERCOVER
>
>   Can travel in Mexico without undue danger
>
>   Communicates with Randolph Robertson and/or consul at Tampico if necessary
>
>   NOTE: Robertson's informant Juan Cisneros and Mennet will thoroughly cover the area General Funston is mainly interested in.
>
> Special Employee Manuel Sorola
>
>   Fluent in Spanish
>
>   San Antonio native
>
>   Public school education
>
>   Alamo Business College
>
>   Bookkeeper
>
>   Insurance agent
>
>   Railroad investigator
>
> Informant Juan Cisneros. Hired @ $2 a day, plus $20 a month for expenses
>
>   Was employed through Vice Consul Randolph Robertson, whose informant he was.
>
>   Mexican
>
>   Knows Plan de San Diego leaders de la Rosa and Nafarrete
>
>   Had "heretofore furnished considerable information, much of which, at least, is believed to be reliable."
>
>   Robertson had great confidence in Cisneros
>
>   Cisneros will report to Robertson, who will handle his compensation and expenses.

> Cisneros' reports will also be promptly transmitted to Agent Barnes
>
> Galveston
> > Local Officer J. L. Webb.
> > He is a well-known attorney
>
> New Orleans (Félix Díaz's intrigues and Máximo Rosales plotting a revolution in Honduras were the reason to hire more people for New Orleans.)
> AIC Forrest C. Pendleton
> Special Employee _____ Spencer
> Special Employee Elmer E. Stoy. Hired @ $4 a day
> 32
> Speaks Spanish
> "good education"
> Spent 6 years in the Marines
> Four years as streetcar conductor in Washington
> Five years as sanitary food inspector in Washington
> Worked in a similar capacity in the Canal Zone, Cuba, Honduras, New Orleans.
> Has many Central American acquaintances in New Orleans.
> (Bielaski was thinking of employing an additional man but had not found him.)

With the State Department providing unlimited funds, the Bureau now enjoyed a force multiplier effect. The agency could afford not just to hire special employees, but these special employees could now hire their own informants.[1016]

In Arizona, for example, Agent Breniman, who was responsible for the entire state, sent Special Employee Arthur A. Hopkins, the former deputy US marshal, his instructions:[1017]

> I enclose herewith copy of instructions recently issued by the Chief of this Bureau for your information and guidance in making investigations of Mexican Matters. Please advise me of your P. O. box number or street address where our office communications will reach you without being handled by

others. I may not have made myself clear when I advised you concerning your reports. It is desired that you send the original and two copies of your reports to Washington, in addition to one copy to the San Antonio office and one copy to me. I expect to be in Bisbee within a week or ten days and will confer with you."[1018]

Hopkins sought information from a variety of people, ranging from the foreman of a mine in Sonora to Francisco Elías, formerly consul general and Carranza purchasing agent in New York, who discussed conditions in Sonora. In his capacity as deputy sheriff, Hopkins also tracked down for the army a reported clandestine telegraph wire in the red-light district running from Douglas to Agua Prieta. He found "two sets of telegraph instruments connected by a wire running through the back doors [of two-room flats occupied by impoverished Mexicans]. They were operated by ordinary small cell storage batteries, producing little power. It was manifest they could not be used for the purpose reported." He so informed Captain M. O. Bigelow, the Intelligence officer.[1019]

Figure 75. Arthur Alva Hopkins
Source: Hopkins Family Tree Ancestry.com, viewed February 2024

Hopkins continued to reopen old and open new channels of information. The sheriff of Cochise County had one of his informants also report to Hopkins. J. Lozano Pérez had been the Carranza consul, and later the Villa consul, at Naco. Hopkins noted that "This is the same man whom I arrested two years ago in company with H. M. Martínez, W. H. Brophy, and the Phelps Dodge Co. for conspiracy in an ammunition case and who plead guilty at Phoenix and paid a fine. His record should be on file in the Bureau, and as I will be reporting considerable information from this source believed the Bureau should know all about him."[1020]

Hopkins next informed Breniman that he had spoken in Douglas with Mateo Ortiz, who had worked in the office of the Mexican consul general and purchasing agency in New York. Ortiz had just arrived from New York on his way to Mexico City, saying that the purchasing agency had been closed and that most of the Carranza government's purchasing was now being done in California. Hopkins had also talked with H. Rivera, a wholesale merchant in Douglas and contractor for the Mexican government. Two years ago, Hopkins had arrested him for conspiracy in connection with ammunition shipments. Rivera told Hopkins confidentially, not knowing of his Bureau connection, that General Calles was not getting any arms and ammunition, that it was impossible to do any business in contraband any more as the present embargo was very effective, and that he personally would not take a chance on smuggling. The difference was that Anglo merchants would not sell munitions or help cross them as they did several years earlier. In view of this, Calles was making no effort to cross contraband.[1021]

Accompanied by a captain of the 14th US Cavalry, Hopkins checked conditions in Naco, Arizona. He also checked Naco, Sonora as well as Bisbee, Lowell, Warren, and San Luís generally for Mexican matters. He also conferred with Breniman. Hopkins reported on the disposition of Mexican troops in northern Sonora from Nogales to the Chihuahua state line, based on information received from several Americans and from his informant, J. L. Pérez. He shared this information with the military and was pleased to report that his information agreed with theirs.[1022]

Agent Breniman went from his Tucson headquarters to Douglas, where he conferred with Captain Bigelow and informant B. M. Pacho, who operated there, reporting on troop strength at Agua Prieta.[1023] Barnes had wired Breniman to "Please make special effort secure all available information concerning distribution and troop movements in Mexico along border. Will endeavor send you another man day or week. Advise whether Mexican informants are giving you their information direct. Reports [are] rather indefinite."

Breniman replied, "Mexican informants mail reports directly to me. I have them read before mailing you for translation. Have instructed informants along lines you refer to. Am doing best possible with them. I am constantly in communication military, Customs, Immigration authorities. All state nothing unusual in situation. Reports all agree about eighteen thousand Mexican troops northern and western Sonora but apparently not active." Breniman mentioned informants Juan Ortiz and Juan Echegaray, who did not know each other and whose information could be cross-checked. Breniman received Ortiz's reports, and he had secured Barnes's authorization to hire Echegaray for not less than $10 per day for ten or fifteen days. Echegaray would be sent to Tucson, where Breniman could keep an eye on him and report on his activities. The agent then sent Echegaray, who was well acquainted with Mexican military affairs, to visit all military camps in northern Sonora and report on conditions. The informant had specific instructions as to what information was desired, and Breniman was confident of getting useful results. He informed Barnes that he would make the best possible arrangements to keep expenses low, but Echegaray would cost more than the expenses for an ordinary informant. Hopkins translated Echegaray's reports, copies of which went to Captain Bigelow.[1024]

Special Employee William Neunhoffer at Tucson handled informant Cirilo Ibarra and took over as informant Juan Ortiz's case officer. He received, translated, and forwarded their reports.[1025]

Bielaski arrived in El Paso on May 21, and the following day conferred with General George H. Bell. The general "has been considerably worried by the frequent rumors and reports which have reached him concerning unneutral activities in the vicinity of El Paso and stated to me that he believed at least three of our agents should be kept at El Paso without interruption solely for this class of work."[1026] Bielaski so arranged.

The Chief stated that "in addition to keeping in touch with all activities on this side of the border, each of the various men has been instructed to secure all available information with respect to military movements in Mexico or other activities in that country which may be directed against this country or its citizens." Furthermore, "Should the conditions along the border grow more serious, we will be in a position to undertake for the army without delay and with a reasonable prospect of success the securing of any detailed information desired from Mexico. All the arrangements made are temporary in character and may be terminated in whole or in part at any time."[1027] Bielaski ended his report to the Attorney General by writing: "Some other matters respecting border conditions which came to my attention during this trip should, I believe, be discussed with you, but I think should, at least at this time, be communicated to you verbally."[1028]

Anxious to improve the Bureau's intelligence capability in El Paso, Bielaski had authorized Barnes to employ up to three informants. Barnes tried to find a Mexican informant who could be trusted.[1029] To his relief, State Department officer George Carothers, who had been attached to Villa, recommended an informant who had been doing confidential work for him and whom he thought could be valuable to the Bureau. Barnes instructed Stone to interview the possible informant, Colonel Dario Silva, who had previously been on Villa's staff. Silva was about twenty-six years old, had been educated in New York City, and spoke English as well as German. Not only that, but Silva was one of the original eight who had followed Villa in March 1913 when he slipped out of El Paso to take up the fight against Huerta.[1030] Barnes interviewed Silva and was impressed with the man's intelligence and his *villista* connections. He notified Bielaski that he had personally hired Silva, who was to receive expense money, his salary to be determined by the value of his information.[1031] To safeguard Silva's identity, Barnes informed the Chief that he gave the informant the creative cover name of AVLIS ("Silva" spelled backwards).[1032] Another instance in El Paso of a Bureau informant's cover name being his name spelled backwards was Tomás Rodríguez—SAMOT.[1033]

Although Barnes considered Silva to be a real prize, the Agent in Charge in El Paso, Steve Pinckney, disagreed. Nevertheless, Barnes asserted his authority and made Pinckney Silva's case officer. Silva delivered not only information about *villista* activities, such as Juan Medina's mission to Japan, but also insights into Villa's character.[1034] The informant provided a great quantity of information, but much of it was couched in vague terms. An exasperated Pinckney commented that "AVLIS is not a worthy informant. He has been instructed time and again to be able to state explicitly the sources of his information, to secure names etc. when asked from time to time; he is seldom able to state things exactly, saying 'Some man whose name I don't know told me so.'"[1035] Pinckney's skepticism had reached Bielaski, who wired Barnes asking whether he had made any effort to check AVLIS's reports, and if he considered AVLIS reliable. If this had not already been done, Bielaski ordered that the informant's movements immediately be checked closely for a short time. However grudgingly, Barnes instructed Pinckney to investigate Silva's reports.[1036]

Pinckney sent Barnes a PERSONAL AND CONFIDENTIAL message regarding Bielaski's telegram. "As you will recall, I stated to you before your leaving El Paso that I had no faith whatever in this informant. You did not agree with me as to his reliability and in taking him over to handle after your departure I dismissed from my mind all suspicion I had of the man and continued from day to day to meet him and report such information as he tendered. However, after several days I was again forced to reassume my first opinions of the man. Upon receipt of the telegram above referred to, I set about to check up this man as nearly as practicable."[1037]

Pinckney's particular concern was that Captain Robert E. Grinstead of Military Intelligence, who was unaware that Silva was working for the Bureau, had been telling Pinckney that one of his informants observed Silva in the company of suspicious Mexicans, and believed he was involved in revolutionary activities. Pinckney decided to test Silva by giving the *villista* captain specific assignments and having Grinstead's people cover his movements. When Silva reported back to Pinckney the following day, the agent realized Silva was lying. Just to be sure, Pinckney repeated the procedure, with the same results.

A triumphant Pinckney informed Barnes that "AVLIS lied totally. I feel that most of the information he has reported during the past two or three weeks was worthless. On Monday I will discontinue his services unless you instruct otherwise. If you want a detailed report of the two days' cheating of him, I will be happy to send it." A mortified Barnes wired back, "Dismiss informant AVLIS."[1038] The affair was a painful reminder that informants' information should be corroborated.

Bielaski met with Agents Frank Garbarino and T. J. McGee at El Paso. who had been sent from Philadelphia to work undercover and assist Stone and Pinckney.[1039] Garbarino registered at the Paso del Norte Hotel under the name of "Frank Greenwood," and McGee presumably also registered under an alias. Garbarino worked on securing relevant telegrams from Western Union, hoping to learn more about the Columbus raid. He cast a wide net, including among others Mayor Tom Lea, Sam Dreben, William Randolph Hearst, Pancho Villa, Felix Sommerfeld, Archbishop José María Mora y del Río. It was a long slog, given the number of persons of interest and the volume of telegrams going through the El Paso office.[1040]

Garbarino and McGee met Special Employee Harry Berliner, whose cover story was that he was going to Mexico to look over some land.[1041] In fact, Berliner's life had taken a most unpleasant turn. The attack on Columbus briefly ripped Harry Berliner away from his comfortable New York City routine when Bielaski had sent him to the border to investigate. Since Berliner was fluent in Spanish, a valuable commodity within the Bureau, he made the rounds in El Paso, offering refreshments and talking to friends and acquaintances. When Garbarino and McGee met him, he was under cover as a real estate investor and considered a *felicista* by people in the know in the Mexican exile community.

Sent to Columbus to investigate several Mexican residents suspected of complicity in the raid, he was dismayed to learn how few of the amenities he was used to were available in that village now transformed into an important army post. To give some idea of the housing situation, the post commander, Lt. Colonel Charles Stewart Farnsworth, described to his wife the shack he was renting for $5 a month; it lacked a porch, closet, running water, and toilet.[1042] Accompanied by a deputy US marshal, Berliner made the rounds of movie houses, dance halls, and the red-light district. He also collected evidence against the suspected residents, but ultimately the prosecutor was decided that the evidence was insufficient, and the matter was dropped.[1043] Thankfully, Berliner's time in purgatory was brief. He returned to El Paso after a few days, then on to San Antonio and back to his beloved New York City and his comfortable routine.

Berliner had encountered Charles Francis Louis Zeilinger Caracristi, a "fellow" *felicista*, when checking into his El Paso hotel. It is unknown whether Berliner and Caracristi had locked horns in the past and over what. Since both were part of the *felicista* faction, it is not hard to imagine that Caracristi, known to be bombastic crook, genius and international celebrity in his own mind, would have had a confrontation with Berliner, the straight-shooting Bureau agent who thoroughly despised pretentious megalomaniacs.

While previous confrontations are not documented, Harry Berliner's disdain for the man surfaced in the chance encounter. Berliner wrote, "He saw me, I looked him straight in the eye as he went past and into the hotel; he ripped out an oath which was intended for me; I returned the compliment. He did not take it up but continued on in towards the desk of the hotel where he asked the clerk something. I was right on his heels. Caracristi then stepped over and spoke to the manager of the hotel, I all the time looking at him. He evidently told the manager something about

Figure 76. *Harry Berliner at the Border*
Source: *Courtesy Kristin Rounds*

me, as they both looked at me. I took out the key to my room to show him I was stopping in the house, so as to let him know where he could find me if he wanted me. He tried to get the girl at the telegraph desk to show him a wire I'd received. He left, and as I had to meet [Agents] Stone and Minck in the room over in the federal Building I had to leave. I asked [Agent] Pinckney if the files had anything about this crook Caracristi. He said there was and got the file out and handed it to me as an assignment, which in due course will be fully covered under separate report."[1044] Clearly, there was no love lost.

Caracristi continued on his path of deluded craziness. He contacted the German consul in Richmond, Virginia, in October 1916, representing himself as a key player in the Mexican Revolution and offering to join the German cause.

> It might be well for some duly accredited agent to see me [...] as I have been the really big factor behind Mexican events for the past five years [...]. You probably do not know that underground diplomacy has been my business for over 20 years and that much that has happened in Latin America during that period, including the Panama Canal, has been due to my work. I will under no circumstances discuss international matters with underlings such as the consuls along the Mexican border. Of course, you know where I stand. I am an Austrian first, last, and always—a fact I have never told in the US, but this is confidential. It might be well for you to see the ambassador and suggest to him that he send me some person of his confidence from Washington [...]. [signed] C. F. Z. Caracristi.[1045]

Caracristi was next heard of in 1917, when he may have briefly become involved in German intrigues, most likely an expendable resource for the Albert office, since at that time, the spring of 1917, Germany had resumed unrestricted submarine warfare, and the Zimmermann Telegram had surfaced. Caracristi was in New York's Ansonia Hotel and contacted a Félix Díaz representative, W. E. D. Stokes, with an offer for "10,000 Winchester carbines with 70,000,000 [rounds of] ammunition [...] 20,000 Mausers and say, about 2,000,000 cartridges." Stokes, who owned the Ansonia, had him watched closely.

Instead of considering the offer, Stokes turned the information over to the State Department. Robert Lansing correctly assumed German intrigue. Indeed, Tauscher and the German military attaché's office were selling their stockpiles before the expected entry of the US into World War I. Caracristi seemed eager to assist, for a sizeable commission, one could assume.[1046] He found the attention he so much craved.

The State Department promptly stripped Caracristi of his citizenship. He appealed but to no avail. He did, however, receive permission to reside in New Mexico. While living in Las Cruces, he continued to spin his endless yarns, even trying to run for the US Senate.[1047] He tried to get mining engineering jobs, but to no avail. He published a book on mining in Venezuela in 1919.[1048] Now an expert on Venezuelan oil, he eventually moved to his new hunting ground, where no one remembered his checkered past, and perhaps even admired the fantastic stories he undoubtedly continued to spread. He died in 1942 in Venezuela. While C. F. Z. Caracristi remains a minor actor in history books covering his era, his niece Anne Zeilinger Caracristi upheld the honor of the family name. She became a celebrated codebreaker and cryptanalyst during World War II and deputy director of the NSA in later years.[1049]

The Bureau continued to introduce technology to gather intelligence. Pancho Villa's second wife, Juanita Torres Villa, passed through El Paso from Los Angeles on her way to Cuba, where Villa's first wife, Luz Corral Villa, was residing along with Villa's brother, Hipólito. Mrs. Villa No. 2 was accompanied by her brother, Zenaido Torres. Agent Barnes instructed Stone to bug Mrs. Villa's room in the Detroit Hotel. Unfortunately, she never left her room, so the best Stone could do was to install a "Holliday Detecto, an instrument similar to the dictograph," in her brother's room. Evidently, they learned nothing of importance.[1050] By the way, this was not some sort of rogue operation. Chief Bielaski himself approved the use of the Detecto device.[1051]

Agents Stone and Pinckney went to the elegant Paso del Norte hoping to eavesdrop on an important meeting in the hotel, where exiled General Luis Terrazas had a suite, with guards at the entrance and at the elevator. Reportedly, Terrazas was meeting with prominent *felicistas*, *científicos*, and *orozquistas*. Major Laubach of Military Intelligence had secured a room on the same floor and was trying to monitor the proceedings. He counted thirteen Mexicans waiting in the hall for admittance. The Bureau agents examined two rooms adjoining the Terrazas suite to determine if a dictaphone could be successfully installed, and conversations from the suite overheard. The rooms looked favorable to Stone, and he said so to Pinckney, for he was experienced with dictaphones and that sort of work. It is not known whether the bug was installed.[1052]

Chief Bielaski met three times at El Paso with Harry Berliner.[1053] The latter was working undercover, having been in San Antonio in early May. There he had registered at the Menger Hotel, and had contacted Barnes, who came to his room and gave him his instructions. Berliner was his usual convivial self, looking up acquaintances from his days in Mexico. One was Captain William A. Burnside, who had been the military attaché. Berliner had gotten to know him during the Decena Trágica. Mainly, though, Berliner was "dangled," circulating in hotels and offices, inviting men to "refreshments" and cigars, intimating that he was a follower of Félix Díaz and open to illegal suggestions. Berliner would call at the Bureau office and dictate his reports.[1054] At El Paso, Berliner also made the rounds of the hotels and clubs. He ingratiated himself with Frank Thayer, who had business dealings with Villa. He and Thayer enjoyed refreshments in the café of his hotel, then lunch there, discussing the ammunition trade. Berliner also looked up his friend the Mexico Northwest Railway official, for information about the Columbus raid.[1055]

It was Special Employee Edward Stone in El Paso who was recruiting and dispatching confidential informants into Mexico. One was José "Joe" Solanos, whose assignment was to observe and report on troop disposition along the railroad from Juárez to Torreón.[1056] On the recommendation of the local Immigration authorities and with Barnes's approval, Stone recruited a Japanese informant, Hidekichi Tuschiya, code name FRANK and designated JAF. Stone's arrangements involved sophisticated tradecraft. Tuschiya, using the alias of "Y. Shinuya," sent his reports to a fictitious Japanese in San Antonio, "S. Tamagi," in care of General Delivery. The reports were written in code, in Japanese, in invisible ink with a letter written over them, to be read by heating the paper. Stone apprised Barnes of these arrangements. At the request of Barnes, who was to be FRANK's handler, Stone sent him a photograph of FRANK and a sample of his handwriting. Tuschiya's mission, beginning on June 27, was to travel from Ciudad Juárez through the city of Chihuahua to Eagle Pass observing troop dispositions and strengths, and report in San Antonio to Barnes.[1057]

During the Plan de San Diego unrest in 1915, Stone had broached the idea of having the Plan's leaders killed and their heads delivered in a sack on the bank of the Rio Grande. Now, on June 13, Stone interviewed two Japanese-Mexicans as possible informants. He discussed the idea with a certain Gemichi (Gustavo) E. Tatematsu, who claimed to have been the personal servant of both Pancho and Hipólito Villa. As proof of his connection with the Villa family, Tatematsu provided a letter and a postcard to him from Hipólito's wife, Mabel S. de Villa, in Havana. Stone also interviewed Tatematsu's partner, Lucas G. Hayakawa, until recently an informant for Military Intelligence at El Paso.[1058] Stone's superior, Agent Barnes, forwarded the proposal to the Chief. Bielaski was cautious, wiring Barnes: "Referring again your telegram fourteenth two Japanese have original letters photographed checkup informants work carefully and ascertain everything practicable concerning reliability which will not prejudice their work for us."[1059]

Stone conferred with the army and secured permission from Immigration for the Japanese to travel in the United States; these officials agreed with Stone that the project was a gamble, but a gamble worth taking. As Stone put it, "their connection and relations with Villa family and their friends are such as to enable them to obtain important confidential information from these sources. In the event they attempt double-cross us, it is a case of weighing our wits against theirs and detecting their duplicity."[1060]

Barnes authorized Stone to employ Tatematsu and Hayakawa, their per diem and expenses to be decided. Hayakawa remained in El Paso for the time being and spied on Carranza troop dispositions in the Juárez area. Tatematsu, wearing glasses and attired in a navy-blue suit, white straw hat, and white shoes, was advanced $100 and dispatched to Los Angeles to work with Agent Blanford, for Hipólito Villa was reportedly going there upon his return from Havana.[1061] Tatematsu informed Blanford that Hipólito Villa had not arrived in Los Angeles, and the Japanese provided additional information about Hipólito's plans. But, Blanford reported, "his replies to questions indicate to me very clearly that he would not give any information against his country or countrymen." Since Tatematsu did not know any of the Japanese in Los Angeles, the Chief directed that he and Hayakawa be used on the border or in Mexico.[1062] Stone was happy to use the Japanese in that capacity, reporting on troop dispositions and on general information from Mexico.[1063] Tatematsu was given the code designation of JAT. Hayakawa was JAH. (The system was: "JA"—Japanese, and first letter of informant's surname.)[1064]

Stone launched an operation in conjunction with the local army intelligence officer. He dispatched Tatematsu and Hayakawa to the city of Chihuahua, their cover story being that they were couriers entrusted with important messages from Hipólito to Pancho Villa. Interestingly, Stone had discussed with Hayakawa "the matter of capturing Villa alive and delivering him on the border to agent; the matter was also taken up of whether or not Villa could be delivered dead, on the border, if same was requested. Agent gave him no instructions whatever in this connection but merely put this proposition up to him view a view of seeing what could be done by them towards capturing Villa if the Department would authorize such action through this office."[1065] Despite his disclaimer, Stone was amenable to having Villa killed. He sent copies of his report to Bielaski and to General Bell.

Armed with letters from Hipólito Villa and villista General Manuel Ochoa, Agent Stone's two Japanese informants arrived in Chihuahua on the afternoon of September 15 and checked into a hotel. As luck would have it, Pancho Villa launched a surprise attack against Chihuahua in the early hours of September 16. The Japanese fled from their hotel over the rooftops. To their great relief, they encountered a *villista* patrol, displayed their credentials, and were escorted off toward Villa's headquarters. Unfortunately, the group ran into a sizeable *carrancista* force and were captured. Jailed as *villistas*, the Japanese managed to rid themselves of their incriminating *villista* letters by stuffing them down a sewer pipe. When interrogated by their captors, they pretended to speak only Japanese, and by September 20, both had been released.[1066] Hayakawa returned to El Paso, while Tatematsu continued the mission and left for the village of San Andrés, Villa's headquarters at the time.

Stone was doubtless intrigued when his agents Tatematsu and Hayakawa reported that there were Japanese peddlers from the State of Chihuahua in Pancho Villa's entourage—Tsutomo Dyo, K. Fuzita, A. Sato, and T. Suzuki. It turned out that the Punitive Expedition's Intelligence section had developed its own network of informants, in this instance settling, as did the Bureau, on Japanese because they could openly interact with both the *carrancistas* and the *villistas*. The difference was that the Punitive Expedition's Japanese had the mission of assassinating Pancho Villa. They evidently tried to poison him, but the plan miscarried (and Villa lived until he was well and truly assassinated in 1923.) The failed attempt resulted in a hurried and successful cover-up by the army. In a noteworthy development, Agent Stone contributed to the cover-up. After speaking with General Pershing, Stone submitted an amended report on February 17, 1917, stating that the Japanese had concocted the poison story out of whole cloth.[1067]

Stone lied, of course. His informant Gustavo Tatematsu had reported to Stone that on September 24, 1916, a friendly *villista* soldier at Santa Isabel had told him that

> some Japanese, a group of four, had attempted to poison General Villa, the latter was now enraged against all Japanese and had threatened to kill any he met. This friendly Villista told me this in confidence and warned me to escape before it was too late. I replied that as I had come as a messenger from Hipólito Villa, I wished to see Villa anyhow and believed that this fact would ensure my personal safety. My friend told me, however, that might be all right at a later date but that in Villa's present mood, he thought an interview would be

> extremely dangerous no matter what claims I might make with reference to myself.

Tatematsu continued to Torreón, gathering intelligence.

> I intended then to proceed directly to El Paso but when I got to Chihuahua, I found the Japanese residents there in great alarm because of the fact that they had learned of General Villa's recent threats towards Japanese.
> While I was engaged in giving what assistance I could in connection with the situation, I ascertained that about ten Carrancista secret service men were investigating my recent actions and weaving a net about me on suspicion that I was aiding the Villistas. To forestall probable apprehension and execution I obtained an interview with General Jacinto Treviño through the assistance of Mr. Scooichi Ishikaroa [sic], the President of the Japanese Chihuahua Association and obtained his assurance as to my personal safety but only on condition that I proceed immediately to the United States accompanied by Mr. Ishikawa [sic] and promise not to return to Mexico.[1068]

Tatematsu arrived in Juárez on October 21 and reported to Stone.

A sequel to Agent Stone's employment of Tatematsu and Hayakawa was that as of May 1917, Tatematsu was living at Hipólito Villa's residence in San Antonio. When brought to the Bureau office for questioning, "he refused to make any statement regarding the actions of the Villa faction, claiming that there was nothing of importance taking place in their circles. He also claimed that his object for being in San Antonio was to secure money from Villa in order to start a produce business." Barnes had Tatematsu turned over to the Immigration Service, who had been looking for him for violating his parole.[1069]

During the war crisis, the Bureau was also dealing with the Carranza intelligence service.[1070] In May, that service was reorganized, bringing the consuls under a central authority. The foreign minister appointed twenty-nine-year-old Jesús María Arriola, an experienced agent, as the "Chief of the Mexican Secret Service in the United States." His assignment was to compile information about the United States military, evaluate the agents attached to each consulate, establish a central headquarters, and develop regulations for the intelligence service. The Carranza administration ordered its consuls along the border secretly to secure intelligence regarding US troop dispositions, lines of communication, strategic points, bases of operation, etc.[1071]

As Arriola embarked on his assignment in the United States, the Bureau of Investigation kept him under surveillance.[1072] Traveling under his own name, Arriola was trying to recruit operatives and distribute a new code to the consuls. Things went awry at San Antonio. One sympathetic historian remarked, "As the result of uncharacteristic carelessness and a lapse of judgment on Arriola's part, one of Barnes's men in San Antonio acquired a copy of the new Mexican code."[1073] It seems that Arriola and an associate, one Eneas Levi, were on a double date with some fast women when Arriola got drunk; Levi picked his pocket, purloined the code, and delivered it to the Bureau.[1074]

Then at El Paso, Arriola tried to recruit Charles E. Minck, a man who had lived in Chihuahua and with whom Arriola was acquainted. But unknown to Arriola, Minck was a special employee of the Bureau and had been assigned to cover him. Arriola showed Minck a telegram signed by the Mexican Minister of Foreign Relations empowering Arriola to completely reorganize the Carranza intelligence service on the border. Having unburdened himself of this sensitive material, he offered Minck the position of working for Carranza intelligence as chief of station at either San Antonio or Los Angeles. Minck reported all this to his superior, Agent Stone, who was, of course, delighted. Stone instructed Minck to play along with Arriola while he apprised Barnes of the matter. Barnes, too, was enthusiastic and approved of Minck appearing to accept Arriola's offer. Minck wrote to Arriola at San Francisco stating that by July 1 he was ready to accept Arriola's offer.[1075] But for reasons unknown, Minck never became an agent of Arriola's.

As for the Mexican spymaster, he had continued on his journey, still under surveillance in Naco, Tucson, and Douglas. When Arriola arrived in Nogales, Agent Neunhoffer and a deputy sheriff waited until he was away from his hotel and

> entered this man's room and took a look at the contents of his suitcase. His papers showed that he was the chief of the Carranza Secret Service. He also had notes which appeared to be information from American informants. I thought it would be best to look this man over and took him to the customs house for examination, calling in an army officer. Arriola presented his commission from Mr. Arredondo and also had letters from Chief of Police Fred Lancaster in San Antonio, Texas, and Special Agent [sic] Tom Ross of Laredo, Texas. While we

were detaining this man I called Special Agent Breniman over long distance telephone, and he advised me that he had examined this man earlier in the day and found nothing against him. Arriola left today for Tucson, stating that he would go to San Francisco, Calif.[1076]

Arriola's apologist writes that "Hostility and suspicion limited the willingness of North American officials to cooperate with the Constitutionalist intelligence operatives," citing as an example that in October 1916, Bureau agents detained Arriola in Phoenix, "treated him with open disrespect, searched his personal belongings, ransacked his room, and seized copies of the new regulations" [...] "The written reports of North American agents clearly reveal the suspicion and low regard in which they held both their Mexican counterparts and the government they represented."[1077] Perhaps they were sending a message. Since the United States had come perilously close to war with Carranza, there was little comradely feeling toward his minions. This attitude was reinforced during World War I, when Carranza's policy was one of pro-German neutrality.

Arriola's problems were not confined to United States authorities. He engaged in a vicious quarrel with the Mexican consuls, who resented having to give up their autonomy in intelligence matters. Arriola's nemesis proved to be Andrés G. García, the Inspector General of Consulates, who orchestrated a campaign of vilification that resulted in Arriola's being dismissed on September 7, 1917.[1078]

El Paso was a center of clandestine activity, but farther down the Rio Grande, at Eagle Pass, Special Employee John H. Lege took a trip to Mexico in March 1916, about which he reported directly to Chief Bielaski. Lege's lengthy "Conditions in Mexico" report covered military, economic, and political matters, and was based on personal observations from the border to Mexico City and on information obtained from Mexican contacts. Overall, Lege painted a grim picture of conditions, and he noted that the Mexican army lacked heavy artillery, and that Carranza was having trouble paying his troops.[1079]

Special Employee J. J. Lawrence at Del Rio worked closely with the army, reporting on Mexican troop dispositions in his area.[1080] Lawrence was also investigating one José Zertuche, suspected of planning a villista expedition to attack the Carranza garrison across the river at Las Vacas (Ciudad Acuña). By unspecified means, Lawrence obtained papers that Zertuche had left in the safe at a local hotel. The deputy collector of customs, an army lieutenant assigned to Intelligence, and Lawrence went through the papers until after midnight. Lawrence was elated, for there was enough evidence to file a criminal complaint, which Lawrence did after returning the incriminating papers to the safe. A deputy marshal arrested Zertuche, who, unable to post $2,500 bail, was jailed. Lawrence sent Zertuche's effects and all the papers on his person at time of arrest to Barnes in San Antonio. And, not coincidentally, more than half of the group of unknown Mexicans, who had gathered in Del Rio, left precipitously.[1081]

Special Employee Adolph Wiseman, who was working undercover at Eagle Pass, made several trips into Mexico and reported directly to Chief Bielaski on conditions there.[1082]

Carranza was engaged in brinkmanship. On May 22, he sent a strongly worded note demanding the withdrawal of the Punitive Expedition, repeating the demand in a blunt note on June 2. He also massed some 30,000 troops in northern Mexico.

The Bureau's sense of urgency increased. Agent Barnes sent a circular letter to all special agents, local officers, special employees, and informants on June 9, supplementing his previous instructions: "It is desired that in the future all information of value concerning troop movements, locations, etc. be immediately given to the nearest commanding officer of the United States troops. It is further desired that you specifically state in your report that this has been done, furnishing the name of the officer to whom you have given the information."[1083]

What particularly concerned the Bureau was the situation in the lower Rio Grande Valley. As noted, within a week after Carranza's recognition on October 19, 1915, all Plan de San Diego raids into Texas ceased. The Plan's leaders had no alternative but to remain in Mexico at Carranza's pleasure. And Carranza kept them under surveillance in case they were ever needed again. Now they were. In his unyielding demand that the Punitive Expedition be withdrawn, Carranza reverted to the strategy that had been so successful in 1915; that unless the Punitive Expedition were withdrawn, serious unrest would break out in South Texas. The reemergence of the Plan de San Diego supported by the Carranza government was a cause for concern.

An effective Bureau operative in South Texas was informant Manuel Sorola, who on April 27, 1916, became a special employee. Sorola, a San Antonio native, had managed the Prudential Insurance office in El Paso.[1084] He worked undercover among Hispanics as an insurance salesman, and was equipped with two commissions that the San Antonio field office had forged for him. One commissioned him as a major in the Plan de San Diego forces, the other as a major in Villa's army. The latter commission was purportedly signed by Pancho Villa himself, but the forger had been sloppy and had signed it not

"Francisco Villa," but "Francis Villa." Fortunately for Sorola, he did not have to use the commission, but it served as an example of the kind of carelessness that gets secret agents killed.[1085] Agent Barnes in San Antonio handled informant GALED [Juan Rodríguez], who reported on Plan de San Diego leaders and on Pablo Burchard, German consul in Monterrey, who allegedly assisted them.[1086]

Vice Consul Randolph Robertson at Monterrey forwarded reports of Plan recruiting going on in the State of Tamaulipas. On his tour of the border, Chief Bielaski arranged through the State Department to confer several times with Robertson concerning the possibility of securing information about conditions in the vicinity of Monterrey, Saltillo, Linares, Ciudad Victoria, Tampico, Camargo, and Reynosa, as well as the contemplated raids against the United States and military activities directed against this country. Information was desired especially on the activities of Pizaña, De la Rosa, and General Nafarrate, "believed to be the leaders of the plan of San Diego."[1087] Robertson, a member of the State Department's Bureau of Secret Intelligence, had been supplying the Bureau with information for years, even when he was just the clerk of the federal court in Laredo.

Figure 77. Manuel Sorola
Source: FBI Media

Hampering coordination between the Bureau and Robertson was American consul Alonzo Garrett in Nuevo Laredo. As an angry Chief Bielaski recorded,

Consul Garrett in Nuevo Laredo is characterized by our agents in Texas as the most indiscreet person imaginable and utterly unfit for this reason for the position which he holds. It is stated that he devotes nearly all of his time to drinking and talking. Recently when arrangements were made for Vice Consul Robertson and one or two men from Mexico to meet agents of the Department at Laredo, Garrett apparently told everybody in the two towns of the proposed meeting. Vice Consul Robertson on June 2 indicated to Agent Barnes, of this Department, that indiscriminate remarks of Consul Garrett had caused the fact of Robertson's conference with Barnes to become known to Mexican officials and made it somewhat dangerous for Robertson to return to his post.[1088]

Robertson's informant Juan Cisneros had become too well known in Nuevo Laredo to operate there. He was sent into Mexico through Brownsville to learn troop dispositions on the railroad from Matamoros to Monterrey, then from Matamoros to La Jarita, back to Monterrey, then to Piedras Negras, where he would cross into Texas and report to Agent Barnes in San Antonio. Barnes informed the Chief of the plan, adding that "I spent practically the entire day questioning this informant and am somewhat more favorably impressed with his information than heretofore. I did not have available at the time that he left anyone who could be sent into Mexico to follow him, but if you desire will arrange to do this when he next comes to US."[1089]

The situation escalated. Plan de San Diego militants and units of the

Figure 78. Robert Lee Barnes, May 1919
Source: Department of State

Carranza army were massing along the lower Rio Grande. Plan de San Diego raids into Texas began on June 12. Raiders struck near Brownsville on June 16, then retreated back across the river. But the US army's rules of engagement had changed; cavalry pursued the raiders across the Rio Grande, and infantry units began crossing as reinforcements. The Mexican garrison in Matamoros slammed into reverse. Having made their point, the Americans withdrew back across the river the next day.

It was this clash that caused President Wilson on June 18 to take the unprecedented step of calling up for federal duty virtually the entire army National Guard, some 150,000 men. By July 31, nearly 111,000 of them were deployed along the border, ready to support the regular army in the event of war with Mexico.[1090] The United States suspended all munitions shipments to Mexico on June 19.

The National Guard mobilization was the main event. It was related to but distinct from the Punitive Expedition, which by comparison was a sideshow. Nevertheless, the Expedition faced its own threats. There was a Mexican troop buildup east and west of the American forces, raising the possibility that the plan was to cut the Expedition's supply line to Columbus. In addition, Carranza ordered that the American incursion was to be resisted if it moved in any direction but north back to the United States. General Pershing decided to test this ultimatum on June 21 and sent two troops of cavalry to the hamlet of Carrizal, east of the Expedition's lines. The Americans launched a frontal attack against superior *carrancista* forces and suffered a disastrous defeat. This clash seemed to be the beginning of a full-scale war.

Immediately after the Carrizal clash, the State Department requested the Department of Justice to stop all code messages between Mexico and foreign countries.[1091] The Bureau arranged for censorship over all telegraphic communications coming in or going out of Mexico. Following up their telephone conversation, Superintendent Offley sent Chief Bielaski a PERSONAL AND CONFIDENTIAL letter enclosing the report of Special Employee Underhill, who had spoken with the top officials of Western Union. They told Underhill that the only direct means of cable and telegraph communications between the US and Mexico went through Western Union, with most of the Mexican business coming over cables from Veracruz and Coatzacoalcos to Galveston. There were four important landlines running from Mexico City to Laredo, Eagle Pass, El Paso, and Douglas. There were also small lines into Brownsville, Naco, Nogales, and into California at Imperial and Tijuana.

The only other method of sending messages from Mexico into the US was to relay them from Tehuantepec to Colón in the Canal Zone and then by

Central and South American telegraph cable to New York City. Western Union made it clear that the company would cooperate with the government to the utmost to protect national security in the present emergency, and it requested that the government provide the censors. Underhill not only submitted a report, but included maps showing how in case of war, Mexico could be isolated from communication with Europe by cutting the cable running down the west coast of Central and South America. At Offley's instruction, Underhill also learned what cable lines connected the Pacific coast with the Far East.[1092]

The United States on June 25 sent Carranza an ultimatum demanding that he repudiate the attack at Carrizal and immediately return all the American corpses, prisoners, and government property captured with them. The next day, President Wilson drafted a speech and a resolution to a joint session of Congress. Although he declined to use the word "intervention," he asked

> that the President be and is hereby authorized and empowered to use the military and naval forces of the United States in any way that may be necessary to guard the southern frontier of the United States most effectively, if necessary to enter on Mexican soil and there require the entire suspension in the Mexican states which touch and border upon our own, of all military activities of every kind on the part of the Mexican authorities and people until by the establishment of a responsible and effective political authority among themselves they are prepared to resume and meet their full obligations towards us as a neighboring and friendly state.[1093]

The Mexicans probably would have considered the United States army suppressing all Mexican military activities in its northern tier of states a warlike act.[1094]

Faced with imminent catastrophe in a disastrous war with the United States, Carranza folded. He abandoned his belligerent attitude and complied with the American ultimatum. He also shut down the Plan de San Diego, this time for good. The war crisis abated, and a joint US-Mexican commission met at New London, Connecticut, to deal with outstanding issues. The most obvious source of controversy was the continued presence on Mexican soil of the Punitive Expedition.

The FBI and American Neutrality, 1914-1917

13

Trust is Good—Control is Better

War with Mexico had been averted, but the United States kept its guard up. Agent Breniman at Tucson asked Barnes, "Do you advise discontinue services Mexican informants?" Barnes replied, quoting a telegram from the Chief: "Advise Breniman Department thinks situation still requires unusual vigilance and that sufficient informants should be kept in service to enable us to learn of any dangerous action in addition impossible anticipate when emergencies may arise and result new developments."[1095]

The New York office of the Bureau was most interested in the matter of the Consolidated Rolling Mills & Foundries Company, and the whereabouts of the machinery and supplies for the plant that had not yet left the United States.[1096] Bielaski impressed on Superintendent Offley in July that it was important for this information to be secured at the earliest possible time "in order to prevent further shipments of this sort."[1097]

The company was in a serious bind. The president, Harry Wright, informed the secretary of state, that Colonel Alfredo Breceda had had a tough conversation with their Mexico City representative. According to Breceda, Consolidated had not fulfilled its contract entered into on December 14, 1914, to supply the machinery, install it in the national cartridge factory, and leave it in operation. Obeying superior orders, the colonel was now filing a suit for breach of contract. He required a complete inventory of machinery and materials in the Mexico City shops, copies of transactions and contracts the firm had, not just with Breceda, but with railroads and the public in general. Furthermore, Consolidated would abstain from making any further transactions without previously obtaining the consent of Breceda, the purchaser.

The company argued that all of the machines sold under this contract had been delivered to Breceda's representative, Rubén Mier, a lieutenant who had graduated from the Chapultepec Military Academy and was the son of a general. Any machines which had not yet been shipped were being held by order of the Department of Justice. If Consolidated's plant were seized, as Breceda was threatening, it would be a rank injustice and the fault of the Justice Department. Wright asked the secretary of state to take action to prevent such a seizure, which would result in the loss of over $1,000,000 invested in the plant and in an irrevocable loss of reputation.[1098] The State Department informed the Carranza administration that Consolidated should not be penalized for non-shipment of the machinery because the collector of customs in New York was holding the machinery (at the New York Dock Company, Brooklyn) solely at the instance of the State Department.[1099]

Agent J. W. Kemp called at the New York Dock Company and learned that on May 22, several boxes of cartridge brass and machinery from Consolidated were stored there for Ward Line shipment to Colonel Breceda, marked "A. B." Six boxes were delivered on August 29 to Mexican representative Rubén Mier, 120 Broadway. There was nothing in storage at the Dock Company, and no information on file as to what disposition Mier made of the boxes.[1100]

Bielaski sent Offley a letter from the State Department dated October 21 that information had been received that the machinery that the Bureau had ordered to be held up, in fact had been smuggled into Mexico piece by piece. The Chief ordered Offley to "Please make immediate investigation of this matter, going direct to Mr. Harry Wright, president of the company, for verification or disapproval of the allegation."[1101] Offley dispatched Agent Kemp to interview Harry Wright again. Kemp reported:

> I contacted Newton D. Wright, 25 Broad Street, who said Mr. Wright is at the factory near Stamford, Conn.; that as stated on a prior occasion the responsibility of Consolidated ceased upon delivery of said machinery to said representative and nothing is known about its disposition. Newton D. Wright appeared to be surprised to know that the machinery had been taken out of the warehouse of New York Dock Company. He said that Rubén Mier, mentioned in preceding reports, has not been seen for about two months. It is thought that Mier has left the city. Mier, it seems, succeeded Colonel Breceda, financial representative of the Carranza government, who placed the original order with Consolidated.[1102]

Offley had dropped the ball. An angry Chief Bielaski wrote to him:

It is very much regretted that the leads in this investigation were not promptly followed up. Because they were not, it appears the cartridge manufacturing machinery, the exportation of which it was desired to prevent, has apparently got away from us. It is not unlikely that it has been, in some manner, smuggled into Mexico piece by piece as alleged. It was necessary to write to you under date of July 31, 1916, calling attention to the fact that Mr. Wright's promise that he would verbally supply specific information when desired, if seen personally, had not been, but should be followed up; and again on September 23 it was urged that special effort be made to get a list of machinery held up at the New York Dock Company which, it was stated in Special Agent Kemp's report for August 3 would be furnished if possible. In his report of September 26, 1916, Mr. Kemp states that certain of this machinery was delivered to Rubén Mier, of 120 Broadway, who was one of the Mexican representatives in New York, and he concludes that 'if it is thought of sufficient value to determine' the disposition of the machinery, 'it appears that Mier himself is about the only man left to see.' There is no reason why this should not have been promptly followed up and Mier interviewed, in view of the requests for action from this office above referred to, and the reports of Special Agent Cantrell in November 1915 indicating unneutral connection for this company. In this connection, it appears that Mr. Cantrell's reports were not followed up, and the matter was taken up again only after the receipt of my letter of April 22, 1916.[1103]

Agent Kemp on November 14 in New York interviewed Howard D. Hodge, one of the consulting engineers for Harry Wright who had passed upon the plans for the cartridge manufacturing plant. Hodge had recently been told by Rubén Mier, whom he had seen within the last three or four days, that the machines had been sent out of the country. He said that a *carrancista* representative was in New York to purchase more cartridge making machinery and was dickering with Harry Wright for the purchase of the machinery itemized in a recent report of Kemp's.[1104]

Offley wrote to Bielaski:

> Referring to the recent reports in this case, please advise me whether you consider it proper that we should endeavor to locate and interview Mier who as you know, is closely connected with the Carranza consulate or, failing in this, whether we should call upon and request information of the General [Álvaro Obregón, Carranza's Minister of War] as to the whereabouts of the missing machinery. I have hesitated to adopt this course until I can ascertain whether you consider it advisable to openly approach any person directly connected with the Mexican government or its diplomatic representatives.[1105]

Offley reported that a Customs Service official had advised him that a shipment of thirty-one cases, consigned by the Oceania Hardware Co. of New York, to its order at Galveston with instructions to a steamship company to notify Rubén Mier at Galveston. The Oceania Hardware Co. was undoubtedly fictitious, and Assistant Division Superintendent Baker conveyed the above information by telephone to the Chief suggesting that the shipment be located and examined.[1106]

Informant SEMAN (J. García) elaborated further on the matter. He had made a trip through Brownsville and Monterrey to Mexico City from November 9 to 30, and gave a breakdown of garrison strength from Laredo to Mexico City and at the capital itself. He also reported on railroad conditions and on the national munitions factory, where he noticed several boxes of machinery stamped "Gobierno de México, Veracruz," from New York. Maximiliano Koch, manager of the factory, said he purchased the machinery in New York in January 1916, and that between him and the broker they had cleared $500 each. Koch claimed the broker and the Ward Line saw to it that the machinery was delivered to Veracruz. Koch claimed the factory's output was 100,000 cartridges per day. Through Francisco Cantú Lara, a Carranza official friend of his in Mexico City, SEMAN attended a banquet for the diplomatic corps, and inspected the arsenal. He also saw four monoplanes and five biplanes in very good condition. Ten more were under construction. Two young men named Salinas were at the head of the factory. He was told they had studied in the United States.[1107]

Agent Clifford G. Beckham wrote from New Orleans that he had noticed a local newspaper article under a Houston dateline of December 16, 1916, to the effect that R. Mier had been vindicated in Houston of charges of fomenting a Mexican revolution, but was being held under a $1,000 bond on a charge of false billing growing out of the shipment of 1,000,000 rounds of ammunition as "corn mill machinery parts" from New York to Galveston. "The foregoing item purported to grow out of an announcement made by US Attorney Green at Houston."[1108]

Superintendent Offley was also investigating the proposed sale to Carranza of the machinery for a $600,000 factory to manufacture rifles. J. T. Mullany informed the Bureau that he was negotiating the sale with Jorge U. Orozco, the colleague of Francisco Elías, the Carranza purchasing agent in New York. Mullany showed Special Employee Underhill an elaborate set of blueprints for the proposed factory, which would produce 300 7-millimeter Spanish Mausers per day, "complete except for bayonets." Mullany asserted that he had seen a letter from General Obregón authorizing Orozco to negotiate for the factory.

A nervous Mullany called Superintendent Offley to his office and explained confidentially that his negotiations with the Mexican government had reached a point where his proposal had been approved by Jorge Orozco, with whom he had been negotiating for some time. Orozco, however, lacked the authority to close the contract and asked Mullany to take the contract to Mexico City and arrange the details with General Obregón, who would actually sign the document. Mullany said Obregón would insist on delivery of the machinery in Mexico, but Mullany would not proceed unless the State Department and the Department of Justice understood and approved the situation. He said it would take from three to six months to complete the machinery, which had to be specially made.

Offley said he would submit the matter to Chief Bielaski with the request that Mullany's approach to the Bureau be kept secret. Mullany needed a quick answer. Offley stated that "It is evident that he is anxious to secure this contract, if possible, but at the same time I feel satisfied he will abandon the effort if he believes there will be objection upon the part of the United States."[1109]

Mullany and his attorney went to Washington to try to persuade the State Department to make an exception in his case. Bielaski also consulted with the State Department, informing Offley to "Advise Mullany State Department at this time would decline to make exception to embargo in favor of contemplated shipment but see no reason why he should not continue negotiations, keeping us advised, pending future developments."[1110] Offley notified Mullany, who "informed me that it will be impossible for him to go further with the negotiations in this case as he has reached a point where the Mexicans have insisted that he either sign the contract or abandon the negotiations."[1111]

Offley met in December with Mullany, who said that he had been advised by his counsel, following a conference with Solicitor Polk of the State Department, that Mullany would not be furnished with a US passport, but that he should secure a safe passage through General Obregón, and following the receipt of the same, visit Mexico City and sign the contact for the cartridge-making machinery, advising the State Department of his departure from this country. Mullany would travel to Mexico through Laredo. He also informed Offley that he believed much of the ammunition going into Mexico was taken there from Spanish ports and not from the US. Mullany promised to keep the Bureau apprised of any developments.[1112]

The State Department's permission for Mullany to sign the contract is noteworthy, because a month earlier, in connection with the proposed shipment to Colonel Cantú in Baja California of a cartridge manufacturing machine, the assistant attorney general had informed Albert Schoonover, US Attorney at Los Angeles:

> Replying to yours of October 19 regarding our reply to Messrs. Wright, Womack, and McKee as to the propriety of a contemplated shipment by their clients of a cartridge manufacturing machine to Lower California, this Department is advised by State Department that it is important that the shipment to Mexico at this time of such articles of machinery should be prevented and that the War Department has been consulted and concurs in this view.[1113]

The Bureau remained interested in weapons manufacturing machinery. A person of interest was Jorge Orozco, who in 1914 as Carranza consul in El Paso had been tried and acquitted of violating the neutrality laws.[1114] Orozco had an office in New York and was a purchasing agent for Carranza. Special Employee Underhill had an informant, Vera Feinberg, in the office of the sixty-two-year-old John H. Siebert.[1115] John Henry Siebert, a first-generation German immigrant, brass worker and chandelier maker, used knowledge of metalworking to establish a lucrative brokerage of munitions manufacturing equipment.[1116] Siebert worked closely with Hans Tauscher, who helped source manufacturing equipment for US companies willing to commit to manufacture munitions for clients other than the Allies.

Feinberg reported that Jorge Orozco had asked her to find him a Spanish-speaking stenographer. Underhill mentioned this to Agent Kemp, who promptly recruited Rosita Micheloni, a young Uruguayan woman of Italian ancestry. An accomplished stenographer who had worked in the Uruguayan minister's office in Washington, she had taken out her first citizenship papers. Kemp called at her home and informed her of the stenographer job opening, delicately hinting that she could be of great value to the government by keeping the Bureau informed of Orozco's transactions. Under the guise that she was a friend of Miss Feinberg, it was arranged for Orozco to interview Micheloni. She got the job, resigning from her current employment, which, coincidentally or not, was with the Mexicans publishing the Bulnes book.[1117] According to Feinberg, Orozco placed implicit trust in Micheloni, which made her feel guilty about betraying him.

Micheloni continued to report on Orozco's business dealings, but with increasing difficulty.[1118] Orozco had become suspicious of the young lady and watched her every move. She reported, "Mr. O seems to be suspicious even of the air and I must act with the utmost circumspection." Orozco even listened in on her telephone conversations.[1119] After working in this hostile workplace environment for two months and reporting on Orozco's business dealings, Micheloni called the Bureau office and informed Underhill that she could learn almost nothing for the Bureau. She resigned her position with Orozco.[1120] A promising operation had ended in failure.

There was excitement on the border. Military Intelligence agents in Nogales, Arizona, heard rumors of two Germans planning to smuggle an airplane "equipped with bombs and other devices [...]" into Mexico for Carranza. Military Intelligence asked Agent Blanford to "give immediate attention" to the matter.[1121] The principal person of interest was one Richard "Ricardo" Schwierz, a German army captain who spent considerable time in and around Los Angeles. Beginning in October 1915, the Bureau had opened a file on Schwierz, and the reports had gone all the way up to Bielaski.[1122] Now, there was a sense of urgency in learning what Schwierz was up to, for he was rumored to be involved in smuggling an airplane into Mexico. Indeed, he was. The Carranza consul in Los Angeles reported that "two German naval lieutenants, one of them named Schwierz," had offered to work for the Carranza government as pilots with a monoplane they owned. Their offer was rejected.[1123]

Blanford assigned informant Emilio Kosterlitzky, the colorful former Mexican colonel, to the case. Kosterlitzky was a natural choice of investigator since he personally knew the suspect. He immediately went to work and interviewed Schwierz's landlady, who said he had left without a forwarding address.[1124] The Bureau could not locate Schwierz in Los Angeles, but only a few days later he turned up in Nogales, where Bureau agents had him arrested on July 5 on suspicion of violating the arms embargo.[1125]

Schwierz made alarming statements when the agents interviewed him. He volunteered that he had been in the German army and had participated in the defense of Kiao Chow, China; had escaped from there prior to its capitulation, made his way to Manila, then got on a freighter to San Francisco. Since his arrival in America, he had been active in secret service work for the Mexican authorities and, for a time, was attached to the staff of General Obregón as an advisory engineer. He had been recently employed by the Mexican consul in Los Angeles for service with the Mexican army, was primarily engaged with thirty other Germans to operate the railroad between Nogales and Guaymas, but got little encouragement from its owners, and later demonstrated his ability to produce asphyxiating gas and liquid fire.[1126] But Schwierz's story changed every day that he was under arrest. When interviewed by Immigration Service agents, he admitted to being a German secret service agent with a mission to organize a German battalion in Mexico to attack the United States. The "thirty Germans" he had claimed to organize earlier in the week now turned into 400, or even 600.[1127] He also claimed to have been a sabotage agent and part of the team trying to destroy the Welland Canal.[1128] That was a brazen lie.

Figure 79. Emilio Kosterlitzky
Source: FBI Media

Most frustrating and embarrassing for the Bureau agents was the fact that the German boasted of his grandiose career as a secret agent for the Emperor not only to the agents, but also to local reporters. Even more frustrating, several days later, on July 12, 1916, while in the custody of a deputy US marshal, Schwierz escaped. The invisible international boundary in Nogales ran down the middle of the street—Schwierz had merely sprinted into Nogales, Sonora, leaving behind a dumbfounded deputy marshal.[1129] The sensational claims of Schwierz appeared in the national press days later.

The Carranza consul in Los Angeles furnished additional information about Schwierz, advising that a German had offered to deliver ammunition monthly in Sonora. Apprehended in Nogales, Arizona, he had escaped and joined, as a military instructor, the command of General Eugenio Martínez in Hermosillo, Sonora.[1130] Schwierz, meanwhile, claimed that General Plutarco Elías Calles, the military governor of Sonora, who was pro-German (or more accurately anti-American, which led to German sympathies), welcomed the expertise of such a professional soldier, conferred the rank of major on him and assigned him as an instructor.[1131]

The investigation into the elusive Schwierz continued for months. Agent Gershon in San Diego discovered a house in Coronado, the peninsula protecting the San Diego harbor, which Schwierz, using the name "Schwind," had rented earlier in the year. The German gave the Masonic Temple in Tacoma, Washington, as the place to forward his belongings and mail. A search of the apartment produced evidence of Schwierz and the Mexican consul Enrique A. González working together.[1132] The Bureau in late July received information from Sonora indicating that Schwierz might be on his way by ship from Mexico to San Francisco, possibly to continue on to Washington state.[1133] He was not. A few weeks later, agents learned he might cross into Nogales, Arizona, by automobile. That tip also failed to materialize. The agents looking out for him had received differing descriptions of Schwierz: "5'- 8," dark hair, small dark mustache, 28 or 30 years old, about 165 pounds," was one description.[1134] Another was "5'-7," 135 pounds, 28 years old, black hair and eyes, short black mustache."[1135] The Bureau finally secured a photo of Schwierz.[1136]

This man, whose real name was Victor Schwierz, born in Marne near Hamburg in 1869, was well into his mid-forties in 1916. Schwierz's claim to have been stationed in China seems to have been true as there is a Captain Schwierz in the German East Asia Detachment listed in 1903. He was a staff officer and interpreter in Tientsin.[1137] Captain Schwierz is listed as discharged from active service when the German East Asia Detachment was dissolved in 1909.[1138] On July 24, 1909, a certain Victor Schwierz, age forty, arrived in San Francisco from China and Japan. He is the only person with the name Schwierz to have appeared in California immigration records in the period of interest. Victor Schwierz appears again in the city directory for Hamburg between 1938 and 1940 as a retired colonel, indicating that this may indeed have been the true identity of the mysterious Richard "Ricardo" W. Schwierz.

Interestingly, while he was based in Hermosillo, Sonora, Schwierz maintained a friendly correspondence with his "old friend," Emilio Kosterlitzky, who translated the letters written in German and delivered them to the Los Angeles field office. For example, Schwierz recounted that he and two other German officers had invited General Calles as their dinner guest. Since Calles had banned liquor in Sonora, the Germans were complaining about their thirst for beer; Calles graciously provided two crates of the beverage. To preclude any criticism, Schwierz and his companions guzzled their beer in a backroom with an orderly barring entry. This gave rise to a rumor that the Germans had been imprisoned. Schwierz also mentioned that he was organizing Calles's forces on the "German plan" [German military doctrine] and was in charge of German colonization in Sonora.[1139]

In his next letter, Schwierz chortled:

> I see by the papers from Los Angeles that I am accused of having had criminal correspondence with the Mexican Government, that I formed a poison gas corps, a foreign legion and German colony and now am chief of a revolution in Lower California, three aeroplanes smuggled, etc. Nobody home in the Gringo noodles [...]. If you see me mentioned in the papers, please send me the clippings, I enjoy those things hugely and serves [sic] me as a distraction for I am working very hard, nightly up to one A. M. and often the whole night. Next week I go to Kino Bay riding a Mexican horse, the American horses can't stand the long ride; when I return will go to Mexico City, getting new armament, munitions and provisions; don't worry [about] us, we have lots.[1140]

Not only did Kosterlitzky know Schwierz personally, but his daughter Emmy had been in a romantic relationship with the German. Schwierz commented on his relations with Kosterlitzky's daughter: "Mrs. K. wrote me that Emmy advised her to notify me that this month she would marry and that was enough for me, so I returned to her the medallion she gave me and that settles it for I won't be made a monkey of by women and I would thank her if she would return the music book to me. I regret to write you this but repeat, if a woman wants to fool me, she must look up someone else."[1141] Kosterlitzky commented to Agent Blanford in 1917 "that when he found what Schwiebs' [sic] intentions toward his daughter were, he broke the matter up."[1142]

The investigation into Schwierz continued well into 1917, when he did consort with notorious German sabotage agents who had gone to Mexico from the United States. Historian Jamie Bisher accords Schwierz full credit as a German agent with the rank of major, who "simultaneously worked with German and Mexican intelligence."[1143] The sources for this assessment and the quoted Mixed Claims Commission report mention him as "Major Schwierz of the Mexican army," and "a major in the Mexican Army."[1144] There is no evidence to link Schwierz to secret service missions into Canada as he had claimed, especially not the extensively investigated attacks against the Welland Canal and Valcartier. The voluntary and public pronouncements of Schwierz as to sensitive clandestine work for Germany when arrested in Nogales seem to discredit his story, or at the very least, his professionalism. Bureau agents in Nogales reported on Schwierz "usually being drunk."[1145]

Conceivably, personal motivation could explain Kosterlitzky bringing to the Bureau new evidence, including personal correspondence, and clearly pushing for Schwierz's arrest. Whatever inducement, the Schwierz matter sent the Bureau on an extensive wild goose chase in the middle of a war crisis. However, events in 1917 and 1918 (covered in volume 3 of this series) showed that Schwierz was a conman who harbored a dangerous and hostile attitude towards the United States, validating Kosterlitzky's dogged pursuit of the man in 1916.

Of immediate concern on the border was General Plutarco Elías Calles, commanding a substantial body of troops in Sonora that might be used to cut the Punitive Expedition's supply lines. It was Agent Breniman who had responsibility for Arizona. He scored a notable success when he acquired the instructions for Mexican secret service agents: "Requirements Which Should Predominate [sic] Mexican Secret Service Agents."[1146] Ably assisting Breniman were Special Employees Hopkins and Neunhoffer, both of whom routinely received reports from their informants, translated the reports, and sent them forward.

Hopkins sent "J. E," informant Juan Echegaray, later MEY (in yet another system for designating informants, ME indicated Mexican, and Y was the last letter in the informant's surname) from Bisbee to Cananea to note troop dispositions. Because the 1st Arizona Infantry of the National Guard had been transferred to Naco, Hopkins could no longer enjoy the use of a sergeant and two corporals to work in plain clothes at night watching hardware stores suspected of smuggling ammunition. Hopkins did arrange for a sergeant in mufti at Naco to meet trains and to observe suspicious freight shipments, for he felt that the smuggling of ammunition was the principal concern at present.[1147]

Under instructions from Major M. O. Bigelow, Military Intelligence officer for the Arizona District, Hopkins went to Naco, conferred with the commander of the 1st Arizona Infantry, and secured the services of a Lieutenant Fred Wright, Intelligence officer, to watch freight and express shipments and baggage.[1148] The Mexicans were also conducting intelligence operations. Echegaray related in a subsequent report that "I am very sure that [General] Calles has about ten special agents for the purchase of arms and ammunition and also these agents are reporting to the Mexican government all the movements of troops in the United States."[1149]

Another informant, Carlos Herminio Echegaray, was transferred to work in El Paso.[1150] Hopkins, at Agent Breniman's instructions, hired a replacement. "I employed him under the name of Antonio Cerna [MER]. This informant has been employed by the de facto government as Cabo [corporal] of the Customs Guards, is intelligent and discreet, is persona grata in Sonora, has been tried out on special work by Major James Ryan, Intelligence Officer of the Pershing Expedition in Chihuahua, and I have considerable confidence in him."[1151] Cerna was to work in Sonora. Hopkins made a tour of various points near the border to see that the arms embargo on Mexico was being observed. He was encouraged because public opinion strongly favored maintaining the embargo.[1152]

Hopkins employed another informant in Douglas. Luke Short, a veteran Customs line rider, was recently made redundant when Customs replaced mounted inspectors with automobiles. He spoke Spanish and had considerable experience dealing with Mexican businessmen and officials. Short's cover was that of an embittered public servant, and Breniman instructed him to let the *carrancistas* know he was available. Although there was initially some interest, the *carrancistas* evidently did not recruit Short.[1153]

Hopkins reported that on September 11, the El Paso and Southwest Railroad would offer for sale at Douglas to pay freight charges, 200,000 7-millimeter cartridges which were under military guard. They were part of a shipment of 300,000 rounds consigned to General Calles before the embargo by the Douglas brokers, Michelena & Lucas, but were refused because of their corroded condition, having been salvaged from a vessel that sank in the harbor of Galveston during the 1900 hurricane. It was estimated that maybe twenty percent of these cartridges would explode. Hopkins knew this because "we tried some of it when it was offered for sale in Douglas before." Interestingly, Michelena & Lucas had recently shipped the defective ammunition to Douglas again. Evidently, the Mexican officials in Sonora had been under the impression that the talks between the United States and Mexico at New London would result in the withdrawal of the Punitive Expedition and the lifting of the embargo, neither of which happened. Hopkins felt that the purchase of this defective ammunition by the same people who had previously refused it was significant.

It reflected the shortage of ammunition in Sonora and the *carrancistas*' failure to smuggle any appreciable amount. But there were no bids, and the ammunition was shipped to El Paso where it was placed under military guard.[1154]

Hopkins also reported that the Douglas office of Western Union had fired a messenger caught reading the files. He suggested that "in view of the conditions in the Douglas office I believe that all messages from the bureau to Agents in Douglas regarding Mexican matters should be in code."[1155] He later wrote that Western Union had conducted an investigation, and a circular letter went to all managers: "Conversation had been had with you a number of times also letter written in connection with the employment of Mexican help at our border offices. In order to relieve the situation and prevent the least possible chance for information leaking out which would be detrimental to our government, this to instruct that if you have any employees of Mexican or Spanish descent in your office, arrangements be made to dispense with their services immediately and only American [Anglo] help be employed. Please acknowledge receipt of this circular and advise action taken by you."[1156]

Some of Hopkins's time was spent complying with the War Department's request for information. Operatives on the border were asked to compile a list of "Persons to be watched or confined in the event of the occupation of Mexico," with a short comment about each one, and a list of "Persons who would be of service in the event of the occupation of Mexico," with comments. Hopkins also assisted Major Bigelow in preparing "War Department Information Route 10"—the [invasion] route along the railroad from Naco to Del Rio Junction, Sonora, with details about this route, as well as general information about conditions in Sonora.[1157]

Hopkins received information from reliable Mexican and American sources that General Calles had a new secret service chief, replacing Enrique Goldbaum, whom the Bureau in San Antonio had recently detained for conspiracy. The newcomer was a certain Dr. Frederick Ketchul, who bore a commission as a lieutenant colonel in the Medical Corps. Hopkins immediately notified one of his informants, G. W. Read, who covered Ketchul's movements from the time he crossed into Arizona at Naco. Read reported to Hopkins and Major Bigelow. The informant tracked Ketchul to Douglas, noting that he called on the Carranza consul and on *carrancista* sympathizers. Hopkins himself shadowed Ketchul when he took the train back to Naco. The Bureau operative detained him, took him to an empty tent at the 1st Arizona camp, and interrogated him on the pretext that he suspected Ketchul of smuggling. Ketchul stoutly maintained that he had just come to purchase medical supplies, of which he had a few. Ketchul "said he was a Mexican, born in Mexico, and a graduate of Columbia University School of Medicine. However, it is very evident that he is a half-breed Negro. He speaks English with a slight Negro accent and not as a Mexican or Spaniard speaks it. My information is that he is a Cuban. He is pretty smooth, but the fact that most of his conferences were with Consul Lelevier, Dr. J. J. P. Armstrong, and H. Rivera and other Carranza agents satisfies me that our information on him is correct."[1158]

Special Employee Neunhoffer's activities were less exciting. He assisted Agent Breniman and interpreted for him, as when Breniman debriefed informant Juan Ortiz. The informant brought news that Carranza was sending emissaries to Europe to determine what Mexico could expect in war materiel from certain countries, having already arranged with Argentina for war materiel. Ortiz claimed that Carranza was only playing for time, and hostilities would be renewed as soon as he had made the necessary arrangements. And Ortiz reported that among the thousands of Mexican exiles and refugees in the United States, Carranza would permit only his own partisans to return to Mexico to fight against the United States in case of intervention. Carranza was also preparing to send 4,000 troops from Guaymas to Baja California to depose Colonel Esteban Cantú for having unpatriotically declared his neutrality during the war crisis.[1159] The slippery Cantú, though, managed to convince Carranza of his loyalty, and the expedition was cancelled.[1160]

Both special employees reported on attempts to form a new Mexican faction, the *Legalista* Party, composed of Huerta, Villa, and Maytorena refugees. It was another example of political "outs" trying to forge an alliance against whoever was "in," namely Carranza. Some of Neunhoffer's information came from Customs inspector at Nogales Jack Noonan, the former *maderista* mercenary and Constitutionalist arms smuggler.[1161] Neunhoffer also handled informant MEZ (José Hernández), using him for *legalista* matters and to make a trip to Mazatlán and report on conditions there.[1162] *Legalistas* were delighted when in August, Colonel Mariano Támez revolted in Ciudad Juárez on August 4 with 100 men of the garrison. The *legalistas* believed this was the beginning of massive defections from Carranza. It was not.[1163] Despite much planning and many juntas, the *legalista* movement failed to become a major player in the Mexican Revolution.

Neunhoffer had difficulty in carrying out the Chief's instructions to secure certain telegrams supposed to have passed between members of a junta at Tucson and juntas in other cities because they were signed by, and addressed to, fictitious names. Since the Bureau had not even approximate dates when the telegrams were sent, it would be impossible to locate them.[1164]

In yet another instance of the military assisting the Bureau, Breniman arranged with the New Jersey National Guard for a lieutenant and a private to be detailed for intelligence work at Douglas. Beniman stated:

> I was requested by their commanding officer to instruct them in the duties they are expected to perform and accordingly gave them a written memorandum of places, names, and subjects which they will be expected to cover. Their duties are principally to detect any efforts made to smuggle ammunition across the border. They will meet all incoming and outgoing trains; observe baggage, freight, and express shipments; checkup daily the receipt and delivery of all munitions of war. They are instructed to observe closely any packages received by freight, baggage, or express which may contain munitions of war, but under another label or classification. I have given these officers the names of those who are believed to be engaged in smuggling operations and secret work for the Mexican army. I acquainted them with railroad employees and government officers who will be in a position to furnish them with information and assist them in the work. In my absence Lt. Quimby will report to Special Employee A. A. Hopkins and Army Intelligence officer Bigelow at Douglas. I have agreed to reimburse them for small items of expenses it may be necessary for them to incur while in the performance of their duties. These officers will be constantly on duty.[1165]

Posted at San Antonio, Barnes, using the accommodation address of "F. Ligardi" received reports from Randolph Robertson's informant MEC [Juan Cisneros], who was currently in Monterrey. The informant had spoken with Basilio Ramos, of the Plan de San Diego, and was about to leave for Mexico City. He traveled to Guadalajara as well, reporting military and general information.[1166]

Meanwhile, Special Employee Victor Weiskopf at Presidio continued to obtain and break Mexican codes. His latest triumph was the cipher code used by Mexican military and consular officers, as well as code messages showing conditions in the State of Chihuahua.[1167]

Special Employee Wiseman at Eagle Pass, working undercover and a veteran of the Madero intelligence service, proposed to learn troop dispositions himself, writing to Barnes:

> The Mexican that I was going to send to Monclova failed to make an agreement with me, as he did not feel safe in going, and being unable to secure a reliable person for that purpose I believe I will take the proposition. I have secured several good passports from friends that are holding responsible positions with the de facto government. I am taking the trip under my own responsibility, and I assure you that should anything happen, my mission shall never become known. Conditions have changed considerably and there is no reason to fear of being troubled by the Mexicans. I have no reason to fear being known as I have worked overcover [sic] here; furthermore, I have passed to the Mexican side on several occasions without being molested. I await your instructions. Trusting that you will give me an opportunity to show you my qualifications, as so far, I have been unable to do so, I remain. I am not sending you any report as there is nothing of importance to report. Conditions are improving.[1168]

Barnes wrote Wiseman that, per their previous correspondence and provided he could do so in safety, it was desired that he travel from Eagle Pass to Monterrey, stopping enroute at Monclova, Saltillo, and any other intermediate points where troops were stationed. Wiseman was to learn their number and how many were infantry, cavalry and artillery. He was also to learn about their equipment, the condition of their horses, the amount of munitions on hand, the location of fortifications in any of the cities visited, the location of any bodies of running water suitable for drinking, the condition of crops, and any other information of value from a military standpoint. Information concerning the financial condition of Mexico, its people, and the present form of government was also desired; also, ascertaining whether the people were returning to peaceful pursuits and what, if any, feeling of unrest was noticeable. He was to give special attention to the activities of Plan de San Diego leaders, several of whom were probably in Monterrey. Wiseman was to return via Laredo and report to Barnes, who reiterated, "I wish to again state, however, that if there is any element of danger to your personal safety attached to this trip, that it is not desired that you undertake the same."[1169]

Wiseman indeed made the trip to Monterrey, ostensibly to bring back an automobile. He arrived in Eagle Pass on September 2. Due to a railroad strike he had not returned through Laredo as instructed. Upon arrival, he met Special Employee Lege, who took him to Captain Comstock, the Intelligence officer. The captain questioned him about military garrisons and the condition of the country. Wiseman mailed a report to Barnes, remarking that most of the information submitted was from personal observation. Captain Comstock, not knowing that Wiseman was undercover, requested that Wiseman prepare a memorandum of what he had seen, hopefully remembering the number of troops in the cities where he had been. Wiseman asked Barnes what to do. Lastly, Wiseman stated that he had experienced no ill feeling toward Americans, and that conditions were very quiet.[1170]

Barnes informed Wiseman that the intelligence officer at Fort Sam Houston had communicated with Captain Comstock at Eagle Pass, advising him confidentially of Wiseman's status. Wiseman was authorized to call on Comstock and ascertain just what information he desired, after which Wiseman was to write to Barnes fully. The matter of authorizing Wiseman's next trip would be considered.[1171]

The next trip was to Mexico City and was quite productive. Wiseman traveled to San Antonio to report directly to the Southern Department Intelligence officer, Major H. L. Laubach. He gave the detailed information Laubach desired, including maps of cities and of states, plans of fortifications, army divisions, brigades, regiments, and if composed of infantry, cavalry or artillery. He also provided data on running water, conditions of railroad bridges and tanks. Regarding Mexico City, the supply of munitions and the output at the arsenal; who supplied its powder; the names of persons friendly toward the United States government and those unfriendly; the names of military commanders and governors; and revolutionary activities.[1172]

Wiseman made yet another trip into Mexico in October, sending his reports to his "Dear Friend," "Miss J. B. Bege" [Agent Robert L. Barnes] at San Antonio. Wiseman wrote from Torreón, giving Mexican troop dispositions and commenting on the dangers of rail travel. It was not just bandit attacks. "Never again for me. I have my share, it must be auto or special next, this traveling on boxcars do [sic] seem no enjoyment for me."[1173] Wiseman also mentioned that Torreón and its surrounding Laguna district were pro-Villa. The informant, complaining about the sporadic rail service, traveled on to San Luís Potosí and planned to go to Aguascalientes. Besides military information, Wiseman reported on conditions such as starvation and disease.[1174]

Barnes notified Wiseman's colleague at Eagle Pass, J. H. Lege, who had been assisting Captain Comstock there, that "I beg to advise that it is our wish that you render assistance to the War Department whenever practicable. Also, report on conditions in Mexico whenever possible. Also, interview parties coming out of Mexico with reference to general conditions, troop movements, etc."[1175] But Barnes also chided Lege for not furnishing the names of his informants in his reports.[1176]

Special Employee Tom Ross at Laredo reported that his confidential informant Rafael Schiraffa had returned from a trip to Monterrey and Matamoros, noting troop movements. Ross later reported on *villista* depredations.[1177]

At Brownsville, Agent J. B. Rogers still used his original informant, Mateo Gomez, commenting that "he occasionally gets useful information from the other side." Rogers's other local informant was Anthony Laulom, hired at $3 per day and expenses when out of town. And to operate in the interior of Tamaulipas, Rogers had informant Eugenio Tapia, an admirer of some Plan de San Diego leaders.[1178] Rogers, by the way, found himself working on one of the Bureau's original assignments—enforcing the Mann Act of 1910, a federal statute criminalizing the transportation of women for immoral purposes across state lines, also known as the "White-Slave Traffic Act." Because of the thousands of National Guardsmen in the Brownsville area, Rogers had to seek the cooperation of the military in trying to enforce the Mann Act.[1179]

Rogers himself undertook a mission in Mexico in September. Reporting from Tampico, he painted a grim picture:

> Great shortage of food, much sickness. Same at Victoria. Very few soldiers at Tampico or Victoria. The bandits, as they call them, are bad around Tula and along the railroad to San Luis Potosí from Tampico. There is no train service on this line. These bandits are said to be Carranza soldiers. They rob and then chase themselves like a cat chasing its tail.[1180]

Barnes sent Rogers a specimen card to give him an idea of the information the War Department was acquiring about persons residing in Mexico. Rogers was to make a report "furnishing similar information concerning any person which you may know who now resides at any point in Mexico."[1181]

Pancho Villa, whom many had overlooked as a has-been, had been making a comeback in Chihuahua by portraying himself as the champion of Mexican nationalism against the Punitive Expedition. Villa exploded into the news in September. Taking advantage of the celebrations of Mexican independence on September 16, he launched an attack against the city of Chihuahua at four a.m., taking the substantial Carranza garrison completely by surprise. He launched simultaneous attacks against the federal building, the state capital, and the penitentiary, freeing the prisoners. The *villistas* not only caused chaos, but they wounded the *carrancista* commander, General Jacinto B. Treviño. They evacuated the city at midmorning, in triumph, with their booty and recruits.[1182]

Not only was Villa back in the limelight, but his cruelty escalated. Among his minor atrocities was giving captured Carranza soldiers the choice of having their ears cut off or being branded with Carranza's initials, V. C., on their cheeks.[1183] Villa's resurgence, of course, put added pressure on Carranza.

What the protracted negotiations at New London finally produced was an arrangement whereby the Punitive Expedition would be withdrawn, and the Carranza regime promised to secure the Mexican side of the border. On February 5, 1917, the last units of the Punitive Expedition crossed back into the United States at Columbus. And on August 31, 1917, the Wilson administration extended formal diplomatic recognition (de jure), and appointed an ambassador to the government of Venustiano Carranza, thus solidifying his control over Mexico.[1184]

14

If He Just Had Money

Brigadier General Félix Díaz was a most unimpressive leader during the Mexican Revolution.[1185] Born in 1868 in Oaxaca, he had a privileged upbringing. His father, Félix Díaz Mori, was Porfirio Díaz' younger brother. The young Díaz attended the Colegio Militar in Mexico City and graduated with a degree in engineering. He served in the Díaz military and unsurprisingly, given his pedigree, rose quickly through the ranks to become a general without ever having seen combat, or for being known for any exceptional achievements during his service other than being a Díaz. His career stations before the revolution included Mexican consul in Chile, inspector general of the Mexico City police force, and Catholic Party deputy in Congress. Young Díaz's ambitions to one day follow in the footsteps of his famous uncle did not transfer into reality. Being a Díaz was an enormous advantage before 1910, but with the advent of the Mexican Revolution, not so much. Moreover, because of his mediocrity, as well as reluctance from within the científico community to support the young upstart, these roadblocks to prominence in Mexican politics aligned the young Díaz with Bernardo Reyes, who briefly challenged Porfirio Díaz for the presidency in 1908, then opposed the Madero government in 1911.

A frustrated Félix Díaz finally took the plunge and rebelled in the fall of 1912, when he tried his luck in the strategic port of Veracruz. The revolt quickly collapsed, and Díaz found himself in a federal prison in Mexico City. The Veracruz fiasco illuminates two threads in Félix Díaz's career: He schemed, schemed some more, waited, and waited some more until his support base had grown weary and melted away. The other thread is the fact that Díaz seemed uninspiring to many of his followers. The corpulent general lacked self-esteem, which he made up with aloofness and grandiose plans that bore little resemblance to reality. The German minister to Mexico, Admiral Paul von Hintze, commented on the military disaster of Díaz's Veracruz revolt: "The Díaz revolution has collapsed because of the incompetence of its leader."[1186]

In February 1913, Díaz was liberated from prison and joined Bernardo Reyes in the coup d'etat against the Madero administration. The coup succeeded but not as Díaz had envisioned. Following Reyes's death in the early hours of the *Decena Trágica*, it was General Huerta who took the presidency. Díaz, who had played a major role in overthrowing Madero, was soon marginalized: Huerta having shunted him off as special ambassador to Japan. Díaz subsequently broke with Huerta and, fearing for his life, fled from Veracruz to Havana in October 1913. There he preoccupied himself with what he did best: scheming, planning, and biding his time. In contemporaneous photographs Díaz is either depicted in ridiculous fantasy uniforms, including saber, headdress, and pounds of undeserved medals weighing down his chest or he appears slumped, potbelly pushed to the fore, shoulders sagging, and his head lowered, reflecting his deep insecurities and lack of self-esteem.

Figure 80. *General Félix Díaz, 1915*
Source: Bain News Service Collection
Library of Congress Prints and Photographs Division

Almost by default—simply because he was still around while Reyes, Huerta, and Orozco had died, Villa was defeated, and Zapata only a regional influence—Díaz now assumed the role of de facto opposition leader. "Nevertheless, many Mexicans remained skeptical. Only when Díaz proved himself in battle, like a medieval knight, would most Porfirians be willing to grant him another opportunity. In the next four years, then, Félix Díaz would fight an uphill battle, not only against the *carrancista* army, but also against his former supporters' fears and trepidations."[1187]

In January 1916, Secretary of State Lansing wrote to Chief Bielaski, transmitting a letter from Carranza's representative in Washington that agents of the Díaz, Mondragón, Navarrete, and Blanquet revolutionary junta in New York City had formed a revolutionary junta in New Orleans.[1188] Rumors contended that all the outs, the stalwart *científicos* Francisco León de la Barra, Manuel Mondragón, and Aureliano Blanquet, as well as Pancho Villa and Emiliano Zapata, had reached an arrangement with Díaz. Agent Cantrell in Cuba confirmed rumors that Gonzalo Enrile had left on a mission to Germany on behalf of the new movement.[1189]

After the US government in 1915 recognized Carranza as the de facto president of Mexico, Pancho Villa had vowed revenge, declaring war on the "common enemy of all Mexicans:" the United States.[1190] But there was more to it than just Pancho Villa's hatred of the United States. The real fear of the American government at the beginning of 1916 was the possibility of Villa gaining access to funding and aligning with other factions, especially that of Félix Díaz. That is indeed what happened.[1191]

The key figure in the alignment of Mexican reactionaries, conservative exile groups, and Pancho Villa was Gonzalo Carlos Enrile Villatoro, who suddenly appeared in New York in December 1915. Born in 1867 in Guanajuato of a Spanish immigrant father and a Mexican mother, Enrile grew up in a devoutly Catholic family. He joined the federal army in his teens and rose to become a colonel. In the years just before the revolution, Enrile joined the diplomatic service with assignments in Costa Rica and Clifton, Arizona as Mexican consul.[1192] Under the interim administration of Francisco León de la Barra in 1911, Enrile took an assignment in Brussels as consul.[1193] His rejection of the new revolutionary administration of Francisco Madero became clear when he sided with Pascual Orozco and became his treasurer in 1912, as the latter mounted a serious uprising against the Mexican president.[1194] Enrile was the key financial connection between Orozco, the extremely wealthy Terrazas family, and the Díaz exile community in the United States, which, to a large degree, financed Orozco's uprising. After General Huerta took the reins of power in a violent coup d'état in the spring of 1913, the forty-six-year-old Enrile joined the Mexican Congress as a Catholic Party deputy.[1195] The Catholic Party supported Félix Díaz whom Huerta had sidelined in his power grab. Huerta had Enrile arrested and exiled in a sweeping ouster of former *maderistas* and *felicistas* from positions of influence. Enrile spent the remainder of the Huerta presidency in Cuba, aligning himself with Félix Díaz and Aureliano Blanquet, plotting a return to Mexico with other exile groups.

Enrile consistently worked against the interests of the United States, and he supported the reactionary element throughout the Mexican Revolution. His specialty remained fundraising. The suspicion of all exile factions, as well as Pancho Villa and Emiliano Zapata, that Carranza had concluded some secret agreement with Washington in the fall of 1915 that threatened the very sovereignty of the country, formed the cornerstone of Enrile's mission in December.

Enrile arrived in New York from Havana on December 19, 1915.[1196] It is difficult to determine exactly who sent him. Felix Díaz, who had operated out of Havana before he moved to New York, had a large contingent of supporters there. It was on Díaz's behalf that Enrile joined the group of prominent conspirators in plotting a new coalition to unseat Carranza. Among the persons of interest were former interim president of Mexico, Francisco León de la Barra, who now lived at the Hotel Astor in New York, as did German naval intelligence agent and Pancho Villa envoy in the US, Félix Sommerfeld, and Heinrich Albert, the head of the German intelligence mission in the US.[1197]

Enrile claimed to German authorities a few months later that he represented the factions of de la Barra, Félix Díaz, Zapata, and Villa. Although this claim sounds ludicrous, these factions all had a common enemy in Carranza, and a common conviction that the First Chief had sold out Mexico to the United States. Bureau agents along the border, who interviewed a *villista* commander in April 1916, confirmed the development that "With the death of Orozco [in the summer of 1915] and Huerta [in January 1916] there has been a fusion of parties recognizing as leader Félix Díaz who, it is said, put himself in accord with Zapata [...] To invade American territory, to murder American citizens, burn American cities and cause all the possible depredations in American territory in order to bring a conflict with this nation [US]."[1198]

The focus of the Bureau on a possible alignment of revolutionaries on the outside to get back into the game, which remained a pattern throughout the Mexican Revolution, took on an added dimension: Germany was suspected of sponsoring the new effort. Although the Bureau could not prove this, rumors abounded along the border and in revolutionary circles that Villa and Díaz, as well as others, had come to an understanding, and that Germany would finance the new faction. The suspicion turned out to be correct.[1199]

While in New York, the German military attaché Franz von Papen, bags already packed for imminent departure after his expulsion, organized meetings on and around December 23 with Enrile, Sommerfeld, and others. The group worked out an offer to the German government. The document Enrile and von Papen drafted in impeccable German for presentation to Berlin was truly staggering in its audacity: The document promised Germany favorable concessions, such as control over railroads, petroleum, and mining. The newly installed government would be "completely supportive of German policy, which is aimed against the interests of the United States." Enrile also promised to start (or rather restart, as this would have been another iteration of the Plan de San Diego) a separatist movement in the US border states in order to subvert the US government. Finally, the new Mexican government would raise an army strong enough to attack the United States. In return, the new movement required 300 million German Marks for implementing the takeover of Mexico. The proposal concluded with the notation [...] "any questions to be directed at Captain von Papen [...]."[1200]

Enrile and Mexico City lawyer Humberto Islas left for their mission in January 1916. Their first stop was Havana. The Carranza consul there monitored their movements and reported on January 20 that Enrile had sailed from Havana for Spain on the liner *Alfonso XII*.[1201] When they arrived in Santander, Spain, German ambassador Maximilian Prinz Ratibor refused to issue Enrile a visa to continue his journey to Berlin, despite, or rather because of, a letter of endorsement from Franz von Papen. The Imperial Foreign Office at the time fought the Imperial War Department tooth and nail on a crucial policy question. The War Department wanted to reimpose unrestricted submarine warfare and risk the entry of the US into the war on the side of the Allies. The main argument was that by the time the US would have troops on European battlefields, the war would be decided for Germany. The Foreign Office wanted to prevent a US entry into the war and was wary of the navy's prediction of defeating Great Britain in a matter of months. The Kaiser's position was undecided, which meant that, for the time being, the policy of abiding by the London Declaration when using submarines remained in place.[1202]

Enrile and his offer to cause a conflict with the US on Germany's behalf did not set well with the German ambassador in Spain. After two months' delay, Prinz Ratibor allowed the Mexican emissary to proceed to Switzerland, and from there to Berlin.[1203] He arrived in Berlin on April 10, 1916, months behind schedule, a fact unknown to his fellow conspirators.[1204] Even if the Imperial War Department had shown a willingness to fund Enrile's proposal to create a distraction for the US at the Mexican border, the Columbus raid had happened over a month earlier, and in the meantime thousands of US troops had entered Mexico. The interest in Enrile's proposals within the German government had cooled markedly by then, if it ever existed.

There was, however, support for Félix Díaz in Chicago. Monsignor Francis C. Kelley supported Félix Díaz not because he admired Díaz but because Kelley opposed Carranza. The monsignor's concern was the Catholic Church and the anticlerical policy of the Carranza administration. Kelley was president of the Catholic Extension Society and editor of *Extension*, a monthly magazine. He bitterly opposed both Carranza and President Wilson's Mexican policy. To counter *carrancista* propaganda, in 1916 Kelley published a booklet, *The Book of Red and Yellow: Being a Story of Blood and a Yellow Streak*, detailing anticlerical violence.[1205] Monsignor Kelley was also involved in raising financial support for Díaz from the Chicago Spearmint chewing gum tycoon William Mills Wrigley Jr.[1206] Wrigley supported Díaz in hopes of receiving a twenty-year concession for a large expanse of chicle-producing trees in Chiapas and the Territory of Quintana Roo.[1207]

The Bureau investigated the question of whether the German government was financing Villa in his attempt to engage the US in a war. Informer Dario Silva reported to the Bureau in the fall of 1915 that the Catholic Church "offered Villa three hundred thousand dollars for protection about September 1915, and that they would continue to support him if he would take the side of the church."[1208] Agent Cantrell separately reported to Chief Bielaski that Hans Tauscher had told him about a payment of $320,000 to Villa.[1209] This roughly matched the reported financial support from the Catholic Church. Was there a connection between the Catholic Church and the German government? Was this the same money?

Albert's financial records document a $300,000 transfer from a commercial account to the Mechanics and Metals National Bank, marked "K.M." at the end of November 1915. "K.M." stood for *Kriegsministerium* or Imperial War Department.[1210] The ledger of the *Kriegsministerium* shows another $200,000 credit von Papen received in the beginning of December.[1211] It was between November 23 and December 4, at the exact time when Villa's army was imploding, that von Papen received $500,000 from Albert. The use of these credits does not appear to have been for the Bridgeport Projectile Company or purchases of smokeless powder.

The ledgers are inconclusive as to the expenditure of this money, and the accounts of the military attaché in 1916 do not document exactly how it was spent. One suspicious payment stands out, however, in the months following the transfer. Wolf von Igel, who took over von Papen's responsibility as provisional military attaché in New York, received $25,000 on December 28, 1915, just one week after Enrile met von Papen in New York and received a letter of introduction to the German government from him.[1212] The likely purpose of the payment was travelling money for the two Mexicans.

Despite the failure of the mission, there are very important aspects of the Enrile proposals that, so far, the large historiography on the Columbus attack has completely ignored.[1213] Villa, whose frame of mind in the months leading up to Columbus some contemporaries and historians have characterized as bordering on insanity, had a clear motivation and strategy for the attack. Historian Friedrich Katz asserted for the first time, in 1978, that indeed Villa was not crazy when he selected Columbus, New Mexico, to provoke an American intervention.[1214] Considering the rationale of the Enrile memorandum, Villa may not just have attacked the United States in a quixotic, single effort. The alienated Mexican exile community, with Villa leading the effort, believed that a military intervention into the United States would create significant German support. Enrile's proposal shows that, in his desperation, Villa clearly had aligned himself with factions of the old elite, especially that of Félix Díaz. Thus, Enrile's claims of representing diverse factions such as Villa, Zapata, Díaz, and de la Barra, which some historians have ridiculed, were true. The suspected existence of a secret agreement between Carranza and the Wilson administration, whether in writing or not, convinced Mexican exiles and Villa that only a confrontation with the United States could serve their ends. It would either sever the friendly relations of the US with Carranza, or rally the majority of Mexicans behind a defender of the homeland in the persons of Pancho Villa or Félix Díaz.

The timing of the document, namely that it had clearly been drafted and agreed upon before the Santa Isabel massacre (January 1916) and Columbus (March 1916), is critical. Villa's ventures may have been the beginning salvo of a much larger campaign that he was to undertake with the agreement and support of the other factions opposed to Carranza. Ultimately, the pressure of the American military chasing him and the *carrancista* forces preventing him from organizing ended his quest to start a war. The launch of Villa's attack before Enrile had received a German commitment of support is further evidence that initial funding from the Catholic Church and the Albert organization was in place. The German government firmly supported Carranza after the United States launched the Punitive Expedition. Carranza, at that juncture, offered a much better chance of causing a war with the US.

Yet, while historians have deemed the Enrile mission as inconsequential, the episode shows that from the perspective of the Bureau at the time, Díaz's alignment with Villa posed a national security threat, especially if large-scale financing from Germany and the Catholic Church was added to the mix.

The Bureau was justified in detailing significant resources to the *felicista* faction to understand and counter the threat that the otherwise notoriously unsuccessful faction posed.

Despite the unimpressive track record of Díaz, information about the Enrile mission confronted Chief Bielaski with a potentially dangerous situation. If the intelligence on the *felicistas* was correct, then by the spring of 1916 the entire Mexican opposition would have aligned and potentially received financial backing from Germany. That possibility elevated the *felicista* conspiracy to a national security issue. Bielaski decided to make the movement a priority and ordered simultaneous investigations in New York and New Orleans.[1215]

The Bureau had two key intelligence assets to investigate the activities of the *felicistas*: Harry Berliner and Charles E. Jones. Both had infiltrated the *felicista* movement deeply, and possessed the necessary credibility with the conspirators.

Berliner had been an embassy messenger in the Decena Trágica in Mexico in 1913 and befriended Félix Díaz. Only a few months later he saved the general's life in Havana. On November 6, 1913, at 9:00 p.m., Díaz and some close friends—Luís Malda, Cecilio Ocón, José Bonales Sandoval, and Harry Berliner were sitting in chairs on the seaside jetty in Havana harbor. They were listening to a band concert when three Mexicans strolled in front of them. The electric lights suddenly went out and one of the three, Pedro Guerrero Méndez, who had earlier yelled, "¡Viva Huerta!" at Díaz, attacked the general with a dagger. Berliner, who was sitting next to Díaz, hit Guerrero Méndez on the arm, spoiling his aim. Ocón whacked him with a cane. There was a shot—Guerrero Méndez was shot in the abdomen and seriously wounded by one of his own companions who was trying to shoot Díaz. The attackers fled. Díaz had suffered stab wounds in the head and neck, but neither proved to be life-threatening. All those subsequently arrested in the intensive Havana police investigation claimed to be *carrancistas*, but the court concluded that Díaz's attackers were Huerta secret policemen.[1216] It has been stated, however, that most contemporaries agreed Guerrero Méndez was a *carrancista*.[1217]

Harry Berliner, by the way, was not at all bashful in describing to the press how he had saved Díaz's life.[1218] And he ostensibly remained a *felicista*—in March 1914, a CONFIDENTIAL letter from the Huerta charge d' affaires in Washington to the Foreign Minister listed Harry Berliner (misspelled as "Harry Balinger") of Mexico City as one of those rumored to be plotting on Díaz's behalf.[1219]

Having survived the assassination attempt with the help of Harry Berliner, Díaz and his wife sailed from Havana to New York, arriving on

February 20, 1914. The general still dreamed of power. So, he schemed, planned, and waited for the perfect moment to launch his next rebellion, centered in southern Mexico in his home state of Oaxaca and neighboring Chiapas.

In July 1915, despite considering himself the strongest man to avoid American intervention, he said, "I will not make a move until two weeks from now when the Washington policy towards Mexico should have been made known. All depends now on that."[1220] He was referring to the Wilson administration's attempts to force Mexican factions to cooperate in selecting a unity government. When he publicly threw his hat in the ring as a presidential candidate, he—for once—achieved unity: all Mexican factions as well as the American government ignored him. The situation for Díaz changed rapidly in the months afterward: In October, Carranza was officially recognized as "de facto President of Mexico," and Villa was defeated, with his Division del Norte disbanded by November. Díaz appeared to be the last man standing.

The Bureau in the fall of 1914 and the spring of 1915 began receiving word that Díaz's followers were up to no good, allegedly planning a counter-revolution with financial aid from Catholic clergy.[1221] There were, for example, rumors that *felicistas* were organizing a military expedition and purchasing a ship for a campaign in southern Mexico.[1222] Initially, the Bureau's problem was trying to sort out just who were *felicistas*, in the midst of all the plotting going on: Villa's southern strategy, which Guatemalan president Estrada Cabrera supported; Carranza supporting exiled Guatemalans against Estrada Cabrera; Huerta's conspiracy; Conservative Mexican exiles trying to organize a new faction, the *legalistas*; and, a conspiracy to detach Yucatán from the rest of Mexico. This separatist conspiracy fizzled in the summer of 1915, and the ammunition they had amassed in New Orleans as well as their vessels, *Kwasind* and *Teresa*, were offered for sale to the Carranza government along with the 4,000 rifles and 1,000,000 rounds the separatists had accumulated. They were now negotiating with Carranza.[1223]

The Bureau, as well as the Villa and the Carranza consuls and their secret agents, were constantly running down rumors and trying to keep track of persons of interest. And there were many interesting persons. Among them were ex-Federal officers who had pledged their allegiance to Félix Díaz. Twenty-one of them met in New Orleans to sign a declaration of support for Díaz and to await his orders. *Carrancista* agents kept the Bureau informed as did the Villa consul, who provided a list of names and addresses of Díaz supporters.[1224]

Things came into focus by August 1915. After the United States crushed Huerta's comeback bid, which eliminated a major rival, Félix Díaz conferred in New York City with Generals Manuel Mondragón and Aureliano Blanquet, both of whom had served in Huerta's cabinet. Acting Chief Horn had notified Superintendent Offley: "The Department desires all the information we can secure concerning General Díaz and his connections, and his movements in New York should be watched for a few days as far as may be practicable by your force."[1225] Superintendent Offley placed a cover on General Mondragón's mail, and sometimes Bureau agents followed Mondragón, having been furnished a photo of the general.[1226]

Félix Díaz was staying at the Aberdeen Hotel. Acting Chief Horn had Offley try to place a special agent or an informant in the hotel to monitor Díaz's activities. Agents Scully and Tucker, passing themselves off as reporters, enlisted the help of a bellboy. But when they met the bellboy on the agreed corner, he came followed by Díaz and several other Mexicans. It seems that instead of the bellboy pointing out Díaz to the agents, he was pointing out the agents to Díaz. Scully and Tucker left hurriedly.[1227]

As part of the Díaz investigation, Offley directed Agent Cantrell to interview Mrs. L. Frances Roemer, a New York resident, who had been mentioned as a possible source of information. Cantrell called on her. She was an attractive thirty-three-year-old, tall, with a good figure, quite accomplished, and speaking several languages fluently. She told him that her maiden name was Lydia Frances Wilkie, that her home was San Antonio, and that for the past eight or nine years she had lived in Mexico as "Irene Barrett."[1228] During that time, she had met many influential Mexicans, for she had operated exclusive brothels in Veracruz and Mexico City, and was now doing so in New York. "She says at present, various Mexican factions' representatives frequent her house, among them [men of the] Díaz movement, who have constantly talked over the situation concerning an uprising or revolution. They've discussed plans, showed her pictures and plans of two ships." She needed money and was anxious to return to Mexico, assuring the agent that she "is sure she can get any information from any of them that the Government desires." Cantrell's opinion of her, however, was "that she is a very shrewd and unscrupulous woman and in dealing with her the Department should be particularly careful as she is undoubtedly out for financial purposes and would probably sell to the one paying her the most money for any information that she had."[1229] Acting Chief Horn regretted that, because of her character, the Bureau could not employ her, but agents should keep in touch and pay her nominal sums for any information provided. Thereafter agents interviewed Mrs. Roemer only in pairs, to preclude the appearance of a single agent slinking off to the brothel for illicit pleasure.[1230]

It was at this point that Harry Berliner entered the intelligence landscape of New York. In July 1915, while working for the Mexican subsidiary of the Oliver Typewriter Company in Veracruz, he had called Carranza a "darned fool," which was reported in the local press. The First Chief considered Berliner's affront unacceptable, and promptly had him deported and banned from Mexico.[1231] He resumed selling Oliver typewriters, this time in New York. With his impeccable *felicista* credentials—for he had saved the general's life, after all—Bielaski hired him as a special employee in December 1915.

The jovial Berliner publicly maintained his cover as a salesman for Oliver Typewriter, a position the company confirmed on occasion to doubters. Berliner encountered José Ratner on Broadway in New York. Ratner, who was going to New Jersey, invited Berliner to come along.

> Agent declined, saying he might sell a couple of typewriters this afternoon. Ratner said, come along and I'll give you an order for one. On ferry to New Jersey, Agent casually asked about Mondragón and Blanquet [...]. Then he changed subject to typewriters, in a manner which was plain that he was rather in doubt as to whether I was really selling same. He said: I see you are doing the same as you were doing in Veracruz, selling the Oliver Typewriter. He asked price of a big machine, thinking he could stump me, so at once I gave him a price on our Model #9 which is the latest. He told Agent to send him an 18" Printype machine to his office COD. To prove to Ratner that Agent was selling typewriters, Agent pulled out his catalogue and papers and on seeing them Ratner was satisfied that I was really working for the typewriter company. Agent believes Ratner knew more about Mondragón and Blanquette [sic] and what is going on.[1232]

Berliner made the rounds of the hotels, buying cigars and "refreshments" for those from whom he tried to elicit information. Amazingly, while some other agents had to get permission for 30-cent trolly car fares, Berliner freely invited his targets to have a drink or a smoke, occasionally even selling them a typewriter. It seems likely, and only fair, that Oliver Typewriter may have paid for Berliner's expenses.

Berliner's intelligence was top notch. For instance, he found out that General Aureliano Blanquet was negotiating through Frank H. Thayer the purchase of 4,500 30-30 rifles. And without blinking an eye, Berliner called at Félix Díaz's residence, 210 West 72nd Street, and had a long conversation with him and his personal representative in the US, Pedro del Villar, whom Díaz had appointed on January 28, 1916.[1233] Berliner reported to the Bureau that he informed Díaz he was ready to help him return to Mexico, to which Díaz replied that, until the Wilson administration realized Carranza was not the man to restore peace in Mexico, and allowed Díaz's party to do what they wanted, namely to go in with an armed force, the *felicistas* would for the present simply start a publicity campaign and publish the truth as to present conditions. Díaz asserted that he had enough followers and could command all the funds required, confirming intelligence the Bureau had received from the border. And, Díaz was having nothing to do with his former friend and follower Cecilio Ocón, for Ocón was "crooked and underhanded." [They would later reconcile.] Ocón was living at 205 Columbus Avenue and was very friendly with General Blanquet.[1234]

Among Berliner's contacts was former Mexican Congressman Emeterio de la Garza, who said that by January 10, 1916, he, along with Díaz and their followers, would begin an active newspaper campaign on conditions in Mexico and the policy of the US government.[1235] The publicity campaign materialized. Reports surfaced on a national scale that Díaz "might marshal nearly 25,000 men," and that Díaz would be "accompanied by Lee Christmas [...]."[1236] Under the headline "Report of Díaz Rising," the *New York Times* reported that "4,000 malcontents are operating near Torreón shouting for Félix Díaz [...]."[1237]

Berliner continued to ingratiate himself with Díaz, reporting that he had telephoned Díaz, and "gave him a stall" to the effect that he had been offered a position in Guatemala and was thinking of taking it and asked if he could do anything for Díaz there. The general said Berliner should come up and see him, but to call first to be sure he was at home. Díaz had had an interview with a reporter of *The New York Sun*, to be published on January 21. He told Berliner the entire story was false, that no reporter had visited him nor anyone else. He did not know who wrote the article. Díaz said he would discuss the story with Berliner when he saw him.[1238] The *Sun* indeed reported on Díaz on Friday, January 21. The article did not mention an interview but rather quoted a State Department official calling the idea that Díaz was planning a revolt "incredible [...] inasmuch as the men on whom Díaz had been accustomed to rely on principally are not in this country to advise him. Gen. Blanquet is in Canada [...]," and the "talk that Díaz is seeking a loan of $10,000,000 in New Orleans [...] [was] grotesque."[1239] As Harry Berliner would confirm shortly, the quoted government official was wrong about Blanquet. The man who as a lieutenant had given the coup de grâce to Emperor Maximilian I of Mexico was in New York, and he was plotting with Díaz.[1240]

Agent Nils Chalmers managed to interview Félix Díaz at his residence on January 23. Díaz's representative, Pedro del Villar, closely examined the agent's credentials before introducing him to his boss. Díaz said he would be happy to answer any questions. When asked if he had received any overtures to ally himself with Huerta, Díaz indignantly rejected the suggestion as being absurd, given the enmity between himself and Huerta. Indeed, it was absurd. Huerta had died in El Paso on January 13. The Bureau agent reported that Díaz and del Villar had treated him with the utmost courtesy and volunteered to provide him with any information they had, which must have given Chalmers a good chuckle. Del Villar told Chalmers confidentially that Díaz received many letters from prominent Mexicans who considered him the savior of the country, and to all he replied, "Wait until the opportune time arrives."[1241]

Berliner continued his accustomed routine: he called at hotels, restaurants, bars, indulged in gossip, cigars, "refreshments," and reported to Offley anything of interest.[1242] He went to the docks to check out passenger lists of Ward Line steamers plying between Mexican and Cuban ports. He also cultivated relations with important *felicistas*. Chief Bielaski chided Offley for not definitively locating *felicista* General Aurelio Blanquet, who had helped overthrow Madero, had been Huerta's Minister of War in 1914, and was reportedly in Toronto. "This matter should be given prompt attention."[1243]

Berliner not only learned that Blanquet had returned from Toronto and was living at 392 Third Street, Brooklyn, but had a long conversation with

Figure 81. Harry Berliner
Source: Courtesy Kristin Rounds

him as they were well acquainted.[1244] They discussed the Mexican situation at Blanquet's home, the general vehemently predicting Carranza's imminent downfall while maintaining that he was politically neutral, and wanted only a quiet life in New York.[1245] Berliner knew well that Blanquet's sojourn in Toronto had been to organize weapons shipments for Díaz; for the ubiquitous Gonzalo Enrile had made several trips between New York and Toronto to confer with Blanquet in preparation of his mission to Berlin. Berliner also reported that Luís Cabrera had been his personal attorney in Mexico City. They were very good friends. Cabrera was now the Minister of Finance in Carranza's cabinet. He had come to New York to check on an order for Carranza currency being printed at the American Bank Note Company, and Berliner hoped to learn from Cabrera what he could regarding the Mexican refugees living in New York and vicinity, as well as Americans who were enemies of the Carranza government.[1246]

The second major undercover intelligence asset Bielaski had at his disposal against Félix Díaz was Charles E. Jones, code name CRESSE. When the Bureau engaged him, Jones aka CRESSE demanded and was granted absolute independence when it came to his business. The *felicistas*, like other Mexican factions, were extremely interested in obtaining arms and ammunition, and CRESSE soon worked his way into their confidence. He had a partner, Dr. W. T. Richards, a surgeon who had spent decades in Chihuahua, who knew many Mexicans in New Orleans and was the personal physician of General Félix Díaz's wife. The *felicistas* entrusted CRESSE with their most sensitive communications, which he dutifully copied, forwarded to the Bureau in part, and kept the rest as a trove of compromising papers to sell to the highest bidder. When it came to collecting documents, CRESSE was a human vacuum cleaner. His archive eventually comprised more than 1,000 pages.[1247] The files CRESSE turned over to the Bureau left few questions open about the personnel, finances, plans, and operations of the *felicista* movement. As such, CRESSE was primarily responsible for the Bureau being able to monitor the *felicistas* to a greater extent than any other Mexican faction.[1248]

One way in which CRESSE was able to hand the innermost secrets of the *felicista* movement to the Bureau on a silver platter was because he obtained their codes. Jones related that "When the Felicista movement first became active, the private secretary of Mrs. Díaz, Guillermo Rosas, was coming to New York, and he and two other parties came up, we were endeavoring at that time to secure the Felicista codes, and so I brought Rosas and these two other Mexicans up and paid all their expenses. We did succeed in lifting the entire code on the trip, which was turned over to the Department of Justice, photostatic copies made and turned over to them. On the way back, after having spent about five or six weeks on the trip up here and in New York, Mr. Pendleton said, 'You are absolutely foolish to continue to pay your own expenses, and you [must] render an account for this trip;' so I did, and from that time on, such expenses as I incurred, I was reimbursed for by the Bureau."[1249]

Alarm bells rang in the Bureau when Berliner reported that Félix Díaz had disappeared from New York on January 31, 1916. Díaz's representative Pedro del Villar said Díaz had gone to New Orleans because his mother had died, and he could be reached at the home of his brother-in-law, Rafael Alcolea, 1210 Octavia Street. Berliner was skeptical, offering to go to New Orleans, or even Havana, to investigate. Superintendent Offley so informed the Chief in a CONFIDENTIAL letter, stating, "It is evident that Berliner has an extensive acquaintance with Mexicans and is probably in a position to secure information from them, as his association with this Bureau is not suspected in any Mexican quarter."[1250] Bielaski felt that Agent Cantrell could handle matters in Havana, and if Berliner were sent to New Orleans, it might cast suspicion on him. Per the Chief's instructions, Agent Pendleton went to the brother-in-law's house and "under a suitable pretext" learned that Díaz's mother had indeed recently died in Mexico City. Pendleton glimpsed Díaz in an adjoining room, recognizing him from his photograph. The agent presumably breathed a sigh of relief.[1251]

Pendleton received a steady stream of information from journalist H. H. Dunn of *The New Orleans Item*, who had been covering Central America for years. Dunn told him that Javier Larrea, who in 1910 had been Minister of Communications in Porfirio Díaz's last cabinet, had arrived in town on January 3 with a letter from Félix Díaz authorizing Larrea as the financial agent of the *felicistas* to collect funds from sympathizers in the United States. Dunn had known Larrea for many years but declined to get involved in *felicista* intrigues. According to Dunn, Larrea had just left for Guatemala, leaving as his agent in New Orleans, one Pánfilo Maldonado. Larrea's mission was to meet with President Estrada Cabrera of Guatemala regarding the 5,000 soldiers Estrada Cabrera had reportedly stationed on the border with Chiapas to support Félix Díaz's campaign to seize the port of Salina Cruz on the Pacific side of the Isthmus of Tehuantepec. The journalist believed that Estrada Cabrera had done so to get even with Carranza for supporting Guatemalan exiles trying to overthrow his administration.

Dunn also said Larrea had told him a large cargo of munitions would be shipped through New Orleans to Guatemala for Díaz. A $5,000,000 loan had been arranged in New York to pay for this. Interestingly, Dunn stated that while Pánfilo Maldonado was the agent putting up the money for the Díaz party, an American [Charles E. Jones] was handling the munitions shipment. Dunn said Félix Díaz's brothers-in-law, Leonardo and Rafael Alcolea, and General Guadencio González de la Llave were active in the Díaz movement. Félix Somellera, the lay head of the Catholic Party in Mexico, and José Mora y del Río, the exiled Archbishop of Mexico currently living in San Antonio, were the principal parties behind the *felicista* movement, and were enlisting the sympathies and financial assistance of Catholics. "Dunn is a Catholic and he thinks that it was for this reason that Larrea came to him, but he states that he is an American citizen first of all and felt it was his duty to give the above information, and he says that he will do anything possible to aid the Government in obtaining information."[1252]

The reported financial offer seems a mix-up of digits as most of the assets of the Catholic Church in America would had to have been liquidated for this level of support. Still, Díaz's sympathetic biographer states that Mexican and American Catholics, headed by the bishop (also refers to him as monsignor) of Oklahoma [sic], Francis C. Kelley, offered Díaz not just moral support but the sum of $20,000,000 [$420,000,000 in today's value!] to begin his campaign. Squabbling over who was to handle whatever funds had been pledged, combined with Díaz declaring that he was solely dedicated to military matters, resulted in the offer being suspended, if it ever existed.[1253]

Chief Bielaski ordered that Díaz be covered closely. Pendleton detailed Agent D. D. Hawkins solely to Díaz, working with a Burns Detective Agency operative the Mexican consul had hired. Two men were not enough.[1254] Díaz dropped out of sight amid a swirl of rumors as to whether he might still be in New Orleans, or New York, or Washington, or St. Louis, or Chicago, or even Havana. Bielaski wired Pendleton in code on February 17: "Please ascertain immediately and wire if Díaz still New Orleans."[1255] Even Charles E. Jones, who in his capacity as manager of the Newspaper Service Company was arranging to handle a publicity campaign for Díaz and visited him several times a day, was unable to say where the Mexican general was. For Jones, acting as Díaz's press agent was purely a business matter; if the Bureau objected, he would decline the job.[1256]

Pendleton stated on February 22, "I have received so many conflicting reports as to Díaz's whereabouts that I will refrain from expressing any opinion as to the truth of any of these statements. I have tried every possible way that I could think of to get some reliable information as to Díaz's whereabouts but must admit that I am perplexed on this point. I hope, however, to get some definite information, and if he is in New Orleans, I feel quite sure that I will be able to locate him in a short time, unless he is confined in some house which he never leaves."[1257]

The Bureau had lost track of Félix Díaz.

As had happened with Reyes, Huerta, and Orozco, Bureau surveillance had failed. Surveillance requires manpower and equipment, and the Bureau consistently lacked both; in a major city such as New Orleans, the field office did not even have an automobile.

Díaz left New Orleans on the night of February 16. He disguised himself, took a Southern Pacific train to Houston, arriving the following day, and was met by three of his followers. The plan was to go to Galveston, where a shipment of munitions was stored, waiting to be loaded on a vessel that had been chartered through a New Orleans firm. Things went wrong. The vessel mysteriously sailed without Díaz and the munitions. The New Orleans firm had decided that it was too risky to be supporting Díaz as planned and had ordered the ship to leave port.

Matters in disarray, Díaz urgently tried to secure another vessel. Through one of his partisans, he bought a small schooner in Corpus Christi. Unfortunately, the schooner, *La Providencia*, was barely seaworthy. Nevertheless, on February 18, Díaz, disguised as a mechanic, and four companions who were disguised as well, set sail. The schooner foundered on the Mexican coast near Matamoros. Now stranded, Díaz assumed the alias of "Francisco Sánchez." *Carrancistas* arrested the group on suspicion of being smugglers and jailed them in Matamoros. On March 9, the day Pancho Villa's forces attacked Columbus, they were transferred to Monterrey to face a military tribunal. Their defense attorney was able to persuade the court that Díaz and his companions were merely inoffensive fishermen. They were released. Díaz took a train for Mexico City on May 3.[1258] Sympathizers there concealed him until he could make it safely to Oaxaca and take command, recovering from the months of intense anxiety fearing execution if he were recognized. He styled himself the "Supreme Chief" of the uninspiringly-named "National Reorganizing Army," issuing a manifesto "To the Nation." The whole affair had been something out of an adventure novel, and the press had a field day reporting it.

Díaz's publicity campaign in the US had kicked into high gear in March 1916. The purpose was not just to attract potential support in this country, but mainly to prove to the German government, as Gonzalo Enrile supposedly made his proposals in Berlin just around this time, that the Díaz movement was active and had a chance of success. Díaz's propagandists fed US newspapers exaggerated accounts of Díaz's rebellion. The *New York Sun* reported on March 1, 1916, under the headline, "Felix Díaz Joins Oaxacan Revolt—He is in Chiapas and soon will lead a large force against the Carrancistas [sic]."[1259] Also on March 1, The Arizona Republican reported, "Reports say Diaz sailed for Veracruz."[1260] The next day, The Sun followed up with "Félix Díaz now in Tuxpam, U.S. hears."[1261] The paper relied on information from the State Department and recounted Díaz's embarrassing disappearance from the Bureau agents detailed to watch his every move.

The New York Tribune reported on March 9, "Felix Diaz, backed by plenty of money and by the influence of the Cientificos, can make plenty of trouble for Carranza in Mexico [...]."[1262] The State Department told reporters of The Evening World, also on March 9, that "Felix Diaz [...] is hiding in New Orleans, and upon their information they are satisfied that he has not landed in Mexico with an armed expedition as has been reported."[1263] To no avail. The Díaz propaganda machine kept churning. The San Miguel Examiner featured Díaz as the "Nephew of Iron Ruler—Will Start New Revolution."[1264] The New York Tribune reported on March 23, "Felix Diaz captures Puebla, is reported: Followers describe big gains against Carranza."[1265] The Sun reported on the same day, "Has 5,000 men between Vera Cruz and Mexico City [...] he is now making his way toward Mexico City, hoping to take the capital at a time when Carranza is busy elsewhere [...]. Members of the Junta say that [...] if the United States has trouble with him [Carranza], the Felicistas will be found fighting on the side of Uncle Sam."[1266] The New York Times reported on March 30, "Diaz is in Mexico for new revolt [...] Expect[ed] to control south [...]. Revolutionists said to have a $5,000,000 fund [...]." According to the article, the money would be raised in New York City and underwritten by the Catholic Church.[1267] On April 12, Díaz's publicity agent in New York, W. E. D. Stokes, who had created all the heroic reports about Díaz and his Oaxaca campaign, was quoted in The Evening World, "Diaz is now in Mexico—I won't say where—and has 23,000 men at his command, as well as abundant funds."[1268]

William Earl Dodge Stokes was no mere publicist. A Yale graduate and a member of the family who owned Phelps, Dodge & Company, he was a property developer in New York City. His masterpiece was the luxurious Ansonia Hotel in Manhattan. He also became the president of the Chesapeake Western Railway. When he died in 1926, his estate was estimated at $10,000,000 (approximately $177 million in today's value).[1269] Stokes was indeed a wealthy supporter of Félix Díaz, but he exaggerated his own importance. In a letter to Secretary of State Robert Lansing, Stokes wrote, "With two others, I have represented the interests of General Díaz of Mexico [...]."[1270] Stokes did not figure prominently in the documentation concerning *felicista* leaders.

Embarrassed by the intelligence failure in keeping Díaz under surveillance, the Bureau now scrambled to learn how Díaz had managed to get to Mexico. Bielaski wired to Barnes: "Ascertain immediately what can be learned in Corpus Christi about Félix Díaz allegedly leaving from there in a yacht or launch."[1271] Agent Calvin Weakley traveled to Corpus Christi and gathered information about Díaz's schooner La Providencia.[1272] Pendleton consulted CRESSE, who had read to him a letter Mrs. Díaz had received from her husband in Oaxaca recounting his adventures from New Orleans to Oaxaca. Informant William Ibs contributed further details of Díaz's journey.[1273] Agent Beckham in San Antonio learned through an informant that one Eduardo Cuesta had been with Díaz on the voyage and in prison. Cuesta, who had carried the letter to Mrs. Díaz, was reportedly in New Orleans and in communication with Antonio Magnón there. Pendleton made locating him a priority.[1274]

Figure 82. William Earl Dodge Stokes, 1917
Source: Creative Commons

A certain Felipe Pérez at Brownsville wrote to F. A. Chapa in San Antonio that his brother, Adolfo Pérez, was a crewman on the *Providencia*; was taken prisoner near Matamoros, was brought to Monterrey, where he and his friends stood trial, and were liberated. Chapa's El *Imparcial de Texas* carried articles about the schooner's crew on June 14 and 15, 1916.[1275]

US Attorney Camp furnished the confidential information regarding Díaz's trip.[1276] Barnes had Agent Richard B. Spencer interview one Victor Noriega, who had been in prison with Díaz and his companions at Monterrey and who provided a wealth of details.[1277] The Bureau also redoubled its efforts to investigate Díaz's followers and financial backers. Superintendent Offley in New York interviewed William Henry Ellis, one of the most exotic figures in our story.

Ellis was born a slave in Texas but reinvented himself as "Guillermo Eliseo" and became a millionaire Mexican entrepreneur.[1278] Offley had Agent J. G. Tucker arrange a mail cover on General Aureliano Blanquet, and the agent persuaded a clerk at the postal Telegraph Company to make copies of all telegrams concerning the general. Special Employee Berliner translated the telegrams. Berliner also called on Díaz's representative Pedro del Villar and learned more about the infighting among Díaz's followers in the United States. In addition, he investigated the rumor that the Catholic Church had contributed $20,000,000 to Díaz's campaign.[1279] No firm evidence ever turned up.

At New Orleans, Pendleton had Agent E. C. Devlin and Local Officer P. Banville take turns surveilling the house of Díaz's brother-in-law, Leonardo Alcolea, at 1828 Melpomene Street because of a report that Díaz was there. He was not.[1280] Pendleton remained in close contact with informant Charles E. Jones, who said he expected to meet with Colonel Rodolfo Basail, Díaz's chief of staff, and would probably learn something valuable about Díaz.[1281]

On another occasion, at Jones's suggestion, Pendleton went to his office, where Jones had Demetrio Bustamante, formerly Villa consul in Guatemala City and now friendly toward President Estrada Cabrera, speak with him through an interpreter Jones provided. Bustamante disclosed little of value but did state that anything Félix Díaz undertook would end in failure. Pendleton later spoke with journalist H. H. Dunn, and the latter stated that one Pedro Grave de Peralta, who lived in New Orleans most of the time, was the man who arranged with Estrada Cabrera to allow the *felicistas* to land munitions at a Guatemalan port.[1282] Pendleton was not proud, for at least on one occasion, he hid behind a filing cabinet in Jones's office to hear Jones converse with an informant.[1283]

The Bureau's man in Havana, Agent Lewis Cantrell, was monitoring the extensive *felicista* activity there. Cantrell, who reported directly to Bielaski, arranged for mail covers on persons Bielaski named. He also arranged with the Cuban secret police to get information about Díaz leaders and *felicista* movements, as well as whatever other information Bielaski might desire. Information from the secret police constituted most of Cantrell's reports. The agent had also been working on getting Felipe Dusart deported to the United States. Moreover, he interviewed the chief of the Cuban army, who told him that Gonzalo Enrile had bid on twelve surplus 75-millimeter Snyder howitzers but had been unable to come up with the money, and the field pieces were still owned by the Cuban government.¹²⁸⁴ Cantrell did not just collect information. At least on one occasion, he and members of the US Legation intercepted and steamed open, copied, translated, and returned a letter from the arms dealer José Santos Chocano to his colleague Rosendo Márquez.¹²⁸⁵

Persistent rumors alleged financing of the *felicistas* through the Catholic Church.¹²⁸⁶ Cardinal James Gibbons of Baltimore "told the press [in March 1916] that Villa and Carranza were a 'disgrace to their country' [...] [and] hinted that there was 'another candidate for the Mexican presidency [...].' It is probable that he meant Félix Díaz."¹²⁸⁷ A CONFIDENTIAL report by State Department Agent George C. Carothers to the secretary of state further revealed the Catholic Church's support of Félix Díaz. Carothers went to San Antonio and called on Archbishops Mora of Mexico City and Gillow of Oaxaca, after being introduced by a mutual friend. The clerics spoke for the rest of the exiled hierarchy residing in San Antonio, saying that the Church supported Díaz not because he was Félix Díaz but because "he is the first man of law and order that took the field." They were advising all Mexicans to support the movement. They opposed the Punitive Expedition and believed that Carranza was preparing for war, evidenced by his massing of troops in Sonora and Chihuahua. "They stated that they detest Carranza because he has not ceased the persecution of the Church since recognition, but to the contrary has increased it." Furthermore, they stated "that to their knowledge an understanding has been reached between all of the factions of expatriated Mexicans, and that they are united in support of Félix Díaz." Significantly, expatriated Mexicans detested Carranza so much that they preferred to see his downfall caused by American invasion, or by the rage of the masses in their indignation at Carranza's having permitted the Punitive Expedition. Carothers "questioned them as to the financiers of the Díaz movement, and they were reticent but smiled meaningfully when they stated that there would be no shortage of funds." Carothers informed General Frederick Funston of the above, concluding that "on account of the unification of the factions in this country in favor of Félix Díaz, I now consider that his movement is very serious and will gather great strength within a very short time."¹²⁸⁸

This raised the possibility of Germany supporting the Díaz movement, which would constitute a serious threat to national security. The danger of Germany weaponizing the Mexican Revolution against the United States was not only manifested in the Enrile mission, which the Bureau had learned about. In February 1916, Adolfo Stahl, representative of Schwartz & Cia. of Guatemala, approached Hans Tauscher, the German agent and representative of Krupp companies in the United States, about a large arms deal.

Stahl's company had a branch office in San Francisco where he met Harry J. Hart, a broker working with Tauscher, who had made the connection. Stahl, born in Germany in 1859 and an American citizen since 1874, had been the senior partner in Schwarz & Cia. since 1880.[1289] Stahl claimed in meetings with Heinrich Albert and Hans Tauscher in New York in February 1916, that he represented the Guatemalan government of Manuel Estrada Cabrera. According to Stahl, the Guatemalan government wanted to purchase arms and munitions to replace "mold-damaged" stocks in their arsenal. The truth was slightly different. Estrada Cabrera, a puppet of United Fruit Company, supported the planned *felicista* rebellion against the government of Venustiano Carranza in Yucatán.[1290] Stahl arrived with $53,000 in cash (approximately $1.1 million in today's value) from unknown sources.

Tauscher sold Stahl 1.5 million cartridges, caliber 45/70, at $32 per thousand, and ten Colt machine guns from stock he had warehoused for the German government. Whereas Harry Hart received $5,500 in commissions, Tauscher proudly reported to the German military attaché, Wolf von Igel, that the sale had generated a "profit of $4,550."[1291] The shipment was to sail in April on the United Fruit passenger steamer *Sixaola*. The vessel's departure, however, was delayed.

The *Sixaola* had just made major national headlines on its last trip from New York to Guatemala when it answered a distress call from a Brazilian freighter off the coast of North Carolina. Captain C. R. Glenn, in the middle of a nasty storm, managed not only to rescue the crew of the stricken freighter, but also to figure out that it was taking on water as a result of sabotage. The *Sixaola* crew closed the seacocks and pumped out the water, resulting in a lawsuit and damage claim against unnamed saboteurs some months later. As luck would have it, the prominent Washington lawyer and lobbyist Sherburne G. Hopkins, now Estrada Cabrera's attorney on his way to Guatemala, witnessed the daring rescue as a passenger.[1292] Since the *Sixaola* engaged in the harrowing high seas rescue in the middle of April, she did not berth in New York until the end of the month. The delay of the munitions shipment by two weeks caused alarm in an unforeseen quarter.

Not knowing what had caused the delay, the parties interested in the shipment had become nervous. Could the Bureau have caught wind of the neutrality law violation? Archival sources are not clear as to who exactly contacted the State Department for help, or whether the State Department had been involved in the sourcing of arms for "Guatemala." It may have been the financiers behind the effort: United Fruit, International Harvester Corporation, the Catholic Church; or, all three.

Evidently, the head of the Division of Mexican Affairs at the State Department, Leon J. Canova, knew all about the shipment. The Bureau had already been alerted in March 1916 about Canova hobnobbing with the general manager of International Harvester, Alexander Legge, with the suspicion that Canova once again leaked confidential information to outsiders.[1293] Not knowing the details of the delay and suspecting involvement by the Bureau, Leon Canova contacted his "old pal," Harry Berliner. Berliner, who indeed had gained the confidence of the State Department schemer, indulged Canova and met him at the latter's urgent request for a confidential meeting at the St. Regis Hotel in New York.[1294]

Canova confided in Berliner that foreign policy within the US State Department was shifting away from Carranza in favor of Félix Díaz. Once Díaz took control of Mexico (with the help of the US), Canova hoped Berliner would be able to return home to Mexico City.[1295] This shift coincided with the fear of the US government of war with Carranza over the Punitive Expedition. Indeed, Canova told Berliner that he thought a war was inevitable.[1296] Finally, after the emergency weekend meeting and three letters, Canova came to the point regarding the *Sixaola* shipment: "The shipment is straight, as it is for the Government [of Guatemala]."[1297] The next day, Canova went even further in his insistence that Berliner somehow would make sure the shipment would go forward, adding, "if there is anything irregular about it [the shipment,] this delay may cause some more which would betray the parties really interested."[1298] The party really interested, according to Bureau agents monitoring Canova, was International Harvester.[1299]

Berliner was concerned about Canova's likely betrayal of the State Department. He recognized immediately how potentially explosive the information about Canova's involvement with shipping weapons and ammunition in support of the *felicista* revolt would be. So, he elected to inform Chief Bielaski directly in a CONFIDENTIAL AND PERSONAL report:

> Enclosed please find letter that I received from my friend Canova, also copy of my reply [...]. I beg also to advise that during the course of my investigations while in conversation with Mr. Charles O. Gilbert and Dr. F. M. Taube both of Zacatecas, they told me of a letter [...] of which Canova was the writer the contents of which was to the effect that the present Administration in Washington was now very much in favor of Félix Díaz and his new movement [...] the letter was sent to a foreigner, I judged an Englishman [...].[1300]

There is no record of activity between Berliner's note and any action on Bielaski's part, but one could safely assume that Bielaski put out some discreet feelers. In due time, Bielaski confided in William Offley, but otherwise kept the information strictly confidential. By July, Canova had become a suspect not only of leaking classified information but of potentially betraying his office by engaging in neutrality law violations. Bielaski had him closely watched by two of the Bureau's crack agents, Pasquale Pigniuolo and Albert G. Adams. The Chief also consulted journalist J. C. Hammond, who had helped the Bureau with information on Canova in the leak investigation of 1915. He had also assisted the Bureau in the extensive investigation of Franz Rintelen in 1915. This time, Canova was actively surveilled. The Chief hired Hammond as a paid informant but admonished Offley to make sure that there would be no entrapment.[301] The investigation did not turn up a smoking gun of Canova's double-dealing with Wall Street, and by the end of July the investigation fizzled out. What cannot be underestimated, however, is the extraordinary risk Bielaski took when he decided to actively surveil Canova. The head of the Mexican Desk in the State Department was a high government official with a direct line to Secretary of State Lansing. Bielaski would have risked immediate dismissal if the investigation, albeit wholly justified, had become known. Bielaski's instincts, despite the fact that the investigation did not yield a tangible result, were right once again.

Also noteworthy is the role Harry Berliner played in this episode. Just as he was able to infiltrate the inner circle of Félix Díaz, Berliner gained the confidence of his "good friend," Leon Canova, extracted all the pertinent information he could, and then reported him to the Bureau. And, politically astute, he elected to approach Bielaski directly and confidentially to preclude leaks. Just as Félix Díaz never considered Berliner untrustworthy or disloyal, neither did Canova, enabling Berliner to continue to extract sensitive information in the future. His skill in gaining the confidence of his targets made him one of the Bureau's most effective secret agents.

CRESSE confirmed to the Chief that: "Leon J. Canova in charge of the Bureau of Mexican Affairs for nearly a year has been intimate friend and adviser of Pedro del Villar according to del Villar's statements. Canova also according to del Villar has been promised certain large concessions when the Díaz party secure control of Mexico; also, according to del Villar he has several times been a visitor and guest at Canova's home. [Guillermo] Rosas also has confirmed del Villar's statements regarding this matter. Canova has also seen del Villar and others of the Díaz leaders several times in New York. You will remember that several months ago copy of telegram sent by del Villar in New York to Rosas in New Orleans stated that Canova has and was helping them all he could."[1302]

Concerned about the two-weeks' delay in the *Sixaola's* departure, Tauscher arranged for the munitions to be stacked alongside the steamer at Pier 1, North River at Hoboken on May 1, 1916.[1303] The shipment was quite sensitive, as the *Sixaola* called at Jamaica before it reached Puerto Barrios on Guatemala's Atlantic coast. Any suspicion about a German involvement in the shipment would cause certain seizure by British authorities in Jamaica.

CRESSE, whom Bielaski heavily relied upon for information about the *felicista* movement, had as his principal source of information Guillermo Rosas, head of the *felicistas* in New Orleans. Jones and Rosas discussed the Pearson Oil Company, which Rosas said was furnishing money and assistance to the Díaz movement. The money was allegedly coming from Europe, and through the good offices of the archbishop of Yucatán, $200,000 had been promised for a Yucatán expedition.[1304]

The most intriguing aspect of Díaz's financial backers was the alleged role of International Harvester. The company had a monopoly in Yucatán on the market for henequen, used to make binding twine in wheat harvests in the United States. Its agent in Yucatán was the wealthy Avelino Montes. Landowners had to sell their henequen production to International Harvester at Harvester's price. Now, however, the price of henequen had increased substantially because of World War I, and Carranza desperately needed the revenue. The "*Comisión Reguladora del Mercado de Henequén*" regulated henequen production, and Carranza's policy was enforced by General Salvador Alvarado, the anti-American military governor of Yucatán. Avelino Montes had fled to Havana, where he and his even wealthier father-in-law Olegario Molina engaged in new conspiracies.[1305] International Harvester was allegedly determined to regain its monopoly by supporting regime change in Yucatán, more specifically by financing a *felicista* expedition to overthrow Alvarado.

General Pedro Cortés, a former governor of Yucatán, was to lead the expedition. Jones arranged for Rosas and Cortés to come to his office, where Pendleton would conceal himself and overhear the conversation. But Rosas came alone, saying he had been unable to locate Cortés. Rosas discussed with Jones the munitions needed for the Yucatán expedition. Jones also had the specifications and photos of a boat which the Díaz crowd were contemplating purchasing from him.[1306] Rosas stated that contingents would start simultaneously from Point San Antonio, Cuba, and from Belize, British Honduras. Félix Díaz had reportedly bought from Charles Jones 1,800 30-30 rifles, 1,000,000 30-30 cartridges, and two field pieces, to be delivered in Belize. Mentioning that Belize would be one of two starting points for the expedition was a valuable piece of information, because Britain, as a wartime measure, surveilled traffic in the Caribbean. The chances that Britain would permit a *felicista* expedition to amass weaponry and to depart from Belize were problematic.

CRESSE informed Pendleton that Pedro Cortés left New Orleans on April 29 for Havana, where he was to go over his plans with the Archbishop of Yucatán and then submit to Guillermo Rosas in New Orleans the data concerning the necessary equipment and the money required. Cortés also told Jones that the Catholic Party was, through the archbishop of Yucatán, to furnish the approximately $200,000 required to finance the expedition. Originally, it had been intended for this money to come from New York, but plans had changed. Jones advised that Pedro Cortés was returning to New Orleans from Havana shortly as he had made successful plans for the financial backing of the Yucatán expedition. Final arrangements would be concluded in Jones's office, and a contract signed for the munitions and supplies for the expedition.[1307]

But, given the extremely grave situation between the US and Mexico, nothing could be done at present; the *felicistas* would wait until the situation cleared up. Several Americans who had agreed to furnish money and arms and ammunition for the campaign in Chiapas were holding back for the moment since it would put them into a very unpatriotic position, but as soon as matters between the United States and Mexico were resolved, "they would start things." The *felicistas* would also wait until the presidential election in November, for they feared the reelection of Woodrow Wilson.[1308]

Jones stated that Pedro Cortés would leave New Orleans shortly for Havana and remain there a short time, then proceed to Belize to prepare the Yucatán expedition.[1309] But, as Cantrell reported from Havana, his sources indicated that the *felicistas* there were broke—they had expected large sums "from a particular source," which had not materialized.[1310]

Pendleton received more information from Jones about the Díaz movement. Pedro del Villar was at 210 West 72nd Street, New York, receiving mail and telegrams under the alias of "Esteban León." In fact, Jones was PREPARING A CODE FOR THE USE OF THE DIAZ FACTION, AND THEY HAD ALREADY BEGUN TO USE THE CODE. General Cortés's code name was "Mr. Polite." Guillermo Rosas received mail and telegrams under the alias of "William Flowers, Jr.," 1210 Octavia Street, New Orleans. The junta's Havana agent was Esteban Maqueo Castellanos, c/o Juan Casiano Petroleum Company, Aguilar 16, Havana.

Jones's most important report was that International Harvester had agreed to finance the entire Yucatán expedition, and one of the directors of the company had left Chicago for Havana a week or ten days earlier. Pendleton suggested that an investigation be made in Chicago to ascertain the name of the director, and in that way the Bureau could probably verify these statements. Avelino Montes and his father-in-law, Olegario Molina, were both in Havana and presumably meeting with the Harvester director. Avelino Montes and Olegario Molina were referred to in the code as "Mills" and "Hills." The code word for International Harvester was "Reapers." Pendleton quoted a cipher telegram Jones provided and translated, dated June 6, 1916, from del Villar in New York to Rosas asking him to confirm the letter mailed to General Cortés from Chicago which advised that the entire affair was successfully consummated with International Harvester. One of their directors was now on the way to meet with Avelino Montes and Olegario Molina, and del Villar would probably join them in Havana.

Jones believed that Cortés was impatient and extremely anxious to start, and that the Mexican situation now was the psychological moment for beginning the Yucatán expedition. He said that they had been waiting until definite arrangements for financing the expedition were made, but now that International Harvester was going to put up the money, Jones did not anticipate there would be any great delay. He furnished Pendleton with copies of a mass of letters and telegrams exchanged between del Villar and himself regarding the former's wife being in prison. It showed why del Villar and the others had confidence in Jones. Pendleton suggested that extreme care be exercised to protect Jones (CRESSE) as the Bureau's source in New Orleans.[1311]

Jones informed Pendleton that Pedro Cortés was supposed to have received a telegram on June 12 from Avelino Montes from Havana regarding the Yucatán expedition. He said the cable was in code. Jones was also informed that Cortés answered the cablegram the same day. Jones had a friend at Western Union and said it was a very easy matter to get a copy of any messages he desired, but that this cablegram was not sent over Western Union. Pendleton would inquire if these messages were sent over Postal Telegraph. Jones advised that he had had a long conference with Cortés, Rosas, and Rafael Alcolea, and that they had gone over the specifications for arms and ammunition and other equipment for the Yucatán expedition: 2,000,000 30-30 rounds, 2,000 30-30 rifles, four Hotchkiss 37-millimeter Gatling guns, 100 Colt automatic pistols, ten 7-millimeter Colt machine guns, etc. totaling $217,000 worth of war materiel. He said the money would be furnished by International Harvester through Montes. Jones expected it would not be very long before they would take decisive action, because they considered the time ripe for the movement to begin. If Díaz were permitted to go ahead in the southern part of Mexico, he would soon have Carranza on his knees, and the latter would not further annoy the US. Jones agreed to keep Pendleton posted, and Pendleton believed that he would, because it would be embarrassing for him to hold back anything now, after having given so much information to the Bureau. Jones advised that Demetrio Bustamante came to his office accompanied by informant William Ibs, and he said Bustamante had 600 men in Guatemala and desired to join Díaz's revolution. The majority of Bustamante's men were said to be the old "Villa crowd," who were involved in the proposed expedition against the State of Chiapas. Jones said he did not believe Díaz would accept aid from Bustamante.[1312]

The Chief sent Cantrell in Havana a copy of Pendleton's June 9 report stating that Esteban Maqueo Castellanos was the Havana agent of the Díaz faction, and that International Harvester had agreed to finance the entire Yucatán expedition, and that one of the Company's directors had gone to Havana a week or ten days earlier. The Chicago field office would inquire about the director. If his name were secured, Cantrell would be notified. Cantrell was to take extreme care to protect Jones as a source.[1313]

Pendleton called on Jones, who advised that Pedro Cortés would probably leave for Havana via Key West. He said Pedro del Villar had been in Washington recently to confer with Congressman William S. Bennett of New York, who he understood was Díaz's representative in Washington. Jones gave Pendleton copies of telegrams, the most important of which was from Del Villar to Rosas stating the International Harvester matter had been working out according to plan. Accordingly, Cortés would leave immediately for Havana to brief Avelino Montes before the arrival there of the Harvester director.[1314] Assistant Superintendent W. L. Furbershaw tried to learn the name of the Harvester director who left Chicago for Havana about ten days or two weeks earlier to confer with Montes and Molina. The district court deputy and a confidential informant in the employ of Harvester assisted by providing information that no officer or director was now in Havana or enroute there. This information was said to have come from the secretary of the corporation, George A. Raney [who would be unlikely to admit that Harvester was involved in a nefarious operation]. They would make further efforts to test the validity of this information.[1315] The Harvester director never showed up, however. Neither did the money the *felicistas* had been expecting.[1316]

The Bureau investigated other potential sources of financing through American sources. Jones reported in July, that Cecilio Ocón, one of the witnesses of the Díaz assassination attempt, went to New York about a year ago and offered his services to Pedro del Villar in any capacity. Ocón had broken with Díaz in 1914 but tried to reconcile, and issued a circular supporting Díaz and repudiating his earlier statements against Díaz. Rosas said Ocón arrived in New Orleans on June 24 with $50,000. Rosas told Jones he had no idea where Ocón had obtained the money. Rosas said on June 29, Ocón sent $10,000 to someone in San Antonio to defray the expenses of certain parties from San Antonio and El Paso going to Guatemala to assist the Díaz crowd. Ocón left New Orleans on June 29 with General Guadencio González de la Llave, the latter's son and several others. Ibs reported that they were going to Guatemala and through Chiapas to join Díaz in Oaxaca.[1317]

Apparently International Harvester was still considering backing the Yucatán expedition. Jones reported to Pendleton that General Pedro Cortés left on July 1 for Havana to join Olegario Molina and Avelino Montes, and to make final arrangements for the expedition. Cortés expected to send money from Havana to Rosas in New Orleans with which to buy the arms and ammunition and a boat; that Cortés would go to Belize, where he had a group of assistants, and expected to receive the supplies and boat near Belize. According to Jones, relating information secured from Rosas, there would also be an expedition against Chiapas and one against the neighboring state of Tabasco. Jones also advised that three Americans had recently arrived in New Orleans: Kimball, Taggart, and Mason; Mason owned large coffee plantations in Tabasco, and Taggart was supposedly an ex-US army officer and went under the title of "Colonel" Taggart. Jones reported that Taggart and Mason had left New Orleans. Kimball was still there, and Jones expected to meet him in a day or two and go over a proposition with Kimball. Jones would supply arms and ammunition for the Díaz movement against the State of Tabasco, to be financed by the three mentioned above. Jones said the three expected to put up $50,000 to back the Tabasco expedition. Jones talked with Kimball, who said he was waiting for Taggart and a certain Wolfe, who were associated with him in Tabasco, and that if these two agreed, Kimball would advance the money to supply the Díaz expedition against Chiapas. It seems that Kimball, Taggart, Wolfe, and others were interested in large coffee plantations and sold machinery in Tabasco and Chiapas. They bitterly opposed the Carranza government and would be glad to give any assistance to overthrow him. Kimball said that if his partners consented, he would have Jones furnish the arms and ammunition.[1318]

Informant Ibs met with Rosas, who claimed that Díaz was gradually placing his forces near the railroads and would not attempt to attack the larger cities until he controlled more of the main lines. Rosas said there would be plenty of money as soon as Díaz made his first real demonstration, and that Rosas would then want Ibs's help in a publicity campaign for Díaz.[1319]

Jones reported that he understood from Rosas that when Cecilio Ocón came to New Orleans he received $25,000 at the Whitney Central Bank in the name of Carlos Landa, and that this amount was supposed to come from one of the executives of the Pearson Oil interests in New York, probably in the form of a check or draft. Pendleton interviewed the bank president, who was unable to find anything having been handled through the bank for either Landa or Ocón. Pendleton spoke with Jones, who said that Rosas had told him the amount was $10,000, instead of $25,000.[1320]

As Díaz's troops in Oaxaca were pushed back and defeated by Carranza's forces, the Yucatán campaign—without money, ammunition, or troops— continued on a path to victory only in the general's imagination. A classic Díaz conundrum was that, if he just had supplies, he would be successful; yet in order to get supplies, he had to show success. In a last-ditch effort to admit the obvious, Díaz wrote to his US representative, del Villar, that he had 20,000 troops distributed as follows: 10,000 in Oaxaca, which he commanded personally; 7,500 in Puebla, divided into one army of 4,500 and one of 3,000; and, 2,500 troops in Veracruz. Díaz claimed that these troops had an abundant supply of artillery, machine guns, rifles, and other equipment, but that they had practically no ammunition at all, and that it was imperative to send at least 5,000,000 rounds as quickly as possible, for the Díaz forces could not do much until they received ammunition. Jones said that Rosas got very confidential with him and showed him copies of contracts that Díaz had with J. P. Morgan & Company bearing the signature of a man named "Strang" or "Strong." Jones got a glimpse of the contracts but was unable to read them. Rosas told him, however, that Díaz was to get $600,000 when he arrived in Mexico and $250,000 additional each fifteen days thereafter that he showed progress, up to five million dollars. Jones said that Rosas had the custody of these papers and all other papers of importance belonging to the Díaz faction.[1321]

Jones told Pendleton that del Villar in New York had written to Rosas advising him that the former had been in Washington in the previous week, accompanied by certain bankers. These bankers had visited the State Department, and officials there had stated that they would like to see some demonstration by Félix Díaz and his party to show their ability to control matters in Mexico before announcing the position of the Department in the matter or making any comment thereon. Jones said that Rosas informed him that del Villar stated in his letter that they stopped at the Ebbet House while in Washington, and claimed he was in Washington four different times. Pendleton suggested checking the register at the Ebbet House for the past two weeks, and for July 13 and 14.[1322] Del Villar had not registered there under his own name.¹³²³ Rather than encouraging the Díaz representatives to show action in Mexico before any consideration, the State Department official actually told the representatives to stay out of Mexican affairs.

The fate of the Yucatán expedition went from bad to worse on August 10, when Jones reported that the designated commander, General Pedro Cortés, had died in Havana on August 9. He thought it was likely that *carrancista* agents had poisoned him. Rosas told him that General Blanquet would probably succeed General Cortés and take charge of the Yucatán expedition. A telegram by Rosas to del Villar ("Esteban León") underscored the disaster: "Unhappily, our good friend 'Polite' died some days ago according to a cablegram just received. Business will be ruined if we do not handle with excessive care. I am fully informed of while details also show how far our negotiations were. I suggest to you the idea to send me immediately to Havana to finish matters with friends to secure absolutely good results consulting also to [with] shareholders for our [illegible word] if you realize I can do something good for our friend. Waiting [for] your orders by fast wire. [signed] William Flowers Jr. [Guillermo Rosas]."¹³²⁴

Despite the valiant efforts of Díaz's adherents in the US, the vaunted Yucatán expedition never happened. Once more, Díaz had proved that he lacked the leadership qualities and wherewithal to pull off such a grandiose plan. From the beginning, he was short of funds. He also could not curb infighting among his partisans. General Salvador Alvarado remained as governor of Yucatán until 1917. Regarding the role of International Harvester, the *felicistas* certainly believed the company would finance the Yucatán expedition. Harvester apparently did offer financial support, only to back out of any arrangement upon mature reflection. While Díaz mounted a significant publicity campaign in the US that lasted into the fall of 1916, the effort never garnered the support he had envisioned. After the Columbus attack of March 9, 1916, and the resulting Punitive Expedition, a war between the US and Mexico loomed large. American financiers avoided supporting Mexican revolutionists for the fear of appearing unpatriotic. Also, unfortunate was the failure of the Enrile mission to Berlin. After being held up in Spain, Enrile finally arrived in Berlin after the Columbus raid had happened and the American military intervention had begun. Germany saw no further need to support a new revolutionary movement.¹³²⁵ Rather, the Albert office in New York received orders to switch financial support to Carranza, who had the best chance of engaging in a war with the US.¹³²⁶

Due primarily to CRESSE, the Bureau was fully abreast of *felicista* activities. But CRESSE's intelligence contributions were by no means limited to the *felicistas*. Chief Bielaski wrote to CRESSE on June 28, 1916:

> With respect to the Dusart case, the Díaz case, the Honduras Revolutionary matter and numerous other similar matters of grave concern to the United States, I am only too glad to testify to the discreet, patriotic and invaluable service which you have rendered. I appreciate very much your assurance that you will continue to aid us as heretofore and assure you that I will be glad to testify to the value of your services at any time such action may seem desirable.[1327]

This view of Jones was reinforced by a meeting that took place in Washington on December 13, 1916. Leland Harrison of the State Department's Office of the Counselor reported the following day to Frank Polk that:

> Last evening, I was asked by Mr. Bielaski to come over to the Department of Justice for a conference with Assistant Attorney General Warren about an important matter. Mr. Warren handed me the attached summaries of information furnished the Department of Justice by Informant Cresse relative to the activities of Félix Díaz'[s] adherents against Mexico, of Máximo B. Rosales against Honduras, of Dr. Carlos F. Dardano against Salvador and of Dr. Julián Irías against Nicaragua. In view of the evidence in the possession of the Department of Justice Mr. Warren believes the moment now is opportune to arrest all those implicated in these various movements. Some are in Douglas, Arizona, others in Laredo, Brownsville and San Antonio, Texas, others in New Orleans and New York City. Before doing so, however, he wished to consult the [State] Department in order to ascertain whether there would be any objection to his proceeding in the matter at this time.

> The most prominent names connected with these various movements are as follows: General Blanquet, General Mondragón, General Gerónimo Villarreal, Doctor González, Doctor Iberri, Arturo M. Elías, Máximo B. Rosales, Doctor Peralta, Mr. Eiseman, Doctor Larrea, Pedro del Villar, Mr.

M[anuel] Peláez, General Manuel Lardizábal, and Guillermo Rosas.

Briefly stated, the plans of the Félix Díaz followers contemplate assistance to the Díaz revolutionary movement in the southeast of Mexico, the sending of General Blanquet and others to take command of the Diacistas [sic] in the southwest, the sending of arms and ammunition to General I. [sic—M.] Peláez operating around Tampico and Tuxpan, the setting on foot of an expedition from the neighborhood of Brownsville of the forces to be commanded by General Villarreal to operate in the State of Tamaulipas and a similar movement from Douglas, Arizona and New Mexico, in an effort to join up with General José Inés Salazar who would desert Villa.

General Rosales hopes to start his expedition against Honduras about the first of the year. He plans to land in Ceiba. Peralta recently visited Mexico City and obtained from Carranza and Obregón $50,000 for the assistance of Rosales on the promise that Rosales after he becomes President of Honduras would arm and equip 10,000 men who were to start a revolution against the government of Guatemala from the territory of Honduras. This revolution was to cooperate with another revolution similarly armed and equipped by Carranza starting from the State of Chiapas. Rosales has also arranged through Peralta that Dr. Carlos F. Dardano of San Salvador will start of movement against Honduras at the time ordered by Rosales. Dardano and his friends will furnish the arms and ammunition. In return, Rosales upon becoming President of Honduras will pay for these arms and ammunition and back Dardano in starting a revolution against Salvador. At the same time that Rosales starts his revolution, he will assist Irías in a similar effort against Nicaragua which will start from Honduras territory [...].

In view of the information in the possession of the Department of Justice indicating that these various movements are now about to take place, I would respectfully recommend that Mr. Warren be informed that the Department has no objection to his proceeding in the matter. There is, however, the possibility that the connection between Carranza and Rosales may become public, that the Mexican Consuls General in New Orleans and New York may be implicated, and that the fact that Carranza has obtained arms and ammunition through Canada may become known; also, Father Kelley may be implicated in the Wrigley-Díaz arrangement. Should you think it desirable for any reason, Mr. Warren might be requested to prevent, if possible, this side of the matter from reaching the newspapers.[1328]

The *felicista* conspiracies of 1916 shed light on another, much more important, development. Despite the continued lack of proper resources for surveillance, which accounted for the embarrassing disappearance of Félix Díaz, Chief Bielaski showed that the Bureau had reached a new level of proficiency of intelligence gathering and counterintelligence work, both on a national and international stage. Harry Berliner and Charles Jones provided a 20/20 vision into the Díaz movement, their personnel, planning, resources, and time schedules. After the Oaxaca campaign withered and the Yucatán project never even got off the ground, Bielaski decided that the potential national security threat had passed. In an unprecedented set of investigations, agents under cover in New Orleans, New York, Mexico, and Cuba not only followed developments in real time, but proved to Bielaski that Germany was only involved initially, and in fact had lost interest as did any other potential supporters of Díaz. The Chief, therefore, was able to allocate resources elsewhere. As 1916 came to a close, war with Germany loomed large on the horizon.

While historians may question why Bielaski committed such significant department resources to the perennial loser of the Mexican Revolution, we see in hindsight that he was right. The possibility of German support of a new movement comprised of all opposition factions was a potential threat to American national security. In an efficient and effective campaign, the Bureau not only determined that Díaz once more had presided over a losing proposition, but also likely deterred further German attempts to support the movement actively. Bureau agents arrested Hans Tauscher on March 30 and charged him with conspiracy for attacking Canada.[1329] While keeping track of the Díaz conspiracy, Agent Cantrell in Cuba also tracked the German bomb maker, Walter T. Scheele, who had fled to Cuba in the spring of 1916.

Yet, while Bielaski monitored the *felicista* movement and committed significant resources to determining the facts, German sabotage efforts in the US homeland escalated. In July 1916, the Allied munitions dump at Black Tom Island in New York exploded, causing an earthquake estimated to be 5.5 on the Richter scale. Insurance companies, as well as fire department investigators, initially ruled the explosion an accident. The Bureau had no leads and did not open an official investigation. The German sabotage agents based in Baltimore, whom the Bureau had investigated in unrelated cases, were not identified as the perpetrators until well into the 1920s and 1930s. During that ill-fated summer of 1916, virtually the entire US military had deployed to Mexico or along the border. The German strategy to tie up US resources preventing an active participation in the European war seemed to have succeeded.

The FBI and American Neutrality, 1914-1917

15

Descent Into War

CARRANZA WAS THE RECOGNIZED HEAD of the Mexican Government as 1917 opened, and the Bureau was engaged in enforcing the neutrality laws against those trying to overthrow him. Agent in Charge Robert Barnes in San Antonio wrote to the Chief on January 5 that

> in view of the many disquieting reports along the border indicting numerous bands operating against the de facto government and the sympathy which these movements are receiving from this side it is believed that some drastic steps will have to be taken in the very near future or the de facto government will no doubt lose a large portion of the territory which they now control. As suggested in my recent letter to you, it is believed that about the only effective way to do this under our present neutrality laws would be to file a complaint charging a conspiracy to violate section ten and thirteen and the President's proclamation against all persons involved. It is realized that at this time the evidence may probably not be sufficient to secure a conviction, but it is believed that a vigorous attempt at prosecution will have a wholesome effect in deterring many of the sympathizers of this movement from further activities. If you think this course advisable, it is desired to include in this complaint practically all of the active leaders now on this side of the border, including those operating in New York, New Orleans, and San Antonio. I might say in this connection that if there are sufficient overt acts in some jurisdictions farther away from the border, like New York, it is probable that more effective prosecution could be secured. I

would be glad to have you advise me upon the receipt of this letter as to the course which we should pursue.[1330]

Bielaski answered the following day:

State Department has been advised through Associated Press that there will be meeting today or yesterday San Antonio of number of Villa officers for purpose selecting officials to govern territory controlled by Villa. Offley advises received information person left New York fourth instant to attend meeting San Antonio Monday or Tuesday to be attended by representatives Félix Díaz, General Villa and eleven generals of different factions now operating against Carranza in field and effort made to agree upon representative government oppose and overthrow Carranza. Representatives Villa will agree he shall not head new government. Information may not be reliable but should be given immediate and close attention. Any person found in this country who has been actively engaged in army of Villa or in field in Mexico for him since Columbus raid should be arrested and held as long as practicable. Might possibly be charged as accessory after fact to murders at Columbus. In any event desire that all such persons be held as long as practicable through cooperation state authorities or on any charge which in any reasonable manner may be brought against them under Federal statutes.[1331]

Bielaski also stated: "In the present situation along the border, Government officers should be willing to take some chances in examining the contents of vehicles going into Mexico for articles which may be carried there in violation of the President's proclamation."[1332]

Pancho Villa remained a problem, but he had been reduced to a regional one, operating primarily in Chihuahua. Arguably, those most at risk were the Chinese, whom Villa enjoyed massacring. Many Chinese, in fear of their lives, accompanied the Punitive Expedition as it crossed back into the United States.[1333] Illustrating the Bureau's having to follow leads no matter how improbable, a Mrs. Jules Cassard in New Orleans claimed to have seen and talked with Pancho Villa in Calatoire's Restaurant. Agent Pendleton reported that on the remote chance she might be right, he instructed Informant Ibs to make a thorough canvass of all the Mexican hangouts.[1334] Villa was not located.

Bielaski continued to take a hard line against *villistas*. When Agent Blanford asked in March for guidance regarding a munitions shipment in which Frank Thayer was involved, Bielaski replied, "Favor aggressive action and taking chances particularly at this time if any reasonable theory possible on which party may be apprehended. Think this should be done if other methods exhausted."[1335] Furthermore, Bielaski saw "no objection to the placing of a military guard in the vicinity of stores that persistently sell ammunition to Mexicans, under the circumstances which reasonably indicate that it is intended to be smuggled into Mexico, providing it can be arranged with the military authorities."[1336]

Agent in Charge Barnes in San Antonio was certainly aggressive. He sent Special Employee E. T. Needham to bring to the field office Ignacio Borrego, a frequent visitor to Villa's brother, Hipólito.[1337] Needham returned to Borrego's room and

> secured codes, letters from Miguel Díaz Lombardo [who had been Villa's foreign minister] and various other men regarding the Villa revolution and a great number of other papers pertaining to the *Felicista* and *Villista* activities. All of the above documents are being translated from the Spanish. On instructions from Agent Barnes had Borrego detained at police headquarters until all evidence secured could be shaped up.[1338]

Needham later interrogated Borrego and conferred with the US attorney about building a case against him.[1339] Borrego's troubles continued, as Needham reported:

> Borrego advised this office on May 5 that after his release from city jail he found on his return to his room at 501 St. Mary's St. that a watch, two tie pins, and a ring or two were missing from his trunk. The articles mentioned, with the exception of the rings, were noticed by Employee when he examined Borrego's effects, and were also seen by the woman who runs the house, who was in the room at the time the examination was made. The house in question is nothing more than an assignation house and in all probability the landlady is the party who obtained the articles.[1340]

Agent Barnes sent Special Employee Willard Utley to the Victoria Hotel to interview Miguel Díaz Lombardo, who reportedly had certain papers from Villa in his possession. Taking with him an interpreter, Utley interrogated Díaz Lombardo, who was sick in bed. Thoroughly browbeaten, the Mexican got out of bed long enough to open two trunks and a briefcase containing papers. Utley went through them, finding nothing from Villa, but decided that a number of the documents were important. He took the papers to the Bureau office to be copied and translated.[1341]

By the time the US entered World War I, Bielaski felt that *villistas* posed no threat. He instructed Barnes: "I beg to advise you that I do not see any particular reason, at this time, for requesting Villa followers to move farther North. The situation does not seem to be especially critical at this time, and we do not desire to take any unusual steps, except when necessary to meet real emergency."[1342]

As for the *felicista* cause, it revived somewhat. With the withdrawal of the Punitive Expedition on February 5, 1917, and the consequent lessening of US-Mexican tensions, American sympathizers of the *felicistas* could worry less about being considered unpatriotic by supporting a Mexican faction. In January, Díaz wrote to his brother-in-law Alcolea that all the cause lacked was money.[1343] As we shall see, there was a revival of intrigues concerning financial support for Díaz.[1344] Barnes at San Antonio sent a circular letter to all agents and special employees, quoting from a report of a confidential informant of the New York office, alerting them that Díaz couriers used messages written in invisible ink on very thin tissue paper sewn into their clothes. A hot iron brought out the message.[1345]

Díaz's grand strategy regarding the US border was twofold; first, General Santos Cavazos was dispatched to Brownsville to try to buy the Carranza garrison in Matamoros. He failed. Secondly, expeditions were to be launched across the border from the United States, one of which had crossed on the night of December 24, 1916, near Laredo. It did not go as intended. Led by attorney Pedro González, sometime mayor of Nuevo Laredo, who now bore the title of "Chief of the Reorganizing Movement in the State of Nuevo León," the expedition numbered less than twenty-five men. The plan was for this to be a nucleus, around which volunteers would rally as the group moved deeper into the interior. The recruits would come from the roving bands which were not so much pro-*felicista* as they were anti-Carranza. González's numbers did increase, but mainly he swept into small towns, levied a forced loan on the residents, and departed. Carranza forces drove the *felicistas* back to the Rio Grande, where US soldiers arrested some of the filibusters. González tried to cross another contingent, on January 23, 1917, but Carranza troops drove them back to the US side of the river.

Chief Bielaski ordered Barnes to ensure that all members of the González expeditions who were caught were indicted. Agent Breniman was assigned exclusively to the González matter, about which he prepared a comprehensive report.[1346] One of his informants was Adolfo Osterveen, Jr., formerly a Bureau informant who was now working for the Mexican consul against the *felicistas*, but who was also once again a Bureau informant. Not only that, but Osterveen had recently applied to Jesús María Arriola, Carranza's intelligence chief in the US, for a position. Osterveen asked Breniman whether it was proper for him to work for the *carrancistas* after having worked for the Bureau. Breniman had confidence in Osterveen's integrity and told him that he "saw no objections to his contemplated action, providing he did not reveal to the Mexicans information obtained while employed by this Department. Osterveen said that under no circumstances would he be disloyal to the United States government."[1347]

Breniman believed that an indictment and conviction could be obtained on a conspiracy charge against González and his band of filibusters, many of whom were in custody. González finally informed his remaining followers that it was useless to continue their efforts since they had received none of the assistance promised. It had been another *felicista* fiasco. On March 17, Agent Breniman and a deputy US marshal took Pedro González into custody at his residence, which had been under surveillance. He posted a $10,000 bond, to the disappointment of the Chief, who had instructed Barnes to make every effort to have González's bail set so high that he would have to remain in custody.[1348]

Pedro González and his followers were tried in May 1917. González was sentenced to a $10,000 fine or twelve months in the Webb County jail. His two lieutenants received a $5,000 fine or twelve months in jail. Eleven men received a $300 fine or three months in the jail. Twenty-five indictments were returned against other members of González's band.[1349] These sentences were hardly draconian.

A major development occurred in New York City. Special Employee Harry Berliner, and Agents Charles Scully and Pasquale Pigniuolo had been surveilling Carranza consul Juan T. Burns on Superintendent Offley's instructions. They arrested Burns on January 3, 1917, as he entered his chauffeured car, charging him with plotting to smuggle arms. They also arrested four of the consul's associates, charging them with the same offense.[1350] Burns, a Notre Dame graduate, had been appointed Carranza consul in Galveston on September 18, 1914, and was promoted to consul general in New York on March 1, 1916, succeeding Dr. Alfredo Caturegli.[351] Harry Berliner investigated, learning that Burns claimed he was innocent, but that the other four were guilty. Moreover, Burns claimed, he was the victim of a plot by certain other Carranza officials, among them Doctor Alfredo Caturegli, financial agent for the Mexican government, and Luís Cabrera, Minister of Finance, to make Burns "persona non grata," and had resorted to any means to get rid of him.[352] However, in a 1925 letter to the Secretary of Foreign Relations describing his career, Burns stated that his principal consular assignment in 1916 was to purchase and ship munitions to Mexico.[353] After the unpleasantness in New York, the Mexican government ordered Burns back to Mexico on October 23, 1917. The US government cancelled Burns's exequatur as consul that same month. Carranza appointed Burns as consul general in Hamburg on November 10, 1917.

On another matter, one S. P. Bradford, a former Treasury Department agent, wrote to Berliner from Los Angeles offering him $1,000 if he could find a buyer in New York for the yacht Sybilla, which could be used to transport munitions to Félix Díaz.[354] Berliner reported this to Superintendent Offley, who notified Bielaski and cautioned agents that

> if any investigation is made of Bradford, who is unknown to Berliner as identified with Mexican activities except insofar as this letter indicates, please caution the agent or agents to be particularly discreet and to avoid it becoming known that Berliner has given any information upon this subject, as the latter will use the original letter to secure entree to Mexican circles here, and will bring the matter to the attention of various of the leaders in furtherance of an effort to ascertain their plans and whether they are in the market for such a purchase.[355]

Berliner's efforts were cut short, however, for Offley received orders for Berliner to proceed immediately to Washington and report to Chief Bielaski, who was sending him on an undercover mission to investigate Germans. Berliner's cover story was that he had been called away to check up on the Cuban branch office of the Oliver Typewriter Company.[356]

Enroute to Cuba, Berliner traveled by train to Key West. Illustrating the man's impressively wide network of friends and acquaintances, the conductor on the train turned out to be an old acquaintance from Monterrey. Berliner bought cigars, and they chatted in an empty compartment about Mexican affairs the rest of the way.[357] Sailing to Havana on the steamer *Governor*

Cobb, Berliner spent the voyage ingratiating himself with several Mexican passengers, inviting them to "refreshments" and pumping them for information about Mexican activities.

Berliner registered at the Plaza Hotel in Havana, and quickly established rapport with a secret agent of the Cuban government, who promised to keep him informed. Indeed, the Cuban agent later told him a large group of Mexicans had recently left for Mexico by way of Guatemala. Berliner also met several times with a certain Julius Wise, who at one time was supposed to be connected with the Carranza faction. "Wise is known to Agent as having been connected with Félix Díaz in Mexico, also in New Orleans, New York and El Paso." A year earlier, Berliner and Agent Scully had called on a bank in New York and had obtained a statement of Wise's account. Wise "seemed to be watching Agent, who asked him to have a refreshment, which he accepted. Agent asked Wise if it wasn't true he was working for Carranza as a spotter. He said he had been working for Carranza in the US but was not doing so here. He is such a dirty lying underhanded rat that Agent believes he is here to do some dirty work."[1358] Although Berliner chatted with Wise at length in the hotel café, Berliner could tell he was lying from the way Wise answered his questions.

To cover his own lies, Berliner called on Rafael Galves, the resident manager for William A. Parker, General Latin American Agent of the Oliver Typewriter Company. Galves had information to contribute: *felicista* Henry Blum was now in Havana, selling fine horses and cows, but also participating in revolutionary matters. That night, at a dance hall and cabaret called The Black Cat, Berliner recognized two *huertista* officers, who asked him to join them. When they asked what Berliner was doing in Havana, he gave them a "stall" that he represented some American manufacturers and was enroute to Central America. "Agent bought some refreshments for the party, and in a casual manner began asking questions." Berliner continued to mine his seemingly inexhaustible circle of friends and acquaintances. "Met Capt. Rice whom Agent has known for a number of years; Rice is related to Pullman of Pullman car and owns large properties in Cuba. Agent obtained from Rice information—covered in another title." They were joined by the assistant police chief of Havana, Duke Estrada, "with whom Agent is also well acquainted. We talked over old times." Estrada confirmed that a large group of Mexicans had recently sailed away.[1359] A few days later, Berliner encountered Rafael Arozarena, a Cuban by birth, but whom Berliner had known for many years in Mexico, and who "Agent knows is an intimate friend of Félix Díaz. He has a sugar estate. Agent asked him to partake of a refreshment; was accepted."[1360]

Berliner sailed for Panama on January 20, on the SS *Tenadores*. He was using the transparent alias of Harry Berliner y Baldwin, "so that in the event that the party whom Agent desires to see should be on board as a passenger he would not get wise to the alias Agent is using. Got a complete passenger list of those who had sailed from New York from the purser but did not find the name sought." Agent sent Bielaski a radiogram: "Have sailed, Yrias not among passengers."[1361] On board the ship, Berliner shadowed Carl Heynen, whom he saw in conversation with three German stewards.[1362] He tried to overhear their conversation from the men's room, but failed. So, he plied Heynen with drink but again failed to learn anything significant.[1363] Heynen was a person of interest to the Bureau because of his work for the Albert office in New York, which became public during the briefcase affair. He was arrested in July 1917, as a suspected German agent in New York and interned in Fort Oglethorpe for the duration of the war.[1364]

Arriving at Colón, Panama, on January 21, Berliner cabled Bielaski, then looked up the port captain, who was an old friend, but who could not provide any information about Mexicans at Colón. Berliner then looked up another intimate old friend, the resident manager of the cable office at Colón. The manager listed a number of Mexicans he and Berliner knew who had passed through Colón bound for other Central American ports.[1365]

The next stop on Berliner's tour was Puerto Limón, Costa Rica, where he received a coded cablegram from Bielaski updating his agent on the movements of Mexican officials. Leaving Limón, he proceeded to the capital, San José, and reported on Carranza providing technical support to the government of El Salvador—with two airplanes, a high-powered radio set, and equipment.[1366]

Returning to Havana, Berliner continued to look up his old friends. One was Carlos Ortega, a successful wine merchant. "Ortega invited Agent to a refreshment in a café. For nearly an hour, Ortega related to Agent and gave the names of every Mexican that Agent has either at one time or another had to investigate or who has ever had any connection with any of the revolutionary movements of Mexico. He is a walking storehouse of information."[1367] Another old friend of Berliner's was Henry Comings, formerly an official in the National Lines of Mexico. Berliner invited him to dinner, knowing the Comings was an intimate friend of Carl Heynen.

> Heynan [sic] told him how he had put it over on the Etna or the Atlas Powder Co. by sewing up a contract for their entire product;[1368] when they found out he had tricked them they were mad as March hares. Heynen told him the Government

was watching him very closely and that one time they very nearly had him in a trap, but that he had managed to keep his nose pretty clean, that he was avoiding insofar as possible to keep from doing anything that would land him in the hands of the law.[1369]

Increasingly, Berliner was focusing on Germans, "checking steamers on the lookout for any of the German element which Agent has under surveillance.[1370]

Berliner provided useful intelligence about individuals, but the Bureau's premier informant was still Charles E. Jones, CRESSE, who provided invaluable intelligence about the *felicista* movement as a whole, getting much of his information from Guillermo Rosas, who trusted him implicitly. Jones, like Berliner, sometimes reported directly to Chief Bielaski. His reports also covered intrigues concerning Guatemala and Honduras.

Jones's lengthy report to Bielaski in February covered not only Mexican affairs in general, but the *felicista* movement in Yucatán after General Cortés's death. Esteban Maqueo Castellanos took up the work.

> As per information given to you when I was in Washington and New York, Mr. del Villar and Rosas at that time had just received information from Mr. Castellanos that he had succeeded in completing all of the financial arrangements and expected at any moment to arrive in the United States and that the only necessary additional thing was for Mr. del Villar to secure the funds agreed upon from the International Harvester Company in Chicago. Mr. del Villar and myself have an engagement to meet in Chicago on any date selected by me where we are to complete the negotiations with the International [Harvester] people and also with Mr. Wrigley, working these two propositions in connection with Father Kelley.

CRESSE continued:

> Mr. Castellanos was expected to arrive in this country during the early part of December, is now due to arrive here with his brother at almost any date. Immediately upon his arrival he is expected to turn over to Rosas the funds received by him in

Cuba, and I am then to receive this money for the purchase of arms and ammunition for the Yucatán and Quintana Roo movement and on or about Dec. 25th to January they expect and hope to move this expedition out of New Orleans. Three days after the ship sails from New Orleans their friends in Yucatán and Quintana Roo are to start an uprising in Mérida and other parts of Yucatán and Quintana Roo.

Unfortunately, through treachery the Carranza authorities in Yucatán "became aware of some of these plans and seized a large number of their officers and supporters in Yucatán, executing many of them." Eternally optimistic, del Villar and Castellanos wrote to Rosas that this incident merely interrupted their plans.[1371]

Normally, though, Jones reported to Agent Pendleton about the above matters.[1372] And Jones had a plan—nothing less than securing the *felicista* archive in the possession of Guillermo Rosas and others.[1373] This became easier when Rosas notified the post office that all mail addressed to Guillermo Rosas, Jr., William Rosas, Jr., William Flowers, William Baker, heretofore delivered to 1801 Constantinople Street, 1820 Melpomene Street, 1522 Prytania Street, c/o Latin American Trading Co., 1324 Whitney-Central Bank Building, respectively, was to be delivered only to the Newspaper Service Company, 738-740 Audubon Building—Jones's office.[1374]

Agent Cantrell at the Hotel Morrison in Chicago, managed to look at the papers whereby Cecilio Ocón was organizing a corporation with his partner, Ramón Díaz, who was Félix Díaz's cousin. The corporation was formed to facilitate supplying Félix Díaz.[1375]

Ramón Díaz arrived in New Orleans on February 21. Jones spent a good deal of time with him, advising Bielaski that he had obtained important information from Díaz. Jones submitted a special report to Bielaski and provided Pendleton with a copy.[1376] He described a meeting at the Hotel Cecil in New York on February 26 between Cecilio Ocón, Generals Manuel Mondragón and Aurelio Blanquet, Leandro R. Alcolea, Ramón Díaz, and Pedro del Villar to discuss the proposed corporation, which would receive funds from American firms and financiers prepared to support Félix Díaz.[1377] Agent Joseph G. Tucker was keeping Mondragón and Blanquet under sporadic observation in New York.[1378]

Jones elaborated in a lengthy report to Bielaski, mentioning that Ramón Díaz, a wealthy attorney with mining and oil interests, was "extremely suspicious and very shrewd, therefore had to handle him with a light touch and did not endeavor to pry into things of the most confidential nature with him too rapidly." Ramón Díaz had been authorized to finance all *felicista* movements on the border as well as reorganizing the Yucatán movement, for which he was to arrange financing and the purchase of armament. "He has for several months been conducting negotiations in New York and Chicago with bankers, oil people, and those interested in the chicle business." Jones suggested that Díaz might secure financing from some bankers in New Orleans. With Bielaski's approval, Jones would arrange this, and "am sure when he has his conversation with the parties here his entire plan of operation, all of those implicated in the new Yucatán movement, likewise those that have prior to this date financially assisted him for this movement could be showed up." [...] "Believe the Special Agent in Charge of your local office and myself could arrange with banker in this city whereby said banker would go into this proposition with Díaz to assist your Department, and in that way Díaz's plans, etc. would be brought out at that meeting.

Jones added that Ramón Díaz had replaced Maqueo Castellanos as director of the Yucatán movement, and General Blanquet was to head the expedition. Jones learned that Rosas had a complete copy of the military maps and plans for the expedition. That grandiose strategy was for Blanquet's expedition to sail from some point on the Texas, Louisiana, or Florida coast and attack Yucatán and the Territory of Quintana Roo from the sea. Simultaneously, a part of the personal forces of General Félix Díaz in Chiapas would work their way from Chiapas into the State of Tabasco and from there to Yucatán. "According to Rosas and Díaz they have sufficient money at this time to carry this expedition through in a very small way, but like all Mexicans they are still after more money and if there is a reasonable chance to secure same then this movement will be detained until all financial prospects have been worked to a finish."

According to Jones,

> Ramón Díaz hopes to put through a proposition of this kind whereby the Villa leaders and financial backers in the United States would work always in perfect harmony with the Félix Díaz leaders, and that while there was now, as there has been for the last six months, a working arrangement by and between the military leaders of Félix Díaz, Zapata, and Villa; that there never has been a perfect understanding by and between the backers of such of these parties in the United States. He told me that he has had many interviews with Hipólito Villa, also

the Madero brothers and many other Villa leaders in New York and elsewhere along these lines.[1379]

Jones sent Bielaski an even longer report in March. Among the highlights, he referred to the New York meeting of *felicista* leaders on February 26, saying they had formed a central committee to manage the movement.

> This committee also was at this time advised by Ramón Díaz and Ocón that the Chicago negotiations had been consummated through the influence of Father Kelley, Mr. Wrigley and others which I have fully mentioned in previous reports, likewise herein, whereby the central committee at an early date will receive approximately half million dollars from these Chicago financial interests as part payment of a total sum of several millions of dollars. This entire sum is to be advanced in amounts of from quarter to one-half million dollars payable as results are produced by the Díaz leaders. Apparently, the Chicago interests are willing to gamble the original amount advanced by them, and if the Díaz movement collapses, undoubtedly, they consider their gamble of this amount would have been well worthwhile. If on the other hand the Díaz movement succeeds, they will have made a good investment. They, however, propose to advance additional sums only as the Díaz forces produce results to justify such additional payments on their part [...] Rosas tells me that the bankers in Chicago with whom Ocón and Father Kelley have been conducting negotiations are directors of the Continental Bank of that city likewise with directors and officers of the International Harvester people as mentioned in many of my previous reports have been promised the exclusive sisal concession from Yucatán. Likewise, some of their directors also at the same time grabbed a concession for mahogany and chicle from the Territory of Quintana Roo and Chiapas. Ocón also with the others implicated have agreed on a concession for twenty years with Mr. Wrigley for an unusually large quantity of chicle from Quintana Roo and Chiapas [...]. The money derived from their negotiations in Chicago, according to Rosas who secured this information from Ramón Díaz, is to be spent in purchasing arms, ammunition, and supplies to the

extent of approximately [a] quarter of a million dollars for the forces of General Félix Díaz in different parts of Mexico. The balance of this money is to be sent to General Díaz and to be used by him in paying his soldiers and in bribing Carranza soldiers and officers to desert to the Díaz forces.

Jones secured letters from Ramón Díaz, written by prominent *felicistas*. "Your New Orleans office will forward you photographic copies of same." Jones noted that

> Ramón Díaz upon his arrival in San Antonio expects to immediately get in touch with Hipólito Villa and at this meeting lay the preliminary plans for an absolute written contract by and between Hipólito Villa, representing his brother, and Ramón Díaz, representing his party. Díaz feels perfectly satisfied of the fact that this can be put through by him whereby all of the leaders of the Villa party in the United States will be forced to come into the Díaz, Zapata, Villa combination.

Jones's brother, Winfield, the journalist in Washington, wrote him regarding Hipólito Villa that "there is no doubt at all but what with the newspaper influence that he and I have in Washington, likewise also due to having strong friends among the Congressmen and Senators that he and I would be able to put the Hipólito Villa matter over as mentioned to you in my previous letters [...]." Jones intended to convince the *villistas* that through his and Winfield's influence and effort in Washington, they had persuaded the attorney general's office and the Department of Justice to allow Hipólito to leave San Antonio and to eliminate the necessity of his reporting to the Bureau every day.[1380]

Superintendent Offley in New York assigned Agents Tucker and Chalmers to proceed to the Ward Line dock to search the baggage and effects of Ramón Díaz, who was said to be about to sail for Mexico. The agents reported that Díaz did not appear.[1381] This was because Díaz went to New Orleans. Still, Bielaski instructed Pendleton that

> If suitable opportunity inspect confidentially Díaz effects arrives take advantage of it otherwise delay inspection until just prior sailing in accordance my previous telegram; keep in as close touch as practicable cover any messenger or other

person who might go in his stead. Trip to Houston may mean he will sail from Galveston or some other point other than New Orleans or New York; cover this possibility cooperating with Barnes as far as necessary.

Pendleton conferred with Jones at the latter's office, listening in as Rafael Alcolea told Jones on the phone that his brother and Ramón Díaz would arrive shortly in New Orleans by train. Pendleton "arranged with Jones whereby he will furnish me immediately any information he may secure from Díaz relative to his future actions and will follow out the instructions contained in Chief's telegram."[1382] Jones advised Pendleton that he and Rosas met Díaz at the depot, and that Díaz was staying in room 304, De Soto Hotel for a few days.

Jones further reported that Ramón Díaz was anxious to meet the president of a New Orleans bank to secure loans on his oil properties in order to help Félix Díaz, and he suggested that if Pendleton could arrange such a meeting, they would obtain valuable information. Pendleton did arrange an appointment for Jones and Díaz with the president of the Whitney Central Bank, who was ready to assist the government in a matter of national importance. Jones reported that Ramón Díaz hoped to borrow $100,000 on a mortgage of his properties for not less than two years at a reasonable rate of interest.[1383]

Meanwhile, Agents Pendleton and Beckham went to the De Soto Hotel, whose manager allowed them to search Díaz's room.[1384] They were unable to open Díaz's locked trunk, but they did hurriedly examine a briefcase containing letters to Félix Díaz and others from General Mondragón. Pendleton reported that "Because of the Chief's telegrams of March 7 and 10, instructing inspection just prior to sailing, I deemed it inadvisable to take any risks that would cause any suspicion on the part of Díaz and, as there was no opportunity to copy or to photograph these letters, I thought it best to leave them unmolested at the present time." The agents had a narrow escape, leaving Díaz's room only a few minutes before he arrived.

Undeterred, the agents returned to Díaz's room the following day. They opened the trunk using a key Pendleton had bought the previous afternoon, removed papers from it and the briefcase, and immediately took them to Special Employee Irby to be photographed and returned. They notified the Chief, who telegraphed: "Telegram received wire from time to time until tomorrow afternoon brief summary as far as you are able get it from documents found, as action will depend largely on material you have."[1385]

Pendleton contacted Jones and arranged for him to take Ramón Díaz and Rosas for an automobile ride and keep them out for enough time for Pendleton to search Ramón Díaz's effects thoroughly. Jones informed Bielaski that

> At 2 p.m. of the afternoon of March 14 I took Ramón Díaz, Rosas, and Alcolea out for an auto ride from 2:30 until 7 p.m. so that your Special Agent would have sufficient time to go through all of his [Ramón Díaz's] papers and baggage at the hotel, and also have all of them photographed. So that there could be no possible chance of getting them back too early I managed to keep them out until 9:20 p. m. and then turned them loose.

The extended search produced incriminating documents that the agents took to a photographer and which informant Ibs translated. Pendleton informed the Chief that the most important document was to the effect that two high officials of a Chicago bank were willing to finance Félix Díaz on a commercial basis. Jones advised that Ramón Díaz would soon leave New Orleans on the Southern Pacific for an unknown destination.

Bielaski instructed that if Díaz did leave, to have someone go on the same train and cover his movements, and that if Díaz's destination were learned to wire the appropriate special agent to cover his arrival. Bielaski added that after careful consideration, Díaz would be permitted to sail without any examination of his person, with the expectation that the Bureau would be able to obtain even more important documents from him on his return.[1386]

Ramón Díaz went to San Antonio to confer with Hipólito Villa about their joint plans against Carranza. Villa stated that if Jones could get the Bureau off his back, he would immediately give Jones a large order for ammunition. Jones believed he could get the details of Villa's plans. Bielaski was most interested, wiring Barnes to question Pedro González with the utmost thoroughness, endeavoring especially to secure information about his connection with New York and other lenders to Félix Díaz, their knowledge and support of González's expedition, and full details of any trips he made to New York or the East.[1387]

But Ramón Díaz remained an object of the Bureau's activities.[1388] Jones reported that Díaz had returned to New Orleans, using the alias, "Duval," when registering at the Hotel De Soto. He carried the original contracts made by Ocón and the other backers of Félix Díaz, taking them in person to the general in Chiapas for his approval and signature. But Ramón Díaz was about to sail for Guatemala the following day. Jones was confident he could get Díaz out of his room for a time so that Bureau agents could photograph documents. A frustrated Pendleton reported that he "got in touch with several photographers but could not find any who has equipment for photographing at night, and the plan was abandoned." Therefore, the best course would be not to search Ramón Díaz's baggage just prior to his departure for Mexico but to search it on his return, when presumably he would be carrying the signed original contracts. Bielaski approved, wiring that unless otherwise instructed, not to detain or search, preferring to do this on Díaz's return.[1389]

Jones wrote to Chief Bielaski that Rosas had told him Ramón Díaz was to arrive on April 30 from Guatemala aboard a United Fruit steamer.

> He left the United States under an assumed name as per information given in my previous reports and the probabilities are that he will return to this port likewise under an assumed name. He will no doubt bring back with him the contracts and agreements that he took to General Félix Díaz for his signature, as per my previous reports covering this matter; therefore suggest that I meet this steamer and in that way either with your special agents here or the Immigration authorities then pick him up on the steamer, and in that way at this time all of the papers, documents, contracts, etc. that he will have with him will in that way pass into your possession for a sufficient time anyway for you to secure photographic copies of same.

Jones so advised Pendleton, who arranged with Immigration to detain Ramón Díaz for a day or so while the Bureau obtained and photographed whatever documents he was carrying.[1390]

Pendleton detailed Agent Beckham to meet the steamer on her arrival. Beckham reported that Ramón Díaz was not a passenger but that a man going under the name of Rodolfo Basail, giving his address as 1828 Melpomene Street, Leandro Alcolea's residence, was. Pendleton had Basail and his luggage brought to the field office.

Charles Jones had advised back in January that Colonel Rodolfo Basail, Félix Díaz's chief of staff, was about to leave for Guatemala with important messages for Díaz. Pendleton wired Bielaski asking, "if you desire him detained and searched, please advise also please suggest proper procedure to follow in matter answer early as boat sails at 11 o'clock." While awaiting instructions, Pendleton intended to ask the police to detain Basail quietly, as it appeared to be the only way to handle the matter without a warrant. However, Bielaski wired "Think inadvisable take any action messenger matter," which solved the problem.[391]

Now, Pendleton advised Basail that because he had entered the country as a military engineer, it was necessary for the Bureau to take the usual precautions of searching him, to which Basail acquiesced.

> His person and baggage were thoroughly searched; quite a number of letters and documents were taken from his pocket [...]. He appeared to take the matter lightly. However, if I am any judge of human nature the man was badly scared. I advised him I'd look over the papers and return them to him tomorrow. He was given his baggage and permitted to leave. Employee Stillson accompanied him to 611 St. Charles Street, where he engaged a room. The documents will be translated by Informant Ibs and photographed by Stillson in the morning then returned to this party.

Interestingly, while in the Bureau office, Basail gave Charles E. Jones as a reference. That evening Jones phoned Pendleton at his residence and said that Basail was in his office, and that he had vouched for him, the conversation being carried on for Basail's benefit. After Basail left, Jones phoned again and told Pendleton that Basail was deeply worried. He also reported that Ramón Díaz probably would arrive in New Orleans within a week.[392] As it turned out, Basail's documents did not contain anything that would justify detaining him.[393]

While dealing with the *felicistas*, the Bureau continued to keep an eye on the *carrancistas*. There was a steady stream of reports on conditions in Mexico, such as one from Special Employee John Perry Sellar Mennet, who spent two and a half months in Monterrey. In addition, the Intelligence officer at Fort Sam Houston received intercepted and decoded Mexican army wireless messages, among them one from General Obregón directing the purchase of all possible munitions in the United States and furnishing funds for this purpose. The army notified Barnes, who instructed H. B. Mock at Nogales and Arthur A. Hopkins at Warren to cover the matter closely. Hopkins also reported on Mexican troop dispositions and continued to compile "War Department Information." J. H. Lege and Victor Weiskopf deciphered Mexican coded messages. The American military attaché in Mexico City reported on wireless plants in Mexico.[394]

The Bureau was also involved in tying up the loose ends regarding the 1915-1916 Carranza-supported Plan de San Diego, which was a discouraging endeavor. Special Employee Mennet reported that

> in my recent investigations in connection with the Plan de San Diego I found it impossible to get persons to give evidence, those who really have evidence, because of fear of the consequences to themselves. They feel that Judge Burns is altogether too sympathetic toward these people (one evidence is his treatment of Basilio Ramos, Jr., one of the principals of this Plan who was released on a ridiculously low bond, as I am informed, his humility and apparent harmlessness deceived the judge.) They believe that even if a man was convicted of taking a part in these activities his sentence would be so light that he would soon be free to take vengeance on those who gave evidence against him.

Given the sensitivity of the subject, Mennet sent all copies of his report directly to Barnes so he could dispose of them as he saw fit.[395]

Bielaski prepared a memorandum for the Attorney General: "I have the honor to invite your attention to the attached confidential report made by Special Employee J. P. S. Mennet, who was temporarily employed in work along the Mexican border and in Mexico. Judge Burns' attitude has been quite well known for a long time, but no practical way has ever suggested itself whereby the situation might be remedied."[396]

It was not just Mexican factions the Bureau was targeting—German activity was increasingly menacing, and the United States worried about German-Mexican intrigues. On February 4, Agent Breniman, the acting Agent in Charge in San Antonio, had wired Local Officer J. L. Webb at Galveston that

> This Department desires that all investigations except those of utmost importance be made subordinate to neutrality investigations. Covering any kind of activity on part of persons connected with European interest, you are requested to investigate and report names of any person whom you suspect might participate in such activity and keep such person under surveillance as much as possible until further instruction. If assistance is needed, advise us.[397]

Chief Bielaski in late 1916 stated his policy regarding cooperation between the Bureau and the military. Writing to Agent Robert E. Lee Barnes, Bielaski said:

> I have received your letter of November 27, 1916, asking me whether you should take the lead in the matter of securing information for the military for reasons of efficiency, or should, for reasons of economy, stand aside and let the military make use of their own funds to secure information. I think, as a general practice, where there is no acute situation and no matter of special importance, you should allow the military to handle matters without suggesting the use of this service. Should matters, however, again become critical along the border, or in any place along the border, or should any situation of importance arise, you should make use of your forces for the purpose of getting the information desired in the most efficient manner. All of this, of course, assumes that our relations with the military authorities are so close and cordial that matters can be handled in these different ways without any possibility of friction. You should bear in mind, of course, that the securing of military information, now that the military have some facilities for obtaining it, is primarily their affair, and, at the same time, we desire to render every possible service, especially in times of real need.[398]

Bureau cooperation with the army became even closer. Barnes sent a letter to all his subordinates:

> The Intelligence Officer of the United States Army for the Southern Department, stationed at San Antonio, desires this office to furnish him with a copy of all reports of employees concerning information of interest to that office. In order that this may be done, please be careful in the future to see that an extra copy of your report covering such investigations is furnished to this office. You should also bear in mind that if the case needs attention at some other points, and you do not furnish copies of your report direct to the investigating agents who should handle the matter outside of this Division, that extra copies should be furnished here in order to be

transmitted to the agents interested. Your careful compliance with these suggestions will materially aid the work in this office.[1399]

Barnes sent another circular letter, regarding the commanding general of the Southern Department having directed radio stations on the border to accept for transmission in emergencies official messages from Bureau employees. "In emergencies this service will of course be desirable, and you may avail yourself thereof."[1400]

Evidencing interagency cooperation, Bielaski sent translations of the documents found in Ramón Díaz's trunk to Leland Harrison, Office of the Counselor, Department of State.[1401] Both agencies were concerned about any German intrigue with the looming US entry into World War I. A disquieting report came from Agent William R. Beckham in New York City. W. E. D. Stokes, owner of the Ansonia Hotel where Victoriano Huerta had stayed, and an acknowledged supporter of Félix Díaz, telephoned him at midnight on April 13 reporting that a fire had occurred in his friend Pedro del Villar's apartment at 210 West 72nd Street. According to Stokes, the fire was arson, started by a Miss Fuchs, a German woman who resided at that address. Stokes claimed that the purpose of the fire was "either to obtain the possession of, or have destroyed, letters from Von Bernstorff, the former German ambassador, to Félix Díaz, offering aid to him and his interests in Mexico, which letters Miss Fuchs believed to be in the possession of Del Villar." Stokes said her efforts were in vain, "as he has possession of these letters and will turn them over to Division Superintendent Offley in the immediate future. He further states that the Fuchs woman was taken into custody during the day on a charge of arson and detained at the 68th St. police station. He further says that she has a sister now interned as a German spy at Ellis Island. He does not know the name of the sister. I reported the foregoing to Division Superintendent Offley."[1402] The alleged letters from the German ambassador never surfaced.

Much more disquieting was the publication of the Zimmermann Telegram. British intelligence had intercepted the infamous offer of the German foreign office to support Mexico in the case of a US entry into the European war. The telegram offered German support of Mexico if it wished to attack the United States. The actual offer has been mis-translated by British intelligence (without much doubt on purpose), and historian Barbara Tuchman in her 1958 monograph made no effort to investigate the translation.[1403] The original German note from Foreign Secretary Arthur Zimmermann offered Mexico "consent on our part [Germany] to reconquer" the lost territories in Texas,

Arizona, and New Mexico. He did not, as Tuchman wrote in The Zimmermann Telegram, offer German support to Mexico in the military effort. Since Tuchman's bestselling monograph, the flawed interpretation of the German offer in the Zimmermann note has dominated the historiography. Whether interpreted correctly or not, and whether British intelligence purposely misled the US government, the telegram was so outrageous that President Wilson initially doubted its authenticity. However, when asked whether he had drafted the note, Zimmermann quickly confirmed his authorship in an interview and a Reichstag speech.[1404] President Carranza, who correctly assessed from the vague language of the telegram that Germany may have only offered to fight to the last Mexican, rejected the note on the advice of his military, most notably General Obregón.[1405]

Tomes have been published on the offer and the US entry into World War I, yet only recently have historians been able to assess the true circumstances of the telegram. Barbara Tuchman and other historians in the 1950s and 60s did not have access to many recently declassified archival documents and had ignored available German sources.[1406]

First and foremost, the note did not cause the United States to declare war against Germany on April 6, 1917. The United States entered the war entirely as a result of the renewed German unrestricted submarine war which threatened American shipping and, in the view of the American government, violated international law. The Zimmermann Telegram, although certainly scandalous in the American public eye, was born from German domestic policy differences. Since the initiation of unrestricted submarine warfare in the spring of 1915, which ended with the sinking of the Lusitania in May of that year, the German government had been divided over the importance of keeping the United States neutral versus breaking British and French supply lines through a war on commerce. The German navy, as well as Generals Ludendorff and Hindenburg, supported an unrestricted commerce war against the Allies, while most of the German foreign office, Chancellor von Bethmann-Hollweg, and other civilian advisers of the Kaiser advocated for appeasing the neutral countries, most importantly, the United States.

A compromise was struck in the latter part of May 1915, when Chancellor von Bethmann-Hollweg and Admiral Henning von Holtzendorff signed off on Felix Sommerfeld's offer to create a US military intervention in Mexico, which would keep the US occupied in its hemisphere and cause military supplies to flow to the US military rather than be sold to the Allies.[1407] The strategy to hamper the United States's ability to enter the war in Europe resulted not only in German financial support for Pancho Villa and Sommerfeld's influence in supporting Villa's decision to attack Columbus in March 1916. The German government also organized a deadly sabotage campaign against US infrastructure and shipping, critical supplies, and manufacturing facilities, which culminated in the explosion of the Black Tom loading terminals in the New York harbor in July 1916. By the summer of 1916, Germany could take some satisfaction in that almost the entire US military was on the border or in Mexico; America's abilities to export war materials were severely hampered by labor unrest, ship fires, and plant explosions. Nevertheless, the German government remained indecisive. The Kaiser would not allow the navy to proceed with the campaign against commerce. It took until January 9, 1917, for the Kaiser to succumb to the military's pressure to declare renewed unrestricted submarine warfare starting February 1, 1917.[1408]

Arthur Zimmermann, who had succeeded Secretary Gottlieb von Jagow in November 1916 and became Foreign Secretary, had grown weary of the Kaiser's vacillations. He sent the telegram to be discovered and publicized, and thus force the Kaiser's hand. Historian Thomas Boghardt correctly assessed that Zimmermann "wanted to please Ludendorff," and was intrigued by "the idea of embroiling the United States in a guerilla war along its southern border."[1409] Not only was Zimmermann "intrigued," but pinning the US down at its southern border had been German policy since May 1915. However, by January 1917 the window of opportunity that German agents such as Heinrich Albert, Hans Tauscher, Felix Sommerfeld, Carl Heynen, Friedrich Hinsch, Paul Hilken, Walter Scheele, Frederico Stallforth, and others had created was closing. Zimmermann

Figure 83. Arthur Zimmermann, 1918
Source: Wikimedia Commons

thus had no illusions of providing actual support for Mexico. Rather than posing a true military threat to the United States, as historians Tuchman, Katz, Patrick Devlin, John Milton Cooper, and Arthur Link, among others, have argued, the true purpose of the note was quite different.[1410] Zimmermann needed international public pressure to force the Kaiser's hand and keep him aligned with German hardliner policies. British intelligence chief Sir Reginald "Blinker" Hall was only too happy to oblige.

Historian Barbara Tuchman, who had not used German sources, misinterpreted the purpose of the telegram and the reasons why Zimmermann was eager to admit his authorship. Historian Friedrich Katz, using limited German archives in his first book on German intelligence in Mexico, also misinterpreted the purpose.[1411] He argued that Germany sincerely wanted to expand its influence in Latin America and sought to establish hegemony over Mexico between 1917 and 1918.[1412] If such a foreign policy ever existed (for which there is no evidence), Germany certainly would have played its trump card of unrestricted submarine war in the summer of 1916, when there was a window of opportunity to check the United States and cut off Great Britain from war supplies.

The Zimmermann note was designed to deny the German emperor any possibility of changing his mind with respect to unrestricted submarine warfare. Boghardt's correctly concluded that the telegram sparked a "U.S. intervention on behalf of the Allies."[1413] Also important is Boghardt's unraveling of Admiral "Blinker" Hall's sophisticated propaganda effort regarding the telegram. The translation was botched, likely on purpose, not only with respect to actively supporting Mexico's effort to attack the US and getting back the lost border states rather than just consenting to Mexico undertaking such a quixotic endeavor, but also concerning the territory to which Zimmermann was referring. Boghardt points to the original text, re-conquering lost territories "in Texas [...]." Did this mean a strip of land along the southwestern US border, or entire states listed in the telegram?[1414]

Despite the irritation over the Zimmermann note, Germany's declaration of unrestricted submarine war would bring the United States into the war on the side of the Allies. Wilson went to Congress to ask for a declaration of war on April 2, 1917. The casus bellum was the sinking of the SS *Vigilancia*, on March 16, 1917. Wilson had hoped that Germany would abandon its confrontational course. It took the fourth sinking of an American freighter since February 1 to finally convince him.

Domestically, the Bureau had uncovered most of the German plots to corner US industries, create trouble at the US-Mexican border, finance and incite labor unrest, and sabotage US production facilities, save for the two big ones: The Villa attack on Columbus, and the sabotage at the Black Tom Island. By the time the US declared war on Germany, the Bureau had arrested, or at least uncovered, most German agents. With the declaration of war in April and the passing of the Espionage Act in June 1917, the Bureau rounded up the remaining German agents. The diplomatic corps had left, including Heinrich Albert, but the Bureau arrested and interrogated the second-tier agents who worked for him and interned them in Fort Oglethorpe as "dangerous enemy aliens." Bureau agents captured fugitives, like bomb maker Walter Scheele in Cuba, and brought them back to be tried in the US. Franz Rintelen and Horst von der Goltz were extradited from England, the former to be tried, the latter to be a star witness for the government. The court cases all hinged upon the Bureau investigations conducted during the neutrality years. When the United States entered World War I on April 6, 1917, the Bureau of Investigation was the premier government intelligence and counterintelligence agency. The major challenge for the Bureau during World War I is evidenced in the fact that the massive "Old German Files" of over 400,000 pages are contained on 596 microfilm rolls in the National Archives.

Figure 84. Horst von der Goltz, 1914
Source: British National Archives

Epilogue

The Neutrality Period of World War I posed a set of fresh challenges for the Bureau. The Wilson administration made the political decision in the fall of 1914 to declare the US's strict neutrality in the European War. Neutrality in thought and action, however, was a theoretical construct and resulted in unprecedented challenges for the Bureau as well as other law enforcement and intelligence agencies. The United States, for example, maintained that any nation could buy American products, including war supplies. Yet, the by international standards illegal British sea blockade of Northern Europe, combined with ever-expanding contraband lists restricted international trade to benefit the Allies only. The German government also perceived the flow of information and access to financial markets in the United States as being decidedly lopsided. The British Royal Navy had severed German transatlantic cables as soon as the war started, thus cutting off Germany's access to US banks, stock markets, and the free flow of information between Germany and the US. Most news about the European war had to pass through British censorship before reaching the American public.

The strict view of the Wilson administration regarding American citizen's rights to travel on British ships, often carrying war supplies in their holds, undermined Germany's desperate attempt to break the British blockade with an unrestricted submarine war on merchant ships. The sinking of the *Lusitania* on May 7, 1915, not only stopped the unrestricted submarine war until February 1917, but it also laid bare the political rifts that had developed in the US within the Democratic Party and the public at large. The resignation of William Jennings Bryan over the tone of the *Lusitania* notes to Germany saw the rise of a vocal peace movement. At the same time, as the US war economy produced huge corporate profits, the labor movement felt empowered to bargain for higher wages and benefits. These political developments combined with the alienation of German, Austrian, Slavic, Irish, Mexican, and Indian minorities, created a fertile soil for German manipulation and agitation.

Between 1908 and 1914, the Bureau had focused on enforcing the US neutrality laws vis-à-vis Mexican revolutionary factions and governments.[1415] In this effort, the Bureau's capabilities had grown significantly, from a handful of special agents, and on a shoestring budget before 1914, to a national network of field offices with over two hundred agents enforcing federal laws with increasing success. Federal special agents also gained experience in infiltrating Mexican factions under cover, working internationally, for example, in Mexico and Cuba, and using newly acquired counterintelligence skills successfully to undermine plots still in their planning stages. Chief A. Bruce Bielaski, who took charge of the Bureau in 1912 deserves credit for leading his agency through such dramatic growth and unprecedented challenges during the neutrality years.

The outbreak of World War I in August 1914 changed the complexities of Neutrality Law enforcement. While the Mexican Revolution still raged across the southern border and required significant investigative resources, the Bureau soon experienced the backlash of the Wilson administration's neutrality policies. The British sea blockade forced German trade and financial activities underground. After initially targeting mostly British interests in the US and Canada, while attempting to spirit German reservists to Europe with falsified passports, the harsh reactions of US law enforcement quickly shifted German energies to target the US directly. Not being able to finance, sell off, or store large enough purchases of war materials to make a difference in the Allied war effort, German agents began to undermine American industry, manipulate supply chains, and sabotage manufacturing and shipping on a grand scale in 1915.

Just as was the case in the beginning of the Mexican Revolution, the Bureau, by 1914, was the only intelligence and counterintelligence agency of the federal government with national and international reach. It took valuable time to grasp the magnitude of German conspiracy. Chief Bielaski virtually ignored German attacks on Canadian installations, and, in the case of the bombing of the Vanceboro Bridge, even sided with German sabotage agent Werner Horn over British demands. Repeatedly, the Bureau, without much fervor, followed up British leads on the German naval supply mission, passport frauds, and smuggling of "conditional" contraband in the Walter Scheele smuggling plot. The Bureau's sluggish approach changed dramatically in the fall of 1915, when the German attacks clearly threatened national security, whether by blowing up American factories and ships, manipulating US labor relations, sowing discord within minority communities, infiltrating the peace movement, or weaponizing the Mexican Revolution (whether real—as in the case of the Columbus raid—or perceived—as in the case of the Plan de San Diego) against US interests.

The Bureau, with the help of British intelligence, especially in the person of British Naval Attaché Guy Gaunt, was tasked to enforce the US government's "strict neutrality" policy, to vigorously combat German intrigue on US soil. While the Bureau built legal cases against a host of German plotters, the Wilson administration expelled German and Austrian diplomats believed to constitute the command and control for German conspiracies. Many of the cases the Bureau brought were successfully prosecuted, but this study shows that, in the process, the Bureau lost its focus or overextended its resources, preventing it from conducting effective counterintelligence work. While vigorously pursuing the legal cases, for example against Werner Horn (convicted and sentenced), Carl Ruroede (convicted and sentenced), Robert Fay (convicted, sentenced, escaped, recaptured), Hans Tauscher (acquitted), Paul König – P. K. (convicted, suspended sentence), Walter Scheele (changed sides), Charles von Kleist (convicted and sentenced), Franz Rintelen (convicted and sentenced), David Lamar and Henry Martin (acquitted), another tier of agents, arguably more skilled and dangerous, continued their missions and wrought unprecedented destruction on the United States during the period of this study.

Despite the Bureau carefully monitoring, infiltrating, and effectively neutralizing the Félix Díaz and Victoriano Huerta factions, Bureau agents missed the true mission of Felix A. Sommerfeld. The German agent used the recognition of Venustiano Carranza as de facto Mexican president in the fall of 1915 to carefully curate the conditions that precipitated Pancho Villa's attack on Columbus, New Mexico, in March 1916. The resulting Punitive Expedition, with General John J. Pershing as commander, and the activation of the US National Guard along the Mexican border in the summer of 1916, effectively hobbled the US's ability to intervene in the World War on the side of the Allies. In the summer of 1916, and to the disappointment of German agents, the US barely averted a major war with Mexico. The arming and supplying of the US army and reserves also absorbed much of the materiel previously sold to Allied buyers, a secondary stated goal of Sommerfeld's mission.[1416]

An even more brazen and unprecedented attack on the United States occurred in July 1916, when the German sabotage cell around Paul Hilken and Friedrich Hinsch caused the explosion of the Allied loading terminal on Black Tom Island in the New York Harbor. The Bureau had missed the plot despite its main actors openly consorting with known German agents under surveillance and investigation. The case of Frederico Stallforth, which will continue to develop in the next two volumes of this study, shows how close both the Bureau and the State Department came to unraveling the Baltimore sabotage cell, yet failed.

The official centennial publication of The FBI: The Centennial History of the FBI, 1908-2008 includes an attempt to obfuscate the unmitigated intelligence failure and national disaster the Black Tom explosion in 1916 represents. Under the heading "Famous Cases," the centennial history emphasizes the investigations in the 1920s and 30s of the Black Tom explosion, which the Mixed Claims Commission lawyers initiated in order to force Germany to admit guilt and pay for the damages. The investigations were successful and, many decades later, after World War II, Germany paid for the destruction it had brought onto the United States.[1417] The text states, "Were the saboteurs ever identified? Oh, yes, The Bureau and other agencies doggedly pursued the case after the war [...]."[1418] Rather than recounting other, truly "famous cases" of World War I, for example the successful investigations into Walter Scheele and Franz Rintelen, or the impressive counterintelligence action that led to the arrests of the passport forgers in 1915, the Black Tom case is clearly not a prime example of investigative prowess. The heading in the centennial publication, "'Black Tom' Bombing Propels Bureau Into National Security Arena" implies that it took until 1916 for the Bureau to work on national security issues. As this and the previous monograph show, the Bureau had been working on national security cases related to the Mexican Revolution before 1914, and cases related to German intrigue as soon as the war broke out.[1419]

The mixed record of success during the neutrality period did not result from a "small and inept force," as historian Don Whitehead proclaimed in the semi-official, J. Edgar Hoover-sanctioned, The FBI Story (1956), but rather in large part from the Bureau operating in a new political environment that produced unprecedented challenges, many beyond the control of the agency:[1420] the "strict neutrality" policies of the Wilson administration; the lack of legal frameworks for registering and pursuing foreign agents; a restless labor movement; weaponization of minority communities; and, shortages of human resources and funding. Overcoming staffing and budget shortages, the Bureau finally received a boost in new funding in 1916, allowing Chief Bielaski to hire dozens of additional special agents, examiners, special employees, and informants to meet the challenges facing the United States.[1421]

The Bureau also coordinated closely with other government agencies to combat the German conspiracies. While the historiography of this period emphasizes interagency conflict and jealousy, this study documents close and largely harmonious cooperation between federal agencies, the

Military Intelligence Division (War Department), Office of Naval Intelligence (Navy Department), Customs (Treasury Department), Immigration (Labor Department), and the State Department (after 1916, the Bureau of Secret Intelligence).[1422] There are some rare instances of cooperation with the United States Secret Service. These contacts either concerned the investigation of counterfeit fraud cases (the predominant mission of the US Secret Service besides protection of the President), or occurred exclusively through Secret Service Chief William J. Flynn, who overstepped his authority and the mission of the Secret Service on a regular basis between 1915 and 1917, when he finally resigned under pressure for meddling in the Justice Department's domain.[1423]

Chief Flynn's role in the investigations of German intrigue during the neutrality period has been widely exaggerated in the historiography, in part as a result of his postwar fiction writings. As research in this study shows, the Albert briefcase affair as told by William J. Flynn, William Gibbs McAdoo, and uncritically adopted by dozens of historians including Barbara Tuchman in The Zimmerman Telegram (1958), Walter S. Bowen and Harry E. Neal in The United States Secret Service (1960), and Ernest Wittenberg in "The Thrifty Spy on the Sixth Avenue EL" (1965) never happened.[1424] Later historians, most notably Rhodri Jeffreys-Jones, The FBI: A History (1973, with an updated 2007 version), went through intellectual contortions to mold disparate historical facts into a seemingly cohesive thesis, resulting in a complete misinterpretation of the mission and role of the United States Secret Service.[1425]

The case of the Albert portfolio is the best example yet of how the Wilson administration—and the president personally and knowingly—permitted a large-scale British propaganda campaign to flourish in the American press. The mis- and disinformation onslaught was designed to convince the American public to support a US entry into the war on the side of the Allies. The publication of the contents of Heinrich Albert's briefcase is linked to the president himself, who helped cover up the true source of the papers, privately supported the British propaganda efforts, and yet publicly upheld the promise of neutrality ("He kept us out of war"). The publication of the Archibald papers (1915), the von Papen papers (1916), the "Sworn Statement of Horst von der Goltz, alias Bridgeman Taylor" (1916), and the close cooperation of John Revelstone Rathom of The Providence Journal with the Bureau and members of the Wilson administration, most notably with Colonel Edward House, were part of the same influencing campaign.[1426] While the US Declaration of War on April 6, 1917, was a direct result of the German resumption of unrestricted submarine warfare and of German threats to US national security (the Zimmermann telegram and the on-going sabotage campaign), the British propaganda campaign sanctioned by the Wilson administration contributed greatly to making the war decision palpable to the American public.

As the United States entered the World War on the side of the Allies, the role of the Bureau assumed even greater importance. Cooperating and working in harmony with the intelligence agencies of the Departments of State and War, the Bureau was in charge of securing the home front, monitoring the southern border, arresting German agents, interning enemy aliens, rounding up slackers (draft-dodgers), and managing an explosion of human resources through the informants of the American Protective League.

Endnotes

1. The lower case "f" in the "federal Bureau of Investigation" is purposeful to show continuity of the history of this federal agency, despite the 1934 name change to a capital "F."
2. New Haven: Yale University Press, 2007, 61.
3. New York: Simon and Schuster, 2022, 43.
4. When J. Edgar Hoover became Director in 1924, he was only the sixth head of the Bureau of Investigation, following: Stanley Wellington Finch (July 26, 1908-April 29, 1912), Alexander Bruce Bielaski (April 30, 1912-February 9, 1919), William E. Allen (February 10, 1919-June 30, 1919), William J. Flynn (July 1, 1919-August 22, 1921), William J. Burns (August 21, 1921-May 10, 1924), J. Edgar Hoover (May 10, 1924-May 2, 1972).
5. Willard M. Oliver, *The Birth of the FBI: Teddy Roosevelt, the Secret Service, and the Fight Over America's Premier Law Enforcement Agency* (Lanham: Rowan & Littlefield, 2019), 261-263.
6. For example, from the FBI's pursuit of civil rights leaders in the 1960s to the controversies surrounding the alleged involvement of Russia in the 2016 presidential elections and the subsequent firing of FBI Director James Comey.
7. Ronald Kessler, *The Bureau: The Secret History of the FBI* (New York: St. Martin's Press, 2002), 10.
8. Raymond J. Batvinis, *The Origins of FBI Counterintelligence* (Lawrence: Kansas University Press, 2007), 1.
9. Kessler, *The Bureau*, 11.
10. Roy Emerson Curtis, "The Law of Hostile Military Expeditions as Applied by the United States," *The American Journal of International Law*, 8, (January, April 1914), 1-37, 224-256.
11. Throughout the text there are US dollar and Mexican peso amounts quoted and mentioned. The value of the Mexican peso in that period was firmly linked to the value of the US dollar at fifty percent, i.e. 1,000 Mexican pesos during that period had a value of 500 US dollars. The 2023 value of 1,000 US dollars in 1910 was approximately 31,000 US dollars. This current value decreased throughout the decade 1910-1920. The current value of 1,000 US dollars in 1920 was approximately 15,000. See "Purchasing Power Today of a US Dollar Transaction in the Past," *Measuring Worth*, 2023, www.measuringworth.com/ppowerus.
12. Library of Congress, "U.S. Neutrality Proclamation;" *Ottumwa Tri-Weekly Courier*, August 6, 1914,
13. Thomas J. Tunney, *Throttled! The Detection of the German and Anarchist Bomb Plotters in the United States*, (Boston: Small Maynard and Company, 1919), 127. Tunney estimated 80 ships had interned in New York alone. The true number is far below that. A total of fifty-four ships sought refuge in all U.S. harbors on August 4. A good portion of those were the North German Lloyd liners moored in Baltimore. *The New York Times*, August 6, 1914, reported 23 ships to be moored in New York with another 30 expected in the following week.

14 Heribert von Feilitzsch, *The Secret War Council: The German Fight Against the Entente in America in 1914* (Amissville: Henselstone Verlag, 2015), 21.

15 According to international law, a blockade had to be specifically targeting an enemy harbor or coastline. In the case of the British sea blockade, the blockade was not specific and restricted access for neutral countries to and from Scandinavia.

16 Admiral Sir Guy Gaunt, *The Yield of the Years* (London and Melbourne: Hutchinson and Co. LTD, 1940), 18-19, and Mark Arsenault, *The Imposter's War: The Press, Propaganda, and the Newsmen who battled for the Minds of America* (New York: Pegasus Books LTD, 2022), 89.

17 Arsenault, *The Imposter's War*, 91.

18 *Otago Daily Times*, May 21, 1913; *Sydney Morning Herald*, May 20, 1913.

19 Gaunt, *The Yield of the Years*, 131.

20 Boy-Ed's rank in the Imperial Navy was "Fregattenkapitän," comparable to Lieutenant Commander in the US Navy.

21 Von Feilitzsch, *The Secret War Council*, 25.

22 Gaunt, *The Yield of the Years*, 132.

23 Von Feilitzsch, *The Secret War Council*, 26.

24 Militärbericht 19, July 14, 1914, Box 27, Albert Papers, RG 65, NARA.

25 Militärbericht 14, 15, May 22 and May 28, 1914, Box 27, Albert Papers, RG 65, NARA.

26 For a historiographic discussion of the arms of the Ypiranga, see Thomas Baecker, "The Arms of the Ypiranga: The German Side," *The Americas*, vol. 30, no. 1 (Jul., 1973), 1–17; Michael C. Meyer, "The Arms of the Ypiranga," *Hispanic American Historical Review*, Vol. 50, No. 3 (August 1970), 543–556; Friedrich Katz, *The Secret War in Mexico: Europe, the United States, and the Mexican Revolution* (Chicago: University of Chicago Press, 1983), 232–235; and, Heribert von Feilitzsch, *In Plain Sight: Felix A. Sommerfeld, Spymaster in Mexico, 1908 to 1914* (Amissville: Henselstone Verlag, 2012), 356 ff.

27 Militärbericht 16, June 4, 1914, Box 27, Albert Papers, RG 65, NARA.

28 Von Feilitzsch, *The Secret War Council*, 29-30.

29 Gaunt also hired Pinkerton detectives, the Mooney and Boland Detective Agency, and detectives of the Thiel Detective Agency.

30 Von Feilitzsch, *The Secret War Council*, 90-91.

31 John Price Jones, *The German Spy in America: The Secret Plotting of German Spies in the United States and the Inside Story of the Sinking of the Lusitania* (London: Hutchinson and Co., 1917), 95-96.

32 Hamburg-American Line Personnel, December 1913, case 8000-156, Old German Files, RG 65, NARA; and, von Feilitzsch, *The Secret War Council*, 98.

33 See, for example, Sommerfeld to Boy-Ed, Nov. 11, 1914, Box 19, Albert Papers, RG 65, NARA.

34 Edwin P. Hoyt, *Spectacular Rogue: Gaston B. Means* (New York: The Bobbs Merrill Company, 1963).

35 Means engaged in paying tender captains in New York to sign affidavits alleging that they supplied the British navy from neutral ports.

36 Thomas Garrigue Masaryk, *The Making of a State: Memories and Observations, 1914-1918* (New York: Frederick A. Stokes Company, 1927), 259. The organization Voska headed was also called the Czech National Alliance. After the Cleveland Agreement in October 1915 the Czech National Alliance and the Slovak League united into the Bohemian National Alliance with Voska as the Vice Chairman.

37 Masaryk, *Making of a State*, 261.

38 Leo Baca, *Czech Immigration Passenger Lists*, volume VII (Richardson: Old Homestead Publishing Co., 1998), 246.

ENDNOTES

39 Passport Application, Sept. 11, 1918, Emanuel Victor Voska, NARA; Naturalization Deposition, May 1, 1900, Southern District of New York, Roll 24, Vol. 92, 745 – Vol. 93, 463; and, Oath of Allegiance, May 1, 1902, Southern District of New York, Roll 24, Vol. 92, 823.

40 Passport Application, Sept. 11, 1918, Emanuel Victor Voska, NARA.

41 Dagmar Hájková, *Emanuel Voska in the Czechoslovak Foreign Resistance in World War II: News and Propaganda*, PhD Dissertation, Charles University, Prague, 2007, translation extracted from https://www.armedconflicts.com/Voska-Emanuel-t94783, viewed 8-31-2023.

42 Masaryk, *The Making of a State*, 259; Victor Emanuel Voska and Will Irwin, *Spy and Counter-Spy* (London: George G. Harrap and Co. LTD, 1941), 38. The most prominent source of information from within the Austro-Hungarian Consulate was Frank Kopecky, who became the first consul of Czechoslovakia in New York after the war.

43 Voska and Irwin, *Spy and Counter-Spy*, 29-31; and, Gaunt, *The Yield of the Years*, 167.

44 Masaryk, *The Making of a State*, 261.

45 Von Feilitzsch, *The Secret War Council*, Chapter 10: "Blind Deaf and Dumb", 145ff.

46 Arsenault, *The Imposter's War*, 95.

47 Case 8000-80773, John R. Rathom, Witnessed Statement, John R. Rathom to Thomas W. Gregory, February 8, 1918, RG 65, BI, NARA.

48 Ibid., Undated memorandum, ca. 1918, RG 65, BI, NARA.

49 Gaunt, *The Yield of the Years*, 137-138.

50 Case 8000-80773, John R. Rathom, Undated memorandum, ca. 1918, RG 65, BI, NARA.

51 Rathom was accused in San Francisco of having poisoned his mistress. Although admitting to having written the address on a package with poisoned fruit, he was acquitted.

52 Arsenault, *The Imposter's War*, 95. Mark Arsenault worked for the *Providence Journal* and uncovered Rathom's history in this new book.

53 See, for example, *New York Times*, June 10, 1915, and *New York Times*, August 4, 1915.

54 Case 8000-80773, John R. Rathom, RG 65, BI, NARA and Department of Justice File 9-5-138; and, correspondence of John R. Rathom between November 1914 to June 1920, including letters to and from A. Bruce Bielaski and Thomas W. Gregory.

55 *Las Vegas Optic*, September 22, 1914; *Manitowoc Pilot*, October 22, 1914; and, *New York Tribune*, March 2, 1915. The first official complaint was lodged in August 1914 by the British Consul General in New York, Sir Courtnay Walter Bennett.

56 The BI file on the HAPAG manifest investigation starts in the spring of 1915. See case 8000-156, "Re HAPAG," RG 65, BI, NARA.

57 Boy-Ed Accounts, Albert Papers, Box 7, RG 65, NARA.

58 The following paragraphs appeared in part in von Feilitzsch, *The Secret War Council*, chapter 5.

59 *New York Times*, November 23, 1915.

60 Naval Records, volume 1 through 16, logbooks of unarmored cruiser SMS *Geier*, RG 45, Naval Records Collection of the Office of Naval Records and Library, NARA.

61 Entry 199, Box 131 file 3221, RG 131, Alien Property Custodian, NARA; and, *Ogden Standard*, October 16, 1914.

62 Boy-Ed Accounts, Albert Papers, Box 7, RG 65, NARA; Boy Ed lists expenses for the *Patagonia*, *Spreewald*, *Praesident*, *Stadt Schleswig*, all HAPAG supply ships for the German raiders in the Atlantic. *The New York Times*, November 23, 1915, lists another supply ship, the *Berwind*, owned by the Gans Steamship Line; *The New York Times*, August 19, 1914, in which the British government warned

349

Cuba not to support the supply operation since the SS *Bavaria* and SS *Praesident* had supplied the SMS *Karlsruhe* from there multiple times; and, New York Times, August 16, 1914.

63 Boy-Ed Accounts, November 7, 1914, Albert Papers, Box 7, RG 65, NARA. D. stands for *Dampfer*, the German word for steamer.

64 Baltimore Sun, January 30, 2010; von Feilitzsch, The Secret War on the United States in 1915 (Amissville: Henselstone Verlag, 2015), 91; and, Chad Millman, The Detonators: The Secret Plot to Destroy America and an Epic Hunt for Justice (New York: Little, Brown and Company, 2006), 33-34.

65 Millman, Detonators, 33-34.

66 Alexandria (Sacramento), Bangor, Bering, Berwind, Fanny Moll, Fram, Gladstone, Greacia, Guita, Heina, Lorenzo, Macedonia, Mahoney, Mazatlán (Jason/Edna), Mowinckle, Navarra, Nepos, Nordpol, Olsen, Patagonia, Praesident, Retriever, Somerstad, Spreewald, Stadt Schleswig, Thor, and Unita. Sources are RG 65 Albert Papers; Entry 199, Box 131 file 3221, RG 131 Records of the Alien Property Custodian, NARA; Poverty Bay Herald, December 24, 1915; New York Times, November 25, 1915; and, Jones, The German Spy in America, 120-129.

67 New York Times, August 22, 1914.

68 Ibid.; New York Times, August 23, 1914.

69 New York Times, February 9, 1916. Also, Spokane Daily Chronicle, October 5, 1914.

70 Marine Crew Chronik MIM620/CREW, Marineschule Mürwik, Flensburg, Deutschland, 45.

71 San Francisco Call and Post, April 14, 1909; February 23, 1912; and, December 2, 1912.

72 San Francisco Call and Post, December 8, 1913.

73 Ibid., August 22, 1913.

74 Ibid., May 30, 1913.

75 Los Angeles Herald, May 29, 1908.

76 Marine Crew Chronik MIM620/CREW, Marineschule Mürwik, Flensburg, Deutschland, 45.

77 New York Times, August 18, 1914.

78 Jamie Bisher, World War I Intelligence in Latin America, unpublished manuscript, 2008, 66.

79 Washington Herald, August 24, 1914; New York Sun, August 24, 1914; Hartford Courant, October 6, 1914; and, United Nations, Reports of International Arbitral Awards, S. S. 'Edna.' Disposal of pecuniary claims arising out of the recent war (1914-1918), United States, Great Britain, volume III (December 1934), 1592-1596.

80 Katz, Secret War in Mexico, 414; and, Bisher, World War I Intelligence in Latin America, 66. Katz cites no source for the white slavery story.

81 It originated in Katz's book and has floated through the Internet ever since.

82 Case 8000-156, John Hanna to John Lord O'Brian, June 21, 1918, Interview with Gustav Kuhlenkampff, RG 65, BI, NARA.

83 Boy-Ed accounting, November 7, 1914, RG 65 Albert Papers, Box 7, NARA.

84 Case 8000-156, John Hanna to John Lord O'Brian, June 21, 1918, Interview with Gustav Kuhlenkampff, RG 65, BI, NARA. The American prosecutor at Kuhlenkampf's trial traced a $135,000 payment to HAPAG in the beginning of the war for the purpose of buying a ship.

85 San Francisco Call and Post, March 13, 1913.

86 United Nations, Reports of International Arbitral Awards, S. S. 'Edna', 1592.

87 New York Times, November 23, 1915.

ENDNOTES

88 Hilken diaries, 1915-1917; and, H. H. Martin to John J. McCloy, December 28, 1935, Box 7, RG 76, Mixed Claims Commission, NARA. These documents not only establish Hilken as one of the main conspirators, but also Stallforth and Albert financing the sabotage efforts.

89 Case 8000-1396, Hindu Conspiracy Matter, Albert Klein alias Fre Jebsen, March 6, 1919; and, case 8000-383, Investigation of C. C. Crowley, RG 65, BI, NARA.

90 New York Times, August 24, 1914; and, New York Times, August 23, 1914.

91 Bennington Evening Banner, August 19, 1914.

92 Evening Public Ledger, January 18, 1915.

93 "Chapter IV, Shipping," Albert Papers, Box 9, RG 65, NARA.

94 Colliers carry coal, while lighters carry supplies from waterfront warehouses to the vessels that are being loaded. Typically lighters stay close to the harbor and are not designed for offshore service. Hence the claim that these lighters supply British vessels one mile offshore.

95 Hoyt, Spectacular Rogue, 36-39.

96 Case 8000-341494, Memorandum to the Attorney General in preparation of Senate testimony, January 27, 1918, BI, Old German Files, RG 65, BI, NARA

97 New York Sun, April 6, 1915.

98 Laramie Republican, April 7, 1915.

99 Dudley Field Malone appears in a host of BI files, but none refer to the case in question.

100 New York Sun, April 7, 1915.

101 Hoyt, Spectacular Rogue, 39-40.

102 Diary entry July 1, 1915, Albert Papers, Box 23, RG 65, NARA.

103 Washington Times, May 2, 1915.

104 Hoyt, Spectacular Rogue, 42.

105 Ibid., 101 ff.

106 New York Tribune, March 2, 1915.

107 New York Times, September 16, 1918; and, Johann Heinrich Count Bernstorff, My Three Years in America (New York: Charles Scribner's Sons, 1920), 86.

108 Karl Boy-Ed, Verschwörer? (Berlin: Verlag August Scherl, 1920), 5.

109 New York Times, August 1, 1914.

110 New York Times, August 4, 1914. "Die Wacht am Rhein," is a patriotic German anthem by Max Schneckenburger (1840).

111 New York Times, August 4, 1914.

112 Case 8000-229 Passport Fraud, Statement of Carl Ruroede, County of Fulton, November 1914, RG 65, BI, NARA.

113 Affidavit of Horst von der Goltz, undated, HO 144/21710, British National Archives, Kew.

114 Ibid.

115 Spring-Rice to Edward Grey, November 27, 1914, HO 144/21710, British National Archives, Kew.

116 Spring Rice to Foreign Office, November 22, 1914, HO 144-21710, Horst von der Goltz, British National Archives, Kew.

117 Case 8000-228, Passport Fraud, Robert Lansing to Thomas Gegory, December 23, 1914, RG 65, BI, NARA.

118 US Army Intelligence Report, Portland, Oregon, Nov. 15, 1918, roll 873, RG 65, BI, NARA.

119 CPI Inflation Calculator, www.in2013dollars.com/us/inflation/1891, viewed January 3, 2024.
120 Case 8000-228, Passport Fraud, Statement of Carl Ruroede, November 21, 1915, RG 65, BI, NARA.
121 Ibid., Statement of Charles Raoul Chattilon, January 16, 1915, RG 65, BI, NARA.
122 Passport Applications, August 8, 1914, RG 85, Immigration and Naturalization Service, NARA.
123 Index to Marriages, New York City Clerk's Office, New York, June 30, 1910.
124 Passenger and Crew Lists of Vessels arriving in New York, July 26, 1910, RG 85, Immigration and Naturalization Service, NARA.
125 Passport Applications, August 8, 1914, RG 59, Department of State, NARA; and, New York County Supreme Court, naturalization petition card for October 1, 1914, RG 65, BI, NARA.
126 1910 Census, New York, Manhattan Ward 12, Hans A. von Wedell.
127 *Guthrie Daily Leader*, January 8, 1915.
128 Case 8000-229, various, German Consulate Rotterdam advising von Wedell trip on behalf of Foreign Office, September 24, 1914, RG 65, BI, NARA.
129 Ibid., von Holtzendorff to H. A. von Wedell, October 8, 1914; and, Ida Albert to H. A. von Wedell, October 1, 1914, RG 65, BI, NARA.
130 Case 8000-228, Passport Fraud, Robert Lansing to Thomas Gregory, December 23, 1914, RG 65, BI, NARA.
131 World War II registration card, April 25, 1942.
132 Case 8000-924, various, Indictment of Carl Ruroede, February 16, 1916; and, of Hans Adam von Wedell, May 15, 1913, RG 65, BI, NARA.
133 Case 8000-228, Passport Fraud, von Wedell to Ambassador Count Bernstorff, December 26, 1914, BI, NARA.
134 US Census 1910, New York, Manhattan, District 205; Census 1920, New York, Syracuse, District 194; and, Lucerne, Pennsylvania, District 1, 1930.
135 Case 8000-228, Passport Fraud, Statement of Carl Ruroede, November 21, 1915, RG 65, BI, NARA.
136 Ibid., Statement of Carl Ruroede, November 21, 1915; and, Jentzer Report, December 30, 1914, RG 65, BI, NARA.
137 Case 8000-924, various, Indictment of Carl Ruroede, February 16, 1916, RG 65, BI, NARA.
138 Case 8000-228, Passport Fraud, Adams Report, December 29, 1914, RG 65, BI, NARA.
139 Ibid., McGee Report, Scully Report, December 31, 1914, RG 65, BI, NARA.
140 Ibid., Grgurevic Report, January 6, 1915, RG 65, BI, NARA.
141 Ibid., Jentzer Report, January 2, 1915, RG 65, BI, NARA.
142 Ibid., LoMedico Report, January 2, 1915, RG 65, BI, NARA.
143 Ibid., Tucker Report, January 2, 1915, RG 65, BI, NARA.
144 Ibid.
145 Ibid.
146 Jones, *The German Spy in America*, 77.
147 One of the reasons historians such as Barbara Tuchman and Rhodri Jeffs-Jones referred to agents of the BI as "secret service agents" was that the term was used to describe agents involved in intelligence work in general. Many original documents, including reports from the Bureau, as well as newspaper articles, call special agents of the BI "secret agents" or "secret service agents." Historians have mistakenly picked up on these sources and concluded that the original documents referred to US Secret Service Agents, creating a whole cotton industry of purported rivalries between the US

Secret Service and the Bureau of Investigation during World War I, despite a clear delineation of mission and responsibility. As the referral of these passport fraud cases from the State Department to the Justice Department show, even in a case of counterfeiting official documents, which may conceivably have touched upon the expertise and mission of the US Secret Service, counterespionage was clearly the purview of the Bureau of Investigation.

148 Johannes Reiling, *Deutschland: Safe for Democracy?* (Stuttgart: Franz Steiner Verlag, 1997), 241.
149 Prison registry, December 4, 1914, HO 144-21710, Horst von der Goltz, British National Archives, Kew.
150 Arrest Sheet, November 16, 1914, HO 144/21710, British National Archives, Kew.
151 Court Order, Recommendation for Expulsion, November 27, 1914, HO 144-21710, Horst von der Goltz, British National Archives, Kew.
152 Prison registry, December 4, 1914, HO 144-21710, Horst von der Goltz, British National Archives, Kew.
153 Minutes, contents of safe deposit box, November 28, 1914, HO 144-21710, Horst von der Goltz, British National Archives, Kew.
154 Horst von der Goltz, *My Adventures as a German Secret Agent* (New York: Robert McBride and Company, 1917), image opposite page 140.
155 Emerson to Home Office, November 27, 1914, HO 144/21710, British National Archives, Kew.
156 Prison governor notes, January 6, 8, 12, 1915, petition H. v. d. Goltz, January 6, 1915, HO 144-21710, Horst von der Goltz, British National Archives, Kew.
157 Admiral Hall to Home Office, January 8, 1915, HO 144/21710, British National Archives, Kew.
158 Affidavit of Horst von der Goltz, undated, HO 144/21710, British National Archives, Kew.
159 Hall to Prison Governor, January 18, 1915, HO 144-21710, Horst von der Goltz, British National Archives, Kew.
160 Affidavit, undated (February 1, 1916), KV 2-519, Horst von der Goltz, British National Archives, Kew.
161 Suspension of Deportation Order, April 9, 1915, HO 144/21710, British National Archives, Kew.
162 *Providence Journal*, December 18 and 26, 1918.
163 Cecil Spring-Rice to Edward Grey, November 27, 1914, HO 144-21710, Horst von der Goltz, British National Archives, Kew.
164 The following passages are synthesized from von Feilitzsch, *The Secret War Council*, 150 ff.
165 Summary of von der Goltz case, February 1, 1916, KV 2-519, Horst von der Goltz, British National Archives, Kew.
166 Affidavit, undated (February 1, 1916), KV 2-519, Horst von der Goltz, British National Archives, Kew.
167 Von Feilitzsch, *Secret War Council*, 150 ff.
168 Affidavit, undated (February 1, 1916), KV 2-519, Horst von der Goltz, British National Archives, Kew.
169 Brian Lee Massey, "A Brief History of the Canadian Expeditionary Force," http://www.rootsweb.ancestry.com/~wwican/cef14_15.htm, 1997 - 2007.
170 There are no German sources as the National Archives in Potsdam burned to the ground in 1945. Many important archival collections, including intelligence files were destroyed. For the Pilenas article, see *New York Tribune*, May 12, 1918.

171 Brixton has a long list of celebrity inmates, including Irish Nationalist Roger Casement and Mick Jagger of the band The Rolling Stones.

172 von der Goltz, My Adventures, image opposite page 196; and, Miscellaneous #6, 1916: Selection of Papers found in the Possession of Captain von Papen (London: Harrison and Sons, 1916), check No. 22.

173 Sworn Statement by Horst von der Goltz, alias Bridgeman Taylor, Miscellaneous No. 13 (1916) (London: Harrison and Sons, 1916); New York Tribune, May 9, 1916.

174 Scotland Yard to Harris, April 17, 1916, von der Goltz interview with the New York Sun, while on the ship carrying him to the US, HO 144-21710, Horst von der Goltz, British National Archives, Kew.

175 Watertown Daily Times, June 29, 1916; and, New Yorik Tribune, May 12, 1918.

176 Case File 8000-5994, Horst von der Goltz, RG 65, BI, NARA.

177 Rocky Mountain News, April 8, 1916.

178 New York Tribune, May 9, 1916.

179 Public Ledger, July 11, 1916. Lüderitz is identified as Paul Hilken's business partner. Lüderitz captured national headlines in 1916 with news about the German merchant submarine U-Deutschland. He also briefly found public mention in 1917, when thieves took his car for a pleasure ride.

180 Case File 8000-1024, von Papen Coded Letter Case, RG 65, BI, NARA; and, Watertown Daily Times, June 29, 1916.

181 Bridgeport Evening Farmer, March 29, 1916.

182 Case File 8000-229, Werner Horn, Statement of Werner Horn, February 7, 1915, RG 65, BI, NARA. Horn recounted the time of the detonation as 1:30 am. The hotel proprietor Aubrey Take, recalled that he was rattled awake at 1:10 am. See Ibid., Statement of Aubrey Take, February 7, 1915, RG 65, BI, NARA.

183 File 3209, Werner Horn Case, Entry 199, undated (likely 1917-1918), RG 131, Alien Property Custodian, NARA.

184 Case File 8000-229, Werner Horn, A. Bruce Bielaski to Attorney General, February 13, 1915, RG 65, BI, NARA.

185 Ibid., Statement of Aubrey Take, February 7, 1915, RG 65, BI, NARA.

186 Ibid., A. Bruce Bielaski to Attorney General, February 13, 1915, RG 65, BI, NARA.

187 Ibid.

188 Ibid., Statement of Werner Horn, February 7, 1915, RG 65, BI, NARA.

189 Ibid., Mental Evaluation, Memo to Frank Burke, August 1, 1919, RG 65, BI, NARA.

190 Ibid., A. Bruce Bielaski to Attorney General, February 13, 1915, RG 65, BI, NARA.

191 Ibid.

192 Ibid., John C. Howard report, June 15, 1917; and, Joseph F. O'Connell, Esqu. to Bielaski, July 13, 1917, RG 65, BI, NARA.

193 Ibid., A. Bruce Bielaski to John Lord O'Brian, September 15, 1918, RG 65, BI, NARA.

194 New York Times, July 23, 1921.

195 Tunney, Throttled! 32. Tunney referred to P. K.'s case record "D-case 277."

196 Selection from Papers found in the Possession of Captain von Papen, Falmouth, January 2 and 3, 1916, Miscellaneous No. 6 (1916) (London: Her Majesty's Stationary Office, February 1916).

197 Mixed Claims Commission Report, December 31, 1928, volume 8 (New York: United Nations, 2006), 260.

198 File 3221, Boy-Ed Accounts, RG 131 Alien Property Custodian, Entry 199, NARA.

ENDNOTES

199 Reinhard R. Doerries, *Imperial Challenge: Ambassador Count Bernstorff and German-American Relations, 1908-1917* (Chapel Hill: University of North Carolina Press, 1989), 180.

200 For details on Boehm's time in Germany, see Reinhard R. Doerries, *Prelude to the Easter Rising: Sir Roger Casement in Imperial Germany* (London: Frank Cass, 2000).

201 *Detroit Times*, December 6, 1917.

202 *Detroiter Abend-Post*, January 8, 1916.

203 Ibid., June 27, 1915.

204 Ibid., September 3, 1915.

205 *Detroit Times*, October 6, 1915.

206 Ibid., October 5, 1915.

207 Case 8000-210, Albert Kaltschmidt, Keene to Bielaski, May 22, 1917, RG 65, BI, NARA.

208 Deposit of $150 to von Reiswitz, August 20, 1915, Transfer of $16,000 to von Reiswitz, January 23, 1917 (marked reimbursements), $5,000 to von Reiswitz (no details), October 5, 1915, RG 65 Albert Papers, NARA.

209 *Detroit Times*, December 6, 1917.

210 Case 8000-210, Albert Kaltschmidt, C. E. Argabright report, September 26, 1919, RG 65, BI, NARA.

211 For a discussion of the Ottawa Parliament fire of 1916, see von Feilitzsch, "The Canadian Parliament Fire of 1916: A Severely Flawed Investigation," FCH *Annals*, vol 28 (Jan 2022), 61-74; and, *Toronto Star*, February 3, 2016, "U.S. historian says it's possible German agents caused 1916 Parliament fire."

212 Bielaski to Blanford, January 19, 1915; Rathbun reports, January 22, 23, 1915; Blanford report, February 1, 1915; Allen reports, February 3, 6, 1915; Timoney report, July 31, 1915; Tucker report, July 31, 1915, roll 858, RG 65, BI, NARA; Webster reports, January 20, 21, 23, 1915, roll 858, RG 65, BI, NARA; and, January 22, 1915, roll 857, RG 65, BI, NARA; Blanford reports, January 21, 27, 1915, roll 857, RG 65, BI, NARA; and, January 27, 1915, roll 855, RG 65, BI, NARA.

213 Blanford reports, January 28, February 1, 8, 1915; Webster report, February 2, 1915, roll 858, RG 65, BI, NARA.

214 Case 8000-80773 John R. Rathom, German-Hindu Plot, undated (1918), RG 65, BI, NARA.

215 Webster reports, February 2, 3, 9-11, 15, November 15, 1915, roll 858, RG 65, BI, NARA; and, Case 8000-1396, German-Hindu Conspiracy, Blanford to Bielaski, December 8, 1917, RG 65, BI, NARA. Agent Webster discovered two years later that the German purchasing agent Hans Tauscher had pocketed a good percentage of the purchase price, as he made the arms dealer W. Stokes Kirk issue an inflated amount to submit to German Military Attaché von Papen. In addition to the hidden profits, Tauscher also charged commissions to the German government.

216 Case 8000-273862, examination of Dr. C. Chakraberty, undated (1917), RG 65, BI, NARA. Chakraberty testified that he had received about $60,000 from the German military attaché Wolf von Igel.

217 Acting Chief to Offley, July 13, 1915, roll 858, RG 65, BI, NARA; and, Tauscher to von Papen, October 26, 1914, Albert Papers, Box 33, RG 65, NARA.

218 Tauscher to von Papen, October 26, 1914, Albert Papers, Box 33, RG 65, NARA.

219 The 239-foot, 1,749-ton, *Maverick* was built in 1890 for the Standard Oil Company in New York. It burnt and sank at her pier in 1899 but was salvaged. After the German government bought her, she had to be refitted to accept the arms and ammunition cargo in her hold. For more details on Frederick Jebsen, see von Feilitzsch, *The Secret War Council*, 74-80.

220 Chief to Blanford, June 15, 1915, roll 858, RG, 65, BI, NARA.

221 Treadway report, July 14, 1917, roll 858, RG 65, BI, NARA.

222 Chief to Blanford, June 15, 1915; Barnes to Horn, July 7, 1915; Acting Chief to Byron, July 27, 1915; Acting Chief to Offley, July 29, 191; Offley report, August 8, 1915, roll 858, RG 65, BI, NARA; Wright report, April 18, 1917, roll 855, RG 65, BI, NARA; and, von Feilitzsch, *Secret War Council*, 179-201.

223 Wright reports, April 13, 18, 1917, roll 855, RG 65, BI, NARA.

224 Case 8000-1396, German-Hindu Conspiracy, Count Bernstorff to Lansing, July 2, 1915, July 29, 1916, October 5, 1916, RG 65, BI, NARA.

225 The following paragraphs are based on descriptions in von Feilitzsch, *In Plain Sight: Felix A. Sommerfeld, Spymaster in Mexico, 1908 to 1914* (Amissville: Henselstone Verlag, 2012), 286-290.

226 Entry 199, Box 95, file 1955, RG 131, Alien Property Custodian, NARA.

227 *Washington Post*, April 16, 1905.

228 Barnes report, May 15, 1913; Matthews report May 20, 1913; Offley report May 23, 1913, roll 853, RG 65, BI, NARA.

229 As a significant sideline, these 500 rifles became part of the arms of the *Ypiranga* that precipitated an American intervention in the spring of 1914. See von Feilitzsch, *In Plain Sight*, 287.

230 Payments to F. Stallforth, February 9, 1914, February 28, 1914, March 4, 1914, Lazaro De La Garza Papers, Box 5, Folder A, Benson Latin American Collection, University of Texas at Austin.

231 Case 8000-1396, German-Hindu Conspiracy, Memorandum to Chief, undated (fall 1917), RG 65, BI, NARA.

232 Ibid., Bielaski to C. J. Scully, August 16, 1917, RG 65, BI, NARA. Bielaski did not exaggerate. A total of 105 conspirators were prosecuted.

233 The *Maverick* was actually purchased by Franz von Papen for the German government. See von Papen to General von Falkenhayn, April 9, 1915, Albert Papers, Box 19, RG 65, NARA.

234 Case 8000-1396, German-Hindu Conspiracy, Albert Klein alias Fred Jebsen, Interview by special employee W. H. Buck, March 6, 1919, RG 65, BI, NARA.

235 Ibid., Fred Jebsen – Fugitive, A. Marr (British Intelligence Service) to Agent Blanford, May 27, 1919, RG 65, BI, NARA.

236 *Ogden Standard*, December 10, 1915; and, Marine Crew Chronik MIM620/CREW, Marineschule Mürwik, Flensburg, Deutschland, 46.

237 Tauscher to von Papen, June 17, 1915, Albert Papers, Box 33, RG 65, NARA. As a matter of fact, the *Maverick* also never returned to Java. British authorities impounded her in Jakarta and found five Indian nationalists, among them Hari Singh, one of the main conspirators of the planned uprising, and propaganda materials on board. She never sailed again and sank at her berth sometime in 1917.

238 Tauscher to von Papen, July 30, 1915, Albert Papers, Box 33, RG 65, NARA.

239 Case 8000-3994, Hans Tauscher, Adams report, June 25, 1915, RG 65, BI, NARA.

240 Ibid.

241 *New York Evening World*, September 25, 1915.

242 Case 8000-3994, Hans Tauscher, Adams report, June 25, 1915, RG 65, BI, NARA.

243 Tauscher to von Papen, July 30, 1915, Albert Papers, Box 33, RG 65, NARA.

244 Ibid.

245 Case 8000-3994, Hans Tauscher, Adams report, August 21, 1915, RG 65, BI, NARA.

246 Case 8000-1024, Franz von Papen, RG 65, BI, NARA.

247 Ibid., Tauscher to War Ministry, February 1, 1916, RG 65, BI, NARA.

248 Ibid., Hans Tauscher, List of sales, February 8, 1916, RG 65, BI, NARA.

249 Ibid.

250 Fritzen to Koenig, March 28, 1916, "received for fare and expenses $200...", Albert Papers, Box 13, RG 65, NARA; and, New York Tribune, April 25, 1916.

251 New York Evening World, June 28, 1916.

252 New York Sun, April 25, 1916.

253 New York Tribune, April 19, 1916. In a great example, why historians confuse the US Secret Service and Bureau of Investigation activities, the paper reported "[...] Agent Baker with three other Secret Service men [...]." Baker and the three men were Special Agents of the Bureau of Investigation.

254 Case 8000-3994, Hans Tauscher, Baker report, April 17, 1916, RG 65, BI, NARA.

255 Bernstorff to Bethmann-Hollweg, April 21, 1916, ADM1-10982, British National Archives, Kew, UK.

256 New York Sun, April 19, 1916.

257 Historian Rhodri Jeffreys-Jones, who theorized in his books that the USSS was the only capable American counterintelligence agency during the World War, credits the Bureau's counterintelligence success to sheer luck. "American intelligence is revealed at its most calculating in the case of the von Igel raid [...]. On the morning of April 18, 1916, von Igel laid out the contents of the safe on a table ready for packaging. At that precise moment—*the coincidence is truly remarkable*—[italics added—our Justice Department agents arrive to take von Igel in for questioning. As one of them held the office guard at gunpoint, another executed a flying tackle on von Igel as he desperately tried to shovel the evidence back into the safe. The two other agents went to the heart of the matter, pouncing on the mass of evidence, weighing seventy pounds, which provided every last detail, down to the telephone numbers, of German and German-American agents in the United States." See Rhodri Jeffreys-Jones, *American Espionage: From Secret Service to CIA* (New York: Free Press, 1977), 63.

258 New York Sun, April 25, 1916.

259 Case 8000-3994, Hans Tauscher, Grgurevich report, April 27; Storck report, April 22, 1916, RG 65, BI, NARA.

260 New York Tribune, April 25, 1916.

261 Bernstorff to Lansing, April 18, 1916, File No. 701.6211/364, RG 59, Department of State, NARA.

262 Case 8000-3994, Hans Tauscher, Grgurevich report, April 21, 1916, RG 65, BI, NARA.

263 Ibid., Offley report, April 26, 1916, RG 65, BI, NARA.

264 New York Sun, April 20, 1916.

265 New York Tribune, April 28, 1916.

266 Case 8000-3994, Hans Tauscher, Offley to Bielaski, June 12, 1916, RG 65, BI, NARA.

267 New York Tribune, April 25, 1916.

268 Doerries, *Prelude to the Easter Rising*, 9.

269 Ibid., 212-214.

270 Nadolny to von Papen, January 24, 1915, Box 2, RG 76 Mixed Claims Commission, NARA.

271 "Von Igel Papers – Relative to Casement and Ireland, No. 307/16 & 308/16. New York 8.4.16," ADM 1-10980, British National Archives, Kew, UK.

272 "Von Igel Papers – Relative to Casement and Ireland, No. 335/16, New York 17.4.16," ADM 1-10980, British National Archives, Kew, UK.

273 Arthur S. Link, ed., *The Papers of Woodrow Wilson*, 69 vols. (Princeton: Princeton University Press, 1966-1994), volume 36, 503.

274 Doerries, *Prelude to the Easter Rising*, 23. Doerries leaves the question open, whether Admiral Hall had already intercepted communication between Devoy, McGarrity, and Casement, or whether the von Igel papers reached British hands and torpedoed the uprising.

275 Case 8000-1396, German-Hindu Conspiracy, Blanford reports August 15, 16, 17, 1917, RG 65, BI, NARA.

276 Ibid.

277 Ibid., Lee Welch report, November 4, 1917, RG 65, BI, NARA.

278 Ibid., Blanford report, August 17, 1917, RG 65, BI, NARA.

279 Ibid.

280 Ibid., Weise report, October 15, 1917, RG 65, BI, NARA.

281 Ibid., Blanford report August 14, 1917, RG 65, BI, NARA.

282 Ibid., Statement of G. P. Boehm, undated (1916), Statement of Friederic Wilhelm Richard Hermann, May 26, 1917, RG 65, BI, NARA.

283 German Consul Mazatlán to von Magnus, February 25, 1920, Auswärtiges Amt, Mexico III, Packet 28, German Foreign Office Archives, Berlin.

284 Case 8000-1396, German-Hindu Conspiracy, RG 65, BI, NARA.

285 Nadolny to Foreign Office, January 24, 1915, Box 2, cables, RG 76, Mixed Claims Commission, NARA.

286 Charles F. Horne, ed., *Source Records of the Great War*, vol. III (New York, National Alumni, 1923).

287 Von Feilitzsch, *Secret War on the United States*, 40, 93.

288 Ibid., 31-33.

289 *New York Times*, April 4, 1915.

290 New York, List of arriving passengers, April 3, 1915, *Kristianiafjord*.

291 Jones, *The German Spy in America*, 153.

292 Rintelen may himself have introduced himself as "von Rintelen" at times, even boasted that he was related to the German Emperor.

293 Von Feilitzsch, *Secret War on the United States*, 77.

294 Case 8000-174 Franz von Rintelen, Chief Bielaski to William Offley, December 20, 1915, RG 65, BI, NARA. Rice had a flax factory in German-occupied Belgium and visited Berling to receive authorization to resume production. He met Rintelen during these negotiations.

295 Link, *The Papers of Woodrow Wilson*, vol. 32, James Watson Gerard to Edward Mandell House, March 6, 1915, 351-353.

296 Case 8000-174 Franz von Rintelen, William Benham report, January 7, 1916, RG 65, BI, NARA.

297 *Sun*, April 24, 1915.

298 Link, *The Papers of Woodrow Wilson*, vol. 32, Woodrow Wilson to Edward Mandell House, March 1, 1915, 300-301.

299 Ibid., Edward Mandell House to Woodrow Wilson, March 9, 1915, 349.

300 Case 8000-174, Franz von Rintelen, William Benham report, January 7, 1916, RG 65, BI, NARA.

301 Ibid., James F. McElhone to Richard M. Levering, Rintelen-Schmidtmann interview transcription, August 20, 1918, RG 65, BI, NARA.

302 Ibid.

303 Case 8000-925, Walter T. Scheele, Interrogation, March 23, 1918, RG 65, BI, NARA.

304 Jones, *The German Spy in America*, 157; Barbara W. Tuchman, *The Zimmermann Telegram* (New York: McMillan Publishing Company, 1958), 79; Michael C. Mayer, *Huerta: A Political Portrait* (Lincoln: University of Nebraska Press, 1972), 217; Friedrich Katz, *The Life and Times of Pancho Villa* (Stanford: Stanford University Press, 1998); and, Reinhard R. Doerries, *Imperial Challenge: Ambassador Count Bernstorff and German-American Relations, 1908-1917* (Chapel Hill: University of North Carolina Press, 1989), 167.

305 Statement of Karl Boy-Ed, February 14, 1928, Box 14, RG 76, Mixed Claims Commission, NARA.

306 Case 8000-925 Walter T. Scheele, Interrogation, March 23, 1918, BI, RG 65, NARA.

307 Ibid.

308 File 9140-626, Synopsis, June 1, 1918, RG 165, MID, NARA.

309 Case 8000-925 Walter T. Scheele, timeline 1915, RG 65, BI, NARA.

310 ADM 1/10978, Scheele to von Papen, December 22, 1915, British National Archives, Kew.

311 Case 8000-925 Walter T. Scheele, Interrogation, March 23, 1918, RG 65, BI, NARA.

312 Ibid.

313 Ibid.

314 Ibid.

315 Voska and Irwin, *Spy and Counter-Spy*, 112. It is not entirely clear what the separation material really was. Some accounts mention aluminum, others lead, zinc, paraffin, or copper. It is safe to assume from the various U.S. agents' reports that the first separators consisted of paraffin that sometimes did not deteriorate, thus making the bomb a dud. Later, Scheele seemed to have used aluminum plates of different thicknesses that corroded in sulfuric acid. According to Scheele's debriefers in 1918, the chemicals used were hexamethylene tetramine on one side, and powdered sodium peroxide on the other. Tunney, *Throttled!*, 138; Tunney of the New York bomb squad described the chemicals as potassium chlorate on one side and sulfuric acid on the other, Case 8000-925, Walter T. Scheele, RG 65, BI, NARA.

316 Investigators and witnesses of the time coined the descriptive words "cigar" and "pencil," when describing the firebombs.

317 File 9140-626, Synopsis, June 1, 1918, RG 165 MID, NARA.

318 Case 8000-925, Walter T. Scheele, Timeline 1915, RG 65, BI, NARA.

319 Ibid., Interrogation, March 23, 1918, RG 65, BI, NARA.

320 Ibid., Bielaski to Pendleton, March 26, 1918, RG 65, BI, NARA.

321 File 9140-626, Synopsis, June 1, 1918, RG 165 MID, NARA.

322 Case 8000-925, Walter T. Scheele, Interrogation, March 23, 1918, RG 65, BI, NARA.

323 Ibid.

324 See Heribert von Feilitzsch and Charles H. Harris III, *The federal Bureau of Investigation, vol. 1: The fBI and Mexican Revolutionists, 1908-1914* (Amissville: Henselstone Verlag, 2023), 150 ff.

325 Pendleton report, June 10, 1916, roll 863, RG 65, BI, NARA.

326 File 9140-626, Synopsis, June 1, 1918, RG 165 MID, NARA.

327 Case 8000-925, Walter T, Scheele, Timeline 1915, RG 65, BI, NARA.

328 Ibid., Interrogation, March 23, 1918, RG 65, BI, NARA.

329 Ibid.

330 Ibid.

331 Ibid., Timeline 1915, RG 65, BI, NARA.

332 Ibid.

333 Ibid., Phone conversation transcript between Agent Levering and Chief Bielaski, March 15, 1918, RG 65, BI, NARA.

334 Tunney, Throttled! 3-4, 127. The original squad had nineteen members.

335 Since cotton and hay can combust as a result of moisture, some of the suspected arsons during this period may have simply been caused by moisture in the holds of these ships. See, von Feilitzsch, Secret War on the United States, 252-257. The author identified ships that certainly were firebombed, others that could have been firebombed, and some that most likely burnt as a result of other causes.

336 Agents Daily Reports, October 20-24, 1915, New York, volumes 46-48, RG 87, US Secret Service, NARA.

337 Ibid. The nature of the special investigation after mentioning Weehawken is not detailed. USSS special investigations covered mostly out of state counterfeit investigations. In this case different agents are included and taken off the "special investigation," which may indicate that numerous cases are covered.

338 Agents Daily Reports, October 26, 1915, New York, Volumes 46-48, RG 87, US Secret Service, NARA.

339 Lansing Papers, 1914-1919, volume 1, Dudley Field Malone to Robert Lansing, April 30, 1915, 434; and, New York Evening World, October 28, 1915, mentioning the Customs Neutrality Squad as having noticed Fay; and New York Herald, February 26, 1922. In an article titled, "How we trapped the Mysterious Lt. Fay," authored by Flynn, he claimed that "we [US Secret Service agents] arrested him."

340 Case 8000-376, Clara Daeche, Examination of Robert Fay, October 24, 1916, RG 65, BI, NARA.

341 New York Evening World, June 22, 1916.

342 The Bureau file on Fay begins with his escape.

343 Case 8000-376, Clara Daeche, Adams reports, September 20-27; Baker report, September 27, 1915; Baker report, September 30, 1915; Solicitor for the State Department to Bielaski, May 6, 1918, RG 65, BI, NARA.

344 New York Evening World, August 16, 1918.

345 New York Herald, September 22, 1922.

346 Case 8000-925, Walter T. Scheele, Mooney and Boland report, July 17, June 22, 1915, RG 65, BI, NARA; Case 8000-3089, Frederico Stallforth, diary entry August 13, 1915, RG 65, BI, NARA. These sources mention the agency by name. Evidence suggests that Mooney and Boland worked for Karl Boy-Ed and Guy Gaunt at the same time, but on different investigations. On the one hand, Boy-Ed was checking behind Rintelen associate David Lamar, who received hundreds of thousands of dollars from the German agent. Gaunt, on the other hand, knew all about the fertilizer when seizing the SS Esrom, having frequent contact with New York police and the Bureau, especially Offley and Bielaski, and having the funds to outsource investigations. He is documented to have hired private detectives from the Burns Agency and Pinkerton's National Detective Agency on other investigations. See for example FO 115/1936 Allan Pinkerton to Cecil Spring Rice, January 27, 1915, British National Archives, Kew. Among other candidates considered as having hired the detective agency is William J. Flynn. However, he neither had the funding nor authority to engage private investigators. In the July 19-20, 1915, report the detective laments lack of interest by the federal government until more evidence is developed. A. Bruce Bielaski also did not have the authority or funding to hire private investigators. He also had a large field office in New York with plenty of

ENDNOTES

resources. Also, the July 19-20 report mentioned that the Justice Department was not investigating at this point. Another possibility would be a large industrialist. The Mooney and Boland manager in New York wrote on July 22, 1915, to a Dupont lawyer and offered information and services for a price. This report comes at the end of the investigation into Scheele and labor leaders. Dupont therefore had not hired the agency. It is also highly unlikely that another industrial leader had hired them, as they would not have been able to sell the results of their investigation to Dupont. Mooney and Boland detectives noted in one of their reports that the Burns agency was watching Samuel Gompers. For whom Burns worked in this case cannot be determined.

347 Case 8000-925, Walter T. Scheele, Mooney and Boland reports, July 12-23, 1915, RG 65, BI, NARA.
348 Tunney, Throttled! 161.
349 "Familienverband derer v. Kleist e.V.," www.v-kleist.com, viewed February 10, 2013.
350 Ibid.
351 Case 8000-925, Walter T. Scheele, Mooney and Boland agent report July 27-28, 1915, RG 65, BI, NARA.
352 Ibid., Mooney and Boland agent report July 17-23, 1915, RG 65, BI, NARA.
353 Tunney, Throttled! 135.
354 Daily Reports of Agents, New York, September 3, 1915, Volume 47,, RG 87, US Secret Service, NARA.
355 Case 8000-925, Walter T. Scheele, Dotzert report, April 27, 1916, RG 65, BI, NARA.
356 Ibid., Offley report, April 29, 1916, RG 65, BI, NARA. Tunney had furnished the names to the BI.
357 Ibid., Bielaski to Offley, September 22, 1915, RG 65, BI, NARA.
358 Ibid.
359 Ibid., Bielaski to Offley, October 7, 1915, RG 65, BI, NARA.
360 Ibid., Offley to Bielaski, November 20, 1915, RG 65, BI, NARA.
361 Ibid., Statement of Dr. Scheele, March 18,1918, RG 65, BI, NARA.
362 Ibid., Mooney and Boland report, July 27, 28, 1915, RG 65, BI, NARA.
363 Ibid., Assistant Attorney General to Secretary of State, November 26, 1915; Scully report, November 24, 1915, RG 65, BI, NARA. The Danish flagged Esrom had sailed from New York for Gothenburg on October 9.
364 File 300.115/6619, Page to Lansing, December 28, 1915, RG 59, Department of State, NARA.
365 Case 8000-925, Walter T. Scheele, Assistant Attorney General to Secretary of State, November 22 and November 26, 1915, RG 65, BI, NARA.
366 Ibid., Offley to Bielaski, November 20, 1915, RG 65, BI, NARA.
367 Ibid., Gregory to Lansing, 17 January 1916, RG 65, BI, NARA.
368 Ibid., Notes taken from a meeting with Charles von Kleist, October 30, 1916, RG 65, BI, NARA.
369 Ibid., Synopsis, June 1, 1918, RG 65, BI, NARA.
370 Ibid., Dotzert report, March 26, 1916, RG 65, BI, NARA.
371 Ibid., Notes taken from a meeting with Charles von Kleist, October 30, 1916, RG 65, BI, NARA.
372 Ibid.
373 Ibid.
374 Case 8000-376, Clara Daeche, Letter to sister Olga, June 21, 1916, RG 65, BI, NARA.
375 Ibid.

376 Case 8000-925, Walter T. Scheele, Grgurevich report, April 13, 1916; Baker report, April 21, 1916, RG 65, BI, NARA; and, *New York Times*, April 15, 1916.

377 Ibid., Offley report, May 6, 1916, RG 65, BI, NARA.

378 Ibid.

379 Ibid., Grgurevich report, April 21, 1916, RG 65, BI, NARA.

380 Ibid., Statements of Becker, Praedel, Paredies, Schmidt, April 21, 1916, RG 65, BI, NARA.

381 Ibid., Dotzert report, April 17, 1916, RG 65, BI, NARA.

382 Ibid., Interrogation, March 23, 1918, RG 65, BI, NARA.

383 Ibid., Offley to Bielaski, April 10, 1917, RG 65, BI, NARA.

384 Ibid., Synopsis, June 1, 1918, RG 65, BI, NARA.

385 Von Feilitzsch, *The Secret War on the US*, 244-245.

386 Franz Rintelen von Kleist, *The Dark Invader* (London: Lovat Dickson, 1934); and *Return of the Dark Invader* (London: Lovat Dickson, 1935).

387 Tunney, *Throttled!* 142.

388 Case 8000-925, Walter T. Scheele, Dotzert report, April 21, 1916.

389 Ibid., Daughton report, April 27, 1916, RG 65, BI, NARA.

390 Ibid., Cantrell report, April 18, 1916; Daughton report, April 19, 1916; Englesby report, April 2, 1916; Dotzert report, April 26, 1916; Examiner Rankin to Bielaski, April 20, 1916; and, Bielaski to Cantrell, April 20, 1916, RG 65, BI, NARA.

391 Case 8000-925, Walter T. Scheele, timeline 1918-1921, RG 65, BI, NARA.

392 Ibid., Bielaski to Cantrell, April 21, 1916, RG 65, BI, NARA.

393 Ibid., Cantrell report, April 21, 1916, RG 65, BI, NARA.

394 Ibid., Bielaski to Cantrell, May 1, 1916, RG 65, BI, NARA.

395 Ibid., Cantrell report, May 3, 1916, RG 65, BI, NARA.

396 Ibid., Lansing to Gregory, May 4, 1916, RG 65, BI, NARA.

397 Ibid., Bielaski to deputy marshal Key West, May 3, 1916, Offley to James H. Curtis, May 3, 1916, RG 65, BI, NARA.

398 Ibid., Cantrell report, May 3, 1916, RG 65, BI, NARA.

399 Ibid., Bielaski to Cantrell, April 21, 1916; Cantrell to Bielaski, undated (April 1916), RG 65, BI, NARA.

400 Ibid., Cantrell to Bielaski, May 4, 1916, RG 65, BI, NARA.

401 Ibid., Bielaski to Cantrell, May 4, 1916, RG 65, BI, NARA.

402 Ibid., Cantrell report, May 3, 1916, RG 65, BI, NARA.

403 Ibid., Cantrell report, May 5, 1916, RG 65, BI, NARA.

404 Ibid.

405 Ibid., Cantrell to American Minister, May 8, 1916, RG 65, BI, NARA.

406 Ibid., Bielaski to unknown [Levering], undated [1917], RG 65, BI, NARA.

407 Ibid., Cantrell report, May 8, 1916, RG 65, BI, NARA.

408 Ibid., Cantrell reports, May 13, 14, 17, 21, 22, June 2, 5, 1916, RG 65, BI, NARA.

409 For example, ibid., Jentzer report, July 23, 1917; and, Dotzert reports, June 6, 14, 1916, RG 65, BI, NARA.

410 Ibid., Bielaski to Offley, June 15, 1916, RG 65, BI, NARA.
411 Ibid., Offley to Bielaski, June 17, 1916, RG 65, BI, NARA.
412 Ibid., Chalmers report, July 7, 1916, RG 65, BI, NARA.
413 Ibid., Chalmers report, July 9, 1916, RG 65, BI, NARA.
414 For example, ibid., Bielaski to Barnes, June 26, 1916; Webster report, June 27, 1916; Pendleton report, June 14, 1916, RG 65, BI, NARA.
415 Case 8000-174, Franz von Rintelen, interview with Waldemar Schmidtmann, August 20, 1918, RG 65, BI, NARA.
416 Case 8000-925, Walter T. Scheele, Van Natta to Van Deman, March 12, 1918, RG 65, BI, NARA.
417 Ibid., Memorandum, May 22, 1918, RG 65, BI, NARA.
418 Ibid., Chemical Assistant, Thomas Edison to Richmond Levering, March 16, 1918, RG 65, BI, NARA. The debriefing went on for months, filling entire filing cabinets with Scheele's information.
419 Ibid., timeline 1916, RG 65, BI, NARA.
420 *New York Times*, October 16, 1920.
421 Case 8000-925, Walter T. Scheele, Levering to Bielaski, June 26, 1918, RG 65, BI, NARA.
422 Ibid., DeWoody to Bielaski, November 30, 1918; Chief Bielaski to F. H. Haggerson, January 2, 1919, RG 65, BI, NARA.
423 Ibid., Valjevec report, June 14, 1919, RG 65, BI, NARA.
424 Ibid., timeline 1918-1921, RG 65, BI, NARA.
425 Cantrell reports, July 10, 1915, roll 858; and, July 15, 1915, roll 859, RG 65, BI, NARA.
426 Assistant Attorney General to Secretary of State, December 9, 1914; Bielaski to Offley, December 9, 1914; Offley report, February 14, 1915; Guy report, April 14, 1915; Baker report, December 14, 1914, roll 857, RG 65, BI, NARA.
427 *New York Tribune*, August 2, 1915.
428 Ibid.
429 Ibid.
430 *Washington Evening Star*, August 5, 1915.
431 Berliner submitted his first report on December 10, 1915, roll 860, RG 65, BI, NARA.
432 Offley to Bielaski, January 24, 1915; Bielaski to Offley, February 12, 1915; Offley report, February 14, 1915, roll 857; and, Offley to Horn, July 18, 1915, roll 860, RG 65, BI, NARA.
433 Philips reports, February 15-21, 25, 26, March 2, 4, 8, 1915, roll 857; and, Offley report, March 20, 1915, roll 854, RG 65, BI, NARA.
434 Cantrell report, February 23, 1915; Scully report, March 1, 1915, roll 857, RG 65, BI, NARA.
435 Meyer, *Huerta*, 216.
436 Ibid., 72-75, 82.
437 Guy reports, April 14, 1915, roll 857; and, June 23, 25, 1915, roll 859; Offley to Bielaski, April 15, 1915, roll 854; Klawans reports, April 20-22, 1915; Klawans to Bielaski, April 21, 1915; Childers reports, April 29, 30, May 1, 4-7, 10-15, 1915, roll 858; Perasler report, April 17, 1915, roll 857, RG 65, BI, NARA.
438 Childers report, May 17, 1915, roll 858, RG 65, BI, NARA.
439 Ibid.
440 Offley to Bielaski, May 13, 1915, roll 858, RG 65, BI, NARA.

441 Agent Cantrell, born in Spartanburg, South Carolina, began his Bureau career on November 24, 1913, serving until November 14, 1919, when he was appointed a special assistant to the attorney general. Cantrell file, NPRC, NARA, St. Louis.
442 Offley to Bielaski, May 27, 1915; and, Offley report, May 28, 1915, roll 858, RG 65, BI, NARA.
443 Cantrell reports, May 28, 29, June 19, 21, 1915; Offley to Bielaski, June 18, 1915, roll 858, RG 65, BI, NARA.
444 Cantrell reports, June 4, 11, 12, 24, 26, 1915, roll 858, RG 65, BI, NARA.
445 Guy reports, June 28, 29, 1915, roll 858; and, July 20, 1915, roll 859, RG 65, BI, NARA.
446 Barnes report, April 13, 1915, roll 859, RG 65, BI, NARA.
447 Barnes reports, May 8, 19, 1915, roll 858; Guy report, May 25, 1915, roll 855, RG 65, BI, NARA.
448 Guy reports, May 2, 27, 1915, roll 854; May 28, June 8, 1915, roll 859; and, June 5, 1915, roll 855, RG 65, BI, NARA.
449 Guy reports, May 17, 28, June 4, 1915, roll 859, RG 65, BI, NARA.
450 Barnes report, July 23, 1914, roll 857, RG 65, BI, NARA.
451 Guy report, June 30, 1915, roll 858, RG 65, BI, NARA.
452 Barnes report, June 2, 1915, roll 859, RG 65, BI, NARA.
453 Chief to Barnes, May 14, 1915; Chief to Beckham, May 14, 1915, roll 854, RG 65, BI, NARA.
454 Pinckney report, May 1, 1915, roll 855, RG 65, BI, NARA.
455 Pinckney reports, April 23, 25, 27, 1915; Beckham report, May 14, 1915, roll 859, RG 65, BI, NARA.
456 Beckham report, May 21, 1915, roll 859, RG 65, BI, NARA.
457 Charles H. Harris III and Louis R. Sadler, *The Secret War in El Paso: Mexican Revolutionary Intrigue, 1906-1920* (Albuquerque: University of New Mexico Press, 2009), 166.
458 Pinckney report, April 23, 1915, roll 859, RG 65, BI, NARA.
459 Beckham report, April 28, 1915, roll 859, RG 65, BI, NARA.
460 Ibid.
461 Beckham report, May 14, 1915, roll 859, RG 65, BI, NARA.
462 Beckham reports, May 18-21, 1915, roll 859; Stone report, January 12, 1916, roll 858, RG 65, BI, NARA.
463 Beckham reports, May 21, 22, 24, 29, 31, June 5, 6, 1915, roll 859, RG 65, BI, NARA.
464 Von Feilitzsch, Felix A. *Sommerfeld and the Mexican Front in the Great War*, 7.
465 Bernhard Dernburg to Admiral Henning von Holtzendorff, May 10, 1915, RG 242, Captured German Documents, NARA. Also, Katz, *Secret War in Mexico*, 334.
466 Case 8000-174, Franz von Rintelen, Offley report, June 29, 1915, RG 65, BI, NARA.
467 Ibid., Benham report, October 1, 1915, RG 65, BI, NARA.
468 Ibid., Offley to Bielaski, June 28, 1915, RG 65, BI, NARA.
469 Ibid., Offley to Bielaski, June 29, 1915, RG 65, BI, NARA.
470 Ibid., Offley to Bielaski, June 26, 1915, RG 65, BI, NARA.
471 *Sun*, May 26, 1915.
472 Ibid.
473 Case 8000-174, Franz von Rintelen, Hammond to Tumulty, May 13, 1915, RG 65, BI, NARA; *New York Times*, May 3, 1917.

474 New York Evening World, October 15, 1912.
475 Case 8000-174, Franz von Rintelen, Hammond to Tumulty, May 13, 1915, RG 65, BI, NARA.
476 Chief to Offley, June 30, 1915; Offley report, June 30, 1915; Cantrell report, June 30, 1915, roll 858; Chief to Barnes, June 30, 1915, roll 856; Cantrell report, July 7, 1915, roll 859, RG 65, BI, NARA.
477 Case 8000-174, Franz von Rintelen, Charles Warren to Horn, July 10, 1915, RG 65, BI, NARA.
478 Cantrell report, June 30, 1915, roll 858, RG 65, BI, NARA.
479 Breckinridge Long had just joined the Wilson re-election campaign as a foreign policy expert. The future Assistant Secretary of State (1917-1920) and Ambassador to Italy (1933-1936) is credited with creating Wilson's winning 1916 campaign slogan "He kept us out of war."
480 W. M. O. [Offley] to Horn, June 23, 1915, roll 858, RG 65, BI, NARA.
481 Ibid.
482 Ibid.
483 Cantrell report, October 26, 1915; Klawans report, January 10, 1916, BI, roll 858.
484 Case 8000-174, Franz von Rintelen, Offley report, September 29, 1915, RG 65, BI, NARA.
485 Ibid.
486 Link, The Papers of Woodrow Wilson, vol. 33, Wilson to Anne Leddell Seward, July 5, 1915, 473.
487 Case 8000-174, Franz von Rintelen, William Offley to Chief Bielaski, September 29, 1915, RG 65, BI, NARA.
488 Ibid., Offley report, June 29, 1915, RG 65, BI, NARA. Chief Flynn reports to Offley that Sommerfeld and Rintelen conferred frequently.
489 Ibid., Offley to Bielaski, June 28, 1915, RG 65, BI, NARA.
490 Von Feilitzsch, Felix A. Sommerfeld and the Mexican Front in the Great War, 90.
491 Cantrell report, September 30, 1915, BI, roll 864.
492 Katz, Life and Times, 503.
493 Tuchman, Zimmermann Telegram, 76.
494 Case 8000-80773, John R. Rathom, Rathom to Gregory, February 8, 1918, 3, RG 65, BI, NARA.
495 Franz Rintelen von Kleist, The Dark Invader (1933), and The Return of the Dark Invader (1938); Supporting British claims for massive German finances are for example John Price Jones and Paul Merrick Hollister, The German Secret Service in America, 1914-1918 (1918); Henry Landau, The Enemy Within: The Inside Story of German Sabotage in America (1937); Barbara Tuchman, The Zimmermann Telegram (1958); Friedrich Katz, Deutschland, Diaz und die Mexikanische Revolution (1964); Katz, Secret War in Mexico; Michael C. Meyer, "The Mexican-German Conspiracy of 1915," The Americas, 23 (July 1966), 76-89; George Jay Rausch, Jr., "Victoriano Huerta: A Political Biography," (Ph.D. dissertation, University of Illinois, 1960) 237; George J. Rausch, Jr., "The Exile and Death of Victoriano Huerta," Hispanic American Historical Review, 42, no. 2 (May 1962) 151; However, historians Reinhard Doerries, Imperial Challenge: Ambassador Count Bernstorff and German-American Relations, 1908-1917 (1989), and Alan Knight, The Mexican Revolution, 2 vols (1990) did not buy into these reports.
496 For more details of the German organization and financials in the United States during 1914 and 1915 see von Feilitzsch, Secret War Council; von Feilitzsch, Secret War on the United States in 1915; and von Feilitzsch, Felix A. Sommerfeld and the Mexican Front in the Great War.
497 Barnes report, August 14, 1915, roll 859, RG 65, BI, NARA.
498 Cantrell report, July 3, 1915, roll 859, RG 65, BI, NARA.
499 As quoted in Katz, Secret War in Mexico, 248.

500 Case 8000-2752, Rudolph Otto, Stone report, May 29, 1917, RG 65, BI, NARA.

501 1 Peso was set at $0.50 exchange; $2,500,000 in 1915 is equivalent in purchasing power to about $72,350,495.05 today, an increase of $69,850,495.05 over 107 years. The dollar had an average inflation rate of 3.20% per year between 1915 and today, producing a cumulative price increase of 2,794.02%; https://www.in2013dollars.com/us/inflation/1915 (viewed July 2022).

502 *Diccionario Porrúa*, 640; Meyer, *Huerta*, 39; Berliner report, January 17, 1916, roll 859, RG 65, BI, NARA; Barnes informed Bielaski that in the Huerta file he found a memorandum that some plates were made by American Bank Note Company and paid for by Abe Ratner. The case file was rather voluminous and would require considerable time to ascertain whether this lead had been followed up. Barnes suggested that the matter be referred to the New York office; Barnes to Bielaski August 21, 1916, roll 858, RG 65, BI, NARA.

503 Beckham reports, June 1, 4, 1915, roll 859, RG 65, BI, NARA.

504 Beckham report, June 4, 1915; see also his report for June 19, 1915, roll 859, RG 65, BI, NARA.

505 Bielaski to Barnes, June 26, 1915; see also his telegram to Barnes on June 28, 1915, roll 858, RG 65, BI, NARA.

506 Cantrell report, June 28, 1915; Jentzer report, June 28, 1915, roll 858, RG 65, BI, NARA.

507 Guy report, June 28, 1915; Barnes report, June 28, 1915, roll 858, RG 65, NARA.

508 Beckham report, June 29, 1915, roll 858, RG 65, BI, NARA.

509 John F. Chalkley, *Zach Lamar Cobb: El Paso Collector of Customs and Intelligence During the Mexican Revolution* (El Paso: Texas Western Press, 1998), 31.

510 Beckham reports, July 1, 1915, roll 859; and July 2, 1915, roll 858, RG 65, BI, NARA.

511 Beckham report, February 16, 1916, roll 858, RG 65, BI, NARA.

512 Harris and Sadler, *Secret War*, 200.

513 Offley report, July 17, 1915, roll 859, RG 65, BI, NARA.

514 Molina report, July 19, 1915, roll 859, RG 65, BI, NARA.

515 Pinckney report, June 28, 1915; Bielaski to Barnes, June 29, 1915, roll 858, RG 65, BI, NARA.

516 Ibid.

517 Guy report, December 29, 1915, roll 859, RG 65, BI, NARA.

518 US v. Victoriano Huerta, Pascual Orozco, Enrique Gorostieta, Sr., Ricardo Gómez Róbelo, José Elgisero [sic — Elguero], Eduardo Cauz, José Alessio Robles, Alberto Quiroz, José Delgado, Rafael Pimienta, José B. Ratner, Ignacio L. Bravo, Mauro Huerta, no. 316, US Commissioner, San Antonio, Tex. FRC-FW. See also nos. 1446, 1449, 1468, and 1536, US Commissioner, El Paso, Tex., FRC-FW.

519 Melrose report, July 10, 1915; Pinckney report, July 12, 1915, roll 859; Stone report, August 2, 1915, roll 858, RG 65, BI, NARA.

520 Details are in Baker report, January 8, 1916, roll 858, RG 65, BI, NARA.

521 Stone report, July 9, 1915; Cantrell report, July 10, 1915, roll 859; Chief to Barnes, August 26, 1915, roll 857, RG 65, BI, NARA.

522 Barnes report, July 16, 1915; Berliner report, January 17, 1916, roll 859, RG 65, BI, NARA.

523 Pinckney report, July 10, 1915, roll 858, RG 65, BI, NARA.

524 Cantrell report, July 7, 1915; Offley report, July 10, 1915, roll 859; Beckham reports, July 5, 1915, roll 858; and July 18, 1915, roll 859; Guy report, July 7, 1915; Offley to Bielaski, July 7, 1915; Horn to Offley, July 8 [?], 1915; Offley to Horn, July 25, 1915; Barnes to Beckham, August 9, 1915; Barkey reports, September 30, November 19, 1915; Munson to Attorney General, August 27, 1915; Munson

reports, September 25, October 2, 9, 14, 16, 18, 25, 1915, roll 858; Ferneler report, July 10, 1915, roll 857, RG 65, BI, NARA.
525 Stone report, July 14, 1915, roll 858, RG 65, BI, NARA.
526 Ibid.
527 Beckham report, July 22, 1915, roll 859, RG 65, BI, NARA.
528 Huerta to German Ambassador, July 26, 1915, roll 859, RG 65, BI, NARA.
529 Huerta to Chief Justice, July 26, 1915, roll 859, RG 65, BI, NARA.
530 Ratner to Huerta, August 6, 1915, roll 859, RG 65, BI, NARA.
531 Beckham report, July 27, 1915, roll 858, RG 65, BI, NARA.
532 Stone report, July 27, 1915, roll 858, RG 65, BI, NARA.
533 Beckham report, July 9, 1915, roll 859; Acting Chief to Barnes, July 23, 1915, roll 858, RG 65, BI, NARA.
534 Beckham report, July 29, 1915, roll 858, RG 65, BI, NARA.
535 Beckham reports, September 2, 4, 1915, roll 858, RG 65, BI, NARA.
536 Guy report, December 15, 1915, roll 856, RG 65, BI, NARA.
537 Harris and Sadler, *Secret War*, 240.
538 Cantrell reports, August 27, November 16, 1915; Breniman report, November 5, 1915; Cantrell report, November 16, 1915, roll 858, RG 65, BI, NARA.
539 Beckham report, December 31, 1915, roll 859, RG 65, BI, NARA.
540 Barnes to Horn, August 3, 1915; Hay to AGWAR, August 3, 1915; Barnes report, August 5, 1915, roll 859; Stone reports, August 6, 9, 1915; Beckham report, August 19, 1915, roll 858, RG 65, BI, NARA.
541 Beckham report, August 27, 1915, roll 858, RG 65, BI, NARA; Harris and Sadler, *Secret War*, 206-207.
542 Beckham report, August 25, 1915, roll 858, RG 65, BI, NARA.
543 Stone report, August 28, 1915, roll 858, RG 65, BI, NARA.
544 See, for example, Pinckney report, November 17, 1915; Guy report, November 18, 1915; Stone reports, November 24, December 8, 1915, January 10, 1916, roll 858, November 25, 26, 1915, roll 857, and December 20, 1915, roll 859, RG 65, BI, NARA.
545 Beckham reports, December 16, 29, 1915, roll 859, RG 65, BI, NARA.
546 Guy reports, November 6, 7, 9, 15, 1915; Breniman report, November 6, 1915; Breniman to Bielaski, November 7, 1915; Pinckney reports, November 8, 10, 11, 14, 17, 19, 1915; Breniman to Guy, November 11, 1915; Blanford report, November 15, 1915, roll 858; Stone report, December 23, 1915, roll 859, RG 65, BI, NARA.
547 Stone report, April 13, 1916, roll 862, RG 65, BI, NARA.
548 Breniman report, December 16, 1915, roll 859, RG 65, BI, NARA.
549 Barnes to Bielaski, December 23, 1915, roll 859, RG 65, BI, NARA.
550 Beckham reports, December 24, 27, 1915; and, Stone to Barnes, December 24, 1915; Stone report, December 25, 1915, roll 859, RG 65, BI, NARA.
551 The indictments included Alberto Quiroz, Roque Gómez, Francisco Escandón, Albino Frías, Vicente Calero, Luis Fuentes, Aristarco Carrascosa, Rafael Pimienta, Enrique Gorostieta, Jr., Jesús Valverde alias Jesús Velarde, José C. Zozaya, José B. Ratner, José C. Delgado, Jesús Guadarrama, Pascual Orozco, and Crisóforo Caballero. No. 2185, US District Court, San Antonio, FRC-FW.
552 Pinckney report, January 1, 1916; Barnes reports, January 14, 17, 1916, roll 858, RG 65, BI, NARA.

553 Meyer, Huerta, 227-228.

554 Barnes report, January 31, 1916, roll 858; Breniman to Flynn, March 22, 1916; Berliner report, February 26, 1916, roll 860; Breniman report, March 24, 1916, roll 857, RG 65, BI, NARA.

555 Breniman report, November 13, 1915, roll 858, RG 65, BI, NARA.

556 Cornelius C. Smith, Jr., Emilio Kosterlitzky: Eagle of Sonora and the Southwest Border (Glendale: Arthur H. Clark, 1970).

557 Emil Kosterlitzky Baptism Certificate from 1853, Evangelische Kirche Oberursel, FHL Microfilm 1272417; and, Kosterlitzky personnel file, courtesy of John Fox, FBI historian.

558 Blanford reports, November 13, December 2, 1915, roll 858, RG 65, BI, NARA.

559 Webster report June 15, 1916; Barnes to Cantrell, February 25, 1916; Cantrell report, June 2, 1916; Chief to Barkey, September 28, 1916, roll 858, RG 65, BI, NARA.

560 White report, January 13, 1919, roll 870, RG 65, BI, NARA.

561 Franz Rintelen von Kleist, *The Dark Invader: Wartime Reminiscences of a German Naval Intelligence Officer, with an introduction by Reinhard R. Doerries* (London: Frank Cass Publishers, 1997), XXII.

562 Memorandum, re.: Stallforth and Company, File 9140-878-129, RG 165, Military Intelligence Division, NARA.

563 United States, Senate Hearings, 74th Congress, 2nd Session, Munitions Industry Hearings," January 7, 8, 1936 (Washington, DC: Government Printing Office, 1937), 7665-6.

564 *Sun*, April 28, 1915.

565 Hall was Vice-President of the American Independence Union, an organization urging the American public to fight for unrestricted trade and eliminate foreign propaganda in the US.

566 Case 8000-174, Franz von Rintelen, Benham report, October 1, 1915, RG 65, BI, NARA.

567 A "bear raid" means that an investor buys large positions in undervalued stock, then promotes it, and finds other investors to take the bait. As a result of the increased sales the stock value increases. The original investor now dumps his holdings at a peak value, causing the stock price to tumble and leaving the other investors with worthless holdings.

568 *New York Tribune*, July 3, 1913, *New York Sun*, July 6, 1913; *New York Evening World*, July 8, 1913.

569 For more detailed information about David Lamar, see von Feilitzsch, "The Real Wolf of Wall Street," *FCH Annals*, vol. 23, 2016.

570 Case 8000-174, Franz von Rintelen, Statement of George Plochman, October 27, 1915, RG 65, BI, NARA.

571 Ibid.

572 Rintelen received the accolade "Tiger of Berlin" in an unnamed memorandum, likely written by Chief Bielaski in 1918.

573 *New York Tribune*, June 12, 1915.

574 *New York Tribune*, June 18, 1915.

575 *New York Tribune*, June 12, 1915.

576 *New York Tribune*, July 16, 1915.

577 *New York Evening World*, July 21, 1915.

578 *New York Tribune*, July 21, 1915.

579 *New York Tribune*, July 19, 1915.

580 Ibid.

581 *New York Evening World*, July 21, 1915.

582 Case 8000-3089, Frederico Stallforth, undated [April 1917] report on interview of A. Bruce Bielaski and William Offley with Frederico Stallforth, RG 65, BI, NARA.
583 Case 8000-925, Walter T. Scheele, Money and Boland report, July 22, 1915, RG 65, BI, NARA.
584 Ibid., July 16, 1915, RG 65, BI, NARA.
585 Ibid., July 17, 1915, RG 65, BI, NARA.
586 Ibid.
587 Ibid., July 19-20, 1915, RG 65, BI, NARA.
588 Ibid., July 18, 1915, RG 65, BI, NARA.
589 Ibid., July 19-20, 1915, RG 65, BI, NARA.
590 Ibid., July 21-25, 1915, RG 65, BI, NARA.
591 Case 8000-174, Franz von Rintelen, In re: Franz Rintelen, undated (1918), RG 65, BI, NARA.
592 Case 8000-925, Walter T. Scheele, Money and Boland report, July 21-25, 1915, RG 65, BI, NARA.
593 Case 8000-174, Franz von Rintelen, Benham report, April 26, 1916, RG 65, BI, NARA.
594 *New York Tribune*, August 1, 1915.
595 Ibid.
596 Sworn Statement of Hatty E. Brophy, US District Court, May 25, 1916, RG 60, Department of Justice, NARA.
597 Case 8000-174, Franz von Rintelen, Cantrell report, September 24, 1915, RG 65, BI, NARA.
598 Ibid.
599 Ibid., September 27, 1915, RG 65, BI, NARA.
600 File 341.112 M49/40, Gasché to Mondragon, August 9, 1915, RG 59, Department of State, NARA.
601 Ibid., Gasché to Charles Douglas, August 8, 1915, RG 59, Department of State, NARA.
602 File 341.112 M49/12, Meloy to Walter Hines Page, August 14, 1915, RG 59, Department of State, NARA.
603 Ibid., Walter Hines Page to Robert Lansing, September 1, 1915, RG 59, Department of State, NARA.
604 WO 32/15542, Larking to Officer commanding Horse Guards, August 18, 1915, British National Archives, Kew.
605 Ibid., Larking to Commandant Prisoners of War, August 24, 1915, British National Archives, Kew.
606 Ibid., September 4, 1915, British National Archives, Kew.
607 Ibid., Major Larking to Admiral Hall, August 30, 1915, British National Archives, Kew.
608 There are multiple reports in the Rintelen case file about the true amount of money Rintelen left in Stallforth's control. Stallforth claimed, that he only received $40,000, while Rintelen claimed that he left him $80,000, which, given Stallforth's history of "sticky hands," is probably the actual amount, also quoted in the investigations of the Mixed Claims Commission after 1922.
609 Case 8000-174, Franz von Rintelen, Offley to Bielaski, August 24, 1915, RG 65, BI, NARA.
610 Ibid., Flynn to McAdoo, August 26, 1915, RG 65, BI, NARA.
611 Ibid., Cantrell report, August 20, 1915, RG 65, BI, NARA.
612 Ibid., Offley report, September 29, 1915, RG 65, BI, NARA.
613 Ibid., Cantrell reports, August 24, 26, September 14, 27, 1915, RG 65, BI, NARA.
614 Ibid., Cantrell report, September 29, 1915, RG 65, BI, NARA.
615 Ibid., Klawans report, September 29, 1915, RG 65, BI, NARA.

616 Ibid., Adams report, September 28, 1915, RG 65, BI, NARA.
617 Ibid., Cantrell report, September 30, 1915, RG 65, BI, NARA.
618 Ibid., Klawans report; Benham report; Tucker report, September 29, 1915, RG 65, BI, NARA.
619 Ibid., United States Circuit Court of Appeals, David Lamar and Henry E. Martin vs. United States of America, April 27, 1917, RG 65, BI, NARA.
620 Case 8000-924, various, indictment of Franz Rintelen and Andrew Meloy for conspiracy to defraud the United States, October 18, 1915, RG 65, BI, NARA.
621 Case 8000-174, Franz von Rintelen, Munson report, January 1, 1916; Benham report, December 10, 1915; Kerr report, December 16, 1915, RG 65, BI, NARA.
622 Ibid., Offley report, January 3, 1916, RG 65, BI, NARA.
623 Ibid., Benham report, October 1, 1915, RG 65, BI, NARA.
624 Interview between Mr. Polk and Mr. Stallforth in Washington, DC, March 15-16, 1916, Stallforth papers, 1916, private collection, courtesy Mary Prevo.
625 William Wherry to Stallforth, June 14, 1916, Stallforth papers, 1916, private collection, courtesy Mary Prevo.
626 See for example New York Tribune, July 16, 1916; Evening Public Ledger, July 10, 1916. Fore a detailed account of the U-Deutschland history, see Dwight R. Messimer, *The Baltimore Sabotage Cell: German Agents, American Traitors, and the U-boat Deutschland During World War I* (Annapolis: Naval Institute Press, 2015).
627 For a detailed study of Dilger's mission, see Robert Koenig, *The Fourth Horseman: One Man's Mission to Wage the Great War in America* (New York: Perseus Books, 2006).
628 The U-Deutschland departed for Germany on August 9, carrying mostly metals. Heinrich Albert, who wanted to return to German abord the submarine was denied passage. The ship returned to the US in October for the second and last time. She was refitted as U-155 to serve in the German navy for the remainder of the war. U-Deutschland had a sistership, the U-Bremen which disappeared on her first voyage to the United States in 1916.
629 For more detailed accounts of the Black Tom explosion, see Jules Whitcover, *Sabotage at Black Tom: Imperial Germany's Secret War in America, 1914-1917* (Chapel Hill: Algonquin Books, 1989), Howard Blum, *Dark Invasion: 1915: Germany's Secret War and the Hunt for the First Terrorist Cell in America* (New York: Harper Collins, 2014); Chad Millman, *The Detonators: The Secret Plot to Destroy America and an Epic Hunt for Justice* (Boston: Little, Brown and Company, 2006).
630 Interview between Mr. Polk and Mr. Stallforth in Washington, DC, March 15-16, 1916, Stallforth papers, 1916, private collection, courtesy Mary Prevo.
631 Case 8000-3089, Frederico Stallforth, undated [April 1917] report on interview of A. Bruce Bielaski and William Offley with Frederico Stallforth, RG 65, BI, NARA.
632 Ibid.
633 Ibid.
634 Ibid., Statement, April 22, 1917, RG 65 BI, NARA.
635 Ibid., Offley to Bielaski, April 24, 1917, RG 65, BI, NARA.
636 New York Index of Deaths, Manhattan, New York, USA, certificate number 3296.
637 Ibid., Sarfaty to Gregory, April 23, 1917, RG 65, BI, NARA.
638 H. H. Martin to John McCloy, December 28, 1935, Box 7, RG 76, Mixed Claims Commission, NARA.
639 Hilken's wife turned the critical 1916 diary over to investigators in December 1931 after she discovered her daughter playing with it.

ENDNOTES

640 Entries for March 23, 1916; July 10, 1916, July 20, 1916, Hilken Diaries, 1914-1917, Box 7, RG 76 Mixed Claims Commission, NARA.

641 Hilken Diaries, 1914-1917, Box 7, RG 76, Mixed Claims Commission, NARA.

642 Entry May 23, 1915, Stallforth Guest Book, private collection, courtesy Mary Prevo.

643 Entry August 3, 1916, Hilken Diaries, 1914-1917, Box 7, RG 76, Mixed Claims Commission, NARA.

644 Entry June 2, 1916, Hilken Diaries, 1914-1917, Box 7, RG 76, Mixed Claims Commission, NARA.

645 Case 8000-174, Franz von Rintelen, Tucker report, December 29, 1915, RG 65, BI, NARA.

646 Ibid., J. J. Timney report, December 4, 1915, RG 65, BI, NARA.

647 Ibid., Offley report, April 15, 1916, RG 65, BI, NARA.

648 Ibid., Tucker report, December 29, 1915, RG 65, BI, NARA.

649 Ibid., undated memo (July 1915); Benham report, July 18, 1915, RG 65, BI, NARA.

650 Ibid., Kelleher report, December 20, 1915, RG 65, BI, NARA.

651 Ibid., Williamson report, April 16, 1916, RG 65, BI, NARA.

652 Ibid., United States Circuit Court of Appeals For the Second Circuit, undated (January 1919).

653 *New York Times*, December 13, 1915.

654 H. S. Hunter to Secretary of Prisoners of War Department, March 11, 1918, FO383-433, British National Archives, Kew, UK.

655 Case 8000-174, Franz von Rintelen, Momorandum re.: Franz Rintelen, undated [1918], RG 65, BI, NARA.

656 Ibid.

657 Ibid.

658 1937 memorandum, Rintelen sentences, KV2/3846, British National Archives, Kew, UK.

659 Conviction of Rintelen, Bureau of Prisons memorandum, March 5, 1918, FO 383-433, also 1937 memorandum, Rintelen sentences, KV2/3846, British National Archives, Kew, UK.

660 Case 8000-174, Franz von Rintelen, Momorandum re.: Franz Rintelen, undated [1918], RG 65, BI, NARA.

661 He sued the German government for his retirement funds in 1926. In the late 1920s, Rintelen also authored two embellished autobiographies, which greatly exaggerated his mission and accomplishments while in the US. Not finding a German publisher willing to take on his work and fearing repercussions from Franz von Papen who rose to become German chancellor in 1932, Rintelen moved to Great Britain. His success as an author and speaker finally gave Rintelen a sense of being noticed and appreciated. However, when World War II started, the British government interned him as an enemy alien for the duration of the war. He died an embittered man in 1949.

662 A version of this chapter appeared in *Studies in Intelligence* in spring 2024: Heribert von Feilitzsch and Charles H. Harris III, "An Early Influence Operation: The Albert Briefcase Affair: A 100-Year Cover-up of a British Propaganda Coup," *Studies in Intelligence*, vol. 68, No. 1 (March 2024).

663 *New York World*, August 15 to August 18, 1915.

664 See for example, Philip H. Melanson, Peter F. Stevens, *The Secret Service: The Hidden History of an Enigmatic Agency* (New York: Carroll and Graf Publishers, 2002), 38.

665 Link, *Papers of Woodrow Wilson*, Vol. 33, House to Wilson, August 10, 1915.

666 Albert Papers, Box 23, König to Albert, undated memorandum, RG 65, BI, NARA. It is reasonable to assume that König found out within a week of July 24, that the World had the papers, because the lawyer hired by Albert had a meeting with President Wilson on August 3, 1915.

667 Albert Papers, Box 23, Memorandum Paul König to Albert, undated (August 1915), RG 65, NARA.

668 For example, New York Evening Telegram, July 27, 1915.

669 Subcommittee of the Judiciary Committee of the US Senate, Testimony of Samuel Untermeyer, Brewing and Liquor Interests and German and Bolshevik Propaganda, vol. 2 (Washington, DC: Government Printing Office, 1919), 1835ff.

670 Ibid., 1866, 1936-1937. Untermeyer saw Wilson on August 3. According to Paul König, the World did not have possession of the papers until August 2. Therefore, the first Untermeyer meeting must have occurred on that date.

671 Link, Papers of Woodrow Wilson, vol. 33, WW to Edith Bolling Galt, August 3, 1915.

672 Ibid. Wilson considered Untermeyer's request (to prevent the publication of Albert's papers in The New York World) "not a matter of general interest at all, but one in which he [McAdoo] thought we might do Mr. Untermeyer a good turn." Link wrote in note #5 that McAdoo informed Wilson that a secret service agent had taken Albert's briefcase. It seems that Link failed to see the connection of Untermeyer as a German emissary to get help on the briefcase issue. The secret service matter, Wilson mentioned in the letter to Galt, was likely the directive to McAdoo to use the secret service to get a hold of the briefcase. Link made an assumption in this case, using the commonly accepted turn of events after 1918, rather than actual notes or evidence.

673 Ibid. US Senate, Testimony of Samuel Untermeyer, 1867. Untermeyer allows for the "possibility" that he had known about Albert's briefcase before the publication and "could" have been hired to prevent its publication. Although there is no available record that proves Flynn's involvement at this juncture, it seems perfectly reasonable for McAdoo to have asked Flynn to get the papers. Another possibility would be that Flynn received the papers from the World without asking after the McAdoo-Wilson meeting.

674 While Lansing is not mentioned specifically by House, the Secretary of State later told the German 2nd Counselor Prinz Hatzfeld, that he had advance notice of the existence of the briefcase.

675 Daily Report of Agent, August 5, 1915, New York: Volumes 46-48 - February 1, 1915-November 30, 1915, RG 87, US Secret Service, NARA.

676 New York Tribune, November 8, 1918.

677 Ibid.

678 Case 8000-24, J. A. Baker report, July 31, 1915, RG 65, BI, NARA.

679 Link, The Papers of Woodrow Wilson, vol. 33, House to Wilson, August 10, 1915.

680 Ibid., Aug 13, 1915; Albert Papers, Box 23, Letter to Wife Ida, August 14, 1915, RG 65, NARA; Memorandum Paul König to Albert, undated (August 1915), RG 65, NARA.

681 Albert Papers, Box 23, Memorandum Paul König to Albert, undated (August 1915), RG 65, NARA.

682 Albert Papers, Box 5, Memorandum from Carl Heynen, Bridgeport Projectile Company, June 30, 1915, RG 65, NARA.

683 Ibid., Box 23, Letter to Wife Ida, January 17, 1916, RG 65, NARA.

684 Ibid, Box 24, Count Bernstorff to Robert Lansing, June 22, 1915, RG 65, NARA; Albert Personnel File, Foreign Office to Bernstorff, October 13, 1915, GFM 33-4186, British National Archives, Kew, UK.

685 Albert Personnel File, von Jagow to Count Bernstorff, October 13, 1915, GFM 33-4186, British National Archives, Kew, UK.

686 Albert Papers, Albert to Secretary Trautmann, December 5, 1915, RG 65, NARA.

687 Albert Personnel File, Chancellor von Bethmann-Hollweg to Hamburg District Court, July 24, 1917, GFM 33-4186, British National Archives, Kew, UK.

688 New York Sun, February 16, 1919.

689 William F. Flynn, Courtney Riley Cooper, *The Eagle's Eye: A True Story of the Imperial German Government's Spies and Intrigues in America from Facts Furnished by William J. Flynn, Recently Retired Chief of the U.S. Secret Service* (New York: Prospect Press, 1919), 133-147.

690 Ibid., 133-147.

691 Ibid; New York Tribune, January 5, 1918.

692 New York Tribune, November 8, 1918.

693 William Gibbs McAdoo, *Crowded Years: The Reminiscences of William G. McAdoo* (Boston and New York: Houghton Mifflin Company, 1931), 327.

694 Ibid., 327-328.

695 Personnel File of Frank Burke, newspaper clippings, NARA, St. Louis.

696 Washington Evening Star, June 3, 1942.

697 James D. Robenault, *The Harding Affair: Love and Espionage during the Great War* (New York: St. Martin's Press, 2009), 150; Chad R. Fulwider, *German Propaganda and U.S. Neutrality in World War I* (Columbia: University of Missouri Press, 2017), 223; Richard A. Hawkins, *Progressive Politics in the Democratic Party: Samuel Untermyer and the Jewish Anti-Nazi Boycott Campaign* (New York, I.B. Tauris, 2022), 89; Edward Mickolus, *The Counterintelligence Chronology: Spying By and Against* (Jefferson: McFarland and Company, 2015), 24; Kathleen Hill, Gerald N. Hill, *Encyclopedia of Federal Agencies and Commissions* (New York: Facts on File, 2014), 196; Marcia Roberts, *Moments in History: Department of Treasury United States Secret Service* (Washington, DC: PU Books, 1990), 12; Barbara Tuchman, *The Zimmerman Telegram* (New York: Ballentine, 1958), 74; Link, *Papers of Woodrow Wilson*, volume 33; Link, *Wilson: The Struggle for Neutrality, 1914-1915* (Princeton: Princeton University Press, 1960), 554-555.

698 Jeffreys-Jones, American Espionage, 62.

699 Jeffreys-Jones, American Espionage, 70.

700 Ibid., 58.

701 Ibid., 48.

702 Ibid., 55.

703 Ibid., 60, 117.

704 Ibid., 61.

705 Ibid., 62.

706 Ibid., 65.

707 Ibid., 53.

708 Bielaski memorandum, June 8, 1916, roll 861, RG 65, BI, NARA.

709 U.S. Senate, *Brewing and Liquor Interests and German and Bolshevik Propaganda*, Senate doc. no. 62, 66th Congress 1st session, 3 vols. (Washington, DC: Government Printing Office, 1920), 2:1388.

710 Jeffreys-Jones, *The FBI: A History* (New Haven: Yale University Press, 2007), 66-68.

711 Ibid., 68. Ever since the publication of Flynn's books and McAdoo's autobiography, historians including Jeffreys-Jones have bought into the alleged rivalry between the US Secret Service and the Bureau of Investigation. The implication of this interagency strife is a presentist view to explain intelligence failures such as the attacks on Pearl Harbor and 911, namely that the US government fell down on its responsibilities for counterintelligence and prosecution of foreign agents attacking the homeland. Archival sources show that there was no such rivalry during World War I. The briefcase affair shows that there was no involvement of the Bureau in snatching the satchel, an illegal

act. However, sources do show that the Bureau had an intelligence and counterintelligence mission, leading to successful investigations of passport frauds, German attacks on Canada, the Hindu plot to name just a few. By November 1915, and with authorization from the Justice Department, the Bureau not the US Secret Service had also tapped Albert, Boy-Ed, and von Papen's phones. And, Phone Records of Albert, Boy-Ed, von Papen, Entry 199, Box 165, RG 131, Alien Property Custodian, NARA.

712   https://www.secretservice.gov/history-espionage, viewed March 21, 2022.

713   See for example, Melanson, Stevens, The Secret Service, 36.

714   Oliver, The Birth of the FBI, 166.

715   Flynn fashioned himself as the German spy hunter of the World War between 1916 and 1917, when Attorney General Gregory forced his firing. See, for example New York Evening World, October 28, 1915; November 1, 1915; October 24, 1917.

716   A few are Jeffrey D. Simon, The Bulldog Detective: William J. Flynn and America's First War against the Mafia, Spies, and Terrorists (Essex: Prometheus Books, 2024); Frank J. Rafalko, ed., A Counterintelligence Reader, Volume I: American Revolution to World War II (Washington, DC: Military Bookshop, 2011); Robenault, The Harding Affair, 150; Chad R. Fulwider, German Propaganda and U.S. Neutrality in World War I (Columbia: University of Missouri Press, 2017), 223; Jamie Bisher, The Intelligence War in Latin America, 1914-1922 (Jefferson: McFarland and Company, 2016), 366; Hawkins, Progressive Politics in the Democratic Party, 89; Mickolus, The Counterintelligence Chronology, 24; Kathleen Hill and Gerald N. Hill, Encyclopedia of Federal Agencies and Commissions, 196; Roberts, Moments in History, 12; Tuchman, The Zimmerman Telegram, 74; Walter S. Bowen and Harry Edward Neal, The United States Secret Service: The Exciting Story of the World's Foremost Crime-Fighting Agencies (Philadelphia: Chilton Company, 1960), 83, 84-92.

717   Federation of American Scientists, Intelligence Resource Program, A Counterintelligence Reader, Vol. 1, Chapter 3, 2005, https://irp.fas.org/ops/ci/docs/ci1/chap3.pdf, 27.

718   https://www.secretservice.gov/about/history/timeline, viewed March 21, 2022.

719   https://www.secretservice.gov/history-espionage, viewed March 21, 2022.

720   Link, The Papers of Woodrow Wilson, vol. 33; AP Dispatches, May 1915, Library of Congress; Library of Congress Digital Collections: Robert Lansing Papers, April to August 1915; US Department of State, Documents Relating to the Foreign Relations of the United States, volume 2 (Washington, DC: Government Printing Office, 1919); Robert Lansing Papers: Private Memoranda, 1915-1922; Originals: 1915-1917, Library of Congress Manuscript Division, mss29454, box 63, reel 1; William Gibbs McAdoo: A Register of His Papers in the Library of Congress, Library of Congress Manuscript Division, 1959); Charles Seymour, The Intimate Papers of Colonel House. 2 vols. (New York: Houghton Mifflin, 1926), 2:339; Edward Mandell House Papers, Correspondence and Letters, 1915, Yale University Archives, MS 466.

721   For example: the disappearance of Bernardo Reyes in 1911, Victoriano Huerta and Pascual Orozco in 1915.

722   Jeffreys-Jones, The FBI, 62.

723   John F. Fox, Jr., "Bureaucratic Wrangling over Counterintelligence, 1917-18," Studies in Intelligence Vol. 49 No. 1 (2005), 15, n.2.

724   The agents were: John J. Henry, Agent in Charge; Agents Burke, Savage, Kavanaugh, Schlamm (who resigned on July 25 and was replaced by James Carvey), Merillat, McCahill, Rubano, Howell, Manasse (Boston, MA), Connolly (Buffalo, NY), and Rich (Cornish, NH, presidential detail); New York: Volumes 46-48 - February 1, 1915-November 30, 1915, Daily Reports of Agents, RG 87, NARA.

725 New York: Volumes 46-48 - February 1, 1915-November 30, 1915, Daily Reports of Agents, RG 87, US Secret Service, NARA.

726 Daily Report, July 20, 1915, RG 87, US Secret Service, NARA.

727 Daily Reports, July 20, 21, 22, 23, 24, 1915, RG 87, US Secret Service, NARA.

728 Daily Report, July 24, 1915, RG 87, US Secret Service, NARA.

729 Ibid.

730 Ibid.

731 McAdoo, *Crowded Years*, 325.

732 For example, Daily Report, July 22, RG 87, US Secret Service, NARA; "At 7 a m sent the following telegrams: W.J. Flynn, Washington D.C. Leave at 7 a m for Marion. Address care postmaster. (signed) Burke."

733 Daily Report, August 5, 1915, RG 87, US Secret Service, NARA.

734 Daily Reports, August 17, 18, 1915, RG 87, US Secret Service, NARA.

735 Daily Report, September 5, 1915, RG 87, US Secret Service, NARA.

736 *Sunday Telegram*, October 24, 1915, RG 87, US Secret Service, NARA.

737 Gaunt, *The Yield of the Years*, 67. Voska's organization comprised the small Slavic countries of Europe, hence the tease.

738 Masaryk, *The Making of a State*, 259; Emanuel Victor Voska and Will Irwin, *Spy and Counterspy* (London: George Harrap and Co. LTD., 1941), 38.

739 On March 20, 1916, British agents torched the house of a Dr. K. O. Bertling who worked for the German embassy in Washington. During the chaos of the fire, sensitive papers were stolen and, low and behold, were published again in the *New York World*. There clearly is a pattern established by British agents using the *New York World* for scandalous exposés. See Bernstorff to Brockdorff-Rantzau, March 20, 1916, ADM 1-10983, British National Archives, Kew.

740 Franz von Papen, *Memoirs* (New York: E.P. Dutton and Company, 1953), 50.

741 Voska, *Spy and Counterspy*, 34.

742 Ibid., 33.

743 Case 8000-80773, John R. Rathom, Bielaski to Charles DeWoody, March 19, 1918, RG 65, BI, NARA.

744 Ibid., undated memorandum, RG 65, BI, NARA. "At the beginning of the War... Rathom met in Washington, D.C. a member of the British Government, at which time it was alleged a fund was set aside by the British Government, guaranteeing the "Providence Journal" against loss through publishing articles exposing German propaganda [...]." Gaunt, *The Yield of the Years*, 138.

745 *New York World*, August 17, 1915.

746 Case 8000-80773, John R. Rathom, RG 65, BI, NARA; There are dozens of letters with leads to Bielaski from Rathom between October 1915, and May 1916.

747 Ibid., Signed and witnessed statement of John R. Rathom, February 6, 1918, RG 65, BI, NARA.

748 Voska, *Spy and Counterspy*, 42, 92-95.

749 Ibid., 96.

750 Ibid., 97.

751 Ibid., 98-99.

752 Gaunt, *The Yield of the Years*, 147.

753 For example, *Seattle Star*, March 14, 1917; *Tacoma Times*, March 19, 1917.

754 Ralph E. Weber, ed., *The Final Memoranda: Major General Ralph H. Van Deman, USA Ret. 1865-1952, Father of U.S. Military Intelligence* (Wilmington: Scholarly Resources Inc., 1988), 54.

755 *New York World*, August 17, 1915.

756 Link, *The Papers of Woodrow Wilson*, vol. 35, President Wilson to Robert Lansing, December 5, 1915.

757 For more information on the battle of Naco, see von Feilitzsch, "Prelude to the Columbus Raid of 1916: The Battle of Naco," *Journal of the Southwest*, 64, No 3 (Autumn 2022), 473-494.

758 Webster reports, February 24, 25, March 1, 1915, roll 858, RG 65, BI, NARA.

759 Llorente to Villa, February 10, 1915, Enrique Llorente Papers, New York Public Library.

760 Orme report, January 15, 1915, BI, roll 855.

761 Barnes reports, March 2, May 31, 1915; Barnes to McDevitt, March 5, 6, 15, 1915; McDevitt reports, March 5-7, 1915; Guy reports, March 10, 12, 1915, BI, roll 858.

762 McDevitt report, January 27, 1915, roll 858, RG 65, BI, NARA.

763 Barnes to Bielaski, February 22, 1915, roll 855, RG 65, BI, NARA.

764 Barnes reports, February 4, 1915, roll 858; and April 19, 1915, roll 855; Barnes to Bielaski, February 22, 1915, roll 855; Breniman report, April 18, 1915, roll 857; Barnes to Green, April 21, 1915, roll 859; Guy report, April 23, 1915, roll 857, RG 65, BI, NARA.

765 Barnes reports, November 20, 27, 1914, January 12, 1915, roll 856; January 20, 1915, roll 857; Breniman report, April 8, 1915, roll 857, RG 65, BI, NARA.

766 Barnes to Taylor, January 6, 1915, roll 855; Barnes reports, January 18, 20, 1915, roll 857; January 12, 1915, roll 856; January 5, 1915, roll 858; Breniman report, December 8, 1914; Barnes to Johnson, January 9, 1915; Guy report, May 2, 1915, roll 857, RG 65, BI, NARA.

767 Breniman reports, December 5, 8, 1914, roll 857; and, Barnes report, December 30, 1914, roll 856, RG 65, BI, NARA.

768 Barkey reports, November 12, 14, 1915, roll 858; Breniman to Guy, November 14, 1915; Breniman to Pinckney, November 19, 1915; Barnes report, November 9, 1915; Breniman report, November 22, 1915, roll 857, RG 65, BI, NARA.

769 Judge Burns has a history of biased adjudication, see von Feilitzsch and Harris, *The History of the federal Bureau of Investigation before Hoover*, volume 1.

770 Barnes to Bielaski, December 14, 1914, roll 857, RG 65, BI, NARA.

771 Breniman report, December 22, 1914, roll 857, RG 65, BI, NARA.

772 Breniman reports, December 15, 1914; December 7, 1915, roll 857; November 7, 1915; Boden report, August 6, 1915, roll 858; Webster reports, November 9, 10, 1915; Rathbun report, November 10, 1915; Breniman to Green, November 17, 1915; Stone report, November 25, 1915; Barnes report, December 3, 1915, roll 857; Blanford report, July 22, 1915, roll 859, RG 65, BI, NARA.

773 Blanford to Gershon, October 28, 1916; Gershon reports, November 4, 28, December 4, 1916; Barnes to Blanford December 2, 1916; Blanford reports, October 20, December 4, 1916, roll 857; Barnes to Green, December 4, 1916, roll 856, RG 65, BI, NARA.

774 Blanford report, June 30, 1915, roll 856, RG 65, BI, NARA.

775 See, for example the May 15 issue of this bulletin, 812.00/15074, RG 59, Department of State, NARA.

776 Guy reports, February 20, 1915, roll 857; October 6, 1915, roll 858; Harris to Hirsch, April 6-8, 1915, roll 858; Pendleton reports, November 27, 1915, roll 859; December 8, 1915, roll 858; Breniman to Pinckney, November 10, 1915, RG 65, BI, NARA.

ENDNOTES

777 Michael M. Smith, "Mexican Secret Service in the United States, 1910-1920," *The Americas*, 59, no. 1 (July 2002), 76.
778 Harris and Sadler, *Secret War in El Paso*, 166, 187.
779 Guy report, January 23, 1915; Barnes to Guy, January 25, 1915; Barnes report, January 25, 1915, roll 856, RG 65, BI, NARA.
780 Beckham report, June 19, 1915, roll 859, RG 65, BI, NARA.
781 Pinckney report, November 4, 1915, roll 856, RG 65, BI, NARA.
782 *San Antonio City Directories* 1916-1919.
783 *El Paso Herald*, August 24, 1917.
784 *Monett Times*, January 14, 1921
785 Probate Court, Oklahoma, Probate Packets 1025-1027, 1921.
786 See for example, Beckham report, May 29, 1915, roll 859, RG 65, BI, NARA.
787 Spencer report, April 10, 1916, roll 862; Pendleton report, July 15, 1915, roll 860, RG 65, BI, NARA. Pendleton mistakenly reported 30-30 as the caliber.
788 Spreadsheets, June 30, August 24, September 28, 1915, roll 862; see spreadsheet for Western Cartridge Company sales from April 1915 to September 28, 1915, for Villa: Quantity, caliber, consignee, destination; Spreadsheet, April 13- September 28, 1915, roll 862, RG 65, BI, NARA.
789 Barnes report, July 6, 1915, roll 858, RG 65, BI, NARA.
790 Stone report, November 5, 1915, roll 855, RG 65, BI, NARA.
791 Von Feilitzsch, Felix A. *Sommerfeld and the Mexican Front in the Great War*, 166.
792 Bielaski to Clabaugh, April 5, 1916, roll 862, RG 65, BI, NARA.
793 Peters Cartridge Co. to De La Garza June 17, 1915, De La Garza Papers, Box 5, Folder E, Latin American Collection, University of Texas at Austin.
794 Von Feilitzsch, Felix A. *Sommerfeld and The Mexican Front in the Great War*, 53.
795 Harris to Hirsch, April 3, 24, 25, 1915, roll 859; April 10, 12, July 30, August 7, 10, 16, 21, 1915; Hirsch to Harris, August 7, 1915; Harris to Camou, May 26, August 18, 1915, roll 858; Webster reports, February 25, March 1, 1915; Barnes report, July 29, 1915; Camou to Falomir, July 26, 30, 1915; Camou to Harris, August 18, 1915, roll 859, RG 65, BI, NARA.
796 Katz, *Life and Times*, 451-452.
797 See Korngold to Bielaski, November 16, 1915; Chief to Pendleton, November 27, 1915; Chief to Korngold, November 27, 1915, roll 859, RG 65, BI, NARA.
798 Camargo to Bustamante, August 21, 1915; and, Velazquez statement, June 30, 1915; Cristerna receipt, August 25, 1915; Cristerna expense account, September 2, 1915; Centurion to Bustamante, December 6, 1915, roll 861, RG 65, BI, NARA; *Diccionario Porrúa de historia, biografía y geografía de México* (México, DF: Editorial Porrúa, 1976), 326; and, Velazquez statement, June 30, 1915, roll 861, RG 65, BI, NARA, regarding villista efforts in the Isthmus of Tehuantepec.
799 Pendleton report, January 18, 1916, roll 859, RG 65, BI, NARA.
800 Ibid., July 6, 1915, roll 858, RG 65, BI, NARA.
801 Ibid.
802 Pendleton reports, July 9, 1915, roll 859; July 13, 15, November 9, 1915; Berliner report, December 22, 1915, roll 860; Barkey report, September 22, 1915, roll 858, RG 65, BI, NARA.
803 Pendleton reports, December 16, 1915, April 14, 1916, roll 859, RG 65, BI, NARA.
804 Pendleton report, August 20, 1915, roll 859, RG 65, BI, NARA.

805 Berliner report, April 13, 1915, roll 861; Arredondo to Lansing, July 14, 1915; Weeks to Collector of Customs, August 21, 1915; Pendleton report, August 21, 1915; Davis to Bielaski, August 26, 1915; Hawkins report, August 27, 1915, roll 859; Beckham report, August 23, 1915, roll 858; Webb report, July 14, 1915, roll 857, RG 65, BI, NARA.

806 Assistant Secretary of the Treasury to Attorney General, July 26, 27, 1915; Malbun to Secretary of the Treasury, July 27, 1915; Hawkins reports, August 24, 27, 28, 31, September 1, 2, 1915; Davis to Chief, August 26, 30, 31, 1915; Davis report, August 28, 1915; Weeks to Hawkins, August 29 [?], 1915; Pendleton report, August 28, 1915; Beall to Hawkins, August 30, 1915, roll 859, RG 65, BI, NARA.

807 Pendleton reports, September 8, 11, 13, 1915; Davis to Chief, September 14, 1915, roll 859, RG 65, BI, NARA.

808 For Jones's background, see www.Ancestry.com, US Census 1900 and 1940; New Orleans City Directories 1912 and 1916.

809 A search of New Orleans business directories between 1916 and 1919 showed no such company in the city.

810 Case 8000-168908, Charles S. Jones, Maximo Rosales to "Secretary of State of the Justice Department," February 8, 1918; Bielaski to Pendleton, April 6, 1918, RG 65, BI, NARA.

811 Charles and Eugene Jones, *Double Trouble: The Autobiography of the Jones Twins* (Boston: Little, Brown and Company, 1952), 30-31.

812 See, for example, Pendleton reports, June 10, 27, September 11, 1916, February 22, 1917, roll 863, RG 65, BI, NARA.

813 Pendleton reports, December 7, 1916, BI, roll 865, December 23, 1916, January 22, 1917, roll 863; Chief to Pendleton, November 26, 1916, roll 864, RG 65, BI, NARA.

814 US Senate, *Investigation of Mexican Affairs*, 2 vols. Senate doc. no. 285, 66th Congress, 2nd session (Washington, DC: Government Printing Office, 1920), 2889-3117, hereafter cited as IMA.

815 IMA, 2890-2892.

816 IMA, 2894; and, Pendleton reports, July 15, 1915, roll 860; October 26, 1915, roll 855; Lloyd report, September 8, 1916, roll 865, RG 65, BI, NARA.

817 Clarence Winfield Jones was born on January 29, 1874, in Missouri, was a sergeant in the Spanish-American War, and was a correspondent for the *San Francisco Chronicle*, the *San Antonio Express*, the *National Tribune*, the *Philadelphia Bulletin*, and the *Atlanta Journal*. Stone report, December 3, 1915, roll 855; Pendleton report, November 4, 1915, roll 859, RG 65, BI, NARA.

818 Jones to Bielaski, December 15, 1916, roll 860, RG 65, BI, NARA.

819 Pendleton report, January 18, 1916, roll 859, RG 65, BI, NARA.

820 Guy report, November 18, 1915, roll 859, RG 65, BI, NARA.

821 Pendleton to Bielaski, October 12, 1915, roll 860; November 22, 1915, roll 859; Pendleton report, February 10, 1916, roll 859, RG 65, BI, NARA.

822 Pendleton reports, October 21, 1915, roll 855; October 13, 26, 1915, roll 858; October 27, 1915, roll 859, RG 65, BI, NARA.

823 Pendleton to Bielaski, October 12, 1915, roll 860; Chief to Canova, October 13, 1915, roll 855; Garza to Díaz Lombardo, October 20, 1915; Díaz Lombardo to Garza, October 24, 1915; Guy report, November 18, 1915, roll 859, RG 65, BI, NARA.

824 Some reports say the 20th, others the 25th.

825 Bryan to Secretary of State, November 16, 1915; Davis to Bielaski, September 18, October 15, November 18, 29, 1915; Peters to Collector of Customs, October 19, 1915; Griggs to Secretary of the Treasury, November 18, 1915; Nevan [?] to Secretary of State, November 18, 1915; Chastain reports,

ENDNOTES

November 19, December 18, 1915; Story memorandum, November 20, 1915; Davis report, April 26, 1916; Assistant Chief to Harrison, May 6, 1916, roll 859, RG 65, BI, NARA.

826 Baley reports, October 22, 23, 1915, roll 859, October 28, 1915, roll 858; Bielaski to Davis, November 18, 1915; Chastain reports, November 19, 20, 25, December 18, 19, 1915; Pendleton reports, October 26, 1915, roll 858, November 22, 23, 27, December 18, 28, 1915 roll 859; Bielaski to Chastain, November 23, December 19, 1915; Bielaski to Offley, November 23, 1915, April 6, 1916; Offley report, November 27, 1915; Story to Horn, November 20, 1915; Davis to Bielaski, December 4, 1915; Offley to Bielaski, December 4, 1915; Bielaski to McLeod, December 20, 1915; McLeod reports, December 20, 22, 1915; Bielaski to Webb, December 11, 1915; Webb reports, December 22, 23, 1915, roll 859, RG 65, BI, NARA; in 1917, Díaz and Lutz were still up to no good: Harrison to Bielaski, May 9, 1917, roll 859, RG 65, BI, NARA.

827 Baley reports, October 23, 1915, roll 858; October 26, 28, 1915, roll 858; Pendleton reports, October 27, 30, November 8, 1915, roll 859; November 3, 1915, roll 860; Chastain report, November 1, 1915, roll 859, RG 65, BI, NARA.

828 Pendleton to Bielaski, November 8, 1915; Guy reports, November 13, 14, 1915, roll 859, RG 65, BI, NARA.

829 Pendleton reports, November 20, 27, 1915, roll 859, RG 65, BI, NARA.

830 Pendleton to Bielaski, November 22, 1915, roll 859; Pendleton report, November 23, 1915, roll 858, RG 65, BI, NARA.

831 Chastain report, November 1, 1915; and, McGee report, November 1, 1915; Daniel report, November 1, 1915, roll 859, RG 65, BI, NARA.

832 Pendleton to Bielaski, November 22, 1915; Chastain reports, November 27, 28, 1915, roll 859, RG 65, BI, NARA.

833 Pendleton report, November 29, 1915, roll 859, RG 65, BI, NARA.

834 Stone report, November 30, 1915; Guy report, December 4, 1915, roll 858; Pinckney report, December 3, 1915, roll 859, RG 65, BI, NARA.

835 Pendleton report, November 29, 1915, roll 859, RG 65, BI, NARA.

836 Bielaski to Chastain, November 29, 1915; Storey to Horn, November 29, 1915; Pendleton report, December 4, 1915, roll 859, RG 65, BI, NARA.

837 Pendleton reports, November 30, December 1-4, 1915; Pendleton to Davis, November 30, 1915; Chief to Davis, December 1, 6, 1915; Chief to Pendleton, December 1, 4, 1915; Pinckney report, December 3, 1915; Pendleton to Bielaski, December 3, 1915; Stone report, December 4, 1915; George to Bielaski, December 6, 7, 1915; Chief to George, December 10, 1915; Davis report, December 30, 1915; Hawkins report, December 31, 1915, roll 859, RG 65, BI, NARA.

838 Pendleton reports, December 7, 18, 1915 and March 3, 1916; Chastain to Bielaski, December 16, 1915; [Chief] to Baley, December 28, 1915, January 8, 1916; Assistant Attorney General to Lowe, December 28, 1915, roll 859, RG 65, BI, NARA.

839 Acting Chief to Baley, May 24, 1916, roll 859, RG 65, BI, NARA.

840 Bielaski to Pendleton, December 21, 1915, roll 859, RG 65, BI, NARA.

841 Pendleton to Bielaski, December 28, 1915; Chief to Pendleton, December 4, 1915; Pendleton reports, December 6, 1915; February 7; April 25, 1916, roll 859, RG 65, BI, NARA.

842 Pendleton reports, February 19, 24, 26, 29, 1916, roll 859, RG 65, BI, NARA.

843 Pendleton report, March 2, 1916, roll 859, RG 65, BI, NARA.

844 Pendleton report, March 3, 1916, roll 859, RG 65, BI, NARA.

845 Stone report, March 7, 1916, roll 859; March 9, 1916, roll 861, RG 65, BI, NARA.

846 Pendleton report, October 30, 1915, roll 859, RG 65, BI, NARA.

847 Cantrell report, January 31, 1916, roll 859, RG 65, BI, NARA.

848 Bielaski to Cantrell, April 19, 28, 1916; Pendleton report, April 19, 1916; Chief to Pendleton, April 19, 1916; Cantrell report, April 27, 1916, roll 859, RG 65, BI, NARA.

849 Cantrell reports, April 28-30, May 1, 3, 4, 5, 12, June 2, 1916, roll 859, RG 65, BI, NARA.

850 Pendleton report, May 11, 16, 1916, roll 859, RG 65, BI, NARA.

851 Cantrell report, June 2, 1916, roll 859, RG 65, BI, NARA.

852 Cantrell report, June 15, 1916; Pendleton report, June 15, 1916, roll 859, RG 65, BI, NARA.

853 Allen report, July 29, 1915, roll 856, RG 65, BI, NARA.

854 Barnes report, July 29, 1915, roll 859, RG 65, BI, NARA.

855 Kain report, July 31, 1915, roll 856; and, Kain reports, August 6, 1915, roll 863; August 27, 1915, roll 855, RG 65, BI, NARA.

856 Pinckney reports, August 25, 27, 1915, roll 859; Agent Pinckney was covering *villista* activity both in Nogales and in Douglas. Pinckney report, November 2, 1915, roll 856, RG 65, BI, NARA.

857 Spreadsheets, September 21, 1915, roll 862, RG 65, BI, NARA.

858 File 10541-272-17, RG 165, Military Intelligence Division, NARA. After the World War, James Manoil would be well known as a business partner in the Manoil Manufacturing Company for making collectible diecast figures and toy soldiers. He died on September 1, 1955.

859 Kennedy to Van Deman, May 20, 1918, file 10541-272-31, RG 165, Military Intelligence Division, NARA.

860 File 10541-272-17, May 7, 1918, RG 165, Military Intelligence Division, NARA.

861 See von Feilitzsch, Felix A. *Sommerfeld and the Mexican Front in the Great War*, 115-117.

862 Webster report, September 17, 1915, roll 855, RG 65, BI, NARA.

863 Obregón's account is in Álvaro Obregón, *Ocho mil kilómetros en campaña* (México, DF: Fondo de Cultura Económica, 1959), 371-377; Another account differs. See Offley to Bielaski, PERSONAL AND CONFIDENTIAL, March 4, 1917, roll 856, RG 65, BI, NARA.

864 Sommerfeld to Olin, May 17, 1915, Box 7, Folder C, Lázaro De La Garza Papers, Benson Latin American Collection, University of Texas at Austin.

865 *El Paso Morning Times*, September 24, 1916; Sommerfeld's shipments from the Western Cartridge Company in Alton, Illinois to the border tell the story: In April, 2.2 million 7-millimeter rounds left the factory ($78,400 at $35 per thousand), in May slightly more, 2.5 million rounds ($88,515 at $35 per thousand). Sommerfeld shipped 3.3 million rounds ($115,465 at $35 per thousand) in June.

866 Katz, *Life and Times*, 488-498; Charles C. Cumberland, Mexican Revolution: *Constitutionalist Years* (Austin: University of Texas Press, 1972), 198-201.

867 Statement of Felix A. Sommerfeld, June 21, 1918, file 9-16-12-5305, RG 60, Department of Justice, NARA.

868 Sommerfeld to Olin, May 17, 1915, Box 7, Folder C; División del Norte en cuenta con L. de la Garza, January 10 to October 11, 1915, Box 9, Folder A; Cuenta de cartuchos, 1915, Box 2, Folder B, Lazaro de la Garza Papers, Benson Latin American Collection, University of Texas at Austin. The accounts contain two entries, $52,000 transferred to De La Garza on September 24, 1915, and $17,431.47 transferred on October 27, both from Carl Heynen aka James Manoil.

869 Harris and Sadler, *Secret War in El Paso*, 241.

870 S. C. De La Garza to Lázaro De La Garza, October 4, 1915, Box 2, Folder G, Lazaro de la Garza Papers, Benson Lain American Collection, University of Texas at Austin.

ENDNOTES

871 Webster report, February 21, 1916, roll 856, RG 65, BI, NARA.
872 Breniman to Pinckney, November 19, 1915, rolls 855, 856, and 859, RG 65, BI, NARA.
873 See von Feilitzsch, Felix A. *Sommerfeld and the Mexican Front in the Great War*, 161-163; Katz, *Life and Times*, 487.
874 Harris and Sadler, *Secret War in El Paso*, 241-245; Pinckney report, November 4, 1915, roll 856; Stone reports, December 21, 1915, roll 856; December 26, 1915, roll 857, RG 65, BI, NARA.
875 Garbarino report, June 9, 1915, roll 854, RG 65, BI, NARA.
876 Barnes reports, January 21, 29, 1915; Barnes to Flynn, January 21, 1915; Pinckney reports, February 18, 19, 24, 1915, roll 858, RG 65, BI, NARA.
877 Barnes report, July 29, 1915, roll 859, RG 65, BI, NARA.
878 Pinckney reports, August 24, 27, 28, 1915, roll 859, RG 65, BI, NARA.
879 Webster reports, February 24, 25, March 1, 1915, roll 858, RG 65, BI, NARA.
880 Barnes to Kain, September 3, 1915; Flynn to Barnes, September 3, 1915; Barnes report, September 12, 1915, roll 858, RG 65, BI, NARA.
881 Barnes to Pinckney, April 14, 1915; and, Barnes to Breniman, March 29, 1915, roll 855, RG 65, BI, NARA.
882 Guy reports, January 22, 26, February 6, 1915, roll 855; March 28, September 15, 1915, roll 858, RG 65, BI, NARA.
883 Guy reports, March 28, 30, 1915, roll 858, RG 65, BI, NARA.
884 Beckham report, May 15, 1915; and, Beckham reports May 16, 1915, roll 859; September 20, 1915, roll 857, RG 65, BI, NARA.
885 Pinckney reports, April 1, 2, 5, 16, 1915; Guy reports, April 1, 14, 1915; Breniman report, April 1, 1915; Breniman to Guilfoyle, April 3, 1915; Barnes reports, April 13, 19, 1915; Blanford report, April 16, 1915, roll 858; Beckham report, September 20, 1915; Barnes report, September 21, 1915, roll 857, RG 65, BI, NARA.
886 Barnes report, September 4, 1915, roll 858, RG 65, BI, NARA.
887 Webster reports, August 11, 13, 26, September 7, 8, 1915, roll 858; August 16, September 10, 1915, roll 856; September 14, 15, 18, 24, 1915, roll 855; September 21, 1915, roll 859; Peters to Secretary of State, August 16, 1915; Bielaski to Barnes, September 24, 1915, roll 859; Allen reports, August 19, 23, 1915, roll 856; September 4, 1915, roll 858; Webster to Davis, September 15, 1915, roll 855; Blanford reports, September 28, October 1, 1915, roll 855; November 1, 1915, roll 858; and, Offley to Bielaski, November 2, 3, 1915, roll 856, RG 65, BI, NARA.
888 Allen reports, May 19, 21, 22, 24, 1915; Webster report, May 21, 1915; Rathbun report, May 26, 1915, roll 856; Acting Chief to Grgurevich July 9, 1915, roll 859, RG 65, BI, NARA.
889 Allen report, July 13, 1915, roll 856, RG 65, BI, NARA.
890 Grgurevich report, July 3, 1915, roll 859, RG 65, BI, NARA.
891 Horn to Pendleton, July 17, 1915, roll 854; and, Pendleton reports, July 19, 20, 1915, roll 859, RG 65, BI, NARA.
892 Webster report, August 31, 1915; McGee report, August 13, 1915, roll 855; Cantrell report, September 14, 1915, roll 857, RG 65, BI, NARA.
893 Phillips report, February 27, 1915, roll 857; McGee report, August 13, 1915, roll 855, RG 65, BI, NARA.
894 Cantrell report, July 22, 1915, roll 856; Offley report, August 7, 1915, roll 857, RG 65, BI, NARA.
895 Adams report, August 18, 1915; Offley report, August 18, 1915, roll 855, RG 65, BI, NARA.

896 See, for example, Adams reports, July 3, 1915, roll 857; September 4, 1915, roll 858; Webster report, August 5, 1915; Bone report, September 3, 1915, roll 858, RG 65, BI, NARA.

897 Barnes report, July 3, 1915, roll 858.; Barnes to Robertson, July 3, 1915, roll 859, RG 65, BI, NARA.

898 Barkey report, July 11, 1915, roll 858, RG 65, BI, NARA.

899 Ibid.

900 See, for example, Jones to Betts Iron Co., October 14, 1915; Samson report, November 27, 1915, roll 859, RG 65, BI, NARA.

901 Pendleton report, July 16, 1915, roll 860, RG 65, BI, NARA.

902 Breniman reports, July 21, 1915, roll 859; July 31, 1915, roll 854; Pendleton report, July 20, 1915, roll 860; Barnes to Horn, July 24, 1915, roll 858; Cantrell reports, July 23, 1915, roll 856; August 4, 1915, roll 857; Barnes reports, July 30, 1915, roll 857; August 11, 1915, roll 858; Brennan report, July 31, 1915, roll 854; Horn to Offley, August 2, 1915; Webster report, August 13, 1915, roll 855; Timony report, September 12, 1915, roll 859, RG 65, BI, NARA.

903 Guy reports, July 30, 31, 1915, roll 857, RG 65, BI, NARA.

904 Pendleton report, May 31, 1915; roll 855; and, Pendleton report June 3, 1915, roll 859, RG 65, BI, NARA.

905 Pendleton report, June 3, 1915; and, Pendleton report June 5, 1915, roll 859, RG 65, BI, NARA.

906 Pendleton to Horn, July 21, 1915, roll 854; and, Pendleton report, July 16, 1915, roll 860, RG 65, BI, NARA.

907 Pendleton report, October 12, 1915, roll 859, RG 65, BI, NARA.

908 Kropidlowski reports, July 31, August 9, 1915; Acting Chief to Offley, August 3, 1915, roll 859, RG 65, BI, NARA.

909 No. 2152, District Court, Brownsville, FRC-FW.

910 This account of the Plan is based on Charles H. Harris III and Louis R. Sadler, *The Plan de San Diego: Tejano Rebellion, Mexican Intrigue* (Lincoln: University of Nebraska Press, 2013).

911 McDevitt report, January 26, 1915; Breniman report, January 30, 1915, roll 858, RG 65, BI, NARA.

912 See, for example, Meyer, *Huerta*, 215, 217n22, 218.

913 Memorandum, December 17, 1915, roll 856, RG 65, BI, NARA.

914 Breniman report, December 12, 1915; Rogers report, December 12, 1915, roll 856, RG 65, BI, NARA.

915 *New York Times*, June 4, 1915.

916 Katz, *Life and Times*, 529; Robert Lansing, *War Memoirs of Robert Lansing, Secretary of State* (New York: Bobbs-Merrill, 1935), 308.

917 Von Feilitzsch, Felix A. *Sommerfeld and the Mexican Front in the Great War*, 128.

918 Link, *Wilson: The Struggle for Neutrality*, 478.

919 Von Feilitzsch, Felix A. *Sommerfeld and the Mexican Front in the Great War*, 135.

920 Hugh L. Scott, *Some Memories of a Soldier* (New York: Century Company, 1928), 414-415.

921 Von Feilitzsch, Felix A. *Sommerfeld and the Mexican Front in the Great War*, 135.

922 *New York Times*, August 30, 1915.

923 Link, *Wilson: The Struggle for Neutrality*, 630.

924 Lansing Private Memoranda, 1915-1917, Memorandum, 7/11/1915, Library of Congress.

925 Wilson to Lansing, August 7, 1915, and Lansing to Wilson, August 9, 1915, 812.00/1575 1//2, RG 59, Department of State, NARA.

926 Von Feilitzsch, Felix A. Sommerfeld and the Mexican Front in the Great War, 146.

927 Rogers report, November 30, 1915, roll 859, RG 65, BI, NARA.

928 Breniman report, October 24, 1915, roll 858, RG 65, BI, NARA.

929 Blanford to Webster, October 20, 1915, roll 855, RG 65, BI, NARA.

930 Blanford report, October 11, 1915, roll 855, RG 65, BI, NARA.

931 See, for example, Guy report, December 9, 1915, roll 856, RG 65, BI, NARA.

932 Katz, Life and Times, 505.

933 Ibid., 508.

934 Von Feilitzsch, Felix A. Sommerfeld and the Mexican Front in the Great War, 156.

935 Katz, Life and Times, 528; In a speech in November 1915, Villa charged that Carranza had agreed to eight concessions: "1. Amnesty for all political prisoners; 2. U.S. rights over Magdalena Bay, Tehuantepec, and an oil zone for 99 years; 3. Mexico's Interior, Foreign Affairs, and Finance ministries would be filled with candidates supported by Washington; 4. All paper money issued by the revolution would be consolidated; 5. All just claims by foreigners for damages caused by the revolution would be paid and all confiscated property returned; 6. The Mexican National Railways would be controlled by the governing board in New York until the debts to this board were repaid; 7. The United States through Wall Street bankers, would grant a $500 million loan; 8. Pablo Gonzalez would be named provisional president and would call for elections within six months."

936 Ibid., 529.

937 Von Feilitzsch, Felix A. Sommerfeld and the Mexican Front in the Great War, 155-157; Louis G. Kahle, "Robert Lansing and the Recognition of Venustiano Carranza," Hispanic American Historical Review, 38, no. 3 (August 1958), 353-372.

938 See, for example, Rathbun reports, October 27, November 1, 1915, roll 858; Blanford report, October 31, 1915; Blanford to Head, November 22, 1915, roll 855, RG 65, BI, NARA.

939 Cantrell report, November 26, 1915, roll 862; Blanford report, December 29, 1915, roll 855, RG 65, BI, NARA.

940 Pendleton reports, October 23, 26, 1915; Blanford reports, November 9, 1915, roll 858; November 23, 1915, roll 855; National Arms Co. to Baum Iron Co., October 28, 1915; Pendleton to Bielaski, October 29, 1915, roll 859; Bielaski to Munson, November 3, 1915; Barkey report, November 14, 1915; Pendleton report, November 18, 1915, roll 855, RG 65, BI, NARA.

941 Pendleton report, December 7, 1915, roll 860, RG 65, BI, NARA.

942 Stone report, December 21, 1915, roll 856, RG 65, BI, NARA.

943 Stone reports, March 18, 25, 1916, roll 857; War Department General Staff, March 11, 1916, report no. 13137, "Report of investigation of raid on Columbus, New Mexico, by Pancho Francisco Villa and fellow-bandits," Records of the War Department General and Special Staffs, RG 165, Military Intelligence Division, NARA.

944 Charles H. Harris III and Louis R. Sadler, "Pancho Villa and the Columbus Raid: The Missing Documents," New Mexico Historical Review, 50, no. 4 (October 1975), 335-346.

945 Berliner reports, May 12, 17, roll 862; Cobb to Secretary of State, March 6, 7, 1916, roll 857, RG 65, BI, NARA.

946 See, for example, Michael C. Meyer, "Villa, Sommerfeld, Columbus y los alemanes," Historia Mexicana, 28, No. 4 (1979), 76-89; Francis J. Munch, "Villa's Columbus Raid: Practical Politics or German Design?" New Mexico Historical Review, 44 (July 1969), 189-214.

947 Katz, Life and Times, 550-557; Col. Frank Tompkins, Chasing Villa: The Story behind the Story of Pershing's Expedition into Mexico (Harrisburg: The Military Service Publishing Company, 1934).

948 They were tried by the State of New Mexico and were convicted of first-degree murder; Stone report, April 30, 1916, roll 857; and, Breniman report, April 3, 1916, roll 859, RG 65, BI, NARA; James W. Hurst, *The Villista Prisoners of 1916-1917* (Las Cruces, NM: Yucca Tree Press, 2000).

949 Stone reports, March 18, 19, 1916, roll 857; April 16, 1916, roll 862; and, Wright report, April 21, 1916, roll 856, RG 65, BI, NARA; In April, Stone obtained a mass of villista telegrams and documents sent between May and August 1915. He obtained them from one Rios, who was formerly in charge of the consular department of the Villa government under Miguel Díaz Lombardo. The Chief had agent L. S. Perkins translate these documents as soon as possible and send him the results in four copies. At the New York field office Perkins spent months translating the material, producing 104 typed pages in English, "Translations of Documents of Villa Govt.," April 1, 1916, roll 856, RG 65, BI, NARA.

950 Offley report, March 16, 1916, roll 862, RG 65, BI, NARA.

951 Spencer reports, April 9-13, 1916, roll 862, RG 65, BI, NARA.

952 Offley reports, April 12, 1916, roll 856; May 5, 1916, roll 862; Blanford report, April 29, 1916, roll 856, RG 65, BI, NARA; von Feilitzsch, Felix A. *Sommerfeld and the Mexican Front in the Great War*, 184-185.

953 For Bulnes see *Diccionario Porrúa*, 231.

954 Chief to Offley, March 18, 1916, roll 862, RG 65, BI, NARA.

955 Underhill reports, May 6, 8, 1916, roll 862, RG 65, BI, NARA.

956 Underhill reports, May 16, 17, 1916, roll 862, RG 65, BI, NARA.

957 Underhill report, May 15, 1916; Offley to Bielski, May 16, 1916, roll 862, RG 65, BI, NARA.

958 Offley report, May 18, 1916; Gregory to Bielaski, May 20, 1916, roll 862, RG 65, BI, NARA.

959 Offley to Bielaski, May 25, 1916, roll 862, RG 65, BI, NARA.

960 Assistant Attorney General to Polk, May 22, 1916, roll 862, RG 65, BI, NARA.

961 Chief to Offley, May 22, 1916, roll 862, RG 65, BI, NARA.

962 Acting Chief to Offley, May 23, 1916, roll 862, RG 65, BI, NARA.

963 Underhill report, September 18, 1916, roll 862, RG 65, BI, NARA.

964 Records of War Department General and Special Staffs - Army War College - General Correspondence, 6474-374, RG 165, Military Intelligence Division, NARA.

965 See for example: Alberto Salinas Carranza, *La Expedición Punitiva* (México, DF: Ediciones Botas, 1936); Eileen Welsome, *The General and the Jaguar: Pershing's Hunt for Pancho Villa, a True Story of Revolution and Revenge* (Lincoln: University of Nebraska Press, 2006); John S. D. Eisenhower, *Intervention! The United States and the Mexican Revolution, 1913-1917* (New York: W. W. Norton and Company, 1993); Joseph A. Stout, Jr., *Border Conflict: Villistas, Carrancistas, and the Punitive Expedition, 1915-1920* (Ft. Worth: Texas Christian University Press, 1999); Edward P. Haley, *Revolution and Intervention: The Diplomacy of Taft and Wilson with Mexico, 1910-1917* (Cambridge: MIT University Press, 1970); Tompkins, *Chasing Villa*; Herbert Molloy Mason, Jr., *The Great Pursuit: Pershing's Expedition to Destroy Pancho Villa* (New York: Smithmark Publishers Inc, 1970).

966 Blanford report, April 6, 1916, roll 862, RG 65, BI, NARA.

967 Barnes to Bielaski PERSONAL AND CONFIDENTIAL, April 9, 1916; Stone report, April 19, 1916, roll 857; Tucker report, April 17, 1916; Underhill reports, April 24, May 5, 1916, roll 861, May 4, 1916, roll 863; May 6, 1916, roll 862; Bielski to Funston, May 23, 1916, roll 861; Garbarino report, June 9, 1916, roll 857; Breniman report, April 4, 1916, roll 856, RG 65, BI, NARA.

968 Bagley report, March 18, 1916; Bagley receipt, March 20, 1916, roll 861; Chief to Bagley, June 6, 1916, roll 859; March 8, 1917, roll 861, RG 65, BI, NARA.

969 Warren Memorandum, March 15, 1916, roll 855; Barnes report, March 14, 1916, roll 856, RG 65, BI, NARA.
970 Pinckney reports, May 24, June 2, 1916; Barnes report, June 5, 1916, roll 862, RG 65, BI, NARA; Katz, *Life and Times*, 212, 267-268.
971 Barnes to Bielaski, March 24, 1916, roll 856, RG 65, BI, NARA.
972 Pendleton report, March 27, 1916, roll 856, RG 65, BI, NARA.
973 Barnes report, March 23, 1916, roll 856, RG 65, BI, NARA.
974 Cantrell report, November 26, 1915, roll 862, RG 65, BI, NARA. Breceda to Carranza, July 12, 1915, file 4878; [Carranza] to Consolidated Rolling Mills, August 15, 1915, file 5394, Elias to Carranza, November 24, 1915, file 6789, Venustiano Carranza Archive, Centro de Estudios Históricos Carso (formerly Condumex), México, DF.
975 Lansing to Secretary of War, April 18, 1916, roll 862, RG 65, BI, NARA.
976 Offley to Bielaski, June 1, 1916; Chief to Offley, June 2, 1916; Offley report, June 3, 1916; Kemp report, June 5, 1916, roll 855, RG 65, BI, NARA.
977 Offley report, May 25, 1916; and, Scully reports, May 25, 26, 29, 1916, roll 862, RG 65, BI, NARA.
978 Rodgers to Secretary of State, June 1, 1916, roll 857, RG 65, BI, NARA.
979 Spencer report, April 13, 1916; Norcom to Bielaski, July 28, 1916, roll 862, RG 65, BI, NARA.
980 Breniman report, June 25, 1916; Bielaski to Breniman, June 26, 1916; Offley report, June 30, 1916; Underhill report, June 30, 1916; Kemp report, May 29, 1916; Blanford reports, May 26, 27, June 1, 1916; Offley report, May 27, 1916, roll 863, RG 65, BI, NARA.
981 JHS [Siebert] to Tauscher, May 15, 1916, roll 862, RG 65, BI, NARA.
982 Offley to Bielaski, June 1, 1916, roll 862; Chief to Offley, June 3, 1916, roll 861, RG 65, BI, NARA.
983 812.113/3644, 3645, 3646, 3647, RG 59, Records of the Department of State, NARA.
984 Ibid.
985 Beckham to Chief, May 12, 1915, roll 859, RG 65, BI, NARA.
986 Cantrell report, November 9, 1915, roll 857, RG 65, BI, NARA.
987 Berliner report, August 3, 1918, roll 877, RG 65, BI, NARA.
988 Being a German citizen "Sommerfeld was advised on account of nationality, being a German subject, that he would stand no chance of being able to win in a lawsuit." Berliner report, August 3, 1918, roll 877, RG 65, BI, NARA.
989 *Baltimore Evening Star*, June 18, 1915.
990 *Der Deutsche Korrespondent*, August 10, 1915.
991 Ibid., September 25, 1915.
992 Ibid., June 3, 1916, Maryland Circuit Court, Morris v Rasst, 1916, Maryland Appelate Court, Morris v Rasst, 1918; Maryland Supreme Court, Morris v. Rasst, 1922.
993 Chalmers report, April 1, 1916, roll 861, RG 65, BI, NARA.
994 Webb report, April 6, 1916, roll 861, RG 65, BI, NARA.
995 Chalmers report, April 7, 1916, roll 861, RG 65, BI, NARA.
996 Offley report, April 1, 1916, roll 861; Stone report, October 27, 1916, RG 65, BI, NARA; file 9700-44, RG 165, Military Intelligence Division, NARA.
997 Webb report, April 11, 1916, roll 861, RG 65, BI, NARA.
998 Harris report, April 11, 1916, roll 858; Webb report, April 12, 1916, roll 861, RG 65, BI, NARA.

The FBI and American Neutrality, 1914-1917

999 Bielaski to Garbarino, May 16, 1916, roll 861, RG 65, BI, NARA.

1000 Daniel report, June 15, 1916, roll 858, RG 65, BI, NARA.

1001 Pigniuolo report, May 5, 1916, roll 861; Daniel report, June 16, July 19, 1916, roll 858, RG 65, BI, NARA.

1002 Case 8000-90481, Doyas reports, December 18, 1918, May 31, 1919, RG 65, BI, NARA; and, case 363727, "Nestor Nikolene," RG 65, BI, NARA.

1003 Pinckney report, April 28, 1916; Swift to Intelligence Officer, May 1916; McComb to Chief Signal Officer, June 1, 1916; Lynch to Hetrick, June 1, 1916; Barnes to Lawrence, June 3, 1916; Lege report, June 13, 1916; Knabenshue to Department Intelligence Officer, June 16, 1916; Barnes to Bielaski, June 24, 1916, roll 857; Weiskopf report, June 25, 1916, roll 862, RG 65, BI, NARA.

1004 Charles H. Harris III and Louis R. Sadler, *Great Call-Up: The Guard, the Border, and the Mexican Revolution* (Norman: University of Oklahoma Press, 2015), 400-401; Charles H. Harris III and Louis R. Sadler, *The Archaeologist Was a Spy: Sylvanus G. Morley and the Office of Naval Intelligence* (Albuquerque: University of New Mexico Press, 2003), 391n69.

1005 Lynch to Hetrick, June 1, 1916, file 8530-14, RG 165, Military Intelligence Division, NARA; Hitt Memorandum, September 27, 1916, file 9434-16, RG 165, Military Intelligence Division, NARA.

1006 David Kahn, *The Codebreakers: The Story of Secret Writing* (New York: Macmillan and Co., 1967), 70ff.

1007 David Kahn, *The Reader of Gentlemen's Mail: Herbert O. Yardley and the Birth of American Codebreaking* (New Haven: Yale University Press, 2004), 30.

1008 Assistant Attorney General to Secretary of War, June 9, 1916, roll 859, RG 65, BI, NARA.

1009 Chief to Special Agents, May 16, 1916, roll 855, RG 65, BI, NARA.

1010 Bielaski memorandum, June 8, 1916, roll 861, RG 65, BI, NARA.

1011 Ibid.

1012 Ibid.

1013 Ibid.

1014 Ibid.

1015 See, also "List of a New [sic] Mexican Informants Working Under Barnes," July 12, 1916, roll 867, RG 65, BI, NARA.

1016 Ibid. See for example, a list of informants working under Agent Robert Barnes as of July 12, 1916.

1017 Guy report, January 24, 1915, roll 863, RG 65, BI, NARA.

1018 Breniman to Hopkins, May 13, 1916, roll 863, RG 65, BI, NARA.

1019 Hopkins report, May 28, 1916, roll 863, RG 65, BI, NARA.

1020 Hopkins report, June 1, 1916; and, Hopkins reports, June 18, 22, 1916, roll 863, RG 65, BI, NARA.

1021 Hopkins report, June 5, 1916, roll 863, RG 65, BI, NARA.

1022 Hopkins report, June 8, 1916, roll 863, RG 65, BI, NARA.

1023 Pacho report, June 13, 1916, roll 862, RG 65, BI, NARA.

1024 Ortiz to Breniman, June 18, 1916; Breniman reports, June 11, 1916, roll 861; June 13, 20, 21, 1916, roll 862; June 17, 18, 1916, roll 863; and June 24, 1916, roll 858; Ortiz report, June 19, 1916, roll 862; Hopkins report, June 8, 1916, roll 863, RG 65, BI, NARA.

1025 Neunhoffer reports, June 13, 16, 1916, roll 863, RG 65, BI, NARA.

1026 Bielaski memorandum, June 8, 1916, roll 861, RG 65, BI, NARA.

1027 Ibid.

ENDNOTES

1028 Ibid.

1029 Barnes report, March 19, 1916, roll 856, RG 65, BI, NARA.

1030 Stone report, March 19, 1916, roll 857, RG 65, BI, NARA; Katz, *Life and Times*, 258.

1031 Stone report, March 23, 1916, roll 862; Barnes to Bielaski, March 24, 1916, roll 856, RG 65, BI, NARA.

1032 Barnes to Bielaski, March 26, 1916, roll 856, RG 65, BI, NARA.

1033 Stone reports, April 6, 7, 1916, roll 857, RG 65, BI, NARA.

1034 Stone report, March 25, 1916; Barnes reports March 25, 1916, roll 856; March 21, 23, 26, 31, 1916, roll 859, RG 65, BI, NARA.

1035 Pinckney report, May 10, 1916, roll 862, RG 65, BI, NARA.

1036 Barnes report, May 10, 1916, roll 859, RG 65, BI, NARA.

1037 [Pinckney] to Barnes, May 13, 1916, roll 859, RG 65, BI, NARA.

1038 Pinckney to Barnes, May 13, 1916; Barnes to Pinckney, May 16, 1916, roll 859, RG 65, BI, NARA.

1039 Frank L. Garbarino was born Vineland, New Jersey, in 1878. He entered the Immigration Service as a stenographer on October 28, 1903. On December 19, 1906, he was promoted to Chinese inspector at Philadelphia. He resigned on March 9, 1910, to join the Bureau as a special employee. As of 1941, he worked as a private detective in Ventnor, New Jersey. Garbarino file, NPRC, NARA, St. Louis.

1040 Garbarino reports, May 25, 1916, roll 856; June 9, 1916, roll 857, RG 65, BI, NARA.

1041 Berliner report, May 17, 1916, roll 862, RG 65, BI, NARA.

1042 Harris and Sadler, *The Great Call-Up*, 358.

1043 Berliner reports, June 16, 1916, roll 857; June 17, 1916, roll 862; June 23, 1916, roll 863; Assistant Attorney General to Secretary of State, July 27, 1916; Stone to Barnes, July 31, 1916; Barnes to Stone, August 3, 1916, roll 862, RG 65, BI, NARA.

1044 Berliner report, May 26, 1916, roll 862, RG 65, BI, NARA.

1045 Chief to Harrison, October 19, 1916, roll 862, RG 65, BI, NARA.

1046 Stokes to Lansing, February 16, 1917, roll 860, RG 65, BI, NARA.

1047 *Washington Evening Star*, August 24, 1922

1048 *El Paso Herald*, March 15, 1919.

1049 *Washington Post*, January 11, 2016.

1050 Stone report, March 29, 1916, roll 857; Devlin report, April 1, 1916, roll 856, RG 65, BI, NARA.

1051 Chief to Barnes, April 12, 1916, roll 855; Stone report, May 19, 1916, roll 857, RG 65, BI, NARA.

1052 Stone reports, April 23, 24, 1916 roll 861; McGee reports, April 29, 30, May 29, 1916, roll 856, RG 65, BI, NARA.

1053 Berliner report, May 24, 1916, roll 862, RG 65, BI, NARA.

1054 Berliner reports, May 2, 1916, roll 863; May 6-9, 11, 13, 1916, roll 862, RG 65, BI, NARA.

1055 Berliner reports, May 12, 17, 1916, roll 862, RG 65, BI, NARA.

1056 Stone reports, June 21, 27, 1916, roll 862; June 23, 1916, roll 863, RG 65, BI, NARA.

1057 Barnes report, June 26, 1916, roll 862; June 27, 1916, roll 863; Fletcher report, June 27, 1916; Stone report, July 1, 1916, roll 863, RG 65, BI, NARA; Harris and Sadler, *Border and Revolution*, 10-11.

1058 Stone to Barnes, June 17, 1916, roll 863; Stone report, June 22, 1916, roll 857, RG 65, BI, NARA.

1059 Barnes report, June 21, 1916, roll 857, RG 65, BI, NARA.

1060 Stone report, June 22, 1916, roll 863, RG 65, BI, NARA.

1061 Stone to Barnes, June 17, 1916; Minck report, June 18, 1916; Stone reports, June 22, 1916, roll 863; June 23, 1916, roll 857; Barnes report, June 27, 1916, roll 863, RG 65, BI, NARA.

1062 Blanford reports, June 22, 23, 26, 28, 1916, roll 857, RG 65, BI, NARA.

1063 Barnes report, June 29, 1916; Stone report, June 30, 1916, roll 863, RG 65, BI, NARA.

1064 Stone report, June 27, 1916, file 5761-1144, RG 165, Military Intelligence Division, NARA; Harris and Sadler, The Border and the Revolution, 8-11.

1065 Stone report, August 9, 1916, roll 864, RG 65, BI, NARA.

1066 "Report of an attempted visit to General Villa by agents of the Department of Justice," file 9700-44, RG 165, Military Intelligence Division, NARA.

1067 Stone report, February 17, 1917, roll 857, RG 65, BI, NARA; Harris and Sadler, Border and Revolution, 11-22; Katz, Life and Times, 609-610, 827.

1068 Stone report, October 27, 1916, file 9700-44, RG 165, Military Intelligence Division, NARA.

1069 Needham report, May 3, 1917, roll 856, RG 65, BI, NARA.

1070 The following account is based on Smith, "The Mexican Secret Service," 69, 71-80; and Harris and Sadler, Secret War in El Paso, 268-271.

1071 Berta Ulloa, ed. Revolución Mexicana 1910-1920: Archivo Histórico Diplomático Mexicano. Guías para la historia diplomática de México. No. 3 (México, DF: Secretaria de Relaciones Exteriores, 1985), 356-357.

1072 "Lee" report, June 18, 1916, roll 863; Devlin report, June 20, 1916, roll 862, RG 65, BI, NARA.

1073 Smith, "The Mexican Secret Service," 72.

1074 Barnes to Bielaski, including the code, June 13, 1916, roll 857, RG 65, BI, NARA.

1075 Webb report, July 19, 1916, roll 862; Minck report, June 25, 1916; Stone to Barnes, June 24, 1916, roll 862; Hopkins report, June 27, 1916, roll 863; Barnes report, June 28, 1916; Minck report, June 28, 1916; Stone report, July 1, 1916; Barnes to Webb, July 5, 1916, roll 862, RG 65, BI, NARA.

1076 Neunhoffer report, June 26, 1916, roll 863, RG 65, BI, NARA.

1077 Smith, "The Mexican Secret Service," 75.

1078 Ibid., 76-79.

1079 [Lege] to Bielaski, March 17, 1916, roll 861, RG 65, BI, NARA.

1080 Barnes to Barnum, June 9, 1916, roll 863, RG 65, BI, NARA.

1081 Lawrence report, June 3, 1916, roll 863; Barnes to Lege, June 19, 1916, roll 862, RG 65, BI, NARA.

1082 [Wiseman] to Bielaski, March 17, 1916, roll 861, RG 65, BI, NARA.

1083 Barnes to Special Agents et al., June 9, 1916, roll 862; and, Barnes report, June 1, 1916, roll 863, RG 65, BI, NARA.

1084 Guy report, November 14, 1915, roll 858, RG 65, BI, NARA.

1085 Harris and Sadler, Plan de San Diego, 211; Theoharis et al., The FBI, 354. On July 1, 1922, Sorola would become the bureau's first Hispanic special agent.

1086 Barnes to Bielaski, June 7, 1916; Rodriguez report, June 13, 1916, roll 863, RG 65, BI, NARA.

1087 Bielaski memo, June 8, 1916, roll 861, RG 65, BI, NARA.

1088 Bielaski memorandum, June 6, 1916, roll 863, RG 65, BI, NARA.

1089 Barnes to Bielaski, June 19, 1916, roll 862, RG 65, BI, NARA.

1090 Harris and Sadler, Great Call-Up, 61.

1091 Wallace memorandum, June 22, 1916, roll 857, RG 65, BI, NARA.

Endnotes

1092 Offley to Bielaski, June 22, 26, 1916, roll 863; and, Rathbun report, June 22, 1916, roll 862, RG 65, BI, NARA.

1093 Link, *The Papers of Woodrow Wilson*, volume 37, 302.

1094 Harris and Sadler, *The Great Call-Up*, 64.

1095 Breniman report, July 14, 1916, roll 861, RG 65, BI, NARA.

1096 For the convoluted history of this machinery see Chief to Bagley, November 2, 1916; Bagley report, November 10, 1916; Kemp report, November 10, 1916, roll 862, RG 65, BI, NARA.

1097 Chief to Offley, July 31, 1916, roll 862, RG 65, BI, NARA.

1098 Wright to Secretary of State, August 2, 1916, roll 862, RG 65, BI, NARA.

1099 Chief to Offley, August 8, 1916; and, Chief to Offley, September 3, 1916; Kemp report, September 25, 1916, roll 862, RG 65, BI, NARA.

1100 Kemp report, September 27, 1916, roll 862, RG 65, BI, NARA.

1101 Chief to Offley, October 24, 1916, roll 862, RG 65, BI, NARA.

1102 Kemp report, October 27, 1916; and, Chief to Bagley, November 2, 1916, roll 862, RG 65, BI, NARA.

1103 Chief to Offley, November 2, 1916, roll 862, RG 65, BI, NARA.

1104 Kemp report November 14, 916, roll 862, RG 65, BI, NARA.

1105 Offley to Bielaski, November 4, 1916, roll 862, RG 65, BI, NARA.

1106 Offley report, December 9, 1916, roll 861, RG 65, BI, NARA.

1107 SEMAN reports, November 30, December 2, 1916, roll 861, RG 65, BI, NARA.

1108 Beckham report, December 18, 1916, roll 863, RG 65, BI, NARA.

1109 Offley to Bielaski, October 30, 1916, roll 862, RG 65, BI, NARA.

1110 Assistant Chief to Harrison, November 2, 1916, roll 862, RG 65, BI, NARA.

1111 Offley report, November 3, 1916; and, Offley report, November 11, 1916; Chief to Flournoy, November 21, 1916, roll 862, RG 65, BI, NARA.

1112 Offley report, December 22, 1916, roll 862, RG 65, BI, NARA.

1113 Assistant Attorney General to Schoonover, November 4, 1916, roll 859, RG 65, BI, NARA.

1114 No. 1816, US District Court, El Paso, FRC-FW.

1115 Underhill report, October 20, 1916, 1916, roll 862, RG 65, BI, NARA.

1116 1900 census, 1910 census.

1117 "Luis Monroy Duran, Adolfo Álvarez, Enrique Fernández Castillo, and Bulnes, Jr. All these people have their offices at 78 Wall Street under the firm's name of Parisian Real Estate Corp. and Mexican Promoting and Investing Corp." Underhill report, October 20, 1916, 1916, roll 862, RG 65, BI, NARA.

1118 Underhill reports, August 21, 25, 29, 31; September 7, 8, 11, 19, 22, 28, 1916, roll 862, RG 65, BI, NARA.

1119 Underhill report, September 7, 1916, roll 862, RG 65, BI, NARA.

1120 Underhill reports, October 14, 17, 1916, roll 862, RG 65, BI, NARA.

1121 Blanford report, July 1, 1916, roll 862, RG 65, BI, NARA.

1122 Simpich to Secretary of State, July 12, 1916, file 9140-38, RG 165, Military Intelligence Division, NARA.

1123 Ulloa, *Revolución Mexicana*, 339.

1124 Schwierz's name appears in the Bureau reports in all kinds of variations, such as Schwind, Schwiebs, Schwiertz, Schwierbs, Swierz.

1125 Blanford report, July 10, 1916, roll 862, RG 65, BI, NARA.

1126 Ibid.

1127 Blanford report, July 13, 1916, roll 862, RG 65, BI, NARA; *Richmond Virginian*, July 11, 1916; *La Prensa*, July 12, 1916.

1128 Blanford report, July 13, 1916, roll 862, RG 65, BI, NARA.

1129 Ibid.; and, *Nogales Daily Herald*, July 12, 1916.

1130 Ulloa, *Revolución Mexicana*, 347; in January 1917, a Military Intelligence informant claimed that Schwierz planned to smuggle ammunition through Nogales using automobiles. The army passed this report on to the Bureau. There is no evidence that such a scheme did occur. See Barnes memorandum, January 5, 1917, roll 864, RG 65, BI, NARA.

1131 Harrison to Van Deman, September 30, 1916, file 9700-28, RG 165, Military Intelligence Division, NARA.

1132 Gershon report, August 2, 1916, roll 862; Webster report, July 12, 1916, roll 862, RG 65, BI, NARA; Van Deman to Harrison, September 30, 1916, file 9700-28, RG 165, Military Intelligence Division, NARA.

1133 Blanford report, July 25, 1916, roll 862, RG 65, BI, NARA.

1134 Gershon report, August 2, 1916, roll 862, RG 65, BI, NARA.

1135 Hopkins report, November 1, 1916, roll 862, RG 65, BI, NARA.

1136 "Ricardo Schwierz, Neutrality Investigation," quoting Bureau Special Agent Don S. Rathbun report, October 11, 1916, file 9700-38, RG 165, Military Intelligence Division, NARA.

1137 *Deutschland und Österreich, Verzeichnisse von Militär- und Marineoffizieren, 1600-1918* (Provo: Ancestry.com Operations, Inc., 2015), 1198.

1138 Problematic with the Prussian military service lists is that first names are typically not provided.

1139 Van Deman to Harrison, September 30, 1916, quoting Bureau Special Agent Ely M. Blanford report, September 22, 1916, file 9700-28, RG 165, Military Intelligence Division, NARA.

1140 "United States vs Ricardo W. Schwiebs," quoting Bureau Special Agent Ely M. Blanford report, October 13, 1916, file 9700-35, RG 165, Military Intelligence Division, NARA.

1141 Quoted from report of Special Agent Ely M. Blanford, October 23, 1916, file 9700-43, RG 165, Military Intelligence Division, NARA.

1142 Blanford report, February 5, 1917, roll 862, RG 65, BI, NARA.

1143 Bisher, *The Intelligence War in Latin America*, 123, 133, 184.

1144 *Reports of the International Arbitral Awards, Mixed Claims Commission*. Vol. 8 (New York: United Nations, 2006), 354, 358.

1145 Mock report, January 2, 1917, roll 862, RG 65, BI, NARA.

1146 Breniman report, October 13, 1916, roll 863, RG 65, BI, NARA.

1147 Hopkins reports, July 14, 19, 23, 1916, roll 863; July 19, 1916, roll 862, RG 65, BI, NARA.

1148 Hopkins report, August 4, 1916, roll 863, RG 65, BI, NARA.

1149 Breniman report, July 25, 1916, roll 862, RG 65, BI, NARA.

1150 Breniman reports, July 30, 31, 1916, roll 863; July 26, 1916, roll 862, RG 65, BI, NARA.

1151 Hopkins report, August 2, 1916, roll 863, RG 65, BI, NARA.

ENDNOTES

1152 Hopkins reports, July 30, August 29, 1916; MER report, August 19, 1916, roll 863; Barnes to Hopkins, August 4, 1916, roll 862, RG 65, BI, NARA.

1153 Short reports, August 4, 15, 1916; Hopkins report, August 9, 1916, roll 863, RG 65, BI, NARA.

1154 Hopkins report, September 17, 27, 1916, roll 863, RG 65, BI, NARA.

1155 Hopkins reports, August 28, September 8, 1916, roll 863, RG 65, BI, NARA.

1156 Hopkins report, October 16, 1916, roll 863, RG 65, BI, NARA.

1157 Hopkins reports, September 12, 17, 20, 24, 30, 1916, roll 863, RG 65, BI, NARA.

1158 Hopkins report, October 31, 1916; and, Hopkins reports September 27, October 3, 1916, roll 863, RG 65, BI, NARA.

1159 Neunhoffer reports, July 15, 1916, roll 861; July 19, 20, 22, 24, 30, 1916, roll 863, RG 65, BI, NARA.

1160 Neunhoffer report, August 14, 1916, roll 862, RG 65, BI, NARA.

1161 Neunhoffer reports, July 15, 26, 28; August 5, 1916, roll 863, RG 65, BI, NARA.

1162 Neunhoffer reports, August 6, 23, 24, 26, 1916; Breniman report, August 23, 1916, roll 863, RG 65, BI, NARA.

1163 Neunhoffer report, August 14, 1916, roll 863, RG 65, BI, NARA; Harris and Sadler, *Secret War*, 272-273.

1164 Neunhoffer report, November 1, 1916, roll 863, RG 65, BI, NARA.

1165 Breniman report, July 29, 1916; and, Breniman reports, August 23, 1916, roll 863; July 27, 1916, roll 858, RG 65, BI, NARA.

1166 MEC to Ligardi, August 5, 1916, roll 858, RG 65, BI, NARA; MEC report, October 3, 1916, file 9700-35, RG 165, Military Intelligence Division, NARA.

1167 Weiskopf report, November 6, 1916, roll 863, RG 65, BI, NARA.

1168 Wiseman report, July 17, 1916, roll 861, RG 65, BI, NARA.

1169 Barnes to Wiseman, August 16, 1916, roll 863, RG 65, BI, NARA.

1170 Wiseman to Barnes, September 4, 1916, rolls 857 and 861, RG 65, BI, NARA.

1171 Barnes to Wiseman, September 13, 1916, roll 862, RG 65, BI, NARA.

1172 Wiseman report, September 21, 1916, roll 862, RG 65, BI, NARA.

1173 Wiseman to Bege, October 17, 1916, roll 861, RG 65, BI, NARA.

1174 Wiseman to Bege, October 18, 1916, roll 861, RG 65, BI, NARA.

1175 Barnes to Lege, September 22, 1916, roll 863, RG 65, BI, NARA.

1176 Barnes to Lege, August 8, 1916, roll 861, RG 65, BI, NARA.

1177 Ross reports, August 2, 1916, roll 863; December 2, 1916, roll 861, RG 65, BI, NARA.

1178 Rogers report, August 14, 1916, roll 861, RG 65, BI, NARA.

1179 Rogers reports, August 15, 1916, roll 856; August 27, 1916, roll 863, RG 65, BI, NARA.

1180 Rogers report, September 24, 1916, roll 861, RG 65, BI, NARA.

1181 Barnes to Rogers, November 2, 1916, roll 861, RG 65, BI, NARA.

1182 Isidro Fabela et al., eds. *Documentos históricos de la Revolución Mexicana* volumen 13 (México, DF: Editorial Jus, 1960-76), 246-251.

1183 Weiskopf report, November 25, 1916, roll 861, RG 65, BI, NARA.

1184 *The American Journal of International Law*, 12, no. 2 (April 1918), 422.

1185 The standard biography of Félix Díaz is by his fervent supporter Luis Liceaga, *Félix Díaz* (México, DF: Editorial Jus, 1958).

1186 Katz, *Life and Times*, 45.

1187 Peter V. N. Henderson, *Felix Díaz, the Porfirians, and the Mexican Revolution* (Lincoln: University of Nebraska Press, 1981), 124.

1188 Chief to Offley, January 15, 21, 1916, roll 859, RG 65, BI, NARA.

1189 Cantrell to Bielaski, March 8, 12, 1916, roll 861, RG 65, BI, NARA.

1190 Katz, *Life and Times*, 557.

1191 Offley report, March 1, 1916, roll 860, RG 65, BI, NARA.

1192 *Oasis*, August 6, 1910.

1193 *Arizona Republican*, February 24, 1912.

1194 *The Copper Era and Morenci Leader*, March 8, 1912; *Weekly Journal-Miner*, May 15, 1912; *Tacoma Times*, June 4, 1912.

1195 *Evening Independent*, October 16, 1913.

1196 Arrival of Gonzalo Enrile in New York, December 19, 1915, New York Passenger Arrival Records, 1789-1957, roll 2445, RG 85, Immigration and Naturalization, NARA.

1197 Offley report, March 1, 1916, roll 860, RG 65, BI, NARA.

1198 Breniman report, April 30, 1916, roll 860, RG 65, BI, NARA.

1199 Cantrell report, March 4, 1916, roll 860; Cantrell report, including Carothers to Lansing, March 3, 1916, roll 857, RG 65, BI, NARA.

1200 Enrile memorandum (likely Count Montgelas of the Foreign Office), unknown date (likely December 23, 1915), roll 20, RG 242, Captured German Documents, NARA. Second memorandum: Enrile memorandum to Foreign Office, June 15, 1916, roll 20, RG 242, Captured German Documents, NARA. The original text of the two proposals is as follows: "The main proposal which I want to submit to the imperial government are [sic] the following:

Mexico needs weapons and munitions in order to defeat the reign of terror of the Carranza administration, as well as enough capital to recreate the old federal army. In addition, the country needs the support of a large power such as Germany to resist the United States. In return we offer:

1) Installation of Mexican policies completely supportive of German policy, which is aimed against the interests of the United States.

2) Granting of concessions to Germany of railroads, petroleum, mines, and commerce.

3) Expulsion of American capital from the country through legal measures [i.e. expropriation].

4) Creation of an army strong enough to attack the United States in a for Germany and Mexico favorable moment.

5) Support of a separatist movement that already exists in several southern states of the United States: namely Texas, Arizona, New Mexico and the south of Upper [U.S.] California.

6) Creation and support of a political race revolution in Cuba, Puertorico [sic], and Haiti.

7) Financial guarantees to Germany for weapons and munitions in a for Germany agreeable form. The total sum, partly in cash, partly in weapons, munitions, and other war materials needed for an invasion of the United States amounts to 300 million marks.

[...] any questions to be directed at Captain von Papen [...]" [.]

In a second proposal, submitted to the German Foreign Office, Enrile went even further:

"[...] heroic and only because of her financial weakness desperate fight against the assaults of North America [...] A continuation of the conflict between Mexico and the United States [since the attack on Columbus] seem inevitable; Germany will be able to preserve the peace with the United States so long as the latter is fully occupied with the Mexican differences. Thus, it could be achieved that:

a) The United States will be weakened enough, to become ineffectual for further [military] excursions.

b) The current manufacturing of weapons and munitions will end as a result of the United States requiring the same for herself [note the exact same argument Sommerfeld made in his proposal to the German government in May 1915].

c) Mexico can save her existence as a result of the thus received support to defend herself.

Should it come to a war between the United States anyway, the support of a Mexican army easily expanding to 200,000 men could help bring about the defeat of the United States on American soil along a 2,000 kilometer [sic] long border [...] (signed) Gonzalo C. Enrile, Colonel."

1201 Hernández Ferrer reports, January 20, 24, 1916, roll 860, RG 65, BI, NARA; Fabela, *Documentos históricos de la Revolución Mexicana*, volumen 17, 737, 739.

1202 The London Declaration of 1909, a treaty signed by Germany, France, the United States, and Japan among others, but not ratified by England, regulated maritime warfare especially with respect to contraband, blockades, and seizing shipping. For example, the treaty required a naval attacker to send a warning shot across the bow of its civilian target, then allow time for passengers and crew to leave the ship and guide the civilians into safety either by taking them aboard or ensuring safe arrival at the nearest port. By their very nature, submarines became vulnerable when surfacing and had no space to take on passengers. Especially when the British navy ordered its merchant marine to ram surfaced submarines, the German navy decided to abandon its war on commerce rather than abide by the rules of the London Declaration.

1203 Von Feilitzsch, *Felix A. Sommerfeld and the Mexican Front in the Great War*, 177 ff.

1204 Kriminalschutzmann Schmidt to Police headquarters Berlin, June 17, 1916, roll 20, RG 242, Captured German documents, NARA.

1205 John A. Adams, Jr., *William F. Buckley Sr., Witness to the Mexican Revolution, 1908-1922* (Norman: University of Oklahoma Press, 2023), 114-115.

1206 Harrison to Polk, December 14, 1916, Office of the Counselor, RG 59, Department of State, NARA.

1207 Cantrell report, July 14, 1916, roll 860, RG 65, BI, NARA.

1208 Blanford report, March 22, 1916, roll 856, RG 65, BI, NARA.

1209 Cantrell report, April 12, 1916, roll 856, RG 65, BI, NARA.

1210 Albert Papers, Box 45, von Papen accounts, 1914 to 1917; and, ibid., Box 24, General Ledger, RG 65, NARA.

1211 Memorandum, December 28, 1916, Albert Papers Box 26, RG 65, NARA.

1212 Ibid.

1213 See, for example Katz, *Secret War in Mexico*; Thomas Boghardt, *The Zimmermann Telegram: Intelligence, Diplomacy, and America's Entry into World War I*, (Annapolis: Naval Institute Press, 2012).

1214 Friedrich Katz, "Pancho Villa and the Attack on Columbus, New Mexico," *American Historical Review*, 83, no. 1 (February 1978), 101-130.

1215 Chief to Offley, January 15, 21, 1916, roll 859, RG 65, BI, NARA.

1216 Liceaga, *Félix Díaz*, 322-335 He described Berliner as an "American journalist.," 328.

1217 Henderson, *Félix Díaz*, 203n3.

1218 Atlanta Georgian, November 7, 1913.
1219 Fabela, Documentos históricos, volume 15, 43.
1220 Molina report, July 29, 1915, roll 858, RG 65, BI, NARA.
1221 Barnes report, November 5, 1914, roll 856; Pendleton report, January 16, 1915, roll 863, RG 65, BI, NARA.
1222 Pendleton report, January 16, 1915, roll 863; Phillips report, March 2, 1915, roll 857; Guy report, April 18, 1915, roll 859, RG 65, BI, NARA.
1223 Molina report, July 29, 1915, roll 858; Pendleton reports, July 15, 25, 26, 31; August 4, 7, 1915, roll 860, RG 65, BI, NARA.
1224 Pendleton reports, June 30, July 10, 14; August 5, 13, 1915, roll 860, RG 65, BI, NARA.
1225 Acting Chief to Offley, July 8, 1915, roll 860, RG 65, BI, NARA.
1226 Tucker report, July 16, 1915, roll 860; Acting Chief to Barnes, July 17, 1915; Molina report July 30, 1915, roll 859; Molina reports, July 28, 29, 1915; Offley report, July 30, 1915; Jentzer report, October 5, 1915; Pigniuolo report, October 7, 1915, roll 858; Chief to Offley, July 30, 1915; Tucker reports, September 8, 11, 1915; Berliner reports, December 17, 30, 1915, roll 860; January 17, 1916, roll 859; Garbarino report, August 13, 1915, roll 855, RG 65, BI, NARA.
1227 Acting Chief to Offley, July 3, 1915, roll 860; Scully report, July 19, 1915; Tucker report, July 19, 1915, roll 858; and, Jentzer report, July 15, 1915, roll 860, RG 65, BI, NARA.
1228 Cantrell report, July 14, 1916, roll 860, RG 65, BI, NARA.
1229 Ibid.
1230 Acting Chief to Offley, July 17, 1915, roll 859; Offley to Horn, July 18, 1915, roll 860; Hazen report, July 29, 1915; Cantrell report, July 29, 1915, roll 858, RG 65, BI, NARA.
1231 Berliner report, December 6, 1916, roll 861, RG 65, BI, NARA; New York Tribune, August 2, 1915.
1232 Berliner report, December 6, 1916, roll 861, RG 65, BI, NARA.
1233 For Díaz's appointment of Del Villar, see Pendleton report, May 20, 1916; Pendleton to Bielaski, May 29, 1916, roll 859, RG 65, BI, NARA.
1234 Cantrell report, September 13, 1915, roll 858; Berliner reports, December 17, 30, 1915, roll 860, RG 65, BI, NARA.
1235 Berliner report, December 15, 30, 1915; Cantrell report, September 7, 1915, roll 860, RG 65, BI, NARA.
1236 Arizona Republican, February 29, 1916.
1237 New York Times, January 21, 1916.
1238 Berliner report, January 22, 1916; and, Berliner report January 17, 1916, roll 859, RG 65, BI, NARA.
1239 New York Sun, January 21, 1916
1240 Harry Berliner to John Embleton, February 18, 1913, courtesy of Kirstin Keller Rounds, private collection.
1241 Chalmers reports, January 24, 26, 1916, roll 859, RG 65, BI, NARA.
1242 Berliner reports January 7, 1916, roll 862; February 3, 1916, roll 860, RG 65, BI, NARA.
1243 Chief to Offley, January 21, 1916, roll 859, RG 65, BI, NARA.
1244 Harry Berliner to John Embleton, February 16 to 19, 1913, courtesy of Kirstin Keller Rounds, private collection; Berliner met Blanquet on multiple occasions in the Decena Trágica in his capacity as messenger for the American Embassy.
1245 Berliner reports, January 26, 1916, roll 859; February 3, 1916, roll 860, RG 65, BI, NARA.

1246 Berliner reports, December 30, 1915, roll 860; March 20, 21, 1916, roll 861; Adams report, March 18, 1916, roll 861, RG 65, BI, NARA.

1247 Frames 662-1736 roll 872, RG 65, BI, NARA.

1248 CRESSE reports, December 15, 1916, January 21, 1917, roll 860, RG 65, BI, NARA.

1249 CRESSE memorandum for Bielaski, March (no date) 1917, roll 860, RG 65, BI, NARA.

1250 Offley to Bielaski, February 2, 1916, roll 860, RG 65, BI, NARA.

1251 Pendleton report, February 4, 1916; CRESSE memorandum for Bielaski, March (no date) 1917, roll 860, RG 65, BI, NARA.

1252 Pendleton report, January 15, 1916, roll 859; CRESSE memorandum for Bielaski, March (no date), 1917, roll 860, RG 65, BI, NARA.

1253 Liceaga, Félix Díaz, 359-360.

1254 Pendleton reports, February 5, 7, 11, 1916, roll 860, RG 65, BI, NARA.

1255 Bielaski to Pendleton, February 17, 1916, roll 860, RG 65, BI, NARA.

1256 Pendleton report, February 28, 1916, roll 860, RG 65, BI, NARA.

1257 Pendleton report, February 22, 1916, roll 860, RG 65, BI, NARA.

1258 Liceaga, Félix Díaz, 361-375.

1259 New York Sun, March 1, 1916.

1260 Arizona Republican, March 1, 1916

1261 New York Sun, March 2, 1916.

1262 New York Tribune, March 9, 1916.

1263 New York Evening World, March 9, 1916.

1264 San Miguel Examiner, March 11, 1916.

1265 New York Tribune, March 23, 1916.

1266 New York Sun, March 23, 1916.

1267 New York Times, March 30, 1916.

1268 New York Evening World, April 12, 1916.

1269 Stokes to Lansing, April 7, 1918, 812.00/21857, RG 59, Department of State, NARA; Wall Street Journal, November 28, 2003; New York Times, May 27, 1926.

1270 Stokes to Lansing, February 16, 1917, roll 860, RG 65, BI, NARA.

1271 Bielaski to Barnes, June 2, 1916, roll 859, RG 65, BI, NARA.

1272 Weakley report, June 9, 1916, roll 859, RG 65, BI, NARA.

1273 Pendleton report, May 29, 1916; Ibs report, May 30, 1916, roll 859, RG 65, BI, NARA.

1274 Beckham report, June 7, 1916; Pendleton report, June 8, 1916; Barkey report, June 16, 1916, roll 859, RG 65, BI, NARA.

1275 Pérez to Chapa, June 15, 1916, roll 860, RG 65, BI, NARA.

1276 Barkey report, June 16, 1916, roll 859; Spencer report, June 21, 1916, roll 860; Barnes reports, July 6, 12, 1916, roll 861, RG 65, BI, NARA.

1277 Spencer report, July 12, 1916, roll 861; see especially Webb report, July 13, 1916, roll 855, RG 65, BI, NARA.

1278 Offley to Bielaski, March 13, 1916, roll 861; Berliner reports, November 2, 9, 1916, roll 860; December 27, 1916, roll 861, RG 65, BI, NARA; Carl Jacoby, The Strange Career of William Ellis: The Texas Slave Who Became a Mexican Millionaire (New York: Norton, 2016), 173.

1279 Berliner reports, March 1, 1916, roll 860; March 3, 1916, roll 861, RG 65, BI, NARA.

1280 Devlin report, March 15, 1916; Pendleton report, March 16, 1916, roll 861, RG 65, BI, NARA.

1281 Pendleton report, March 6, 1916, roll 861, RG 65, BI, NARA.

1282 Pendleton report, January 20, 1916, roll 859, RG 65, BI, NARA.

1283 Pendleton report, March 13, 1916, roll 855, RG 65, BI, NARA.

1284 Menocal to Carranza, July 20, 1915, file 4995, Venustiano Carranza Archive, Centro de Estudios Históricos Carso (formerly Condumex), México, DF.

1285 Cantrell reports, March 3, 4, 1916, roll 860; March 6-8, 11, 13, 16, 19, 1916; Cantrell to Bielaski, March 8, 12, 1916, roll 861, RG 65, BI, NARA.

1286 Barnes report, November 5, 1914, roll 856; Pendleton report, January 16, 1915, roll 863, RG 65, BI, NARA.

1287 Robert E. Quirk, *The Mexican Revolution and the Catholic Church, 1910-1929* (Bloomington: Indiana University Press, 1973), 69. While Quirk briefly mentions that American Catholics, at least tacitly, supported Díaz at one point, he does not provide any evidence of financing or other support of Díaz by the Church or any members of it. His bibliography does not include any Catholic Church archival records or personal papers of the main US Catholic church officials, especially those of Francis Kelley and Richard Tierney who were actively involved in Mexican affairs and allegedly raised money for Mexican factions.

1288 Carothers to Secretary of State, April 12, 1916, roll 861, RG 65, BI, NARA.

1289 Maximo Soto Hall et al., *El "Libro Azul" de Guatemala* (New Orleans: Searcy & Pfaff, 1915), 210.

1290 Paul J. Dosal, *Doing Business with the Dictators: A Political History of United Fruit in Guatemala, 1899-1944* (Oxford: Rowan and Littlefield, 2005), 45.

1291 Tauscher to von Igel, Box 33, Albert Papers, RG 65, NARA.

1292 *Evening Star*, April 9, 1916; *Washington Herald*, April 10, 1916; *Evening Star*, April 14, 1916; *Evening Star*, April 17, 1916

1293 Ault report, March 4, 1916, Roll 952, RG 65, BI, NARA; Note: Canova was already suspected of leaking State Department and Justice Department information to third parties in the Huerta affair of 1915. The BI briefly investigated but did not take any action against Canova at the time. See Offley report, July 23, 1915, roll 952, RG 65, BI, NARA.

1294 Offley report, April 10, 1916, roll 952, RG 65, BI, NARA.

1295 Canova to Berliner, April 10, 1916, roll 952, RG 65, BI, NARA.

1296 Canova to Berliner, May 4, 1916, roll 952, RG 65, BI, NARA.

1297 Canova to Berliner, April 11, 1916, roll 952, RG 65, BI, NARA.

1298 Canova to Berliner, April 12, 1916, roll 952, RG 65, BI, NARA.

1299 Ault report, March 4, 1916, roll 952, RG 65, BI, NARA.

1300 Berliner to Bielaski, May 10, 1916, BI, roll 952.

1301 Bielaski to Offley, July 20, 1916, roll 952, RG 65, BI, NARA.

1302 CRESSE report, December 15, 1916, roll 860, RG 65, BI, NARA.

1303 Tauscher was arrested and went to court for storing munitions in a warehouse without proper insurance. The case was dismissed, when he produced an insurance certificate. The munitions remained with Tauscher.

1304 Pendleton reports, April 15, 19, 1916, roll 861, RG 65, BI, NARA.

1305 IMA, 2939-2941.

1306 Pendleton reports, April 24, 26, 1916, roll 861, RG 65, BI, NARA.

1307 Pendleton reports May 1, 6, 1916, roll 861, RG 65, BI, NARA.

1308 Ibs reports, May 10, 12, 1916, roll 861; May 16, 17, 27, 1916, roll 859, RG 65, BI, NARA.

1309 Pendleton report, May 30, 1916, roll 859, RG 65, BI, NARA.

1310 Cantrell report, June 2, 1916, roll 862, RG 65, BI, NARA.

1311 Pendleton report, June 10, 1916, roll 859, RG 65, BI, NARA.

1312 Jones estimate, June 15, 1916, roll 861; Pendleton report, June 14, 1916, roll 860, RG 65, BI, NARA.

1313 Chief to Cantrell, June 15, 1916, roll 860, RG 65, BI, NARA.

1314 Pendleton report, June 19, 1916, roll 860, RG 65, BI, NARA.

1315 Furbershaw report, June 25, 1916; Ambrees report, June 25, 1916, roll 860, RG 65, BI, NARA.

1316 See, for example, Garcia to Rosas, July 15, 1916, roll 860, RG 65, BI, NARA.

1317 Pendleton report, July 1, 1916, roll 860, RG 65, BI, NARA.

1318 Pendleton reports, July 16, 11, 1916, roll 861, RG 65, BI, NARA.

1319 Ibs report, July 6, 1916, roll 861, RG 65, BI, NARA.

1320 Pendleton report, July 8, 1916, roll 861, RG 65, BI, NARA.

1321 Pendleton report, July 15, 1916, roll 861, RG 65, BI, NARA; Henderson, *Félix Díaz*, 134.

1322 Pendleton report, July 17, 1916, roll 861, RG 65, BI, NARA.

1323 Lillard report, July 26, 1916, roll 861, RG 65, BI, NARA.

1324 Pendleton report, August 10, 1916, roll 860, RG 65, BI, NARA.

1325 For a brief description of Enrile's career, see Raymond Caballero, *Orozco: The Life and Death of a Mexican Revolutionary* (Norman: University Of Oklahoma Press, 2017), 236. Enrile returned from Europe and settled in Cuba where he continued to engage in pro-German agitation. He was arrested in 1917 in Cuba, in 1919 in Mexico. After engaging in a pro-Félix Díaz uprising in 1921 to overthrow Mexican president Obregón he was arrested and killed "while attempting to escape."

1326 Von Feilitzsch, *Felix A. Sommerfeld and the Mexican Front in the Great War*, 231-236.

1327 Bielaski to Jones, June 28, 1916, Albert. Bacon Fall Family Papers, MS 8, Box 5, Rio Grande Historical Collections, New Mexico State University, Las Cruces, New Mexico.

1328 Harrison to Polk, December 14, 1916, Office of the Counselor, RG 59, Department of State, NARA.

1329 *Sacramento Daily Union*, March 31, 1916.

1330 Barnes to Bielaski, January 5, 1917, roll 860; and "Memorandum of Actual and Attempted Smuggling of Arms and Ammunition into Mexico. From December 1st., 1916 to February 10, 1917. With Particulars," roll 867, RG 65, BI, NARA.

1331 Bielaski to Barnes, January 6, 1917, roll 857, RG 65, BI, NARA.

1332 Chief to Barnes, January 6, 1917, roll 864, RG 65, BI, NARA.

1333 Edward Eugene Briscoe, "Pershing's Chinese Refugees in Texas," *Southwestern Historical Quarterly*, 62, no. 4 (April 1959), 467-488; Stone report, January 16, 1917, roll 857, RG 65, BI, NARA.

1334 Pendleton report, January 19, 1917, roll 857, RG 65, BI, NARA.

1335 Blanford report, March 29, 1917, roll 862, RG 65, BI, NARA.

1336 Chief to Barnes, February 19, 1917, roll 864, RG 65, BI, NARA.

1337 Swift report, May 11, 1917, roll 857, RG 65, BI, NARA.

1338 Needham report, April 30, 1917, roll 856, RG 65, BI, NARA.

THE FBI AND AMERICAN NEUTRALITY, 1914-1917

1339   Needham report, May 2, 1917, roll 856, RG 65, BI, NARA.

1340   Needham report, May 20, 1917, roll 857, RG 65, BI, NARA.

1341   Utley report, May 1, 1917, roll 856, RG 65, BI, NARA.

1342   Chief to Barnes, May 14, 1917, roll 857, RG 65, BI, NARA.

1343   Needham report, January 6, 1917, roll 860, RG 65, BI, NARA.

1344   See Pendleton reports, January 26, 27, February 8, 1917; Munson report, February 3, 1917, roll 860, RG 65, BI, NARA.

1345   Barnes to All Agents, February 16, 1917, roll 860, RG 65, BI, NARA.

1346   Breniman report, January 20, 1917, roll 860, RG 65, BI, NARA.

1347   Breniman to Barnes, January 18, 1917, roll 863; and, Breniman report, January 17, 1917; Mennet reports, January 20, 1917, roll 860; February 9, 1917, roll 863, RG 65, BI, NARA.

1348   Breniman reports, January 1, 1917, rolls 860 and 861; January 3, 6, 9, 12, 14, 19; February 3, 13, 15, 19, 20, 22, 23, 24, 27, April 3, 1917, roll 860; March 19, 20, 22, 27, 28, 1917; Marks reports, January 7, 1917, roll 861; January 12, 1917, roll 860; Weiskopf report, January 1, 1917; Bielaski to Barnes, January 10, 1917; Barnes reports, January 15, February 10, 1917; Garcia report, February 1, 1917; Webb report, February 7, 1917; Mennet report, February 7, 1917, roll 860; Barnes report, March 21, April 2, 1917; Needham report, March 23, 1917, roll 861; Rogers report, January 14, 1917, roll 866, RG 65, BI, NARA.

1349   Secretary of War to Secretary of State, June 4, 1917, 812.00/20980, RG 59, Department of State, NARA.

1350   *New York Evening Sun*, January 3, 1917; *The World*, January 4, 1917.

1351   Juan T. Burns file, 1-16-29, expediente 1/31/280, AREM.

1352   Berliner reports, January 2, 3, 5, 6, 8, 9, 1917, roll 860; and, Baker report, January 17, 1917, roll 866; Offley report, January 18, 1917, roll 862, RG 65, BI, NARA.

1353   Burns to Saenz, October 19, 1925, Burns file, Exp. 1/131/280, AREM.

1354   Bradford to Berliner, January 3, 1917; Berliner report, January 9, 1917, roll 860, RG 65, BI, NARA.

1355   Offley to Bielaski, January 9, 1917, roll 860, RG 65, BI, NARA.

1356   Berliner reports, January 14, 16, 1917, roll 866, RG 65, BI, NARA.

1357   Berliner report, January 14, 1917, BI, roll 866, RG 65, BI, NARA.

1358   Berliner report, January 15, 1917, BI, roll 866, RG 65, BI, NARA.

1359   Berliner report, January 14, 1917, BI, roll 866, RG 65, BI, NARA.

1360   Berliner report, January 18, 1917, BI, roll 866, RG 65, BI, NARA.

1361   Berliner report, January 20, 1917, BI, roll 866, RG 65, BI, NARA.

1362   Carl Heynen and Richard Everbusch co-owned a commercial shipping agency representing Hapag and North German Lloyd in Mexico before World War I. As the shipping agent for HAPAG, Heynen was in charge of the *Ypiranga*, *Bavaria*, and *Kronprinzessin Cecilie* freight that caused an American military intervention in April of 1914. The German businessman was accused of manipulating the situation and cause the delivery of trainloads of weapons and ammunition to Huerta. As Senate hearings later showed, Heynen actually tried to cooperate with American military authorities, but was ignored. In January 1915, the German businessman moved to New York to work as Heinrich Albert's main administrator. While in New York, Heynen was in charge of the Bridgeport Projectile Company, blockade running efforts against the British, cornering strategic US industries, and purchase of commerce ships. After detention as a "dangerous enemy alien" in Fort Oglethorpe, he moved back to Mexico in 1919 and resumed his shipping business. He died in 1950.

ENDNOTES

1363 Berliner report, January 23, 1917, roll 866, RG 65, BI, NARA.

1364 *Olean Evening Herald*, July 1, 1917; July 31, 1917; *Syracuse Herald*, July 7, 1917.

1365 Berliner report, January 23, 1917, roll 866, RG 65, BI, NARA.

1366 Berliner reports, January 24; February 2, 12, 1917; Hariber cable, February 3, 1917, roll 866, RG 65, BI, NARA.

1367 Berliner report, March 5, 1917, roll 861, RG 65, BI, NARA.

1368 This was a true story and one of the most successful German clandestine successes in the United States; see "The Bridgeport Projectile Company," memo by Carl Heynen, September 30, 1915, Albert Papers, Box 5, RG 65, NARA.

1369 Berliner report, March 9, 1917, roll 866, RG 65, BI, NARA.

1370 Berliner report, April 10, 1917, roll 860, RG 65, BI, NARA.

1371 [Jones] to [Bielaski], undated but February 1917, roll 860; see also [Unsigned [Jones] to Del Villar, February 3, 1917, roll 855, RG 65, BI, NARA.

1372 See, for example, Pendleton to Bielaski, January 22, 1917; Pendleton reports, February 6, 19, 1917, roll 860; February 22, 1917, roll 862, RG 65, BI, NARA.

1373 Pendleton report, January 17, 1917, roll 860, RG 65, BI, NARA.

1374 Rosas et al. to Postmaster, February 16, 1917, roll 860, RG 65, BI, NARA.

1375 Cantrell report, February 17, 1917; Pendleton report, February 19, 1917, roll 860, RG 65, BI, NARA.

1376 Pendleton reports, February 23, 24, 1917, roll 860, RG 65, BI, NARA.

1377 CRESSE memorandum, February 26, 1917, roll 861; a slightly different version is dated February 26, 1917, roll 860, RG 65, BI, NARA.

1378 Tucker report, February 27, 1917, roll 860, RG 65, BI, NARA.

1379 CRESSE to Bielski, undated but February 1917, roll 861, RG 65, BI, NARA.

1380 CRESSE memorandum for Bielaski, undated but March 1917, roll 860, RG 65, BI, NARA.

1381 Chalmers report, March 9, 1917; and, Ibs report, March 9, 1917; Irby report, March 9, 1917, roll 861, RG 65, BI, NARA.

1382 Pendleton report, March 12, 1917; and, Ibs report, March 12, 1917, roll 861, RG 65, BI, NARA.

1383 Pendleton report, March 13, 1917, roll 861, RG 65, BI, NARA.

1384 Bureau agents not infrequently arranged with the management of a hotel for permission to enter an individual's room and examine his belongings. See for instance, Tucker report, March 1, 1917, roll 856, RG 65, BI, NARA.

1385 Beckham report, March 15, 1917; and, Irby report, March 16, 1917, roll 861, RG 65, BI, NARA.

1386 Pendleton report, March 16, 1917; Beckham report, March 16, 1917, roll 861; Pendleton to Bielaski, March 19, 1917, roll 860, RG 65, BI, NARA.

1387 Bielaski to Barnes, March 17, 1917, roll 861, RG 65, BI, NARA.

1388 Examiner L. G. Munson in New York City analyzed the bank accounts of Ramon Díaz and his associates. Munson report, March 24, 1917, roll 861, RG 65, BI, NARA.

1389 CRESSE memorandum for Bielaski, undated [March 1917]; another CRESSE memorandum for Bielaski listing arms and ammunition for Yucatan expedition, undated [March 1917]; Pendleton reports, March 20, 22, 1917, roll 861; CRESSE memorandum, undated but March 1917, roll 860, RG 65, BI, NARA.

1390 CRESSE to Bielaski, undated [April 1917], roll 860, RG 65, BI, NARA.

1391 Pendleton reports, January 4, 5 1917, roll 860, RG 65, BI, NARA.

1392 Pendleton report, May 6, 1917, roll 860, RG 65, BI, NARA.

1393 Pendleton report, May 10, 1917, roll 860, RG 65, BI, NARA.

1394 Barnes report, January 12, 1917; Fletcher to Secretary of State, March 14, 1917, roll 866; Hopkins reports, January 10, 1917, rolls 862 and 863; February 4, 1917, roll 863; Weiskopf reports, January 19, 20, 21; March 3, 23, 25; April 4, 27, 1917; Lege report, January 21, 1917; Lege to Barnes, March 31, 1917; Chief to Van Deman, February 5, 1917; Chief to Harrison, May 9, 1917, roll 857; May 10, 1917, roll 861; Weiskopf reports, January 27, 1917, roll 855; February 13, 1917, roll 866; Swift report, May 11, 1917, roll 857, RG 65, BI, NARA.

1395 Mennet report, January 28, 1917, roll 860, RG 65, BI, NARA.

1396 Bielaski memorandum, February 12, 1917, roll 860, RG 65, BI, NARA.

1397 Webb report February 4, 1917, roll 863, RG 65, BI, NARA.

1398 Chief to Barnes, December 2, 1916, roll 864, RG 65, BI, NARA.

1399 Barnes circular letter, February 16, 1917; and, Mennet report, January 26, 1917, roll 863, RG 65, BI, NARA.

1400 Barnes circular letter, February 15, 1917; Barnes to McFarland, January 16, 1917, roll 866, RG 65, BI, NARA.

1401 Chief to Harrison, April 16, 1917, roll 860, RG 65, BI, NARA.

1402 Benham report, April 16, 1917; and, Stokes to Lansing, February 16, 1917, roll 860, RG 65, BI, NARA. The alleged letters from the German ambassador never surfaced.

1403 Tuchman, *Zimmermann Telegram*.

1404 Michael C. Meyer, "The Mexican-German Conspiracy of 1915," *The Americas*, 23, no.1 (July 1966), 76–89.

1405 Katz, *Secret War in Mexico*, 364.

1406 Boghardt, *The Zimmermann Telegram*, 14-15.

1407 Von Feilitzsch, *Felix A. Sommerfeld and the Mexican Front in the Great War*, 98-100.

1408 In the infamous War Council Meeting at Pless, Germany.

1409 Boghardt, *Zimmermann Telegram*, 64-72.

1410 Ibid., 15-16.

1411 Katz researched only archives in formerly East Germany.

1412 Katz, *Secret War in Mexico*, 389-391; Boghardt, *Zimmermann Telegram*, 15.

1413 Boghardt, *Zimmermann Telegram*, 246.

1414 Ibid., 74.

1415 Von Feilitzsch and Harris, *The federal Bureau of Investigation before Hoover, volume 1: The fBI and Mexican Revolutionists, 1908-1914*.

1416 For a detailed discussion of the Sommerfeld mission in World War I, see von Feilitzsch, *Felix A. Sommerfeld and the Mexican Front in the Great War*.

1417 The Federal Republic of Germany (West Germany) made its final payment in 1979.

1418 *The FBI: A Centennial History, 1908-2008* (Washington, DC: Office of Public Affairs, Federal Bureau of Investigation, 2008), 10.

1419 The centennial history also cites the non-existent presidential order of May 1915, through which the US Secret Service supposedly received authority for expanding its mission, and buys into the Albert briefcase affair myth created by Flynn, McAdoo, and Burke.

1420 Don Whitehead, *The FBI Story; A report to the People* (New York: Random House, 1956).

1421 Theoharis, The FBI, 4-8; According to Alan Theoharis the number of special agents and support staff (not including paid informants) went from 260 in 1916 to 570 in 1917.
1422 For example, Jeffreys-Jones, The FBI, 66-68; John F. Fox Jr., "Bureaucratic Wrangling over Counterintelligence, 1917–18," Studies in Intelligence, vol. 49 No 1 (2005).
1423 Simon, The Bulldog Detective, 108. Although buying into the McAdoo/Flynn/Burke story that the US Secret Service stole Heinrich Albert's briefcase, Simon is one of the few scholars who correctly defined the Bureau of Investigation having the "leadership role in counterintelligence during the war years."
1424 Tuchman, The Zimmermann Telegram; Bowen and Neal, The United States Secret Service; Ernest Wittenberg "The Thrifty Spy on the Sixth Avenue EL," American Heritage (August 1965).
1425 Jeffreys-Jones, The FBI.
1426 The best scholarly work on Rathom is by Arsenault, The Imposter's War.

Bibliography

Archives

Ancestry.com, various online archives.

National Archives and Records Administration, Washington, DC and College Park, Maryland.

RG 59 Records of the Department of State.

    Decimal Files, Internal Affairs of Mexico, 1910-1929, Microcopy no. 274.

    Numerical and Minor Files, 1906-1910, Microcopy M-862.

RG 60 Records of the Department of Justice.

RG 65 Records of the Federal Bureau of Investigation: Investigative Case Files of the Bureau of Investigation, 1908-1922.

    Old Mex 232 Files, Microcopy.

    Old German Files, 1909-21, Microfilm Publication No. M1085.

    Miscellaneous Files, 1909-21, Microcopy.

    Papers of Heinrich F. Albert.

RG 76 Records of Boundary and Claims Commissions and Arbitrations. Mixed Claims Commission.

RG 85 Department of the Immigration and Naturalization Service.

    Passenger and Crew Lists of Vessels.

    Selected Indexes to naturalization Records of the U.S. Circuit and District Courts, Northern District of California.

RG 87 Records of the United States Secret Service.

    Daily Reports of Agents, 1875 Thru 1936, Microcopy.

RG 92 Records of the Office of the Quartermaster General.

RG 131 Records of the Alien Property Custodian.

RG 165 Records of the War Department General and Special Staffs.

    Army War College, General Correspondence.

    Military Intelligence Division.

RG 242 Collection of Foreign Records.

    Captured German Documents.

RG 393 Records of United States Army Continental Commands, 1821-1920.

    General Correspondence, Department of Texas, 1870-1913.

National Personnel Records Center, Civilian Personnel Records, St. Louis, Missouri.

Federal Records Center, Fort Worth, Texas.
> US Commissioner, Del Rio, El Paso, Marfa.
>
> US District Court, San Antonio, Austin, Brownsville, El Paso, Laredo.

Federal Records Center, Denver, Colorado.
> US Commissioner, District of New Mexico.
>
> US District Court, Santa Fe.

Federal Records Center, Laguna Niguel, California.
> US Commissioner, Douglas.
>
> US District Court, Phoenix, Tucson.

Library of Congress, Washington, D.C.

Lansing Private Memoranda, 1915-1917.

Archivo Histórico Diplomático Mexicano de la Secretaria de Relaciones Exteriores, México, DF.

Auswärtiges Amt, Politisches Archiv Berlin, Mexiko V.

National Guard Registers, vol. 72, Unattached Companies 2nd and 3rd Brigades Enlisted Men, 1880 – 1894.

National Archives, Kew, Great Britain, Records of the
> Home Office (HO)
>
> Admiralty (ADM)
>
> Foreign Office (FO)
>
> Military Intelligence (KV)
>
> War Office (WO)
>
> German Foreign Ministry (GFM).

Miscellaneous #6. 1916: *Selection of Papers Found in the Possession of Captain von Papen.* London: Harrison and Sons, 1916.

Miscellaneous #13. 1916: *Sworn Statement by Horst von der Goltz, alias Bridgeman Taylor.* London: Harrison and Sons, 1916.

Private Collections and Personal Papers

Albert Bacon Fall Family Papers, Rio Grande Historical Collections, New Mexico State University, Las Cruces, NM.

Berliner, Harry, Letters to John Embleton, courtesy of Kirstin Keller Rounds, private collection.

Papers of Lazaro De La Garza, Nettie Lee Benson Latin American Collection, University of Texas at Austin.

Papers of Enrique Llorente, New York Public Library.

Papers of Emil Holmdahl, Bancroft Library, University of California at Berkley.

Government Documents

Annual Report of the Attorney General of the United States for the Year 1907, 2 vols. Washington, D.C.: Government Printing Office, 1907.

Annual Report of the Attorney General of the United States for the Year 1908. Washington, D.C.: Government Printing Office, 1908.

Lansing Papers, 1914-1920. 2 vols. Washington D.C.: Government Printing Office, 1939.

Birth Registrations, Zaragoza, Puebla Mexico, December 11, 1907.

Boletín Oficial de la Secretaria de Relaciones Exteriores, Tomo VII, Noviembre de 1898 a Abril de 1899. México: Salvador Gutiérrez, 1898.

Death Registrations for Zaragoza, Puebla, Mexico, April 18, 1899.

Deutschland und Österreich, Verzeichnisse von Militär- und Marineoffizieren, 1600-1918. Provo: Ancestry.com Operations, Inc., 2015.

El Derecho, Quinta época, sección de Jurisprudencia, Tomo II. México: Talleres de la Ciencia jurídica, 1898.

Kansas City, Missouri, City Directory, 1912.

Maryland Appellate Court, Morris v Rasst, 1918.

Maryland Circuit Court, Morris v Rasst, 1916.

Maryland Supreme Court, Morris v. Rasst, 1922.

Reports of the International Arbitral Awards, Mixed Claims Commission. Vol. 8 New York: United Nations, 2006.

The FBI: A Centennial History, 1908-2008. Washington, DC: Office of Public Affairs, Federal Bureau of Investigation, 2008.

US Census 1880 to 1960.

US City Directories, 1880-1942.

US Senate, Investigation of Mexican Affairs. 2 vols. Senate doc. no. 285, 66th Congress, 2nd session. Washington, DC: Government Printing Office, 1920.

US Senate, Revolutions in Mexico: Hearing before a Subcommittee of the Committee on Foreign Relations. 62nd Congress 2nd session Washington, DC: Government Printing Office, 1913.

Books

A Twentieth Century History of Southwest Texas. 3 vols. Chicago, New York, Los Angeles: Lewis Publishing Company, 1907.

Albro, Ward S., Always a Rebel: Ricardo Flores Magon and the Mexican Revolution. Fort Worth: Texas Christian University Press, 1992.

Almada, Francisco R., Diccionario de historia, geografía, y biografía Chihuahuenses. 2nd ed. Chihuahua: Universidad de Chihuahua, 1968.

Arsenault, Mark, The Imposter's War: The Press, Propaganda, and the Newsmen who battled for the Minds of America. New York: Pegasus Books Ltd., 2022.

Atwater, Elton, American Regulation of Arms Exports. Washington, D.C.: Carnegie Endowment for International Peace, 1941.

Baca, Leo, Czech Immigration Passenger Lists, vol. VII. Richardson: Old Homestead Publishing Co., 1998.

Batvinis, Raymond J., The Origins of FBI Counterintelligence. Lawrence: University Press of Kansas, 2007.

Beezley William H., Insurgent Governor: Abraham González and the Mexican Revolution in Chihuahua. Lincoln: University of Nebraska Press, 1973.

Bernstorff, Johann Heinrich, Count, My Three Years in America. New York: Charles Scribner's Sons, 1920.

Bisher, Jamie, The Intelligence War in Latin America, 1914-1922. Jefferson: McFarland, 2016.

Blaisdell, Lowell L., *The Desert Revolution: Baja California, 1911*. Madison: University of Wisconsin Press, 1962.

Blum, Howard, *Dark Invasion, 1915: Germany's Secret War and the Hunt for the First Terrorist Cell in America*. New York: Harper Collins, 2014.

Boghardt, Thomas, *The Zimmermann Telegram: Intelligence, Diplomacy, and America's Entry into World War I*. Annapolis: Naval Institute Press, 2012.

Bowen, Walter S., and Neal, Harry Edward, *The United States Secret Service: An Exciting Story of the World's Most Foremost Crime-Fighting Agencies*. Philadelphia: Chilton Company, 1960.

Boy-Ed, Karl, *Verschwörer?* Berlin: Verlag August Scherl, 1920.

Brands, H. W., *T. R. The Last Romantic*. New York: Basic Books, 1997.

Bryan, Anthony Templeton, "Mexican Politics in Transition, 1900-1913: The Role of General Bernardo Reyes." Ph.D. dissertation, University of Nebraska, 1970.

Byrne, Gary J., *Secrets of the Secret Service: The History and Uncertain Future of the US Secret Service*. New York: Hachette Book Group, 2018.

Caballero, Raymond, *Orozco: The Life and Death of a Mexican Revolutionary*. Norman: University of Oklahoma Press, 2017.

Case, Henry Jay, *Guy Hamilton Scull: Soldier Writer, Explorer and War Correspondent*. New York: Duffield, 1922).

Castillo, Víctor et al., *Revista de legislación y jurisprudencia, El delito de quiebra*. México, D.F.: Imprenta del Gobierno Federal, 1898.

Chalkley, John F., *Zach Lamar Cobb: El Paso Collector of Customs and Intelligence During the Mexican Revolution*. El Paso: Texas Western Press, 1998.

Clendenen, Clarence C., *The United States and Pancho Villa: A Study in Unconventional Diplomacy*. Ithaca: Cornell University Press, 1961.

Cockcroft, James D., *Intellectual Precursors of the Mexican Revolution, 1900-1913*. Austin: University of Texas Press, 1968.

Cumberland, Charles C., *Mexican Revolution: The Constitutionalist Years*. Austin: University of Texas Press, 1972.

Devitt, Steven, *The Pen that Set Mexico on Fire: The Betrayal of Ricardo Flores Magón During the Mexican Revolution*. Amissville: Henselstone Verlag, 2017.

Diaz, George T., *Border Contraband: A History of Smuggling Across the Rio Grande*. Austin: University of Texas Press, 2015.

Diccionario Porrúa de historia, biografía y geografía de México. México, D.F.: Editorial Porrúa, 1965-1976.

Doerries, Reinhard, *Imperial Challenge: Ambassador Count Bernstorff and German-American Relations, 1908-1917*. Chapel Hill: University of North Carolina Press, 1989.

_____, *Prelude to the Easter Rising: Sir Roger Casement in Imperial Germany*. London: Frank Cass, 2000.

Dosal, Paul J., *Doing Business with the Dictators: A Political History of United Fruit in Guatemala, 1899-1944*. Lanham: Rowman and Littlefield, 2005.

Eisenhower, John, S. D., *Intervention! The United States and the Mexican Revolution, 1913-1917*. New York: W. W. Norton and Company, 1993.

Emery, Theo, *Hellfire Boys: The Birth of the U.S. Chemical Warfare*. New York: Little, Brown, 2017.

Fabela, Isidro et al., *Documentos históricos de la revolución mexicana*, 28 vols. México, DF: Editorial Jus, 1960-1976.

Federation of American Scientists, Intelligence Resource Program, *A Counterintelligence Reader*, Vol. 1, Chapter 3, 2005. https://irp.fas.org/ops/ci/docs/ci1/chap3.pdf, 27.

Fenwick, Charles Ghequiere, *The Neutrality Laws of the United States*. Washington, DC: Carnegie Endowment for International Peace, 1913.

Flynn, William F. and Cooper, Courtney Riley, *The Eagle's Eye: A True Story of the Imperial German Government's Spies and Intrigues in America from Facts Furnished by William J. Flynn, Recently Retired Chief of the U.S. Secret Service*. New York: Prospect Press, 1919.

Fulwider, Chad R., *German Propaganda and U.S. Neutrality in World War I*. Columbia: University of Missouri Press, 2017.

Furlong, Thomas, *Fifty Years a Detective*. St. Louis: C. E. Barnett, 1912.

Gaunt, Guy, *The Yield of the Years*. London and Melbourne: Hutchinson and Co. Ltd, 1940.

Gamboa, Leticia, *Los empresarios de ayer: El grupo dominante en la industria textil de Puebla, 1906-1929*. Puebla: UAP, 1985.

Graff, Garrett M. *Watergate: A New History*. New York: Simon and Schuster, 2022.

Grann, David, *Killers of the Flower Moon: The Osage Murders and the Birth of the FBI*. New York: Doubleday, 2017.

Grayson, Robert, *The FBI and National Security*. Broomall: Mason Crest, 2010.

Guzmán, Martin Luís, *Memorias de Pancho Villa*. México, DF: Compañía General de Ediciones, 1951.

Hagedorn, Dan, *Conquistadors of the Sky: A History of Aviation in Latin America*. Gainesville: University Press of Florida, 2008.

Hájiková, Dagmar, "Emanuel Voska in the Czechoslovak Foreign Resistance in World War II: News and Propaganda." PhD Dissertation, Charles University, Prague, 2007.

Haley, Edward P., *Revolution and Intervention: The Diplomacy of Taft and Wilson with Mexico, 1910-1917*. Cambridge: MIT University Press, 1970.

Harris, Charles H. III and Louis R. Sadler, *The Great Call-Up: The Guard, the Border, and the Mexican Revolution*. Norman: University of Oklahoma Press, 2015.

_____, *The Secret War in El Paso: Mexican Revolutionary Intrigue, 1906-1920*. Albuquerque: University of New Mexico Press, 2009.

_____, *The Archaeologist Was a Spy: Sylvanus G. Morley and the Office of Naval Intelligence*. Albuquerque: University of New Mexico Press, 2003.

_____, *The Border and the Revolution: Clandestine Activities of the Mexican Revolution: 1910-1920*. Silver City, NM: High-Lonesome Books, 1988.

_____, *The Plan de San Diego: Tejano Rebellion, Mexican Intrigue*. Lincoln: University of Nebraska Press, 2013.

Hawkins, Richard A., *Progressive Politics in the Democratic Party: Samuel Untermeyr and the Jewish Anti-Nazi Boycott Campaign*. New York, I.B. Tauris, 2022.

Henderson, Peter V. N., *Felix Diaz, the Porfirians, and the Mexican Revolution*. Lincoln: University of Nebraska Press, 1981.

Hill, Kathleen and Gerald N. Hill, *Encyclopedia of Federal Agencies and Commissions*. New York: Facts on File, 2014.

History of the Bureau of Diplomatic Security of the United States. Washington, DC: Global Publishing Solutions, 2011.

Horne, Charles F., *Source Records of the Great War*, volume III. New York: National Alumni, 1923.

Hoyt, Edwin P., *Spectacular Rogue: Gaston B. Means*. New York: The Bobbs Merrill Company, 1963.

Hurst, James W., *The Villista Prisoners of 1916-1917*. Las Cruces, NM: Yucca Tree Press, 2000.

Jacoby, Carl, *The Strange Career of William Ellis: The Texas Slave Who Became a Mexican Millionaire*. New York: Norton, 2016.

Jeffreys-Jones, Rhodri, *American Espionage: From Secret Service to CIA*. New York: Free Press, 1977.

_____, *The FBI: A History*. New Haven: Yale University Press, 2007.

Jensen, Joan M., *The Price of Vigilance*. New York: Rand McNally, 1968.

Johnson, David N., "Exiles and Intrigue: Francisco I. Madero and the Mexican Revolutionary Junta in San Antonio, 1910-1911," M. A. thesis, Trinity University, 1975.

Jones, Charles and Eugene Jones, *Double Trouble: The Autobiography of the Jones Twins, Cameramen – Correspondents*. Boston: Little Brown, 1952.

Jones, John Price and Paul Merrick Hollister, *The German Secret Service in America, 1914-1918*. Boston: Small, Maynard, 1918.

Jones, John Price, *The German Spy in America: The Secret Plotting of German Spies in the United States and the Inside Story of the Sinking of the Lusitania*. London: Hutchinson and Co., Ltd, 1917.

Kahn, David, *The Reader of Gentlemen's Mail: Herbert O. Yardley and the Birth of American Codebreaking*. New Haven: Yale University Press, 2004.

_____, *The Codebreakers: The Story of Secret Writing*. New York: Macmillan, 1967.

Katz, Friedrich, *Deutschland, Diaz und die Mexikanische Revolution: Die Deutsche Politik in Mexiko, 1870-1920*. Berlin: VEB Deutscher Verlag der Wissenschaften, 1964.

_____, *The Life and Times of Pancho Villa*. Stanford: Stanford University Press, 1998.

_____, *The Secret War in Mexico: Europe, the United States, and the Mexican Revolution*. Chicago: University of Chicago Press, 1981.

Kerig, Dorothy Pierson, *Luther T. Ellsworth: U. S. Consul on the Border During the Mexican Revolution*. El Paso: Texas Western Press, 1975.

Kessler, Ronald, *The Bureau: The Secret History of the FBI*. New York: St. Martin's Press, 2002.

Knight, Alan, *The Mexican Revolution*, 2 vols. Lincoln: University of Nebraska Press, 1986.

Koenig, Robert, *The Fourth Horseman: One Man's Mission to Wage the Great War in America*. New York: Perseus Books, 2006.

Landau, Henry, *The Enemy Within: The Inside Story of German Sabotage in America*. New York: G. P. Putnam's Sons, 1937.

Lansing, Robert, *War Memoirs of Robert Lansing, Secretary of State*. New York: Bobbs-Merrill, 1935.

Liceaga, Luis, *Félix Díaz*. México, DF: Editorial Jus, 1958.

Link, Arthur S., *Papers of Woodrow Wilson*. 69 vols. Princeton: Princeton University Press, 1966-1994.

_____, *Wilson: The Struggle for Neutrality, 1914-1915*. Princeton: Princeton University Press, 1960.

Logan, Keith Gregory, *Homeland Security and Intelligence*. Santa Barbara, CA: Praeger Security International Textbook, 2017.

Lomnitz-Adler, Claudio, *The Return of Comrade Ricardo Flores Magón*. New York: Zone Books, 2014.

MacLachlan, Colin M., *Anarchism and the Mexican Revolution: The Political Trials of Ricardo Flores Magón in the United States*. Berkeley, Los Angeles, Oxford: University of California Press, 1991.

McAdoo, William Gibbs, *Crowded Years: The Reminiscences of William G. McAdoo*. Boston and New York: Houghton Mifflin Company, 1931.

Masaryk, Thomas Garrigue, *The Making of a State: Memories and Observations, 1914-1918*. New York: Frederick A. Stokes company, 1927.

Mason, Herbert Molloy, Jr., *The Great Pursuit: Pershing's Expedition to Destroy Pancho Villa*. New York: Smithmark Publishers Inc, 1970.

Melanson, Philip H. and Stevens, Peter F., *The Secret Service: The Hidden History of an Enigmatic Agency*. New York: Carroll and Graf Publishers, 2002.

Messimer, Dwight R., *The Baltimore Sabotage Cell: German Agents, American Traitors, and the U-Boat Deutschland During World War I*. Annapolis: Naval Institute Press, 2015.

Meyer, Michael C., *Huerta: A Political Portrait*. Lincoln: University of Nebraska Press, 1972.

_____, *Mexican Rebel: Pascual Orozco and the Mexican Revolution, 1910-1915*. Lincoln: University of Nebraska Press, 1967.

Mickolus, Edward, *The Counterintelligence Chronology: Spying By and Against*. Jefferson: McFarland, 2015.

Millman, Chad, *The Detonators: The Secret Plot to Destroy America and an Epic Hunt for Justice*. New York: Little, Brown, 2006.

Naranjo, Francisco, *Diccionario biográfico Revolucionario*. México, DF: Imprenta Editorial "Cosmos" edición, 1935.

Niemeyer E. V., Jr., *El General Bernardo Reyes*. Monterrey: Universidad de Nuevo León, 1966.

Obregón, Álvaro, *Ocho mil kilómetros en campana*. México, DF: Fondo de Cultura Económica, 1959.

Oliver, Willard M., *The Birth of the FBI: Teddy Roosevelt, the Secret Service, and the Fight Over America's Premier Law Enforcement Agency*. Lanham: Roman & Littlefield, 2019.

Peden, Edward Andrew, *Peden – 1965*. Houston: Premier Printing Company, 1965.

Preston, William, Jr., *Aliens and Dissenters: Federal Suppression of Radicals, 1903-1933*. New York: Harper & Row, 1963.

Quirk, Robert E., *The Mexican Revolution and the Catholic Church, 1910-1929*. Bloomington: Indiana University Press, 1973.

Raat, W. Dirk and William H. Beezley, eds. *Twentieth-Century Mexico*. Lincoln and London: University of Nebraska Press, 1986.

Raat, W. Dirk, *Revoltosos: Mexico's Rebels in the United States, 1903-1923*. College Station: Texas A & M University Press, 1981.

Rafalko, Frank J., ed., *A Counterintelligence Reader*, volume I: American Revolution to World War I. Washington, DC: Military Bookshop, 2011.

Rausch, George Jay, Jr., "Victoriano Huerta: A Political Biography," PhD dissertation, University of Illinois, 1960.

Reiling, Johannes, *Deutschland, Safe for Democracy?* Stuttgart: Franz Steiner Verlag, 1997.

Rintelen von Kleist, Franz, *The Dark Invader: Wartime Reminiscences of a German Naval Intelligence Officer*. London: Lovat Dickson Ltd, 1933.

_____, *The Return of the Dark Invader*. London: Peter Davies Ltd, 1935.

Robenault, James D., *The Harding Affair: Love and Espionage during the Great War*. New York: St. Martin's Press, 2009.

Roberts, Marcia, *Moments in History: Department of Treasury United States Secret Service*. Washington, DC: PU Books, 1990.

Salinas Carranza, Alberto, *La Expedición Punitiva*. México, DF: Ediciones Botas, 1936.

Scott, Hugh L., *Some Memories of a Soldier*. New York: Century Company, 1928.

Scull Guy H., *Lassoing Wild Animals in Africa*. New York: Frederick A. Stokes, 1911.

Seymour, Charles, ed., *The Intimate Papers of Colonel House*. 2 vols. Boston, New York: Houghton Mifflin, 1926-1928.

Simon, Jeffrey D., *The Bulldog Detective: William J. Flynn and America's First War Against the Mafia, Spies, and Terrorists*. Essex: Prometheus Books, 2024.

Smith, Cornelius C., Jr., *Emilio Kosterlitzky: Eagle of Sonora and the Southwest Border*. Glendale, CA: Arthur H. Clark, 1970.

Soto Hall, Máximo et al., *El "Libro Azul" de Guatemala*. New Orleans: Searcy & Pfaff, 1915.

Stout, Joseph A., Jr., *Border Conflict: Villistas, Carranzistas, and the Punitive Expedition, 1915-1920*. Ft. Worth: Texas Christian University Press, 1999.

Taylor, Lawrence D., *La gran aventura en México: El papel de los voluntarios extranjeros en los ejércitos revolucionarios, 1910-1915*. 2 vols. México, D.F.: Consejo Nacional Para la Cultura y las Artes, 1993.

Theoharis, Athan G. with Tony G. Poveda, Susan Rosenfeld, and Richard Gid Powers, *The FBI: A Comprehensive Reference Guide From J. Edgar Hoover to The X-Files*. New York: Checkmark Books, 2000.

Tompkins, Frank, *Chasing Villa: The Last Campaign of the U.S. Cavalry*. 2nd ed. Silver City, NM: High-Lonesome Books, 1996.

_____, *Chasing Villa: The Story behind the Story of Pershing's Expedition into Mexico*. Harrisburg: The Military Service Publishing Company, 1934.

Tuchman, Barbara, *The Zimmermann Telegram*. New York: MacMillan, 1958.

Tunney, Thomas J. and Paul M. Hollister, *Throttled! The Detection of the German and Anarchist Bomb Plotters*. Boston: Small, Maynard, 1919.

Ulloa, Berta, *Revolución mexicana, 1910-1920. Archivo histórico diplomático mexicano. Guía para la historia diplomática de México, No. 3*. México, DF: Secretaria de Relaciones Exteriores, 1985.

Ungar, Sanford J., *FBI: An Uncensored Look Behind the Walls*. New York: Atlantic-Little, Brown, 1975.

Von der Goltz, Horst, *My Adventures as a German Secret Agent*. New York: McBride and Co., 1917.

Von Feilitzsch, Heribert, *In Plain Sight: Felix A. Sommerfeld, Spymaster in Mexico, 1908-1914*. Amissville: Henselstone Verlag, 2012.

_____, *The Secret War Council: The German Fight Against the Entente in America in 1914*. Amissville: Henselstone Verlag, 2015.

_____, *The Secret War on the United States in 1915: A Tale of Sabotage, Labor Unrest, and Border Troubles*. Amissville: Henselstone Verlag, 2015.

_____, *Felix A. Sommerfeld and the Mexican Front in the Great War*. Amissville: Henselstone Verlag, 2014.

Von Feilitzsch, Heribert and Harris, Charles H., III, *The federal Bureau of Investigation before Hoover, Volume 1: The fBI and Mexican Revolutionists, 1908-1914*. Amissville: Henselstone Verlag LLC, 2023.

Voska, Emanuel, and Irwin, Will, *Spy and Counter-Spy*. London: George G. Harrap and Co., Ltd, 1941.

Weber, Ralph E., *The Final Memoranda: Major General Ralph H. Van Deman, USA Ret., 1865-1952: Father of U.S. Military Intelligence*. Wilmington: Scholarly Resources, 1988.

Welsome, Eileen, *The General and the Jaguar: Pershing's Hunt for Pancho Villa, a True Story of Revolution and Revenge*. Lincoln: University of Nebraska Press, 2006.

Whitcover, Jules, *Sabotage at Black Tom Island*. Chapel Hill: Algonquin Books, 1989.

Whitehead, Don, *The FBI Story: A Report to the People*. New York: Random House, 1956.

Articles

Baecker, Thomas "The Arms of the *Ypiranga*: The German Side," *The Americas*, 30, no. 1 (July 1973), 1-17.

Blaisdell, Lowell L., "Harry Chandler and Mexican Border Intrigue, 1914-1917," *Pacific Historical Review*, 35, no. 4 (November 1966), 385-393.

Briscoe, Edward Eugene, "Pershing's Chinese Refugees in Texas," *Southwestern Historical Quarterly*, 62, no. 4 (April 1959), 467-488.

Cumberland, Charles C., "Mexican Revolutionary Movements From Texas, 1906-1912," *Southwestern Historical Quarterly*, 52 (January 1949), 301-324.

Curtis, Roy Emerson, "The Law of Hostile Military Expeditions as Applied by the United States," *The American Journal of International Law*, 8, (January 1914), 1-37.

Fox, John R. Jr., "Bureaucratic Wrangling over Counterintelligence, 1917-1918." *Studies in Intelligence*, volume 49, No. 1 (2005).

_____ "The Birth of the Federal Bureau of Investigation," Federal Bureau of Investigation website, July 2003 (www.fbi.gov/ history/history-publications-reports/the-birth-of-the-federal-bureau-of-investigation.)

Grams, Grant W., "Karl Respa and German Espionage in Canada during World War One," *Journal of Military and Strategic Studies*, 8, no. 1 (Fall 2005), 1-17.

Harris, Charles H. III and Louis R. Sadler., "The 1911 Reyes Conspiracy: The Texas Side," *Southwestern Historical Quarterly*, 83, no. 4 (April 1980), 325-348.

_____, "Pancho Villa and the Columbus Raid: The Missing Documents," *New Mexico Historical Review*, 50, no. 4 (October 1975), 335-346.

_____ "The Underside of the Mexican Revolution: El Paso 1912," *The Americas*, 39, No. 1 (July 1982), 69-83.

Kahle, Louis G., "Robert Lansing and the Recognition of Venustiano Carranza," *Hispanic American Historical Review*, 38, no. 3 (August 1958), 353-372.

Katz, Friedrich, "Pancho Villa and the Attack on Columbus, New Mexico," *American Historical Review*, 83, no. 1 (February 1978), 101-130.

Meyer, Michael C., "The Mexican-German Conspiracy of 1915," *The Americas*, 23, no. 1 (July 1966), 76-89.

_____, "The Arms of the *Ypiranga*," *Hispanic American Historical Review*, 50, no. 3 (August 1970), 543-556.

_____, "Villa, Sommerfeld, Columbus y los Alemanes," *Historia Mexicana*, Vol. 28, No. 4 (April – June 1979), 546-566.

Munch, Francis J., "Villa's Columbus Raid: Practical Politics or German Design?" *New Mexico Historical Review*, 44 (July 1969), 189-214.

Niemeyer E. V., Jr., "Frustrated Invasion: The Revolutionary Attempt of General Bernardo Reyes from San Antonio in 1911," *Southwestern Historical Quarterly*, 67, no. 2 (1963), 213-225.

Paxman, Andrew, "The Rise and Fall of Leon Rasst, the Jewish-Russian Merchant of Puebla," unpublished paper, May 1, 2017.

Peters, Gerhard and John T. Woolley, Woodrow Wilson, Proclamation 1263 — Concerning the Shipment of Arms into Mexico Online by, *The American Presidency Project* (https://www.presidency.ucsb.edu/node/317582, viewed June 2022).

Rausch, George J., Jr., "The Exile and Death of Victoriano Huerta," *Hispanic American Historical Review*, 42, no. 2 (May 1962), 133-151.

Smith, Michael M., "The Mexican Secret Service in the United States, 1910-1920," *The Americas*, 59, no. 1 (July 2002), 65-85.

Stone, Michael, "The Fall Committee and Double Agent Jones," *Southern New Mexico Historical Review*, 6, no. 1 (January 1999), 45-49.

Taylor Hansen, Lawrence Douglas, "Los Orígenes de la Fuerza Aérea Mexicana, 1913-1915," *Historia Mexicana*, 56, no. 1 (July-September 2006), 175-230.

Vigil, Ralph H., "Revolution and Confusion: The Peculiar Case of José Inés Salazar," *New Mexico Historical Review*, 53, no. 2 (April 1978), 145-170.

Von Feilitzsch, Heribert, "Prelude to the Columbus Raid of 1916: The Battle of Naco," *Journal of the Southwest*, 64, No 3 (Autumn 2022), 473-494.

_____, "The Real Wolf of Wall Street," *FCH Annals*, 23 (June 2016), 25-38.

_____, "Leon J. Canova and Pancho Villa's Columbus Raid of 1916," *FCH Annals*, 25 (June 2019), 9-22.

_____, "The German Sabotage Campaign of 1915/16 revisited," *FCH Annals*, 26 (June 2020), 1-16.

_____, "Questionable Loyalty: Frederico Stallforth and the Mixed Claims Commission," *FCH Annals*, 27 (January 2021), 17-26.

_____, "The Canadian Parliament Fire of 1916: A Severely Flawed Investigation," *FCH Annals*, 28 (January 2022), 61-74.

Von Feilitzsch, Heribert and Harris, Charles H., III, "An Early Influence Operation: The Albert Briefcase Affair: A 100-Year Cover-Up of a British Propaganda Coup." *Studies in Intelligence*, volume 68, No. 1 (March 2024).

Wittenberg, Ernest, "The Thrifty Spy on the Sixth Avenue EL." *American Heritage* (August 1965).

Newspapers

Albuquerque Morning Journal
Arizona Oasis
Arizona Republican
Atlanta Georgian
Atlanta Journal
Audubon County Journal
Baltimore Evening Star
Baltimore Sun
Bennington Evening Banner
Billings Gazette
Bisbee Daily Review
Bismarck Daily Tribune
Breckenridge News
Bridgeport Evening Farmer
Brownsville Daily Herald
Buffalo Evening News
Commoner
Crónica
Daily Missoulian
Daily Press
Daily Sentinel
Day Book
Daily Yellowstone Journal
Der Deutsche Korrespondent
Detroit Times
Detroiter Abend-Post
East Oregonian
El Paso Daily Herald
El Paso Herald
El Paso Morning Times
Evening Independent
Evening Standard
Fatherland
Fresno Bee
Garland Globe
Guthrie Daily Leader
Hartford Courant
Honolulu Star-Bulletin
Hopkinsville Kentuckian
Imperial Valley Press
Jersey City News
La Prensa
Laremie Republican
Las Vegas Optic
Lewiston Evening Teller
Los Angeles Herald
Maryland Suffrage News
Minneapolis Journal
Monett Times
National Tribune
New Britain Herald
New York Evening Sun
New York Evening Telegram
New York Evening World
New York Sun
New York Times
New York Tribune
New York World
Nogales Daily Herald
Oasis
Ogden Standard
Olean Evening Herald
Omaha Daily Bee
Owosso Times
Palestine Daily Herald
Parma Herald
Pensacola Journal
Philadelphia Bulletin
Pine Bluff Daily Graphic
Producers News
Providence Journal
Public Ledger
Richmond Virginian
Rocky Mountain News
Sacramento Daily Union
San Antonio Light

San Antonio Express
San Bernardino County Sun
San Francisco Call and Post
San Francisco Chronicle
San Francisco Examiner
San Miguel Examiner
Santa Fe New Mexican
Saratoga Sun
Seattle Star
South Bend News-Times
St Landry Clarion
Syracuse Herald
Tabor Independent
Tacoma Times
The Copper Era and Morenci Leader
Topeka State Journal
Toronto Star

Trenton Evening Times
Tulsa Daily World
Valdez Daily Prospector
Vinita Daily Chieftain
Wall Street Journal
Walsenburg World
Washington Evening Star
Washington Herald
Washington Post
Washington Times
Waterbury Evening Democrat
Watertown Daily Times
Weekly Journal-Miner
Wheeling Daily Intelligencer
White Pine News
Weekly Mining Review

INDEX

A

A. Baldwin & Company 185, 186
Aberdeen Hotel 290
Abraham and Company 211
Abraham, Pedro...... 100, 118, 127, 211, 212, 229, 405
Abteilung IIIb, see Imperial General Staff
Acapulco, City of 54, 57
Adams, Albert Garfield 32, 33, 34, 35, 58, 59, 60, 61, 211, 304, 352, 356, 360, 370, 381, 382, 393, 395
Aero Club of America 213
Aetna, see E.I. DuPont, Aetna Smokeless Powder Division
AFL, see also American Federation of Labor 139, 149
Ahearn, Morris J...............................58
Albert, Heinrich Friedrich .... vii, 5, 6, 9, 14, 20, 21, 23, 31, 32, 48, 49, 57, 58, 64, 74, 76, 77, 79, 87, 108, 110, 116, 133, 144, 148, 149, 153-165, 167-175, 182, 190, 201, 202, 208, 247, 266, 284, 286, 287, 302, 304, 311, 324, 338, 340, 345, 348, 349-352, 355, 356, 357, 370, 371, 372, 374, 393, 396-398, 399-401, 403, 404, 412
Albert, Ida .... vii, 5, 6, 9, 14, 20, 21, 23, 31, 32, 48, 49, 57, 58, 64, 74, 76, 77, 79, 87, 108, 110, 116, 133, 144, 148, 149, 153-162, 164, 165, 167-175, 182, 190, 201, 202, 208, 247, 266, 284, 286, 287, 302, 304, 311, 324, 338, 340, 345, 348-352, 355-357, 370-372, 374, 393, 396-401, 403, 404, 412

Alcazar Theater 123
Alcolea, Leandro, see Alcolea, Leonardo
Alcolea, Leonardo .. 295, 296, 300, 307, 320, 326, 330, 331, 332
Alcolea, Rafael 295, 296, 300, 307, 320, 326, 330-332
Alderete brothers, see Alderete, Ike, and Alderete, Frank
Alderete, Frank................... 107, 123, 129
Alderete, Ike 107, 123, 129
Alexandria, SS 16, 350
Alfonso XII, SS 285
Alien Property Custodian . 43, 349, 350, 354, 356, 374, 403
Allen, Arthur M.199, 209, 234, 347, 355, 380, 381
Alpine, Town of............................. 236
Alsace-Lorraine, State of.................... 29
Alton, City of 182, 201, 223, 228, 380
Alvarado, Pedro 178
Alvarado, Salvador 227, 305, 311
Alvarado, SS .... 210American Bank Note Company 117, 118, 124, 294, 366
American Federation of Labor....... 135, 137
American National Bank 52
American Protective League 346
American Smelting and Refining Company 239
American Truth Society 133
Annie Larsen, Schooner. ...52, 54, 57, 58, 66, 67, 70, 157
Ansonia Hotel 114, 247, 298, 336
Anti-Trust League 134, 135
Appenrade, City of 16
Archibald, James 170, 174, 175, 345

415

Arenas, I. 209, 210
Argüello, M. Robelo 193
Arizona Republican . 298, 392, 394, 395, 413
Armada, Canadian 37, 39
Armstrong, John J., Dr. 274
Arozarena, Rafael 323
Arredondo, Eliseo 253, 378
Arriola, Jesús María 252, 253, 254, 321
Arsenault, Mark 10, 348, 349, 401, 405
ASARCO, see American Smelting and Refining Company
Associated Press 110, 127, 222, 318
Astor Hotel 148, 174, 181
Astoria, BC, City of 11
Atlanta, SS 24, 46, 85, 91, 151, 210, 378, 394, 413
Atlas Line, see Atlas Shipping Line 79
Atlas Shipping Line 79
Aucher, John, see Adams, Albert Garfield 32, 33, 34, 35
Austin, City of .. 122, 356, 377, 380, 404, 406
Austro-Hungarian Empire 8
Auswärtiges Amt ... 5, 20, 30, 37, 38, 69, 285, 351, 352, 358, 372, 392, 404
AVLIS, see Silva, Dário

B

Baja California 51, 54, 179, 266, 274, 406
Baker, Joseph A 33, 35, 61, 62, 63, 91, 157, 230, 264, 326, 357, 360, 362, 363, 366, 372, 398
Baker, William, see also Rosas, Guillermo.... 33, 35, 61-63, 91, 157, 230, 264, 326, 357, 360, 362, 363, 366, 372, 398
Baldwin Locomotive Company 71
Baley, Lewis J 191, 379
Balinger, Harry, see Berliner, Harry
Ballesteros, Indalecio 105
Ballin, Albert 14, 31
Baltimore, City of 15, 26, 27, 28, 29, 30, 34, 39, 41, 42, 82, 85, 140, 144, 145, 147-149, 210, 229-231, 301, 315, 344, 347, 350, 370, 385, 409, 413
Baltimore Country Club 148
Bangor, City of 43, 44, 350

Banville, P. 300
Barkey, A. L. 211, 366, 368, 376, 377, 382, 383, 395
Barnard, Melville, C. 140, 144
Barnes, Robert E. Lee ....
 v, 56, 104, 105, 118-121, 124, 128, 131, 178, 180, 206, 207, 211, 212, 216, 222, 226, 227, 233, 236, 240, 242-245, 248, 249, 250, 252, 253, 255, 256, 257, 261, 275-278, 299, 317, 319, 320, 321, 330, 331, 333-336, 356, 363-368, 376, 377, 380-382, 384-388, 390, 391, 394-400
Barnitz, George 85
Barrett, Irene, see Wilkie, Lydia Frances
Barth, Henry 89, 90
Basail, Rodolfo 300, 332, 333
Batavia, SS 37
Battle of Naco, 1914 .... 376, 412
Bayer Corporation, see Bayer and Company 76
Becker, Ernst 90, 362
Beckham, Clifford Godwin 105-108, 118-129, 180, 192, 208, 236, 264, 299, 330, 332, 336, 364, 366, 367, 377, 378, 381, 385, 389, 395, 399
Bege, J. B., see Barnes, Robert E. Lee
Belgium, Country of 9, 74, 358
Bell, George H. 226, 227, 243, 250
Beltrán, Teódulo R 105, 125
Benham, William R 140, 144, 358, 364, 368-371, 400
Bennett, William S. 308, 349
Bergensfjord, SS 35
Berlin, City of 19, 26, 29, 40, 55, 59, 66, 69, 72-76, 115, 132, 135, 140-143, 151, 170, 285, 294, 297, 311, 351, 358, 368, 393, 404, 406, 408
Berliner, Harry ... 97-99, 184, 185, 222, 245, 246, 248, 249, 288, 291-295, 300, 303, 304, 314, 321-325, 363, 366, 368, 377, 378, 383, 385, 387, 393-396, 398, 399, 404
Berliner y Baldwin, Harry, see Berliner, Harry
Bernstorff, Johann Heinrich Count von ...5, 9, 21, 23, 30, 31, 39, 47, 54, 62, 64, 65,

74, 148, 150, 154, 155, 159, 163, 167, 336, 351, 352, 355-357, 359, 365, 372, 375, 405, 406
Bielaski, Alexander Bruce xii, xiii, 12, 22, 23, 28, 29, 32, 34, 43-46, 50, 51, 57, 59, 64, 66, 85, 87, 88, 91-94, 95, 97, 99, 102, 105, 108, 118, 121-124, 131, 139, 140, 142-144, 146, 147, 149, 151, 163, 170, 171, 182, 185, 187-191, 193-195, 198, 213, 215, 219, 220, 222-228, 230, 232, 233, 240, 243-245, 248, 249, 250, 254, 255, 256, 258, 261-263, 265, 267, 283, 286, 288, 291, 293-296, 299, 300, 303-305, 312, 314, 318-322, 324-329, 331-336, 342, 344, 347, 349, 354-370, 373, 375-381, 383-389, 392, 394-400
Big Bend region 232
Bigelow, M. O. 241-243, 271, 273, 275
Bisbee, Town of . 234, 235, 241, 242, 271, 413
Bisher, Jamie 271, 350, 374, 390, 405
Black Tom Island, 1916 Explosion of . vi, xii, 15, 20, 42, 73, 82, 145, 314, 340, 343, 410
Blanford, Ely Murray ....
    51, 57, 66, 67, 234, 250, 267, 270, 319, 355, 356, 358, 367, 368, 376, 381, 383-385, 388-390, 393, 397
Blanquet, Aureliano 117, 140, 283, 284, 289, 291-294, 300, 311, 312, 313, 326, 327, 394
Bliss, Tasker H. ... 106, 120-123, 125-128, 131, 225, 226
Blum, Henry 323, 370, 406
Bode, Eno 79, 80, 87, 90, 148, 149
Boehm, Hans Walter Luigi ... 26, 29, 30, 47, 50, 65, 145, 149, 355, 358
Boghardt, Thomas ... 338, 339, 393, 400, 406
Bohemian National Alliance 7, 169, 348
Bohemia, State of 8
Bohm, Ernest 135, 137, 149
Bonales Sandoval, José 288
Bonaparte, Charles J. ix
Bonney, W. Leonard 213, 214
Bopp, Franz 53, 67
Borrego, Ignacio 319

Boston, City of 6, 44, 46, 67, 83, 125, 142, 166-168, 347, 370, 373, 374, 378, 408, 410
Bowen, Juan Bernardo .. 51, 52, 66, 345, 374, 401, 406
Bowen, Walter S. 51, 52, 66, 345, 374, 401, 406
Boxer Rebellion 3, 29
Boy-Ed, Karl ...... 1, 3, 4, 7, 13-16, 18-24, 47, 73-76, 82, 108, 110, 111, 116, 117, 132, 137, 140, 144, 154, 167, 174, 348, -351, 354, 359, 360, 374, 406
Bradford, S. P. 322, 398
Brandenburg, SS 16
Bravo, Ignacio R. 104, 366
Breceda, Alfredo 261, 262, 385
Breniman, Charles Edward 179, 208, 228, 234, 240, 242, 243, 254, 261, 271, 272, 274, 275, 321, 334, 367, 368, 376, 381-386, 389-392, 398
Bridgeport, City of ....
    59, 74, 136, 137-139, 143, 149, 154, 158, 183, 286, 354, 372, 398, 399, 413
Bridgeport Manufacturing Company ... 136
Bridgeport Projectile Company . 59, 74, 149, 154, 183, 286, 372, 398, 399
Bridgeport Strike, *see* Great Bridgeport Strike, 1915
Brincken, Wilhelm 53, 67
British Honduras, Country of 13, 305
Brooklyn Bridge 70
Brophy, Hatty E. 141, 143, 241, 369
Brophy, W. H. 141, 143, 241, 369
Brown, Lawrence M. . 154, 213, 350, 370, 378, 406, 408, 409, 410
Brownsville, City of ... 125, 178, 179, 212-215, 233, 238, 256-258, 264, 278, 299, 312, 313, 320, 382, 404, 413
Bruchhausen, Peter 111, 112
Brussels, City of 8, 283
Bryant, Edward 130
Bryan, William Jennings ... 133, 135, 136, 153, 154, 162, 166, 172, 216, 341, 378, 406
Buchanan, Frank 135, 138-140, 143, 149, 150

417

Buenz, Carl, *see* Bünz, Karl Gottlieb
Buffalo, Town of 65, 107, 166, 374, 413
Bulnes, Francisco 223-225, 267, 384, 389
Bulnes, Mario .. 223, 224, 225, 267, 384, 389
Bünz, Karl Gottlieb 14, 19, 24
Bureau of Investigation, German...vii, ix, xi, xiii, 6, 23, 40, 41, 94, 126, 136, 157, 160, 162, 163, 165, 166, 169, 186, 187, 188, 220, 253, 340, 347, 353, 357, 359, 373, 376, 400, 401, 403, 405, 410, 411
Bureau of Secret Intelligence...46, 119, 144, 149, 256, 345
Burgess, John 10
Burke, Frank C. 84, 153, 156, 159-162, 164-169, 173, 354, 373-375, 400, 401
Burns Agency, *see also* William J. Burns International Detective Agency...22, 360
Burns Detective Agency, *see also* William J. Burns International Detective Agency 20, 22, 87, 138, 228, 296
Burns, Juan T. 6, 7, 12, 20, 22, 23, 87, 137, 138, 154, 178, 216, 228, 296, 321, 322, 334, 347, 360, 361, 376, 398
Burns, Waller T. 6, 7, 12, 20, 22, 23, 87, 137, 138, 154, 178, 216, 228, 296, 321, 322, 334, 347, 360, 361, 376, 398
Burns, William J. 6, 7, 12, 20, 22, 23, 87, 137, 138, 154, 178, 216, 228, 296, 321, 322, 334, 347, 360, 361, 376, 398
Busby, George 87, 90, 91
Bustamante, Demetrio 300, 308, 377

C

Caballero, Cristoforo 130, 367, 397, 406
Caballo, León, *see also* Garza, Agustín S .. 215
Cabrera, Luís .. 183, 189, 197, 289, 294, 295, 300, 302, 322
Calais, Maine, City of 45
Calatoire's Restaurant 318
Calexico, City of 57
Cal Hirsch & Sons Iron & Metal Company .. 179

Calles, Plutarco Elías 109, 177, 200, 205, 206, 208, 213, 242, 269, 270, 271, 272, 273
Calvert, George 154
Canada, Country of .... xiii, 13, 37, 39, 42, 44, 46, 47, 49, 50, 55, 67, 69, 165, 271, 292, 314, 342, 374, 411
Canadian Pacific Railway 43
Canadian Parliament, Ottawa 355, 412
Canova, Leon .. 114, 190, 219, 303, 304, 305, 378, 396, 412
Cantrell, Louis Means 35, 92, 93, 94, 102, 103, 113, 117, 118, 125, 141, 143, 157, 198, 228, 229, 263, 283, 286, 290, 295, 300, 301, 306, 308, 314, 326, 362-370, 380-383, 385, 392-394, 396, 397, 399
Cantú, Esteban ... vii, 51, 179, 219, 264, 266, 274
Cantú Lara, Francisco 264
Cape Trafalgar, SMS 14
Caracristi, Anne Zeilinger 246, 247, 248
Caracristi, Charles Francis Louis Zeilinger . 246, 247, 248
Cárdenas, Tomás 185, 186, 191, 195
Carnegie Hall 135, 136
Carothers, George C. 243, 301, 392, 396
Carranza, Venustiano .... xiii, 51, 54, 97, 98, 105, 111, 118, 121, 124, 130, 131, 141, 177-180, 183-185, 189-198, 201-203, 205-213, 215-223, 225, 227, 228, 230, 231, 241, 242, 250, 252-255, 257-259, 262, 264-267, 269, 273, 274, 278, 279, 283-287, 289, 291, 292, 294, 295, 298, 301-303, 305, 308-311, 313, 314, 317, 318, 320-324, 326, 329, 331, 334, 337, 343, 383-385, 392, 396, 409, 411
Carrizal, Village of 258
Casement, Roger, Sir ... 65, 69, 354, 355, 357, 358, 406
Cassard, Jules 318
Castillo Corzo, Teófilo 193, 197
Catholic Church 286, 287, 296, 298, 300-302, 396, 409

418

Catholic Party, Mexico...73, 281, 283, 296, 306
Caturegli, Alredo, Dr. 60, 322
Cauz, Eduardo M. 104, 105, 366
Central Federated Union 135
Central Intelligence Agency....162, 357, 408
Central Park, New York 81, 167
Central Powers 1, 7, 25
Centurion, HMS............................2, 377
Centurión, Manuel 183
Cerna, Antonio........................ 272, 391
Chakraberty, Chandra, Dr......53, 64, 67, 355
Chalmers, Nils... 94, 103, 230, 293, 329, 363, 385, 394, 399
Chamberlain, William C. 238
Chandra, Ram............................ 53, 68
Chapa, Francisco A..................... 299, 395
Chapultepec, Castle of 129, 261
Chapultepec, Military Academy.... 129, 261
Charleston, SC, City of...................... 92
Chastain, Sion Edward191, 192, 193, 378, 379
Chattilon, Charles Raoul 30, 352
Chavarría, Nicolás........................... 130
Chavez, Francisco........................... 130
Chesapeake Western Railway 298
Chiapas, State of 183, 185, 186, 190, 192-194, 197, 227, 286, 289, 295, 297, 306, 308, 309, 313, 327, 328, 331
Chicago, City of............................... 8, 11, 26, 29, 49, 57, 67, 69, 138, 140, 149, 212, 226, 286, 296, 307, 308, 325, 326, 327, 328, 331, 348, 405, 408
Chihuahua, City of..........................26, 37, 39, 116, 121, 182, 193, 203, 210, 217, 219-221, 225, 242, 249, 250-253, 272, 275, 278, 279, 294, 301, 318, 405
Chihuahua, State of 26, 37, 39, 116, 121, 182, 193, 203, 210, 217, 219-221, 225, 242, 249, 250-253, 272, 275, 278, 279, 294, 301, 318, 405
Childers, H. H. 100, 363
Chocano, José Santos...... 183, 184, 197, 301
Church Bros. of Tiffany 86
CIA, *see* Central Intelligence Agency
Cisneros, Juan 239, 240, 256, 275, 391
City of Tampico, SS 213
Ciudad Juárez, City of ... 107, 108, 181, 183, 191, 193, 202, 203, 222, 249, 274
Ciudad Victoria, City of 215, 256
Clabaugh, H. C..........................149, 377
Clan na Gael............................64, 65
Clifton, Arizona, Town of................. 283
Coahuila, State of.......................... 117
Coaster, SS 208
Cobb, Frank I... 119, 120, 129, 155, 156, 157, 179, 222, 226, 323, 366, 383, 406
Cobb, Zach Lamar ... 119, 120, 129, 155, 156, 157, 179, 222, 226, 323, 366, 383, 406
Cohalan, Daniel F. 65, 66
Colegio Militar 281
Cole, Jay Herbert............................. 49
Columbia Law School...................... 30
Columbia University School of Medicine... 274
Columbus, New Mexico, Town of........ xii, 130, 207, 211, 221-223, 225, 226, 245, 249, 257, 279, 285, 287, 292, 297, 311, 318, 338, 340, 343, 376, 383, 393, 411, 412
Columbus Raid, 1916 by Villistas .. 376, 383, 411, 412
Comings, Henry 324
Comisión Reguladora del Mercado de Henequén.............................. 305
Comstock, Captain 277, 278
Conners, James E., *see* Conners, Maurice D.
Conners, Maurice D. 80, 81, 82, 212, 213
Conners, Wilhelm J., *see* Conners, Maurice D.
Consolidated Rolling Mills Company, *see also* Consolidated Rolling Mills & Foundries Company 227
Consolidated Rolling Mills & Foundries Company 261
Continental Guano Works 77
Convention government 177
Cooper, John Milton 339, 373, 407
Corn Exchange Bank 103
Cornish, Town of 166, 217, 374
Coronado, Alfonso 206, 269
Corrigan, John Patrick 34

419

Cortés, Pedro 199, 305-309, 311, 325
Covani, Constante 61
Crawford, R. E................................ 127
CRESSE, see also Jones, Charles Eugene .....
  188, 189, 220, 294, 299, 304-307, 312,
  325, 395, 396, 399
Cuesta, Eduardo 299
Cummings, Matthew...................... 142
Customs Neutrality Squad 84, 360

D

Dardano, Carlos F., Dr. 312, 313
Dark Invader, see also Rintelen, Franz
  Dagobert Johannes 73,
  116, 362, 365, 368, 409
Dávalos, Enrique G., see Dusart Quintana,
  Felipe, Dr.
Dávalos, Felipe, see also Dusart Quintana,
  Felipe, Dr........................ 194, 197
Davis, Arthur W............. 185, 378, 379, 381
Dayal, Har 52
De Berri, Camille 66
Decena Trágica............ 249, 282, 288, 394
Deiches, Maurice 32, 34, 35
De la Garza, Emeterio 117, 202
De la Garza, Lázaro....................117, 202
DELAG, see also Fuentes, Salvador A. 103-
  105, 208
De la Rosa, Luís....................... 215, 256
Delgado, Fred .. 100, 104, 131, 208, 366, 367
Delgado, José... 100, 104, 131, 208, 366, 367
Del Villar, Pedro......293, 308, 310, 336, 394,
  399
DeNegri, Ramón P. 51, 209
Denham, G. C. 66, 67
Der Deutsche Korrespondent.. 229, 385, 413
Derna, SS... 2
Dernburg, Bernhard....5, 10, 109, 112, 113,
  133, 174, 175, 364
De Soto Hotel 212, 330
Detroit Hotel.............................. 248
Deutsche Bank, Berlin 116, 142, 155
Deutsche Bank, Havana 116, 142, 155
Deutscher Flottenverein 75
Deutscher Verein, New York.......... 73, 148

Deutschland, SMS....3, 145, 350, 353-356, 365,
  370, 390, 405, 408, 409
Deutschland, U 3, 145, 350, 353, 354, 356,
  365, 370, 390, 405, 408, 409
Deutz Bros. Hardware Company......... 212
Devlin, E. C........... 300, 339, 387, 388, 396
Devlin, Patrick 300, 339, 387, 388, 396
Devon City, SS...............................72
Devoy, John 38, 64, 65, 358
Díaz, Félix 131, 140,
  184, 191, 195, 197, 220, 221, 230, 240,
  247, 249, 281-284, 286-290, 292-301,
  303-314, 318-320, 322, 323, 326-333, 336,
  343, 378, 379, 384, 392-397, 399, 408
Díaz, I. J....131, 140, 184, 191, 195, 197, 220,
  221, 230, 240, 247, 249, 281-290, 292-
  301, 303-314, 318-320, 322, 323, 326-333,
  336, 343, 378, 379, 384, 392-397, 399,
  408
Díaz Lombardo, Miguel .. 319, 320, 378, 384
Díaz Mori, Félix............................ 281
Díaz, Porfirio........................... 131, 140,
  184, 191, 195, 197, 220, 221, 230, 240,
  247, 249, 281-284, 286-290, 292-301,
  303-314, 318-320, 322, 323, 326-333, 336,
  343, 378, 379, 384, 392-397, 399, 408
Díaz, Ramón 131, 140,
  184, 191, 195, 197, 220, 221, 230, 240,
  247, 249, 281-284, 286-290, 292-301,
  303-314, 318-320, 322, 323, 326-333, 336,
  343, 378, 379, 384, 392-397, 399, 408
Die Wacht am Rhein 25, 351
Dilger, Anton Dr................. 145, 149, 370
Dinkins, Lin................................. 194
División del Norte 37, 380
Division of the North, see also División del
  Norte 177, 182, 201, 202, 220
Division of the Southwest 183, 185
Djember, SS......................... 57, 58, 59
Donald MacLeod and Company, see also
  Rice, Melvin A. 74
Donington Hall............................. 142
Dotzert, Henry.......... 88, 91, 143, 361, 362
Dougherty, George S................ 141, 160
Dougherty, Harry 141, 160

420

Douglas, Charles A. 141, 142, 199, 205, 206, 208, 213, 216, 222, 234, 241, 242, 253, 258, 272, 273, 275, 312, 313, 369, 380, 404, 412
Douglas Hardware Company............. 205
Dreben, Sam 180, 245
Dresden, SMS 13, 20, 117
Dresdner Bank 29
Dubose, Deputy Marshal................. 127
Dunn, H. H. 295, 296, 300
Dupont, Carney's Point 71, 74, 158, 361
Dupont, Hopewell 71, 74, 158, 361
Dupont, *see* E. I. DuPont de Nemours and Company
Durango, State of........................... 140
Dusart Quintana, Felipe, Dr. ...92, 189, 190, 192, 286, 326, 327, 328
Dutch East Borneo 57
Dutch West Indies 94
Dyo, Tsutomo............................. 251

E

Eagle Pass, Town of .218, 227, 236, 237, 249, 254, 255, 258, 276, 277, 278
Eastern Forwarding Company 145
Eastern Hotel, New York................... 22
Easter Rising, 1916 Irish 26, 64, 65, 68, 70, 355, 357, 358, 406
Eber, gunboat.............................. 14
Echegaray, Carlos Herminio... 243, 271, 272
Echegaray, Juan 243, 271, 272
Edison, Thomas...................95, 158, 363
E. I. DuPont de Nemours and Company. 71, 74, 158, 361
Eleanor, SMS 14
Elías, Arturo M. 60, 109, 177, 200, 205, 206, 210-212, 241, 265, 269, 271, 312
Elías, Francisco "Pancho" S..... 60, 109, 177, 200, 205, 206, 210-212, 241, 265, 269, 271, 312
Eliseo, Guillermo, *see* Ellis, William Henry
Elks Lodge, No. 1, New York 32
Ellis Island 72, 145, 336
Ellis, William Henry . 72, 145, 300, 336, 395, 408

El Norte, SS......................................56
El Paso, City of...49, 104-108, 118-132, 177-181, 183, 193, 194, 196, 197, 200, 203, 206-209, 211, 220-222, 226, 229, 235, 236, 243-246, 248-255, 258, 266, 272, 273, 293, 309, 323, 364, 366, 377, 380, 381, 387-389, 404, 406-408, 411, 413
El Paso Herald.......... 128, 180, 377, 387, 413
El Paso Morning Times 128, 380, 413
Emden, SMS................................. 14
Emerson, Robert, Dr. 37, 347, 353, 411
Empire Trust Company 212
Enrile Villatoro, Gonzalo Carlos 283
Equitable Powder Manufacturing Company 182
Eron, Charles A. 125, 131
Escandón, Francisco 131, 132, 367
Espionage Act, 1917 340
Esquer, Joaquín...................... 206, 207
Esrom, SS...........................88, 360, 361
Esteban León, *see also* Del Villar, Pedro . 306, 311
Estrada Cabrera, Manuel 183, 197, 289, 295, 300, 302
Estrada, Duke . 183, 189, 197, 289, 295, 300, 302, 323
Etappendienst of the German Navy 368, 409
E.V. Gibbons Company 133
Expeditionary Force, Canadian 40, 353
Expedition, *see* Punitive Expedition, 1916.. 225-227, 232, 251, 255, 257-259, 271, 272, 278, 279, 287, 301, 303, 311, 318, 320, 343, 383, 384, 409, 410

F

Fabyan, George 231
Falkland Islands, 1914 Battle of 19
Falmouth, City of 40, 59, 61, 170, 354
Farnsworth, Charles Stewart............. 245
Fay, Robert 83, 84, 85, 343, 360
FBI, *see also* Federal Bureau of Investigaton vii, ix, x, 164, 165, 344, 345, 347, 368, 373, 374, 388, 400, 401, 405, 407-410

Federal Bureau of Investigation ..... ix, 400, 403, 405, 411
Feinberg, Vera 266, 267
Finch, Stanley W. ....ix, 347
Fisher, W. H. 205
Fletcher, Lloyd 235, 387, 400
Flores, Adeodato.... 193, 194, 405, 406, 408
Flottenverein, see Deutscher Flottenverein
Flowers, William, Jr., see Rosas, Guillermo
Flynn, Thomas A. .. 84, 85, 91, 92, 112, 142, 143, 153, 156, 159-168, 171-173, 207, 345, 347, 360, 365, 368, 369, 372-375, 381, 400, 401, 407, 410
Flynn, William J. ... 84, 85, 91, 92, 112, 142, 143, 153, 156, 159-168, 171-173, 207, 345, 347, 360, 365, 368, 369, 372-375, 381, 400, 401, 407, 410
Folsom, A. T. S......................... 178, 180
Folsom, C. S. T.......................... 178, 180
Foreign Office, British ..5, 20, 30, 37, 38, 69, 285, 351, 352, 358, 372, 392, 404
Foreign Office, German, see Auswärtiges Amt
Forest Hills, Town of..... 100, 102, 103, 114, 118, 121
Fort Bliss ... 106, 120, 121, 123, 125-128, 131, 226
Fort Hancock........................... 129, 235
Fort McIntosh................................177
Fort Oglethorpe 149, 324, 340, 398
Fort Sam Houston... 199, 206, 226, 277, 333
Fowler, H. Robert ... 135, 139, 140, 143, 149, 150
Franke, Kuno 10
FRANK, see Tuschiya, Hidekichi
Friedman, William 231
Friedrich der Grosse, SMS............ 80, 89, 90
Friedrich Krupp AG...... 38, 53, 55, 108, 301
Fritzen, Alfred 39, 61, 357
Front Royal, Town of 145
Fuehr, Karl 167
Fuentes, Salvador A. 103, 367
Fuller, Paul 163
Funch, Edye and Company 58
Funston, Frederick 4, 226, 233, 239, 301, 384
Furbershaw, W. L. 308, 397

Fuzita, K. 251

G

Gadski, Johanna, see also Tauscher, Johanna iv, 55, 56
Gadski, Lotte............................iv, 55, 56
GALED, see Rodríguez, Juan
Galt, Edith Bolling 155, 372
Galves, Rafael 323
Galveston, City of 51, 72, 153, 230, 240, 258, 264, 265, 272, 297, 334
Gans Steamship Line....................... 349
Garbade, Ernst Friedrich 90
Garbarino, Frank L. 205, 230, 245, 381, 384, 386, 387, 394
García, Andrés G..... 93, 129, 207, 212, 254, 264
García, Juan. 93, 129, 207, 212, 254, 264, 389
García, Melquíades ... 93, 129, 207, 212, 254, 264
García Menocal, Mario......................93
Garger, Frank............................. 22
Garibay, Antonio 129, 131
Garrett, Alonzo....................ix, 256, 407
Garrison, Lindley M. 216
Garza, Agustín S. 117, 181, 184, 185, 190-192, 195, 201, 202, 215, 292, 356, 377, 378, 380, 404
Garza, Manuel........................... 117, 181, 184, 185, 190-192, 195, 201, 202, 215, 292, 356, 377, 378, 380, 404
Gasché, Victor Emile, see also Rintelen, Franz Dagobert Johannes 72, 73, 141, 369
Gates, Edward Victor, see also Rintelen, Franz Dagobert Johannes ... 133, 140-142, 151
Gaunt, Guy Reginald Archer.......... 2, 3, 6, 7, 9-12, 38, 64, 85, 87, 88, 137, 139, 140, 142, 147, 169, 170, 172, 343, 348, 349, 360, 375, 407
Gavira, Gabriel............................ 222
Gaynor Manufacturing Company 136
Gegory, Thomas Watt 351
Geier, SMS 14, 349
Geneva, Illinois, Town of.................. 231
Georg Luger 55

Gerard, James W. 75, 358
German Club, New York, see Deutscher Verein, New York
German East Asia Detachment............269
German Naval Intelligence, see Etappendienst of the German Navy
Germantown, Town of......................35
German West Africa........................54
Germany's Just Cause 133
Gershon, Dave......... 66, 234, 269, 376, 390
Gibbons, James.....................76, 133, 301
Gilbert, Charles O...........................303
Gill, John....................................139
Gillow, Eulogio 301
Glenn, C. R..................... 220, 232, 302
Glenn Springs, Town of................... 232
Gneisenau, SMS 13
Goltz, Otto, see also Von der Goltz, Horst....
    26-28, 37-42, 50, 59, 60, 144, 340, 345, 351, 353, 354, 404, 410
Gómez Farias, Manuel 197
Gomez, Mateo 105, 124, 125, 278
Gomez Robelo, Ricardo 105, 124, 125
Gompers, Samuel 137-139, 149, 150, 361
González, Arturo... 202, 208, 217, 269, 296, 309, 312, 320, 321, 331, 405
González de la Llave, Guadencio ...296, 309
González, Enrique A. ... 202, 208, 217, 269, 296, 309, 312, 320, 321, 331, 405
González, Pablo 202, 208, 217, 269, 296, 309, 312, 320, 321, 331, 405
González, Pedro.... 202, 208, 217, 269, 296, 309, 312, 320, 321, 331, 405
Gorostieta, Enrique 104, 105, 366, 367
Gothenburg, Sweden, City of... 88, 112, 361
Governor Cobb, SS 322
Grand Central Station, New York 72, 168
Grantwood, Town of....................83, 84
Grave de Peralta, Pedro 300
Gray, Edward, Sir 54, 125, 180, 220
Gray, Henry N. 54, 125, 180, 220
Gray's Harbor, Town of.....................54
Great Bridgeport Strike, 1915 136
Great Northern Hotel 81
Greenwood, Frank, see Garbarino, Frank L.

Grgurevich, John J. 62, 64, 91, 210, 357, 362, 381
Grindon Hall, SS 71
Grinstead, Robert E. 244, 245
Guanajuato, State of 197, 283
Guaranty Trust Company 200, 201
Guatemala, Country of ....
    26, 44, 45, 183, 189-191, 193, 194, 197, 199, 292, 295, 300-303, 305, 308, 309, 313, 323, 325, 331, 332, 396, 406, 410
Guaymas, City of 18, 268, 274
Guerra, Deodoro..................... 104, 178
Guerra, Fernando.................... 104, 178
Guerrero, SS 209, 210, 288
Guillén, Flavio 190
Gunter Hotel 130
Gupta, Haramba L. 53
Guy, Frederick.......... 2, 3, 9-12, 38, 85, 88, 104, 105, 119, 129, 130, 137, 140, 142, 169, 170, 172, 180, 207, 208, 212, 343, 348, 360, 363, 364, 366, 367, 376-379, 381-383, 386, 388, 394, 406, 407, 409

H

Hacienda de Bustillos 221
Hackensack, City of..........................95
Hahn, Ferdinand.............................87
Hale, British Agent 67
Hall, Reginald "Blinker"...23, 38, 40, 52, 65, 71, 133-136, 142, 201, 202, 208, 339, 353, 358, 368, 369, 396, 410
Hall, R. L. 23, 38, 40, 52, 65, 71, 133-136, 142, 201, 202, 208, 339, 353, 358, 368, 369, 396, 410
Hall, Thomas C..............23, 38, 40, 52, 65, 71, 133-136, 142, 201, 202, 208, 339, 353, 358, 368, 369, 396, 410
Hamburg-Amerikanische-Paketfahrt-Aktien-Gesellschaft, see HAPAG
Hamburg, Germany, City of 5, 14, 56, 57, 79, 179, 184, 269, 322, 348, 372
Hammond, Jack, see Hammond, John C.
Hammond, John C... 112, 113, 114, 115, 116, 143, 304, 364, 365
Hansa Haus 15, 41, 82

Hansen, Frederick, see also Rintelen, Franz Dagobert Johannes 76, 112, 113, 133, 142, 148, 412
HAPAG 5, 6, 9, 14, 15, 19-22, 24, 31, 79, 157, 201, 349, 350, 398
Harding, Warren G. 85, 373, 374, 409
Harris, Billups 3, 4, 28, 29, 42, 81, 83, 85, 145, 236, 354, 359, 364, 366, 367, 371, 376, 377, 380-383, 385-389, 391, 400, 407, 410-412
Harris, Hyman 3, 4, 28, 29, 42, 81, 83, 85, 145, 236, 354, 359, 364, 366, 367, 371, 376, 377, 380-383, 385-389, 391, 400, 407, 410, 411, 412
Harrison, Leland. 46, 163, 312, 336, 354, 379, 387, 389, 390, 393, 397, 400, 404
Hart, Harry J. 302
Hartridge School 115
Haulloway, SS 86
Havana, City of 20, 71, 76, 92-94, 97, 116, 131, 132, 185, 192, 193, 197-199, 224, 249, 250, 282, 284, 285, 288, 295, 296, 300, 305-309, 311, 322, 323, 324
Hawaii, Islands of 14
Hawkins, Donald D. . 185, 296, 373, 374, 378, 379, 407
Hayakawa, Lucas G. 249-252
Hearst, William Randolph 245
Helm, Ernest, see Bohm, Ernest
Henequén 305
Henjes, Frederick 88
Hernández, José 104, 274, 393
Hernández, Luís 104, 274, 393
Herrmann, Fred .... iv, 149
Heynen, Carl ... 20, 149, 182, 200-202, 324, 338, 372, 380, 398, 399
Hibbard Spencer & Bartlett Company ... 212
Hidalgo County 178
Hilken, Henry Gerhard 15, 20, 27, 28, 41, 42, 82, 144, 145, 148, 149, 338, 343, 351, 354, 370, 371
Hilken, Paul Gerhard 15, 20, 27, 28, 41, 42, 82, 144, 145, 148, 149, 338, 343, 351, 354, 370, 371

Hill, Benjamin 205, 355, 359, 370, 373, 374, 406, 407, 410
Hindustan Ghadar, see also Ghadar Party .. 52
Hinsch, Friedrich Carl 82, 144, 145, 149, 338, 343
Hitt, Parker 231, 386
Hizar, J. 52
Hoboken, City of . 47, 77, 81, 82, 85, 86, 88, 91, 148, 305
Hodge, Howard D. 263
Holden, lawyer 22
Holland-America Line 58
Holland House 115
Holland Line, see Holland-America Line
Holliday Detecto 248
Hoover, J. Edgar ..... vii, ix-xi, 344, 347, 376, 400, 410
Hopkins, Arthur A. 99, 115, 234, 240, 241-243, 271, 272, 273, 275, 302, 333, 386, 388, 390, 391, 400
Hopkins, Sherburne G. 99, 115, 234, 240-243, 271-273, 275, 302, 333, 386, 388, 390, 391, 400
Hoquiam, Town of 54
Horn, Raymond G. 26, 43-47, 50, 70, 113-115, 123, 129, 198, 210, 290, 342, 343, 354, 356, 363, 365-367, 379, 381, 382, 394
Horn, Werner 26, 43-47, 50, 70, 113-115, 123, 129, 198, 210, 290, 342, 343, 354, 356, 363, 365-367, 379, 381, 382, 394
Hossenfelder, Erich 167
Hotel Morrison 326
Houghton, William 161, 166, 168, 169, 373, 374, 408, 410
House, Edward Mandell .... ix, 74, 75, 112, 115, 134, 154, 156, 158, 166, 172, 310, 345, 358, 371, 372, 374, 400, 410
Houser, H. A. 179
Howe, Harland B. 90
Howell, Agent 84, 168, 374
Huerta, Victoriano 4, 56, 97, 98, 100, 102-105, 107, 110, 111, 113-132, 140, 141, 157, 179, 184, 209, 221, 228,

229, 244, 274, 282-284, 288-290, 293, 297, 336, 343, 359, 363, 365-368, 374, 382, 396, 398, 409, 412
Hughes, Charles Evans......... 51, 54, 58, 223
Hughes, Walter C. 51, 54, 58, 223

I

Ibarra, Cirilo 243
Ibs, William... 184, 189, 194, 299, 308, 309, 318, 331, 333, 395, 397, 399
Imperial General Staff, see also Abteilung IIIb.................................. 29, 82
Imperial Navy Department 140
Imperial War Department.. 4, 50, 59, 69, 73, 74, 76, 285, 286
Indian Independence Committee 53
International Harvester Corporation... 302, 307
International Longshoremen's Union... 142
International Union of Iron Workers 135
International Workers of the World 52
Interstate Bank & Trust Company . 194, 198
Irby, Special Employee............... 330, 399
Irías, Julián, Dr. 312, 313
Isidoro, SS......................... 185, 186, 191
Islas, Humberto 285
Isthmus of Tehuantepec 295, 377
IWW, *see* International Workers of the World
Jahnke, Kurt................................ 149
Jason, SS 18, 350
Jebsen, Frederick "Fred" .. 16-20, 54, 57, 351, 355, 356
Jebsen, Michael... 16-20, 54, 57, 351, 355, 356
Jeffreys-Jones, Rhodri. ix, 164, 345, 352, 357, 373, 374, 401, 408
Jentzer, Harry J. 33-35, 118, 149, 352, 362, 366, 394
John A. Roebling's Sons Company..... 70, 71
Johnson, M. E. 167, 376, 408
Jones, Charles Eugene....................... ix, 6, 95, 162-164, 183, 184, 186-195, 197, 212, 213, 220, 235, 288, 294, 296, 300, 305-312, 314, 325-333, 345, 348, 350, 352, 357-359, 365, 373, 374, 378, 382, 397, 399, 401, 408, 412

Jones, Charles Octavius .... ix, 6, 95, 162, 163, 164, 183, 184, 186-195, 197, 212, 213, 220, 235, 288, 294, 296, 300, 305-312, 314, 325-333, 345, 348, 350, 352, 357-359, 365, 373, 374, 378, 382, 397, 399, 401, 408, 412
Jones, Clarence Winfield.................... ix, 6, 95, 162-164, 183, 184, 186-195, 197, 212, 213, 220, 235, 288, 294, 296, 300, 305-312, 314, 325-333, 345, 348, 350, 352, 357-359, 365, 373, 374, 378, 382, 397, 399, 401, 408, 412
Jones, Gustave T. "Buster" .... ix, 6, 95, 162-164, 183, 184, 186-195, 197, 212, 213, 220, 235, 288, 294, 296, 300, 305-312, 314, 325-333, 345, 348, 350, 352, 357-359, 365, 373, 374, 378, 382, 397, 399, 401, 408, 412
Jones Point Experimental Laboratory..... 95
Jones, Winfield, *see* Jones, Clarence Winfield
Juan Casiano Petroleum Company....... 306
Justice Department, United States ... 21, 28, 39, 88, 116, 149, 157, 163, 187, 262, 345, 353, 357, 361, 374, 378, 396

K

Kain, Fred....................... 199, 380, 381
Kaiserkeller................................... 148
Kaltschmidt, Albert C. 48, 49, 50, 355
Kansas City, City of............. 119, 226, 405
Karachi, City of 57
Karlsruhe, SMS......................... 13, 350
Katz, Friedrich 219, 287, 339, 348, 350, 359, 364, 365, 377, 380-383, 385, 387, 388, 392, 393, 400, 408, 411
Kavanaugh, John S. 84, 374
Keating, John P. 65, 69
Keene, Agent 49, 355
Keily, Dan, see Kiely, Daniel J. 91
Kelley, Agent ... 94, 224, 286, 296, 314, 325, 328, 396
Kelley, Francis C. 94, 224, 286, 296, 314, 325, 328, 396

Kemp, James Wallace 61, 262, 263, 266, 267, 385, 389
Kennebunkport, Town of 115
Ketchul, Frederick, Dr. 273
Kiao Chow, China 268
Kiel, City of 13
Kiely, Daniel J. 87
Kienzle, Herbert O. 83
Kingfisher, Town of 181
Kirkoswald, SS 83
Klawans, Agent .. 34, 35, 143, 363, 365, 369, 370
Klein, Albert, see also Jebsen, Frederick ... 57, 351, 356
Knutsford, SS 72
Koch, Maximiliano 264
Köhler, Captain SMS Dresden 117
Komogata Maru, SS iv
König, Paul "P. K." ... 6, 22, 39, 47, 154, 168, 343, 371, 372
Kopecky, Francis 169, 349
Kosterlitzky, Emilia "Emmy" 131, 132, 226, 267, 270, 271, 368, 410
Kosterlitzky, Emilio ... 131, 132, 226, 267, 270, 271, 368, 410
Kramp, Henry 106, 107, 118, 180, 207
Kriegsministerium, see Imperial War Department
Kristianiafjord, SS 72, 97, 358
Kropidlowski, J. F. 213, 214, 382
Krum Heller, Arnoldo, Dr. 238
Krupp, see Friedrich Krupp AG
Kueck, Otto 39
Kulenkampff, Gustav 19
Kutna Hora, Town of 8
Kwasind, SS 289

L

Labor's National Peace Council ... 135, 137, 139, 140, 142, 143, 149, 150
Lady Liberty, see Statue of Liberty
Lafon, Ms. 236
Lake Erie 27, 38
Lake Huron 50
Lake Ontario 27, 38

Lamar, David, see also Levy, David M. .. 119, 134-140, 143, 147, 149, 150, 343, 360, 366, 368, 370, 406, 412
Lancaster, Fred 180, 253
Landa, Carlos 310
Lansing, Robert 28, 32, 64, 66, 88, 93, 114, 150, 156, 158, 164, 166, 172, 174, 216-218, 247, 283, 298, 304, 351, 352, 356, 357, 360, 361, 362, 369, 372, 374, 376, 378, 382, 383, 385, 387, 392, 395, 400, 404, 405, 408, 411
La Providencia, schooner 297, 299
Lardizábal, Manuel 313
Laredo, City of . 105, 177, 178, 181, 211, 212, 218, 237, 238, 253, 256, 258, 264, 266, 276-278, 312, 320, 404
Larrea, Javier 295, 296, 312
Las Cruces, Town of ... 248, 384, 397, 404, 408
La Tourraine, SS 71
Laubach, H. L. 248, 277
Lawrence, John Jay ... 39, 213, 236, 254, 255, 347, 386, 388, 405, 410, 412
Lea, Tom 120, 122, 123, 130, 226, 245
Lecardis, J. C. 205
Lefler, William 48-50
Lege, John Henry 237, 254, 277, 278, 333, 386, 388, 391, 400
Legge, Alexander 303
Le Havre, City of 71, 83
Lehigh University 15
Lelevier, Ives G. 205, 274
León, City of ... 201, 215, 283, 284, 306, 311, 320, 409
Lepe, Filemón 130
Levering, Richmond Mortimer 94, 95, 358, 360, 362, 363
Levi, Eneas 253
Levy, David M. 58, 60, 134
Levy, Felix H. 58, 60, 134
Libau, SS 65
Liberating Army of Races and Peoples, see Plan de San Diego
Ligardi, F. 275, 391
Limburg, City of 65

INDEX

Link, Arthur S... 162, 339, 358, 365, 371-374, 376, 382, 389, 408
Llorente, Enrique.... 106, 114, 177, 376, 404
LoMedico, Agent 35, 352
London, City of.... 8, 28, 37, 40, 55, 71, 142, 145, 259, 272, 279, 285, 348, 349, 354, 355, 362, 368, 375, 393, 404, 406-410
Long Island 100, 102, 167
Long, Samuel Miller Breckinridge 100, 102, 114, 167, 207, 365
Longshoremen's Union, *see* International Longshoremen's Union
Los Angeles, City of 29, 51, 52, 54, 57, 125, 131, 132, 177, 201-203, 208, 234, 248, 250, 253, 266-270, 322, 350, 405, 408, 413
Love, Dick...... 128, 373, 409
Lucy H, schooner 186, 191, 192, 195
Ludendorff, Erich 337, 338
Lüderitz, Carl August. 27, 28, 29, 38, 41, 42, 354
Lusitania, SS..71, 108, 113, 115, 133, 154, 158, 161, 166, 173, 175, 337, 341, 348, 408
Lutz, M. 191, 379

M

Machias, City of...... 44, 46
Mackay-Smith, Virginia......3, 4
Maclovio Herrera, SS...... 210
Madero, Alfonso 37, 56, 100, 110, 111, 116, 117, 179-181, 183, 197, 220, 221, 237, 238, 276, 281-283, 293, 328, 408
Madero Brothers Company 181
Madero, Francisco I. .. 37, 56, 100, 110, 111, 116, 117, 179-181, 183, 197, 220, 221, 237, 238, 276, 281-283, 293, 328, 408
Magnón, Antonio...... 299
Maguire, Bernard 58
Maine Central Railroad 43
Malda, Luís 288
Maldonado, Pánfilo 295
Mallory Line, *see* Mallory Shipping Line
Mallory Shipping Line 230
Malone, Dudley Field ... 22, 23, 84, 351, 360
Manila, City of 19, 209, 268

Manila, SS 19, 209, 268
Mann Act, *see also* White-Slave Traffic Act, 1910 ...... x, 278
Manoil, James, *see* Heynen, Carl
Maqueo Castellanos, Esteban .306, 308, 325, 327
Marfa, Town of...... 236, 404
Margaín, Arturo 179
Maritime Building, Brooklyn 34
Market Street National Bank...... 73
Marks, Fred E. 237, 285, 398
Márquez, L. 183, 184, 212, 301
Márquez, Rosendo...... 183, 184, 212, 301
Marseille, City of...... 30, 83, 87
Marshall, Hudson Snowden.... 22, 143, 144, 149
Martínez, Eugenio...... 52, 241, 269
Martínez, H. M. 52, 241, 269
Martin, Henry B. 135, 138-140, 143, 148-150, 220, 343, 347, 351, 370, 373, 407-409
Martin, Herold H.135, 138-140, 143, 148-150, 220, 343, 347, 351, 370, 373, 407-409
Masaryk, Thomas 8, 348, 349, 375, 408
Matthews, Agent......56, 356
Matzet, Mike 87
Maverick, SS 57
Maximilian I, Emperor of Mexico 293
Maytorena, José María ... 109, 177, 183, 199, 200, 203, 205, 206, 274
Mazatlán, City of . 16, 18, 19, 208, 274, 350, 358
Mazatlán, SS.... 16, 18, 19, 208, 274, 350, 358
McAdoo, William Gibbs 143, 153-156, 160, 161, 164, 166, 168, 172, 345, 369, 372-375, 400, 401, 408
McAllen, Town of...... 178
McCahill, Miles C. 156, 168, 374
McCoy Hotel 124, 129
McDevitt, F. J. 178, 376, 382
McDonald, John A. 209
McElhone, James F. 112, 114, 358
McGarrity, Joseph 65, 358
McGee, Thomas J... 33-35, 245, 352, 379, 381, 387
McGuire's Café 138

427

McHenry, John 156
Means, Gaston B. 7, 22, 23, 92, 348, 407
Mebus, Edgar W. 235
Mechanics and Metals National Bank... 286
MEC, see Cisneros, Juan
Medina Barrón, Luís 104
Medina, Juan 104, 226, 244
Melbourne, City of 11, 348, 407
Meloy, Andrew D. .. 116, 133, 140-144, 148, 369, 370
Méndez, Alberto 184, 209, 288
Méndez, Pedro Guerrero...... 184, 209, 288
Menger Hotel............................... 248
Mennet, John Perry Sellar 239, 333, 334, 398, 400
Mérida, City of 197, 326
MER, see Cerna, Antonio
Mexican Secret Service 180, 252, 271, 377, 388, 412
Mexico City, 1914 Battle of.... 4, 45, 97, 98, 100, 130, 177, 180, 194, 196, 201, 227, 235, 238, 242, 254, 258, 261, 264-266, 270, 275, 277, 281, 285, 288, 290, 294, 295, 297, 298, 301, 303, 313, 333
Mexico Northwest Railway 249
Mexico Western Railway 140
Meyerhofer, Richard 87
MEY, see Echegaray, Juan
MEZ, see Hernández, José
MI-8 231
Micheloni, Rosita 266, 267
MID, see Military Intelligence Division
Mier, Rubén 261, 262, 263, 264
Military Intelligence Division . xi, 162, 164, 173, 345, 359 368, 380, 383-386, 388-390, 391, 403
Minck, Charles E. 235, 247, 253, 388
Mississippi Valley Trust Company 200
MIT University 384, 407
Mixed Claims Commission 20, 70, 146, 148, 271, 344, 351, 354, 357, 358, 359, 369, 370, 371, 390, 403, 405, 412
Mock, H. B. 333, 390
Moeller, unknown, see Barth, Henry
Molina, Olegario..... 305, 307-309, 366, 394

Monclova, Town of 276
Mondragón, Manuel 140, 141, 143, 283, 289-291, 312, 326, 330
Monett, Frank 135, 143, 149, 150, 377, 413
Monterrey, City of............. 103, 177, 178, 180, 197, 211, 215, 228, 235, 238, 256, 264, 275-278, 297, 299, 322, 333, 409
Monterrey, SS 103, 177, 178, 180, 197, 211, 215, 228, 235, 238, 256, 264, 275- 278, 297, 299, 322, 333, 409
Montes, Avelino.......... 305, 307, 308, 309
Montgomery, Joseph W. 196, 213
Mooney and Boland Detective Agency..... 6, 85, 137, 348
Mora y del Río, José María 245, 296
Morelos, State of 221
Morgan, John Pierpoint 134, 135, 310
Morgenthau, Henry 162
Morin, José 215, 216
Morris, Abbott 58, 226, 230, 385, 405
Morro Castle, SS 98, 210
Mr. Polite, see Cortés, Pedro
Muck, Henry 58
Muensterberg, Hugo 10
Mullany, J. J. 265, 266
Muñoz, Rafael............................... 93
Munson, L. G. .. 144, 366, 370, 383, 398, 399
Murphy, Joseph E. 162
Muskogee, City of 124

N

Nadolny, Rudolph.............. 70, 357, 358
Nafarrate, Emiliano P. 256
Naples, Italy, City of..................... 71, 72
National Arms Company 186, 189
National Labor Union, see Labor's National Peace Council
National Reorganizing Army 297
National Secret Police, Cuban 93
National Security Agency 248
Navarrete, Rubio Guillermo 283
Navy Yard, Brooklyn............ 31, 228, 229
Navy Yard, New York 31, 228, 229
Navy Yard, Philadelphia 31, 71, 228, 229
Neal, Harry E. 345, 374, 401, 406

INDEX

Neckar, SS 82
Needham, E. T. 319, 388, 397, 398
Neunhoffer, William W. ...234, 243, 253, 271, 274, 386, 388, 391
Newfoundland Regiment 40
New Jersey Agricultural Chemical Company 91
New London, Connecticut, Town of.... 145, 259, 272, 279
Newman, New Mexico, Town of ... 120, 125
New Orleans, City of 28, 29, 45, 56, 80-83, 95, 125, 132, 183-195, 197, 198, 210, 212, 213, 220, 240, 264, 283, 288, 289, 292, 294-300, 305-307, 309, 310, 312-314, 317, 318, 323, 326, 327, 329-331, 333, 378, 396, 410
New Orleans Item 295
Newspaper Service Company . 186, 296, 326
New York Dock Company 262, 263
New York Evening News 155, 158
New York Evening World ...134, 356, 357, 360, 365, 368, 374, 395, 413
New York Herald 30, 112, 213, 360
New York Metropolitan Opera 55
New York Sun ...59, 63, 112, 133, 292, 297, 350, 351, 354, 357, 368, 373, 394, 395, 413
New York Times 12, 16, 20, 170, 292, 298, 347, 349-351, 354, 358, 362-364, 371, 382, 394, 395, 413
New York Tribune 134, 154, 156, 298, 349, 351, 353, 354, 357, 363, 368, 369, 370, 372, 373, 394, 395, 413
New York World .. 154-158, 161, 170, 172, 173, 371, 372, 375, 376, 413
New York Yacht Club 73, 111, 134, 144
Niagara Falls 27
Nicasio Idar, Clemente 238
Niles, Charles, F. 214
Nogales, 1913 Battle of 131, 177, 183, 199, 200, 205, 206, 228, 234, 242, 253, 258, 267-269, 271, 274, 333, 380, 390, 413
Nogales, Arizona, City of 131, 177, 183, 199, 200, 205, 206, 228, 234, 242, 253, 258, 267-269, 271, 274, 333, 380, 390, 413

Nogales, Sonora, City of 131, 177, 183, 199, 200, 205, 206, 228, 234, 242, 253, 258, 267-269, 271, 274, 333, 380, 390, 413
Noordam, SS 141
Nordhaus, M. A. 226
Norfolk, City of 13, 71, 145
Noriega, Victor 299
Northampton, City of 35
Northern and Southern Navigation Company 16
North German Lloyd.. 15, 16, 19, 25, 27, 80, 82, 145, 347, 398
NSA, see National Security Agency
Nuevo Laredo, Town of .. 178, 212, 256, 320
Nürnberg, SMS 14, 18

O

Obregón, Álvaro108, 131, 201, 202, 217, 264-266, 268, 313, 333, 337, 380, 397, 409
O'Brian, John Lord 46, 350, 354
Ochoa, Manuel 207, 250
Ochoa, Victor 207, 250
Ocón, Cecilio288, 292, 308-310, 326, 328, 331
O'Connor, Thomas Ventry 142, 143
Oelrichs and Company 32
Office of Naval Intelligence ...162, 164, 231, 345, 386, 407
Offley, William 33, 42, 58, 59, 61, 63, 64, 87, 88, 91, 93, 94, 97, 99, 102, 103, 112-115, 117, 118, 139, 142, 143, 146, 147, 149, 150, 210, 211, 213, 222-225, 227, 228, 230, 258, 261-266, 290, 293, 295, 300, 304, 318, 321, 322, 329, 336, 355-358, 360-366, 369-371, 379, 380-382, 384, 385, 389, 392-396, 398
Ojinaga, Battle of 118
Ojinaga, City of 118
O'Leary, Jeremiah 65, 69, 81, 82
O'Leary, Michael 65, 69, 81, 82
O'Leary, Norton, see O'Leary, Michael
Olin, Franklin Jr. 182, 183, 380
Olin, Franklin, Sr., see Olin, Franklin Walter
Olin, Franklin Walter 182, 183, 380
Olin, John 182, 183, 380

Oliver, George B...98, 99, 127, 291, 322, 323, 347, 374, 409
Oliver Typewriter Company .. 98, 291, 322, 323
Omaha, City of 134, 413
ONI, *see* Office of Naval Intelligence ....
Ornelas, Tomás 203
Orozco, Jorge U..... 100, 104, 105, 110, 111, 116, 118, 120, 122-125, 128-132, 140, 143, 179, 211, 230, 265-267, 282-284, 297, 366, 367, 374, 397, 406, 409
Orozco, José .. 100, 104, 105, 110, 111, 116, 118, 120, 122-125, 128-132, 140, 143, 179, 211, 230, 265, 266, 267, 282-284, 297, 366, 367, 374, 397, 406, 409
Orozco, Pascual 100, 104, 105, 110, 111, 116, 118, 120, 122-125, 128-132, 140, 143, 179, 211, 230, 265-267, 282-284, 297, 366, 367, 374, 397, 406, 409
Ortega, Carlos 324
Ortiz, Mateo 185, 242, 243, 274, 386
Osterveen, Adolfo, Jr. 321
Otto, Rudolph........ 27, 39, 79, 90, 117, 366

P

Pacho, B. M. 242, 386
Packard Automobile Company 71
Padilla, Fernando 104, 105, 119
Padrés, Gustavo 206
Page, Walter Hines........... 30, 88, 361, 369
Palmer, A. Mitchell 134
Panama Canal 3, 166, 247
Pan-American Conference, 1915 .... 216, 217, 218
Paradies, Wilhelm............................ 90
Parker, William A. 98, 209, 231, 323
Paso del Norte Hotel 126, 245
Pastrana, Diógenes 193
Patagonia, SS 15, 349, 350
Peabody Leather Label Overall Company 48
Peace Council, *see* Labor's National Peace Council
Pearson Oil Company 305
Pederson, Charles A. 236
Peláez, Manuel 313

Pendleton, Forrest Currier . 29, 81, 183-189, 191-197, 212, 213, 220, 240, 295, 296, 299, 300, 305-310, 318, 326, 329-333, 359, 363, 376-383, 385, 394-400
Pensacola, City of 184, 185, 186, 191, 193-195, 197, 198, 413
Pérez, Adolfo 193, 241, 242, 299, 395
Pérez, Felipe 193, 241, 242, 299, 395
Pérez Figueroa, Angel 193
Pérez, J. Lozano 193, 241, 242, 299, 395
Pershing Expedition, *see* Punitive Expedition, 1916
Pershing, John J. ...107, 222, 225, 226, 251, 258, 272, 343, 383, 384, 397, 409-411
Peters Cartridge Company 182
Phenol 158
Philadelphia, City of 1, 6, 16, 54, 59, 69, 71, 73, 142, 190, 230, 231, 245, 374, 378, 387, 406, 413
Philadelphia Naval Yards, *see* Navy Yard, Philadelphia
Phillips, Harvey . 99, 114, 115, 210, 381, 394
Piedras Negras, Town of 178
Pier Division, German, *see also* Bureau of Investigation, German 6
Pigniuolo, Pasquale... 35, 304, 321, 386, 394
Pilenas, Casimir 40, 353
Pinckney, Stephen Lee..................... 105, 106, 119, 121-124, 126, 180, 206-208, 226, 235, 244, 245, 247, 248, 364, 366, 367, 376, 377, 379, 380, 381, 385-387
Pinkerton Agency, *see* Pinkerton Detective Agency
Pinkerton Detective Agency................ 163
Pino Suárez, José María 100
Pizaña, Aniceto....................... 215, 256
Plan de San Diego ...214-218, 232, 233, 239, 249, 255-257, 259, 275, 276, 278, 285, 334, 343, 382, 388, 407
Planet, SMS.................................. 14
Plaza Hotel.................................. 323
Plochman, George 368
Polk, Frank L.....144, 146, 224, 266, 312, 370, 384, 393, 397
Ponce, Victoriano 216

Pontus, SMS 14
Portland, City of 29, 30, 54, 351
Postal Telegraph............................ 307
Praedel, George........................ 90, 362
Prague, City of 8, 349, 407
Präsident, SS 15, 20
Prenzlau, City of 55
Prince Albert, SS 190, 208
Prinz Eitel Friedrich, SMS 13, 14
Prinz Hatzfeld zu Trachenberg, Hermann .. 158
Prinz Ratibor, Maximilian 285
Providence Journal ... 10- 12, 38, 116, 117, 158, 170, 171, 174, 345, 349, 353, 375, 413
Prudential Insurance 255
Puerto Cortés, City of 199
Punitive Expedition, 1916 225, 227, 232, 251, 255, 257, 259, 271, 272, 278, 279, 287, 301, 303, 311, 318, 320, 343, 384, 410
Punjab uprising, 1915 68

Q

Quebec, State of............................. 39
Quintana, Felipe D., see Dusart Quintana, Felipe, Dr.
Quintana Roo, Territory of .. 286, 326, 327, 328
Quiroz, Alberto 100, 103, 105, 121, 130-132, 366, 367

R

Ramos, Basilio 106-108, 131, 180, 203, 207, 208, 214, 275, 334
Ramos, Hector ...106-108, 131, 180, 203, 207, 208, 214, 275, 334
Ramsgate, Harbor of........................ 141
Raney, George A. 308
Rasmussen, Erich, see von Steinmetz, Erich
Rasst, Elisa 100, 228-231, 385, 405, 411
Rasst, Leon...... 100, 228-231, 385, 405, 411
Rathom, John Revelstone..... 10-12, 23, 116, 117, 170, 171, 345, 349, 355, 365, 375, 401
Ratner, Abraham Z. .. 97-100, 118, 121, 124, 127, 129, 228, 229, 291, 366, 367

Ratner, José B. .. 97-100, 118, 121, 124, 127, 129, 228, 229, 291, 366, 367
Read, George W. 239, 273
Reapers, see International Harvester Corporation
Reichstag................................73, 337
Reilly, Edward John 80-82, 197, 373, 407
Remington Arms Company.............. 211
Respa, Franz 48-50, 411
Respa, Karl F. 48- 50, 411
Reyes, Bernardo 104, 179, 239, 281, 282, 297, 374, 406, 409, 411
Reyes Conspiracy, see Reyes Revolution
Reyes Revolution 411
Reynosa, Town of..................... 178, 256
Rheinfelder, Walter Theodor, see Scheele, Walter Theodor
Rice, Melvin A. ... 2, 28, 39, 74, 75, 113, 323, 351, 353, 358, 360
Richards, W. T., Dr. 294
Riga, SS...88
Riley, John, see Reilly, Edward John
Rintelen, Franz Dagobert Johannes.......... 73-76, 80-82, 85, 91, 95-97, 110-113, 115-117, 132-137, 140-144, 146-151, 157, 304, 340, 343, 344, 358, 360, 362-365, 368-371, 409
Rintelen von Kleist, Franz, see Rintelen, Franz Dagobert Johannes
Rio Grande Valley Bank, see Rio Grande Valley Bank & Trust Company
Rio Grande Valley Bank & Trust Company . 194, 200
Risse, Anita 148
Rivera, H. 242, 274
Riverbank Laboratories 231
Robertson, Randolph 105, 211, 212, 215, 239, 256, 275, 382
Roberts, Powell 106, 180, 373, 374, 409
Rodríguez, Adrián.............. 195, 244, 256
Rodríguez, Juan............................ 256
Rodríguez, Tomás 195, 244, 256
Roebling, see John A. Roebling's Sons Company
Roemer, L. Frances 290

431

Rogers, J. B. 215, 237, 238, 278, 382, 383, 391, 398
Room 40, *see* Hall, Reginald "Blinker"
Roosevelt, Franklin Delano .. 162, 224, 347, 409
Roosevelt, Theodore 162, 224, 347, 409
Rosales Betancourt, Máximo.............. 186
Rosas, Guillermo..... 294, 304-311, 313, 325, 326-328, 330, 331, 332, 397, 399
Ross, George W. 43-45, 237, 253, 278, 391
Ross, Thomas M. "Tom" ... 43-45, 237, 253, 278, 391
Royal Canadian Mounted Police ix
Royal Navy, British 2, 145, 341
Rubano, Peter 167, 168, 374
Ruroede, Carl, Jr. ... 32-35, 88, 166, 343, 351, 352
Ruroede, Carl, Sr. ... 32- 35, 88, 166, 343, 351, 352
Ryan, Detective 65, 87, 272
Ryan, James 65, 87, 272
Ryan, John 65, 87, 272

S

Saenz, Consul.......................... 189, 398
Saint Croix River 42, 43
Saint John, NB, City of...................... 43
Saint Lawrence River 39
Salazar, José Inés 313, 412
Salina Cruz, Town of................ 197, 295
Salinas, Alberto 213, 214, 264, 384, 409
SAMOT, *see* Rodríguez, Tomás
San Andrés, Village of 251
San Antonio, City of ....
29, 49, 95, 103-106, 118, 119, 124, 125, 130, 131, 178, 180, 184, 211, 212, 216, 222, 226, 233, 236, 237, 239, 241, 246, 248, 249, 252, 253, 255-257, 273, 275, 277, 290, 296, 299, 301, 305, 309, 312, 317-320, 329, 331, 334, 335, 366, 367, 377, 378, 404, 408, 411, 413, 414
San Antonio Traction Company.......... 236
Sánchez, Amador 181, 297
Sanderson, Town of 178, 236

San Francisco, City of . 11, 16-19, 26, 28, 30, 37, 51-53, 57, 66, 67, 125, 190, 199, 208, 209, 234, 253, 254, 268, 269, 302, 349, 350, 378, 414
San Guglielmo, SS 72
San José del Cabo, Town of................ 54
San Miguel Examiner 298, 395, 414
Santa Isabel, Village of 251, 287
Santibáñez, Arturo 190, 193, 194
Santos Cavazos, General 320
Santos Chocano, José...... 183, 184, 197, 301
Sapulpa, Town of 181
Sarfaty, William 147, 149, 370
Sato, A. 251
Savage, Henry E. 84, 168, 182, 374
Scharnhorst, SMS........................... 13
Scheele, Oswald T. 47
Scheele, Walter Theodor 3, 4, 44, 47, 50, 76-82, 85-89, 91-95, 149, 154, 198, 314, 338, 340, 342-344, 359, 360-363, 368, 369 377, 388, 410, 412
Scheidemann, Oswald.................. 88-90
Schleswig-Holstein, State of................ 30
Schmid, Frederick P. 46, 223
Schmidt, Carl.................... 90, 362, 393
Scholz, Walter 84
Schone, B. 195
Schoonover, Albert 266, 389
Schultheis, Herman J. 135, 139, 143
Schweitzer, Hugo, Dr. 158
Schwierz, Richard "Ricardo" W., *see* Schwierz, Victor
Schwierz, Victor 267-271, 390
Scotland Yard..................... ix, 142, 354
Scott, Hugh Lenox .. 109, 177, 217, 219, 382, 409
Scull, Guy 85, 406, 409
Scully, Charles J. ... 33, 34, 88, 143, 210, 211, 290, 321, 323, 352, 356, 361, 363, 385, 394
Seaconnet, SS 88
Seattle, City of.... 17, 26, 54, 67, 71, 375, 414
Second Cavalry Brigade............. 199, 206
Secret Service, German ... 6, 35, 66, 84, 85, 87, 91, 92, 94, 112, 142, 153, 156, 159, 160, 162-169, 173, 180, 199, 230, 252,

253, 271, 345, 347, 352, 353, 357, 360, 361, 365, 371-375, 377, 388, 400, 401, 403, 406-409, 412
Seese, George L. 222, 226
SEMAN, *see* García, Juan
Serrano, Pedro................. 184, 211, 212
Sewell, Anne Leddell 115, 143
Sewell, William.......................115, 143
Shelton, W. H. 181, 202
Sherman Anti-Trust Act................. 144
Shetland Islands........................... 57
Shinuya, Y., *see* Tuschiya, Hidekichi
Short, Luke 272, 391
Siebert, John Henry 228, 266, 385
Sierra Blanca, Town of 128, 129
Silliman, John R...................... 98, 219
Silva, Dário 244, 245, 286
Simpich, Frederick................. 206, 389
Sixaola, SS 302, 303, 305
Slocum, Herbert Jermain..................222
Smith, George H. 3, 4, 44, 95, 154, 368, 377, 388, 410, 412
Smith, Michel Hoke .. 3, 4, 44, 95, 154, 368, 377, 388, 410, 412
Smith, Walter Theodor, *see* Scheele, Walter Theodor
Smyth, Herbert C. 41
Snell, H. B. 195
Snelling, Milton........................... 135
Socorro Island........................... 54
Solanos, José "Joe" 249
Solomon, John, *see* Rathom, John Revelstone
Somellera, Félix 296
Sommerfeld, Felix Armand 7, 60, 108-112, 114, 116-118, 125, 131, 132, 142, 143, 149, 151, 175, 177, 180-183, 201, 202, 219, 222-225, 228-230, 237, 245, 284, 337, 338, 343, 348, 356, 364, 365, 377, 380-385, 393, 397, 400, 410, 411
Sonora War Tax Commission 205, 210
Soriano, C. G. 205
Sorola, Manuel 239, 255, 256, 388
Southwestern Steamship Company..... 208
Spanish-American Trading Syndicate .. 229

Spanish American War, 1899-1900.. ....210, 234
Special Detail Division, German 6
Spencer, Richard B.. . 212, 223, 240, 299, 377, 384, 385, 395
Spreewald, SS 15, 349, 350
Sprio, Rosato, *see* Von Wedell, Hans Adam
Staats Zeitung, Jacksonville 92
Stadt Schleswig, SS................. 15, 349, 350
Stahl, Adolfo................... .... 301, 302
Stallforth, Frederico...................... 116, 133, 142-149, 151, 238, 338, 343, 351, 356, 360, 368, 369, 370, 371, 412
Stanchfield and Levy 58
St. Anthony Hotel 104, 211
Stark, Dr. 30, 32, 33
State Department, United States .... x, xi, 21, 28, 30-32, 34, 35, 38, 46, 64, 75, 88, 93, 94, 97, 106, 113-115, 119, 120, 141, 144, 146, 149, 150, 162-164, 179, 188, 190, 198, 215, 216, 219, 222, 224, 227, 233, 240, 243, 247, 248, 256, 258, 262, 265, 266, 292, 298, 301-304, 310-312, 318, 344, 345, 353, 360, 396
Statue of Liberty 145
Sterett, James 87
Sternberg, Erich, *see* von Steinmetz, Erich
Stevens, Charles........ 105, 131, 371, 374, 409
St. Louis, City of .... vii, 116, 179, 200, 296, 364, 373, 387, 403, 407
St. Michel, Town of 186
Stokes, William Earl Dodge 54, 59, 67, 190, 247, 298, 336, 348, 355, 387, 395, 400, 408, 409
Stone, Edward B. 123-127, 129, 196, 197, 215, 220, 222, 235, 244, 245, 247-253, 364, 366, 367, 376-379, 381, 383-385, 387, 388, 397, 412
Storck, George W...................... 62, 357
Storms, Jene 87
Stoy, Elmer E. 240
St. Regis Hotel.......................... 89, 303
Sullivan, James Francis.................73, 142
Sullivan, Lita 73, 142
Sullivan, R. Livingston 73, 142

433

Sunday Telegram 168, 375
Supreme Court, United States .. 24, 66, 127, 230, 352, 385, 405
Surabaya, City of........................ 58, 59
Sutherland, W. J. 138
Suzuki, T. 251
Sybilla, SS 322

T

Tague, Aubrey............................... 43
Tamaulipas, State of........ 215, 256, 278, 313
Tammany Hall 23
Tampico News Agency, *see* Tampico News Company
Tampico News Company 97
Tapia, Eugenio 278
Tatematsu, Gemichi "Gustavo" E. . 249-252
Taube, F. M. 303
Tauscher, Hans 38-42, 53- 61, 63-67, 108, 163, 228, 247, 266, 286, 301, 302, 305, 314, 338, 343, 355-357, 385, 396
Tauscher, Johanna 38-42, 53-61, 63-67, 108, 163, 228, 247, 266, 286, 301, 302, 305, 314, 338, 343, 355-357, 385, 396
Taylor, Bridgeman, *see* Von der Goltz, Horst
Taylor, Hannis...27, 28, 37, 40, 42, 59, 135, 143, 149, 150, 345, 354, 376, 404, 410, 412
Taylor, Jacob C. 27, 28, 37, 40, 42, 59, 135, 143, 149, 150, 345, 354, 376, 404, 410, 412
Teresa, SS 289
Terrazas, Luís.......................... 248, 283
Texas Rangers .... ix, 216
Thayer, Frank H. 249, 291, 319
The Black Cat 323
Thiel Detective Agency.......... 106, 180, 348
Thiel Detective Service, *see* Thiel Detective Agency
Thomas A. Edison Corporation 158
Thomas Hardware Company 227
Thompson, Eck 106, 130, 180
Thompson, Hyman A. 106, 130, 180
Tidwell, Agent.............................. 199
Tierney, Richard 224, 396

Tiger of Berlin, *see* Rintelen, Franz Dagobert Johannes
Tijuana, City of 179, 258
Tilbury Docks, London 37
Timney, Agent........................ 149, 371
Topolobampo, City of 52, 66
Transatlantic Trust Company......... 76, 112
Treasury Department, United States...... 21, 84, 119, 155, 199, 219, 232, 322, 345
Trenton, City of....................... 70, 414
Treviño, Jacinto...................... 252, 279
Tuchman, Barbara Wertheim .. 76, 116, 162, 336, 337, 339, 345, 352, 359, 365, 373, 374, 400, 401, 410
Tucker, Charles J. . 33-35, 290, 300, 326, 329, 352, 355, 370, 371, 384, 394, 399
Tucker, Joseph G. . 33-35, 290, 300, 326, 329, 352, 355, 370, 371, 384, 394, 399
Tucson, City of...124, 199, 228, 234, 242, 243, 253, 254, 261, 274, 404
Tumulty, Joseph 112, 140, 364, 365
Tunney, Thomas...83-85, 87, 89-92, 347, 354, 359-362, 410
Turney, W. W. 222
Tuschiya, Hidekichi 249

U

U-36.. 57
U-*Bremen* 370
U-*Deutschland*.................... 145, 354, 370
U.M.C. Cartridge Company 60
Underhill, E. S. ... 62, 91, 143, 223-225, 258, 265-267, 384, 385, 389
Union Iron Works 209
United Fruit Company 199, 302
United States Secret Service 84, 159, 161, 164, 165, 170, 345, 357, 360 373, 374, 401, 403, 406, 409
Untermeyer, Samuel....... 155, 156, 158, 166, 172, 372
Urrutia, Aureliano.................... 104, 105
US Declaration of War, 1917 .... 146, 345
USSS, *see* United States Secret Service
U.S. Steel Corporation 134
Utley, Willard................... 236, 320, 398

434

V

Valcartier Camp 39
Valley Inn 123
Vanceboro Bridge 342
Vanceboro, City of ... 42-44, 46, 47, 70, 157, 342
Vanceboro Exchange Hotel 43
Van Deman, Ralph H. ... 173, 363, 376, 380, 390, 400, 410
Van Horn, Town of 129
Vasconcelos, José 117
Vaterland, SS 14
Vázquez, P. O., *see* Orozco, Pascual
Venegas, Colonel 103, 118
Ventura, SS 192, 193, 194, 198, 199
Veracruz, 1914 Occupation of ... 4, 20, 45, 51, 97, 98, 177, 191, 205, 208, 210, 213, 228, 258, 264, 281, 282, 290, 291, 298, 310
Verdi, Guiseppe 56
Viereck, George Sylvester ... 133, 134, 142, 155, 161, 167, 169
Vigilancia, SS 339
Villa Agency, *see* Villa Purchasing Agency
Villa, Francisco "Pancho" 37, 60, 104, 106, 108, 109, 111, 118, 121, 124, 129, 131, 132, 140, 171, 175, 177-186, 190-195, 197, 199, 200-203, 205-210, 212, 213, 216-223, 225-229, 241, 243-245, 248-252, 255, 256, 274, 277-279, 282-284, 286, 287, 289, 297, 300, 301, 308, 313, 318-320, 327-329, 331, 337, 338, 340, 343, 359, 376, 377, 383, 384, 388, 393, 406-412
Villa, Hipólito 180, 181, 191, 203, 210, 248-252, 319, 327, 329, 331
Villa, Juanita Torres 248
Villa, Luz Corral 248
Villa Purchasing Agency 108, 181, 191, 202, 208
Villarreal, Gerónimo 178, 179, 312, 313
Villavicencio, Francisco R. 185, 192, 196-199, 212, 213, 220
Virginia, SS 3, 4, 13, 71, 92, 93, 145, 247

Von der Goltz, Horst 27, 28, 37-42, 59, 60, 135, 143, 149, 150, 345, 354, 376, 404, 410, 412
Von Holtzendorff, Henning 109, 175
Von Igel, Wolf Walter Franz .. 61, 64, 65, 357
Von Kleist, Hermann Ewald Carl "Charles" 88-91
Von Kleist, Olga 88-91
Von Kleist, William 88-91
Von Papen, Franz 5, 25-27, 30, 33, 39, 42, 47, 57, 59, 61, 74-76, 78-80, 110
Von Reiswitz, Kurt 67
Von Steinmetz, Erich 79, 80
Von Wedell, Hans Adam 30, 31, 35
Voska, Emanuel Viktor 7- 9, 12, 78, 169-173, 348, 349, 359, 375, 407, 410
Voska, Villa ... 7, 8, 9, 12, 78, 169-173, 348, 349, 359, 375, 407, 410

W

Wachendorf, Franz Robert, *see* Von der Goltz, Horst
Waffenfabrik Mauser 55
Wagner, Richard 56
Walker Bros. Frontier Hardware Company. 212
Walker Brothers-Hancock Company 212, 213
Walker, George F., *see also* Walker Brothers-Hancock Company 212, 213
Walker, H. B., *see also* Walker Brothers-Hancock Company 212, 213
Walkertown, ON, City of 48
Walsh, Timothy 154
Ward Line, *see* Ward Shipping Line
Ward Shipping Line 210, 211, 227, 262, 264, 293, 329
Warren, Charles ... 85, 113, 124, 233, 234, 242, 312-314, 333, 365, 385
Washington, DC, City of 2, 3, 11, 22, 28, 39, 54, 55, 59, 64, 69, 92, 106, 107, 118, 123, 124, 126, 137, 138, 140, 141, 144, 158, 166, 168, 177, 187, 188, 218, 222, 228, 232, 233, 240, 241, 247, 265, 267, 269, 283, 284, 288, 289, 296, 302, 303, 308, 310, 312, 322, 325, 329, 350, 351,

356, 363, 368, 370, 372-375, 378, 383, 387, 396, 400, 403-405, 407, 409, 414
Washington Post 55, 356, 387, 414
W. Curry Sons 192
Weakley, Calvin S. 236, 299, 395
Webb, John L. ... 240, 321, 334, 378, 379, 385, 388, 395, 398, 400
Webster, Frank P. 51, 52, 201, 202, 234, 355, 363, 368, 376, 377, 380-383, 390
Weckstein, Isidore 32
Weehawken, Town of 83, 84, 360
Weise, Feri F. 67, 358
Weiskopf, Victor...231, 235, 275, 333, 386, 391, 398, 400
Weiss, T. F. 236
Welland Canal...27, 38-40, 42, 50, 60, 61, 64, 157, 268, 271
Wessels, Kulenkampff and Company 19
Western Cartridge Company 181, 182, 201, 202, 223, 228, 377, 380
Wherry and Mygatt 142
Whitehead, Don 344, 400, 410
White House........................ 74, 75, 112
White-Slave Traffic Act, 1910, *see also* Mann Act.. 278
Whitney Central Bank 310, 330
Wilhelm II, Kaiser 29
Wilhelmshaven, City of....................... 13
Wilkie, Lydia Frances 290
Willard Hotel 140
William J. Burns International Detective Agency..................................... 6
Willis, William............................... 112
Wilson, Woodrow .... vii, xiii, 1, 22, 66, 73-75, 112, 113, 115, 121, 133, 135, 136, 140, 143, 147, 153-156, 158, 161, 163-166, 172, 174, 216-219, 223-225, 257, 258, 279, 286, 287, 289, 292, 306, 337, 339, 341-346, 358, 365, 371- 374, 376, 382, 384, 389, 407, 408, 411
Winchester Repeating Arms Company .. 183
Windsor Armory............................. 48
Wise and Seligsburg 30
Wise, Julius 30, 323

Wiseman, William Adolph ...237, 255, 276-278, 388, 391
Wittenberg, Ernest 345, 401, 412
Woerndle, Joseph D., *see also* Boehm, Hans Walter Luigi 30
Wolf of Wall Street, *see* Lamar, David
Wolpert, Otto.............................. 79, 90
Wolverton, Charles B. 144
Woodhouse, Henry................... 213, 214
Wörmer, SMS................................ 14
Wren, John................................... 207
Wright, Fred...34, 215, 216, 227, 230, 261, 262, 263, 266, 272, 356, 384, 389
Wright, Harry 34, 215, 216, 227, 230, 261-263, 266, 272, 356, 384, 389
Wright, Howard Paul 34, 215, 216, 227, 230, 261-263, 266, 272, 356, 384, 389
Wright, Newton D. ...34, 215, 216, 227, 230, 261-263, 266, 272, 356, 384, 389
Wrigley, William Mills Jr. . 286, 314, 325, 328
W. Stokes Kirk Company 190

Y

Yorktown, USS 54
Ypiranga, SS 100, 348, 356, 398, 411
Ysleta, Village of 123
Yucatán, State of 185, 197, 208, 227, 289, 302, 305-311, 314, 325-328

Z

Zapata, Emiliano 177, 217, 221, 222, 282-284, 287, 327, 329
Zertuche, José 254, 255
Zimavilla, Muñecas........ 193-195, 197, 199
Zimmerman, Arthur.............345, 373, 374
Zimmerman Telegram 345, 373, 374
Zozaya, José Z. 108, 120, 122, 131, 367

www.ingramcontent.com/pod-product-compliance
Lightning Source LLC
Chambersburg PA
CBHW071940220426
43662CB00009B/926